Communications in Computer and Information Science 1011

More information about this series at http://www.springer.com/series/7899

Lorna Uden · Dario Liberona ·
Galo Sanchez · Sara Rodríguez-González (Eds.)

Learning Technology for Education Challenges

8th International Workshop, LTEC 2019
Zamora, Spain, July 15–18, 2019
Proceedings

Springer

Editors
Lorna Uden
Staffordshire University
Stoke-on-Trent, Steiermark, UK

Dario Liberona
Universidad Tecnica Federico Santa Maria
Valparaiso, Chile

Galo Sanchez
Universidad de Salamanca
Salamanca, Spain

Sara Rodríguez-González
Universidad de Salamanca
Salamanca, Spain

ISSN 1865-0929 ISSN 1865-0937 (electronic)
Communications in Computer and Information Science
ISBN 978-3-030-20797-7 ISBN 978-3-030-20798-4 (eBook)
https://doi.org/10.1007/978-3-030-20798-4

This Springer imprint is published by the registered company Springer Nature Switzerland AG
The registered company address is: Gewerbestrasse 11, 6330 Cham, Switzerland

Preface

The 8th International Workshop on Learning Technology for Education Challenges (LTEC 2019): How Technologies Help us to Learn to Meet Future Learning, was held at the University of Salamanca, Zamora, Spain, during July 15–18.

The conference was preceded by one day of free tutorials for participants who wished to learn about the state of the art of research relating to the topics of LTEC. The tutorials were held on July 15, 2019. The conference itself commenced on July 16, 2019.

There is a shift in attitudes from having a job for life to continuous learning at work. Skills that businesses require today are changing. Individuals that succeed in the future will be those who adopt the philosophy of lifelong learning. A continuous learning culture needs to be at the heart of universities and all organizations. Technology is absolutely central to the future of the learning community, particularly as we move into the age of the Internet of Things (IoT), artificial intelligence (AI), big data, smart cities, and blockchain.

Businesses must work with universities to provide work experience for students, and universities must ensure they produce the employees that businesses want. A host of learning tools are being used as the technology continues to mature, including personalization, gamification, social media, and micro-learning, which allows students to absorb ideas and lessons in bite-sized information chunks. Artificial intelligence is used to provide intelligent and personal learning for students. Virtual-reality technology is exciting because it allows both educational establishments and employers to prepare people in a far more engaging and realistic way than traditional classroom methods.

Higher education institutions are changing their roles, from focusing on research and teaching to having focus on research, teaching, and more effective learning. It is important to investigate teaching and learning approaches aimed at empowering students to handle their lives during their education and toward an occupational life.

Co-creative processes are a trend that is going to grow in the future, together with the growing of interest in creative solutions for future education and organization. We must think of universities as an “indivisible whole” in which teaching, research, and social impact work together for the benefits of all: an inclusive system. To achieve this, universities need to partner within their ecosystem to facilitate value creation like the natural ecosystem. This means adopting an e-learning ecosystem.

In today’s digital world, a web of learning resources surrounds every individual. It is an environment where in each resource connects to others, creating an overall structure in which all learning takes place. The e-learning ecosystem is the combination of technologies and support resources available to help individuals learn within an environment. This new revolution focuses on agility and integration of multiple solutions. A learning ecosystem will make the most of digital transformation using a stack of technology to facilitate learning.

The 8th LTEC (2019) examined how these technologies and pedagogical advances can be used to change the way teachers teach and students learn while giving special emphasis to the pedagogically effective ways we can harness these new technologies in education. The aim is to provide a platform for research in the very broad area of educational technology that bridges theory, research, practice, and policy.

The proceedings consist of 40 papers covering various aspects of technologies for learning including:

Learning technologies
Learning tools and environment
E-learning and moocs
Learning practices
Machine learning and evaluation support programs

The authors of the papers come from many different countries including Austria, Bosnia, Brazil, Colombia, Ecuador, Estonia, Finland, France, Germany, Greece, Indonesia, Italy, Malaysia, New Zealand, Oman, Poland, Portugal, Russia, Singapore, Slovakia, Slovenia, Spain, Switzerland, Taiwan, the UK, and the USA.

We would like to thank our authors, reviewers, and Program Committee for their contributions and the University of Salamanca for hosting the conference. Special thanks to the authors and participants at the conference. Without their efforts, there would be no conference or proceedings. Particular thanks to Dr. Fernando De La Prieta for dealing with the websites and local arrangements.

July 2019

Lorna Uden
Dario Liberona

Organization

General Conference Chair

Lorna Uden	Staffordshire University, UK

Program Chair

Dario Liberona	Universidad Tecnica Federico Santa Maria, Chile

Local Chairs

Galo Sánchez	Universidad de Salamanca, Spain
Sara Rodríguez	Universidad de Salamanca, Spain

Local Organizing Committee

Juan Manuel Corchado Rodríguez	University of Salamanca, Spain
Galo Sánchez Sánchez	Universidad de Salamanca, Spain
Fernando De la Prieta Pintado	University of Salamanca, Spain
Sara Rodríguez González	Universidad de Salamanca, Spain
Javier Prieto Tejedor	University of Salamanca, Spain
Juan Carlos Matos Franco	University of Salamanca, Spain
José Escuadra Burrieza	University of Salamanca, Spain
José Luis Pérez Iglesias	University of Salamanca, Spain
María Luisa Pérez Delgado	University of Salamanca, Spain
Pablo Chamoso Santos	University of Salamanca, Spain
Alfonso González Briones	University of Salamanca, Spain
Jesús Angel Román Gallego	University of Salamanca, Spain
Manuel Pablo Rubio Cavero	University of Salamanca, Spain
Alberto Rivas Camacho	University of Salamanca, Spain
Roberto Casado Vara	University of Salamanca, Spain
Elena Hernández	University of Salamanca, Spain
Ines Sitton	University of Salamanca, Spain
María Cruz Sánchez Gómez	University of Salamanca, Spain
Antonio Sánchez Martín	University of Salamanca, Spain
Iago Ramos Fernández	University of Salamanca, Spain
María Victoria Martín Cilleros	University of Salamanca, Spain
Eva González Ortega	University of Salamanca, Spain

Program Committee

Dale Rose Baker	Arizona State University, USA
Birgit Feldmann	FernUniversität in Hagen, Germany
D'Arcy Becker	University of Wisconsin, USA
Dario Liberona	Universidad Tecnica Federico Santa Maria, Chile
I Hsien	National University of Kaohsiung, Taiwan
Jane Sinclair	University of Warwick, UK
Jeremiah Sullins	Harding University, USA
Lorna Uden	Staffordshire University, UK
Michael Vallance	Future University Hakodate, Japan
Sabine Seufert	Universität St.Gallen (HSG), Switzerland
Viktorija Florjančič	University of Primorska, Koper, Slovenia
Fotini Paraskeva	University of Piraeus, Greece
Debora Nice Ferrari Barbosa	Universidade Feevale, Brazil
Fernando Moreira	Univ Portucalense, Aveiro, Portugal
Alberth Alberth	Universitas Halu Oleo, Sulawesi, Indonesia
Anat Wilson	Swinburne University of Technology, Australia
Sunnie Lee Watson	Purdue University, USA
Alberto Magreñán	Universidad de La Rioja, Spain
Reneta Barneva	SUNY Fredonia University, USA
Hui Min Lai	Chienkuo Technology University, Taiwan
Kelley Reinsmith-Jones	East Carolina University, USA
Eric Lau	Open University of Hong Kong, Hong Kong
Fernando de la Prieta	Universidad de Salamanca, Spain
Rein Smith	East Carolina University, USA

Contents

Learning Technologies

The Use of Gamification Technique in Agile Development Methodology. . . . 3
Rula Al-Azawi, Sebastin Antony Joe, Mohaned Al-Obaidy, and Jonathan Westlake

Exploring the Impact of Artificial Intelligence in Music Education to Enhance the Dyslexic Student's Skills 14
Michele Della Ventura

Otowik: Mining Text from Wikis to Mind Maps. 23
Vinothini Kasinathan, Aida Mustapha, and Mohamad Firdaus Che Abdul Rani

Exploring the Potential of Using Augmented Reality and Virtual Reality for STEM Education 36
Rula Al-Azawi, Ali Albadi, Raziyeh Moghaddas, and Jonathan Westlake

Boosting Motivation Through Process Gamification: Evidence from Higher Education 45
Julia Bilinkis, Alexander Gromoff, and Yaroslav Gorchakov

Health Student Using Google Classroom: Satisfaction Analysis. 58
Amadeu Sa de Campos Filho, Webber de Souza Fantini, Mirelly Atanázio Ciriaco, Joelton dos Santos, Fernando Moreira, and Alex Sandro Gomes

Gamification Design Framework Based on Self Determination Theory for Adult Motivation 67
Stavroula Karra, Vasiliki Karampa, and Foteini Paraskeva

Designing a Video Course. The Case of the Online Course of Mathematical Olympiads 79
Lucía Rotger and Juan M. Ribera

Learning Tools and Environment

Evaluation of the Disciplinary Competences of the Students of the Bachelor's Degree in Physiotherapy at "Sapienza" University of Rome Through the TECO: A Cross-Sectional Study 93
Giovanni Galeoto, Anna Berardi, Cecilia Pizzi, Ilaria Farina, and Julita Sansoni

The Use of Digital Devices in the University Classroom: Exploring and Comparing Students' Perceptions and Practices 103
Maria Rabl, Juliana Pattermann, Stephan Schlögl, and Niki Canham

A Preliminary Review of Blockchain-Based Solutions in Higher Education . . . 114
Aida Kamišalić, Muhamed Turkanović, Saša Mrdović, and Marjan Heričko

EduBrowser: A Multimodal Automated Monitoring System for Co-located Collaborative Learning 125
Yi Han Victoria Chua, Preman Rajalingam, Seng Chee Tan, and Justin Dauwels

Internet-Based Immersive Learning (IIL): Applying Ubiquitous Web 1.0 and Web 2.0 Resources in EFL Learning 139
Yun-Hsuan Huang

Towards Successful Implementation of a Virtual Classroom for Vocational Higher Education in Indonesia 151
Bayu Rima Aditya, Irawan Nurhas, and Jan Pawlowski

Computer Application for the Evaluation of Mathematical Competence in Secondary Education: A Case Study 162
Lara Orcos, Rosario Arias, Alberto Magreñán, Juan Antonio Sicilia, and Íñigo Sarría

E-learning and MOOCS

Teachers' Beliefs Towards Blended Learning in Higher Education: A Mixed-Methods Study 177
María Cruz Sánchez-Gómez, Antonio V. Martín-García, and Juanjo Mena

Motivating Engineer Students in E-learning Courses with Problem Based Learning and Self-Regulated Learning on the apT^{2}CLE4'Research Methods' Environment 189
Foteini Paraskeva, Aikaterini Alexiou, Hara Bouta, Sofia Mysirlaki, Dimitrios J. Sotiropoulos, and Aikaterini-Maria Souki

Developing a MOOC to Foster Information Literacy (IL) by Means of a Conjecture Map 202
Sabine Seufert, Josef Guggemos, Luca Moser, and Stefan Sonderegger

Variations in Self-Regulation of Learning On-Line Versus On-Campus 214
Jonathan Kaplan

Let's Digitize It: Investigating Challenges of Online Education 224
Stephan Schlögl, Christian Ploder, Teresa Spieß, and Franziska Schöffer

Implementing Blended Learning in Mathematics Classrooms: Perspectives of Two South African Educators Working in an International School in Saudi Arabia. 234
Ilhaam Abrahams, Lawrence Meda, and Eunice Ivala

Learning Practices

Context Analysis of Teachers' Learning Design Practice Through Activity Theory, Distributed Cognition, and Situated Cognition. 247
Leandro M. Queiros, Carlos J. P. Silva, Alex S. Gomes, and Fernando Moreira

Opening Spaces for the Development of Human Agency with Problem Based Learning in Palestinian Higher Education 260
Karl Royle

Facing a Digital Challenge at a Traditional University 279
Viktorija Florjančič

Math Anxiety Analysis in Indonesian Elementary School. 292
Nurhayati, Dina Anika Marhayani, Chih-Hung Chang, and Marja Naaranoja

Co-creation Workshops for Work Life Oriented ICT Education 302
Anne-Maria Aho and Jane Sinclair

Developing Entrepreneurship Education: Case of the University of Žilina. . . . 313
Anna Závodská, Veronika Šramová, and Vladimír Konečný

The Digital Literacy of Business Students with Evidence from Poland and Slovenia. 325
Viktorija Florjančič and Łukasz Wiechetek

Using Digital Resources to Boost English Writing Development. 337
Ângela Musskopf, Débora Nice Ferrari Barbosa, Patrícia Brandalise Scherer Bassani, and Amanda Jefferies

Social Media Learning Tools

Using Social Media to Enhance Learning and Motivate Students in the Higher Education Classroom 351
Eva Lahuerta-Otero, Rebeca Cordero-Gutiérrez, and Vanessa Izquierdo-Álvarez

Fostering Foreign Language Learning Through a Telecollaborative Social Media-Based Tandem Language Learning Approach 362
Alberth, Yun Wang, and William Yu Chjung Wang

Social Media Services Ecosystem for Marginalized Youth to Access Adult Education 369
Kai Pata and Sille Paas

The Effect of Social Media on the Emotional Intelligence of Teachers in Indonesia 381
Andi Mursidi, Yudi Darma, Rustam, Suherdiyanto, T. Yani Achmad, and I-Hsien Ting

Machine Learning and Evaluation Support Programs

Design for System Change: Developing Digital Competences of Vocational Teachers 393
Sabine Seufert, Josef Guggemos, and Eric Tarantini

Teaching Data Analytics to Sport Management Majors: A Practical Approach. 408
Reneta P. Barneva and Valentin E. Brimkov

A Teaching-Learning Model of Collaborative Assessment in Computer Engineering Studies. 418
Ana B. Gil-González, Ana de Luis Reboredo, Sara Rodríguez González, and Fernando de la Prieta Pintado

Students Performance Analysis Based on Machine Learning Techniques 428
Alberto Rivas, Jesús M. Fraile, Pablo Chamoso, Alfonso González-Briones, Sara Rodríguez, and Juan M. Corchado

A Report on the Application of Adaptive Testing in a First Year University Course. 439
Anna Maria Angelone and Pierpaolo Vittorini

Teaching Effectiveness: An Innovative Evaluation Model. 450
Walter Orozco, Miguel Ángel Rodríguez-García, and Alberto Fernández

Machine Learning for the Identification of Students at Risk of Academic Desertion 462
Leidy Daniela Forero Zea, Yudy Fernanda Piñeros Reina, and José Ignacio Rodríguez Molano

Evaluation of Computer Assisted Qualitative Data Analysis Software (CAQDAS) Applied to Research. 474
M. C. Sánchez-Gómez, M. V. Martín-Cilleros, and G. Sánchez Sánchez

Author Index 487

Learning Technologies

The Use of Gamification Technique in Agile Development Methodology

Rula Al-Azawi[1(✉)], Sebastin Antony Joe[1], Mohaned Al-Obaidy[2], and Jonathan Westlake[3]

[1] Gulf College, Muscat, Oman
rulaalaazawi@yahoo.com, Sebastin@gulfcollege.edu.om
[2] Modern College of Business and Science, Muscat, Oman
Mohanad.alobaidi@mcbs.edu.om
[3] Staffordshire University, Staffordshire, UK
j.c.westlake@staffs.ac.uk

Abstract. Students motivation and engagement difficulties are present in higher education. Between many technologies to increase student motivation and engagement, we found that Gamification technique is the most suitable case. This paper presents our experiment of using Gamification in learning process and based on the use of the Agile methodology in-order to obtain the best results and engagements from the students.

Applying Gamification in software engineering is not as straight to move as it may appear. Current research in the area has already recognized the possible use of Gamification in the context of software development. It is still an open area of research about how to design and use Gamification in this context.

Higher education universities, especially in the Middle East are sometimes facing problems to get students engagement and motivation as a group structure.

This paper supports the proposed idea; we presented a preliminary experiment that shows the effect of gamification on the performance of students involvement in a funded project from TRC (The Research Council) in Sultanate of Oman.

1 Introduction

Nowadays, motivation and engagement is a very common problem in lecturers, especially when they don't find the purpose of learning activities [1]. Therefore, as an academic lecturer, we faced a daily problem to motivate and develop students skills. Actually, learning strategies related to the use of game components look like an appropriate contribution to the development of these skills. Thus, gamification, understood as the use of game design and game elements in non-game contexts [2] becomes a relevant technique for increasing student motivation and engagement. By applying gamification into the classroom, students could be motivated to learn in new ways or become engaged in otherwise tedious tasks [3]. According to these principles, different experiences are being carried out [4, 5].

In this paper, we introduced the concept of gamification to show how it may be successfully applied to the process of Agile development methodology. Our final purpose is to improve software education/training and to improve the quality of project

L. Uden et al. (Eds.): LTEC 2019, CCIS 1011, pp. 3–13, 2019.
https://doi.org/10.1007/978-3-030-20798-4_1

development for team. The aim of using gamification in Agile was to increase the engagement, motivation and to add fun to their work in the project. The gamification includes setting the comfort level of members in the workplace.

Agile methodology is commonly used in terms of software development by making the building process easy and efficient, thanks to iterative and incremental tasks including permanent testing and corrections. The attention to the human motivation and engagement issues gives Agile projects a particular relevance.

Through our course-work experiment, the method of Gamification was applied as Final Year Projects (FYPs). The method was deployed after the funding approval of project proposals by The Research Council of Oman (TRC). Agile methodology has been assigned in the project proposal as a research methodology. We integrated gamification technology as a part of our check-points by counting the students engagement and motivation in all Agile iteration process.

This paper is structured as follows: Sect. 2 presents the best practice for higher education. Agile methodology and Gamification in education are sub-sections. Section 3 introduces our framework to integrate gamification technology in Agile methodology. Section 4 aims at explaining the findings and observations of the study. Section 5 shows the results related to our experiment. Finally, Sect. 6 presents conclusion and suggestion for further studies.

2 Best Practices Recommend for Higher Education from the Literature

In this section, we highlight various ways in higher education to enhance the production of software and furthermore how to increase engagement and motivation of the students.

In this experiment, the students should create a mobile application with the title "Scientific and Numerical Miracles in the Holy Quran" using Android studio.

The following subsections are covering first, the main methodology used in mobile application (Agile Methodology) and secondly, the new trend in higher education learning strategy to increase students motivation (Gamification).

2.1 Agile Methodology

In mobile software engineering, we have found that Agile methodology is an appropriate for mobile application development [6]. Agility means having the capacity to move rapidly and effectively. Utilizing Agile methodologies in software development process improvement makes the procedure sufficiently adaptable to adjust rapidly and effectively to the changing patterns and innovations. In mobile software engineering, methodology is of extraordinary significance, since software applications are perpetually changing and developing in view of quick client prerequisites. For the team concentrated on customer satisfaction by means of advancement of a very much composed application by methods of generation procedure. Agile methodology was adopted. Projects were produced through arrangement of emphases called "sprints" Projects are developed through series of iterations called sprints. Each sprint was in a perfect world a pack of low level SDLC (Systems development life cycle) forms where a little sub highlight is driven from thought origination, arranging till testing stage, which took around two to four weeks to finish. Short meeting were hung once a day to talk about announcements of the group's sprint undertakings. In our case we proposed weekly meetings. Post sprint review meetings led to reporting the shortcomings and improvements. It has been found that agile-scrum process is most appropriate for project development scenarios with highly emerging or quickly changing requirements as in the case of mobile software development.

The Agile methodology as mentioned earlier is an iterative and incremental approach and it achieves the quality and productivity through iterations. Each iterations of sprint phase includes a software development team working through a full software development cycle including planning, requirements analysis, design, coding, unit testing, and acceptance testing as shown in Fig. 1 [7].

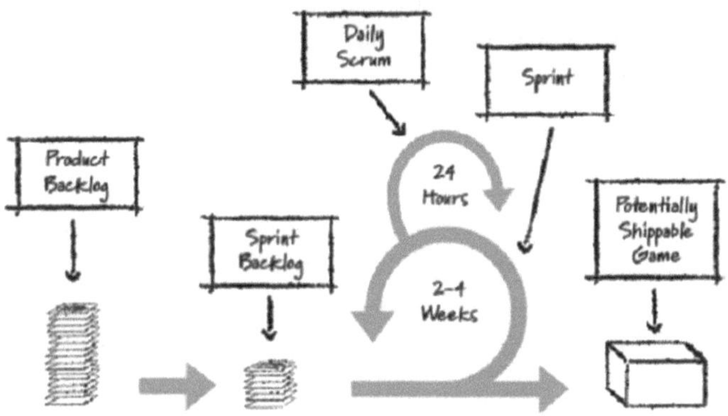

Fig. 1. Agile methodology diagram

The Agile phase approach diagram which is used by Keith [8] as shown in Fig. 2 shows that Agile methodology is based on iterations that could start new iteration before completing the previous iteration. Agile methodologies aim to improve the efficiency and quality of the final developments, having the ability to respond to changes and new definitions and by providing the greatest possible satisfaction to the final user and continuous feedback. Therefore, in contrast to traditional methodologies, Agile relies on incremental developments with very short iterations, giving greater value to the individual issues with high effectiveness in unclear and changeable environments. Agile development encompasses a broad set of principles and methodologies [5].

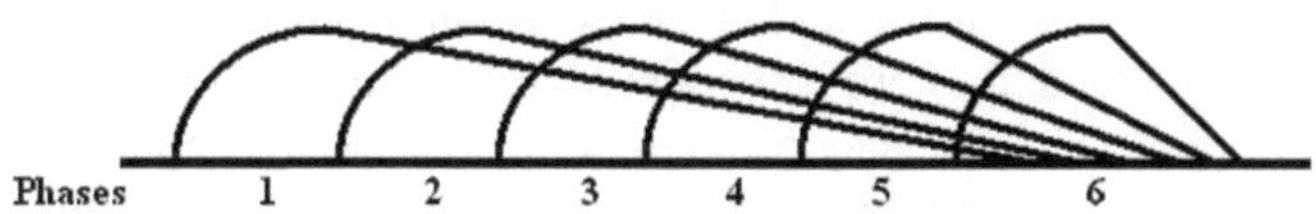

Fig. 2. Agile phases approach

2.2 Gamification in Education

In this section, we have Gamification analysis as an educational technique. Gamification appears as a good match for education [9].

Gamification is defined as the use of game design elements in non-game contexts [10]. The most elementary gamification element consists of a rewarding mechanism that awards people in response of the accomplishment of certain activities (also known as challenges) that need to be encouraged.

We see gamification as using social gaming elements such as team-work, game thinking, and game mechanics, in non-game environments (e.g. higher education). Figure 3 shows the actual relation between Gamification concept and different types of game. The main promise of gamification is that it gives the educator a number of powerful and predictable tools for influencing human motivation and behavior and, when done right, to activate various types of students in pursuing learning activities. The main concern is to make technically and conceptually challenging courses interesting for classroom of students with various personalities and skill-levels [11].

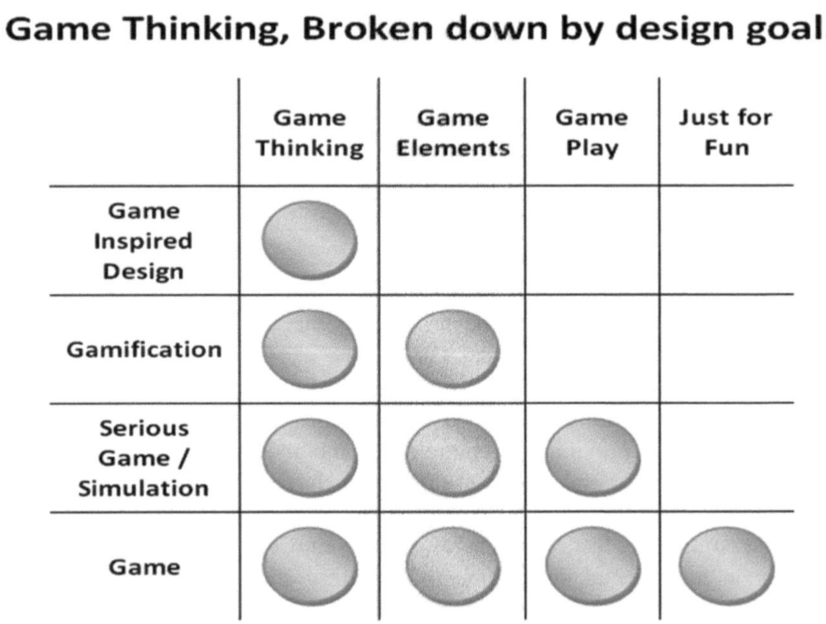

Fig. 3. Relation between gamification and game

There are many reasons for this (1) Games are built on sound learning principles. Play is an important element to provide concept of learn through play, as digital games can provide an opportunity for play through simulated environments. (2) Games provide an environment where failure can happen without consequence, allowing learning to happen. (3) Games provide personalized learning opportunities. As games support the use of levels, games can provide students with the ability to learn at their own pace and at a level that suits where they are. (4) Games provide more engagement for the learner. Games contain the pieces necessary to engage students and help them enter a state of flow [12], where they are fully immersed in their learning environment and energized and focused on the activity they are involved in (5) Games teach 21st century skills. Teaching and assessing 21st century skills frequently require exposing learners to well-designed complex tasks, affording them the ability to interact with other learners and trained professionals, as well as providing them with appropriate diagnostic feedback that is seamlessly integrated into the learning experience [13].

Gamification can be divided into two main categories: internal and external [14]. Internal gamification focuses on motivation of internal employees in some company. It has several types of use in internal environment such as company development, Human resource improvement and work efficiency; while external Gamification is customer-oriented and it focuses on building strong connections between customers and a company. Propagation is a part of external gamification when it is implemented into web pages to motivate visitor to be more interested in a board. Education is another part of external Gamification. It is mainly used in e-learning courses or as a part of the software user guides.

3 Approach to a Conceptual Framework in Education Context Based upon Agile Methodology

This section focuses on the use of game elements in Agile methodology. We have a previous experience of using Gamification in higher education classes [15]. Our previous experiment results show a very positive feedback from students and the pass rate was increased, as well.

In this experiment, we have created a framework to include gamification technique in Agile methodology life-cycle. Many gamification frameworks exist in the literature and most of them were developed with business, as shown in the bibliographic review [16]. Gamification in learning focuses on specific experiences [15, 17]. The approach to a conceptual framework in education context based upon Agile methodology also presented in the literature [5, 9, 14, 18].

In Agile, gamification is often used as part of release planning [19]. The release planning requires a high level estimation to give the business an indication of what stories to include in a release and how to prioritize them. However, when faced with the need to produce an estimation, the team were spend a significant amount of time, discussing the low level detail, and how the story would be implemented, rather than giving an estimate. These discussions were often only of interest to the development team, or sometimes specific members of the development team, with others in the meeting quickly losing interest. The release planning session was used to estimate and prioritize many stories [9].

From the previous definition, we have noticed that gamification is a great tool to increase peoples interests. That is why game became very common to use in Software Engineering as well as our experiment used same concepts of Agile methodology and we added the gamification technique in the proper phase or iteration in Agile.

For the followings, we explained some of the game concepts and how we have integrated in the Agile methodology life-cycle.

1. **Team profile**
   It is important to the team to understand that team success can always be a good motivation element for all team members. Each team member can publish their profile status, results and evaluation, gain experience point, team velocity, gain budget, etc.
2. **User profile**
   Since we are dealing with mobile application, it is important to know some of the main data such as contact information and relevant information expertise, skills and user feedback.
3. **Experience points**
   With the end goal of users motivation, exertion spent by utilizing Agile structure must be compensated. Picking up experience points is an exceptionally valuable method for users evaluation with the end goal of reward framework. Experience points should be received during whole development process for teams achievements. As an inspiration apparatus, experience point ought to be increased just for significant exercises. Framework gamification is intended to contain these point-gaining possibilities:

   a. **Points for work time**
      Teams and their members get experience points for every week for work in the environment using Agile framework. Prototype is designed to give every person 2 points for every week spent in the team assigned to some projects.
   b. **Points for finished user stories**
      Every user story should be evaluated, with its completion being rewarded. Main parameter of this evaluation type is sum of really finished (state Done) user stories compared to sum of user stories planned to be finished during current sprint. Both team and its members get 0 to 5 points according to ratio mentioned above for every week spent in previous sprint, after it ends.
   c. **Points for efficient work**
      If sprint ends and all finished user stories from sprint backlog are approved by product owner, the team gets 1 point multiplied by average product owner evaluation of customer satisfaction for every week of such sprint.
   d. **Points for integrated work**
      Each team member is responsible to integrate his/her work with other team member in a Drop-Box file. For each correct integration activity they get 1 point.
4. **Progress bar**
   People always like to see their progress in visual forms and not just as a number, so the framework should also contain a progress bars which display how much experience points user/team currently has and how much points are left.
5. **Badges**
   Team evaluation by experience points is a good approach; more can be done more for their motivation increase, such as system of gaining badges for some achievements. There exist lots of opportunities, for which users and teams can gain some badges.

Badges are evaluated regularly as mentioned at every badge description. Gamified Agile framework should contain at least these team badges:

a. **Hard workers**
All sprints of given team in last semester have been completely finished (with no undone user stories), evaluated once at the end of each semester.
b. **Stable workers**
Velocity of sprints in the last semester, evaluated once at the end of each semester.
c. **Completion masters**
All user stories of one project has been finished before end of the project, evaluated after end of the project.
d. **Customer importance**
Product owner is satisfied with the team work, evaluated after end of the project.

6. **Attendance holder**
Team average attendance. Evaluated once at the end of each semester.
7. **Team leader board**
Agile is based on the rule of team as an individual. People are typically motivated by comparison with others, so the prototype should contain leader board which compares results of all teams.
8. **Rewards**
It is really great to have a system, which can show differences in efficiency and work effort between people and teams, but all of that is only in virtual world. For better motivation of all members of development teams, there is also a need of some tangible thing they can get.

The main purpose of this experiment is to integrate gamification into Agile framework in a way that it increased the motivation and engagement of all the team member. We have selected Agile because it is defined as a way to increase motivation among the whole team as a unit and gamification to motivate individual team member. In our experiment, each student should submit two products. First, as his/her individual work to be evaluated as a final year project. Second, an integrated project with other team member as a FURAP (Faculty Mentored Undergraduate Research Award Program) scholarships are granted by The Research Council of Oman (TRC) through higher education institutes, colleges and universities in Oman project. The challenge was how to evaluate both products in a separate measurement procedure. A team member should communicate with other members and at the same time, must be careful about submitting similar projects.

For motivation increase, we have used the following modification and its gamification improvement:

- Unit tests
Unit tests are good for fast and efficient software development. It can improve team effort to maintain framework rules and it can be based on their importance.
- Test-driven development

uses a very simple process for test creation and product implementation. This process can be very easily adapted on creation of unit tests and helps to maintain the order and clear work-flow.

- Pair programming
  Pair programming belongs to often used development methods in Agile approach. It has several advantages such as increase in the team members substitutability, more educated employees with wider knowledge and more efficient development with fewer mistakes.

4 Observation and Finding

This section tends to discuss our observation in applying Agile Gamification in this mobile project and the practical experience faced in developing our Android application. Today's smart phones support many different programming options. We focused on the Android platform, since it is one of the most prominent platforms so far [20], with the largest number of available devices [6].

The present study aimed at finding suitable answer the following questions

(1) **Can gamification used with Agile project and improve the tracking of Agile?**
(2) **Can gamification improve the efficiency of the team and what are the impact on the team motivation?**

There was a positive result of our experiment. Our observation has focus on four main areas:

1. **Engage**
   Adapting gamification in the different phase of Agile methodology life-cycle increases team engagement. Students notice that their individual work will be integrated with other team members work and this issue increase their challenge to submit high quality work. We have noticed that engagement has been increased in the integration activities. For those activities, we propose target environments such as dealing with same Android studio version and using Drop-Box to store the latest integrated version of their practical work.
2. **Train**
   The final objective of the study was to improve both software education and training. In addition we aimed at improving developments activities frameworks. Actually, using pair programming increases training among the team members. They have created also Whats-up group to share their knowledge, information and to support team member to solve any technical issues.
3. **Monitor**
   It was a confusing task to be a student supervisor and at the same time, a team leader for group project. This was the main reason to search for a technique to be assisted in that complicated task. The gamification technique facilitates the monitor tasks and gave us an easy indicator to monitor the students behavior and performance both individually and as a team work.

4. **Motivate**
   Points system and rewards with points increase the students motivation. Furthermore, level access and power increase their achievements. For example, students may get access to additional materials. As the project was funded, budget was also a reason to increase students motivation, since this was the first time for students to avail funds for their work.

5 Results

Finding of the experiment revealed several benefits of using Gamification integrated with Agile methodology through Android Studio. Some examples may include (a) project risk minimization, (b) better productivity, (c) High range of quality assurance, and (d) on-time project release.

Our basic idea was to develop a light weight mobile application as shown in Fig. 4. We have achieved the requirements to be easy to use and understandable in two languages Arabic and English. The software is still under the evaluation phase with different customers. Our application is available on the Google store under the name numerical and scientific miracle of Quran and the application icon and link shows below: https://play.google.com/store/apps/details?id=cm.exa.admin.nnq11848alkhatab

The team members in this experiment got the highest marks in their final year project grade in comparison with normal students.

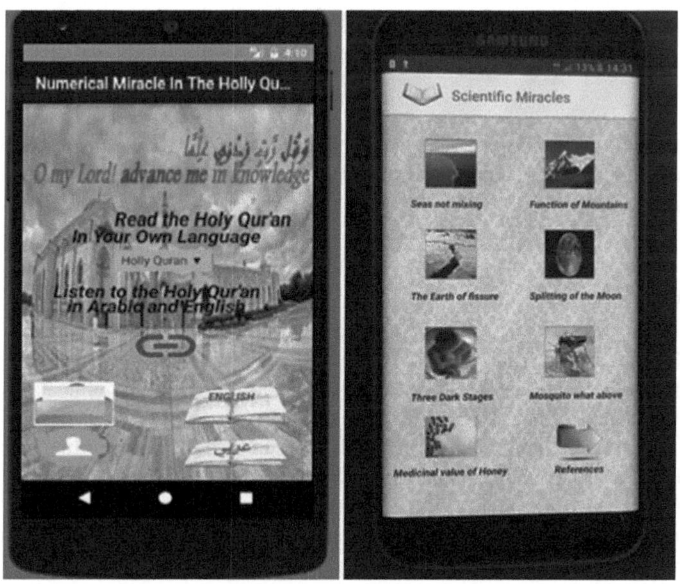

Fig. 4. Mobile application environment

6 Conclusion and Future Work

Several research about gamification success in driving desired behavior already exist [21–23]. Gamification does not necessarily mean success [24]. It also depends on the form of gamification integration, used elements and target domain.

By using Gamification Agile in our experiment, we have been able to increase students engagements and motivation and increase the project quality. Finally, it gave us a good benchmark to evaluate team individually and as a team work. The application was developed using important features from (Agile), technique from (gamification), and software application by using (Android studio).

The Mobile industries need to adopt software development methodologies that provide a balance between market-oriented and technical activities in order to sustain in today's market.

It is conceivable to enhance the current experiment by augmenting the project and running it over a more extended period. Through this approach, the information could be analyzed crosswise. This would in turn diminish the probability that the outcome was identified distinctively A further augmentation to this would run the gamification in more than one group.

Another area of research would be searching for a way to acquaint observing with a group in a convincing way. As talked about in the evaluation, the group profited from exact estimation of the venture, yet at the same time opposed observing to help them to accomplish exactness. In summary, education and gamification turned out to be good fits. Gamification helps to increase the engagement in a fun way.

The aim of this paper was not only to report on the outcomes of the research project, but also to describe our experience with an approach for a teaching and a learning method.

Acknowledgment. The authors would like to thank Raya Al Hajri, Majed Almaqbali and Al Khatab Alghawi for their participating in this experiment and providing with us all the required information and material.

References

1. Glover, I.: Play as you learn: gamification as a technique for motivating learners. In: World Conference on Educational Multimedia Hypermedia and Telecommunications (2013)
2. Dixon, D., Khaled, R., Nacke, L., Deterding, S.: From game design elements to gamefulness: defining gamification. In: 15th International Academic MindTrek Conference: Envisioning Future Media Environments, pp. 9–15. ACM (2010)
3. Fox, J., Hanus, M.D.: Assessing the effects of gamification in the classroom: a longitudinal study on intrinsic motivation, social comparison, satisfaction, effort, and academic performance. Comput. Educ. **80**, 152–161 (2015)
4. Mora, A., Gonzalez, C.: Methodological proposal for gamification in the computer engineering teaching. In: Computers in Education (SIIE), 2014 International Symposium, pp. 29–34. IEEE (2014)

5. Mora, A., Zaharias, P., González, C., Arnedo-Moreno, J.: FRAGGLE: A FRamework for AGile gamification of learning experiences. In: De Gloria, A., Veltkamp, R. (eds.) GALA 2015. LNCS, vol. 9599, pp. 530–539. Springer, Cham (2016). https://doi.org/10.1007/978-3-319-40216-1_57
6. Kaleel, S., Harishankar, S.: Applying agile methodology in mobile software engineering: android application development and its challenges. Comput. Sci. Tech. Rep. pp. 1–11 (2013)
7. Al-Azawi, R., Ayesh, A., Obaidy, M.A.: Towards agent-based agile approach for game development methodology. In: 2014 World Congress on Computer Applications and Information Systems (WCCAIS), pp. 1–6. IEEE (2014)
8. Keith, C.: Agile Game Development with Scrum. Signature Series. Addison-Wesley, Boston (2010)
9. Mcclean, A.: An Exploration of the Use of Gamification in Agile Software Development. Dissertations, p. 180 (2015)
10. Deterding, S., Khaled, R.: Gamification: toward a definition. In: CHI 2011 Gamification Workshop. ACM (2011)
11. Iosup, A., Epema, D.: An experience report on using gamification in technical higher education. In: Proceedings of the 45th ACM Technical Symposium on Computer Science Education - SIGCSE 2014, no. 2008, pp. 27–32 (2014)
12. Csikszentmihalyi, M.: Flow: The Psychology of Optimal Experience. Harper Perennial, New York (1991)
13. Rupp, A.A., Gushta, M., Mislevy, R.J., Shaffer, D.W.: Evidence-centered design of epistemic games: Measurement principles for complex learning environments. J. Technol. Learn. Assess. **8**(4) (2010)
14. Martin, B.: Gamification in the SCRUM Software Development Framework. Ph.D. thesis, Masaryk University, Faculty of Informatics (2016)
15. Al-Azawi, R., Al-Faliti, F., Al-Blushi, M.: Educational gamification vs. game based learning: comparative study. Int. J. Innov. Manag. Technol. **7**(4), 131 (2016)
16. Mora, A., Riera, D., Gonzalez, C., Arnedo-Moreno, J.: A literature review of gamification design frameworks. In: VS-Games 2015 - 7th International Conference on Games and Virtual Worlds for Serious Applications (2015)
17. Nah, F.F.-H., Telaprolu, V.R., Rallapalli, S., Venkata, P.R.: Gamification of education using computer games. In: Yamamoto, S. (ed.) HIMI 2013. LNCS, vol. 8018, pp. 99–107. Springer, Heidelberg (2013). https://doi.org/10.1007/978-3-642-39226-9_12
18. Patary, C.L.: Gamifying agile projects to drive employee engagement and increase performance. PM World J. **3**(11), 1–18 (2014)
19. Grenning, J.: Planning poker or how to avoid analysis paralysis while release planning. Hawthorn Woods: Renaiss. Softw. Consult. **3**, 22–23 (2002)
20. Gartner report on smartphone sales
21. Why does gamification work: a look into successful examples (2012)
22. Zichermann, G.: Intrinsic and extrinsic motivation in gamification. In: Gamification Summit, San Francisco, vol. 27 (2011)
23. Dale, S.: Gamification: making work fun, or making fun of work? Bus. Inf. Rev. **31**(2), 82–90 (2014)
24. Seaborn, K., Fels, D.: Gamification in theory and action: a survey. Int. J. Hum.-Comput. Stud. **74**, 14–31 (2015)

Exploring the Impact of Artificial Intelligence in Music Education to Enhance the Dyslexic Student's Skills

Michele Della Ventura(✉)

Department of Music Technology, Music Academy "Studio Musica", Via Andrea Gritti 25, 31100 Treviso, Italy
michele.dellaventura@tin.it

Abstract. This paper explores the impact of the use of Artificial Intelligence (AI) it the dyslexic student's learning process in higher music education. Music involves almost every cognitive ability: not only the auditory and motor systems involved in perception and music production (performance), but also attention, memory and learning, language, social intelligence, creativity and (last but not least) emotions. It is important for teachers to understand the different cognitive abilities and challenges of each student to help him/her to reach the aims of the learning process. It is necessary to avoid over-fatigue and psychological distress of the student that can lead him/her to the loss of confidence and personal motivation. The paper investigates the educational implications of the use of the software CAMA (Computer Added Musical Analysis) designed with the explicit purpose of managing the student's motivation in order to promote effective, active, efficient and satisfactory learning. Finally, some challenges for teachers of Musical High-Schools in the adoption of AI-technologies are identified and further directions for research are explored.

Keywords: Artificial Intelligence · Dyslexia · Intelligent tutoring system · Learning motivation · Music education

1 Introduction

Many, perhaps too many, words are written about the concept of Artificial Intelligence (AI) with the paradox that many people do not understand their meaning and importance. Technology based on Artificial Intelligence is a part of our everyday lives and it is also changing the way we acquire information, think, work and learn. Indeed, among its main objectives there are the ones related to simulating on a computer the cognitive process [1, 2], behaviour [3], the human brain relationships [2, 4], so as to better understand the human mind [5–7].

The recent Artificial Intelligent Technologies (AIT) attracted the teachers' attention for their potential to enhance traditional teaching and learning methods and improve the learning process quality. This kind of technologies make it possible to personalise the learning of the students on the base of their needs [8, 9]: every student learns differently and technology may allow teachers to meet the students' learning style on a case-by-case basis [9]. AIT represents a support for students with learning disabilities and it

L. Uden et al. (Eds.): LTEC 2019, CCIS 1011, pp. 14–22, 2019.
https://doi.org/10.1007/978-3-030-20798-4_2

helps them to reach the learning goals by individualized training and focusing on the area which they need to improve [10]. In this way it could be possible to increase student engagement, motivation and therefore independence in carry out a task [11, 12]. AIT can support and help the student's participation with learning disabilities, overcoming the barriers created by traditional educational methodologies: they are one of the most relevant elements for the realization of an inclusive pedagogy [13].

The use of the AIT must be done with *responsibility* and *critical sense* from both teacher and student.

It is the responsibility of every single teacher, for their own discipline, to understand what technology is better to use (to help students to reach their academic goals) in relation to the class group [9], and on the base of the individual strengths and needs of each student [14]. The presence of dyslexic students imposes on the teacher the need to have knowledge of the technology developments and reflect on what effects these might have on their learning process.

The teacher has to find the right balance between providing direct instruction (or texts, notes, examples, exercises, ...) to improve areas of weakness and the use of AIT to compensate for the identified learning difficulties. The teacher must verify: (1) that their use helps the student in the learning process and allows him/her to become more independent [15]; (2) if the student has the prerequisite skills necessary to develop a learning strategy [16]. This means that in some periods of the learning process, the teacher should work in cooperation with the student to be sure that he/she is learning and able to use the strategy in different contexts. At the same time this collaboration work provides the teacher the possibility to know the student understanding and supplies the necessary information (corrective feedback) to him/her in order to carry out a task.

AIT must represent a support tool for the student with learning disabilities and not become an instrument of dependency. The student should not feel disoriented in the absence of this kind of technology because the aim of its use is to lead him/her to become independent; he/she has to work at increasing independence in a supportive environment. The student has to believe that his/her learning strategy allow him/her to reach the learning goals [17].

In a Learning process supported by AIT the operation of monitoring and analysis are essential. Without them the learning process will barely be able to guarantee efficiency and effectiveness: the monitoring and analysis of the learning processes assume an indispensable role for the development of quality processes. On the basis of the above considerations, in Table 1 there are some indicators that the teacher could consider to evaluate the learning process.

In order to explore the possibilities of the Artificial Intelligence Technologies to support the dyslexic student learning process in a Music High School, a software has been design, developed and released by the author: CAMA (*Computer Added Musical Analysis*). The main objective was to assist the dyslexic students in the individual study of the *Theory, Analysis and Composition* discipline. The software has agents capable of mapping the student's sequences of actions and guiding him/her in order to avoid running into the same errors.

The structure of the paper as follow. Section 2 introduces the concepts of dyslexia and provides a brief review of the strengths and weaknesses of the student with

Table 1. Learning indicators

• Learning tasks the student find manageable
• Learning activities the student find manageable
• How the student applies new concepts
• How the student follows the guidelines of the teacher
• How long the student remains focused on a concept
• Time required by the student to start an activity
• The student is able to answer the questions of the teacher
• How the student asks the teacher's attention
• Clarifications required by the student
• Types of errors make by the student
• The student ask help to the classmates to solve a problem
• The student's strengths are enhanced to mitigate the weaknesses
• The student transfers the acquired problem-solving skills to new problems
• While using technology student appears to be more engaged or more receptive to the learning process
• The teacher uses the appropriate approaches for each student
• The teacher has an adequate planning for learning process with a back-up plan
• The teacher uses the appropriate words on the base of the needs' student
• The teacher keeps student's expectations high
• The teacher promotes dialogue with the student
• The teacher offers to the student several forms of the material
• The teacher provides the student with examples of satisfactory work
• The teacher encourages the student to use more often the type of activity where he/she has particular success
• The teacher provides the student with prompts to lead him/her
• The teacher uses the student's mistakes to allow and promote learning
• The teacher makes sure that AIT does not stimulate technology addiction

learning disability. Section 3 details the software architecture for providing teacher and students with personalized feedback. Afterwards, Sect. 4 presents a case study to illustrate the effectiveness of the use of AIT. Finally, Sect. 5 provides some remarks on the current issues and future research possibilities.

2 Dyslexia: Strengths and Weaknesses in Music Education

In this paragraph the concept of dyslexia is analysed from the musical point of view, trying to highlight the strengths and weaknesses of a student.

Dyslexia is defined as a Specific Learning Disorder (SLD): a reading disorder which affects *intelligent* people who have difficulties automatizing the graphic signs interpretation process [18, 19]. Dyslexia has nothing to do with intelligence but it simply describes a different kind of cognitive processing.

Dyslexic people have normal or even higher intelligence. They can be creative (strength), the most important characteristic of a composer or of a performer; they have interconnected reasoning (strength), the ability to make connections between things (i.e. relationships of similarity, analogy), which allows them to shift perspective and view an object from multiple perspectives [20]: this represents a fundamental need in the analysis of a music piece, where it is required to find the pre-thematic elements (i.e. the elements that will characterize the entire musical piece) and the connections among them; they have the ability to think critically (strength) and to synthesize information (strength): in musical analysis one of the most important thing is to define what is intended by motif repetition, more specifically which of the textual repetitions in the score could be associated to the definition of musical theme, when there are different repetitions and which criteria to adopt in order to select only the part that can be considered "meaningful" by an expert [21]; they have the ability to think outside the box, that means they have problem-solving abilities (strength): to better understand a composition it is necessary to recognize the thematic elements that are never such clearly expressed on the score by the musician (this lack of explanation can identify the musical language as a meta-language, without rules about syntactic and semantic elements of the compositions, that make art mysterious) [22].

People with dyslexia also have weaknesses. They have difficulties in reading (weakness) which entails difficulties in comprehending the content of the (musical) text (weakness); they can write and read, but they manage to do so using their capacities and energies at the maximum (weakness), given that they cannot do it automatically; they grow tired quickly (weakness), they make errors (weakness), fall behind and do not learn (weakness).

One of the major issues of the dyslexic student is the lack of autonomy in the learning process, which leads the individuals to disesteem and educational failure.

Most dyslexic students remember facts as experiences.

Focusing on weaknesses reduces their self-confidence, motivation and performance. That doesn't mean that the points of weakness must not be considered. Working on the weaknesses contributes to personal growth: improving something hard even slightly can make huge change in the student performance [23].

It is equally important to understand both the strengths and weaknesses. It is essential for self-development and personal growth. Students who are self-aware understand their abilities, interests and needs.

3 CAMA Software

The main aim of the software CAMA (*Computer Added Musical Analysis*) is to help students with learning disabilities to reach the learning goals, with the explicit purpose of managing the student's motivation in order to promote effective, active, efficient and satisfactory learning. The use of the software should offer the possibility for dyslexic students to work independently and successfully revising, practicing and learning new skill.

Fig. 1. Example of musical analysis

CAMA is able to read a music score from a MIDI file and identity the musical themes (see example in Fig. 1), through an algorithm based on the Entropy principle [24].

The final analysis will be shown on the video and it will be possible to print it on a sheet. The different musical objects identified by the algorithm, will be highlighted in a different color so as to allow putting emphasis on its own features (that may be rhythmic or melodic). This way an attempt is made to take advantage of the dyslexic student's visual thinking in order to reduce fatigue during studying.

CAMA is based on the concept of "discovery learning": learning through discovery provides opportunity for students to explore and experiment. The software also permits the student to select a musical segment within the music score read from the MIDI file and then highlight within the same score other segments that it considers to have the same characteristics (see Fig. 2). This kind of analysis is based on three musical operators regarding melodic transposition (the process of moving a sequence of notes up or down in pitch by a number of semitones), melodic inversion (the process through which a melody is transformed by inverting the direction of its single intervals in relation to the initial note, so that every ascending interval becomes descendent and vice versa) and melodic retrogradation (the process that consists in representing the melody backwards, from the last to the first note). The student can ask the software to find the segments that are subject to one of these characteristics (such as a transposed segment) or more than one of them (such as a segment with transposition and inversion), only clicking on the corresponding button of the CAMA interface.

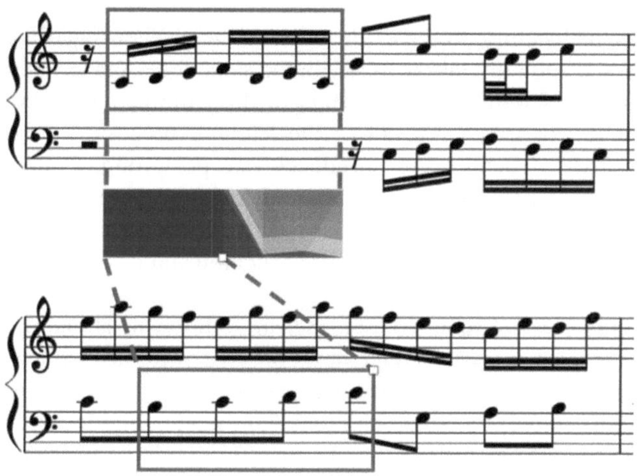

Fig. 2. Example of musical analysis

At the same time, the students can select two different segments and ask the algorithm to compare them, and display an isometric diagram that illustrates their differences through different colors. The colors are used to help the student to understand possible differences among the selected segments, taking thus advantage of the visual thinking of the dyslexic student in order to reduce fatigue during studying.

The interface has been designed as a set of buttons (see Fig. 3) every one of them with a specific musical function. After reading a score, the buttons of musical operators and analysis are enabled. The main area of the screen is a sort of musical editor where is shown the musical score and the corresponding analysis.

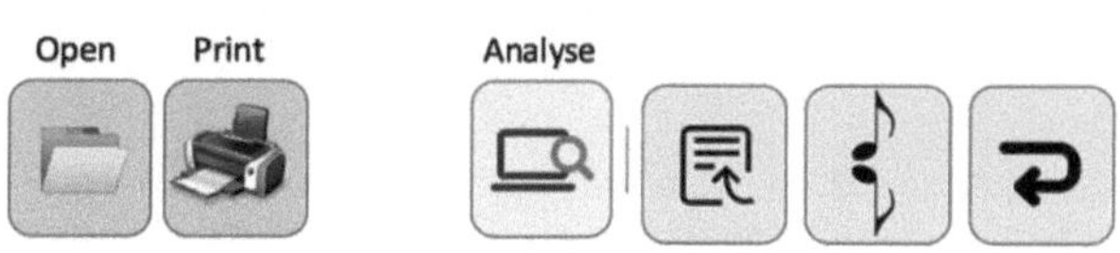

Fig. 3. CAMA interface

4 Application and Analysis

This research presents a case study referred to a pilot project realized in a Musical High-School where the Headmaster and all teachers were interested for the integration of innovative technologies in the learning process. In addition, attention was also taken to this kind of school due to its attention to dyslexic students.

The discipline forming the object of the project was Theory, Analysis and Composition. The project was conducted for a time period of 8 months (from October 2017 to May 2018) and it involved 51 students (aged 17 to 19) of witch 7 dyslexic students.

The project consisted of three phases.

In the first phase (2 months) characterized by classroom lessons, students participated in the lessons listening to the explanation of the teacher regarding new concepts of musical analysis, and only taking notes. In the same time, the teacher introduced the use of the CAMA software asking students to do some activities (only in class) to familiarize with it. For a better result of the learning process, 7 work groups were created: the dyslexic students were introduced one per group. Collaboratively work help all students (but particularly the dyslexic students) because they not only work on the assignments, cooperating by sharing ideas and experiences, but also enhance their skills. Moreover, it can reduce the risk of disorientation and consequently the anxiety in dyslexic students.

In the second phase (4 months), students in addition to attending the classroom lessons (where the teacher explained the new concepts of his academic program) had to participate in an online activity: a forum was created (using the computer environment *Moodle*) to permits students to share opinions, information and ideas, to collect and to analyse data, to draw conclusions, … During this period, dyslexic students were allowed to use, at home, CAMA for their personal study, sharing and comparing the results of their analysis with their classmates, on the forum.

In third phase (2 months), the teacher alternated group activities with individual activities helping students to work alone. At the end of this phase an examination was passed in the classroom, identical for all students (non dyslexic and dyslexic student) and the results were very satisfactory.

During the whole learning process the teacher observed a positive behaviours of the dyslexic students, including the desire to attempt analysis tasks in third phase. All students were actively involved in collaborative activity. Despite the difficulties, they managed to complete their tasks in a highly collaborative process. All of them said that "*the result of the work was a collaborative product and that the environment contributed to their collaboration*": they were all highly motivated to know the main potentialities of the new tool. Finally, students found CAMA more interesting, challenging and enjoyable, as well as it allows self-directed learning and makes them be proud of their work.

5 Discussion and Conclusions

The student with learning disabilities is not a person who does not want to learn or who is not committed enough. He/she has average to above average intelligence and has the same desire to learn like all other students. There is not only one type of disability for all students but each student can have a specific situation and the skills involved can be different and of different levels. Compensatory tools should not be perceived as an "excuse" by students and teachers. The goal is always to learn independently.

It is important to monitor the situation of each student to permit him/her to reach together with his classmates the educational objectives, that are common to the whole class. Teacher can use different approaches to satisfy the learning needs of all students, and can support students with compensatory tools including any technology that permits to increase, maintain or improve the abilities of a student affected by any kind of disability (and, indirectly, of any person).

In other words, teachers can use Assistive Technology that is certainly a very complex field even if sometimes the solution of problems may seem relatively simple. This means that teachers must reflect on/reconsider their own didactic methodologies.

This article highlights the opportunity offered by the AI systems: an opportunity that should be more thoroughly integrated into didactics, with formal and informal learning environments, with the teachers and their methodologies, with the existing resources and the activities performed by the students. The new AI-based technologies alone cannot improve a teaching/learning process. Teachers must be able to understand which technology to use and how to use it: the technology must support the student with learning disabilities and help him/her to become autonomous in carrying out specific tasks. For these reasons teacher must monitor dyslexic students during the whole learning process and not delegate the AI-based technology the task to solve a problem.

The development of technologies requires teachers with an innovative training in line with the times, able to lead students during the learning process.

References

1. Lieto, A., Radicioni, D.P.: From human to artificial cognition and back, new perspectives on cognitively inspired AI systems. Cogn. Syst. Res. (2016). https://doi.org/10.1016/j.cogsys.2016.02.002
2. Sousa, D.: How the Brain Learns, 4th edn. Corwin, Thousand Oaks (2011)
3. Macbeth, J.C.: Conceptual primitive decomposition for knowledge sharing via natural language. In: Proceedings of The Joint Ontology Workshops, Episode 3: The Tyrolean Autumn of Ontology. The International Association for Ontology and its Applications, Bolzano-Bozen, Italy (2017)
4. Andrea, K., Holz, E.M., Sellers, E.W., Vaughan, T.M.: Toward independent home use of brain-computer interfaces: a decision algorithm for selection of potential end-users. Arch. Phys. Med. Rehabil. **96**(3), S27–S32 (2015). https://doi.org/10.1016/j.apmr.2014.03.036
5. Popenici, S., Kerr, S.: Exploring the impact of artificial intelligence on teaching and learning in higher education. Res. Pract. Technol. Enhanced Learn. **12**, 22 (2017). https://doi.org/10.1186/s41039-017-0062-8

6. Hessels, M.P., Hessels-Schiatter, C., Bosson, M.S., Balli, Y.: Metacognitive teaching in a special education class. J. Cogn. Educ. Psychol. **8**(2), 182–201 (2011). https://doi.org/10.1891/1945-959.8.2.182
7. Mclaren, B.M., Scheuer, O., Mikkátko, J.: Supporting collaborative learning and e-discussions using artificial intelligence techniques. Int. J. Artif. Intell. Educ. **20**, 1–46 (2010). IOS Press
8. Differ. Improve teaching and learning with chatbots. https://www.differ.chat/bots. Accessed 2 Dec 2017
9. Della Ventura, M.: Creating inspiring learning environments by means of digital technologies: a case study of the effectiveness of whatsapp in music education. EAI Endorsed Trans. e-Learn. **4**, 1–9 (2017). https://eudl.eu/pdf/10.4108/eai.26-7-2017.152906
10. Holstein, K., McLaren, B.M., Aleven, V.: Intelligent tutors as teachers' aides. In: Proceedings of the Seventh International Learning Analytics & Knowledge Conference on -LAK 2017, New York, USA, pp. 257–266. ACM Press (2017)
11. Wang, F.H.: An exploration of online behaviour engagement and achievement in flipped classroom supported by learning management system. Comput. Educ. Pergamon **114**, 79–91 (2017)
12. Della Ventura, M.: Twitter as a music education tool to enhance the learning process: conversation analysis. In: Deng, L., Ma, W.W.K., Fong, C.W.R. (eds.) New Media for Educational Change. ECTY, pp. 81–88. Springer, Singapore (2018). https://doi.org/10.1007/978-981-10-8896-4_7
13. Graham, S., Harris, K.: Writing Better: Effective Strategies for Teaching Students with Learning Difficulties, 1st edn. Paul H Brookes Publishing Co., Inc., Baltimore (2005)
14. Ventura, M.: Using twitter to enhance the students' skills: motivation – a disregarded factor in educational design. In: Liu, S., Glowatz, M., Zappatore, M., Gao, H., Jia, B., Bucciero, A. (eds.) eLEOT 2018. LNICST, vol. 243, pp. 338–345. Springer, Cham (2018). https://doi.org/10.1007/978-3-319-93719-9_46
15. Busemann, S., Horacek, H.: Generating air quality reports from environmental data. In: Proceedings of the DFKI Workshop on Natural Language Generation, pp. 15–21
16. Pecore, J.L.: Beyond beliefs: teachers adapting problem-based learning to pre-existing systems of practice. Interdisc. J. Probl.-Based Learn. **7**(2), 6–33 (2013). https://doi.org/10.7771/1541-5015.1359
17. Leyser, Y., Greenberger, L., Sharoni, V., Vogel, G.: Students with disabilities and teachers education: changes in faculty attitudes toward accommodation over ten years. Int. J. Spec. Educ. **26**(1), 162–174 (2011)
18. Saccomanni, L.: Disturbi di apprendimento e Disturbo da deficit di attenzione/iperattività. In: Giornale Neuropsichiatria dell'Età Evolutiva, n. 19, pp. 93–104. Pacini Editore, Pisa (1999)
19. Lyon, G.R., Shaywitz, S.E., Shaywitz, B.A.: A definition of dyslexia. Ann. Dyslexia **53**, 1–14 (2003)
20. Lomas, T., Hefferon, K.: Positive Psychology Volume 5: Positive Psychology in Applied Settings. SAGE Publications, Thousand Oaks (2015)
21. Della Ventura, M.: Similarity measures for music information retrieval. In: Le, N.-T., Van Do, T., Nguyen, N.T., Thi, H.A.L. (eds.) ICCSAMA 2017. AISC, vol. 629, pp. 165–174. Springer, Cham (2018). https://doi.org/10.1007/978-3-319-61911-8_15
22. Della Ventura, M.: DNA Musicale: Matematicamente Suono. ABEditore, Milano (2018)
23. Sockalingam, N.: The relation between student satisfaction and student performance and blended learning curricula. Int. J. Learn. **18**(12), 121–134 (2012)
24. Della Ventura, M.: Relations between melody and rhythm on music analysis: representations and algorithms for symbolic musical data. In: Proceedings of the 3rd International Conference on Applied Physics and Mathematics, Hong Kong, China (2013)

Otowik: Mining Text from Wikis to Mind Maps

Vinothini Kasinathan[1(✉)], Aida Mustapha[2], and Mohamad Firdaus Che Abdul Rani[1]

[1] School of Computing, Asia Pacific University of Technology and Innovation, Technology Park Malaysia, 57000 Bukit Jalil, Kuala Lumpur, Malaysia
[2] Faculty of Computer Science and Information Technology, Universiti Tun Hussein Onn Malaysia, Parit Raja, 86400 Batu Pahat, Johor, Malaysia

Abstract. The impact of the Internet on education has been recognized for decades in which learners or students are able to access educational resources cross borders and languages. However, exposure to or provision of too much information or data will lead to information overload, which dampens understanding and effective decision making. In this paper, we share a software named Otowik that is able to extract keywords and keyphrases from wiki pages and automatically construct a mind map based on the keywords and keyphrases extracted. Otowik was evaluated via a User Acceptance Test and was highly recommended by the participating respondents.

Keywords: Text mining · Keyphrase extraction · Wikipedia

1 Introduction

The world-wide web (WWW or the web) is an information space or storage of various documents, text contents, images and a variety of other web resources are identified by Uniform Resource Locators (URLs). Due to the vast growing information and knowledge which is obtainable through the world-wide web, it is often the preferable channel of choice for students to obtain information on their education or relevant topics for their assignments. Especially with the help of various great search engines which exist in the current high-tech world such as Google, Yahoo, Bing and many more, it is significantly easier and faster for students to obtain information on a specific topic or their relevant field of studies in the web. This, in turn, leads to the new form of distance learning features where the idea of "global school" surfaced because courses and content can always be reached despite the location and time. This also means that school/college space, time and organization will no longer be a limitation for people to decide on the configuration of their own learning [1]. Besides than being just a form of distance learning, the world-wide web provides information on extensive range of topics including those that are highly specific and rare, which are often not easily obtainable if searched from the variety of existing books. This is the easiest, fastest, and cheapest ways of accessing necessary information cited in [2].

Although the world-wide web as an education tool has been a very beneficiary and indispensable source for students, the issue of whether the information provided by

L. Uden et al. (Eds.): LTEC 2019, CCIS 1011, pp. 23–35, 2019.
https://doi.org/10.1007/978-3-030-20798-4_3

these web pages on any relevant topics are all important and are students able to effectively gasp the information hurled to them in a huge amount of text content is raised. For example, a given scenario where a student searches for a particular topic in the world-wide web and the big amount of data obtained as results often drowns the students with huge amount of information which may or may not be important for the searched topic which only leads to the doubt of how well students are able to use this method of text learning to learn effectively. Prior to [1], findings back then stated that the vast majority of the existing educational websites are still heavily based on text where 93% of the sites included multiple amount of text fields in all of its pages, 58% included one image per page, 96.1% did not include interactive images, 81.9% did not included interactive animation or sound which only describes how heavily dependent web pages are to text and wordings.

Wikis such as Wikipedia and other Wikis are becoming the latest trend of tools being used for knowledge structuring and sharing. The common processes of knowledge formation are exploration, tentative guessing and trial-error conduct where knowledge formation works hand to hand with regular knowledge revising. In the Wiki environment, the knowledge content and structure evolves and grow by the supporting community [3]. As time goes by, large structures of articles, content and categories are formed which eventually requires the attention of manual refactoring. Refactoring is a process of amending the internal structure without changing it external behaviors. Wiki refactoring can provide changes to Wiki internal structure in terms of how well its navigation is while maintaining the original content and authorship of the content.

During the 10 years of observing how people use the web, [4] observed that there was a significant difference between how website owners think people use the web and how they actually use them. What most people actually do most of the time is glance at the web page, scan some text and clicks the first link that catches their interest or vaguely resembles the thing they are looking for. This well-known fact about web use is that most users tend to only spend a small amount of time "reading" websites, instead they scan websites for words or any sort of phrases which is relevant to what they are looking for. These issues raise the concern of how effective will it be for students to use the websites for learning without missing out on the large part of the pages, important information or keywords they are looking for. Such situation often leads students to move on to different web pages which they think they have a better chance finding a particular information and without doubt the same mistakes of missing out on large part of the web pages is prone to recur, hence resulting an ineffective learning experience. To assist users or learners to get better results in learning via the world wide web, this work proposes a mechanism to the represent the content of unstructured information in websites into a structured form with the use of mind map techniques.

Mind maps or mind mapping is a method which you can make notes or take notes that helps your memory to remember. Mind map a diagram in which information is represented visually, usually with a central idea placed in the middle and associated ideas arranged around it. The literature revealed that there are major advantages of applying the mind mapping technique in education regardless of web-based or conventional way. As mind mapping is well-known for the collaboration and combination of imagery, color and visual arrangements, it has been proven that it can significantly improve information recalling compared to the conventional way of note taking and learning. Mind mapping has been proven to increase recall rate up to 32% [5, 6] and improve long-term memory of facts in their participants by 10%. It is reported by the participants also have a deeper level of processing and understanding. Finally, integrating mind mapping into learning comprehension skills boost student's understanding and memory of comprehension passages [7]. Mind maps also provide creativity boosts. Common issues that occur during a session of brainstorming among students are scenarios like brain freeze and writer's block. These issues are the effect of handling big amount of information and the inability for students to sort and organize the information that are absorbed during web-based learning process. One of the best mechanism of mind maps is the spatial layout characteristic that is able to provide students a better overview and makes connections between facts. This is ideal in fostering creativity and generation of new ideas as infinite amount of thoughts, ideas and associations on topics can be created [5].

The remainder of this paper is structured as follows. Section 2 presents the related areas from which the work is proposed and developed. Section 3 presents the proposed extraction system called Otowik (automatically extract keywords and keyphrases from wiki pages). Section 4 presents the evaluation findings and finally Sect. 5 concludes with some indication for future work.

2 Related Areas

Text mining is a sub-process of data mining, which is commonly used to identify patterns that are hidden and important information from big amount of unstructured text materials [8]. A supporting definition by [9], stated that text mining is a field that seeks to extract useful information from unstructured textual data through the identification and exploration of interesting patterns. It is essential to understand why these text mining approach is used specifically for these hidden significant information and patterns to be analyzed. Text mining approach is used towards analyzing texts that are different compared with the kind of data stored in databases, text is unstructured, amorphous, and difficult to deal with algorithmically [10]. In order to identify certain specific patterns or significant information, text mining uses several approaches and techniques in order to achieve that as understood by the researcher.

According to [8], text mining uses techniques of different fields like machine learning, visualization, case-based reasoning, text-analysis, knowledge management and information extraction to identify these patterns and important information. On the other hand, [11] stated that the several techniques that are proposed to text mining also includes conceptual structure, association rule mining, episode-mining, decision trees and rule induction method. This information provides the researcher with a wide scope to evaluate in understanding the main key techniques to be considered and evaluated. As stated in [8], the main three steps that are taken place after any sort of data in stored in the form of text are the preprocessing of data, the application of a text mining technique and the bare analysis of results. Figure 1 shows the general processes of text mining.

Within text mining, various technology premises included are Summarization, Information Extraction, Categorization, Visualization, Clustering, Topic Tracking and

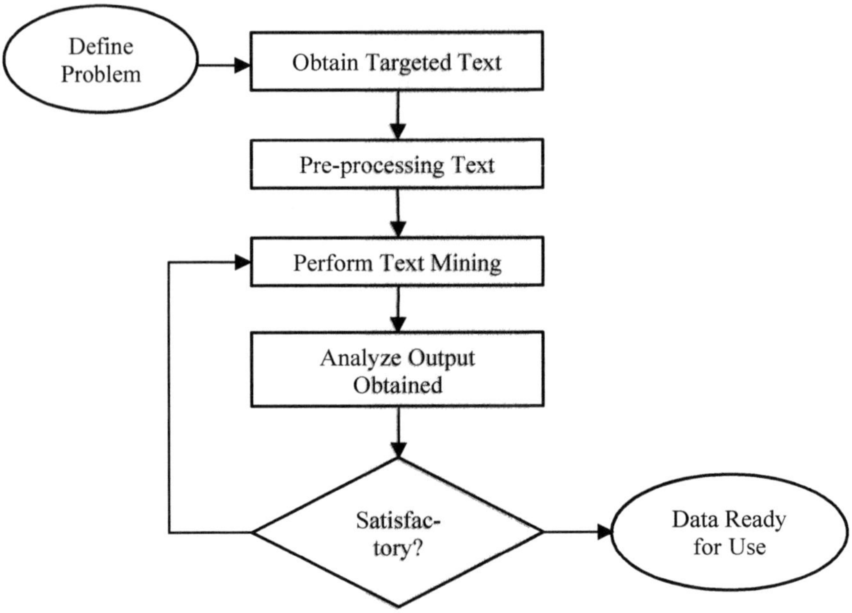

Fig. 1. General processes in text mining [21]

Sentiment Analysis [8]. This work focuses on Information Extraction in order to represent the unstructured form of wiki content into a structure form of mind maps with relations. Onto understanding the purpose of information extraction within the text mining implementation, [8] reasoned out that when data is in unstructured form, information cannot be extracted out by ease. It is explained in the source that in Information Extraction, natural language documents are first converted into structured documents allowing the information to be extracted. However, it is stated as the aim of Information extraction is to create structured view to represent information which is understood by machines [12].

One of the common information extraction tasks include Named Entity Recognition (NER). The general understanding of Named Entities are real world entities such as "Malaysia", "John" and "Google Inc. The task of named entity recognition, often abbreviated as NER, is to identify named entities from free-form text and to classify them such as organizations (e.g., 'World Health Organization'), persons (e.g., 'Muammar Kaddafi'), place names (e.g., 'the Baltic Sea'), temporal expressions (e.g., '1 September 2011'), numerical and currency expressions (e.g., '20 Million Euros') [13]. This information will be taken down as a key information to the researcher in understanding the representation of data within the applied information extraction technique. Although there are more tasks related to information extraction, it is essential to focus on the name entity recognition as entity recognition is probably the most fundamental task in information extraction. Figure 2 illustrates the steps undertaken commonly in the process of information extraction as adopted from [8].

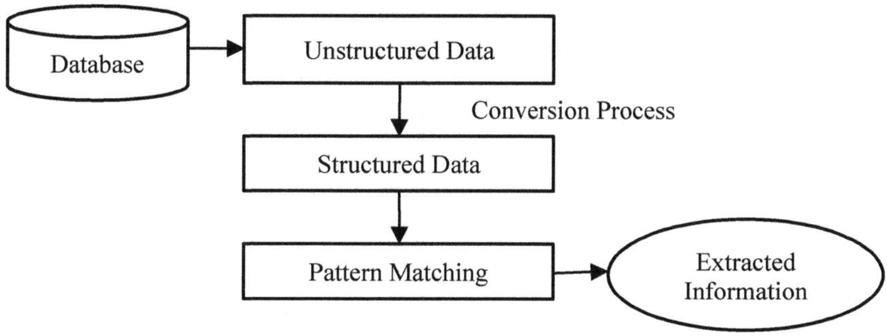

Fig. 2. Steps of information extraction [8]

Based on these premises, Otowik will be a tool for students to insert URL of websites contain knowledge revolving their preferred area of studies. Then, Otowik will convert these texts based knowledge representation into useful form of mind maps in a PowerPoint slide. Otowik as an idea proves that there are various benefits to be integrated within the web-based learning education of students. Otowik could be used as an application to redefine the structure of information and knowledge represented within the websites that are available. Students will find Otowik useful as it would convert the text representation of knowledge and information of knowledge base websites such as Wikipedia, ordinary web-pages and relevant informative content into structured form of knowledge representation with high quality information which is mind maps. With the text mining technology, Otowik will be able to filter necessary important information from a huge amount of text based content into structure form knowledge which is the mind map. This means important knowledge and information can be extracted from big amount of text-based content, hence students will worry less on information which they are unsure of its importance and about missing parts of web pages.

3 Otowik

Otowik provides a mechanism to automatically convert text-based knowledge representation in webpages (in specific wiki pages) into structural form of knowledge in the form of mind maps. Otowik uses libraries containing PowerPoint tools to generate these mind maps as output. In this case, the generated mind map will be displayed in form of PowerPoint slides which allows user interaction as well. For this instance, the Otowik can be a powerful tool because students will be able to move key-points, recolor important key-points and even connect them to different key-points which proves how Otowik can surpass the method of text reading as an educational tool. This overall will provide students authority, preferences and likings in interacting (managing) these generate mind maps to best suit their studying style. By using Otowik, student will be given a more like “privilege” to avoid high amount of text reading but instead put some sort of “reliability” in the key-points obtained through the generated mind maps. Students will be able to avoid spending vast amount of time huge amount of information which is scattered all over a web-page but instead understand the relation of each information to each other in the form of a mind map "connectors". The feature of pairing a visual image/diagram corresponding to the information consist in the map will allow students to understand certain non-familiarized terms/words.

The targeted user of the Otowik system will be primarily undergraduate students due to their common practice of accessing the Internet and WWW on sites such as Wikipedia, informative web-pages for information regarding their education purposes. Although the target users are isolated as a priority, but as the Otowik system works for generally any sort of websites, therefore its usage could be benefited for a wide variety of crowd as well. For instances, the intended learning based Otowik Mind mapping tool can also be used for the group of educators and home use as well to in fact generate any form of text based content into a summarize structured. As one of the additional features of the generated mind maps in terms of key-points is to be guided along with a sample picture of the specific key, this will further improve users understanding of Key-points generated by the Otowik mind maps. Figure 3 shows the steps involved in build Otowik.

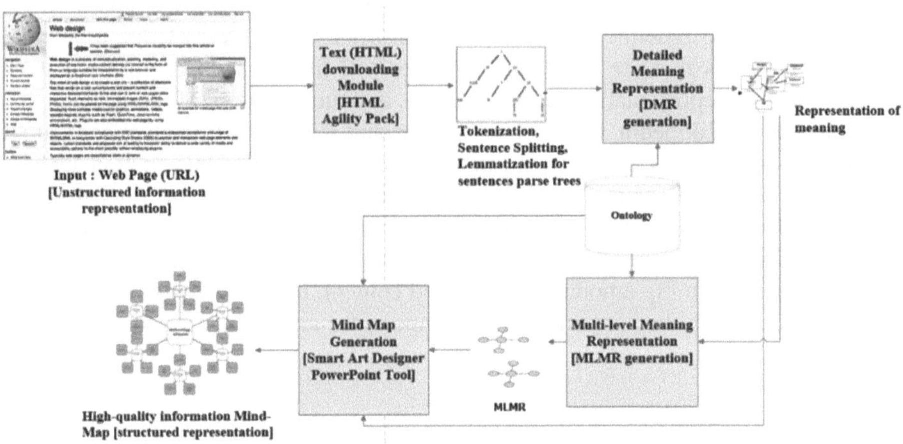

Fig. 3. Framework of Otowik

Basically, the URL on the Wikipedia page is pasted into system user interface, the HTML codes are then changed into, the keyphrase extraction algorithm called MiKe [14, 15] extract the keywords and keyphrases, and finally Otowik generates the mind map in the form is PowerPoint. Next, Fig. 4 shows the user interface for Otowik. Note that there is only one page that is used for user interaction. As shown the figure, only four components will require action-driven event and to interact with the Otowik system. Users are firstly required to input a preferred website link (URL) in the "Insert URL" text box. Then users are required to click the "Download Web Content" button which is proceed to download the necessary HTML content from the web page of the provided URL. Once a message box displays "web page content is downloaded. please proceed to generate mind-map", users can then click the "Generate MindMap" button which will make the system to scan quality information and form a fully formed mind map. After mind map is successfully generated, users can click "Open Mind Map" button which will make the system direct the users to Microsoft PowerPoint where the generated mind map will be ready for users to refer as shown in Fig. 5.

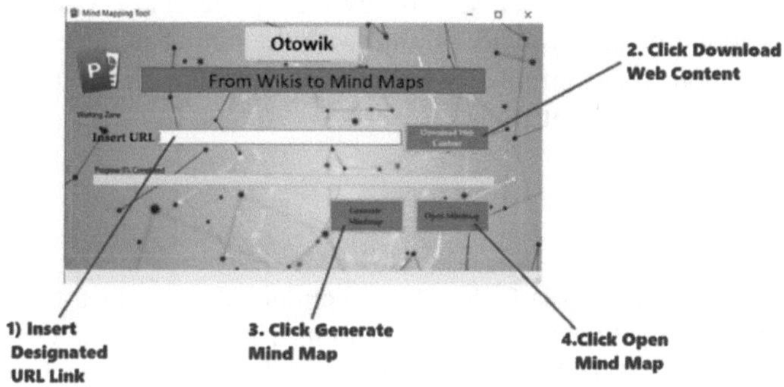

Fig. 4. User interface of Otowik

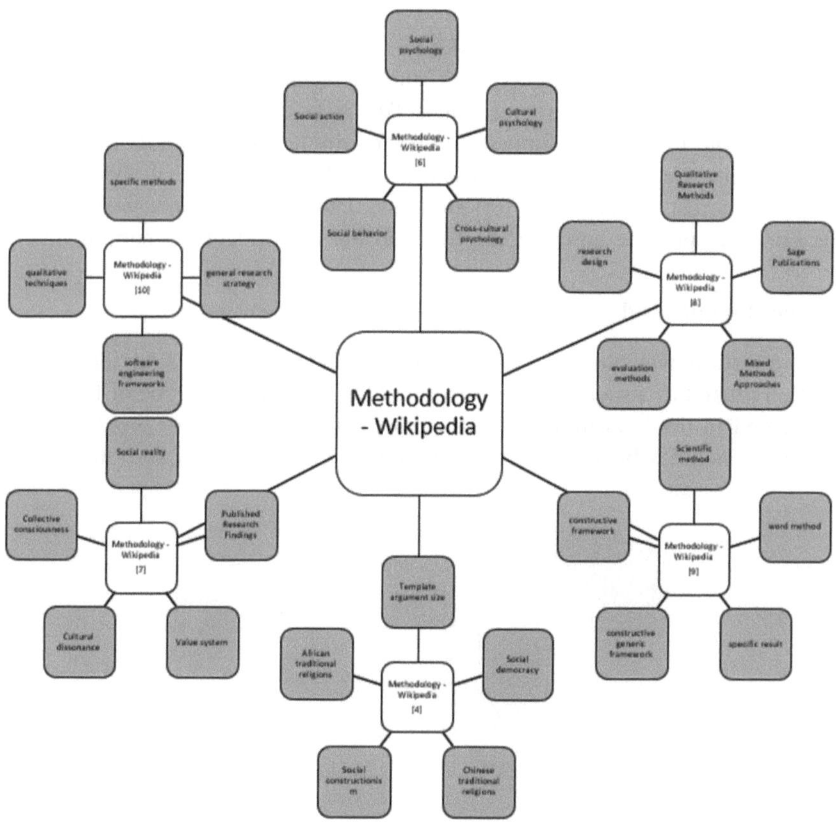

Fig. 5. Output of Otowik

The generated mind map of Otowik will be displayed in Microsoft PowerPoint. The structure of the mind map involves objects that are created using PowerPoint Library tools to fit in the high-quality information that is generated. In addition to that, users are allowed to interact with the output as this work-around is within the Microsoft PowerPoint environment. This allows amendments or further editing in information on the mind map to allow users to actively use by their preferences. Users can even add any other PowerPoint objects to work-around with the output of generated mind-map. This provides a more like "infinite" work-around with the generated mind-map of Otowik which users can benefit from.

4 Results and Testing

The User Acceptance Test (UAT) has been conducted according to the Test Plan strategized. UAT involved the targeted users of Otowik, which are university students. This students are from Asia Pacific University of Technology and Innovation. The university has huge number of international students around 12, 000 from more than 130 countries studying in the campus where this study was conducted. With the cosmopolitan learning environment, the undergraduate level 1 students were used in the testing of OtoWik system. Age between 19 to 21 years old. All participants were briefed on the mechanics of Otowik and how it can be used in their daily task within their studying environment. The pool of students will be selected and divided into category depending on the course of study. This is to ensure that the Otowik system will be applicable to not only limited number of domain information, but rather as a generic tool to be used for students across different disciplines. The number of students involved as the respondents was 100 students. The questionnaires were built using Google Forms to provide an easier approach to the respondents or participants.

4.1 User Background

The first question was the background of the students. This is to identify which information related to a specific course is limited to; in terms of scope of knowledge to be represented in the final mind map. As shown in Fig. 6, each of the 20% from the domain areas includes business, computing, engineering, medical and other areas.

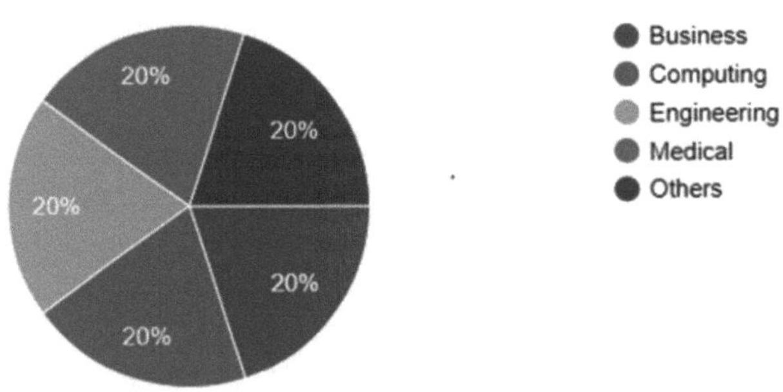

Fig. 6. User background

4.2 User Acceptance

The second question was on to identify how difficult is it for students to use the Otowik system. This will allow the rooms for improvement in understanding whether any changes in terms of user interface. In Fig. 7, all the respondents agreed and rated at max scale of 5 stating that Otowik system is easy to use. This will provide an insight to researcher that the current interface suffices to allow users understanding of the workflow.

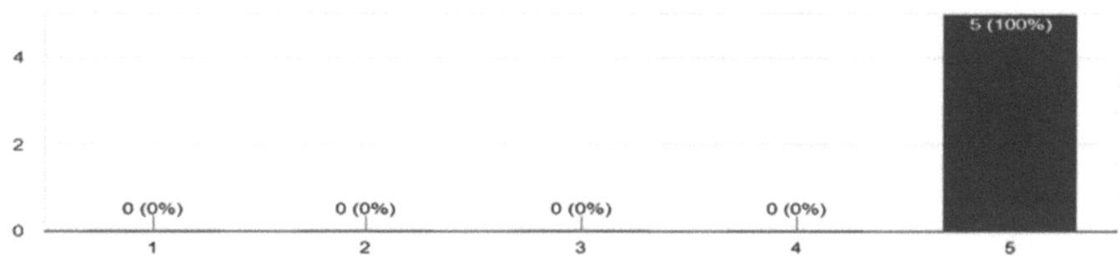

Fig. 7. User acceptance the Otowik

4.3 Accuracy of Output

The third question is to identify the accuracy level of output from Otowik. This will allow to receive feedbacks on whether information that is being represented are all relevant to students. Based on Fig. 8, the respondents [60%] agreed that Otowik system generated a mind-map with accurate and high-quality information while 2 respondents [40%] agreed that it only generated averagely accurate information. No respondents found that the information generated by Otowik system is invalid or irrelevant to the subject topic.

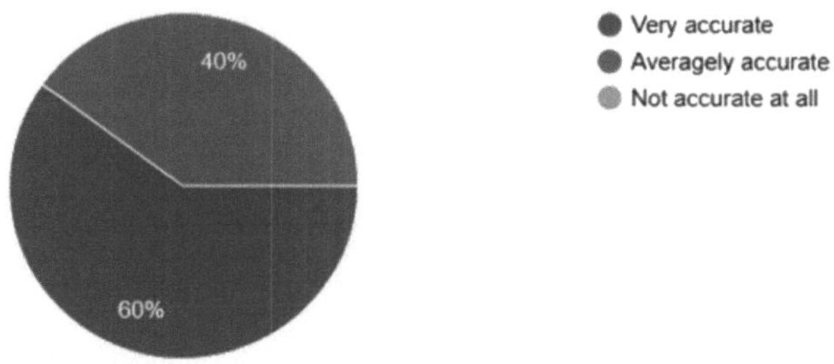

Fig. 8. User satisfaction of using Otowik

4.4 Quality of Output

The fourth question was to identify whether any unwanted or replicated information are being represented in the generated mind map. This provides an insight on whether amendments are required for a better quality of information. From Fig. 9, the respondents [40%] rated the scale of 4, 2 respondents [40%] rated the scale of 3 and while 1 rated the scale of the completely disagree that the mind-map generates unnecessary and redundant information. This shows that the information that are being generated somehow plays a role in the subject topic and the relevance is maintained as most of them rated towards disagreeing. This provides assurance that the theoretical understanding of high-quality information is being practically implemented successfully.

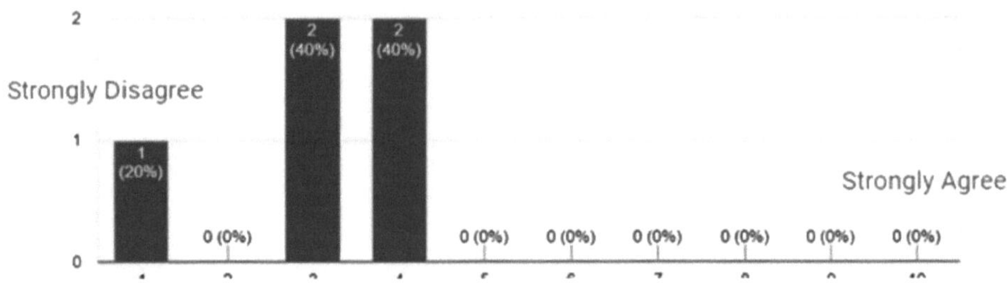

Fig. 9. User input on redundant information by Otowik

4.5 Overall Acceptance

The fifth question was to identify the overall acceptance level of Otowik to be present as a studying tool to be used in a daily basis. Based on Fig. 10, the scale results indicate the overall acceptance of the Otowik system by the pool of students involved in the User Acceptance Test. 4 of the respondents [80%] rated 4 out of 5 stating the system's usefulness if it is integrated with students daily studying routine. While 1 rated 3 out of 5 for its usefulness. Overall, the feedback received in terms of acceptance rate is above average and considered good. This provides that the entire Otowik system is ready to be brought to the real-world application.

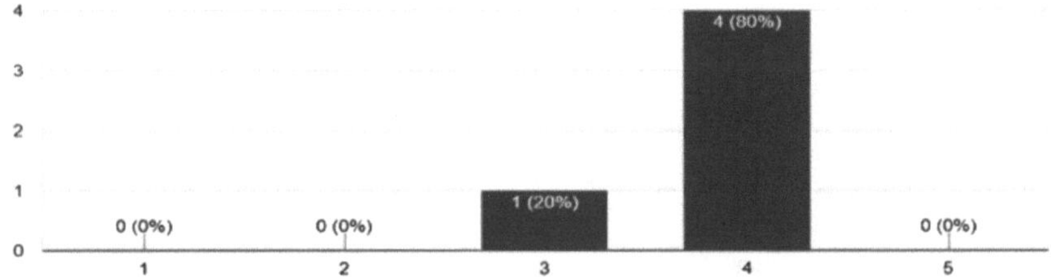

Fig. 10. User acceptance of Otowik as a studying tool

5 Conclusion and Future Development

The advancement of technology today enables information to flow across various means, be it through digital media or printed materials. Similar concerns were also expressed by [16] that too much data or information is impossible to be process by any database. Websites contain too much text information, which not only require user's patience and time to digest all required information but such huge amount of information may pose a challenge to the users to be focused and interested in the information presented before them. Thus, there is indeed a need to create applications to help people better manage information [17]. In this regard, websites are better to be represented as structured, giving users the required information in a simpler structured form, thus focusing on only what's necessary, relevant and current, as requested. However, as pointed by [18], that with limited time in hand, there is a need to find ways to process information in a more efficient way and structure the data in a timely fashionable manner. In this regard, building an effective tool such as Otowik that can covert huge web-based information content into high-quality structured information becomes necessary.

Otowik is an extraction system that is capable to automatically extract keywords and keyphrases from websites (in specific wiki pages) and generate a mind map based on the keywords and keyphrases extracted. There are several limitations that the current Otowik system. One of the limitation of Otowik is that it is designed based on Wikipedia pages as a foundation. Therefore, the generated mind map is highly suitable only for such wiki pages. Although Otowik can be used for just any websites and various websites that exist, there is no best way to understand all the existing websites design and how their HTML contents are organized. As the result, Otowik provides unorganized information or inaccurate information depending on different websites. As these intelligent systems are built in different environments or for different input types, integrating such intelligent systems to work with web pages is indeed a difficult one. Further development of Otowik must take into consideration of the amount of content a web page may have and to understand simply because any web page design is equally challenging. These challenges and factors may affect the quality of generated keywords and keyphrases. OtoWik words the same way as how a mind map is design and used. Due to information overload OtoWik helps by automatically drawing main concept or idea and the rest of the map revolves around it, it starts from the middle point with the main topic or chapter topic. From that main node, create branches not more than 5 for the human brain to remember and that each represent a single word that relates to the main topic. Then it creates the sub-branches that stem from the main branches to further expand on ideas and concepts. These sub-branches will also contain words that elaborate on the topic of the branch it stems from. This helps develop and elaborate on the overall theme of the mind map. Visual thinking is a learning style where the learner better understands and retains information when ideas, words and concepts are associated with images. Research tells us that the majority of students in a regular classroom need to see information in order to learn it. Some common visual learning strategies include creating graphic organizers, diagramming, mind mapping, outlining and more.

Nonetheless, Otowik promises saving of cost, money and Internet resources due to avoidance of manually loading web pages which could consume big amount of Internet data for small plan Internet users. Saving cost in contact of now usage of papers and students can understand the topic and ideas much faster and accurately instead of them spending time drawing a mind map which leads to miss understanding of the points. The final mind map drawn into powerpoint helps students use as learning piece of work and they can add in more information from their readings which helps them as outline into difficult topics. As the student does not need to waste time brainstorming the idea or concepts. They have more time to do critical thinking and adding on new ideas and process thoughts. This helps them recall they keywords and keyphrases for exams.

As various web-pages that exist contains different elements such as advertising, pop-ups and elements that utilizes a decent amount of Internet data consumptions. In addition, students can avoid wasting papers on redundantly writing notes based on the information in the Internet or web-pages but instead interact with the generated mind maps in the PowerPoint slides to perform their form of studying. Students who do not have access to Internet that uses Internet café to access the Internet to collect notes on their studies can significantly reduce the amount time (money) spent at these Internet cafés (paid service) by avoiding the necessity to read all these web-pages but instead use Otowik to convert all these web-pages into generated mind maps in forms of PowerPoint slides which to be studied at home later. Huge amount of papers and printing usage is done in common scenarios of printing big amount of web pages in order to study their knowledge content, this can be avoided as the Otowik is able to generate mind maps of the content of a single web-page into a single PowerPoint slide.

There are several ways the Otowik system can be upgraded as a future enhancement in providing a better experience and better results to the users. The enhancements include (1) picture representation; to provide a sample picture as an assisting element to each generated high-quality information in the mind-map, (2) color representation; to use different color in different category in order to get high quality information. The (3) to have a mobile version so students could excess with their hand held devices. The new version will include combination for slides extraction into mind map and Wikipedia extraction mind map. The prototype in progress.

Acknowledgement. This research is supported by Asia Pacific University of Technology and Innovation.

References

1. Mioduser, D., Nachmias, R., Tubin, D., Forkosh-Baruch, A.: Models of pedagogical implementation of ICT in Israeli schools. J. Comput. Assist. Learn. **18**(4), 405–414 (2002)
2. Davinson, N., Sillence, E.: It won't happen to me: promoting secure behaviour among internet users. Comput. Hum. Behav. **26**(6), 1739–1747 (2010)
3. Brailas, A., Koskinas, K., Dafermos, M., Alexias, G.: Wikipedia in education: acculturation and learning in virtual communities. Learning, Culture and Social Interaction **1**(7), 59–70 (2015)
4. Krug, S.: Don't Make Me Think: A Common Sense Approach to the Web, 2nd edn. New Riders, San Francisco (2005)
5. Buzan, T.: Mind Maps for Kids: Max Your Memory and Concentration. Harper Collins, New York (2005)
6. Toi, H.: Research on how mind map improves memory. In: International Conference on Thinking, Kuala Lumpur, Malaysia (2009)
7. Moi, W.A., Lian, O.L.: Introducing mind map in comprehension. In: Annual Meeting of the Redesigning Pedagogy International Conferences: Culture, Knowledge and Understanding (2007)

8. Kaushik, A., Naithani, S.A.: Comprehensive study of text mining approach. Int. J. Comput. Sci. Netw. Secur. **16**(2), 69 (2016)
9. Radovanovic, M., Ivanovic, M.: Text mining: approaches and applications. Novi Sad J. Math. **38**(3), 227–234 (2008)
10. Tsai, F.S.: A tag-topic model for blog mining. Expert Syst. Appl. **38**(5), 5330–5335 (2011)
11. Frank, E., Chui, C., Witten, I.H.: Text categorization using compression models
12. Saggion, H., Poibeau, T.: Automatic text summarization: past, present and future. In: Poibeau, T., Saggion, H., Piskorski, J., Yangarber, R. (eds) Multi-source, Multilingual Information Extraction and Summarization, Springer, Heidelberg (2013). 10.1007/978-3-642-28569-1_1
13. Aggarwal, C.C., Zhai, C. (eds.): Mining Text Data. Springer Science & Business Media, Berlin (2012)
14. Kasinathan, V., Mustapha, A., Murad, M.A.A., Rahmat, R.W., Mansor, E.I.: Presentation mining tool: from slides to mind maps. Information **19**(7B), 3003 (2016)
15. Kasinathan, V., Mustapha, A., Murad, M.A.A., Rahmat, R.W., Mansor, E.I.: The mechanics of the presentation mining framework. Jurnal Teknologi **78**(8–2), 80–88 (2016)
16. Kudelic, R., Malekovic, M., Lovrencic, A.: Mind map generator software. In: 2012 IEEE International Conference on Computer Science and Automation Engineering (CSAE), 3, pp. 123–127 (2012)
17. Kudelic, R., Konecki, M., Malekovic, M.: Mind map generator software model with text mining algorithm. In: Proceedings of the ITI 2011, 33rd International Conference on Information Technology Interfaces (ITI), pp. 487–494 (2011)
18. Ingersoll, G.S., Morton, T.S., Farris, A.L.: Taming Text: How to Find, Organize, and Manipulate It. Manning Publications Co., Shelter Island (2013)

Exploring the Potential of Using Augmented Reality and Virtual Reality for STEM Education

Rula Al-Azawi[1(✉)], Ali Albadi[1], Raziyeh Moghaddas[1], and Jonathan Westlake[2]

[1] Gulf College, Seeb, Oman
rulaalaazawi@yahoo.com,
{aalbadi,raziyeh}@gulfcollege.edu.om
[2] Staffordshire University, Staffordshire, UK
j.c.westlake@staffs.ac.uk

Abstract. The purpose of this article is to focus on the potential of using new technologies such as Augmented Reality and Virtual Reality in science education in general and in STEM education in particular. Although Augmented Reality and Virtual Reality as a technology have strength and weaknesses, this article focus to show how those technologies may facilitate STEM education and how to improve the area of weaknesses. In this research, we address the need for STEM education and training, which is currently either limited or not interested for students. It is also overcome the distance limitation that students face in STEM education. Furthermore, Augmented Reality and Virtual Reality environments are an effective platform to encourage and attracting the new generation technology to STEM field. Technology virtualization has been used in a various way in STEM classroom to encourage creatively and innovation. However, it is also important to take in our consideration that students learning in this environment can be difficult in many directions.

1 Introduction

This article aims to study the assess impact of the next generation Virtual Reality (VR) and Augmented Reality (AR) to increase the engagement, effectiveness and the quality of student learning contents of STEM education.

STEM training specialists are required to be at the forefront of technology and how it may fit into their classroom. This is particularly essential on the grounds that undeniably, instructors are getting themselves encompassed by new students that hope to be engaged with participatory, intelligent, interactive with opportunities for students to be more creative [1].

Previous work discussed the STEM (Science, Technology, Engineering and Math) education needs for suitable learning tools to enhance the quality of engineering education.

This prospect combined with the way that technological advancements and mobile devices have turned out to be pervasive parts of our lives, roused the creators to investigate the likelihood of utilizing cell phones and tablet as instrumental guides to

L. Uden et al. (Eds.): LTEC 2019, CCIS 1011, pp. 36–44, 2019.
https://doi.org/10.1007/978-3-030-20798-4_4

enhance the quality of classroom educating and learning. In particular, a context- aware augmented reality application was used to create a pop-up book by superimposing 3D graphics (virtual models, animations) and multimedia (images, videos, sounds) over the pages of a construction engineering textbook. This empowered students to watch, connect with, and learn abstract topics in development methods and techniques in different settings [2].

The new generation of students is technology savvy with high knowledge of and interest in social media, mobile technologies, and strategy games [3]. Several school systems have recently initiated plans to deploy various types of classroom technology aimed at providing students with higher quality education with long-lasting impact. However, studies indicate that using technology without a suitable pedagogical structure may not yield desired outcome and can even have negative impact on student learning and long-term knowledge retention [4]. Therefore, having a technology-based pedagogical learning tool besides traditional learning methods could potentially enhance the learning quality [5].

It is very likely that within the next several years, instructional techniques that benefit from new emerging technologies such as virtual reality (VR) and augmented reality (AR) will become standard components of STEM education. Such techniques will better assist teachers to be more effective when explaining abstract topics, while providing students with a means to collaborate on a common problem which ultimately strengthens their teamwork, communication, and critical thinking skills. This paper presents the latest results of an on-going research project which aims at exploring the potential of mobile context-aware AR in STEM education [2].

This paper is structured as follows: Section two presents a brief introduction of AR and the usage of AR in education. Section three describes a brief introduction of VR and the usage of VR in education. Section four explains the STEM education in details. Section five and six explain the potential of using VR and AR in STEM education. Section seven presents the conclusions and future work.

2 Augmented Reality: A Brief Introduction

The latest development technologies are Augmented Reality which can be easily applied in many different tools such as computers, tablet and smart phone. AR also can be utilized through wearable components such as glasses [6].

Augmented Reality (AR) is defined based on three characteristic [7]:

1. The combination of virtual and real objects in a real environment through mobile devices.
2. Runs intuitively and in real time.
3. Virtual and real objects are combining together in the same environment.

Currently, most of the smart phone, tablet equipped with many of latest technology such as sensors, camera, accelerometer and gyroscope. These sensors and extra features allows the smart-phone to form a virtual perception of the real world and deal with augmented layer of information on the real world as a simple motivation way. Augmented Reality has a great potential to be used as a new technology in education. Many studies focus on the application of AR in the real life, only few studies conducted in the educational field. Actually, the number of studies for using VR in education has been increased recently and AR has been used in different field of education [8].

The next section explains AR in education field and showing the benefit and limitation that mention from the literature review.

2.1 Augmented Reality in Education

Technology in education can affect students to learn adequately and can encourage them, prompting a suitable method of learning. Past research has perceived the issue that innovation will make by not included learning process if the innovation used does not advance promote critical thinking and meaning-making. Since its introduction, Augmented Reality (AR) has been seemed to have extraordinary potential in impacting the learning procedure more dynamic, successful and important [9].

Augmented Reality used to improve the teaching and learning knowledge by connecting with the student to investigate the world by utilizing interactive media components to help the examination of the encompassing.

The students trusted that the integration of technologies would help them in their learning process. Hence, instructors have started to look for technology that can possibly be incorporated in training keeping in mind the end goal to enable students to learn effectively and to enhance their seeing particularly in Science subjects [9]. Augmented Reality is a new way to improve the 3D shape instead of using wood object. Many advantage of Augmented reality are highlight it by many authors as shown below [10]:

1. Provide an easy communication among real and virtual environments [11].
2. Give teachers an approach to fortify students understanding in the classroom by Augmenting physical props with Virtual explanations and outlines [12].
3. Makes a learning knowledge that is connected to the formal classroom, so students can learn outside of class hours and outside of school limits [13].
4. Enables the visualization of interactions among static 2D/3D images and 3D dynamic images (animations) [14].

AR technology has picked up a following in the educational market for its capacity to bridge gaps and convey a more substantial way to deal with learning. Student-centered exercises are improved by the incorporation of virtual and real-world experience [8].

AR offers another type of intuitiveness between the physical and virtual world and improves users perceptions of actual world. As indicated by Wu et al's review [15], AR enables students to create essential practices and has become one of the key emerging technologies in education [16].

3 Virtual Reality: A Brief Introduction

It's an unpredictable type of technology that utilization closeness 3D imaging to trick the brain into trusting that the user is immersed in the virtual reality world, and exceptionally tools to enable user to associate with that reality to fluctuating degrees.

Achieving the concept immersion is the main objective of Virtual Reality. Jennett [17] defines immersion as the involvement with the Virtual condition which causes the absence of consciousness of the real time and real world, causing an affair of "being" in this Virtual universe. Jennet worked on this definition considering game context, yet the embodiment of such definition could be investigated while examining any Virtual Reality environment. "Immersion" in Virtual Reality is usually utilized as a part of regard of "spatial immersion", the impression of quality in a non- physical world, which is caused by the stimulation of images, animations, sounds and others interactivity aspects. The user can investigate the Virtual environment in 360 degrees. Virtual Reality technology does not include other human detects, for example, taste, smell, and touch.

In the previous decades, the beginning time of Virtual Reality has been integrated development in view of the intelligent 3D designs, UI, and visual simulation [18]. Virtual Reality draws in individuals' consideration, and the technology has been connected in pharmaceutical, industry, education, computer games, tourism and other industries [19].

3.1 Virtual Reality in Education

In education field, a new term has been arisen and used widely in education which is Computerized learning environments. In such case, the students are given the chance to solve well-defined problems using technology and technological resources particularly intended for the learning environment [20]. Simulations, similar to critical thinking, give students the chance to follow up on what they are learning, to get input in light of their own decisions, and to give real-world relevance [21] thus empowering learning. Virtual reality (VR) simulations have been utilized to upgrade the web based learning condition by expanding the realism of the learning condition. Furthermore, mobile technology has been presented and has discovered across the board utilize particularly in gaming applications. To date endeavors have been made in a few separate directions which have led to significant development, as follows:

1. More realistic, engaging and immersive games (e.g. Xbox).
2. E-learning that takes advantage of the Internet, simulation, multimedia, and virtual reality (VR).
3. Advanced visualization and immersive environment for increased realism [22].

Virtual Reality is utilized to break the limits of formal education. Virtual Reality has been utilized as a part of education sector so as to enhance the on-line learning. A few perspectives give students the feeling of essence in an immersive world, and carrying another approach to cooperate with associates and teachers when they are not in a similar place [23].

4 STEM Educational

So what is STEM? STEM stands for science, technology, engineering, and math. These four symbols represent the different areas of STEM education.

The definition of STEM has not reached a solid conclusion, but it can be defined as a broad area encompassing many disciplines and epistemological practices [24] or as using trans-disciplinary knowledge and skills in solving real-world problems. Furthermore, the extending definition of learning STEM is the acquisition of knowledge and skills through experience and study integrated through multiple lenses allowing for the appreciation of the encompassing complexity and crosscutting ideas across the STEM disciplines as a whole [24]. It is noted that successful STEM learning is the total effect of the interaction of affect, cognition, and application of ideas [25]. Background highly qualified Science, Technology, Engineering, and Mathematics (STEM) professionals will be needed for worldwide innovation and global economics [25, 26] STEM education will help students develop their understanding of social issues. In many countries, STEM is viewed as a means of developing the national economy and citizens scientific literacy, but there seems to be decreasing readiness and motivation on the part of students to pursue STEM majors and careers. Educators need to ensure that human capital for STEM professions is well-trained for the workforce [16].

STEM education could take place in a separate STEM class or be incorporated into practically any subject and grade level. Of course science and math classes would be able to directly implement STEM-related lessons. In a social studies class learning about the industrial revolution, however, students may design their own assembly line. Or, in an English class, students may be keeping a journal about their thinking and research processes while designing a realistic bridge from a fictional novel.

Provide learning experience in STEM is a major challenge that will be meaningful to students with different need. Therefore, we selected new technologies (AR and VR) to integrate knowledge and practical skills in the visualization form.

In the next section, we will explain the potential of using AR and VR in the STEM education and highlight the strength and area which of improve which need to improve to activate those technologies as a part of STEM learning experience.

5 Potential of AR in STEM

AR has the potential to change education to be more efficient in the same way that computers and Internet did in the previous generation of educational method.

Researchers noted that providing case studies and opportunities for participant feedback extended the wealth of knowledge available and provided key insights to the quantitative data Engagement was also found while using augmented books through a qualitative research study [8]. Surveyed user studies concerning elementary and high school students to determine if AR enhances the learning experience. The authors found that, AR educational media could be a valuable and engaging addition to classroom education and overcome some of the limitations of text- based methods, allowing students to absorb the material according to their preferred learning style [8].

Actually combining AR with STEM is activating complex problem solving and increase the team work. As good results, AR increases the engagement, motivation and involvement during STREM education.

AR tools are becoming more user-friendly and require less programming skills making them more pointed out that AR platforms could be employed that allow an author to create augmented reality games and experiences with no programming experience required. In addition, [27] predicted that by the year 2030, students will be building AR educational content on a regular basis to connect collaboratively with the outside world from within their classroom attractive to the common educator. Overall, students reacted positively to using AR technology both in and outside of the classroom [8].

6 Potential of VR in STEM

The significant gap in STEM skills cannot be bridged quickly enough by relying solely on classroom teaching and physical laboratory training. Among the different STEM fields/subjects, advanced manufacturing has received special attention as a US national interest area. There are currently more than 600,000 unfilled manufacturing positions, due to the lack of skilled workers, and this number is anticipated to reach 2 million by 2025 [28].

Students learning in an AR environment is more stimulating and appealing than viewing a traditional slide presentation (i.e., Microsoft Power Point, Smart Notebook) because they preferred the audio, video, and feeling as if they were part of the 3D model that was transposed into a real physical space AR is continuously growing and improving every day, and using students feedback allows AR technology developers to incorporate these helpful tips to improve user experience [8].

One of good example is VR technology to bridge the gap in STEM is VOTE (Virtual reality based On line Technology and Engineering) platform as shown in 1. Its only a matter of time before virtual reality becomes a fixture in schools. Imagine a technology that will allow students to virtually walk through museums on the other side of the world, or swim with marine life in their natural habitat! It's got so many possible applications in education in general, and in STEM studies in particular, including: Fig. 1

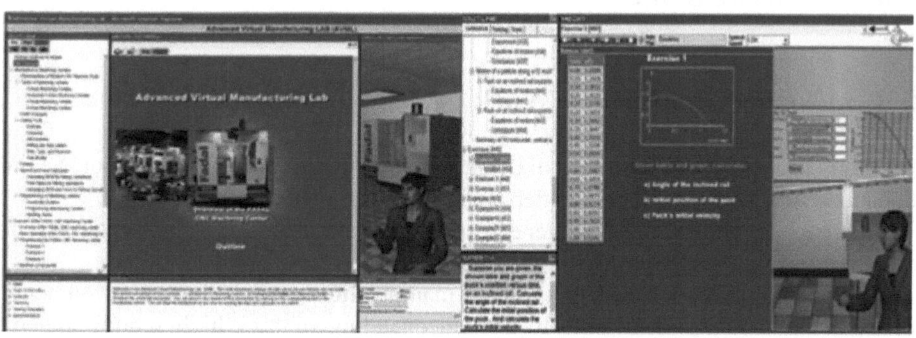

Fig. 1. VOTE (Virtual reality based Online Technology and Engineering) [22]

- A cruelty-free way to conduct dissection on a variety of critters, or just to see what they look like inside!
- The perfect way to conduct experiments that may otherwise be too dangerous for the school science lab.
- A great way to test engineering and physics in simulated realities, and even in hard to replicate environments like zero gravity or vacuums.
- The ideal way to conduct field trips to impossible to reach places. Imagine using the footage from the Mars rover with VR to take a stroll on the red planet?
- An amazing way to model mathematical concepts in a digital reality, so kids can see their formula at work, and manipulate them in real time!
- Access to the best teachers and experts from around the world, in a virtual reality setting. Imagine if your kids could attend lectures by the leading lights in STEM education from around the world, without leaving their classrooms?

The truth is, virtual reality is going to allow students to explore this world and others in ways that we have never imagined possible. It's going to let kids do things they would never be able to do otherwise, and it will undoubtedly even find its way into tertiary and high level medical, engineering and scientific study.

7 AR and VR Limitation in Education

In this section, we consider some limitation of using those new technologies as educational tools generally. We have identified the following three general and potentially serious drawbacks that have limited or restricted the general application of VR and AR in education [29]:

- Potentially high financial costs of acquiring a system.
- Lack of realism/fidelity/skill transfer issues.
- Physical effects on end-users.
- No Curriculum Content.
- Requires Mobile Device.

8 Conclusion and Future Work

This study proposes the possibility of using AR and VR technologies to support STEM education and increase students understanding, engagement, enrolment.

This paper highlight the next generation of education by integrates technology to take engineering, science, technology education to the next level.

AR technology can facilitate students manipulation of experiments in authentic contexts. The findings contribute to an understanding of how high school students perceive STEM lessons and the possible influence of STEM lessons on students career trajectories.

However, there is still limitation of such research to effect STEM by using new technology have a good experience with mobile application and new technologies.

As a future work, it is important to find ways to create a seamless transition between the outside world and the classroom environment. Surprisingly, a large percentage of students already have a good knowledge of terms such as VR and AR, but cannot or do not know how to relate these tools to their learning experience.

References

1. Birt, J., Cowling, M.: Toward future' mixed reality' learning spaces for steam education. Int. J. Innov. Sci. Math. Educ. **25**(4), 1 (2017)
2. Shirazi, A., Behzadan, A.: Assessing the pedagogical value of augmented reality-based learning in construction engineering 1, pp. 30–31 (2013)
3. Friedrich, K.A., Sellers, S.L., Burstyn, J.N.: Thawing the chilly climate: inclusive teaching resources for science, technology, engineering, and math. Improve Acad. **26**(1), 133–141 (2008)
4. Cristia, J., Ibarrarán, P., Cueto, S., Santiago, A., Severín, E.: Technology and child development: evidence from the one laptop per child program. Am. Econ. J.: Appl. Econ. **9** (3), 295–320 (2017)
5. Echeverría, A., Améstica, M., Gil, F., Nussbaum, M., Barrios, E.L.S.: Exploring different technological platforms for supporting co-located collaborative games in the classroom. Comput. Human Behav. **28**(4), 1170–1177 (2012)
6. Swensen, H.: Potential of Augmented Reality in Sciences Education a Literature Review, pp. 2540–2547 (2016)
7. Azuma, R., Baillot, Y., Behringer, R., Feiner, S., Julier, S., Mac-Intyre, B.: Recent advances in augmented reality. IEEE Comput. Graph. Appl. **21**(6), 34–47 (2001)
8. Antonioli, B.M, Blake, C., Sparks, K.: Augmented Reality Applications in Education, no. 2009, pp. 96–107 (2013)
9. Saidin, N.F., Halim, N.D.A., Yahaya, N.: A review of research on augmented reality in education: advantages and applications. Int. Educ. Stud. **8**(13), 1 (2015)
10. Al-Azawi, M., Shakkah, R.: Embedding augmented and virtual reality in educational learning method: present and future. In: 2018 9th International Conference on Information and Communication Systems (ICICS), pp. 218–222 (2018)
11. Singhal, S., Bagga, S., Goyal, P., Saxena, V.: Augmented chemistry: interactive education system. Int. J. Comput. Appl. **49**(15), 1–5 (2012)
12. Coffin, C., Bostandjiev, S., Ford, J., Hollerer, T.: Enhancing classroom and distance learning through augmented reality. In: EdMedia: World Conference on Educational Media and Technology, pp. 1140–1147, Association for the Advancement of Computing in Education (AACE) (2010)
13. Burton, E.P., Frazier, W., Annetta, L., Lamb, R., Cheng, R., Chmiel, M.: Modeling augmented reality games with preservice elementary and secondary science teachers. J. Technol. Teacher Educ. **19**(3), 303–329 (2011)
14. Medina, E., Chen, Y.-C., Weghorst, S.: Understanding biochemistry with augmented reality. In: EdMedia: World Conference on Educational Media and Technology, pp. 4235–4239, Association for the Advancement of Computing in Education (AACE) (2007)
15. Wu, H.-K., Lee, S.W.-Y., Chang, H.-Y., Liang, J.-C.: Current status, opportunities and challenges of augmented reality in education. Comput. Educ. **62**, 41–49 (2013)
16. Hsu, Y.-S., Lin, Y.-H., Yang, B.: Impact of augmented reality lessons on students' STEM interest. Res. Pract. Technol. Enhan. Learn. **12**(1), 2 (2017)

17. Jennett, C., Cox, A.L., Cairns, P., Dhoparee, S., Epps, A., Tijs, T., Walton, A.: Measuring and defining the experience of immersion in games. Int. J. Human-Comput. Stud. **66**(9), 641–661 (2008)
18. Zyda, M.: From visual simulation to virtual reality to games. Computer **38**(9), 25–32 (2005)
19. Martín-Gutiérrez, J., Mora, C.E., Añorbe-Díaz, B., González-Marrero, A.: Virtual technologies trends in education. EURASIA J. Math. Sci. Technol. Educ. **13**(2), 469–486 (2017)
20. Abdelraheem, A.Y.: Computerized learning environments: problems, design challenges and future promises. J. Interact. Online Learn. **2**(2), 1–9 (2003)
21. Selwyn, N.: Education and Technology: Key Issues and Debates. Bloomsbury Publishing, London (2016)
22. El-mounayri, H.A.: Assessment of STEM e-Learning in an Immersive Virtual Reality (VR) Environment (2016)
23. Cortiz, D., Silva, J.O.: Web and virtual reality as platforms to improve online education experiences. In: 2017 10th International Conference on Human System Interactions (HSI), pp. 83–87. IEEE (2017)
24. Lamb, K., Akmal, R., Petrie, T.: Development of a cognition-priming model describing learning in a STEM classroom. J. Res. Sci. Teach. **52**(3), 410–437 (2015)
25. Oppezzo, M., Schwartz, D.L.: A behavior change perspective on self-regulated learning with teachable agents. In: Azevedo, R., Aleven, V. (eds.) International Handbook of Metacognition and Learning Technologies. SIHE, vol. 28, pp. 485–500. Springer, New York (2013). https://doi.org/10.1007/978-1-4419-5546-3_31
26. Eisenhart, M., Weis, L., Allen, C.D., Cipollone, K., Stich, A.: High school opportunities for STEM: comparing inclusive STEM-focused and comprehensive high schools in two US cities. J. Res. Sci. Teach. **52**(6), 763–789 (2015)
27. Billinghurst, A., Duenser, M.: Augmented reality in the classroom. Computer **45**(7), 56–63 (2012)
28. El-Mounayri, H., Wasfy, T., Fernandez, E., Peters, J.: Innovative online course using an integrated virtual reality based e-learning tool with course management tool. In: Iskander, M. (ed.) Innovative Techniques in Instruction Technology, E-learning, E-assessment and Education, pp. 183–189. Springer, Berlin (2008). https://doi.org/10.1007/978-1-4020-8739-4_33
29. Christou, C.: Virtual reality in education. In: Affective, Interactive and Cognitive Methods for e-Learning Design: Creating an Optimal Education Experience, pp. 228–243. IGI Global (2010)

Boosting Motivation Through Process Gamification: Evidence from Higher Education

Julia Bilinkis(✉), Alexander Gromoff, and Yaroslav Gorchakov

National Research University Higher School of Economics, ul. Myasnitskaya, 20, Moscow 129000, Russian Federation
yuliastavenko@mail.ru, agromov@hse.ru, yar-gorchakov@yandex.ru

Abstract. Boosting motivation is a challenging task on the way of additional productivity, especially considering new generations Y and Z. In this paper we combine set of methods from process management, pedagogics and psychology to develop an interactive gamification process and test it for generations Y and Z currently studying in the leading Russian university. The efficiency of approach is demonstrated on several models and authors suggest ways how to implement them.

Keywords: Gamification · S-BPM · E-learning

1 Introduction

Theory of generations claims the current and future employees (Y and Z) differ from their previous peers (X) [3]. Their engagement into working processes requires new approaches to boost motivation, such as *gamification*. Kevin Werbach, an Associate Professor at University of Pennsylvania, defines *Gamification* as '*the application of game elements and digital game design techniques to non-game problems, such as business and social impact challenges'*. Gamification focuses efforts on inner motivations and autonomy in a controlled environment, where the contents of specific areas subdivided and treated as stage in a surrounding context by cognitive, social and emotional correlating [9, 10]. As the major part of generation Z are currently studying in higher education institutions (HEIs) we decide to create and test our process approach in the leading Russian University.

Educational systems there currently still are driven by the conventional offline lecturing style content. However, the main content type students consume is much more interactive than proposed by lecturers. Video and computer games (now followed with mobile gadgets apps) has shaped so called Generation Y looking at reflexivity and impact. Self-expression, interactivity and freedom of choice is a must for Y-s, while traditional methods, such as installation of responsibilities are not efficient. Various marking formulas (training attendance, activity, etc.) do not raise a slight interest in the subject, rather it is perceived by students as a boring fulfilment of formal requirements.

L. Uden et al. (Eds.): LTEC 2019, CCIS 1011, pp. 45–57, 2019.
https://doi.org/10.1007/978-3-030-20798-4_5

Luckily, is one of the most important indicators of Higher Education quality perceived by students [1, 2].

2 Literature Review

There are earlier evidences that gamification has positive effects on engagement, knowledge mediation and dissemination of knowledge. Papers devoted to gamification are growing rapidly. From 2011 to 2014 according to Gartner, gamification has been at the peak of increased interest, along with the Internet of things, big data and 3D printing, and Gartner predicts only 5-10 years to reach a '*plateau performance*', indicating that the little-studied phenomenon gamification. In the 2015 Seaborn C. and Fels D [11] considering more than 700 articles and scientific works, one way or another affect the issue gamification [12, 13]. Based on the definitions of gamification in various studies gives the following definition: gamification - it is *purposeful and intentional use of game elements and game design techniques in the context of non-fiction* [14]. This term came after the realization by many researchers that the creation of a game to teach students is too expensive task, both in terms of development of software to support the game, and from the point of view of its design [15]. Gamification is the intersection of the best methods and practices of game mechanics, loyalty programs, and behavioural economics. To draw an analogy with the process of learning the game, then during the game expects student awards and achievements (assessment), each task considering how to stage a specific purpose (such as the level in the game), and the road to the goal must be clear.

Traditionally the problem of involvement and motivation to learn was considered in pedagogy and psychology, but in recent years it has increasingly become a technological challenge, especially with the new technologies in education and the transition to the so-called digital economy [6–8]. *Student Engagement* is often seen as a multi-dimensional construct and a large body of research is based on the definition of its three components: *Behavioural engagement* (responsibility, commitment, perseverance, attitude, habits, discipline, social skills), *Emotional engagement* (interest, motivation, curiosity) and *Cognitive engagement* (improved academic performance, test scores, assimilate information, skills) [4]. Recent work on the engagement shows that setting goals and provide opportunities for joint activities in planning, assessment and decision-making help making students more active participants in their education processes [5]. Most often external motivation is achieved by creating a *community* which consists of students sharing *common interests, norms, behaviour and objectives*, and improving their training based on experience and shared knowledge.

In this paper we investigate gamification combined with process management and test the solution in the the leading Russian University. We aim at better students' involvement in the educational process by proposing a workflow oriented towards a student comprising variety of tools, which student may select to impact the learning process, depending on personal preferences. This ultimately contributes to improve the quality of personalised education to obtain the necessary set of theoretical and practical capabilities. By proposing a process-oriented solution [20–23] to cluster student groups as communities in accordance with their needs and preferences we implement gamification components in the learning process to for better involvement of Generation Y and Z students. Thus, this study has the following research question:

RQ1: How can process management facilitate gamification of the conventional learning process as perceived by students?

In order to answer this RQ we (1) assess gamification techniques for creating a community of students; (2) analyze the current learning process and develop process model supporting gamification techniques; (3) evaluate the efficiency of the` learning process as compared to the traditional process of learning.

3 Process Management

Mastering disciplines in the educational program comprise measurable learning process to obtain a degree. This requires the maintenance of a consistent trend of knowledge acquisition and demonstration of obtained capabilities via exchange of 'messages' – tasks and answers. Figure 1 describes the conventional learning process:

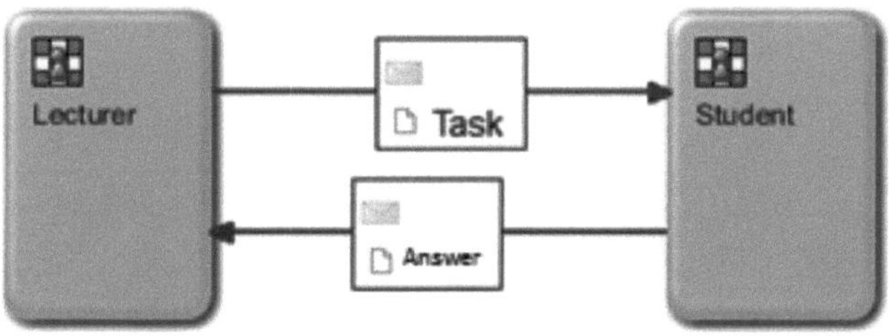

Fig. 1. Conventional learning process through communication with a teacher

Regarding this model most of the students report longer feedback on task implementation, lack of interaction, unclarity of tasks, which leads to lower exam scores. To improve the model, many teachers are taking the following steps mentioned above (see Fig. 3):

1. Strengthening interpersonal relationships with students (unofficial social media channels, such as chats in WhatsApp, Skype).
2. Creating a more flexible model of interaction. Tasks are not attached to student but to students' teams where more detailed division is done by members.
3. Proposing to execute a project rather than to accomplish a set of tasks. Project manager inside the team divides tasks into smaller sub-tasks and distributes them between members. Additional tasks here comprise coordination and quality assurance.
4. Discussing projects with the presence of a lecturer to better understand the problems and the resulting marks.

After these changes the interaction scheme could be redrawn as follows:

However, still this scheme also has disadvantages. Such team are often created out of students presented with different knowledge and motivation for learning, but

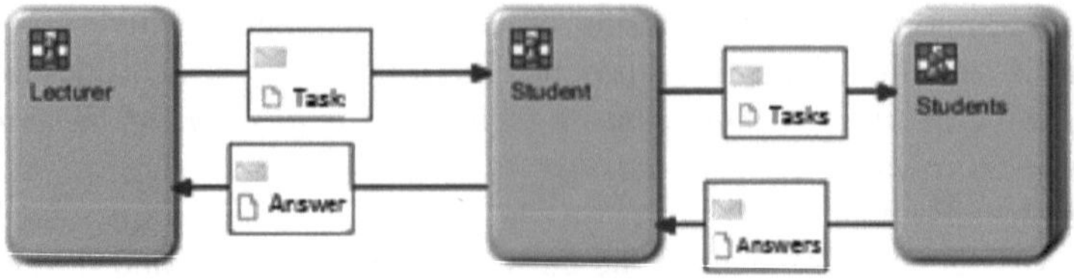

Fig. 2. Model of creating a learning community of students

granting a common grade for team work. Thus, it is not a personalized learning process, and many students feel the injustice after the common mark is issued. To create an effective learning community we add cognitive, emotional and behavioral (social) components [16], that affect the learning process, that results in exchanging of tasks (having different readiness) for getting feedback on what was done for the project and clarifying messages from with the pool of students.

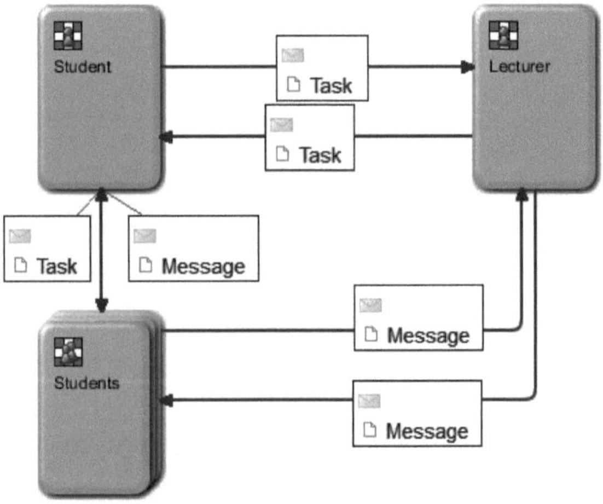

Fig. 3. The training model through the creation of a learning community of students and gamification with constant feedback

Creating a community of students allowed us to use motivation to measure a social group and to run educational projects to achieve common goals. We facilitate common problems solving using interactive feedback in a process environment, team spirit, and contribution to the common deliverable. To improve cognitive component, we support independent and team work fully compatible with the student interest in the course and its current knowledge and experience. Student's expression of emotions is also fully supported: curiosity, the joy of victory, elements of gamification: scores, badges, awards, progress bars, levels, avatars, quests leader board. Kevin Verbahom developed one of the most popular gamified systems, abbreviated as 6D:

1. Define Business Objectives (identify business goals) - which is used for introducing gamification;
2. Delineate target behaviour (delineate the target behaviour). The system should be constructed in such a way as to give feedback to players, thereby stimulating the desired behaviour.
3. Describe your players (describe the players). At this point, you can determine which types of elements are preferred for one or another group of players (e.g., supporting an atmosphere of competition and cooperation).
4. Devise activity loops (develop active loop) - how the system will give feedback on the results of the behaviour of the player how a player can be motivated to advance in the game, and how to grow his skill.
5. Don't forget the fun (do not forget about the fun). It can operate without winning a game, whether it will be interesting. The element of fun design is complex. Considering the preferences of the target audience need to understand what its main interest will be.
6. Deploy appropriate tools (add the appropriate tools)

Mapping of these elements in the learning process additionally improves the effectiveness of the latter [see also 17].

4 Gamification Tools

The system for one of the process management courses has been developed based on Fig. 3 and Table 1. Teacher checks student's introduction essays and forms several communities of students (5-6 persons), depending on students' knowledge and skills

Table 1. Gamification elements

Type of involvement	Motivation	Gamification elements
Emotional	Monitoring learning progress	Experience Points; Reputation; Skills and 'Karma'
Social	Demonstration of the achievements of others and the pursuit	Group assignments, awards and badges The recommended model consists of: 1. *Status* (titles) 2. *Access*. Providing exceptional features, such as lunch with the Rector or an internship in a company. 3. *Power*. Implementation of control over other people in the real or virtual world, for example, the role of team leader in the project 4. *Prizes* and gift cards
Cognitive	Call	Quests during assignments

that can be modified further. At the same time another group of students follows traditional approach described in Fig. 2. In the traditional approach, the team is formed out of the list of students. After courses have been finished we surveyed students. The comparison between traditional and gamification approach is shown in the Table 2.

A student needs to go through four levels of "game" by analogy with the four practical tasks to achieve a common goal. Each level proposes several missions. During the execution of each "mission" students get badges with achieved results. It is impossible to complete second-level missions, without completing first. The levels provide difficulty thresholds (from simple to hard). Each new mission requires to more immersion and the development of professional skills. This is necessary for the

Table 2. Comparison of two approaches

	The traditional approach	The gamification approach	
1	**Personal Job. Simulation of the business process modelling.**		
	Student gets a task, and sends a report via e-mail for marking. Communication occurs in the class.	1. Selection and confirmation of modeling notations.	20 points
		2. Modeling "as is" process. Feedback from the lecturer.	20 points
		3. Repeat ways to optimize processes.	20 points
		4. Modeling "as is" process. Feedback from the teacher.	20 points
		5. Create report, evaluation. Badges: • « The best Optimizer" - for the best work • « Early bird" -this first work done Awards: Free access to the master class	20 points
2	**Personal Job. Search processes to find bottlenecks using 6 sigma, lean and other methods.**		
	Student gets a task, and sends a report via e-mail for marking. Communication occurs in the class.	1. Recap of process enhancement methods	20 points
		2. Process Analysis. Feedback from the teacher.	20 points
		3. Report, Evaluation. Badge "Star" - for the best presentation Awards: Free access to the master class, organized by the University	

(*continued*)

Table 2. (*continued*)

	The traditional approach	The gamification approach	
3	**The group task. First level problem solving using analysis tools.**		
	After the task distribution team makes a presentation in class. Communication occurs in the classroom or during team selection (online).	1. Case analysis, defining roles	20 points
		2. Participants implement their parts	20 points
		3. Re-examination of the case all together	20 points
		4. Preparation of presentations	20 points
		Protection of the presentation. Evaluation Badges: "Helping Hand" -The best student in the community "Quality Mark" - for the best presentation	20 points
4	**The group task. Second level problem solving, using all the knowledge gained.**		
	After the task distribution team makes a presentation in class. Communication occurs in the classroom or when team prefers.	1. Case analysis, defining roles	20 points
		2. Participants implement their parts	20 points
		3. Re-examination of the case all together	20 points
		4. Preparation of presentations	20 points
		5. Presentation in front of lecturer. Receiving evaluation Badge "Star" - for the best presentation	20 points
	Exam	Evaluation based on the answers to questions and cumulative assessment for the course. Badges: "Legend" - the best student - for the maximum number of points	Accumulated points

calculation of progress that shows the percentage of the degree of the passage of each level. Personal effectiveness charts allow obtaining an instant feedback on how well the work is performed in comparison with others. Using the system also encourages social interaction in the team.

5 Evaluation of the Proposed Solutions

Based on the survey with students (Appendix 1) the following diagrams have been drawn (Figs. 4, 5 and 6).

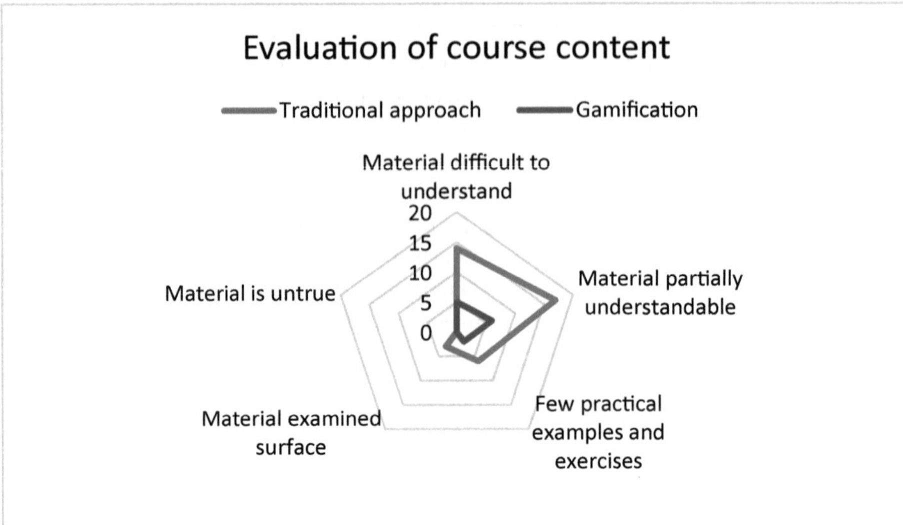

Fig. 4. Evaluation of course content (40)

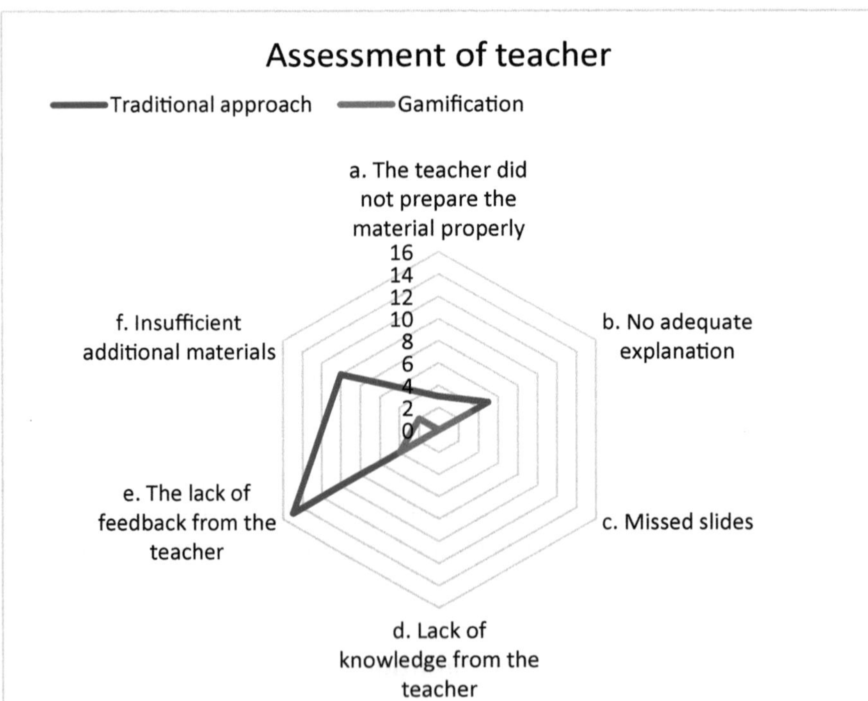

Fig. 5. Evaluation of the teacher (40)

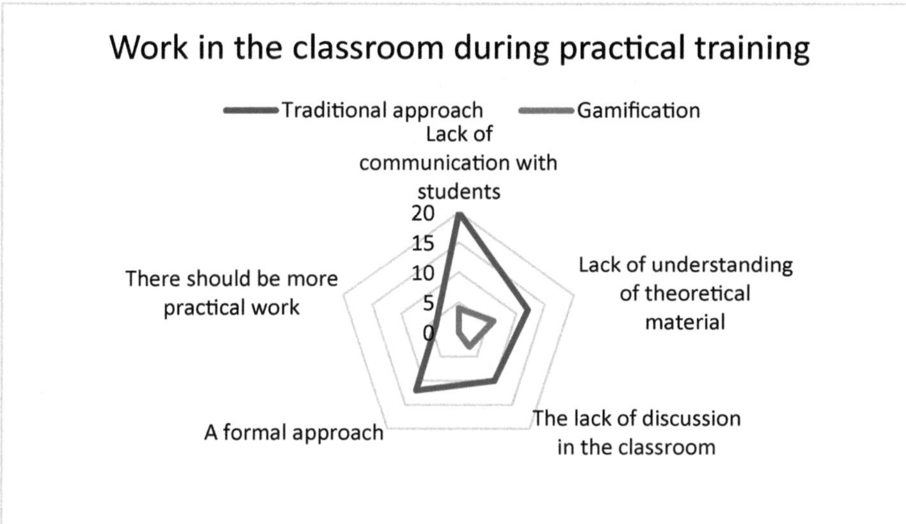

Fig. 6. Assessment of practical training (40 people)

6 More Application of Gamification Tools for Raising Generation Z

A tremendous potential of gaming methods is used in other areas as well. Classical learning approaches are being substituted to better cope with new generations [1, 18, 19].

First, the private school 'Kodvards'[1] installed an educational platform to teach children the basics of software engineering to prepare them for the interconnected world of digital economy [1]. Children who have been trained under the program, got computer science skills, logical thinking, problem solving and software engineering in a gamified manner. In contrast to classical approach of basic syntax learning much discouraging students, authors have taught children and how to use the key concepts in a language independent way. This course was created using a storytelling format to broadcast programming concepts more interactively. It also allows students to remember texts in an easier way and motivates them for a further study recognizing the importance of programming skills in today's world. Program "Kodvards" intends to engage a wide audience of schools, art centres, centres of additional education in the implementation of their educational program.

Second, the course has been implemented inside "Engineering Power" project (Samara) that currently is still in progress of negotiation with other regions of the Russian Federation. They plan to be a worthy alternative educational program in computer science in the elementary school by interconnecting hundreds of schools and summer camps embracing 15 000 children.

[1] http://codewards.ru (accessed 03.03.2019).

Third, the extracurricular activities of "Elementary School 2100" program– aim at development of substantive skills, universal educational actions and personal qualities of students. The authors believe that the challenge is to know what information is needed but how to request it. The educational system 'School 2100'[2] is the first and only modern experience of creating an integrated educational model which offers a systematic and continuous training of children from preschool age until their graduation at the high school in Russia and CIS countries.

7 Conclusion

In this work, we considered Gamification not only as an obvious trend for new generation, but as a tool for enhancing learning process in universities, supported by ICT. It has a high potential to change the behavioural patterns of students and support the learning process. Once generations get older, more research is needed to analyse potentials of gamification in their industrial working environments. We derive several key aspects to consider gamification in learning processes:

1. Companies/Universities must develop Key Performance Indicators (KPIs) regarding employees/students engagement into learning (e.g. participation in research projects) and regarding lecturers' performance (such as student feedback after the course), mapping them to the business strategy. Such indicators motivate both lecturers and students for better engagement into learning process, boost motivation inside gamification roles and lead to higher creativity.
2. Learning process owner must always analyse feedback from its execution in real-time, that makes students and teachers more active and flexible, e.g. during subject-oriented process interaction. Gamification tools such as bonuses, grade levels that are integrated with coaching and e-learning tools for further performance management and training. Feedback from processes and users should be updated on a regular basis, corresponding to the efficiency of the processes: for example, once an hour, once a day, once a week, once a month, etc.
3. Learning process participants need additional motivation for their own contribution to creative games and for reconsideration of their involvement. Accordingly, the role of mentoring increases, when experienced "players" can help "beginners" to show themselves from their best side. Achieving milestones and goals makes each employee a hero of his own game. It's important to avoid competition: better to reach mutual involvement in the objective achievement than pursue personal survival. Therefore, the comparison between personal "percentage" within result demotivating people and leads to a failure in achieving the effectiveness of training. In gamification (as in any game at all) a positive emotional mood is an important success factor.
4. There is a need for cooperation and exchange of knowledge between all participants of the "game". The system of involvement scoring in the "game" should support updating of knowledge, its storage and the ability to remote access at anytime from

[2] http://school2100.com/school2100/about/pedagogika.php (accessed 01.03.2019).

anywhere. Within a short time, a common knowledge platform or knowledge center should be created for the exchange of experience, rapid involvement in the learning process, answers to frequently asked questions and standard solutions.

5. There is a need for support for business process roles in the "game". One "player" can take several roles, but these roles should be developed in each process and contribute to the achievement of goals. For example, the role of the Manager can be performed by the" owner " of the process, the role of content managers is to update the "mechanics" and content of the game. Technical support managers identify system failures and errors, update the database, and provide solutions to problems. "Communicator" sends announcements about new versions of the "game", its stages and changes, updates the scenario. Depending on the level of game and involvement, the role of PR (GR) Manager can also be created, who establishes and maintains contacts with the official government structures involved in the game, heads of interested organizations.

Appendix A1

After completing the course, the students were asked to undergo a survey consisting of the following questions from the perspective of cognitive, psychological and social characteristics:

1. Evaluate the course content:
   (a) Material difficult to understand
   (b) Material partially understandable
   (c) Few practical examples and exercises
   (d) Material examined surface
   (e) Material is untrue
2. Evaluate a course instructor:
   (a) The teacher did not prepare the material properly
   (b) No adequate explanation
   (c) Skipped slides
   (d) Lack of knowledge from the teacher
   (e) The lack of feedback from the teacher
   (f) Insufficient additional materials
3. Work in the classroom during practical training
   (a) Lack of communication with students
   (b) Lack of understanding of theoretical material
   (c) The lack of discussion in the classroom
   (d) A formal approach
   (e) There should be more practical work.

References

1. Itsakov, E., Kazantsev, N., Yangutova, S., Torshin, D.: Digital Economy in the Russian Federation: The Missing Priority for Continuous Education (2018). https://www.researchgate.net/publication/327209762_Digital_Economy_in_the_Russian_Federation_The_Missing_Priority_for_Continuous_Education
2. Kazantsev, N., Gorchakov, Y., Bilinkis (Stavenko), Y., Torshin, D.: Best practices for a scientific seminar in business process management for master students at russian university. In: Kavoura, A., Sakas, Damianos P., Tomaras, P. (eds.) Strategic Innovative Marketing. SPBE, pp. 629–633. Springer, Cham (2017). https://doi.org/10.1007/978-3-319-33865-1_77
3. Mehralizadeh, Y., Pakseresht, M.J., Baradaran, M., Shahi, S.: The dilemma of internal evaluation in higher education: a longitudinal case study. Qual. Assur. Educ Int. Perspect. **15**, 352–368 (2007)
4. Schunk, D.H., Mullen, C.A.: Self-efficacy as an engaged learner. In: Handbook of Research on Student Engagement, pp. 219–235. Springer, US (2012). https://doi.org/10.1007/978-1-4614-2018-7_10
5. Fletcher, A.: Meaningful Student Involvement Guide to Students as Partners in School Change. SoundOut, Olympia (2005)
6. Chen, G., Kumar, V., Kinshuk, Huang, R., Kong, S.C. (eds.): Emerging Issues in Smart Learning. LNET. Springer, Heidelberg (2015). https://doi.org/10.1007/978-3-662-44188-6
7. O'Brien, H.L., Toms, E.G.: What is user engagement? A conceptual framework for defining user engagement with technology. J. Assoc. Inf. Sci. Technol. **59**(6), 938–955 (2008)
8. Uskov, A., Sekar, B.: Smart Gamification and Smart Serious Games Fusion of Smart, Multimedia and Computer Gaming Technologies Volume 84 of the series Intelligent Systems Reference Library, pp. 7–36 (2015)
9. Busarello, R.I., Ulbricht, V.R., Fadel, L.M., de Freitas e Lopes, A.V.: Gamification approaches to learning and knowledge development: a theorical review. New Advances in Information Systems and Technologies. AISC, vol. 444, pp. 1107–1116. Springer, Cham (2016). https://doi.org/10.1007/978-3-319-31232-3_105
10. Вербах, К.: Вовлекай и властвуй: игровое мышление на службе бизнеса. – М.: Манн, Иванов и Фербер (2015)
11. Seaborn, K., Fels, D.I.: Gamification in theory and action: a survey. Int. J. Hum. Comput. Stud. **74**, 14–31 (2015)
12. Huotari, K., Hamari, J.: Defining gamification – a service marketing perspective. In: Proceedings 15th MindTrek Conference, Tampere, pp. 17–22 (2012)
13. Deterding, S., Dixon, D., Khaled, R., Nacke, L.: From game design elements to gamefulness: defining gamification. In: Proceedings 15th MindTrek Conference, Tampere, pp. 9–15 (2011)
14. Werbach, K.: (Re)Defining gamification: a process approach. In: Spagnolli, A., Chittaro, L., Gamberini, L. (eds.) PERSUASIVE 2014. LNCS, vol. 8462, pp. 266–272. Springer, Cham (2014). https://doi.org/10.1007/978-3-319-07127-5_23
15. Bredl, K., Bösche, W.: Serious Games and Virtual Worlds in Education, Professional Development, and Healthcare (2013)
16. Illeris, K., Reader, D., Malone, M.: The Three Dimensions of Learning: Contemporary Learning Theory in the Tension Field between the Cognitive, the Emotional and the Social, Roskilde University Press, Frederiksberg (2002)

17. Su, C.-H.: The effects of students' motivation, cognitive load and learning anxiety in gamification software engineering education: a structural equation modeling study. Multimed. Tools Appl. **75**, 10013–10036 (2016). https://doi.org/10.1007/s11042-015-2799-7
18. Kazantsev, N., Zakhlebin, I.: Measuring influence of internationalized universities on smart city development in terms of human capital and urban aspects. Knowl. Manage. E-Learn. Int. J. **6**(4), 410–425 (2014)
19. Kazantsev, N., Korolev, D., Torshin, D., Mikhailova, A.: An approach to automate health monitoring in compliance with personal privacy. In: Zheng, X., Zeng, D.D., Chen, H., Leischow, Scott J. (eds.) ICSH 2015. LNCS, vol. 9545, pp. 26–30. Springer, Cham (2016). https://doi.org/10.1007/978-3-319-29175-8_3
20. Gromoff, A., Kazantsev, N., Shapkin, P., Shumsky, L.: Automatic business process model assembly on the basis of subject-oriented semantic process mark-up. In: 2014 11th International Conference on e-Business (ICE-B), pp. 158–164. IEEE August 2014
21. Komarov, M., Kazantsev, N., Grevtsov, M.: Increasing the adoption of social collaboration software. In: 2014 IEEE 16th Conference on Business Informatics (CBI), pp. 54–59. IEEE, July 2014
22. Anna, K., Nikolay, K.: Survey on big data analytics in public sector of russian federation. Procedia Comput. Sci. **55**, 905–911 (2015)
23. Gromoff, A., Kazantsev, N., Schumsky, L., Konovalov, N.: Business transformation based on cloud services. In: 2014 IEEE International Conference on Services Computing (SCC), pp. 844–845. IEEE, June 2014

Health Student Using Google Classroom: Satisfaction Analysis

Amadeu Sa de Campos Filho[1(✉)], Webber de Souza Fantini[2], Mirelly Atanázio Ciriaco[3], Joelton dos Santos[3], Fernando Moreira[4,5], and Alex Sandro Gomes[6]

[1] Medical Science Center, Federal University of Pernambuco, Recife, PE 50000, Brazil
amadeu.campos@nutes.ufpe.br
[2] Telehealth Center, Federal University of Pernambuco, Recife, PE 50000, Brazil
wsfantini@gmail.com
[3] Unissaomiguel, Recife, PE 50000, Brazil
mirelly.atanazio@gmail.com, joeltonds57@gmail.com
[4] REMIT, IJP Universidade Portucalense, Porto, Portugal
fmoreira@uportu.pt
[5] IEETA, Universidade de Aveiro, Aveiro, Portugal
[6] Informatic Center, Federal University of Pernambuco, Recife, PE 50000, Brazil
asg@cin.ufpe.br

Abstract. Currently, the expressive growth of educational technologies has made health education institutions discuss new pedagogical forms with the reorientation and reorganization of teaching, being considered of utmost importance the presence of information technology in the course of student training and pedagogical practices. In this context, Google Classroom has emerged as an educational platform that can be used as a technology innovation to make academic activities more dynamic and effective. The objective of this study was to evaluate the usability and user satisfaction of Classroom as a tool to support the process of teaching learning. The methodology used was based on a qualitative and quantitative approach through the method of usability analysis and user perception. The qualitative and quantitative variables used to analyze usability were the effectiveness, time of use and user perception through the Attrakdiff questionnaire. The sample used in the study was 110 students from a Faculty in the city of Recife, state of Pernambuco, Brasil, during the 2nd semester of 2017. From the results, we can noted that the platform is relevant to the learning process but improvements can be made to a greater identification and interaction of the user. The student satisfaction analysis showed that Classroom can be a great tool used in pedagogical practice as a support to the teaching learning process and also to evaluate the benefits of its use. This study can serve as a starting point for research in this area, and for the development of new technologies related to education.

Keywords: Usability · Google Classroom · Satisfaction

L. Uden et al. (Eds.): LTEC 2019, CCIS 1011, pp. 58–66, 2019.
https://doi.org/10.1007/978-3-030-20798-4_6

1 Introduction

Teaching requires that the teacher have students participate in lessons, to keep their attention and to develop the subjects addressed. The integration of new technologies into teaching serves as a different and innovative pedagogical approach that provides the student with a better environment for acquiring and building knowledge [1].

Academic institutions are ideal places to research, develop and test new technologies. This site of knowledge-creation arouses interest in seeking the new and improving the old, especially in the area of healthcare information management, where it is necessary to maintain and routinely update information about patient care precisely to ensure correct treatment. Upon graduation, students must be able to apply what they have learned in real life applications [2].

The technological changes occurring in the teaching-learning process, which focus on contextualization in health education, has facilitated the formation of critical students capable of interfering in decisions on these aspects. Understanding the relationship between Science, Technology and Society, means broadening the possibilities of understanding and effective participation in the world.

Thus, the use of Information and Communication Technologies (ICT) has become increasingly an immediate necessity in the construction and transmission of knowledge. Society must live with the opportunities created by technology which bring information at high speeds, reducing the boundaries of the world and facilitating social relations [3].

According to [4, 5], technologies are like bridges that open the classroom to the external world. Besides being forms of representation of reality—in a more abstract or concrete, static or dynamic, linear or parallel form they combine and integrate different learning processes, favoring the potential of students.

Therefore, it is worth noting that students easily adapt to technological resources, but teachers find it more difficult to adapt to the use of technologies in the classroom. [3] states that the great difficulty is that many teachers were not born in the information age, nor were they indoctrinated early in the utility of these digital resources in the same way that their students have been since the beginning of their formal education. With this, these difficulties become obstacles to the use of this important teaching instrument.

In health, educators face many challenges not only in using technology in the learning environment, but also finding the right technology to use. [3, 6] found that health educators need more technology skills training, because it is essential to be able to operate new technologies to engage students in the classroom.

Several new technologies are currently used in the classroom, such as laptop computers, projectors and smartphones, as well as collaborative learning platforms and virtual learning environments such as Google Classroom and Moodle. These learning environments allow for student interaction, knowledge sharing and collaboration beyond the walls of the classroom. When used during class time in an educational context, it enables the transmission of knowledge through its attention-attracting capabilities. In addition, the rapid emergence of educational applications is uniting interest in technology with the teaching process.

On the other hand, teachers have a variety of educational platforms to assist in students' teaching and learning processes and to provide a collaborative learning environment for them. In this context, Google Classroom has emerged as an innovative educational platform that makes academic activities more dynamic and effective.

Google Classroom is a free-to-use platform developed by Google, to help the teacher in the classroom. With it, the teacher can create a virtual classroom to share various materials, exercises, and activities, and where students can submit assignments and receive teacher feedback and grades. This saves time and paper, as it is used through smartphones, tablets, and laptops. It also develops a vibrant, interactive online collaborative space to support and complement face-to-face classes. The platform can be accessed from any device that has internet access and has a browser, there is also a mobile version available to download for Android and IOS platforms [7].

All new technologies and educational platforms should be tested to identify possible errors before they are released. Verifying speedy operation, a user-friendly and simple interface and the presence of all desired features that operate effectively for the end user, thus guarantees usability and user satisfaction [8]. The goal of usability research is to analyze whether the application is easy to understand and use and if it has a dynamic and interactive format for the intended population, and to compare the real benefits to those claimed by the producer, and evaluate the quality of their inclusion in the learning teaching process [9].

In this context, the objective of this study was to evaluate the usability and satisfaction of Classroom users as a tool to support the process of teaching learning.

1.1 Usability and Satisfaction Analysis

There are many kinds of Usability and satisfaction analysis protocols. According to [10] there are three characteristics that will enable a positive user experience: (a) Functionality: the artefact needs to match the function it proposes, otherwise it will be considered useless and the user will be dissatisfied; (b) Usability: the artefact has correct and easy to use; (c) Satisfaction: In addition to the above mentioned benefits, users expect positive feelings when using a product. Among existing validated protocols to analyze usability and satisfaction (NASA [11], QUIS [12], SUPR-Q [13], CSUQ [14], SUMI [15], ATTRAKDIFF [10]), these characteristics above fit to both hedonic and pragmatic quality of AttrakDiff questionnaire. This questionnaire is based on the same user experience evaluation criteria proposed by [10].

In this experiment, AttrakDiff was selected to evaluate the users experience in the proposed system, as it allows one to evaluate the attractiveness through the different aspects of an application. This type of testing becomes increasingly important, given its ability to help developers understand the product from users' perspectives [10]. The questionnaire is divided into three dimensions: Pragmatic Quality (PQ); Hedonic quality - in this dimension there is a subdivision where one part focuses on the Stimulus (QH-E) in the Identity (QE-I); and Attractiveness.

The pragmatic quality refers to the objective use of the product by an individual and is more related to the characteristics of functionalities and usability, that is, they will analyze how good or bad is the experience that the product provides the user.

This dimension describes the quality of an application and indicates the degree of success that users achieve by using the application [10].

2 Materials and Methods

The methodology used in this study was based on a qualitative and quantitative exploration of usability and user perceptions of the technology. The qualitative and quantitative variables used to analyze usability were the effectiveness and perception of the user through the Attrakdiff questionnaire [10, 16]

AttrakDiff measures the user's perception about the intended object, and according to [10] "allows assessing attractiveness through different aspects of an application." The questionnaire was divided into three dimensions: (I) the Pragmatic Quality (QP), referring to the quality of the application and the desired objectives achieved by the user; (II) the Hedonic Quality, that is divided into Stimulus (HQ-S), indicating how much the object meets the needs of the user and promotes interest, motivation, etc., and the Hedonic Quality of Identity (HQ-I), identifying of the user's need with the application; and, (III) Attractiveness (ATT), that indicates the general value of the application based on the user's perception of quality. AttrakDiff is composed of twenty-eight-word pairs grouped in dimensions where each pair of words are placed at the ends of a scale with a semantic differential of seven points (−3 to 3, with 0 as the neutral point).

The number of items evaluated, are distributed as follows: seven items for Pragmatic Quality dimension; fourteen items for Hedonic Quality (seven evaluate the Stimulus and seven evaluate the Identity); and seven items for Attractiveness. It is available on the AttrakDiff website [16] all explanations about the analyzed dimensions and are therefore easily interpreted by commercial developers and/or non-usability specialists.

2.1 Scenario

The usability and satisfaction evaluation were performed in the Google Classroom application, a content management platform for educational institutions that seek to simplify the creation, distribution and evaluation of educational content. The study was conducted with the voluntary participation of 110 students from different academic programs in the health informatics discipline at the same college, in Recife City, Brazil, in 2017. The students used the google classroom during the second semester of 2017 accessing the pedagogical content (ebook, video, podcast, website and text) and doing activities.

The usability evaluation occurred during the second semester of 2017 and was divided into two stages. In the first stage, students used the Google Classroom for six months, where it was possible to track the user's immersion time and interaction with the platform. In the second stage, students completed the AttrakDiff standardized satisfaction test aimed at identifying usability issues, analyzing the user experience, and determining the participant's satisfaction with the product. Additionally, all participants completed a single-question, open ended questionnaire about their perception of the Google Classroom platform.

3 Results and Discussion

The AttrakDiff questionnaire was answered by 110 students from different academic programs at the higher education institution in the city of Recife, Brazil, in 2017. In the portfolio presentation (Fig. 1), horizontal axis represents the value of the pragmatic quality (i.e., the left = a low value). The hedonic quality values are represented on the

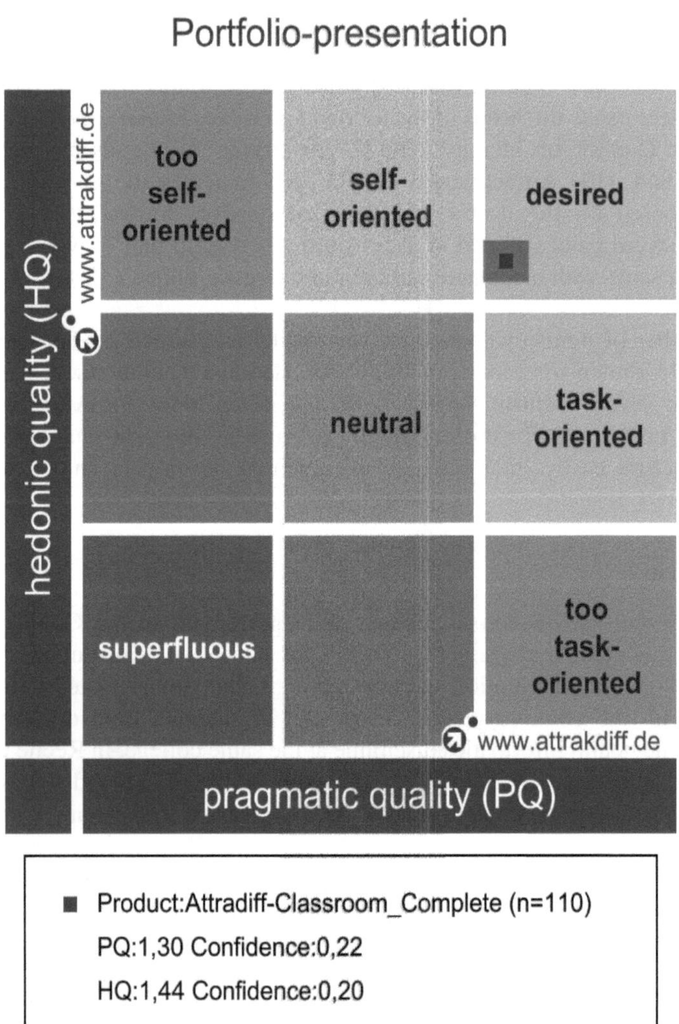

Fig. 1. Mean values of confidence dimensions and rectangles of portfolio-representation

vertical axis (bottom = low value). Depending on the dimension values, the product will be in one or more "character regions". The higher the confidence rectangle, the less sure which region belongs. A small rectangle of confidence is an advantage because it means that the results of the research are more reliable and less coincident. The confidence rectangle is displayed, if the users are in a in evaluating the product. The higher the confidence rectangle, the more variable the rating scores.

According to AttrakDiff and the portfolio-representation, the application is Desirable in the pragmatic and hedonic dimensions. The results of the measurement are clearly situated in this quadrant, indicating that the product assists users, arouses their interest and stimulates users as well as decreases the cost of teaching materials in and outside the classroom. The confidence interval of pragmatic quality (0.22) is higher than that of hedonic quality (0.20), although it is only located in a single quadrant. This can be attributed to the different classifications given by the users, indicating that there are still spaces for improvement of the product in terms of its pragmatic and hedonic quality.

The results of the 3 dimensions can be visualized in the Fig. 2

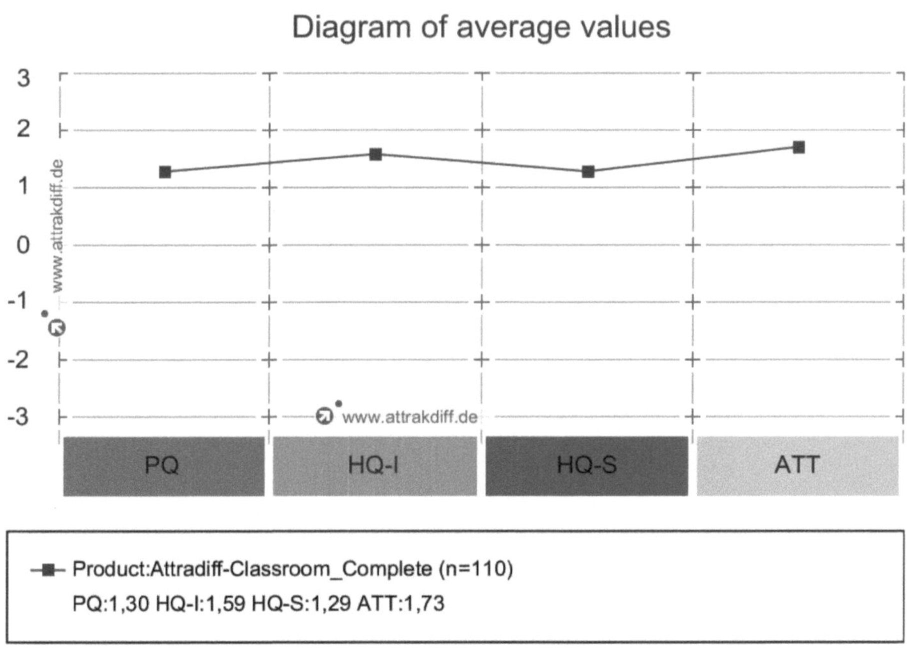

Fig. 2. Mean values of each dimensions

According to Fig. 2, the Pragmatic Quality (PQ) describes that the user has achieved all the desired learning goals, despite having the lowest score (1.30), thus denoting that it meets the needs of a classroom. The Hedonic Identity Quality (HQ-I) that indicates the level of user identification with the application has a score of 1.59. Through this score, we observe that the application is a recommended tool for students of different age groups seeking a more dynamic knowledge. The Hedonic Quality of Stimulus (HQ-S), which evaluates if the application is original, interesting and stimulating, had a score of 1.29. The main items that stood out were ingenuity and creativity, demonstrating that the application is innovative and brings a different encouragement for students to study. Attractiveness (ATT), which says how attractive the Google Classroom is to the user, has a score of 1.73, very close to the maximum value. According to the questionnaire responses, this is due to the application's ease of use and accessibility.

In Fig. 3, the AttrakDiff scale indicates user associations of word pairs on a seven level, semantic differential scale. With the center point at 0, the values positioned to the right are 1, 2, and 3, and the values to the left are −1, −2, and −3. The methodology

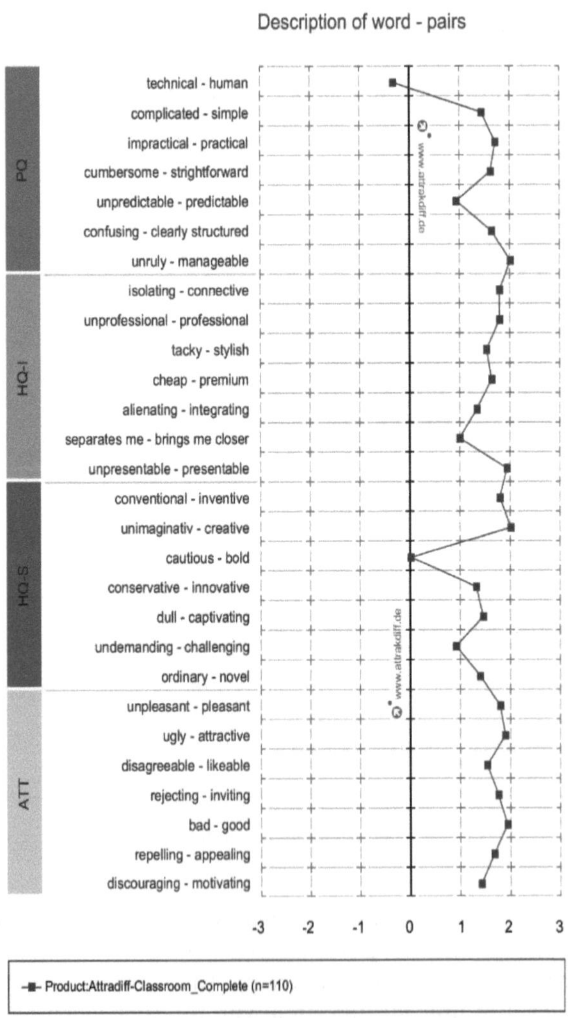

Fig. 3. Mean values of word pairs

recommends attention to the points in the extremities, because they are very well resolved or critical issues. We expect that most points will be positioned to the right of the dividing line; i.e., values above 0 and, where possible, close to 3.

According to the Description of Peer Words in Fig. 3, in the Pragmatic Quality dimension (PQ), the Technical - Human item has a value close to −0.50, showing that the application has a less colloquial language, and in the Hedonic Quality of Stimulus (HQ-S), the Caution - Bold item has a score of 0, a neutral value indicating that Google Classroom had a good acceptance. Of all the AttrakDiff word pairs, these are the only ones with non - favorable values that gave zero or below zero. In contrast, we obtained other items with more positive scores. Under Pragmatic Quality (PQ), the Manageable item has a positive score of 2, indicating that students felt extremely willing to work with the application because it was easy to use, aligning with the Hedonic Quality - Identity (HQ-I). The item Presentable has a value close to 2,0 denoting that the interface of the application is quite interesting to users. Also, under the Hedonic Quality - Stimulus (HQ- S), the Creative item has a very satisfactory value of 2, the application is both creative and available at no cost. Finally, the Good item in the Attractiveness dimension has a positive value very close to 2,0 thus highlighting the high level of user satisfaction.

4 Conclusion

This article presented an evaluation of usability and user satisfaction regarding the use of google classroom. The results found from the analysis of the data collected by AttrakDiff showed that improvements can be made to promote a greater identification and interaction of the user with the classroom. According to Pragmatic Quality, the results showed that users exhibited a greater focus on the task to be performed, and the predictability could be improved so that participant frustration is not caused. In the dimension of Hedonic Quality, we can see that we have a captivating and connective platform, bringing user motivation and satisfaction. With the results obtained in the Practicality item, we can infer that the classroom fulfills its objectives: facilitating student understanding of the content and making learning less dense. Improvements still need to be made, in order to provide the most technical and fun educational game. A difficulty reported by the participants was the process of responding to a task suggested by the teacher, since the students did not know how to post the answers due to a low proficiency with the technology.

When technology and education are applied together, everyone involved benefits. The student, because the classroom is an easy-to-use platform that is quickly accessible anywhere, and the teacher, because they can interact with the students, offer activities, and track who has answered on the platform itself. The student satisfaction analysis through AttrakDiff is a useful measure of the benefits of the Classroom platform, and has showed that Classroom can be a great tool used in pedagogical practice as a support to the teaching learning process. This study can serve as a starting point for research in this area, and for the development of new technologies related to education.

In addition, the analysis of results obtained through tests with voluntary users demonstrates the high degree of attractiveness, satisfaction and willingness to work with the application because it is easy to manipulate and customize the Google Classroom. To corroborate this argument, we highlight the fact that the Classroom uses different types of interactive devices than the most commonly used ones, allowing for new ways of interacting and contributing to student immersion into the material.

References

1. Cruz, J.A.S., Bizelli, J.L.: Educação contemporânea e as tecnologias : educar para os meios. X Conferência Bras. Mídia Cid. e V Conferência Sul-Americana Mídia Cid., September 2015
2. Costa, I., Gaspar, W., Conte, T., Gadelha, B., Oliveira, E.: Melhor prevenir do que remediar: Avaliando usabilidade e UX de software antes de levá-lo para a sala de aula. An. do XXVII Simpósio Bras. Informática na Educ. (SBIE 2016) Melhor, no. Cbie, p. 806 (2016)
3. Sinkinson, M.: Technology devices and social media as determinants of youth health and well-being: pre-service health education teachers interpret implications for their own practice. Int. J. Heal. Promot. Educ. **52**(5), 235–244 (2014)
4. Lemos, W., Junior, I., Filho, A.C.: Uma Proposta de um Serious Game no Auxílio do Aprendizado da Anatomia Humana. In: Anais do XXVIII Simpósio Brasileiro de Informática na Educação (SBIE 2017) Uma, 2017, no. Cbie, p. 655 (2017)
5. Silva, A., Valerio, M., Albuquerque, P., Filho, A.C.: Anatomia Digital: Um ambiente virtual de apoio ao processo ensino-aprendizagem. In: Brazilian Symposium on Computers in Education (Simpósio Brasileiro de Informática na Educação - SBIE), vol. 28, no. 1, p. 745 (2017)
6. Harrison, B., et al.: Through the eye of the master: the use of virtual reality in the teaching of surgical hand preparation. In: 2017 IEEE 5th International Conference Serious Games Applications Health SeGAH 2017 (2017)
7. GOOGLE. Google Classroom | Google for Education (2018)
8. Simão, J.P.S., et al.: Inovação Educativa e Usabilidade em Ambientes Virtuais de Aprendizagem. Rev. Tecnol. na Educ., vol. 21, no. Sited, pp. 1–12 (2017)
9. Santana, E.C., Pereira, C.E.: ANÁLISE DE USABILIDADE EM AMBIENTES VIRTUAIS DE APRENDIZAGEM. *Rev.* Científica Interdiscip. Pensar Saber, pp. 7–17, 2015
10. Hassenzahl, M., Burmester, M., Koller, F.: AttrakDiff: Ein Fragebogen zur Messung wahrgenommener hedonischer und pragmatischer Qualität. Mensch Comput., pp. 187–196 (2003)
11. TLX @ NASA Ames – Home. https://humansystems.arc.nasa.gov/groups/TLX/. Accessed 02 Mar 2019
12. Slaughter, B., Norman, L., Shneiderman, K.: Assessing Users' Subjective Satisfaction with the Information System for Youth Services (ISYS). In: VA Tech Proc. of Third Annual Mid-Atlantic Human Factors Conference, pp. 164–170 (1995)
13. Sauro, J.: SUPR-Q: a comprehensive measure of the quality of the website user experience. J. Usability Stud. **10**(2), 68–86 (2015)
14. Lewis, J.R.: IBM computer usability satisfaction questionnaires: psychometric evaluation and instructions for use (1995). http://hcibib.org/search:quest=J.IJHCI.7.1.57. Accessed 02 Mar 2019
15. SUMI Questionnaire Homepage. http://sumi.uxp.ie/. Accessed 02 Mar 2019
16. AttrakDiff. http://attrakdiff.de/index-en.html#hello. Accessed 25 Feb 2019

Gamification Design Framework Based on Self Determination Theory for Adult Motivation

Stavroula Karra(✉), Vasiliki Karampa(✉), and Foteini Paraskeva(✉)

Department of Digital Systems, University of Piraeus, Karaoli Dimitriou St. 80, 185 34 Piraeus, Greece
stavri_k7@hotmail.com, {bkarampa, fparaske}@unipi.gr

Abstract. It is particularly important to understand the role of motivation in digital learning environments so that designers taking advantage of design principles can encourage trainee's engagement and, by extension, the learning process and further contribute to reducing the drop-out rates. This study aims to add evidence to the context of e-learning motivational design, based on Gamification and motivational strategies of Self Determination Theory (SDT), by integrating them appropriately into Moodle Learning Management System. Judging from the initial positive results of the research conducted through an e-learning course for adult trainees and where the combination of SDT and Gamification played a key role, the proposed framework seems to have great impact on trainees' motivation and satisfaction, leading us to describe it as a "well-designed" solution. However, a further rigorous analysis on the results is considered necessary in the future.

Keywords: Self Determination Theory (SDT) · Gamification · Education · Game elements · Intrinsic motivation · Moodle

1 Introduction

Nowadays, the way one learns, is constantly transforming. The rapid development of technology, as well as the variety of human needs, have necessarily shaped a different approach to the educational process. The entry of digital technologies and social media has changed the way trainees are involved, creating, sharing, discussing and reforming experiences. Increasingly, e-learning environments are developed and applied to sectors, including the entrepreneurial. More and more, business recognize the multiple benefits of e-learning and empower such training solutions in order to have in workforce efficient and expertized employees. From the other hand and with no doubt employees easily and fast can improve their knowledge and skills, as to become more competitive, paving the way to their future career development.

However, in e-learning settings a major problem that continuous to involve many researchers is drop-outs that appear in higher rates than in face to face settings, especially in adult education. Obviously, this fact is justified, since adult trainees dispose specific features like self-regulation, orientation to goals, familiar contexts etc. [14]. Lately, literature research has highlighted e-learning drop-out factors [10] but with a vague documentation about their comprehension. Nevertheless, most researchers

L. Uden et al. (Eds.): LTEC 2019, CCIS 1011, pp. 67–78, 2019.
https://doi.org/10.1007/978-3-030-20798-4_7

advocate to factors such as lack of time, lack of supervision of management, problems with technology, inexperienced operators, badly designed courses and mainly to lack of motivation – satisfaction [5].

Focused on the last two abovementioned factors, there is a crucial need for constructing e-learning courses that will be well-designed under motivational guidelines, capable to provide trainees motives for engagement, real participation and course completion [21]. In addition, motivation boosts trainees' satisfaction and attitudes towards educational process [1] and drive them to accomplish their tasks, presenting better outcomes. Based on this perspective, the article attempts to present a well-orchestrated framework tailored on practices which incorporate the Self Determination (SDT) theoretical background and motivational gamified techniques. The rest of this document is structured as follows: Sect. 2 contains the theoretical background, namely a literature review with our contribution to the theoretical knowledge. Section 3 refers to the Methodology. Section 4 concerns SDT, Gamification and Moodle and finally, Sect. 5 presents the Discussion and the Conclusions.

2 Theoretical Background

In order to enhance e-learning courses, designers are mainly based on motivational design principals, aiming to empower intrinsic motivation. It is widely accepted that when trainees are intrinsically motivated, they will have greater learning outcomes than those who are not and consequently will be more motivated to do so in the future [12].

The emergence of intrinsic motivation arises from the coverage of three basic human needs: (1) competence, (2) autonomy and (3) relatedness. Initially, the term competence has been linked to many other terms such as self-efficacy [3] and strategies for success [6]. Deci et al. [7] argue that the positive feedback is an indisputable factor in the competence of the individual. Werbach and Hunter [22] also point out that every person feels competent when it deliberately influences the environment in which it interacts. When the person feels that can face and solve problems at that time feelings of pleasure are created. Additionally, autonomy concerns someone' s need to control his actions and choices and implies his psychological freedom and will to fulfill a task. Research results [22] revealed greater growth of intrinsic motivation, when trainees were asked to define time frames and activities that wanted to carry out, in contrast with the imposition of limits and the creation of possible fear assessment that led to its undermining. Finally, relatedness represents the basic desire of the individual to be integrated by the social environment [4, 8]. It refers to the inherent need of the individual to develop social ties and feel part of a group.

Across the viewpoint of the three above human needs, Self Determination Theory SDT [8, 18], a long-term theory of human motivation, emotion and development, focuses on factors that either facilitate or prevent assimilation and development processes in humans. SDT can be studied more in the field of motivation in education as it creates a two-way relationship between motives and learning.

From the other hand, gamification takes advantage of technological means and game elements, practices and methods, stimulating engagement, affecting behaviors in performing a task or achieving a goal via game-like systems [1]. It includes a variety of game elements [22], namely game components such as among others, badges, points, levels and quests; mechanisms such as collaboration, discovery and feedback; dynamics such as emotions, progress, narrative and relationships as well. By exploiting game design elements in non-gaming contexts like work or learning environments, motivation is enhanced effectively [13] and as a result, performance increases. According to Zichermann [23], gamification techniques could grow skill acquiring new knowledge up to 40%. In general, surveys converge to the fact that if design and implementation are done properly, gamification will have positive effects on learning [9].

Table 1. SDT and gamification

SDT		Gamification techniques (e-courses)	Gamification elements		
Core components	Strategies		Components	Mechanisms	Dynamics
Competence	C1 – Scaffolding	Inform users for their progression through messages		Instant Feedback	
	C2 – Fun learning activities	Integrate interactive digital material	Quests Content Unlocking Battles/Boss fight	Challenges Luck	Emotions Constraints
	C3 – Control of learning process	Integrate visual elements for game levels and user's progression	Levels Progress Bar Ranking/ Leaderboards		Progress
		Provide users measurement of success	Points Virtual Goods/Assets		Emotions
Autonomy	A1 – Clear learning goals	Present main learning goals and guide users achieve them	Narrative/Scenario (Syllabus)		Emotions
	A2 – Customization of the environment	Provide the possibilities to customize their profile and dashboard	Avatar		Emotions Progress
	A3 – Feedback	Inform users for their progression through messages or visual elements	Levels Progress Bar Ranking/ Leaderboards	Instant Feedback	Emotions Progress
	A4 – Meaningful choices	Provide opportunities for choices with consequences	Quests	Challenges Transactions	Emotions
Relatedness	R1 – Collaboration	Provide opportunities for teams' creation	Teams	Transactions	Emotions Relationships
	R2 – Interaction and communication	Provide opportunities for socializing	Competition		
	R3 – Mutual Assistance	Provide possibilities for help (Co-Solver users)	Gifting/Sharing Resources		
	R4 – Social status	Give conspicuous rewards (Marks/Certifications/Badges)	Points Badges Achievements Collections Ranking	Resources Rewards	

However, in order to create a gamified e-course and evaluate the levels of efficiency based on the intrinsic motivation, there is a need to combine motivational theories with gamified practices [20]. SDT components directly seems to get linked to the games, since games enable autonomy (mode and game type), competence (end of the game) and relatedness (sharing success to friends). As a result, the following table (Table 1) is emerged through a literature review, [1, 2, 7, 8, 17–19] as an attempt of matching in detail SDT theory (human needs displayed as theory's core components and theory's strategies), as well as gamification (techniques and elements), in order to orchestrate robust solutions of well-designed e-courses.

As can be seen, gamification mechanisms and dynamics are shaping up a more exciting and participatory experience that encourages trainees to carry out concrete actions. They also rely on user's wishes for reward.

3 Methodology

This article aims to present the high impact of a well-designed conceptual framework on the motivation of adult trainees. Particularly, it presents how gamification techniques are tailored to the SDT guidelines by providing capabilities for customization of an e-learning environment such as Moodle, while increasing its potential, thereby positively affecting trainees' engagement and performance. According to that purpose the Research Questions are formed as follows:

RQ1: Is there an effect on the motivation of adult trainees by designing an educational scenario based on Self Determination Theory (SDT), adapting appropriately gamification techniques/elements?

RQ2: How Moodle could be customized upon the guidelines of Self Determination Theory (SDT) and gamification in order to serve effectively the proposed framework?

In order to find answers to the above research questions, an online training course for customer communication and training was developed based on a well-orchestrated educational scenario. The name "Lord of the Riiiings" was chosen for the course as a variant of the famous trilogy by J. R. R. Tolkien, "The Lord of the Rings". This choice is entirely justified, because either the course refers to trainees involved in a customer service department or the enjoyment was attempted to be increased. Besides, the scenario/narrative is encompassed by the gamification dynamics which is related to users' behavior and interaction and provokes their greater urge.

Specifically, in this game-based scenario, the powerful Lord Sauron has stolen all communication skills that belong to the Hobbits and has closed them on an object called the "golden" earpiece. A little hobbit called Frodo asks each trainee to help the Hobbits find the pieces of the golden earpiece and destroy them, releasing the stolen skills. As a result, all trainees, having been informed about their mission, pass through all the main stations of the journey in Middle Earth, from Hobbiton to Mountain Doom (Fig. 1), learning basic facts and facing various challenges. If they deal with them successfully, they will reach their destination and defeat Lord Sauron.

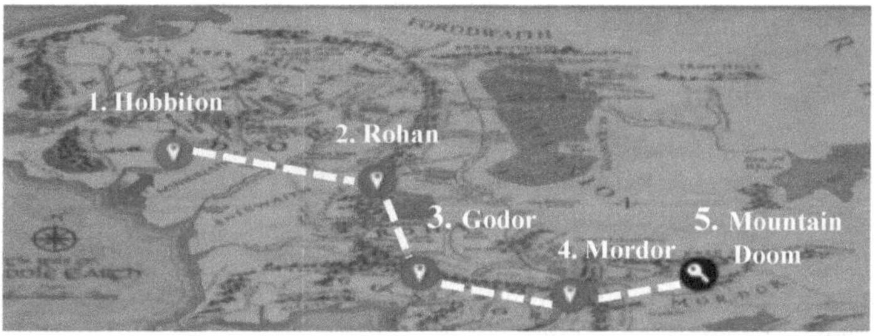

Fig. 1. The journey in Middle Earth (modules of the macro-script design)

4 Instructional Design

Since the SDT Theory doesn't include specific steps for the instructional design the macro-script was set in accordance with the gamified scenario. Thus, the training course was composed of five different modules. Each module serves different learning objectives (Table 2), corresponds to a station of the abovementioned journey and includes a four-step micro-script design of (1) Goals, (2) Material, (3) Activities and (4) Assessment. Furthermore, the Fig. 3 presents at the same time the macro-script (the five modules) and the micro-script (the four steps) of the design. The procedure (numbered tasks), the interaction (individual, group) as well as the components/strategies of the SDT theory are clearly imprinted.

Table 2. E-course main learning objectives – Step 1. Goals

ID	Learning objectives
LO1	Identify the characteristics of good customer service
LO2	Identify different types of customers and choose the appropriate management mode depending on the corresponding type
LO3	Learn ways to communicate effectively with all kinds of customers
LO4	Apply real-world knowledge and connect knowledge with incidents that are encountered
LO5	Make decisions and work with others
LO6	Develop communication skills

However, a brief description follows:

Module 1. Hobbiton (Estimated time: 1 day): This module is preparatory and concerns tasks such as the announcement of the e-course learning objectives and syllabus (goals) as well as instructions for Moodle's environment functionality (material) and avatar creation (activities). It aims to join trainees to the learning process in order to be part of the story as individuals.

Module 2. Rohan (Estimated time: 3 days): In this module trainees deal with the concepts of good/bad customer service. After they have get informed for the learning goals (goals – LO1, LO4) and the learning content (material), initially they are asked to define the features of an efficient customer service by brainstorming. In addition, they accomplish interactive activities (activities) like a case-study analysis. A positive feedback is given for their correct answers and at last they test their knowledge through quiz (assessment).

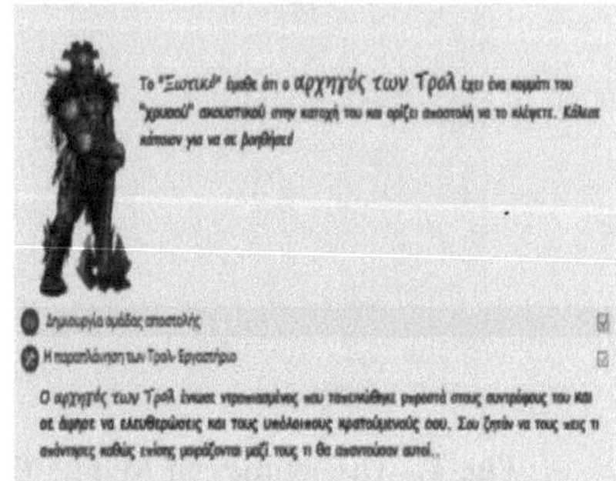

Fig. 2. Screenshot of narrative and activities in Moodle (Module 3)

Module 3. Godor (Estimated time: 3 days): The concept of effective customer management is highlighted in this module. Once again, the learning goals (goals –LO2, LO4, LO5, LO6) and the learning content (material) are announced, including further information about the collaborative technique of Think-Pair-Share. Therefore, pair-teams are formed by user's free choice and a collaborative case-study activity takes place (activities). The module ends up with both peer-to-peer and self-assessment (assessment).

Module 4. Mordor (Estimated time: 3 days): A similar procedure is repeated as in the previous module. However, the difference refers to the learning content, namely the concept of effective customer complaints management (goals – LO3, LO4, LO5, LO6/material). In addition, the activities include two case studies (activities) with the second being decisive for the progress of the trainees, since the trainees must be evaluated (assessment) based on all learning concepts they have been taught, as well as they must overcome a grading limitation of 80%.

Module 5. Mountain Doom (Estimated time: 1 day): In this module, trainees gain their certification for the course completion as an instant feedback which is a visual recognition of their achievement.

Figure 3 also presents the Moodle tools that were incorporated by the design and will be described in detail in the next section. For example, in Module 3, in "Godor", a page was used to announce learning objectives to the trainees. In accordance with the narrative, the "Elf", through a SCORM and a lesson activity, helped trainees study the digital material. Then, in order to deal with the threat of the Trolls' chief (Fig. 2), who trapped them in a case-study workshop activity about effective customer management, they collaborated with peers. At the end, through a quiz, namely a challenge, trainees managed to escape from Sauron and through access restriction & activity completion settings, they discovered a piece of the "golden" earpiece.

It is worth to be mentioned that while the story evolves during modules, trainees have opportunities for free choice, social interaction as they ask and give help,

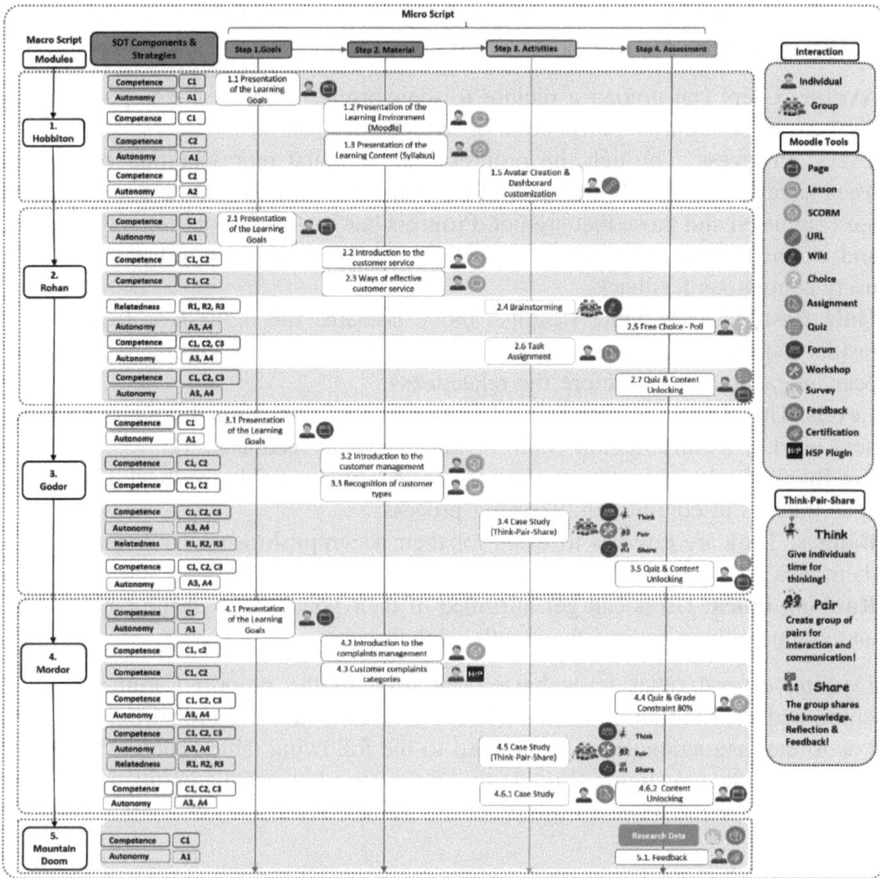

Fig. 3. Instructional design of the e-course "Lord of the Riiiings"

communicate, discuss in order to collaborate, share their experience, gain enjoyment and recognition. Through this dynamic process, autonomy, competence and relatedness get enhanced. At the same time motivation and satisfaction get empowered.

5 SDT, Gamification and Moodle

O'Donovan et al. [16] argue that there is a lack of technological support in formulating properly a gamified activity as well as there is no effective management system learning that could provide what is considered necessary in gamified courses. Nevertheless, Moodle is one of the Learning Management Systems (LMS) that dispose elements customized easily and simple, facilitating gamification, aiming at trainees' active participation and motivation. Researchers [11, 15] outline that Moodle can offer the following capabilities for gamification:

- **Avatar**: Users can upload a picture to their profile. Avatars are important, since they cover autonomy's perspective of free choices [2].
- **Users' Progress**: Through the progress bar, a visual representation of progress, users have the ability get informed of the number of activities to be done, those that are completed and those that are not. Progress bar is a useful tool for self-regulation and empowers the components of competence and autonomy, given that it offers users continuous feedback.
- **Quiz Results**: The "Quiz Results" block contains the highest or lowest scores results and strengthens the competitive users' nature, whereas they enhance peer to peer interaction and therefore the relatedness.
- **Levels**: The "Level Up" block displays the level of trainees and the progress to the next level. This information could be considered as feedback, too.
- **Feedback**: Both quiz and assignment, among others enable feedback that encourages trainees to continue the learning process.
- **Badges**: They are rewards to users for their accomplishments. Trainees can share them as a means of social recognition.
- **Ranking block**: Users can get informed of their points through the ranking tables and compare them against the results of their peers.

Despite, several other tools have been used in the proposed framework. The matching and distribution of all used Moodle tools to the theoretical background as well as to the instructional design is listed to the following table (Table 3).

In addition, the next figure (Fig. 4) shows the most important gamification elements that were used for the needs of the proposed framework.

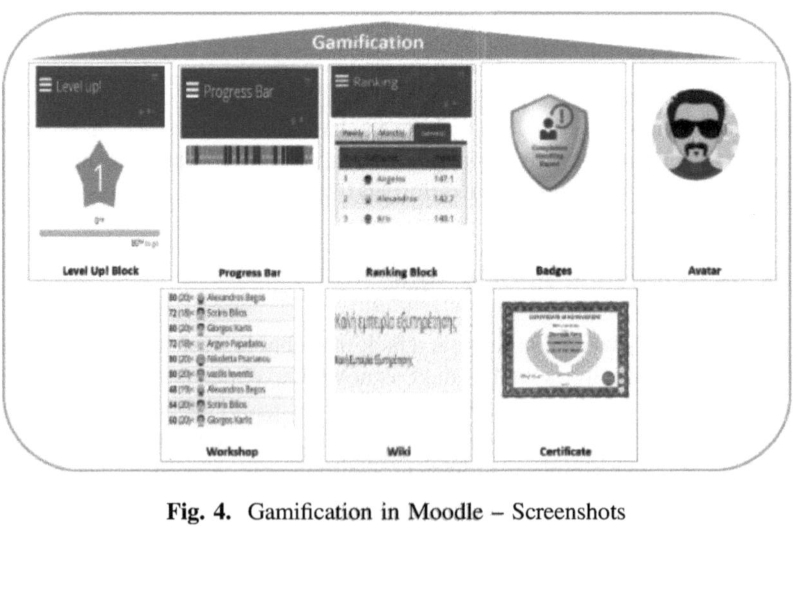

Fig. 4. Gamification in Moodle – Screenshots

Table 3. Design, theoretical background and moodle

Instructional design			Moodle tools	Core	Plugin	Aim/ gamification technique	SDT strategies	Gamification elements
Macro-Script	Micro-Script	1. Goals	Page	✓		Presentation of main learning goals	C1, A1	Narrative/ Scenario (Syllabus)
		2. Material	Lesson	✓		Provision of different learning paths for the learning material	C2, A1	Challenges
			SCORM	✓		Presentation of Interactive Content		
			H5P		✓			
		3. Activities	URL	✓		Access to external websites	A2	Avatars
			Wiki	✓		Brainstorming	R1, R2, R3	Quests Teams Collaboration
			Assignment	✓		Individual/ Collaborative tasks	C1, A4, R1	
			Choice	✓		Free user's choice on queries for customer service	A3, A4	Instant Feedback
		4. Assessment	Workshop	✓		Collaborative tasks and peer-to-peer assessment	C1, A4, R1	Quests Teams Collaboration
			Quiz	✓		Formative cognitive assessment	C1, A4	Challenges
Macro-Script			Badges	✓		Provision ofrewards	A3, R4	Badges/ Achievements Rewards Instant Feedback
			Certification		✓			
			Progress Bar Block		✓	Visualization of progression	C3, A3	Progress Bar
			Level Up Block		✓			Levels
			Ranking Block		✓		C3, A3, R4	Ranking
			Forum	✓		Interaction Communication	A4, R2, R3	-
			Chat	✓				
			Dashboard Customization	✓		Integration of free choice	A2	Avatars
			Access Restriction	✓		Integration of constraints	C2	Content Unlocking Challenges
			Activity Completion	✓				
			Survey	✓		*Collection of research data*	-	-
			Feedback	✓				

The research was conducted with the participation of sixteen adult trainees without previous experience on customer communication and training. All of them completed the e-course successfully and gained the certification of accomplishment. The initial research findings can give a clear picture for the impact of the design on their motivation (RQ1). The research data collected by a post-test (an improvised questionnaire with twelve questions in likert scale 1–5, where 1 = Absolutely Disagree, 5 = Absolutely Agree), shown greater means than mean test-value 3 (Table 4), for all SDT components.

Therefore, the presented framework attempted to support an e-course for adult trainees by combining SDT strategies with gamification elements and incorporating them appropriately into Moodle Learning Management System, aiming to enhance their motivation. As one can find out, from the abovementioned (Table 3), the three components of SDT theory, competence, satisfaction and relatedness seems to be supported by the instructional design sufficiently.

From the other hand, Moodle can be customized effectively under the guidelines of SDT and gamification (RQ2), by installing third-party plugins and exploiting appropriately a variety of educational tools that disposes (Table 3). This assumption is confirmed by the research data collected by COLLES questionnaire (Table 5). COLLES (Constructivist On-Line Learning Environment Survey) is a Moodle survey with twenty-four questions grouped into six scales (Relevance, Reflection, Interactivity, Tutor Support, Peer Support, Interpretation) in likert scale 1–5 (where 1 = Almost Never, 2 = Seldom, 3 = Sometimes, 4 = Often, 5 = Almost Always) and evaluates the quality of the on-line environment by presenting the preferred and the actual perceptions of trainees about the e-course.

Table 4. Motivation means

	N	Minimum	Maximum	Mean	Std
Competence	16	3.8	5	4.3	0.3
Autonomy	16	3.8	5	4.4	0.3
Relatedness	16	4	5	4.5	0.3
Motivation	16	4	4.9	4.4	0.2

Table 5. Trainees' perception - COLLES means

	N	Minimum	Maximum	Mean	Std
Relevance actual	16	3.25	5	4.3438	0.63819
Relevance preferred	16	3	5	4.3594	0.59839
Reflective thought actual	16	1	5	1.7188	1.05623
Reflective thought preferred	16	1	4	1.6875	0.75
Interactivity actual	16	3	5	4.0781	0.71716
Interactivity preferred	16	2.5	5	4.0313	0.67004
Tutor support actual	16	2.75	5	4.2031	0.64691
Tutor support preferred	16	2.5	5	4.2031	0.72583
Peer support actual	16	2.75	5	4.1094	0.81122
Peer support preferred	16	2.5	4.75	3.9531	0.57893
Interpretation actual	16	3	5	4.1406	0.57712
Interpretation preferred	16	3.25	5	4.3594	0.5625

It is obvious that most means referring to actual perceptions such as the relevance of are greater than the preferred, and as a result, trainees expressed a pleasant learning experience. Overall, the e-course enhances trainees to engage, provides satisfaction and empowers motivation, confirming thus the well-designed framework.

6 Discussion and Conclusions

Non-gaming environments can be more entertaining when game elements are incorporated, but at the same time can offer the achievement of learning goals effectively. The imitation of games should be an integrated part of instructional motivational design, since games model the real world and refer to human psychological needs and behaviors. Recent research [9] highlights the term "good gamification" implying the transformation of the learning by students, when they by themselves after immediate feedback for their failure, redefine the goals and move towards to their accomplishment. In addition, the intrinsic motivation becomes stronger when they perceive learning experience with a sense of autonomy, competence and relatedness.

Despite, in a standardized system, improving user's engagement is achieved by enhancing both extrinsic and intrinsic motivation, but an inappropriate use of extrinsic motivation will probably reduce the intrinsic motivation of the user. Since intrinsic motivation can affect the user internally and improve his engagement for a long time, we must pay more attention to its promotion. According to SDT, the encouragement of intrinsic motivation succeeds in, when gamification keeps up with the three basic psychological needs - autonomy, competence and relatedness.

Moreover, a well-designed framework based on a motivational theory as SDT and gamification, contributes to the empirical evidence of motivational design, providing an integrated and robust solution against drop-out rates' decrease. However, the research limitations of the quite small sample of responders as well as the limited time range pave the way for further investigation. From the other hand, the completed research statistical analysis which will confirm exactly the proposed design framework and the research methodology is not presented currently, therefore our commitment is to do so in a future paper.

Acknowledgment. This work has been partly supported by the Research Center of the University of Piraeus.

References

1. Alafouzou, A., Lamprinou, D., Paraskeva, F.: Gamified Project based learning environment for motivation improvement. In: ECEL 2018 17th European Conference on e-Learning, p. 10. Academic Conferences and Publishing Limited (2018)
2. Anneta, A.L.: The "I's" have it: a framework for serious educational game design. Rev. Gen. Psychol. **14**(2), 105–112 (2010)
3. Bandura, A.: Self-efficacy: toward a unifying theory of behavioral change. Psychol. Rev. **84** (2), 191–215 (1977)

4. Baumeister, R.F., Leary, M.R.: The need to belong desire for interpersonal attachments as a fundamental human motivation. Psychol. Bull. **117**, 497–529 (1995)
5. Cheyung,Y. Winiecki, D.J., Fenner, J.A.: A case study: increase enrolment by reducing dropout rates in adult distance education, Madison, WI (1998)
6. Deci, L.E., Vallerand, R.L., Pelletier, L.G., Ryan, R.M.: Motivation and education: the self-determination perspective. Educ. Psychol. **26**(3–4), 325–346 (1991)
7. Deci, E., Koestner, R., Ryan, R.: A meta-analytic review of experiments examining the effects of extrinsic rewards on intrinsic motivation. Psychol. Bull. **125**(6), 627–668 (1999)
8. Deci, E.L., Ryan, R.M.: Intrinsic and extrinsic motivations: classic definitions and new directions. Contemp. Educ. Psychol. **25**, 54–67 (2000)
9. Dichev, C., Dicheva, D., Angelova, G., Agre, G.: From gamification to gameful design and gameful experience in learning. Cybern. Inf. Technol. **14**(4), 80–100 (2014)
10. Gortan, A., Jereb, E.: The dropout rate from e-learning courses and the satisfaction of students with e-learning. Organizacija **40**(6), 248–257 (2007)
11. Henrick, G.: Gamification - What is it and What it is in Moodle. Retrieved from SlideShare (2013). http://www.slideshare.net/ghenrick/gamification-what-is-it-and-what-it-is-in-moodle
12. Hodges, C.B.: Designing to motivate: motivational techniques to incorporate in e-learning experiences. J. Interact. Online Learn. **2**(3), 1–7 (2004)
13. Kapp, K.M.: The Gamification of Learning and Instruction: Game-based Methods and Strategies for Training and Education. Wiley, New York (2012)
14. Knowles, M.: La práctica moderna de la educación de adultos. Traducción de Marcos Faudez. Chicago, USA (1980)
15. Muntean, C.: Raising engagement in e-learning through gamification. In: 6th International Conference on Virtual Learning ICVL, pp. 323–329 (2011)
16. O'Donovan, S., Gain, J., Marais, P.: A case study in the gamification of a university-level games development course. In: Proceedings of the South African Institute for Computer Scientists and Information Technologists Conference, pp. 242–251. ACM (2013)
17. Rigby, S., Ryan, R.M.: Glued to Games: How Video Games Draw us in and Hold us Spellbound: How Video Games Draw us in and Hold us Spellbound. AbC-CLIo, Santa Barbara (2011)
18. Ryan, R.M., Deci, E.L.: Intrinsic and extrinsic motivations: classic definitions and new directions. Contemp. Educ. Psychol. **25**, 54–67 (2000)
19. Sailer, M., Hense, J., Mandl, J., Klevers, M.: Psychological perspectives on motivation through gamification. Interact. Des. Architecture **19**, 28–37 (2014)
20. Shi, L., Cristea, A.I.: Making it game-like: topolor 2 and gamified social e-learning. In: The 22nd Conference on User Modeling, Adaptation and Personalization, pp. 61– 64 (2014)
21. Tyler-Smith, K.: Early attrition among first time eTrainees: a review of factors that contribute to drop-out, withdrawal and non-completion rates of adult trainees undertaking eLearning programmes. J. Online Learn. Teach. **2**(2), 73–85 (2006)
22. Werbach, K., Hunter, K.: For the Win: How Game Thinking Can Revolutionize Your Business. Wharton Digital Press, Philadelphia (2012)
23. Zichermann, G., Cunningham, C.: Gamification by Design: Implementing Game Mechanics in Web and Mobile Apps. O'Reilly Media, Sebastopol (2011)

Designing a Video Course. The Case of the Online Course of Mathematical Olympiads

Lucía Rotger(✉) and Juan M. Ribera

University of La Rioja, Logroño, Spain
{lucia.rotger, juan-miguel.ribera}@unirioja.es

Abstract. Current secondary and university students use their technological devices not only in playtime but also in study time. Our proposal makes use of this fact to create educational content that can be viewed on any smartphone or computer. These videos can be used to teach new concepts, mathematical procedures or problem-solving resolutions. Although there is a wide variety of educational videos and MOOCs, on many occasions these videos do not fit in terms of content or notation. With this in mind, in this article, we define the detailed process that we should follow if we are interested in creating our own educational videos. We devote special attention to giving advice on video creation from a methodological point of view. This process is enhanced with an example of learning unit collection that we created at the University of La Rioja. The project that we present is a collection of math Olympiad problem-solving strategies that can be used as complementary learning materials.

Keywords: Educational videos · Video creation · Mathematics education · Mathematical olympiads

1 Introduction

Nowadays, our Secondary School students use many social networks. First we want to put emphasis on the use of Instagram due to its popularity. In this social network, users create and share stories of their own experiences in diverse ways, for instance, they can upload videos that are deleted after one day. On the other hand, there are more elaborated videos that are usually viewed and shared through YouTube. The main topics of these videos in particular are opinions, game strategies and music.

As we have just pointed out, short videos have become another source of information and tutorials for our students (Tan 2013). Currently, the majority of university students use videos predominantly to cover the content (Howard et al. 2017). Moreover, (Trenholm et al. 2012) showed that students enjoy and value online learning. This is the reason why we want to take advantage of the interest shown in this communication channel for the transmission of teaching content in mathematics. For this purpose, we should study the main features of those videos that attract students.

L. Uden et al. (Eds.): LTEC 2019, CCIS 1011, pp. 79–89, 2019.
https://doi.org/10.1007/978-3-030-20798-4_8

2 Video Creation Process

The use of video requires the application of a different teaching methodology from the usual live lectures. We can differentiate three processes which involve teaching contents at organizing our standard face-to-face lectures: the structuring and timing of the sessions in which we are going to impart this content, the teaching on these sessions and the subsequent reflection of the effectiveness of our teaching organization proposal. These three processes are closely related and are a sign of the dynamism of our lectures. In fact, what happens often is that our initial planning is not analogous to the final structure of the sessions that we impart. Moreover, in many cases we make some modifications in the structure of the teaching sessions once we have taught that lesson, especially when that content has not been correctly comprehended by our students, to keep it in mind in future courses.

In the case of the creation of video teaching content, those three processes are modified when organizing the videos through which we want to present that content. Thus, we differentiate three new processes related with the production of teaching content in the video. Planning, structuring, timing, and preparing video pills constitute the first process. The second one consists in the recording of formerly designed video pills. The last one is the edition of raw videos recorded during the second process.

The first process has higher relevance in terms of the organization of the video sequences, even more relevance that in the face-to-face teaching. In this process, a large number of decisions are made that are associated with the teaching content and how that content is created. In addition, the difficulties brought about the modification of the video sequences once they have been recorded and edited makes necessary to analyze concisely all the possible difficulties that the students may find when they visualize the contents.

Afterwards, the video recording of the content differs in some aspects from the teaching methodology of the face-to-face lectures. For instance, in our on-site lectures we have exclusively one opportunity to release our teaching content while, when recording, we can make as many recordings as we want to until we get a correct presentation of the planned teaching content. Even so, this causes more pressure on the teacher who is being recorded. Typically, teachers who are recorded try to achieve perfection on its content presentation. Recording video content process also makes us take into account other details related to verbal communication that we usually do not consider in face-to-face sessions. In these classes, non-verbal communication is more widely used than in video lessons. Those examples show a clear difference between these two teaching processes. What makes recorded material very rewarding is the fact that it can be used as many times as desired, enabling the students to review the explanations and the teachers to reuse video lessons.

Finally, video edition is a very useful process that allows us to perfect our teaching pills in different ways. On the one hand, the editing process can be useful in order to select the best versions of our recordings, allowing us to choose our best speeches. On the other hand, our recording viewings may reveal the need to add visual elements or graphics that make a clearer presentation of the contents. These graphic elements can be added in the editing process and can be part of the previous sessions planning.

In addition, the teacher can observe the necessity of graphic elements after viewing all recordings of the content. This process, as has seen shown, is closely related to the reflections made by teachers after their classes. In the design of video lessons, one of the most important processes is the creation of teaching content.

In the following sections, we will discuss in detail the factors that have to be taken into account in the process of generating video teaching content.

2.1 Planning

The preparation of lessons in face-to-face lectures needs not only contents but also methodology. When we are interested in the creation of teaching videos, the planning process has an even greater relevance. In this case, we should pay more attention to the communication of contents by making a point to make an exposition of contents that are as clear and self-contained as possible. To achieve that, the first thing we should know is the aim of each one of our video lessons. Here we present some objectives related to each part of the teaching-learning process (motivation and introduction, presentation and explanation and finally application):

- Short texts that aim to guide or motivate a mathematical definition or basic practical examples that contribute to the understanding of a certain concept or situation.
- Graphic animations that allow contextualizing some concepts. In this way, we can have both symbolic and graphic elements for content presentation.
- Real examples of the use or application of some mathematical proceedings. We can present the most characteristic examples.

In addition, we should take into account a greater number of factors than in face-to-face teaching. An example of that is the analysis of the situation, the planning, the timing of the process and the creation of complementary documentation.

First, we should select the topic of our videos, while we determine the technical equipment that we have. The technical features of the equipment are closely related to the methodology that we will follow for the presentation of the content in our videos. It is very important to maximize the use of the technical features of recording and edition equipment to allow our presentation to be as clear and didactic as possible. We can found an example of this previous analysis in videos of mathematical calculations, since the correct visualization of the steps followed in the resolution is needed to understand the process. Therefore, a previous study of the recording form it is necessary, especially, to provide the most comfortable visualization of each resolution step. A common problem found in mathematical teaching videos is the partial covering of the steps or the writing of the formulas. These blocks prevent having a general overview of the process followed.

Once we select the subject and analyze the situation, we sequence and sketch our content, organizing the information. This previous work has multiple applications in obtaining a quality video teaching material. In the first place, the sketching content process will allow us to organize our content by selecting the right order to present it. In addition, sketching will allow us to separate those contents that can be set apart from others, thus enabling the production of self-contained recordings. In the same way, it will facilitate to show existing connections among different parts of our teaching content. An example of the importance of the sketching process can be seen in the recording of the mathematical procedure known as conversion factors. This recording can be used not only in the teaching unit of measurements, which belongs to mathematics, but also in teaching units of physics and chemistry. Therefore, it is useful in different moments of the educational process.

In parallel to the sequencing and schematization, we would create a script, but we may require other complementary materials besides the recordings. This need is one of the factors that should be taken into account in the planning of the video teaching contents. Not only is it important to have a well-defined scheme and sequence, but also to take into account all the details that we want within the recording. It depends on the teachers' knowledge of the subject, the conciseness of the script and its length. For example, in our face-to-face sessions, we usually have special cases planned to present the mathematical contents in a meaningful way. In addition, another element that can facilitate the comprehension of the video contents is the creation of graphics or visual elements. Moreover, we can mention the visual elements in the recordings and then add these elements later on in the video-edition process. Teachers should prepare these graphic elements previously to mentioning them when it is appropriate in the recording.

The selection of the recording methodology of the content is also part of the planning process. Depending on the content and on the financial availability, we recommend different content recording methods. Here we present some possibilities:

- Directly recording to teacher with a good quality camera. This recording method is the one that most resembles classroom teaching. In this type of recordings, sound quality requires especial attention since the farther the teacher is from the camera the worse the audio quality of the recorded content is. In this case, we recommend the use of complementary microphones to solve any sound issue. Another detail to consider is the added difficulty that we may found when we are recording the teacher and the blackboard at the same time. To solve any problem that this situation may bring, we recommend using a secondary support camera when the teacher is using the board.
- Screen recording. This method is also known as Screencast, a name that is similar to the trademark of the software that we recommend to perform this task, Screencast-O-Matic. When we use this type of software we can capture the contents on the computer screen while we are commenting in the screen movements. With this recording methodology, you can use elements of live lectures (such as a PowerPoint) combined with audio, videos, subtitles, visual demonstrations or interactive components (Farkas 2007). The possibility of re-visualizing the recordings helps to adapt them to the different learning paces of the students. Since we can split the video and audio of a recording in the edition process if necessary, we could record the sound separately from a video that has already been recorded. We recommend this content recording method for the acquisition of using procedures for mathematical programs such as Geogebra constructions, data statistics collection and handling and arithmetical calculations.
- Document camera. This recording device mixes aspects of teacher's camera recording with the screen recording. In this case, recording with a document camera enables to record videos of the movements that are made throughout a sheet of

paper from an overhead perspective. Thus, it is possible to record both handmade operations and sequences of actions of manipulative elements of mathematics. This recording method is widely used because it is the most similar to the notes taking recording. If no camera of this type is available, you can use a camera on a tripod so that you can record from above.

2.2 Recording

In consonance with the video requirements that students are used to nowadays, Pérez-Navío et al. (2015) recommend some characteristics that we can adapt to the math videos recording process:

- Creating videos of approximately 5 min in length. Several studies show that people begin to lose interest in videos when they last longer than 10 min.
- Introducing narrative elements. In this aspect, it is important for the video to include a summary at the beginning of the content that we are going to explain. We also recommend the inclusion of another summary at the end of the video with the main ideas covered in it. In the particular case of procedural videos, it is advisable to sequence correctly the steps followed in the resolution of the exercises and problems.
- Introducing symbolic elements such as tables, graphs and other forms of presenting mathematical content while we narrate the explanations needed. They can be added in the edition process as additional digital graphic elements. We can also consider the use of physical manipulative materials to support our explanations.

All these recommendations show how important the previous planning is to the teaching content recording.

In addition, we should take some aspects related to verbal communication into consideration. In order to get closer to the students and be as clear as possible, we recommend:

- Speak slowly, taking care of your diction, especially on those words that are specificaly mathematical. Define new and abstract terms using a more familiar vocabulary. Even write these terms or leave them on the screen.
- Avoid double negations and passive voice in the resolution of procedures and in the steps of transitions in operations.
- Vary the tone of voice, putting emphasis on the main points or the most important mathematical properties used in the resolution processes.
- Use nouns instead of pronouns to refer to the elements that appear in the presented content. In this way, we will improve the acquisition of new mathematical terms.

2.3 Edition

Last but not least, we will elaborate the final phase of the creation of videos with mathematical content: the edition process. The main purpose of the edition process is to add the visual and graphical complements that we have previously recommended and that help to facilitate knowledge building. (Lucas et al. 2015). Furthermore, the editing process should be used to check on other visual and narrative elements.

Concerning the visual aspects, we should examine the frames, the composition, the lighting, etc.; this means that we would check if everything on the screen can be read. In the same way, the teacher should take care of the movements in front of the camera avoiding oscillating and other rough movements. The controlled use of gestures also prevents monotony in our speech. Hand gestures are the most frequently suggested ones, although the teacher should avoid performing repetitive or excessive gestures (Cáceres and Martínez 2017).

On the other hand, concerning the narration, we should verify the use of affirmations that indicate the beginning and end of the topics explained. These affirmations are a guide in the scheme and link the parts of the presentation (Cáceres and Martínez 2017). The use of these narrative elements will aid the students to realize what the purpose of the video that are visualizing is and to relate it to other visualized contents.

For the edition of the video content, we recommend paid software such as Camtasia like other authors such as Abassian and Sieben (2015). There are free alternatives, such as OpenShot, which can be used for editing short videos. However, they frequently cause problems when working with high quality or long duration videos.

2.4 Evaluation

There are different methods that we can use for the evaluation of the students visualizations of the video, many of them related to the Flipped Classroom or inverted class (https://www.theflippedclassroom.es/). It is necessary to implement these evaluations in order to check not only the visualization but also the meaningful learning of the contents. One of the tools we have used to get this feedback is the EdPuzzle platform. In this platform, we can enrich the edited videos as well as use other existing videos in the network. Thus, we can enrich our video recordings by adding audio explanations throughout the recording or references to the web. Another interesting action provided by the platform is the possibility to incorporate questions throughout the video. The use of these questions can be multiple: the evaluation of the video viewing, the evaluation of some strategy or procedure displayed in the video or the demand for further reasoning by the student. These multiple options allow us to register both the viewing of the video and to check the comprehension of the contents. Moreover, this platform offers the possibility of checking the number of visualizations of the video by every student, thus allowing us to know the most difficult aspects of the displayed content. A methodological proposal using EdPuzzle in the classroom can be checked in Orcos Palma et al. (2018)

Based on our experience, we recommend recording our own content before exploring the web for more content that satisfies our interests, especially in the case of mathematical learning content. Some factors such as differences in notation or the degree of the abstraction of the vocabulary used in these videos can generate a contradictory effect among the students. In addition, some educational videos in mathematics show procedures which are formally incorrect as Beltrán-Pellicer et al. (2018) analyzed.

3 An Implementation Case

We will illustrate the implementation of the characteristics of educative videos presented and studied previously with an example of use that we have developed.

The Online Course of Mathematical Olympiads is a course that includes a collection of learning units and their evaluations developed by a group of mathematics professors at the University of La Rioja. This course is currently formed by a set of 12 learning units that present different classic methodologies for solving math Olympiad problems. This online course aims to be complementary to the Seminar on Mathematics Problems that takes place weekly at the University of La Rioja.

3.1 Planning

In a first meeting, we established the contents that we wanted to cover in the recordings made by the members of the project. We singled out the topics that can be found among the classic problems of mathematical Olympiads. In this way, we tried to cover the ins and outs of the varied range of mathematical problems that students may be confronted with in a Mathematical Olympiad.

Once we determined the topics, we also defined the format of the video learning units that we want to create. We decided to design a minimum of four videos per learning unit: introduction and motivation for the use of the problem-solving strategy, theoretical elements associated with the problem-solving strategy, examples of a direct application of the problem-solving strategy, and examples of application of the problem-solving strategies in a real Mathematical Olympiad.

At the same time that we planed the sessions, we developed the teaching content of the mathematical problem-solving strategies. This educative content consists in slide presentations that supplement the video recordings, the collections of problems that we used in the videos, and the formative texts with theoretical content that summarize the contents studied in the learning units (Table 1).

Table 1. Mathematical topics in the Online Course of Mathematical Olympiads.

Pigeonhole and maximal principle	Induction principle
Plane geometry	The Theorems of Ceva and Menelaus
Game theory	Modular arithmetic
Series summation	Probability and combinatory
Polynomials	Recurrences relations
Inequalities of real numbers	Functional equations

3.2 Recording

In this phase, we assign the corresponding recordings to the teachers explaining the topics that they had planned in the first phase of the project.

Recording methods were of different types, depending on the content. It was possible to use existing recording equipment in the University consisting of two video cameras. In addition, it was possible to use computer screen-capture software, being able to observe the resolution processes by the teacher on the screen. All the recordings made by the group had followed the previous recommendations (Fig. 1).

Fig. 1. Example of recording method: two video cameras, a microphone and a computer in order to check the content scheme.

3.3 Edition

In order to make all the content available to learners interested in it, it was convenient to edit the recordings using video editing software. We purchased some licenses of the payment software Camtasia since our recordings were high-quality videos. Besides, we plan a workshop with the members of the project to know how to use the software and its possibilities. In this sense, teachers edited their own videos working with the software mentioned above (Fig. 2)

It was advisable to perform a revision of the content to correct the errata. This was also a good moment to suggest improvements by the colleagues of the innovation group. Subsequently, we had to re-record some of the videos because of the need to complete some examples or the correction of some errata found after the visualization. Additionally, revision task checked introduction and conclusion had the same style.

3.4 Evaluation

The process of evaluation of the educational contents was arranged in face-to-face lectures by solving math problems in a written test. In this test, we evaluated the problem-solving processes presented in the videos. In this way, we review not only the visualization of the videos but also the significant learning of the problem-solving processes.

Fig. 2. Example of edition method using Camtasia software.

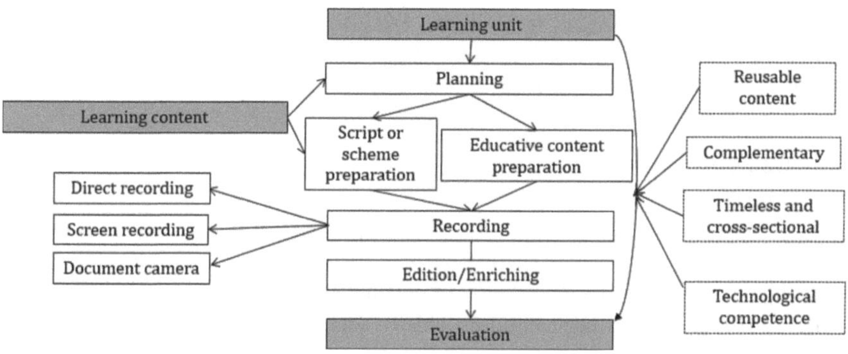

Fig. 3. Diagram of the video creation process.

On the other hand, students gave us their feedback concerning the learning units. We make emphasis on the fact that the students' visualization allowed us to unify the format among the different sequences. At the same time, we received positive answers related to the application of our educational course.

Moreover, we have proposed one open problem per learning unit to allow students to be able to self-evaluate their learning. These problems are proposed in one video and the solutions are provided in another video. The characteristics of these types of problems allow the students to practice the mathematical procedures they have learned in different ways since partial solutions are available on many occasions.

4 Conclusions and Future Work

The use of video has become a resource to be taken into account in mathematics teaching. Since devices allow audiovisual content visualization, it may be useful to provide teaching content that can be visualized, adapting it to the different learning rates of the students.

We present the following diagram that summarizes all the factors to be taken into account in the creation of video teaching content (Fig. 3)

At the moment, after having recorded 12 learning units, we are evaluating the usefulness of the content created. To do this, we establish some research evidences that evaluate students' perception and interest. Furthermore, a large number of students who have provided their feedback confirm its application.

On the other hand, we are also investigating other content recording methodologies. We are interested in determining the most valuable recording methodology for students. Moreover, we are interested in creating other recordings within other recording methodologies.

Thus, the analysis presented here has been a good starting point to achieve an adequate design of the learning unit.

Acknowledgements. The present research was partially supported by the project "Mejora y ampliación del Curso Online de Olimpiadas Matemáticas (MACOOM)" of the proyectos de Innovación Docente de la Universidad de La Rioja.

References

Abassian, R., Sieben, J.: Creating math videos: comparing platforms and software. PRIMUS. **26** (2), 168–177 (2015)

Beltrán-Pellicer, P., Giacomone, B., Burgos, M.: Online educational videos according to specific didactics: the case of mathematics/Los vídeos educativos en línea desde las didácticas específicas: el caso de las matemáticas. Cult. Educ. **30**(4), 633–662 (2018)

Cáceres, P.A., Martínez, S.: Plan Docencia en Red 2017–2018 de la Universitat Politècnica de València (2017)

Farkas, M.: Social Software in Libraries: building collaboration, communication and community online. Information Today Inc., Medford (2007)

Howard, E., Meehan, M., Parnell, A. : Live lectures or online videos: students' resource choices in a first-year university mathematics module. Int. J. Sci. Math. Educ. (2017) https://doi.org/10.1080/0020739x.2017.1387943

Lucas, S. et al.: Utilización de recursos software y mini-videos docentes como herramientas didácticas en asignaturas de ingeniería industrial. XXIII Congreso Universitario de Innovación Educativa en las Enseñanzas Técnicas (2015)

Orcos Palma, L., Blázquez Tobías, P.J., Curto Prieto, M., Molina León, F.J., Magreñán Ruiz, Á. A.: Use of *Kahoot* and *EdPuzzle* by smartphone in the classroom: the design of a methodological proposal. In: Uden, L., Liberona, D., Ristvej, J. (eds.) LTEC 2018. CCIS, vol. 870, pp. 37–47. Springer, Cham (2018). https://doi.org/10.1007/978-3-319-95522-3_4

Pérez-Navío, E., Rodríguez, J., García, M.: El uso de mini-videos en la práctica docente universitaria. EDMETIC. Revista de Educación Mediática y TIC, **4**(2), 51–70 (2015)

Tan, E.: Informal learning on YouTube™: exploring digital literacy in independent online learning. Learn. Media Technol. **38**, 463–477 (2013)

Trenholm, S., Alcock, L., Robinson, C.L.: Mathematics lecturing in the digital age. Int. J. Math. Educ. Sci. Technol. **43**(6), 703–716 (2012)

Learning Tools and Environment

Evaluation of the Disciplinary Competences of the Students of the Bachelor's Degree in Physiotherapy at "Sapienza" University of Rome Through the TECO: A Cross-Sectional Study

Giovanni Galeoto[1(✉)], Anna Berardi[2], Cecilia Pizzi[3], Ilaria Farina[1], and Julita Sansoni[1]

[1] Department of Public Health, "Sapienza" University of Rome, Rome, Italy
{giovanni.galeoto, ilaria.farina, julita.sansoni}@uniroma1.it

[2] "Sapienza" University of Rome, Rome, Italy
aberardi96@gmail.com

[3] San Camillo Hospital of Rome, Rome, Italy
cecilia.pizzi@uniroma1.it

Abstract. The objective of the study is to evaluate whether the TECO-D is a useful tool for measuring the skills acquired by students during three years of the physiotherapy bachelor's degree course at the "Sapienza" University of Rome. The sample was recruited between October and December 2017. To be included in the study, the participants had to be enrolled in the bachelor's degree course in physiotherapy at the "Sapienza" University of Rome and had to be on track with the course's prescribed completion timeframe. The distribution of the scores for the TECO-D shows an increasing average (Standard Deviation) from 147.1 $\pm$ 34.5 in the first year up to 227.1 $\pm$ 17.8 for graduating students. Progress testing is a form of assessment in which groups of learners of different seniority (i.e., different classes in a curriculum) are given the same written test. The test is comprehensive by sampling all relevant disciplines in a curriculum, usually determined by a fixed blueprint. The total score of the TECO-D exponentially increased between the first and second years of the course. In fact, the score, at the first year of the course, was averaged at 147 $\pm$ 34.5 and increased up to 204 $\pm$ 23.2 in the second year. Regarding the third year of the course and the undergraduates, there was an increase, but the latter was less significant. Because of this, we can say that the TECO-D is a great tool for measuring student's knowledge in order to evaluate study programs.

Keywords: TECO-D · Progress test · Physiotherapy

L. Uden et al. (Eds.): LTEC 2019, CCIS 1011, pp. 93–102, 2019.
https://doi.org/10.1007/978-3-030-20798-4_9

1 Introduction

Progress testing is a longitudinal testing approach invented by the University of Missouri, the Kansas City School of Medicine and the then University of Limburg in Maastricht [1, 2]. The main advantage of the progress test is that it breaks the link between learning and revision [3]. It is widely believed that what is asked in examinations drives what students learn [3, 4]. In 2012, the Italian National Agency for the Evaluation of Universities and Research Institutes (ANVUR) started a project evaluating the learning outcomes of the Italian undergraduates through a test (Test on skills, TECO), holding that analyzing skill levels is an important tool for monitoring the quality of the educational process [5].

European Union recommendations have been particularly interested in integrating citizenship and lifelong learning skills in national policies for the educational field, while the actions of institutions in the European Higher Education Area (EHEA) are progressively moving towards didactics centered on the student and on competences (European Standards and Guidelines for Quality Assurance (ESG), 2015) [6].

In line with the ESG, Ministerial Decree number 987/2016 clarifies that TECO results, once fully operational, will become part of the system of indicators for evaluating teaching (self-assessment, periodic evaluation, accreditation—AVA). It is further clarified that collecting new data related to the Transversal and/or Disciplinary skills acquired by students will allow the development of indicators that will be used for periodic evaluation and accreditation of Study Centers and Courses [7]. In 2016, the ANVUR reset the complete research design, including reference areas, the methodological approach and the means of detection, for both Transversal Competencies (TECO-T) and Disciplinary Competencies (TECO-D).

Transversal Competencies (TECO-T) are skills that college students can develop independent of the specific study route taken, and, therefore, they may be compared between different courses of study. Disciplinary Competencies (TECO-D) are closely related to capacity-specific training content in university studies, and, therefore, they can only be compared with study courses that are similar in nature.

Currently, the TECO project aims to construct indicators reflecting the skills of college students in the first and third years of a bachelor's degree program or a single cycle in Italian universities.

The objective of the study is to determine if the TECO-D is a useful tool for measuring the Disciplinary Competencies acquired by students over three years in the physiotherapy bachelor's degree program at the "Sapienza" University of Rome.

2 Materials and Methods

2.1 Population and Procedures

The sample was recruited between October and December 2017. To be included in the study, the participants had to be enrolled in the bachelor's degree course in physiotherapy at the "Sapienza" University of Rome. They were also required to be in side of the prescribed timeframe for the course of study that is, not progressing through the course at a slower or faster rate than the standard tree year timeframe. Participation in the TECO project was voluntary for universities, courses and students, and, at the time of recruitment, the participants were informed about the modalities and objectives of the project.

The test was administered digitally in university computer rooms during 170-min sessions [8]. The results of the tests were communicated individually to the participating students and did not affect the evaluation in progress or the final evaluation, while the aggregated data were transmitted to the coordinators of the study courses involved and to the university referents.

2.2 Instrument

The Transversal test (TECO-T) was divided into Numeracy and Literacy section.

The first section, Literacy, consisted of 30 reading comprehension questions (compilation time, 35 min) divided into the following categories:

- A piece followed by 10 closed-answer questions.
- A short passage from which 20 words were missing (Cloze test).

The second section, Numeracy, consisted of 25 questions (compilation time, 45 min) asking participants to understand and solve logical-quantitative problems divided into the following categories:

- A short piece with graphs and tables, followed by five questions.
- An infographic followed by five questions.
- Five short questions of logical reasoning.

The Disciplinary test (TECO-D) for the physiotherapy bachelor's degree course used in this study was a single file consisting of 100 closed questions with five alternative answers each. It was divided into ten macro areas, as shown in Table 1.

Table 1. Macro areas divided by year of course (TECO-D)

Number macro areas	Learning	Year of course	Number questions
1	Biology, Anatomy and Physiology	1	21
2	Physics and Radioprotection	1	2
3	Statistics and Research Methodology	1	4
4	Physiotherapy in skeletal muscle disorders	2	23
5	Health organization and occupational medicine	2	4
6	Physiotherapy in cardio-respiratory and internist pathologies	3	11
7	Psychology and Pedagogy	1	6
8	Pathology and pharmacology	1	8
9	Physiotherapy of neuromuscular disorders	2	12
10	Physiotherapy in childhood	3	9

2.3 Data Collection and Data Analyses

For each year of study, data was collected for each of the main areas of the TECO-D, and, through SPSS-23 software, the data were registered in terms of the mean and standard deviation of the score distributions.

3 Results

3.1 Population

The sample for the study was composed of 404 students of the physiotherapy bachelor's degree course. Of these, 90 (22.3%) were excluded because the students were out of the course timeframe; they had not completed their university exams within the set time period. Demographic characteristics of the population are reported in Table 2.

Table 2. Demographic characteristics of the population

	Sample = 314
Age mean (SD)	22,2 (3,4)
Gender Male n (%)	250 (79,6)
Year of course n (%)	
First year	103 (32,8)
Second year	110 (35)
Third year	84 (26,8)
Fourth year	17 (5,4)

The distribution of the TECO-D scores shows an increasing average from 147.1 in the first year to 227.1 for graduating students (Fig. 1).

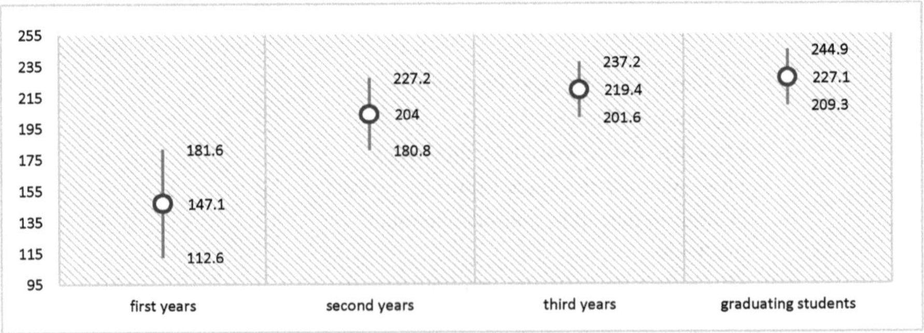

Fig. 1. The mean of the total scores for year of course (TECO-D).

The distribution of the scores for the first macro area shows an increasing average from 6.4 in the first year of the course to 12.4 for graduating students. The population data are shown in Fig. 2.

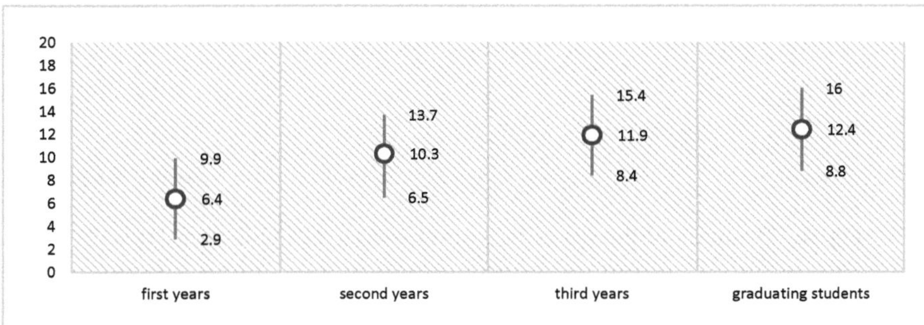

Fig. 2. The mean of the scores for year of course (TECO-D-macro area 1)

The distribution of the scores for the second macro area shows a constant average of 0.7 in the four studied cohorts. The population data are shown in Fig. 3.

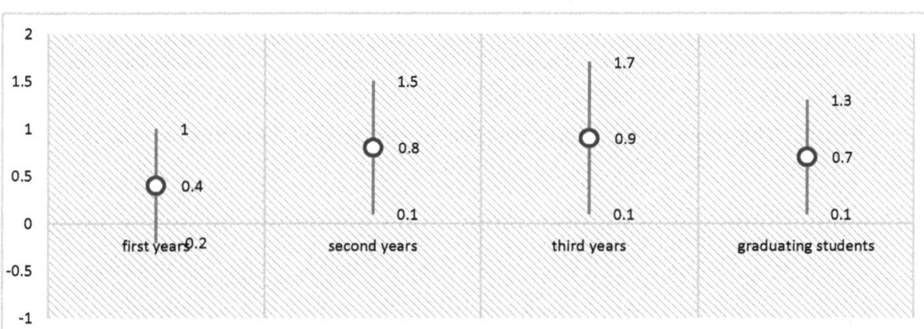

Fig. 3. The mean of the scores for year of course (TECO-D-macro area 2)

The distribution of the scores for the third macro area shows an increasing average from 0.8 in the first year of the course to 2.3 for graduating students. The population data are shown in Fig. 4.

The distribution of the scores for the fourth and fifth macro area shows an exponential growth from the first to the second year of course; while a minor growth at the third year of course and graduating students. The population data are shown in Figs. 5 and 6.

The distribution of the scores for the sixth macro area shows an exponential growth from the first to the second year of the course, which continues increasing until the third year, as the questions relate to skills acquired in the second and third years of the course. The population data are shown in Fig. 7.

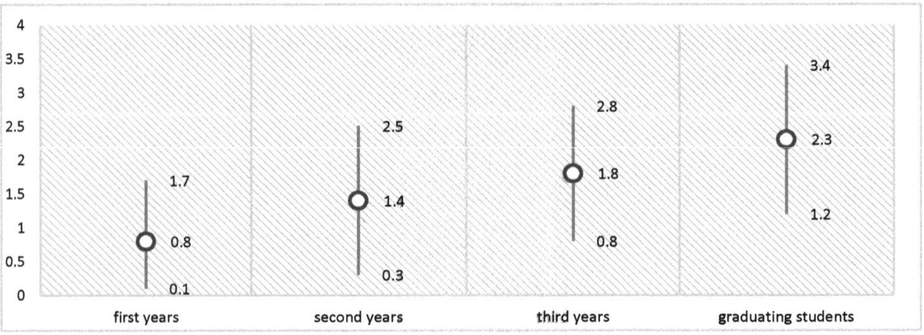

Fig. 4. The mean of the scores for year of course (TECO-D-macro area 3)

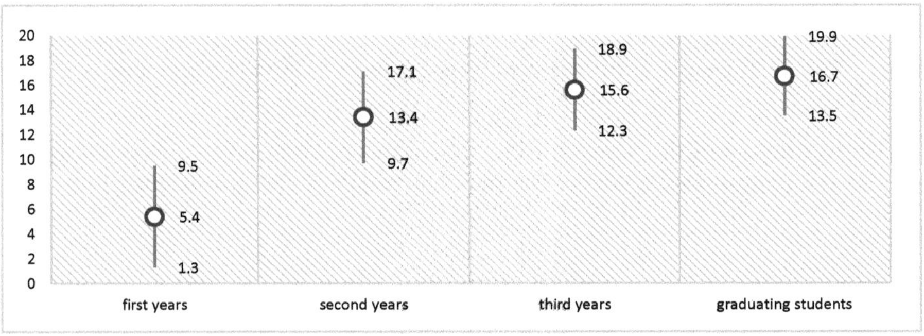

Fig. 5. The mean of the scores for year of course (TECO-D-macro area 4)

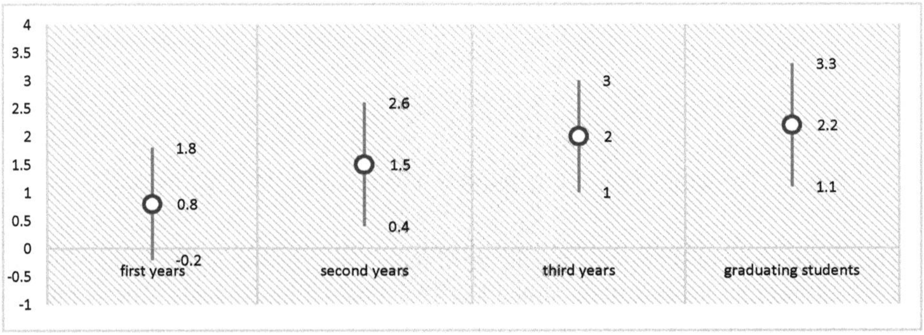

Fig. 6. The mean of the scores for year of course (TECO-D-macro area 5)

For the seventh macro area, the distribution of the scores shows an increasing average from the first to the second year, while the knowledge remains stable at the third year and for graduating students. The population data are shown in Fig. 8.

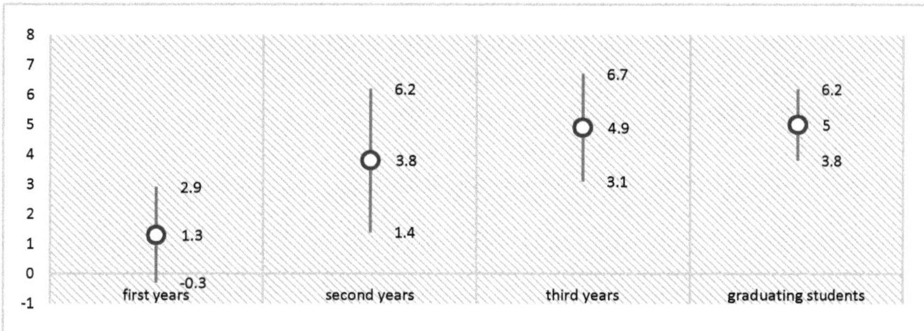

Fig. 7. The mean of the scores for year of course (TECO-D-macro area 6)

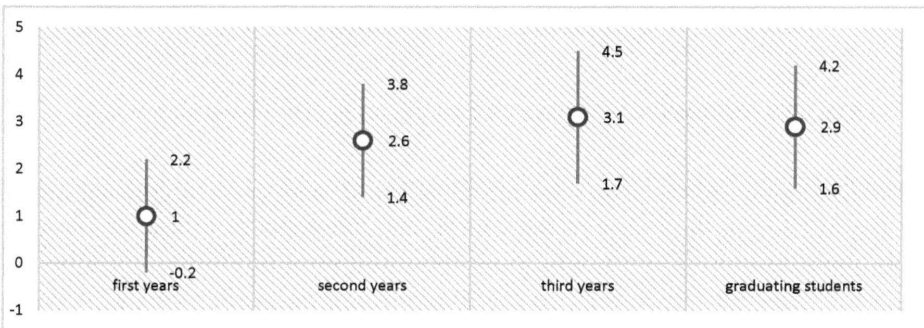

Fig. 8. The mean of the scores for year of course (TECO-D-macro area 7)

The distribution of the scores in the eighth macro area shows an exponential growth from the first to the second year, which remains stable in year three but increases again in graduating students. These population data are shown in Fig. 9.

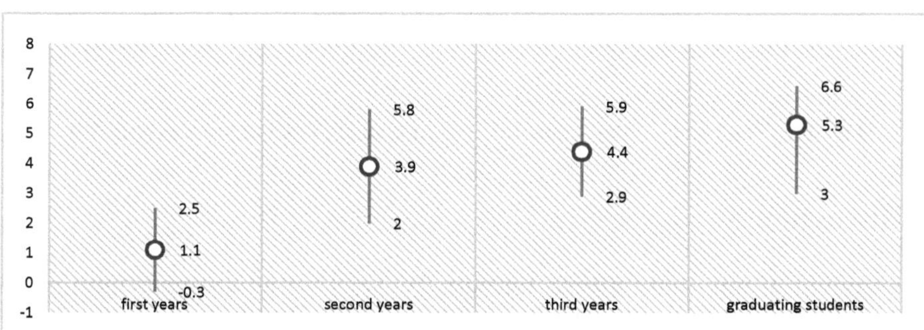

Fig. 9. The mean of the scores for year of course (TECO-D-macro area 8)

For the ninth macro area, the distribution of the scores shows exponential growth from the first to the second year of the course. This remains stable at the third year, but, as with the eighth macro area, it increases again in graduating students. The population data are shown in Fig. 10.

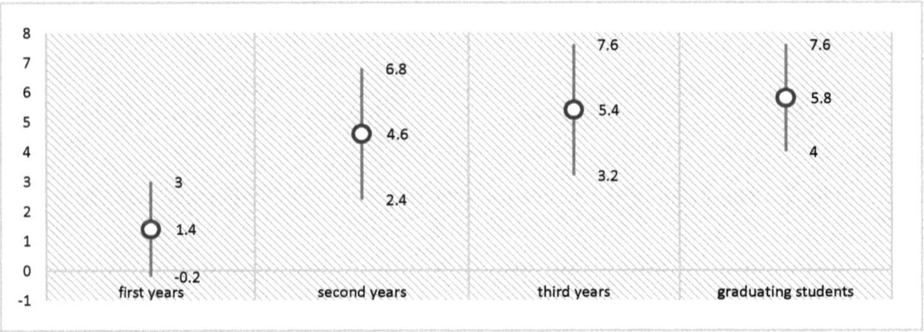

Fig. 10. The mean of the scores for year of course (TECO-D-macro area 9)

The distribution of the scores for the tenth macro area shows a growing average from the first to the third year of the course, and the population data are shown in Fig. 11.

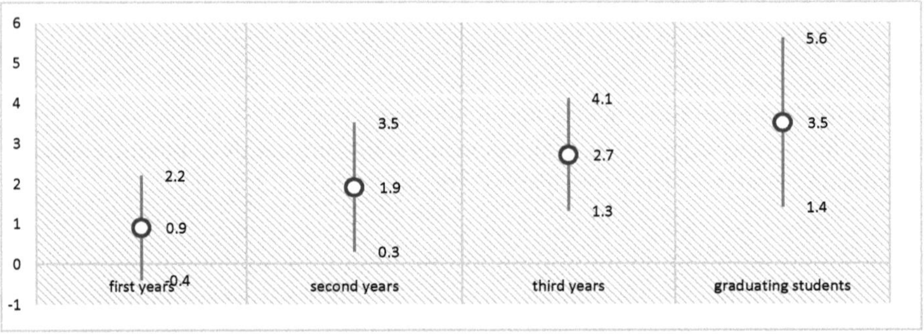

Fig. 11. The mean of the scores for year of course (TECO-D-macro area 10)

4 Discussion

The objective of this study was to evaluate the TECO-D as a measurement tool to assess the skills acquired, over three years, by students in the physiotherapy bachelor's degree course at the "Sapienza" University of Rome.

The progress of individual students can be modelled, giving a sequence of test results, and the effects of rules for progression and remediation can also be modelled [9].

Progress testing is a form of assessment in which groups of learners of different seniority (i.e., different classes in a curriculum) are given the same written test. The test is comprehensive by sampling all relevant disciplines in a curriculum, usually determined by a fixed blueprint. Because of the need for wide sampling, questions are typically of the multiple-choice type. The test is repeated at regular intervals [10].

The total score of the TECO-D exponentially increased between the first year and the second year of the course. In fact, the mean score, at the first year, was 147 ± 34.5, and it increased to 204 ± 23.2 in the second year of the course. Regarding the third year of the course and the undergraduates, there was an increase, but the latter was less significant. This data could mean that the TECO-D is much better at evaluating the basic training given to students in the first year of the course, while its assessment of Disciplinary Competencies in the second and third years is less significant.

The first macro area showed that students enrolled in the first year of the course have a basic knowledge of their discipline, assessed with a mean score of six. That score increased by an average of four points in the second year, a competency that remained for final year students. This score showed that students already have specific skills on these topics from previous studies.

The evaluation of the single macro areas showed statistically significant data reflecting increasing knowledge regarding the progression of the skills received during the university course. Because of this, we can say that the TECO-D is a great tool for determining student's knowledge in order to evaluate study programs.

This study was conducted by a research group composed by medical doctors and rehabilitation professionals from the "Sapienza" University of Rome and from "Rehabilitation & Outcome Measure Assessment" (R.O.M.A.) association. R.O.M.A. association in the last few years has dealt with several systematic reviews and the validation of many outcome measures in Italy [11–21].

Conflict of Interest. The authors declare that they have no conflict of interest.

Financial Disclosures. All authors have no commercial associations or disclosures that may pose or create a conflict of interest with the information presented within this manuscript.

References

1. Van der Vleuten, C.P.M., Verwijnen, G.M., Wijnen, H.F.W.: Fifteen years of experience with progress testing in a problem-based learning curriculum. Med. Teach. **18**, 103–109 (1996). https://doi.org/10.3109/01421599609034142
2. Arnold, L., Willoughby, T.L.: The quarterly profile examination. Acad. Med. **65**, 515–516 (1990)
3. Newble, D.I., Jaeger, K.: The effect of assessments and examinations on the learning of medical students. Med. Educ. **17**, 165–171 (1983)
4. Frederiksen, N.: The real test bias: influences of testing on teaching and learning. Am. Psychol. **39**, 193–202 (1984)
5. http://www.anvur.it/attivita/ava/teco-test-sulle-competenze/. Accessed 18 Dec 2018
6. https://enqa.eu/wp-content/uploads/2015/11/ESG_2015.pdf. Accessed 18 Dec 2018
7. http://attiministeriali.miur.it/anno-2016/dicembre/dm-12122016.aspx

8. Galeoto, G., Rumiati, R., Sabella, M., Sansoni, J.: The use of a dedicated platform to evaluate health-professions university courses. In: Di Mascio, T., Vittorini, P., Gennari, R., De la Prieta, F., Rodríguez, S., Temperini, M., Azambuja Silveira, R., Popescu, E., Lancia, L. (eds.) MIS4TEL 2018. AISC, vol. 804, pp. 275–284. Springer, Cham (2019). https://doi.org/10.1007/978-3-319-98872-6_33
9. McHarg, J., Bradley, P., Chamberlain, S., Ricketts, C., Searle, J., McLachlan, J.C.: Assessment of progress tests. Med. Educ. **39**(2), 221–227 (2005)
10. Freeman, A., Van Der Vleuten, C., Nouns, Z., Ricketts, C.: Progress testing internationally. Med. Teach. **32**(6), 451–455 (2010)
11. Culicchia, G., et al.: Cross-cultural adaptation and validation of the Jebsen-Taylor hand function test in an Italian population. Rehabil. Res. Pract. (2016)
12. Castiglia, S.F., et al.: The culturally adapted Italian version of the Barthel Index (IcaBI): assessment of structural validity, inter-rater reliability and responsiveness to clinically relevant improvements in patients admitted to inpatient rehabilitation centers. Funct. Neurol. **32**(4), 221 (2017)
13. Marquez, M.A., et al.: Cross-cultural adaptation and validation of the "Spinal Cord Injury-Falls Concern Scale" in the Italian population. Spinal Cord **56**, 712–718 (2018)
14. Galeoto, G., et al.: A psychometric properties evaluation of the Italian version of the Geriatric Depression Scale. Depression Res. Treat. (2018)
15. Murgia, M., et al.: Inter-and intra-interviewer reliability of Italian version of pediatric evaluation of disability inventory. Ann. Ig. **30**, 153–161 (2018)
16. Berardi, A., et al.: The wheelchair use confidence scale: Italian translation, adaptation, and validation of the short form. Disabil. Rehabil. Assistive Technol. **13**(6), 575–580
17. Tofani, M., et al.: The psychosocial impact of assistive device scales: Italian validation in a cohort of nonambulant people with neuromotor disorders. Assistive Technol., 1–6 (2018)
18. Galeoto, G., et al.: Validation and cross-cultural adaptation of the Van Lieshout test in an Italian population with cervical spinal cord injury: a psychometric study. Spinal Cord Ser. Cases **4**(1), 49 (2018)
19. Parente, M., Tofani, M., De Santis, R., Esposito, G., Santilli, V., Galeoto, G.: The role of the occupational therapist in disaster areas: systematic review. Occup Ther. Int. (2017)
20. Galeoto, G., et al.: Quality of life in Parkinson's disease: Italian validation of the Parkinson's Disease Questionnaire (PDQ-39-IT). Neurol. Sci. **39**(11), 1903–1909 (2018)
21. Galeoto, G., et al.: Construction and validation of a tool for the evaluation of environmental risks and limitations to the manual handling of loads: cross-sectional study. La Clinica Terapeutica **168**(6), e349–e356 (2018)

The Use of Digital Devices in the University Classroom: Exploring and Comparing Students' Perceptions and Practices

Maria Rabl[1(✉)], Juliana Pattermann[1], Stephan Schlögl[2], and Niki Canham[3]

[1] Department Business Administration Online, MCI Management Center Innsbruck, 6020 Innsbruck, Austria
{maria.rabl, juliana.pattermann}@mci.edu
[2] Department Management, Communication and IT, MCI Management Center Innsbruck, 6020 Innsbruck, Austria
stephan.schloegl@mci.edu
[3] Department of English, University of Innsbruck, 6020 Innsbruck, Austria
niki.canham@uibk.ac.at

Abstract. Dealing with students' use of digital devices and the resulting interruptions and distractions in university classrooms has become part of the daily challenges for teaching faculty in higher education. This exploratory study ($N = 46$) investigated first semester students' perceptions, experiences, and time estimates regarding their use of digital devices for non-course-related activities. Questionnaire data were complemented with and compared to tracking data from the students' laptop use in class through logs generated by the time management software RescueTime. Results indicate that approximately a quarter of class time is lost to non-course-related activities and that students underestimate their own laptop use in comparison to the tracking data. Nevertheless, they are aware of the distractive potential of digital devices, and this awareness increased over the ten-week research period. However, the study suggests that this awareness has little effect on the students' actual behavior and that they give in to the digital temptations despite knowing the potential for distraction.

Keywords: Digital devices · Interruptions · Distractions · Higher education · Laptop use · Mobile phone use

1 Introduction

The use of laptops, tablets, and mobile phones in the classroom has become a permanent fixture in today's higher education landscape. The mindset that taking out a mobile phone or laptop in class signals a lack of respect or attention has changed through initiatives such as Bring Your Own Device (Kong and Song 2015; Song 2016). Today, learning management systems (e.g., Moodle, Sakai), learning platforms (e.g., Kahoot!), and other educational tools (e.g., PINGO, AnswerGarden) are widely used and often necessitate the use of technology in class. In fact, digital media – "always-on,

L. Uden et al. (Eds.): LTEC 2019, CCIS 1011, pp. 103–113, 2019.
https://doi.org/10.1007/978-3-030-20798-4_10

socially interactive, technologically mediated communication artifacts" (Le Roux and Parry 2017, p. 86) – enable new forms of social interaction and may contribute to increased student engagement. Consequently, students remain connected with their peers and friends via social media and texting applications, such as WhatsApp, at all times (Felisoni and Godoi 2018), even during self-study or class time. However, it remains to be seen whether students are aware of their own multitasking habits and effects as studies indicate varying levels of awareness in students. While May and Elder (2018) observe that students have a poor level of awareness, McCoy (2016) suggest that 89% of students actually know that using digital devices during class diminishes their attention.

Members of the *net generation*, born after 1984 (Kirschner and de Bruyckere 2017), are supposedly used to rapidly switching between several media and non-media activities (Judd 2013; Le Roux and Parry 2017; Rosen et al. 2013). However, Kirschner and de Bruyckere (2017) highlight the lack of evidence for the common belief that members of the net generation, or *digital natives*, are better multitaskers than so-called *digital immigrants*. As a matter of fact, for first semester students coming from school contexts, where the use of technology is typically restricted, there is the particular challenge of managing the freedom and expectations connected with the use of technology in university classes. This exploratory study investigates how first-semester university students use digital devices during class and how their perceptions regarding the use of technology in class develop over the course of the first semester.

2 Digital Devices in University Classrooms

The incorporation of digital devices in the university classroom poses many potential advantages. Students are able to use mobile phones and laptops to look up additional information, check facts, and take pictures of class content (Berry and Westfall 2015). Laptops and even tablets can be used to take notes, to organize materials, and to provide access to lecture materials (Carter et al. 2017).

Even though digital media provide a great opportunity for students to enhance their learning, several studies have revealed that students who use digital media in class typically perform worse than students who do not use technology (Aguilar-Roca et al. 2012; Fried 2008; Wei et al. 2012; Wood et al. 2012). While data on how much students actually use mobile devices in class vary, the distracting effect of media use for non-course-related activities cannot be denied (Kraushaar and Novak 2010; Wei et al. 2012). Kay et al. (2017) noted, for example, that 8 out of 10 secondary school students were simultaneously using their mobile devices while carrying out tasks in class. Instant messaging could be particularly problematic for learning environments as it is "difficult to ignore when an auditory, visual, or tactile notification signals the arrival of a new message" (Lebbon and Sigurjónsson 2016, p. 434).

2.1 Interruptions, Task Switching, and Multitasking

Interruptions are defined as breaks from an activity due to the introduction of a new activity on top of the ongoing one (Miyata and Norman 1986), with the intention of returning to the main activity at a later point in time (Altmann and Trafton 2002; Baethge et al. 2015; Brixey et al. 2007). Contrary to distractions, which are activities that do not contribute to the achievement of the learning goals (Kay et al. 2017, p. 976) and are caused exclusively by external stimuli (Jett and George 2003), interruptions can either have an external or internal origin (Baethge et al. 2015; Katidioti et al. 2016). External interruptions are initiated by an outside element (Katidioti et al. 2016), such as a colleague's phone. They are typically unintended, uncontrollable, and they force the person to switch to the interrupting activity (Baethge et al. 2015). Internal interruption refers to the act of self-interruption, where a person's physical needs, mental state, or own thoughts, such as the decision to check social media during class, lead to an interruption of an ongoing activity (Baethge et al. 2015). Katidioti et al. (2016) conclude that internal interruptions are generally more disruptive than external ones as they add a period of decision or preparation before the interruption takes place. While external interruptions are always uncontrollable, self-initiated interruptions may either be controllable or uncontrollable (Baethge et al. 2015). Students oftentimes justify their interrupting behavior because of its self-inflicting nature and argue that "they should be allowed to do whatever they wanted as long as it did not negatively affect other people" (Langan et al. 2016, p. 107).

It has been well documented that interruptions negatively affect the performance of the main activity in four main ways (Gupta and Irwin 2016; Katidioti et al. 2016; Rosen et al. 2011; McFarlane 2002; Monk et al. 2008). First, it takes longer to finish the main task (Katidioti et al. 2016; Ratwani et al. 2008). Second, the longer an interruption lasts, the more difficult it will be for the person to resume the main task (Katidioti et al. 2016). Third, errors in the main task, once it has been resumed, appear to be more frequent (McFarlane 2002; Ratwani et al. 2008). Fourth, the additionally required time for the main task can result in increased levels of stress and anxiety (González and Mark 2004; Ratwani et al. 2008).

Another consequence of interruptions is the increased engagement in task switching and multitasking. Task switching is a cognitive ability (Darmoul et al. 2015) where a person needs to complete a main and an interruptive task, in addition to dealing with an interruption and resumption lag (Rosen et al. 2013). The term multitasking is typically discussed from contrary viewpoints. Some researchers define it as the simultaneous execution of at least two activities (Demirbilek and Talan 2018; Dzubak 2008; Kirschner and Karpinski 2010), while others believe that multitasking is merely a function of dividing attention between several tasks (Fried 2008; Gupta and Irwin 2016; Junco 2012; Le Roux and Parry 2017; Sana et al. 2013). Considering that cognitive resources are limited, attention filters stimuli and postpones the processing of one task until another is finished (Broadbent 1958; May and Elder 2018). Advocates of the *bottleneck theory* argue that "attention can be allocated to only one task at a time" (May and Elder 2018, p. 87). Thus, multitasking involves rapidly switching between various ongoing activities creating continuous attention shifts and disruptions (Chen and Yan 2016; Fried 2008; Le Roux and Parry 2017).

2.2 Students' Perceptions and Awareness About the Use of Digital Devices

While university faculty are aware of the implications of technology use in the classroom, students' practices and perceptions about the effects vary. May and Elder (2018) observed in their study on media multitasking and academic performance that students overall exhibited "poor awareness of how media multitasking affects their learning" (p. 95). In an exploratory study by Clayson and Haley (2012), 68% of students insisted that they were capable of texting and keeping up with a lecture at the same, which was, in fact, negatively associated with their class grade. What is more, Kraushaar and Novak (2010) noted that students generally underestimate the time they spend on non-course-related activities in class, for example believing that they spend 40% less time on instant messaging than they actually do. In a study by Kirschner and Karpinski (2010), 73.8% of students claimed that Facebook had zero impact on their learning; a small percentage of students even felt that Facebook had a positive impact. On the contrary, McCoy (2016) established that 89% of students are aware that using digital devices in a classroom results in a lack of attention.

These findings suggest that students, on the one hand, have an inaccurate impression of their own interrupting behavior, and, on the other hand, do not grasp the extent of the negative consequences resulting from this behavior.

3 Context and Methods

We conducted this study among Bachelor students. To explore their perceptions and practices concerning the use of digital devices during their first semester, we chose two methods for data collection. Firstly, students completed a self-assessment questionnaire at the beginning of a specific course and an exit questionnaire 10 weeks later. The questionnaires generated mainly quantitative data, enriched by open-ended questions, which helped to expand on the quantitative results through thematic content analysis (Braun and Clarke 2006). Secondly, students voluntarily installed personal analytics and time management software on their laptops for the duration of the semester.

3.1 Sample

Seventy-five students enrolled in a Bachelor program on *Business & Management* were asked to participate in this study, of whom 68 consented to participate and answered at least one of the two questionnaires. The following analysis focuses on the $N = 46$ students (29 female) who completed both the entrance and the exit questionnaire (Note: of those 46 students, 13 also installed the personal analytics software on their laptops). Participants were aged between 18 and 29 ($M = 20.43$ years, $SD = 2.38$), and the majority of them (i.e. 91%) had never studied at tertiary level before.

3.2 Instruments

In the entrance questionnaire, we asked students about their non-course-related activities during high school. Next, we focused on non-course-related activities on mobile phones and laptops/tablets during their first classes at university. For both questionnaires, the item development was based on a survey by Ravizza et al. (2017). We asked students about their usage of digital devices for the following activities: check social media, send SMSs, message on WhatsApp, shop online, read the news or check sports scores, watch videos, play games, and other activities. In addition, we inquired how students thought the use of digital devices affected their learning during class. Furthermore, we asked them to estimate the time they spent per day on the abovementioned activities. Finally, students answered two open-ended questions relating to the advantages and disadvantages of technology use in university classrooms. The exit questionnaire posed the same questions in retrospect.

To track how students really used their computers and for how long, we encouraged them to install RescueTime (www.rescuetime.com), a personal analytics software, which tracks time spent on applications and websites. A weekly email report summarizes users' activities. Participants were asked to disable the report function during the 10-week period to avoid a change in behavior triggered by the reports.

3.3 Data Collection and Analysis

Following ethical clearance, participants were recruited from the course "Principles of Academic Work". The project was introduced to them on the first day of their studies, and they were given a week to consider their participation. The time span between the entrance and the exit questionnaire was 10 weeks. Questionnaires were completed online during class time.

We used a frequency analysis to provide an overview of the students' engagement in non-course-related activities. For the open-ended questions, we used inductive coding and conducted a thematic analysis. At the end of the ten-week period, participants voluntarily shared their RescueTime log files, and we categorized the data using labels such as email and social networking and calculated the mean time spent during class.

4 Results

4.1 Non-Course-Related Activities at School

At school, 44% of the students were not allowed to use mobile phones and 52% were not allowed to use laptops or tablets during class. For those who were allowed to use their digital devices at school, the most frequently reported non-course-related activities were using WhatsApp (52.5% on mobile phones, 13.0% on laptops), checking other social media such as Facebook (47.8% on mobile phones, 23.9% on laptops), and sending SMSs (41.3% on mobile phones, 32.6% on laptops). In general, mobile phones were used more frequently for non-course-related activities than laptops in school.

4.2 Digital Device Usage on an Average Day

In the entrance questionnaire, respondents estimated spending 201 min on average per day on their mobile phone and 117 min on average per day on their laptop for non-course-related activities. At the end of the 10-week period, these values dropped to an average of 163 min on the phone and an average of 114 min on the laptop.

In the exit questionnaire, by far the biggest proportion of time on mobile phones was, according to students' self-assessment, spent on checking social media (47.2% of the estimated use on an average day) and using WhatsApp (42.3%), followed by reading the news or checking sports scores (11.7%). Laptops were thought to be used for watching videos (56.1%), followed by emails (15.8%) and checking social media (10.5%).

The time reduction on mobile phones was caused by less time for SMSs (−68.2%) and for reading the news and checking sports scores (−40.0%). The major time reduction on laptops was caused by less time spent on playing games (−41.2%) and sending emails (−35.2%). Despite the general reduction of time spent on both devices, students indicated that they spent 5.6 times more on WhatsApp and 1.6 times more on checking social media on their laptops than estimated in the entrance questionnaire.

4.3 Digital Device Use in an Average Class

For an average class (180 min), students estimated spending 20.6% of the time on non-course-related activities on their phone and 17.9% on their laptop/tablet. The most preferred activities are similar to the previously described activities: social media (8.6% of the total class-time on phones and 6.1% on laptops) and WhatsApp (7.8% on phones and 3.9% on laptops) rank first on mobile phones and laptops.

In comparing the students'self-assessment of digital device use during class time in the exit questionnaire to data from the tracking software RescueTime, we can see that students slightly underestimate the time spent on laptops for non-course-related activities. RescueTime showed an average of 25.7% of class-room time spent on non-course-related activities.

4.4 Critical Reflection on Technology Use

When asked about the impact of non-course-related activities on their learning, the majority of students – and a larger proportion of the students compared to the entrance questionnaire – stressed at the end of the 10-week period that it somewhat disrupted their learning of course material (see Table 1). It is also remarkable that the number of students who stated that they never used phones, laptops, or tablets in class decreased from 32.6% to 2.2% after the 10-week period.

Overall, in both the entrance and the exit questionnaires, students viewed the use of mobile phones more critically than the use of laptops. At the end of the 10-week period, 50% of students perceived the use of their phones as too high, whereas only 8.7% of students indicated that they used their laptop too much. The percentage of students who were uncertain about their laptop use increased from 13% (entrance questionnaire) to 32.6% (exit questionnaire).

Table 1. Impact of using technology on learning.

Impact on learning	Entrance questionnaire	Exit questionnaire
It strongly helped my learning of course material	4.3%	4.3%
It somewhat helped my learning of course material	8.7%	15.2%
It made no difference to my learning of course material	19.6%	60.9%
It somewhat disrupted my learning of course material	34.8%	17.4%
I never use my phone/laptop/tablet in class	32.6%	2.2%

We also investigated the perceived effect of other students using technology on learning, where 80.4% of students reported that the use of digital devices by other students in the class made no difference to their learning. Only 6.5% of students conceded that their learning was strongly influenced by their peers' use of technology in class.

5 Discussion

Our study found that for approx. half of the first semester students it is new that the use of mobile phones and laptops is permitted in class. While 44% of them were not allowed to use their mobile phones in school, the other 56% of participants stated that they had mostly used their phones in school to stay connected via WhatsApp (52.5%), to use social media (47.8%), and to send text messages (41.3%). Only 48% of students indicated that they had been allowed to use laptops during their school years, possibly suggesting that the use of laptops for educational purposes has not been fully established in secondary education. This tentative conclusion corroborates the findings of other studies which question the existence and characteristics of the so-called net generation (Kirschner and de Bruyckere 2017; Margaryan et al. 2011).

On the question of digital device use, the entrance and exit questionnaires revealed divergent results. The self-assessment survey indicated an overall reduction of mobile phone and laptop use on an average day within the 10-week period of the course. Students reported a reduction of 38 min per day on their mobile phones as well as three minutes less on their laptops. A possible explanation for the major reduction in phone time might be a hesitancy to take out their phones during classes, while laptops are generally accepted as note-taking devices and possibly seen as less suspicious.

Another possible explanation for the reduction of phone time is a shift between devices. Checking social media (77 min) and using WhatsApp (69 min) accounted for the highest amount of time spent on mobile phones, while laptops were mainly used for entertainment purposes (64 min). Most interestingly, the results from the exit questionnaire revealed that students spent 5.6 times more time on WhatsApp and 1.6 times more time on social media on their laptops than at the beginning of the semester.

Instant messaging apps, such as Facebook Messenger and WhatsApp, are nowadays available on laptops as well, and these allow students to hide behind their screens.

While we cannot draw a conclusion on the realistic self-assessment of students' mobile phone use, the results from the tracking software RescueTime allow us to make the following observation. Comparing students' estimations, we see that they slightly underestimated the time spent on laptops for non-course-related activities (17.9% compared to 25.7%). Overall, however, 25.7% of class-time spent on non-course-related activities is still lower than described in other studies. Kraushaar and Novak (2010), for example, reported that 42% of class time was spent on computers for non-course-related activities. Nonetheless, this still means that a quarter of class-time is lost to course-irrelevant topics.

In contrast to earlier findings (Clayson and Haley 2012; Kraushaar and Novak 2010; May and Elder 2018), students seem to become more aware of the effects of technology use in the classroom. That is, we found that at the end of the 10-week period, 78.3% of students considered the use of mobile phones and laptops during class as interruptions, signaling a change in mindset for 23.9% of students. Several students also realized at the end of the 10-week period that they used their phones and laptops too much.

Nevertheless, an increased level of awareness does not automatically lead to corrective measures and changed behavior. In fact, the number of students who indicated the use of phones and laptops in class increased dramatically between the entrance and the exit questionnaires, from 67.4% to 97.8%. Another blind spot for the participants seemed to be the distracting effect of digital devices on their peers, as 80.4% of students did not see any effect on their own learning. Even though several studies have revealed that students are aware of what their peers are doing on their digital devices (Berry and Westfall 2015; Fried 2008; Sana et al. 2013), it is possible to conclude that students have not grasped the full extent of the consequences of these possible interruptions.

6 Conclusion

This study set out to investigate first semester students' digital device use in university classrooms and their perceptions regarding this use. The research shows that about a quarter of class-time was lost to non-course-related topics and that students slightly underestimated their digital device use. Despite its exploratory nature, these results offer some insight into the challenges of changing one's behavior in class. On the one hand, it was shown that students' awareness of the distractive potential of digital devices in classrooms increased over the 10-week period. On the other hand, this awareness had very little impact on students' actual behavior. It seems that checking social media and staying connected with peers via WhatsApp has merely shifted from mobile phones to laptops and remains irresistible.

Although some studies have discussed a laptop ban (Fried 2008; Yamamoto 2007), prohibiting them is not a viable solution. The use of laptops in a university context poses many advantages and students have integrated them into their lives. We simply need to accept that they are here to stay. The bottom line is that we have to accept that students do engage in multitasking in our classrooms. Considering the fact that social media and instant messaging are considered important enough by students that they draw away students' attention from what is happening in class, lecturers need to ask themselves what options there are to deal with this situation in the future.

One of the major goals of higher education is to support students in making active use of critical and reflective thinking in physical and digital contexts, combined with the development of the competence to act, which in case of digital distractions means to set corrective measures in an active manner. One way of guiding our students in this direction could be to educate them to become higher-level self-regulated learners. This includes the self-regulation of behavior, such as the active control of available resources (e.g. time). It also refers to controlling one's motivation and effectiveness by changing motivational beliefs such as self-efficacy or goal orientation to improve learning outcomes. Finally, self-regulation also addresses the control of cognitive learning strategies, such as deep processing strategies (Pintrich 1995). Various classroom tasks can foster self-regulation and increase the awareness of students' own behavior, motivation, and cognition. Research shows that the higher the self-efficacy of students is, the more likely they are to link bad marks to an inappropriate learning strategy, which sets the basis for changes in future behavior (Ledermüller and Fallmann 2017).

The major limitation of this exploratory study was the small sample size, particularly for the data collected from the tracking software. Nevertheless, the study lays the groundwork for future research on students' behavior and their handling of digital interruptions. Thus, an essential next step will be to continue the study with a higher number of participants. The issue of self-regulation in the context of dealing with digital interruptions is also intriguing, and it too could be explored in further research.

References

Aguilar-Roca, N.M., Williams, A.E., O'Dowd, D.K.: The impact of laptop-free zones on student performance and attitudes in large lectures. Comput. Educ. **59**(4), 1300–1308 (2012). https://doi.org/10.1016/j.compedu.2012.05.002

Altmann, E.M., Trafton, J.G.: Memory for goals: an activation-based model. Cogn. Sci. **26**(1), 39–83 (2002). https://doi.org/10.1016/S0364-0213(01)00058-1

Baethge, A., Rigotti, T., Roe, R.A.: Just more of the same, or different? An integrative theoretical framework for the study of cumulative interruptions at work. Eur. J. Work Organ. Psychol. **24**(2), 308–323 (2015). https://doi.org/10.1080/1359432X.2014.897943

Berry, M.J., Westfall, A.: Dial D for distraction: the making and breaking of cell phone policies in the college classroom. Coll. Teach. **63**(2), 62–71 (2015). https://doi.org/10.1080/87567555.2015.1005040

Braun, V., Clarke, V.: Using thematic analysis in psychology. Qual. Res. Psychol. **3**(2), 77–101 (2006). https://doi.org/10.1191/1478088706qp063oa

Brixey, J.J., Robinson, D.J., Johnson, C.W., Johnson, T.R., Turley, J.P., Zhang, J.: A concept analysis of the phenomenon interruption. Adv. Nurs. Sci. **30**(1), E26–E42 (2007). https://doi.org/10.1097/00012272-200701000-00012

Broadbent, D.E.: Perception and Communication. Pergamon Press, London (1958)

Carter, S.P., Greenberg, K., Walker, M.S.: The impact of computer usage on academic performance: evidence from a randomized trial at the United States military academy. Econ. Educ. Rev. **56**, 118–132 (2017). https://doi.org/10.1016/j.econedurev.2016.12.005

Chen, Q., Yan, Z.: Does multitasking with mobile phones affect learning? A review. Comput. Hum. Behav. **54**, 34–42 (2016). https://doi.org/10.1016/j.chb.2015.07.047

Clayson, D.E., Haley, D.A.: An introduction to multitasking and texting: prevalence and impact on grades and GPA in marketing classes. J. Mark. Educ. **35**(1), 26–40 (2012). https://doi.org/10.1177/0273475312467339

Darmoul, S., Ahmad, A., Ghaleb, M., Alkahtani, M.: Interruption management in human multitasking environments. IFAC-Pap. Online **48**(3), 1179–1185 (2015). https://doi.org/10.1016/j.ifacol.2015.06.244

Demirbilek, M., Talan, T.: The effect of social media multitasking on classroom performance. Act. Learn. High. Educ. **19**(2), 117–129 (2018). https://doi.org/10.1177/1469787417721382

Dzubak, C.M.: Multitasking: the good, the bad, and the unknown. Online J. Assoc. Tutoring Prof. **1**, 1–12 (2008)

Felisoni, D.D., Godoi, A.S.: Cell phone usage and academic performance: an experiment. Comput. Educ. **117**, 175–187 (2018). https://doi.org/10.1016/j.compedu.2017.10.006

Fried, C.B.: In-class laptop use and its effects on student learning. Comput. Educ. **50**(3), 906–914 (2008). https://doi.org/10.1016/j.compedu.2006.09.006

González, V.M., Mark, G.: Constant, constant, multi-tasking craziness: managing multiple working spheres. In: CHI Letters, vol. 6. Association for Computing Machinery, New York (2004)

Gupta, N., Irwin, J.D.: In-class distractions: the role of facebook and the primary learning task. Comput. Hum. Behav. **55**, 1165–1178 (2016). https://doi.org/10.1016/j.chb.2014.10.022

Jett, Q.R., George, J.M.: Work interrupted: a closer look at the role of interruptions in organizational life. Acad. Manag. Rev. **28**(3), 494–507 (2003)

Judd, T.: Making sense of multitasking: key behaviours. Comput. Educ. **63**, 358–367 (2013). https://doi.org/10.1016/j.compedu.2012.12.017

Junco, R.: In-class multitasking and academic performance. Comput. Hum. Behav. **28**(6), 2236–2243 (2012). https://doi.org/10.1016/j.chb.2012.06.031

Katidioti, I., Borst, J.P., van Vugt, M.K., Taatgen, N.A.: Interrupt me: external interruptions are less disruptive than self-interruptions. Comput. Hum. Behav. **63**, 906–915 (2016). https://doi.org/10.1016/j.chb.2016.06.037

Kay, R., Benzimra, D., Li, J.: Exploring factors that influence technology-based distractions in bring your own device classrooms. J. Educ. Comput. Res. **55**(7), 974–995 (2017). https://doi.org/10.1177/0735633117690004

Kirschner, P.A., de Bruyckere, P.: The myths of the digital native and the multitasker. Teach. Teach. Educ. **67**, 135–142 (2017). https://doi.org/10.1016/j.tate.2017.06.001

Kirschner, P.A., Karpinski, A.C.: Facebook® and academic performance. Comput. Hum. Behav. **26**(6), 1237–1245 (2010). https://doi.org/10.1016/j.chb.2010.03.024

Kong, S.C., Song, Y.: An experience of personalized learning hub initiative embedding BYOD for reflective engagement in higher education. Comput. Educ. **88**, 227–240 (2015). https://doi.org/10.1016/j.compedu.2015.06.003

Kraushaar, J.M., Novak, D.C.: Examining the affects of student multitasking with laptops during the lecture. J. Inf. Syst. Educ. **21**(2), 241–251 (2010)

Langan, D., et al.: Students' use of personal technologies in the university classroom: analysing the perceptions of the digital generation. Technol. Pedagogy Educ. **25**(1), 101–117 (2016). https://doi.org/10.1080/1475939X.2015.1120684

Rosen, L.D., Lim, A.F., Carrier, L.M., Cheever, N.A.: An empirical examination of the educational impact of text message-induced task switching in the classroom: educational implications and strategies to enhance learning. Revista de Psicología Educativa **17**(2), 163–177 (2011). https://doi.org/10.5093/ed2011v17n2a4

Le Roux, D.B., Parry, D.A.: In-lecture media use and academic performance: does subject area matter? Comput. Hum. Behav. **77**, 86–94 (2017). https://doi.org/10.1016/j.chb.2017.08.030

Lebbon, A.R., Sigurjónsson, J.G.: Debunking the instant messaging myth? Int. J. Inf. Manag. **36** (3), 433–440 (2016). https://doi.org/10.1016/j.ijinfomgt.2016.02.003

Ledermüller, K., Fallmann, I.: Predicting learning success in online learning environments: self-regulated learning, prior knowledge and repetition. Zeitschrift für Hochschulentwicklung **12** (1), 79–99 (2017). https://doi.org/10.3217/zfhe-12-01/05

Margaryan, A., Littlejohn, A., Vojt, G.: Are digital natives a myth or reality? University students' use of digital technologies. Comput. Educ. **56**(2), 429–440 (2011). https://doi.org/10.1016/j.compedu.2010.09.004

May, K.E., Elder, A.D.: Efficient, helpful, or distracting? A literature review of media multitasking in relation to academic performance. Int. J. Educ. Technol. High. Educ. **15**(1), 86 (2018). https://doi.org/10.1186/s41239-018-0096-z

McCoy, B.: Digital distractions in the classroom phase II: student classroom use of digital devices for non-class related purposes. J. Media Educ. **7**(1), 5–32 (2016)

McFarlane, D.C.: Comparison of four primary methods for coordinating the interruption of people in human-computer interaction. Hum.-Comput. Interact. **17**, 63–139 (2002)

Miyata, Y., Norman, D.A.: Psychological issues in support of multiple activities. In: Norman, D. A., Draper, S.W. (eds.) User Centered System Design. New Perspectives on Human-Computer Interaction, pp. 265–284. Lawrence Erlbaum Associates Inc, Hillsdale (1986)

Monk, C.A., Trafton, J.G., Boehm-Davis, D.A.: The effect of interruption duration and demand on resuming suspended goals. J. Exp. Psychol. Appl. **14**(4), 299–313 (2008). https://doi.org/10.1037/a0014402

Pintrich, P.R.: Understanding self-regulated learning. New Dir. Teach. Learn. **1995**(63), 3–12 (1995). https://doi.org/10.1002/tl.37219956304

Ratwani, R.M., Andrews, A.E., Sousk, J.D., Trafton, J.G.: The effect of interruption modality on primary task resumption. Proc. Hum. Factors Ergon. Soc. Annu. Meet. **52**(4), 393–397 (2008). https://doi.org/10.1177/154193120805200441

Ravizza, S.M., Uitvlugt, M.G., Fenn, K.M.: Logged in and zoned out. Psychol. Sci. **28**(2), 171–180 (2017). https://doi.org/10.1177/0956797616677314

Rosen, L.D., Mark Carrier, L., Cheever, N.A.: Facebook and texting made me do it: media-induced task-switching while studying. Comput. Hum. Behav. **29**(3), 948–958 (2013). https://doi.org/10.1016/j.chb.2012.12.001

Sana, F., Weston, T., Cepeda, N.J.: Laptop multitasking hinders classroom learning for both users and nearby peers. Comput. Educ. **62**, 24–31 (2013). https://doi.org/10.1016/j.compedu.2012.10.003

Song, Y.: We found the 'black spots' on campus on our own: development of inquiry skills in primary science learning with BYOD (Bring Your Own Device). Interact. Learn. Environ. **24** (2), 291–305 (2016). https://doi.org/10.1080/10494820.2015.1113707

Wei, F.-Y.F., Wang, Y.K., Klausner, M.: Rethinking college students' self-regulation and sustained attention: does text messaging during class influence cognitive learning? Commun. Educ. **61**(3), 185–204 (2012). https://doi.org/10.1080/03634523.2012.672755

Wood, E., Zivcakova, L., Gentile, P., Archer, K., de Pasquale, D., Nosko, A.: Examining the impact of off-task multi-tasking with technology on real-time classroom learning. Comput. Educ. **58**(1), 365–374 (2012). https://doi.org/10.1016/j.compedu.2011.08.029

Yamamoto, K.: Banning laptops in the classroom: is it worth the hassles? J. Leg. Educ. **57**(4), 477–520 (2007)

A Preliminary Review of Blockchain-Based Solutions in Higher Education

Aida Kamišalić[1](✉), Muhamed Turkanović[1], Saša Mrdović[2], and Marjan Heričko[1]

[1] Faculty of Electrical Engineering and Computer Science, University of Maribor, Koroška c. 46, 2000 Maribor, Slovenia
{aida.kamisalic,muhamed.turkanovic,marjan.hericko}@um.si
[2] Faculty of Electrical Engineering, University of Sarajevo, Zmaja od Bosne bb, Kampus Univerziteta, 71000 Sarajevo, Bosnia and Herzegovina
smrdovic@etf.unsa.ba

Abstract. Blockchain technology is showing its potential to disrupt established business processes. Four types of blockchain initiatives have been identified: Record keeper, efficiency play, digital asset market, and blockchain disruptor. Many different applications have also been emerging within the educational domain, following a student or institution-centric approach. Student-centric solutions simplify the validation process of received credentials, while institution-centric solutions facilitate mainly operational activities of educational institutions. In this paper, we present several use cases addressing different aspects within the educational domain, such as streamlining the process of diploma verification, virtual lifetime learning passport, securing the issued certificates permanently, verifying the accreditation process, automatic recognition of credits, etc. A preliminary review and analysis of identified projects and initiatives show that most of them follow a student-centric approach while facilitating record-keeping.

Keywords: Blockchain-based solution · Higher education innovation · Certificate management

1 Introduction

Blockchain is an emerging technology that has the potential to optimize, transform and disrupt established and traditional business processes, products and services. Its key features provide space for innovative technological approaches, and differentiate it from others on multiple levels. Kandaswamy [17] identified four types of blockchain initiatives: (1) Blockchain disruptor, (2) Digital asset market, (3) Efficiency play, and (4) Record keeper. The "blockchain disruptor" initiative relies on a technology foundation in order to achieve decentralization of business. New markets that facilitate the creation and trading of new digital

L. Uden et al. (Eds.): LTEC 2019, CCIS 1011, pp. 114–124, 2019.
https://doi.org/10.1007/978-3-030-20798-4_11

assets form part of a "digital asset market" initiative. "Efficiency play" is the initiative which gathers those companies or industries that attempt to improve efficiency in their existing business processes using the blockchain technology. Finally, companies or institutions ensuring that records cannot be corrupted, and that they can be audited on demand, are gathered under the "record keeping" initiative. Blockchain technology is slowly integrating itself in different domains, such as logistics, energy, manufacturing, life sciences and healthcare, digital identities, retail, etc. One of the domains suitable for adopting blockchain technology is the Higher Education (HE) domain, where the principles of document authenticity, transparency, immutability, and trust, are the key advantages which make it a perfect match [12]. We have identified two basic types of approaches adopted when implementing blockchain-based solutions within the HE environment. The first one is a student-centric approach, which gives a student control over his/her data. The second one is an institution-centric approach, the primary goal of which is to facilitate and streamline activities of educational institutions. The aim of the paper is in presenting the differences between those two approaches, as well as to analyze and present key features of selected blockchain-based projects and initiatives within the educational domain. Additionally, projects will be classified considering the two types of approaches, as well as regarding the purpose of the solution provided and the impact it might have. Furthermore, we will present characteristics of our project, named EduCTX, as well as the implementation challenges that other implementers of blockchain-based solutions within the HE domain might also be facing.

The rest of the paper is organized as follows. Section 2 provides descriptions of different types of blockchain initiatives and solutions in HE. Analysis of existing use cases applying blockchain technology within the educational domain is presented in Sect. 3. The EduCTX initiative is detailed in Sect. 4, presenting the challenges faced during its implementation. Finally, Sect. 5 presents conclusions and directions for future work.

2 Blockchain Initiatives and Solutions in HE

This section provides a brief classification of blockchain-based solutions for HE, based on the entity focus and on the Kandaswamy classification. Student-centric blockchain-based solutions facilitate and simplify the student activities related to validation of received credentials, since blockchain-based services accelerate and facilitate administrative procedures where a validation process is required. Credentials are Certificates awarded to students in order to recognize achieved learning objectives, such as participation in formal or informal education, completion of courses or Study Programs (e.g., with ECTS (European Credit Transfer System) points awarded), completion of an apprenticeship or work-experience, etc. [12]. Blockchain-based student-centric solutions place the responsibility and control over received credentials on students, thus eliminating the need for a verification process by an intermediary (e.g., Higher Education Institution (HEI)). Consequently, the processes for stakeholders (e.g., potential employers) interested in the evidence of a student's achievements can be streamlined [25]. On the other hand, an institution-centric approach facilitates mainly management and operational activities of HEI for payment management (e.g., receipts of students' payments), international collaboration management (e.g., automatic recognition of awarded ECTS points), accreditation processes (e.g., a Certificate issued by government that the HEI is licensed to carry out specific tasks), etc. Blockchain-based institution-centric solutions can provide a wide range of benefits for HEIs. For example, the process of internationalization of HEIs through the Student Exchange Programs or joint degrees, can be facilitated avoiding long-lasting administrative procedures, which are a financial and time-consuming burden. Another example is blockchain-based gamification of learning, which would facilitate the management of the issued Certificates for the achievements of intermediate learning goals. Both approaches are faced with different challenges, e.g. organizational, legal, administrative, etc., whereby special attention should be placed on the data privacy challenge. Another classification of blockchain-based solutions within the educational domain can be provided considering the four types of blockchain initiatives identified by Kandaswamy [17]. Blockchain as a disruptor has the potential to be used as an education and academic publishing platform. Receiving students' payments, providing student funding and tokenized educational rewards are some use cases of the blockchain digital asset market initiative. Streamlining Diploma verification and virtual lifelong learning passport are use cases within the initiative for efficiency improvement. The blockchain record-keeping initiative for HEIs covers several use cases, such as securing the Certificates permanently, verifying the accreditation, automatic recognition of credits and intellectual property management [12,25]. A good overview of current trends and existing implementations of blockchain for education can be found in [8,15].

3 Analysis of Existing Blockchain-Based Solutions in HE

Taking into account the two previously described classifications, a preliminary literature review was performed related to the HE domain, and focusing on reports published by the European Commission [12] and Gartner [25]. We performed a detailed analysis of published articles, white papers and project web pages. The chosen applications are grouped considering four types of blockchain initiatives. There is a significant difference in the number of different projects, regarding their implications. For example, we detected many projects related to issuing new digital credentials, while just one dedicated to academic publishing. Nevertheless, here, we will present a few use cases considering different approaches taken for implementation of blockchain technology - ones related to the student-centric approach, and others to the institution-centric approach.

3.1 Selected Use Cases

As representatives of the student-centric approach related to issuing new digital credentials, the following universities can be considered due to their existing projects on this topic: (1) University of Nicosia, (2) Massachusetts Institute of Technology (MIT) and (3) University of Maribor. The University of Nicosia presented a project on issuing a blockchain verifiable credential for completion of a digital currency course [23]. Blockchain-verifiable Diplomas were issued by MIT [21]. The University of Maribor presented a blockchain-based platform named EduCTX, which enables managing, assigning and presenting any type of digital micro-credentials [26]. Loci, Bernstein and Binded are projects addressing the field of Intellectual Property Management. Loci developed a blockchain-based platform for facilitating the invention process, where ideas can be verified as unique and could be claimed as one's own [20]. Bernstein provides a Blockchain-as-a-Service solution for registration of intellectual property assets [1], while Binded offers a blockchain-based copyright registration service for images [2]. All the above-mentioned projects form part of the "record keeping" blockchain initiative. Typical representatives of the "efficiency play" initiative with institution-centric approaches are a joint project of three Greek universities: Aristotle University of Thessaloniki, Democritus University of Thrace, and Athens University of Economics and Business, as well as a joint project of the Government of Dubai and EduChain. The first is addressing a process of streamlining Diplomas' verification [7], while the second is dealing with the creation of a lifelong academic passport [10]. King's College [18], the University of Nicosia [23], Simon Fraser University [6] and the University of Cumbria [31] are among educational institutions which accept bitcoin cryptocurrency for student payments [25]. Tokenized educational rewards are addressed by the Extra Credit and Bitcoin Homework projects. Extra Credit is a cryptocurrency learning platform [11], while Bitcoin Homework is designed as a learning portal for sharing ideas [3]. Use cases where a blockchain technology serves as a disruptor are Bitdegree, Woolf University and Ledger (University of Pittsburg). Bitdegree is an online education platform offering gamified learning experience and scholarships based on cryptocurrency [4]. Woolf University develops a platform where the relationship between students and professors is backed up with smart contracts and blockchain technology [30]. Finally, the only blockchain-based platform detected as an academic publishing use case is Ledger, which supports peer review process with published reviews, together with accepted manuscripts [19]. All those disruptor projects followed the institution-centric approach. Some additional projects are presented briefly in Table 1, and included in the final data analysis presented in Figs. 1 and 2.

3.2 Summary of Preliminary Analysis Results

Overall, we have identified 25 projects, whereby 13 can be classified into a record-keeper blockchain initiative. Only two projects are part of the efficiency play. Six belong to the digital asset market, and four to the blockchain disruptor initiative. Only four out of 25 are detected as institution-centric, while 11 as only student-centric projects. Ten projects are following both approaches, student- and institution-centric. Most of the projects within the educational domain deal with record-keeping issues while taking student-centric approaches. Only four

Table 1. Use cases in the educational domain.

Project	Owner	s-c	i-c	Initiative
Verifiable credential for completion of a digital currency course	University of Nicosia [23]	x		R
An open standard for applications that issue and verify blockchain-based Certificates (Blockcerts)	MIT Media Labs [5]	x		R
Blockchain-based Diplomas' verification	Malta College of Arts Science and Technology [12]	x		R
	MIT [21]			
	Univ. of Melbourne [28]			
	Southern New Hampshire University [24]			
	Central New Mexico Community College [29]			
	Ngee Ann Polytechnic [22]			
Managing, assigning and presenting any type of digital micro-credentials	University of Maribor [26]	x	x	R
Invention process; determining the uniqueness of an idea and providing a possibility to claim own ideas	Loci [20]	x	x	R
Registration of intellectual property assets	Bernstein [1]	x		R
Copyright registration service used for images	Binded [2]	x		R
Intellectual property rights for artists	Zhejiang University, Shenzhen University, Chinese Academy of Sciences [9]	x		R
Student Diplomas' verification	Three Greek universities [7]		x	E
Facilitating the creation of a lifelong academic passport	Government of Dubai and Educhain [10]	x	x	E
Accepting payment with bitcoins	King's College [18]	x	x	A
	University of Nicosia [23]			
	Simon Fraser Univ. [6]			
	University of Cumbria [31]			
Learning platform for cryptocurrency courses	Extra Credit [11]	x	x	A
Learning portal promoting a sharing of ideas	Bitcoin Homework [3]	x	x	A
Online education platform offering gamified learning experience and cryptocurrency-based scholarships	BitDegree [4]		x	D
A digital platform providing a complete record of everything ever learned	Ledger [14]	x	x	D
Platform connecting learners and educators	Woolf University [30]		x	D
Ledger - open publishing platform that supports the peer review process	Univ. of Pittsburgh [19]		x	D

s-c: Student-centric, i-c: Institution-centric
R: Record-keeping, E: Efficiency play, A: Digital asset market, D: Disruptor

projects set up an institution-centric approach. Nine out of 25 projects follow both approaches – student- and institution-centric, which indicates the tendency of using blockchain additionally in order to support organizational processes within institutions.

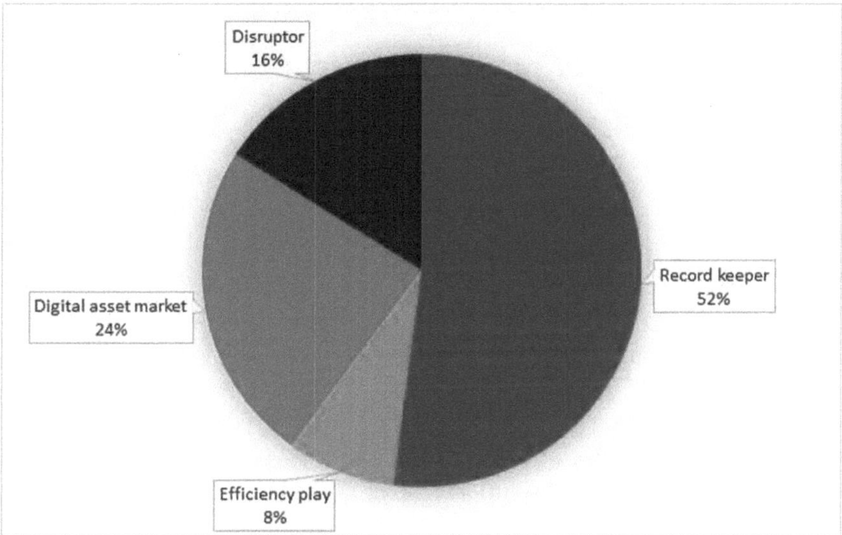

Fig. 1. The share of applications within the educational domain classified into four blockchain initiatives.

4 Characteristics and Implementation Challenges of the EduCTX Project

In this section, we provide a detailed insight into the EduCTX project, which is a global decentralized blockchain-based platform that, primarily, follows a student-centric approach, while demonstrating a strong potential to solve organizational issues of HEIs. We will present the challenges that other implementers of blockchain-based solutions within the HE domain might also be facing. With its student-centric approach, EduCTX offers a comprehensive and unified digital environment for managing students' credentials, giving students control over which data to share [26]. Educational institutions, as well as other potential stakeholders such as companies, institutions, and organizations, are certified authorities issuing credentials. It aims at creating an effective and simplified digital environment to avoid linguistic and administrative barriers. It is a perfect solution to address internationalization challenges of HEIs, such as joint degrees, Student Exchange Programs, etc. Additionally, the platform contributes to the modernization of processes, and supports the development and deployment of innovative digital services. Through publicly accessible APIs, it provides organizations with the possibility to develop their own intelligent services in order

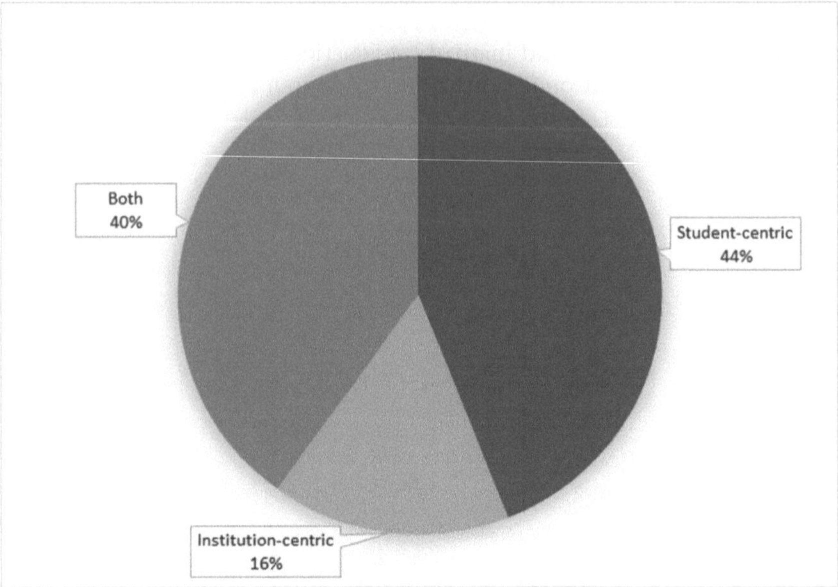

Fig. 2. The share of applications within the educational domain classified into two approaches to blockchain-based solutions.

to automate the evaluation of individuals' skills and knowledge, which can be used for ranking job candidates. A student sends the credential to the potential employer, which uses the publicly accessible API of the EduCTX platform to validate the content of the received credential. The validation process is time constrained by the student. We refer readers interested in more technical details to the original EduCTX articles [16,26]. HEIs that use EduCTX do not have to devote resources for answering inquiries about their students' achievements. Instead, that data is publicly available to interested parties through reference provided by student. Using EduCTX educational organizations thus shorten this process that can be time-consuming, costly and burdensome. Therefore, it also shows the potential to be as well considered as an institution-centric solution. Another important aspect of the platform lies in its social importance, as it enables individuals to have the equal possibility to share their competences with potential employers. Based on our experience, we have identified various challenges related to: (1) Addressing process-organizational aspects, (2) Assigning previously issued certificates, (3) Deciding on an adequate type of data storage, (4) Identity management, (5) GDPR compliance, and (6) Dealing with the immutability of blockchain records. Further, we present how the afore identified challenges were addressed within the EduCTX project. In order to develop and deploy blockchain-based solutions successfully, it is necessary to establish cooperation with the IT Departments of educational institutions to provide resources, network operation, etc. In addition, successful implementation of blockchain-based solutions is accompanied by innovations in existing business processes, thus requiring the collaboration of all involved actors inside and outside the HEI. Certain authorities (such as a Notary's office, a Ministry of Education, etc.) should be determined to deal with the challenge of assigning credentials issued in the past. This task could be attributed to the authority that issued a specific credential or, in the case that the issuing institution is no longer active, the task is passed to those general authorities which would verify the credential and assign it to the blockchain-based platform.

The new version of the EduCTX platform is implemented with Ethereum as the backbone and deployed on a consortium-based P2P network [16]. The platform manages ECTX tokens and transactions, which represent a trusted and transparent evidence of acquired skills and knowledge of individuals in the form of digital micro-credentials [13]. EduCTX enables all types of credentials to be stored in a JSON-format file, encrypted, and pushed into a distributed file system like IPFS, while storing the hash of such an encrypted file on the blockchain ledger. A student's certificate JSON file can only be decrypted by its owner. A student that wants to prove the possession of a certificate can download the decrypted version of the JSON file and send it to anyone. The recipient of the decrypted JSON file can verify its integrity and authenticity using the platform, where the decrypted JSON file can be uploaded, and the verification result obtained, i.e., the certificate is not valid (see Fig. 3). Furthermore, the platform also generates a user-friendly version of the certificate by generating its PDF version. The platform facilitates the anonymous storage of personal data, thus being compliant with the GDPR requirements, considering the right to be forgotten [27].

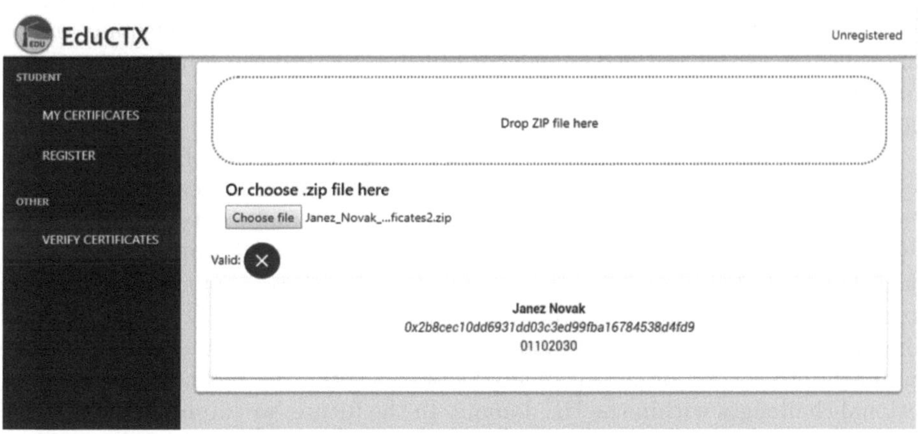

Fig. 3. Certificate verification process on the EduCTX platform.

The EduCTX platform does not provide connectivity with identity management systems to support obtaining a student's identity. Therefore, anyone who wants to use the platform needs to create a classic Ethereum account, store the account keys and run a plugin for managing the account. Another important issue to deal with is the immutability of records within the blockchain network. Since an institution has the possibility to withdraw issued credentials for Degrees, Diplomas, Certificates, etc., this is inconvenient for a blockchain-based solution where none of the processed transactions could be deleted. In order to solve this problem, the EduCTX platform enables issuing of annulled transactions i.e. credentials, which are bound automatically to existing revoked transactions.

Blockchain-based solutions should be a generic and global as possible in order to take advantage of the most important blockchain features. Those solutions should be integrated with existing Student Information Systems (SIS). Blockchain-based solutions are not supposed to substitute existing SIS, since there is no benefit of data replication, while additionally having to comply with privacy concerns. Therefore, EduCTX promotes itself as being only a blockchain-based platform for managing credentials, while enabling traditional SIS to integrate with it through publicly available APIs.

5 Conclusions and Future Work

In this paper, we have presented a thorough overview of blockchain initiatives and solutions in higher education. Main strengths and opportunities of this approach have been identified, as well as particular ongoing projects related to this domain. We have shown how blockchain is used to immutably store student achievement data, while making it available for authorized users. Through the systematic analysis of identified projects, we have been able to classify them into four blockchain initiatives and two approaches to blockchain-based solutions. This provides the basis for future research and development. Experience from implementation of EduCTX was used to identify and present main practical challenges. The identified challenges of EduCTX and the solutions for those, could help other researchers with their projects and enable further advances in blockchain projects for education.

Existing solutions and initiatives clearly demonstrate that Blockchain technology has enormous potential to disrupt current higher educational systems. Due to the nature of blockchain features (e.g., immutability, permanence), several challenges need to be addressed for a successful implementation of blockchain-based services. Process-organizational and socio-cultural aspects are crucial for the successful introduction of any technology and IT-based services. The protection of sensitive personal data and the incorporation of the disruptive approach into settled organizational processes are the key technical and organizational challenges within the HE domain. In the future, we intend to contact the authors of identified projects through prepared questionnaires, in order to identify common challenges and issues on implementing blockchain-based solutions, and discover how different authors address them. In that manner, an initial set of best practices could be identified and documented, as well as possible reference models and architectures defined, including detailed implementation scenarios for blockchain-based solutions within HE environments.

Acknowledgments. The authors acknowledge the financial support from the Slovenian Research Agency (research core funding No. P2-0057 Information Systems and project No. BI-BA/19-20-020 Implementation challenges of blockchain technology in higher education).

References

1. Bernstein. https://www.bernstein.io/. Accessed 30 Jan 2019
2. Binded. https://binded.com/. Accessed 30 Jan 2019
3. Bitcoin Homework. https://bitcoinhomework.com/. Accessed 2 Feb 2019
4. BitDegree. https://www.bitdegree.org/. Accessed 2 Feb 2019
5. Skriba, D.: The potential of blockchain in education and health care. Nurs. Educ. Perspect. **38**(4), 220–221 (2017). https://doi.org/10.1097/01.NEP.0000000000000190
6. Canadian University Enables Bitcoin Payments On Campus, 28 May 2015. http://digitalmoneytimes.com/canadian-university-enables-bitcoin-payments-on-campus/.
7. Cardano Blockchain's First Use Case: Proof of University Diplomas in Greece, 2 January 2018. https://bitcoinmagazine.com/articles/cardano-blockchains-first-use-case-proof-university-diplomas-greece/.
8. Chen, G., Xu, B., Lu, M., Chen, N.S.: Exploring blockchain technology and its potential applications for education. Smart Learn. Environ. **5**(1), 1 (2018). https://doi.org/10.1186/s40561-017-0050-x
9. China develops a blockchain intellectual property, 28 Febuary 2018. https://hype.codes/china-develops-blockchain-intellectual-property.
10. Educhain. https://educhain.io/. Accessed 30 Jan 2019
11. Extracredit. https://extracredit.io/. Accessed 2 Feb 2019
12. Grech, A., Camilleri, A. F.: Blockchain in education. JRC science for policy report (2017). https://goo.gl/gG4F1w, https://doi.org/10.1109/EAEEIE.2018.8534284
13. Hölbl, M., Kamišalić, A., Turkanović, M., Kompara, M., Podgorelec, B., Heričko, M.: EduCTX: an ecosystem for managing digital micro-credentials. In: IEEE, Mentasetriõ viõ Lækinn 28th EAEEIE Annual Conference, pp. 1–4. Hafnarfjörõur, Iceland (2018)
14. Institute for the Future. http://www.iftf.org/learningisearning/. Accessed 2 Feb 2019
15. Jirgensons, M., Kapenieks, J.: Blockchain and the future of digital learning credential assessment and management. J. Teacher Educ. Sustain. **20**(1), 145–156 (2018)
16. Kamišalić, A., Turkanović, M., Heričko, M.: A decentralized system for managing micro-credentials based on blockchain 2.0. In: 10th International Workshop on Data Analysis Methods for Software Systems, p. 39. Vilnius University Press. cop., Druskininkai (2018)
17. Kandaswamy, R.: Pay Attention to These 4 Types of Blockchain Business Initiatives. Gartner (2018)
18. King's College Becomes First U.S. School to Accept Bitcoin, 13 June 2014. http://time.com/2871764/kings-college-accept-bitcoin/.
19. Ledger. https://ledger.pitt.edu/ojs/index.php/ledger/about/editorialPolicies. Accessed 2 Feb 2019
20. Loci. https://loci.io/. Accessed 30 Jan 2019

21. MIT Has Started Issuing Diplomas Using Blockchain Technology, 19 October 2017. https://futurism.com/mit-has-started-issuing-diplomas-using-blockchain-technology.
22. Ngee Ann Polytechnic to issue blockchain diplomas in first for Singapore, 26 May 2018. https://www.techinasia.com/ngee-ann-blockchain-diplomas.
23. Sharples, M., Domingue, J.: The blockchain and kudos: a distributed system for educational record, reputation and reward. In: Verbert, K., Sharples, M., Klobučar, T. (eds.) EC-TEL 2016. LNCS, vol. 9891, pp. 490–496. Springer, Cham (2016). https://doi.org/10.1007/978-3-319-45153-4_48
24. Southern New Hampshire U Issues Blockchain Credentials to College for America Grads. https://campustechnology.com/articles/2018/06/11/southern-new-hampshire-u-issues-blockchain-credentials-to-college-for-america-grads.aspx. 11 Jun 2018
25. Thayer, T.-L.: 4 Promising and Ambitious Blockchain Initiatives for Higher Education. Gartner (2018)
26. Turkanović, M., Hölbl, M., Kšič, K., Heričko, M., Kamišalić, A.: EduCTX: a blockchain-based higher education credit platform. IEEE access 6(1), 5112–5127 (2018). https://doi.org/10.1109/ACCESS.2018.2789929
27. Turkanović, M., Kežmah, B., Kamišalić, A., Heričko, M., Podgorelec, B., Heričko, M.: Method and device for controlling the re-identification of pseudonymized data in a permanent immutable distributed decentralized storage. Patent application (2019)
28. University of Melbourne to issue recipient-owned blockchain records, 9 October 2017. https://about.unimelb.edu.au/newsroom/news/2017/october/university-of-melbourne-to-issue-recipient-owned-blockchain-records.
29. Using Blockchain, New Mexico Community College Becomes First Community College to Issue Student-Owned Digital Diplomas, 16 November 2017. https://www.prnewswire.com/news-releases/using-blockchain-new-mexico-community-college-becomes-first-community-college-to-issue-student-owned-digital-diplomas-300557931.html.
30. Woolf: Building a Borderless University. https://woolf.university. Accessed 2 Feb 2019
31. World first: UK public university to accept bitcoin, 21 January 2014. https://www.rt.com/news/cumbria-bitcoin-university-fee-977/.

EduBrowser: A Multimodal Automated Monitoring System for Co-located Collaborative Learning

Yi Han Victoria Chua[1(✉)], Preman Rajalingam[2], Seng Chee Tan[3], and Justin Dauwels[1]

[1] School of Electrical and Electronic Engineering, Nanyang Technological University, Singapore, Singapore
vicchuayh@gmail.com

[2] Medical Education Research and Scholarship Unit (MERSU), Lee Kong Chian School of Medicine, Singapore, Singapore

[3] National Institute of Education, Singapore, Singapore

Abstract. Majority of learning analytics systems are designed to monitor and analyze students' online interactions during collaborative learning. In the case of co-located collaborative learning, student interactions take place in the physical space as well as online. While existing learning management systems provide specific logs and snapshots of students' online responses that are automatically captured, the potential of insights that can be derived from students' non-digital face-to-face interactions during collaborative discourse remains untapped. In this paper, we propose an architecture for data acquisition and processing from co-located face-to-face collaborative learning, designed to be scalable beyond dyadic and triadic collaborative learning and across different curricula. We outline the system design, current experience of deployment across 4 sessions of co-located collaborative learning sessions, as well as brief examples of acquired data.

Keywords: Collaborative learning · Multimodal learning analytics · Physical spaces

1 Introduction

Collaboration is often emphasized as an important education outcome and key 21st century skill [2]. Collaborative learning provides opportunities to hone communication skills, sharpen understanding through mutual knowledge building and cultivate social emotional skills [4]. The value of collaborative learning lies within the interactions that occur during team tasks, as students discuss, and build upon their ideas and conceptions [17].

Currently, in co-located classrooms that adopt collaborative learning methods, facilitators may leverage Learning Management Systems to support all phases of collaborative learning: digital delivery of learning materials, administration of assessment procedures, and real-time collection of students' responses (e.g., large-scale team-based learning implementation [23]. These systems allow fine-grained recording of

L. Uden et al. (Eds.): LTEC 2019, CCIS 1011, pp. 125–138, 2019.
https://doi.org/10.1007/978-3-030-20798-4_12

students' online responses, from response time, number of attempts, to number of correct answers. However, the physical interactions (via facial expression, speech and gestures) among students are often overlooked in such systems. Facilitators may monitor these cues and reciprocate accordingly in real-time, but the task of monitoring students' interactions becomes more complex and difficult as the size of the classroom increases [7].

As the face-to-face collaborative discourse contains a wealth of information of team dynamics [17], such discourse is often analyzed via observational methods, which are labor-intensive and infeasible to employ at a larger scale. This is because analyzing discourse qualitatively is subjective as discussions are heterogeneous and diverse due to group composition and group expertise. In addition, the number of observers required per team increases as the size of a team increases. In a typical team-based learning (TBL) situation, the optimal team size is 6, with up to 20 teams participating in a single TBL session [20, 23]. In such large-scale implementation of collaborative learning, assessment of team dynamics is limited to objective team test scores. On top of that, as a stopgap, team dynamics are also often assessed via self-reports, which are limited by responses biases, such as social desirability bias [35].

Our objective is to understand how elements of team dynamics and interactions make collaborative learning a successful learning paradigm as well as incorporate assessment of team dynamics to improve learning outcomes in collaborative learning using technology. As such, we present a study aimed at scaling and adapting multi-modal learning analytics to large-scale co-located collaborative learning classrooms. We design and test a setup that collects raw audio and video data during face-to-face collaborative learning discussions. We then present examples of interpretable metrics that can be computed by algorithmic methods and be utilized by facilitators, to better understand and monitor collaborative group dynamics, and by learners, to monitor and review their participative roles and processes.

The rest of the paper is structured as follows: we review similar studies on automated co-located collaborative learning analysis in Sect. 2, followed by a description of our system design and framework for data processing in Sect. 3. We then share our current experience of deployment and propose hypotheses for automated analysis of collaborative learning dynamics in Sect. 4; finally, we discuss limitations, lessons learnt and our future work in Sect. 5.

2 Related Work

To date, there is a limited number of studies on automated analysis of co-located collaborative learning [6, 39]. We briefly review studies that apply learning analytics to face-to-face, co-located collaborative learning scenarios in Sect. 2.1, as well as systems designed to harness non-digital data from these scenarios in Sect. 2.2.

2.1 Learning Analytics for Co-located Collaborative Learning

Most studies that investigate face-to-face collaborative learning were laboratory studies, recruiting students in realistic educational tasks that matched their target curriculum to test specialized equipment such as digital user interfaces [27, 40]. In terms of the types of multimodal indicators collected during co-located collaboration, a review by Praharaj et al. [22] observed multiple multimodal indicators ranging from speech-based cues, hand and body movements, eye gaze, and digital interaction logs. These findings seem to extend beyond non-learning contexts.

In our previous review of co-located learning analysis [6], we found that many collaborative learning studies also attempt to delineate common collaboration dimensions such as *synchrony* and *proximity* from physical indicators. Synchrony is defined as how coordinated and synchronized the behaviours of each team members are [3]. For example, when one member is swaying their body during conversation, others who are in sync may follow as well [5]. On the other hand, proximity refers to the similarity between group members [5]. These dimensions are often computed at individual continuous points in time, over the entire course of collaborative interaction.

Between collaborative programming dyads, Grover et al. [12] observed that synchrony in body position and eye gaze towards the computer screen were useful indicators in predicting the level of collaboration. While analysing two-person collaborative learning dialogues, Lubold and Pon-Barry et al. [15] found that synchrony and proximity of pitch on a turn-to-turn basis correlate strongly with high levels of rapport. Besides speech-based and movements, Schneider and colleagues demonstrated that synchrony in eye gaze (i.e., Joint Visual Attention) is a good predictor of collaboration quality [28]. A small subset of studies detected *synchrony* and *proximity* beyond dyads. When studying students' Collaborative Problem Solving (CPS) behaviours, Cukurova et al. [8] showed that high levels of synchrony displayed through hand position and head direction were good predictors for students' CPS competencies. Similarly, Spikol et al. [29, 30] found that, within project-based learning groups, proximity between students' hands and faces strongly predicted the quality of artefact built by students collaboratively.

2.2 Automated Systems for Co-located Collaborative Learning Analysis

In a co-located collaborative learning scenario, the face-to-face interactions that occurs contains a wealth of information. While systems that rely solely on digital traces have reported considerable success (e.g. MTFeedback [16]), our focus is on systems that analyse physical interactions during collaborative learning. Thus, we focus on systems that harness at least one aspect of physical interaction (i.e., speech, hand gestures, body movements, eye gaze, etc.) and may include—but do not rely solely on—digital data sources such as keyboard strokes and mouse clicks. In addition, such automated systems should be able to collect data from collaborative teams beyond dyads.

For instance, one such unimodal system was developed by Bachour et al. [1]. They employed audio cues to develop a system that gave students real-time feedback of speaking time during their collaborative discussion, and reported success in promoting equal speaking participation within students. A multimodal system designed by Ruffaldi et al. [25] leveraged the use of video, audio, interactions with specialized equipment (i.e., button clicks) and multimedia content uploaded by students to model, analyse and monitor co-located hands-on collaborative tasks. The system was specifically tailored to hands-on collaborative learning and they were able to integrate data from multiple sensors to identify distinctive features in [29, 30]. Similarly, Praharaj et al. [22] created a multimodal setup that includes audio, video and human annotated data for modelling real-time participation time during in-the-wild collaborative discussions within PhD students. As a preliminary prototype, they showcased a real-time dashboard of speaking time, generated based on human-annotated data only.

3 Experimental Design

To test our data collection setup, we employed both laboratory and in-the-wild studies. As our express purpose is not only to test the viability of our setup in-situ, but to investigate elements of team dynamics that contribute to collaborative learning, we first focus on teams that have worked together for a while, rather than recruiting newly formed teams, i.e., strangers randomly assigned to team. The teams that participated in our studies were from different faculties and underwent different curriculums, which we outline in Sect. 3.1. We then explain the design of our study as well as the multimodal data collection setup in Sect. 3.2.

3.1 The Learning Contexts

The laboratory studies were conducted in conjunction with Lee Kong Chian School of Medicine, which established TBL as its principal teaching strategy, in place of face-to-face lectures [23]. TBL is a type of collaborative learning paradigm developed by Michaelsen which emphasizes student engagement and knowledge application [20]. In the Lee Kong Chian School of Medicine, students are assigned to teams of six at the start of semester and take part in TBL sessions in their assigned team for one whole academic year.

In each TBL session, students are expected to individually study materials pre-class, and participate in a myriad of individual and team assessments in-class [20, 23]. In-class session starts off with students answering a set of closed-book multiple-choice questions (MCQs) individually i.e., the Individual Readiness Assurance (iRA). The iRA tests whether the students have completed the pre-lesson study materials assigned as well as give students an overview on the important foundational concepts of each lesson [20]. Following which, they then answer the same set of MCQs as a team, i.e., Team Readiness Assurance (tRA). During the tRA, students submit one answer as a team, facilitated by their appointed leader, receive immediate feedback and can attempt the question multiple times. The peer discussion that takes place during tRA enables knowledge exchange and clarification of questions and misconceptions, while the immediate feedback given facilitates the team's decision-making process [20]. Both the iRA and tRA are processes carefully designed to ensure individual and team accountability and facilitate understanding of high-level concepts [20].

Lastly, they move on to the application phase and work on open-book open-ended application exercise (AE) together as a team, which encourages them to apply the concepts they have learnt in the previous stages to realistic clinical use cases and problems [20, 23]. The team is then required to report and defend their answers at the class level. The entire in-class sequence is managed and delivered via a learning management system.

For the in-the-wild studies, we focused on a class conducted by National Institute of Education (NIE) Singapore. The facilitators employed collaborative discussions for a designated portion of the curriculum time each week and students in this class were assigned to groups of five. Before the class, students would prepare for class by reading assigned materials. During the allocated discussion time, students worked on collaborative tasks in their designated group, assigned to them at the start of the semester. The tasks included MCQs or open-ended questions which sometimes culminated into a presentation.

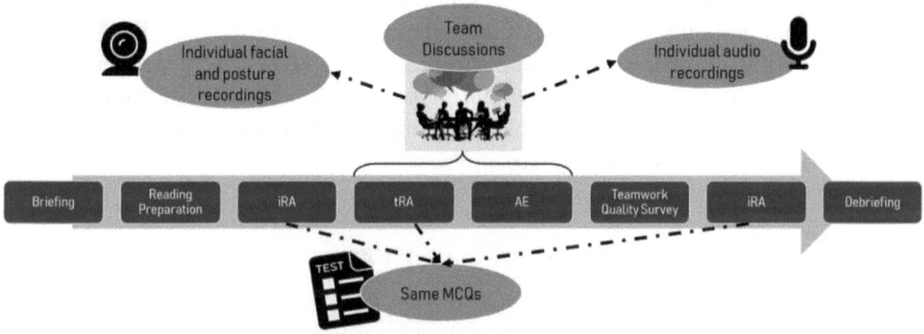

(a) For laboratory sessions

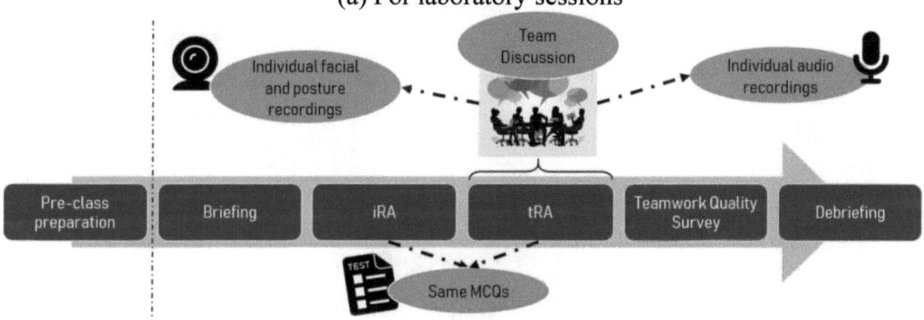

(b) For in-the-wild

Fig. 1. Procedures for laboratory and in-the-wild collaborative learning sessions.

3.2 Study Design and Multimodal Data Collection

Study Design. For the laboratory sessions, we recruited students in their existing TBL teams to participate in simulated TBL sessions. The aim is to test the viability of our data collection setup while TBL teams are engaged in similar TBL curriculum and materials. The study also took place in a similar classroom where actual TBL sessions were conducted. The simulated TBL process is as follows: students recruited read a passage on a related medical education subject matter, underwent a short iRA, collectively selected a leader representative, attempted tRA as a team and answered one AE (see Fig. 1a). After which—for the purpose of correlating video and audio features to perceptions of team dynamics—students were required to answer a Teamwork

Quality Survey (adapted from [36]). The survey consisted of items regarding students' perceptions of their team dynamics during the session (e.g., "My team communicated frequently when completing the tasks."). Students indicated their responses on a 5-point Likert scale ranging from 1 (Strongly Disagree) to 5 (Strongly Agree). To measure learning gains, students worked on the iRA again and individual learning gains could be computed by comparing the two iRA scores. Each portion of the process had varying lengths of duration depending on students' speeds at which they finished the task, but most teams finished within one and a half hours.

During the in-the-wild sessions, due to limitations in curriculum time and variation in curriculum context, student teams were sent pre-class preparation materials as part of their curriculum and only went through one attempt of iRA (instead of twice). For the team portion, the number of attempts allowed during tRA was dependent on the available curriculum time. For example, during one of the recordings, a student arrived late, and the student team was only able to attempt the tRA once. Lastly, the students did not work on any AEs (see Fig. 1b).

Fig. 2. Audio and video data collection setup.

Data Collection Setup. For the collaborative learning contexts in our study, students are seated most of the time and refer to their individual laptops or tablets. Hence, for video data collection, we were interested in collecting individual facial data and body posture (see Fig. 2). We set up a 360 camera in the middle of the table that clearly captured students' faces (see Fig. 2). We also installed 3 GoPro cameras around the table. Each GoPro camera is focused one student pair in order to capture their sitting posture. For the audio setup, we attach individual lapel microphones and collect separate audio streams from each student via an H6 N recorder with a sample rate of

48 kHz. Activity that corresponded to the collaborative discussion was recorded, i.e., during the leader selection, tRA and AE (only for laboratory sessions). A total of 17 students across 4 collaborative learning sessions were recorded.

Taken together, for laboratory sessions, we were able to collect assessment scores on the individual level (2 sets of iRA scores; pre and post), team level (tRA) and self-reported Teamwork Quality Survey responses. For in-the-wild sessions, we have the iRA, tRA test scores and self-reported Teamwork Quality Survey responses.

4 Analysis

As team interactions are an important part of collaborative learning, it is important to capture, analyze and monitor these interactions. In order to do that, we will adapt and augment audio and video processing algorithms to automatically extract relevant metrics of student behaviours from these recordings and investigate correlations between these extracted metrics and: (i) objective learning test scores and (ii) subjective team dynamics indicators outlined by existing frameworks. The objective iRA and tRA test scores are measures of team success while responses to the Teamwork Quality Survey are subjective measures of team dynamics. In this way, we leverage the combination of audio/video analytics, objective test scores, and subjective observational measures to build and validate our automated system.

To scaffold our analysis and explore potential mappings between features and team dynamics indicators, we focus on the types of data collected, that is, audio (cf. Sect. 4.1) and video (cf. Sect. 4.2) data, following by the types of relevant analyses that could be conducted. We include challenges encountered in the initial attempts of processing the data for some hypotheses. In Sect. 4.3, we explore potential analyses of detection of leadership, expertise and team diversity with the purpose of understanding the effect of team composition on team success. Lastly, in Sect. 4.4 we discuss the potential of applying the interaction adaptation theory to extract and understand the social dynamics during collaborative learning.

4.1 Audio Analysis

As demonstrated by many studies, audio-based cues, especially in terms of speaking time, can be a useful indicator of individual participation and team dynamics (e.g., [1, 22]). Beyond extracting speaking participation time from audio data, we present examples of the potential of using audio data collected in our setup to explore dynamics of team interactions.

Preliminary Analysis. Keeping in mind the importance of collaborative discourse, we adopted the framework identified by Mercer [17], which outlines features of collaborative dialogue that are important in the understanding of collaborative learning dialogues. Mercer outlines two types of talks, *disputational* and *exploratory*; the former features short utterances, rarely accompanied by explicit reasoning, and characterized by disagreement, while the latter features coordinated forms of co-reasoning, accompanied by exchange of ideas and characterized by rational decision-making.

Between the 2 TBL groups recorded in controlled settings, we conducted a preliminary qualitative analysis of the collaborative discourse. We uncovered significant differences between the number of occurrences in *disputational* and *exploratory* talk between a high- and low-performing group (dependent on their team scores). For the low-performing group, team members asserted their answers, with little to no reason. Often, team members would insist the correct answer was wrong by articulating their answer repeatedly (e.g., "It's A, it's A, it's A") and gave insubstantial explanations when challenged (e.g., "It's just the way it is."). This type of interaction was repeated several times, resulting in a lower team score. In comparison, the high-performing group engaged in active discussion, back-and-forth justifications and rebuttal of one another's answers, resulting in a higher team score.

Conversational Features. For detecting and monitoring of such speech-based phenomena, conversational patterns such as turn-taking, mutual silence, number of overlaps, length of utterances can be useful indicators. As short utterances are characteristic of insistences with little elaboration, automatic detection and segmentation of utterance can potentially be a useful predictor in the level of epistemological contributions by each team member. In addition, Oviatt et al. [19] studied groups of students working collaboratively to solve math problems and found the frequency of overlapped speech increased during the "moment of insight" (i.e., the moment when a student proposes a correct solution to when the group submits it as answer). Hence, for effective collaborative dialogues to occur, we could expect an interaction of mutual silence, turn-taking and increasing speech overlaps as the discussion for each question progresses. However, prolonged speech overlaps could indicate to the facilitator and students that less collaboration is occurring as students are talking over one another.

Linguistic Features. Apart from monitoring conversational cues, the linguistic content of team discussions contains potential insights as well. Existing dictionary-based natural language processing toolkits such as Linguistic Inquiry and Word Count (LIWC) [21], could be applied to automatic transcripts of team discussion derived from automatic speech recognition software. Such linguistic content analysis could be beneficial in providing an overview of the linguistic trends of team discussions. For example, the nature of *exploratory* talk [17] suggests that as students engage in active exchange of ideas, the discussion would feature more unique words as well as a larger distribution of words. On the other hand, as *disputational* talk consists of less ideas being elaborated [17], we would expect the opposite: a smaller distribution of words as well as less unique words.

4.2 Video Analysis

Facial Emotional Cues. In a recent review by Chua et al. [6], it was observed that while widely studied in computer-supported learning scenarios, emotions of learners are rarely investigated during co-located face-to-face learning scenarios. We observe that in observational studies, displays of positive affect during learning have mixed effects on the success of collaboration [33]. We predict a curvilinear relationship between positive affect and team scores, as over-engagement in off-task humorous talk can impede task completion [33]. On the other hand, for the laboratory sessions, students can attempt the questions multiple times with instantaneous feedback in the team task. Given the hypothesized relationships between learning and positive affect [9], we may observe a linear relationship between individual learning gains (computed by pre and post iRA). As such, we anticipate further examination of the relationship between displays of positive affect and team scores, as well as individual scores.

Many learning analytics studies in computer-based educational systems showcase the potential of capturing and analyzing students' emotions in order to understand the trajectory of students' learning processes, e.g., the cognitive disequilibrium theory. In a series of studies on students' interactions with an intelligent tutor, D'Mello et al. [10] found that transitions between confusion and engagement predict learning gains. Worsley and Blikstein [40] replicated similar findings within a co-located collaborative hands-on learning scenario and demonstrated that number of transitions between confusion and engagement correlated with high post-test scores. These studies illustrate the importance of modelling students' affect in the understanding of co-located learning environments.

As such, in our setup, we included the capture of facial images from individual students. In the context of the cognitive disequilibrium theory, we hypothesize more frequent alternation between confusion and engagement would correlate with higher individual learning gains as well as higher team scores. In addition, continuous detection of frustration and disengagement within team members over time could indicate individuals that are not benefitting from team discussion. Detection of such moments is useful as facilitators can be notified and intervene when appropriate.

Posture. Posture is another important non-verbal information channels in human communication. For instance, the state of engagement is presented through, among other indicators, the shifting of postures [34], while mirroring and repetitions of posture has been observed as manifestations of rapport building [14, 34]. Thus, in our current learning contexts, while students in the current learning contexts may be sitting down the majority of the time, we hypothesize that detection of postures such as leaning in and leaning away, could correlate with self-reported perceptions of team dynamics by the students in our sessions. A team with members who are closely clustered physically and leaning in would indicate higher team engagement and team cohesion [20].

4.3 Team Composition and Success

Team composition is one of the most commonly investigated variables in team performance research [38]. Successful teams are composed of members who have expertise in relevant but diverse domains but must be sufficiently aligned to engage in collaborative planning for effective performance [37]. As such we outline two important areas for future analyses of our data: the domain of expertise and dominance, as well as team diversity and agreement.

Expertise and Dominance. In our qualitative analysis, we observe that in the low performing group, a team member was particularly dominant in the discussions, but due to his lack of domain expertise, he often misled the team to submit the wrong answers. Prosodic and speech cues are useful indicators of social dominance, leadership and expertise [19, 24, 26, 32]. When combined with measures of speaking time, the detection and monitoring of expertise and dominance is potentially useful in ensuring equity of participation between experts and non-experts.

Team Diversity and Agreement. In experimental studies, it has been observed that successful teams not only have functional diversity, but also engage explicitly in knowledge coordination [37]. This is also emphasized in TBL, as teams that relied on majority-voting often underperform compared to those who shared explanations and came to a consensus afterwards [20]. This suggests that while teams should be sufficiently diverse, gradual agreement is an important indicator of successful team performance. This is reflected in observational studies where acquiescence talk occurred more frequently in successful dyads working on computer-supported collaborative tasks, compared to their unsuccessful counterparts [33].

As such, detection of agreement within teams could be a useful indicator of collaboration success. We hypothesized a curvilinear relationship between agreement and team success, as groups who agree all the time with little to no discussion could be engaged in biased decision making and groups that are too diverse and display continual conflict would be counterproductive [38]. Our previous work on dyads have shown that prosodic cues could serve as an automated metric of agreement [24, 32] and we intend to extend such analysis to our dataset.

4.4 Interaction Coordination and Team Dynamics

As discussed in Sect. 2, collaboration quality is often assessed via dimensions of *synchrony* and *proximity.* These underlying concepts are common themes in the interaction adaptation theory, which posits that during social interactions, humans monitor, observe and adapt to their counterparts in their verbal and nonverbal communication [3]. Similar ideas of such an interactive adaptive process has been referred to in concepts such as *mirroring, accommodation, entrainment, matching, mimicry* across different disciplines. Behavioral adaptation via verbal or non-verbal behaviors have been found to increase social cohesion and facilitate effective communication, but majority of studies have focused on dyads [5].

Automated Detection of Interaction Coordination. While speech style accommodation of prosodic cues [13, 15] and mirroring of posture and gestures [5, 14, 34] have been observed with rapport and collaboration success, research has been largely limited to dyads as well as relying on observational methods. We intend to extend our analysis to automatically detect such phenomena in larger groups of 5 to 6 members. With separate audio channels, it is possible to extract prosodic cues of each team member over a predefined window length (e.g., 30 ms) and monitor the dynamics of *synchrony* and *proximity* over the entire course of collaborative discussion. In addition, we intend to apply similar analyses to the postures of students to detect mirroring. A preliminary hypothesis would be that the speed (i.e., defined by how long into the discussion) and degree (i.e. defined by the number of members that exhibit the phenomenon) at which teams display *synchrony* and *proximity* are significant predictors of their collaboration quality. We also intend to extend similar forms of analysis to explore ideas of *convergence* (i.e. actors behaviors become more like one another over time). For example, high performing teams may converge more quickly in terms of adjusting their postures and prosodic cues compared to low performing teams.

5 Lessons Learnt

Challenges. Feature extraction of acoustic-prosodic cues from audio data can be done via existing toolkits such as openSMILE [11] and DisVoice [18]. Similarly, previous works [24, 32] have demonstrated the process of automatically extracting conversational features from dialogues. However, the audio data used to generate these features may include classroom noise and interference from other concurrent team discussions especially during the in-the-wild sessions. Even in laboratory sessions, speaker diarization (i.e., detecting who spoke when) can be challenging, as students are situated close to one another and each speaker channel contains interference from other speakers. This problem becomes more complex as the number of speakers increases, as observed from our dataset of groups of 6. While conversation patterns and audio-based cues can inform co-located, face-to-face collaboration processes, we anticipate several challenges to acquire clean data, even in a laboratory environment.

Moreover, while existing toolkits for facial emotion and pose recognition could generate students' affect states and postures automatically, capture of students' faces may be impeded by logistic difficulties. For instance, we found that during sessions where collaborative learning was facilitated by electronic devices such as laptops, students' faces were sometimes partially obscured. In addition, unforeseen events can occur in face-to-face learning scenarios. For example, students may leave the table halfway through the class, arrive late to class and join the discussion, one by one. We expect more effort in considering such events in future designs of our setup.

Finally, it is well-known that emotion recognition and speech recognition toolkits are trained largely on Caucasian faces and speakers and have limited cross-cultural applicability for non-Caucasian faces [31] and non-native English [41]. Thus, we anticipate more work to be done in terms of ensuring the accuracy and validity of outputs from these toolkits, when applied to non-Caucasians, as in our recordings.

Data Management and Ethics. In co-located, face-to-face educational settings, privacy, consent and data management have to be taken into consideration. This is particularly important for setups, like our case, where raw data involves video and audio recordings. Our study has been cleared by the ethics committee of the university and students that participate in our studies have given full consent to the collection and use of their data.

6 Conclusion

In this paper, we outline our setup for collecting physical data from co-located face-to-face collaborative learning scenarios. This study proposes a novel approach to understanding and assessing team dynamics in collaborative learning in an automated fashion. We anticipate a deeper understanding of what team dynamics elements indicate the effectiveness of a collaborative team and contribute to better learning outcomes. Although there are existing projects that utilise digital devices (e.g., tablets) to monitor collaborative work, none have looked at leveraging both nonverbal and verbal communication through audio and video to monitor team dynamics in an automated fashion. This proposed project would tackle long-standing bottlenecks in assessment and monitoring of team dynamics.

Acknowledgements. This project is supported by grants M4081917 and M4081918 from the Centre for Research and Development in Learning at NTU (CRADLE@NTU).

References

1. Bachour, K., Kaplan, F., Dillenbourg, P.: An interactive table for supporting participation balance in face-to-face collaborative learning. IEEE Trans. Learn. Technol. **3**(3), 203–213 (2010)
2. Bereiter, C., Scardamalia, M.: Education for the knowledge age. In: Alexander, P.A., Winne, P.H. (eds.) Handbook of Educational Psychology, 2nd edn, pp. 695–713. Lawrence Erlbaum Associates, Mahwah (2006)
3. Burgoon, J., Dunbar, N.E., Giles, H.: Interaction coordination and adaptation. In: Social Signal Processing, pp. 78–96. Cambridge University Press, Cambridge (2017)
4. Chai, C.S., Lim, W.Y., So, H.J., Cheah, H.M.: Advancing Collaborative Learning with ICT: Conception, Cases and Design. Ministry of Education, Singapore (2011)
5. Chartrand, T.L., Lakin, J.L.: The antecedents and consequences of human behavioral mimicry. Annu. Rev. Psychol. **64**, 285–308 (2013)
6. Chua, Y.H.V., Dauwels, J., Tan, S.C.: Technologies for automated analysis of co-located, real-life physical learning spaces: where are we now? In: Proceedings of the International Conference on Learning Analytics and Knowledge (LAK 2019), pp. 11–20. ACM (2019)
7. Dillenbourg, P.: Design for classroom orchestration. Comput. Edu. **69**, 485–492 (2013)
8. Cukurova, M., Luckin, R., Millán, E., Mavrikis, M.: The NISPI framework: analyzing collaborative problem-solving from students' physical interactions. Comput. Edu. **116**, 93–109 (2018)
9. D'Mello, S., Graesser, A.: Dynamics of affective states during complex learning. Learn. Instr. **22**(2), 145–157 (2012)
10. D'Mello, S., Lehman, B., Pekrun, R., Graesser, A.: Confusion can be beneficial for learning. Learn. Instr. **29**, 153–170 (2014)
11. Eyben, F., Wollmer, M., Schuller, B.: Opensmile: the munich versatile and fast open-source audio feature extractor. In: Proceedings of the 18th ACM International Conference on Multimedia (MM 2010), pp. 1459–1462. ACM (2010)
12. Grover, S., Bienkowski, M., Tamrakar, A., Siddiquie, B., Salter, D., Divakaran, A.: Multimodal analytics to study collaborative problem solving in pair programming. In: Proceedings of the 6th International Conference on Learning Analytics and Knowledge (LAK 2016), pp. 516–517. ACM (2016)
13. Gweon, G., Jain, M., McDonough, J., Raj, B., Rosé, C.P.: Measuring prevalence of other-oriented transactive contributions using an automated measure of speech style accommodation. Int. J. Comp-Supp. Coll. **8**(2), 245–265 (2013)
14. La France, M.: Postural mirroring and intergroup relations. Pers. Soc. Psychol. Bull. **77**(11), 207–217 (1985)

15. Lubold, N., Pon-Barry, H.: Acoustic-prosodic entrainment and rapport in collaborative learning dialogues. In: Proceedings of the 2014 ACM Workshop on Multimodal Learning Analytics Workshop and Grand Challenge (MLA 2014), pp. 5–12. ACM (2014)
16. Martinez-Maldonado, R., Clayphan, A., Yacef, K., Kay, J.: MTFeedback: providing notifications to enhance teacher awareness of small group work in the classroom. IEEE Trans. Learn. Technol. **8**(2), 187–200 (2015)
17. Mercer, N.: Talk and the development of reasoning and understanding. Hum. Dev. **51**, 90–100 (2008)
18. Orozco-Arroyave, J.R., Vsquez-Correa, J.C., et al.: NeuroSpeech: an open-source software for Parkinson's speech analysis. Digit. Signal Process. **77**, 207–221 (2017)
19. Oviatt, S., Hang, K., Zhou, J., Chen, F.: Spoken interruptions signal productive problem solving and domain expertise in mathematics. In: Proceedings of 2015 ACM on International Conference on Multimodal Interaction (ICMI 2015), pp. 311–318. ACM (2015)
20. Parmelee, D., Michaelsen, L.K., Cook, S., Hudes, P.D.: Team-based learning a practical guide: AMEE guide no. 65. Med. Teach. **34**(5), 275–287 (2012)
21. Pennebaker, J.W., Boyd, R.L., Jordan, K., Blackburn, K.: The development and psychometric properties of LIWC2015 (2015)
22. Praharaj, S., Scheffel, M., Drachsler, H., Specht, M.: Multimodal analytics for real-time feedback in co-located collaboration. In: Pammer-Schindler, V., Pérez-Sanagustín, M., Drachsler, H., Elferink, R., Scheffel, M. (eds.) EC-TEL 2018. LNCS, vol. 11082, pp. 187–201. Springer, Cham (2018). https://doi.org/10.1007/978-3-319-98572-5_15
23. Rajalingam, P., Rotgans, J.I., Zary, N., Ferenczi, M.A., Gagnon, P., Low-Beer, N.: Implementation of team-based learning on a large scale: three factors to keep in mind. Med. Teach. **40**(6), 1–7 (2018)
24. Rasheed, U., Tahir, Y., Dauwels, S., Dauwels, J., Thalmann, D., Magnenat-Thalmann, N.: Real-time comprehensive sociometrics for two-person dialogs. In: Salah, A.A., Hung, H., Aran, O., Gunes, H. (eds.) HBU 2013. LNCS, vol. 8212, pp. 196–208. Springer, Cham (2013). https://doi.org/10.1007/978-3-319-02714-2_17
25. Ruffaldi, E., Dabisias, G., Landolfi, L., Spikol, D.: Data collection and processing for a multimodal learning analytic system. In: Proceedings of 2016 SAI Computing Conference, pp. 858–863. IEEE (2016)
26. Scherer, S., Weibel, N., Morency, L.P., Oviatt, S.: Multimodal prediction of expertise and leadership in learning groups. In: Proceedings of the 1st International Workshop on Multimodal Learning Analytics (MLA 2012). ACM (2012)
27. Schneider, B., Blikstein, P.: Unraveling students' interaction around a tangible interface using multimodal learning analytics. J. Educ. Data Min. **7**(3), 89–116 (2015)
28. Schneider B., Sharma, K., Cuendet, S., Zufferey, G., Dillenbourg, P., Pea, R.: Detecting collaborative dynamics using mobile eye-trackers. In: Proceedings of the 12th International Conference of the Learning Sciences, pp. 522–529 (2016)
29. Spikol, D., Ruffaldi, E., Dabisias, G., Cukurova, M.: Supervised machine learning in multimodal learning analytics for estimating success in project-based learning. J. Comput. Assist. Learn. **34**(4), 366–377 (2018)
30. Spikol, D., Ruffaldi, E., Landolfi, L., Cukurova, M.: Estimation of success in collaborative learning based on multimodal learning analytics features. In: Proceedings of the 17th IEEE International Conference on Advanced Learning Technologies (ICALT 2017), pp. 269–273. IEEE (2017)
31. Stöckli, S., Schulte-Mecklenbeck, M., Borer, S., Samson, A.C.: Facial expression analysis with AFFDEX and FACET: a validation study. Behav. Res. Methods **50**(4), 1446–1460 (2018)

32. Tahir, Y., et al.: Real-time sociometrics from audio-visual features for two-person dialogs. In: 2015 IEEE International Conference on Digital Signal Processing, pp. 823–827. IEEE (2015)
33. Tan, J.P.-L., Caleon, I., Ng, H.L., Poon, C.L., Koh, E.: Collective creativity competencies and collaborative problem-solving outcomes: insights from the dialogic interactions of singapore student teams. In: Care, E., Griffin, P., Wilson, M. (eds.) Assessment and Teaching of 21st Century Skills. EAIA, pp. 95–118. Springer, Cham (2018). https://doi.org/10.1007/978-3-319-65368-6_6
34. Taylor, R.: The multimodal texture of engagement: prosodic language, gaze and posture in engaged, creative classroom interaction. Think. Skills Creat. **20**, 83–96 (2016)
35. Villar, A.: Response bias. In: Lavrakas, P.J. (ed.) Encyclopedia of Survey Research Methods, pp. 752–753. Sage Publications Inc., Thousand Oaks (2011)
36. Weimar, E., Nugroho, A., Visser, J., Plaat, A., Goudbeek, M., Schouten, A.P.: The Influence of teamwork quality on software team performance. arXiv preprint arXiv:1701.06146 (2017)
37. Woolley, A.W., Gerbasi, M.E., Chabris, C.F., Kosslyn, S.M., Hackman, J.R.: Bringing in the experts: how team composition and collaborative planning jointly shape analytic effectiveness. Small Group Res. **39**(3), 352–371 (2008)
38. Woolley, A.W., Aggarwal, I., Malone, T.W.: Collective intelligence in teams and organizations. In: Handbook of Collective Intelligence, pp. 143–168 (2015)
39. Worsley, M., Blikstein, P.: Leveraging multimodal learning analytics to differentiate student learning strategies. In: Proceedings of the 5th International Conference on Learning Analytics and Knowledge (LAK 2015), pp. 360–367. ACM (2015)
40. Worsley, M., Blikstein, P.: Using learning analytics to study cognitive disequilibrium in a complex learning environment. In: Proceedings of the 5th International Conference on Learning Analytics and Knowledge (LAK 2015), pp. 426–427. ACM (2015)
41. Zapata, J., Andreas S.K.: Assessing the performance of automatic speech recognition systems when used by native and non-native speakers of three major languages in dictation workflows. In: Proceedings of the 20th Nordic Conference of Computational Linguistics (NODALIDA 2015), pp. 201–210. Linköping University Electronic Press (2015)

Internet-Based Immersive Learning (IIL): Applying Ubiquitous Web 1.0 and Web 2.0 Resources in EFL Learning

Yun-Hsuan Huang(✉)

Chia Nan University, Tainan 71710, Taiwan ROC
ninisunday321@yahoo.com.tw

Abstract. Authentic language materials are always considered ideal language acquisition resources. Today's generation lives with the Internet, surfing over Internet resources every day. Web 1.0 and Web 2.0 provide authentic and learner-directed resources and platforms with accessible and ubiquitous features, which greatly benefits English as a Foreign Language (EFL) learners living in non-English speaking countries. Despite abundant English resources available, most EFL learners usually still rely on the Internet resources of their first language. Therefore, this study aimed to devise a course adopting an immersive approach guiding students to live in an authentic English Internet life as native speakers do, thereby promoting EFL acquisition in real life. This study involved 62 college students around low intermediate levels in Taiwan, simulating a realistic English Internet life. Nine theme-based Internet resources were selected and task-based learning was employed. A survey was conducted at class end. Results show that four out of the five thematic websites considered the easiest to navigate and comprehend were presented via Web 1.0. Regarding the top five thematic websites that the students reported to browse after taking this course were related to recreation (music, movie, and travel), living consumption (shopping), and online community interaction (social media). Usefulness and interest are two major reasons motivating them to browse English websites. 61.3% and 38.7% of the students reported that they would "Strongly recommend" and "Recommend" this course respectively, demonstrating the effectiveness of the course. Qualitative results and implications were elaborated in the study.

Keywords: Immersive learning · Ubiquitous Internet · Task-based learning

1 Introduction

1.1 Background and Problems

For English as a foreign language (EFL) learners, authentic English materials and environments are two major factors in successful, enjoyable, and natural foreign language acquisition. The major disadvantage for EFL learners in English learning is that they are not surrounded by English-speaking environments to naturally interact with the target language in daily life. In addition, most EFL curricula use textbooks which contents are planned, unauthentic, and limited in learning contexts. Therefore, seeking

L. Uden et al. (Eds.): LTEC 2019, CCIS 1011, pp. 139–150, 2019.
https://doi.org/10.1007/978-3-030-20798-4_13

authentic, practical, and ubiquitous English learning materials as well as natural English contexts is significant. Internet resources happen to meet these criteria as English websites on the Internet provide authentic English information that native English speakers interact with in daily life, and that is also accessible for non-English speakers worldwide.

Applying Internet resources into English learning lies in both characteristics of the Internet and today's young generation. These characteristics are elaborated as follows.

The Characteristics of the Internet. With advanced development of Web technology, the Web has evolved from Web 1.0 to Web 2.0. Web 1.0 provides the static information based on a one-way approach—Users are passive information receivers. However, Web 2.0 not only further provides multimedia information delivery but also offers the features of interaction for users: user-website and user-user [1]. Such features promote the user's activeness in interacting with information and net communities.

The Characteristics of Today's Young Generation. Regarding today's young generation, they are netizens living and growing up with the Internet, and unable to live without it. Internet resources provide ubiquitous learning via the Internet, and the digital natives are already used to accessing to Internet resources through the smartphone in addition to the computer. Thus, the convenience of using Internet resources and ubiquitous learning can be greatly promoted through mobile devices today.

1.2 The Purpose of the Study

Grounded on the above reasons, this study aimed to employ the immersion approach to immerse EFL learners in authentic and ubiquitous English environments through using English websites for any information of real-life purposes as native English netizens do in their life. Based on the immersion theory, the devised EFL course in the study also integrated the approaches of theme-based learning and task-based learning in order to optimally foster immersive learning. Therefore, this study attempted to investigate how EFL learners perceived the approach of thematic task-based immersion using ubiquitous Internet resources, as well as its effectiveness.

1.3 Immersive Learning

Since immersion teaching methods first appeared to teach French to English-speaking children in Canada in the 1960s, immersive learning has been extensively applied worldwide. The core characteristic of the immersion approach lies in the combination of language, content, and culture of the target language instead of the first language [2].

Past studies have found many advantages and benefits of immersive learning. For example, the immersion approach exposes language learners to actual language contexts, effectively engaging them to practice authentic language, interactions and skills for real-life purposes in the real world [3]. Immersion education promotes cognitive skills such as metalinguistic awareness (e.g., sounds, words, and syntax) [4, 5], executive control [4, 6], critical thinking and problem solving [7], and so forth. In addition, immersive learning elevates motivation, especially intrinsic motivation such as enjoyment, curiosity, and achievement [8, 9]. With such benefits, immersion methods have been widely adapted to various kinds of learning.

1.4 Theme-Based and Task-Based Learning

Theme-based instruction or learning is one type of three content models which emphasize learner interests and needs, authentic materials and tasks, and eventual language uses. The main features of theme-based learning are that topics of high interest to learners are important, and that the units involve language skills [10]. Theme-based learning has been demonstrated to meet learner needs and improve learner achievement [11], more effective to both high- and low-interest students [12], foster learning, and promote comfort with learning new materials [13].

Task-based instruction or learning is primarily grounded on constructivism which characterizes with the following features. Learners use and interact with authentic language meaningful to them, have more control in what they learn, and learning mainly takes place in social contexts [14]. Task-based learning is thus learner-centered and can develop language skills through completing meaningful language tasks relevant to contents [15].

Task-based learning has been found to have a significant effect on the motivation and engagement of learners [16]. Task-based instruction has been applied in four language skills and demonstrated effective learning [14, 15, 17, 18] as it provides learners with opportunities of constructing personal knowledge and experience, thus facilitating personalized learning. With the development of technology, some studies also investigated how task-based learning was implemented through technology such as computer-mediated contexts and online courses [15, 17, 19, 20].

1.5 Ubiquitous Learning

Ubiquitous learning emerged from the combination of the Internet and digital technology. The Internet provides ubiquitous connections with open and accessible digital information and resources via computing devices [21, 22]. With these characteristics, past research has demonstrated that these Internet resources not only remove the digital divide but also can be used as open educational resources to improve teaching-learning environments as well as promoting ubiquitous learning [22].

Ubiquitous learning has been advancing with emerging digital technologies such as notebook computers, smartphones, and tablets which facilitate flexible learning time and unconstrained location [23]. Thus, learners can access and retrieve updated Internet resources in a more effective and convenient way. Research has also found and categorized four major factors influencing adoption of ubiquitous Internet among students: efficiency, information, performance, and techno [24]. Additionally, research has demonstrated the correlated effects of ubiquitous learning and flipped learning in that the higher the ubiquitous rate is, the higher the flipped rate learners attain in the learning environments [25]. Such a finding implies the contribution of ubiquitous learning to flipped learning.

2 Methods

2.1 Participants

This study involved 62 non-English majors who took the class "The Internet for English Learning" offered in General Education Center at a university in Taiwan. The students' English proficiencies were around low intermediate levels. This course was a semester long, 18 weeks, and 2 h per week. The lessons were theme-based, comprising the websites of nine different themes: online music, online movie, net community interaction, online weather, online shopping, travel booking, online English learning, Taiwanese culture, and social media. One to three commonly-used websites were selected for each theme. The selected websites are listed in Table 1 as below.

Table 1. The websites selected for each lesson theme.

Theme	Web technology features	Selected websites
1. Online music	Web 1.0	• Billboard; Yahoo Music
2. Online movie	Web 1.0	• Movies.com; Yahoo Movies
3. Net community interaction	Web 2.0	• Yahoo! Answers
4. Online weather	Web 1.0	• The Weather Channel; Yahoo Weather
5. Online shopping	Web 2.0	• eBay; Amazon
6. Online travel booking	Web 2.0	• Expedia.com; Hostelworld.com; Airbnb
7. Online English learning	Web 2.0	• TED.com; Youtube Education
8. Taiwanese culture	Web 1.0	• The China Post; Taiwan.net
9. Social media	Web 2.0	• Flickr; Facebook; Twitter

2.2 Procedure

This course was conducted through three stages for each lesson theme: demonstration, hands-on task, and oral report. At the demonstration stage, the instructor introduced selected thematic websites, guided the students to explore the websites, explained important vocabulary and phrases, etc. At the hands-on task stage, the students started self-exploring interested information according to the task requirements for the lesson theme. At the oral-report stage, the students orally reported in English what they found in the task.

In the lesson theme of online travel booking, for instance, the task required that the students plan a trip to one destination respectively in Asia, America, and Europe. They must search for the travel information through the English websites introduced in the lesson, including their desired airlines, airfare, flight information, stopover city, flight duration, luggage information, hotel/hostel room type, fees, accommodation information, etc.

On midterm and final examinations, the students took an on-site task examination to find out the information on the assigned websites according to the task requirements of each theme. At semester end, each students filled out a course survey to reflect on the course learning.

The entire procedure was grounded upon the model of Internet-based Immersive Learning (IIL) proposed in this study. Three major elements in this IIL model: theme-based or thematic instruction, task-based instruction, and Internet technology. Theme-based instruction aims to promote motivational learning. Task-based instruction is to implement constructivist learning. Internet technology facilitates ubiquitous learning. Figure 1 manifests this IIL model as below.

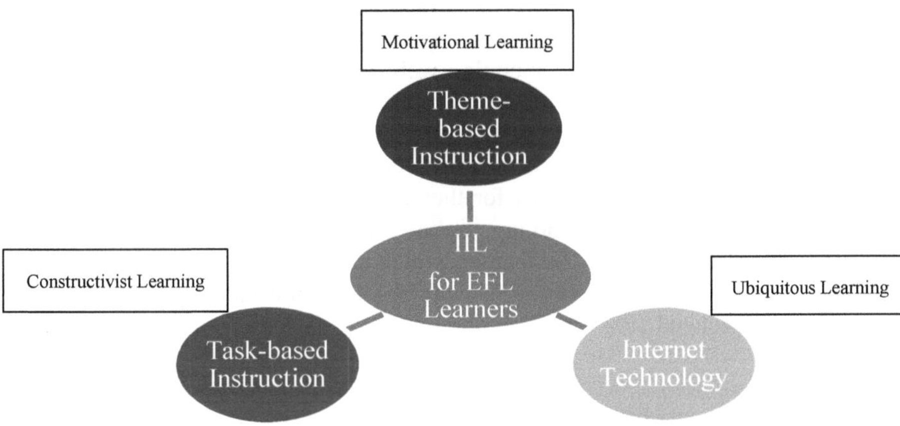

Fig. 1. The proposed model of Internet-based Immersive Learning (IIL).

2.3 Instrument

The instruments in this study included Internet materials and a course survey. The Internet learning materials were from selected websites of nine themes. This semi-open-ended survey mainly investigated the following questions: Which thematic websites do the students think easy and comprehensible in navigation? Which thematic websites would they start using after this course? Whether they would recommend this course? What are the reasons for the above questions?

2.4 Data Collection and Analysis

The data collected were mainly from the semi-open-ended survey. Thus, the data included quantitative and qualitative data. The data analysis aimed to understand which thematic websites were easy and comprehensible for the EFL students in navigation, which thematic websites interested them most, how they thought of those websites, whether this course was useful, and the reasons. All in all, the analysis attempted to understand the effectiveness of theme-based immersive learning through ubiquitous Web 1.0 and Web 2.0 authentic English materials and environments.

3 Results and Discussion

Survey results are discussed in the following. Regarding which thematic websites introduced in the course were easy to navigate and comprehend, results show that 69.4% of the respondents found the thematic websites of online music easy to navigate and comprehend; 74.2%, online movie; 19.4%, net community interaction; 41.9%, online weather; 48.4%, online shopping; 27.4%, online travel booking; 35.5%, online English learning; 53.2%, Taiwanese culture; and 38.7%, social media (See Fig. 1).

The five easiest to navigate and comprehend thematic websites were online movie, online music, Taiwanese culture, online shopping, and online weather. Interestingly, four out of the five are presented via Web 1.0; only the websites of online travel booking are presented via Web 2.0. The information of music, movie, weather, Taiwanese culture (Web 1.0) is delivered mainly for the user to read without any interactive needs. The reason why the shopping websites (Web 2.0) were also considered easy to navigate and comprehend might be because these students are used to online-shopping activities in daily life. Even though the shopping websites are English and Web 2.0, the concepts of interface and content display are not too different from browsing Chinese shopping websites for them. For the other four thematic websites (social media, online English learning, online travel booking, and net community interaction), they involved Web 2.0 features which required more understanding on the interactive interfaces and contents. Thus, the students considered more complex to browse and comprehend (Fig. 2).

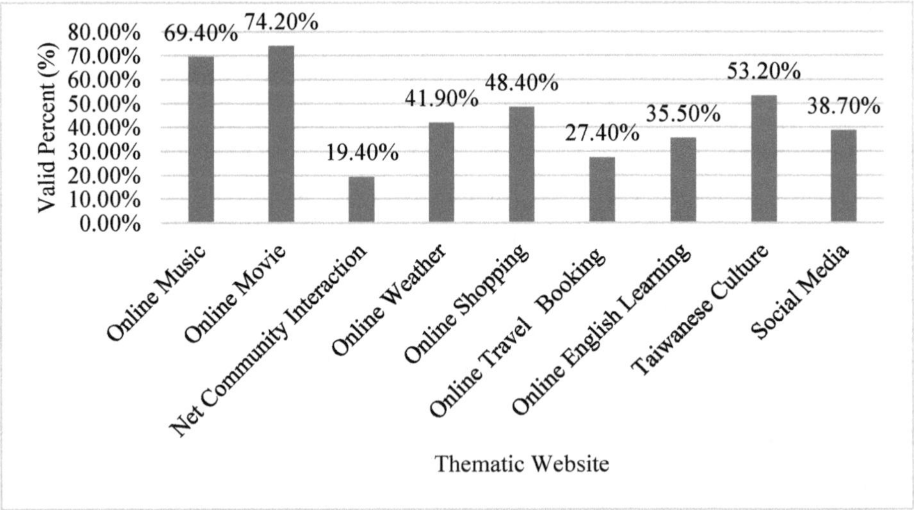

Fig. 2. Which of the following thematic websites introduced were easy to navigate and comprehend? (Multiple Choice)

Regarding the question which thematic websites the students would start browsing after taking the course, 66.1% of the respondents chose online music; 69.4%, online movie; 14.5%, net community interaction; 16.1%, online weather; 41.9%, online shopping; 51.6%, online travel booking; 30.6%, online English learning; and 35.5%, social media (See Fig. 3).

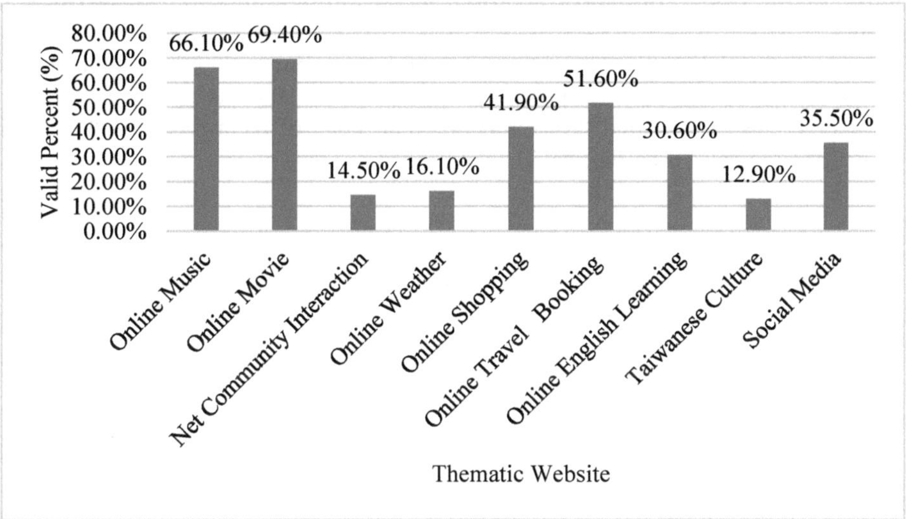

Fig. 3. After taking this course, which of the following thematic websites introduced would you start browsing? (Multiple Choice)

It is found that top five thematic websites that the students would start browsing are online movie, online music, online travel booking, online shopping, and social media. Three out of the five thematic websites that more than 50% of the students chose are related to recreation (music, movie, and travel). The other two out of the five are related to living consumption (shopping) and social relationships (social media).

According to the responses in Question 2, the investigation for the reasons reveal that 80.6% of the students responded the reason of "useful"; 74.2% responded "interesting"; 32%, easy; and other, 1.6% (See Fig. 4).

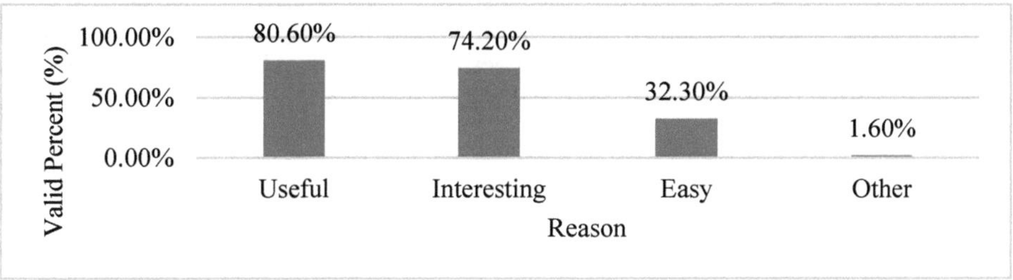

Fig. 4. According to Question 2, what were the reasons? (Multiple Choice)

Such findings show that for these EFL students, whether the English websites are useful in life and the themes of websites interesting are two major reasons motivating them to browse English websites. Whether the websites are easy to navigate is a minor factor. One other reason reported is from a consumer's perspective in that using English websites is a convenient approach to directly reaching foreign products in person.

Regarding whether they would recommend this course to other students, the responses were all positive. Surprisingly, 61.3% of the students reported "Strongly recommend;" 38.7% reported "Recommend;" and none of them reported "Fair" and "Do not recommend" (See Fig. 5).

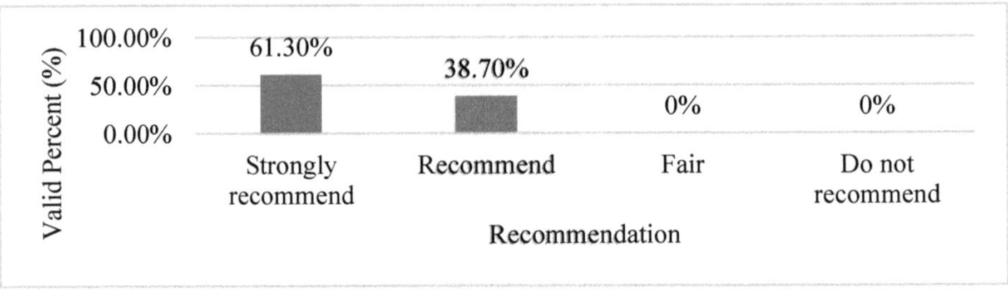

Fig. 5. Would you recommend this course to other students?

The results imply that using English websites are not only useful in daily life but also interesting to these EFL students. Such findings suggest that the EFL learners hold both 'instrumental motivation' and 'integrated motivation' in using English websites.

According to the preceding results, the results about Question 5 thus account for why they would recommend this course. Such results are further categorized into nine dimensions with selected responding examples: (1) cultural understanding; (2) practicality and authenticity; (3) interest; (4) confidence; (5) unconventionality; (6) world knowledge and language competence; (7) autonomous and personalized learning; (8) latest and updated materials; and (9) ubiquitous learning. These nine dimensions exactly indicate what the EFL learners are concerned about regarding to their EFL learning using Internet resources. Table 2 manifested the results.

From such results, it implies that the EFL learners' reasons of wanting to take an English course which immersed them in authentic learning English environments through English websites involve a wide spectrum of factors. All these types of factors contribute to EFL learners' enjoyment of English learning.

Table 2. According to the preceding question, why?

Category	Selected Examples
Cultural Understanding	• This course helps me understand which websites are commonly used by English speakers.
Practicality and Authenticity	• I can learn and use English in real life. • Authentic materials are closely related to our daily • I can obtain latest information when I travel abroad. • These websites are helpful to our life. • A lot of vocabulary learned from the websites cannot be seen in the textbook. • Practical assignments and assessment
Interest	• This course is very interesting and easy. • I am more motivated by learning from the thematic websites.
Confidence	• This course guided students not to be afraid of browsing English websites.
Unconventionality	• This course is not like traditional English courses.
World Knowledge and Language Competence	• My English improved a lot. • I gained a lot of knowledge in addition to English ability. • If I did not take this course, I would have never known so many English websites from which I could learn English in daily life.
Autonomous and Personalized Learning	• We can self-explore interested thematic contents and learn different vocabulary based on our self-exploration, very flexible.
Updated Materials	• I can get first-hand information without reading translated news.
Ubiquitous Learning	• The website information can be retrieved via the smartphone. • I can interact with English information anytime and anywhere.

4 Conclusion

This study used ubiquitous Web 1.0 and Web 2.0 Internet resources as well as integrating thematic and task-based approaches to facilitate immersive and ubiquitous learning for EFL learners. Such blended approaches take the advantages of each method to benefit EFL learning to the utmost. Thematic learning promotes learner motivation and interest. Task-based learning emphasizes self-exploration and personal experience construction, facilitating personalized learning. Internet resources offer ubiquitous learning as well as direct connections to the real world of the target culture and language. All the above approaches in combination greatly contribute to EFL immersive learning.

The major findings have contributed valuable information to the literature and EFL instructors: (1) Interesting themes and real-life purposes are two major factors that motivate EFL learners to use and learn Internet resources as open ubiquitous learning materials. (2) Taking the different advantages of Web 1.0 and Web 2.0 in selecting Internet resources best facilitate EFL learners' navigation of Web interfaces as well as comprehension of learning contents. (3) Successful immersive learning using Internet resources must use meaningful tasks for real-life purposes so as to fully engage and immerse EFL learners into the real-world language and culture. (4) All the thematic task-based, ubiquitous, and immersive approaches greatly promoted learner-centered and -directed learning. All in all, these are important pedagogical implications for EFL instructors in curriculum design based on the Internet-based Immersive Learning (IIL) model which applies Internet technology and resources through thematic tasks for ubiquitous immersive learning.

Moreover, this IIL model emphasizes the significance in that technology cannot simply stand alone to best promote learning. Any technology requires integrating with appropriate instructional methods or theories in order to create its optimal effectiveness in promoting and facilitating learning. Encouragingly, this study has demonstrated the success of applying the IIL model in the course. 81% of the participants achieved final scores above 60 points and 59% of them achieved final scores above 80 points. This indicates that the students not only have acquired a satisfactory amount of practical vocabulary and expressions but also are able to use English Internet resources for real-life purposes.

To conclude, the study results have demonstrated how Web 1.0 and Web 2.0 technologies ubiquitously deliver various types of Internet resources for learners to use and interact with for their real-life purposes in English learning. The value of web technology for teaching and learning is its ubiquity, accessibility, interactivity, personalization, etc. Thus, the language instructor should be ready for fast-evolving Web technology like 3.0 or 4.0 in the future in order to understand and apply its features and resources in language teaching and learning.

Despite the findings, there were two limitations in the study. One limitation was that this study involved only non-English majors of low intermediate levels. The other was that the semi-structured tasks and pre-selected themes in the study might limit the students to explore Internet learning materials at their preference. Therefore, future research will include English majors and offer learners more freedom in open-ended tasks as well as preferred website themes.

References

1. Hiremath, B.K., Kenchakkanavar, A.Y.: An alternation of the Web 1.0, Web 2.0, and Web 3.0: a comparative study. Imperial J. Interdisc. Res. **2**(4), 705–710 (2016)
2. Reyhner, J.: Native language immersion. http://jan.ucc.nau.edu/~jar/NNL/NNL_1.pdf. Accessed 18 Dec 2018
3. Immersive Learning: Explained. https://raccoongang.com/blog/immersive-learning-explained/. Accessed 15 Dec 2018
4. Grosjean, F.: Cognitive advantages of second language immersion education, https://www.psychologytoday.com/us/blog/life-bilingual/201401/cognitive-advantages-second-language-immersion-education. https://www.psychologytoday.com/us/blog/life-bilingual/201401/cognitive-advantages-second-language-immersion-education. Accessed 11 Dec 2018
5. Asnawi, M., Merza, A.: The effectiveness of immersive multimedia learning with peer support on English speaking and reading aloud. Int. J. Instruction **10**(1), 203–218 (2017)
6. Puric, D., Vuksanovic, J., Chondrogianni, V.: Cognitive advantages of immersion education after 1 year: effects of amount of exposure. J. Exp. Child Psychol. **159**, 296–309 (2017)
7. Benefits of Immersion. https://hwis.org/dayschool/immersioneducation/. Accessed 18 Dec 2018
8. Tanaka, Y., Kutsuki, A.: Motivation for learning English in the immersion environment of an international school in Japan. Int. J. Bilingual Educ. Bilingualism, 729–743 (2016). https://doi.org/10.1080/13670050.2016.1210566. Accessed 11 Dec 2018
9. Grant, S.: Effects of intensive EFL immersion programmes on willingness to communicate. Lang. Learn. J. (2018). https://doi.org/10.1080/09571736.2017.1422274. Accessed 11 Dec 2018
10. Different models of content-based instruction, https://zh.scribd.com/document/61046077/Different-Models-of-Content-Based-Instruction. Accessed 18 Dec 2018
11. Brannigan, S.: Meeting 10–12 year olds' English language learning needs through a theme-based approach. e-J. Teacher Educ. Appl. Lang. Stud. **2**, 12–26 (2011)
12. Rosyita, U.: The effect of theme-based instruction compared to competence-based language teaching to teach reading comprehension to students with IDGH and low interest. Engl. Educ. J. **7**(1) (2017). https://doi.org/10.15294/eej.v7i1.14692. Accessed 18 Dec 2018
13. Tessier, L, Tessier, J.: Theme-based courses foster student learning and promote comfort with learning new material. J. Learn. Arts **11**(1) (2015), https://eric.ed.gov/?id=EJ1087088. Accessed 18 December 2018
14. Zhou, Y.: Application of task-based instruction to college English teaching for non-English majors in Leshan Normal University, Sichuan, China. Theor. Pract. Lang. Stud. **7**(2), 153–157 (2017)
15. Huang, Y.H., Chuang, T.Y.: Technology-assisted sheltered instruction: Instructional streaming video in an EFL multi-purpose computer course. Comput. Assist. Lang. Learn. **29**(3), 618–637 (2016)
16. Kafipour, R., Jafari, S., Khojasteh, L.: The effect of task-based instruction on L2 grammar learning and motivation of Iranian EFL learners junior high school students. Riv. Publicando **5**(16), 769–795 (2018)
17. Lee, L.: Autonomous learning through task-based instruction in fully online language courses. Lang. Learn. Technol. **20**(2), 81–97 (2016)
18. Derakhshan, A.: The effect of task-based language teaching instruction on the Iranian intermediate EFL learners' writing performance. Int. J. Instruction **11**(4), 527–544 (2018)

19. Pierson, S.J.: Bridges to Swaziland: using task-based learning and computer-mediated instruction to improve English language teaching and learning. Teach. Engl. Technol. **15**(2), 105–119 (2015)
20. Baralt, M., Gomez, J.M.: Task-based language teaching online: a guide for teachers. Lang. Teach. Technol. Forum **21**(3), 28–43 (2017)
21. Loke, S.W.: Ubiquitous connections: The Internet of people and things. Crowd-Powered Mobile Computing and Smart Things. https://doi.org/10.1007/978-3-319-54436-6_1. Accessed 15 Dec 2018
22. Banerjee, K.: How to incorporate Open Educational Resources (OER) into the infrastructure and pedagogy for promoting ubiquitous learning. In: Li, K.C., Yuen, K.S., Wong, B.T.M. (eds.) Innovations in Open and Flexible Education. EIS, pp. 177–184. Springer, Singapore (2018). https://doi.org/10.1007/978-981-10-7995-5_16. Accessed 15 Dec 2018
23. Moser, S.: Linking virtual and real-life environments: Scrutinizing ubiquitous learning scenarios. Digital Tools for Seamless Learning. https://doi.org/10.4018/978-1-5225-1692-7.ch011. Accessed 15 Dec 2018
24. Juned, M., Adil, M.: Factors influencing adoption of ubiquitous Internet amongst students. International J. Inf. Commun. Technol. Educ. **11**(3). https://doi.org/10.4018/ijicte.2015070106. Accessed 15 Dec 2018
25. Uosaki, N., Ogata, H., Mouri, K.: Towards flipped learning using ubiquitous learning log system in L2 learning class. In: Chen, G., Kumar, V., Kinshuk, Huang, R., Kong, S.C. (eds.) Emerging Issues in Smart Learning. LNET, pp. 353–360. Springer, Heidelberg (2015). https://doi.org/10.1007/978-3-662-44188-6_49

Towards Successful Implementation of a Virtual Classroom for Vocational Higher Education in Indonesia

Bayu Rima Aditya[1(✉)], Irawan Nurhas[2,3], and Jan Pawlowski[2]

[1] Telkom University, Bandung, Indonesia
bayu@tass.telkomuniversity.ac.id
[2] Institute of Positive Computing, Ruhr West University of Applied Sciences, Mülheim, Germany
irawan.nurhas@hs-ruhrwest.de
[3] University of Jyväskylä, Jyväskylä, Finland

Abstract. The virtual classroom continues to grow, but it is becoming more and more the norm, and it is fundamentally different from the vocational students at the Indonesian university. With the promised benefits of the virtual classroom, many challenges and difficulties come in the implementation. Although there are already successful design principles for virtual classrooms that support organizations in overcoming the challenges, the approach to implementing the design principles of virtual classroom at the vocational higher education in Indonesia is still lacking. In this study, we aim to answer the research gap and used the design sciences research by interviewing the lecturers to design the solutions. The proposed design approaches were implemented in a course and evaluated with students from two different groups. Overall, the evaluation of the proposed approaches shows 1 significant results as an indicator of the benefits of the implementation of a virtual classroom for vocational students in Indonesia.

Keywords: Online learning · Design challenges · Design principles · Vocational education · Indonesian higher education

1 Introduction

A virtual classroom is a technological approach mainly used in the educational world. Chen and Liu [1] define the virtual classroom as "synchronous learning model in ICT based", while Clark and Mayer [2] include the virtual classroom as part of e-learning to illustrate what is meant by virtual classroom. In this study, we define the virtual classroom as learning with the use of various digital media (e-learning) that support digital presence and real-time interaction between students and instructors. Some advantages of a virtual classroom are presented [3], among others are to improve the interaction between teachers and students, to enable immediate and fast reactions to students and to give students the feeling of being connected with the instructors [3].

L. Uden et al. (Eds.): LTEC 2019, CCIS 1011, pp. 151–161, 2019.
https://doi.org/10.1007/978-3-030-20798-4_14

The integration of technology into classrooms is important in preparing instructors and students for the 21st century and push the implementation of the virtual classroom can support teaching and learning in the digital age. In the context of a virtual learning environment, which focuses on real-time interaction between instructors and their students, the use of virtual classroom must be supported by the readiness of stakeholder, user capabilities and access on technology to implement the virtual classroom. Therefore, evaluating the implementation of the virtual classroom is an essential factor for the sustainability of the virtual classroom.

Although the virtual classroom has many advantages for the world of education, there are various obstacles to its implementation. These challenges include for students: Lack of skills and bad experiences with digital tools. For instructors: Lack of technological and didactic skills and the intention to allow more face-to-face meetings and for fear of change [4]. General strategies have been developed to overcome obstacles to the implementation of virtual classrooms by establishing online community learning or the use of wiki systems [5]. However, barriers tend to evolve over time and context. For example, specific barriers for educational institutions in Indonesia require more attention to the availability of software and hardware [6], barriers related to Indonesian regulations for virtual classrooms with a maximum share of 50% of online classrooms [7] or culture-specific barriers based on the cultural dimension of the Hofstede [8], e.g. unequal power distances and lower values for individualism, which can hinder the establishment of a virtual classroom for individual trainers.

Reports on higher education in Indonesia show that there are 80.6% of a total of 3276 public and private campuses offering vocational education programs [9]. Several studies have tried to implement virtual classroom to support teaching and learning activities in vocational higher education institute in Indonesia [10, 11]. Although some studies show the positive impact of implementing a virtual classroom, the lack of a general approach that can be used by vocational higher education as a guide for the integration of a virtual classroom in Indonesia remains an obstacle for various vocational institutions in Indonesia. Some of the ideas used to support the implementation of virtual classroom are the use of Moodle and Edmodo software in the teaching and learning process integrated into a blended learning environment. To our knowledge, however, there is no research discussing how to implement virtual classroom for vocational students in Indonesia. Using Google Scholar as a search engine using the search keywords "Virtual Classroom" AND "vocational" AND "Indonesia" queries in English (results in 342 sources) and Indonesian translation of keywords (21 sources) from the search results does not yet offer any form of the proposed design approaches within the context of the vocational higher education in Indonesia. Therefore, we want to fill the gap by proposing design approaches on how the implementation of virtual classroom will be carried out in this context. To answer the research gap, in this study, we used the Design Science Research (DSR) [12], starting with an initial first problem, such as lack of the applicable concept to implement virtual classroom in Indonesian higher education. Then we used [13] as basic principles in the preparation of proposed design approaches, which we discussed with university lectures from three different higher educational institutes. We then applied the proposed approaches in a lecture module of the vocational school and evaluated the results with 100 students. The proposed approaches show the potential both for new students as well as the students that other vocational higher educational institutions in Indonesia can use the approaches as guidelines for the implementation of the virtual classroom that comply with the regulation for the institutions of higher education in Indonesia.

In this work, first, we present literature and information related to our study and the explanation of principles for successful implementation of virtual classrooms [13]. Then, we give a short description of the steps that we have taken in the Methods section. Next, the results of the research including the proposed implementation design and the evaluation of the proposed design. Finally, we provide information about the limitations of the study, conclusions and future steps that can be taken with the results of our research.

2 Theoretical Foundation

2.1 Overview Learning Theory

In the development of learning theory, the learning process has undergone a paradigm shift in the learning approach, from pedagogy to andragogy and now heutagogy [14]. Heutagogy learning emphasizes that students learn independently (self-determined learning), in this case, the student can determine what they want to learn, manage teaching material in a format beloved by students, a wide variety of digitally learning resources, and the use of educational social platforms such as Edmodo, Youtube, and Whatsapp [15]. To support these developments, educational institutions need to provide a learning environment that can make it easier for students to develop their own knowledge anytime and anywhere. In other words, learning technology should be an integral part of the current learning model [16].

2.2 Design Principles of Successful Virtual Classroom

A virtual classroom is an online class that enables students to communicate, present lessons, interaction with teaching materials, and works in groups [17]. The virtual classroom is not a novelty, the discussion about e-learning at the end of 1990 became the gateway to the integration of digital materials into the educational world. The web-based learning management system at the university level was used at the beginning of 2000 as a tool to promote learning [18]. As time goes by, advances in technology and infrastructure become more sophisticated to support real-time digital interaction between students and instructors. A holistic approach of educational institutions using digital learning materials is proposed to support as many learning activities as possible [19]. One of the main challenges in online learning is interactivity in the virtual classroom [20]. Referring to the research conducted by [13], the seven basic principles for a successful interactive virtual classroom can be seen in Fig. 1.

Fig. 1. Seven basic principles for successful virtual classroom based on [13].

Based on Fig. 1, to be able to effectively implement virtual classroom, it is essential to pay attention to the seven basic principles of successful virtual classroom including: (1) Pre-engineering lessons: advance planning and preparation of all the major elements of the event; (2) Include diverse media: diverse delivery media complement one another; (3) Be job relevant: good virtual events are explicitly relevant job; (4) Be interactive: learning is interactive; (5) Consider social presence: social presence promotes learning; (6) Combine the visual and verbal: appropriate visual and verbal modalities; (7) Manage cognitive load: cognitive load must be managed in all instructor-led events. The advantage of design principles of a virtual classroom by [13] is the ability of the design principles to adapt into different context and cultures [21–23] which is relevant with multicultural characteristic of Indonesian society. Furthermore, the design approaches [13] focuses more on the technique of developing a learning environment. We, therefore, used these principles [13] as a basis for our research.

3 Method

In this study, we applied design science research (DSR) process [12] aiming to tackle the initial research problem and evaluate the proposed solution close to the object of the study and their environment. Lack of available design approach to implementing virtual classroom for a vocational university in Indonesia is the initial research problem that guiding our research study in the next step of the DSR. For a phase of a solved definition, in this study, we used qualitative research on the phase of design solution by using an interview with university lectures from three different universities in Indonesia who had 10 to 16 years of teaching experiences, and it was not involved in the writing of this paper. The interview was conducted both in form face-to-face meeting as well as an online interview. Each result of the interview is recorded and documented in written format. We had adapted the design principles [13] for the virtual classroom, combined with the interview and the study literature, a set of design approaches for the implementation of the virtual classrooms for vocational students and presented in the results section. The proposed design approaches were then implemented and tested for a one-course semester of selected study module of the vocational program at one of a private university in Indonesia. The course modules consist of two different groups of students. The first group consists of students of the 5th semester and the second group for the first semester students. Two different groups are selected to show a general effect of the proposed approach for vocational students. At the end of the semester, the student was asked questions about the implemented design approaches in the form of blended learning. We used Likert scale (1: very poor - 5: very good) online questionnaire consisted of 9 questions required by the institution where the solution approaches were implemented (see Table 1) to meet our study purpose. The proposed approaches, as well as the result of the evaluation, are presented in the following section.

Table 1. Items question (Adapted from [24]).

No	Questions
1	Availability of teaching content (material, discussion, assignments, etc.)
2	Use of tools (Edmodo, Kahoot, etc.)
3	Compatibility with the teaching and learning process
4	Support for increasing learning motivation
5	Support for improving learning methods
6	Support for improving learning outcomes
7	Supporting facilities (guidelines, instructors, etc.)
8	Overall evaluation

4 Result and Discussion

In this section, we present two main findings of the study. The first results are related to the proposed design approach and the second results is the evaluation of the proposed approaches.

4.1 Proposed Approaches

Our study proposed seven design approaches for a vocational private university in Indonesia to implement a virtual classroom. The seven approaches can be seen in Fig. 2.

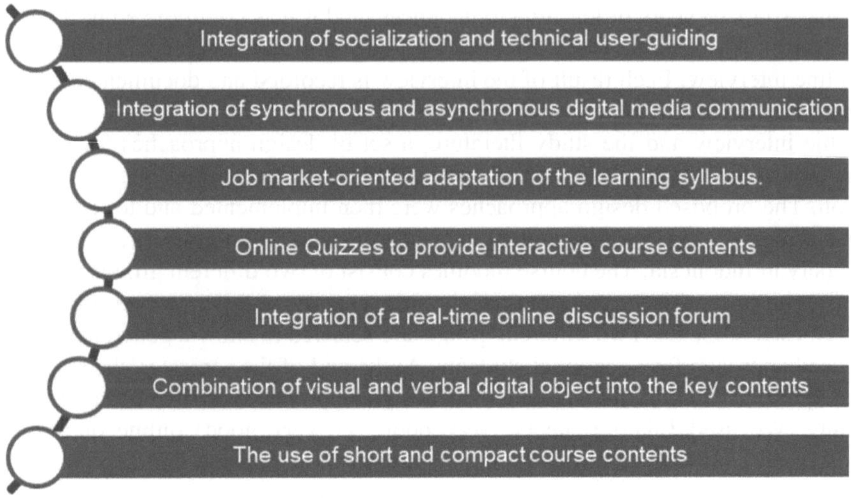

Fig. 2. Proposed design virtual classroom.

More details are explained as follows:

Integration of Socialization and Technical User-Guiding Features for New Users. The first design approach is based on principles of pre-engineering lessons that focus on the planning and preparation of the virtual class both by providing digital and printed guideline book for the students about how to use the virtual class. The printed book was made to give information of module handbook and the printed book, as well as the digital version were socialized among the students at the first course meeting. The guideline book included information about the method in the blended learning, explanation about the course contents and how to use the required tools and procedures of the courses. The importance of the virtual class is also stated in the interview for instance: "…a virtual class is still a new thing for the students; therefore, it is important to socialize the guideline how to use the virtual classroom…".

Integration of Synchronous and Asynchronous Digital Media Communication. The use of different media is the second principle of a successful virtual class. We elaborated the second principle and focused on the integration of several digital media as well as the use of open source tools that can utilize synchronous and asynchronous virtual learning activities. For this second approach, we used different digital learning media, including digital slide presentations, video tutorials uploaded to the YouTube platform and other open source platforms to store the digital learning content. In addition, social media such as Facebook group and WhatsApp group were used to support synchronous communication. The importance of the multichannel media to support learning activities for a virtual class is also mentioned in the interview: "…there is a need for media that can support synchronous and asynchronous learning activities…".

Job Market-Oriented Adaptation of the Learning Syllabus. The third approach to implement virtual classroom is by adapting the course syllabus based on the need of the current job market. Identifying relevant contents based on the analysis of the job market collected from industry and available job vacancy that listed in any online job portal. The solution approach focus on relevancy between the activities in the virtual classroom with the targeted competencies for students. We customized the course syllabus also by adding more detail information to the learning plan that includes design activities and teaching content, design content of course descriptions, a design of task content, draft discussion forum, a design of quiz content, design of learning videos and design of blended learning activities. Based on the interview, some notable comments related to the proposed design solution are "...We need to have a detailed blended learning plan..." other interviewee stated that "...The activities that are taught must be relevant and clear..." and "...The design of blended learning activities must be explicit...".

Online Quizzes to Provide Interactive Course Contents. This fourth solution relies on the "Be interactive" principle, which explains the importance of interaction between teacher and student and between students in a virtual class. Based on the results of interviews with the teaching team to increase the interactive activities, we conducted an online quiz with Kahoot's game-based learning tools in one session (See Fig. 3). The proposed solution is also supported on the basis of an interview that there are no online quiz questions yet for the learning content.

Fig. 3. The use of Kahoot platform to provide an interactive quiz.

Integration of a Real-Time Online Discussion Forum. This fifth approach embodies the principle of taking social presence into account and the approaches are also still related to the second proposed design approach. The fifth approach aims to integrate social activities into virtual class-based learning activities. Based on the results of interviews, social media-based tools are needed to increase social activities in learning. The tools used are Edmodo LMS and WhatsApp applications. Edmodo LMS is used to create discussion forums related to learning materials and related tasks that are assigned online. In addition to social activities, the WhatsApp group is also used to facilitate social activities in the teaching and learning process.

Combination of Visual and Verbal Digital Object into the Key Contents. The sixth solution follows the principle of the importance of combining visual and verbal techniques in the teaching content used. Based on the results of interviews to improve the effectiveness of the students' competence performance, the learning content is not only created in the form of texts but also made interesting by adding pictures, graphics and videos. The proposed approach supports the result from an interview "...Activities and digital content must be made more interesting in relation to topics considered important...".

The Use of Short and Compact Course Contents. For the last proposed solution, the principle of controlled cognitive stress is applied. The principle describes the importance of cognitive load control for all learning activities. Based on the results of the interviews, the summarized learning content, which highlights the main points of the learning materials supported by the instructor's narrative, accessible anytime and anywhere, is important for students to facilitate discussion and repetition of self-learning. The proposed solution is also related to the proposed second approaches related to the selection of the online repository. Based on the interview, some notable comments related to the proposed design solution are "...the choice of content depends on whether the subject is interesting/not..." and "...must pay attention to the level of difficulty of the material to be taught.....".

Next, we present the assessment result of the implemented proposed approach.

4.2 Analysis of Evaluation

Evaluation of the results is done by involving 100 students (32 for the first group, 68 for the second group, 60% male students, 40% female students, age 18–19th: 32 respondents, age 20–21 years: 68 respondents) who are registered as active students in the virtual classroom that has been created. The evaluation method used a survey method with a questionnaire tool, containing 8 items of questions that represent the student's perceptions of the results of the design of the virtual classroom that have been made. A summary of the results of student evaluations is shown in Table 2.

Table 2. Relative numerical distribution of all variables.

Score	All			Old students			New students		
	Y	R	Rk	Y	R	Rk	Y	R	Rk
Teaching content	3,86	77,20	8	3,94	78,82	5	3,69	73,75	7
Tools	4,22	84,44	2	4,25	85,00	1	4,19	83,75	2
Compatibility in learning	4,23	84,60	1	4,22	84,41	2	4,25	85,00	1
Learning motivation	4,00	80,00	4	3,96	79,12	4	4,09	81,88	3
Learning method	3,97	79,40	5	3,96	79,12	4	4,00	80,00	4
Learning outcome	3,93	78,60	6	3,91	78,24	6	3,97	79,38	5
Supporting system	4,14	82,80	3	4,12	82,35	3	4,19	83,75	2
Overall evaluation	3,90	78,00	7	3,91	78,24	6	3,88	77,50	6

Y: Mean, R: Relative Weight; Rk: Rank

Table 2 shows that compatibility in learning and tools are the two highest score for student perceptions, while teaching content is in the lowest score from the result of student assessment of the design of the virtual classroom. On the one hand, for the old student tools availability of the proposed design approaches is evaluated at the top, on the other hand, for the new student shows the compatibility in learning is in the first place and as an indication of how helpful the student experiences on technology for the implementation of the proposed approaches for virtual classrooms. Overall, the findings of the evaluation indicate that the overall assessment of students in the design of virtual classroom shows positive results. This can be seen from the average range of all variables between 3, 86 (77, 2%) and 4.23 (84, 60) with all mean score above 3, 41 (68, 2%). Thus, it can be said that the design of the virtual classroom can be well received by the student in order to support the effectiveness of blended learning activities.

5 Discussion

Interestingly considering to the results of this study compared to previous studies, some points of discussion appear. The first is related to the barriers that exist in Indonesia, previous studies mentioned about the barrier related to the implementation associated with infrastructure, the availability of supporting software and hardware [4, 6]. We also found this out through the results of the interviews, so that there are suggestions for the use of open platforms, open source software, and social media. Second, the use of social media as a learning medium is also consistent with research on the role of social media in supporting the teaching, learning, and knowledge transfer process [25, 26]. The popularity of WhatsApp in Indonesia [27] as the way of group communication can be used to enhance real-time feedback that can be seen to all students.

Next, we also utilized the well-known platform for learning such as Edmodo, Kahoot, and the use of YouTube to 24 h online available video tutorial to provide individual learning as part of the solution. Interestingly, lack of infrastructure [6] to access the video platform was not mentioned in the interview. Instead, the interviewee recommended such video open platform to enhance virtual learning. Fourth, the use multiple media channels resulting on the overall score; however, the results of the interview show that there is still a need for guidance on how to integrate the implementation and use of these different tools, and also support prior research on the obstacles related to skills in the use of tools [6]. Therefore, it is still necessary to provide information on guidelines in a face-to-face format at the first session of a course. Finally, the use of design principles [13] are also supported as a general approach that is in line with the needs of the instructors as the result of the interview, moreover the proposed approaches also providing an overall accepted score for the implementation for vocational students.

6 Outlook and Future Work

Based on the literature review, current research in the field of online learning is leading to increasing the effectiveness of a virtual classroom. The main key to create an effective learning in the virtual classroom is to develop teaching and learning design.

Therefore, this research tries to develop a proposed design for the implementation of a virtual classroom, especially for a vocational university in Indonesia. The development process is focused on the interaction between students and instructors in an online learning environment.

From the theoretical perspective, the result of this study provides an insight into the needs of different approaches to how a virtual classroom can be integrated into vocational education modules in Indonesia. Moreover, the study also shows the successful implementation of the basic principle of designing a virtual classroom. While in practice, the results of this study can be utilized by higher education institutions to design and improve existing online learning services.

The results of this research have shown that the virtual classroom can support online learning at the higher education sector, especially for a vocational university in Indonesia. In addition, this study also shows that student can interact with instructors as a real. That is, the focus of a virtual classroom is not only on the use of the technology but also on the virtual learning environment. Therefore, the result of this study can be used as a starting point for further research.

In our future work, we are going to analyze the factors that influence the success of a virtual learning environment. The results also can provide us with basic approaches to support us analyzing the impact of using virtual classroom both on improving student and instructor performance. Finally, we will incorporate the proposed design to institutional curricula for various higher vocational study programs or subjects.

References

1. Chen, R.C., Liu, S.C.: Applying concept mapping on the influent learning in virtual classroom. In: International Conference on Hybrid Intellelligent System IEEE Computer Society Press (2009)
2. Clark, R.C., Mayer, R.E.: E-Learning and the Science of Instruction: Proven Guidelines for Consumers and Designers of Multimedia Learning, 3rd edn. Wiley, San Francisco (2011)
3. Wang, A.Y., Newlin, M.H.: Online lectures: benefits for the virtual classroom. The Journal **29**(1), 17–18 (2001)
4. Barajas, M., Owen, M.: Implementing virtual learning environments: looking for holistic approach. Educ. Technol. Soc. **3**(3), 39–53 (2000)
5. Palloff, R.M., Pratt, K.: Building Online Learning Communities: Effective Strategies for the Virtual Classroom. Wiley, Hoboken (2007)
6. Hendrastomo, G.: Dilema dan Tantangan Pembelajaran e-Learning. Majalah Ilmiah Pembelajaran **4**(1), 32–35 (2008)
7. Ristek Dikti Website. http://kelembagaan.ristekdikti.go.id/wp-content/uploads/2016/11/permen24tahun2012.pdf. Accessed 08 Jan 2019
8. Hofstede Website. https://www.hofstede-insights.com/country-comparison/indonesia/. Accessed 08 Jan 2019
9. Kopertis Website. Indonesian government institution for private higher education. http://kopertis3.or.id/v5/wp-content/uploads/Buku-Statistik-Pendidikan-Tinggi-2017.pdf. Accessed 08 Jan 2019

10. Ambarita, A.: Implementasi sistem e-learning menggunakan software moodle pada politeknik sains dan teknologi wiratama maluku utara. IJIS-Indonesian J. Inf. Syst. **1**(2) (2017)
11. Silanegara, I.: Penerapan konsep reengineering untuk mengidentifikasi kebutuhan teknologi informasi (studi kasus: progam studi teknik energi di politeknik negeri). Jurnal Poli-Teknologi **9**(3) (2013)
12. Hevner, A.R.: A three cycle view of design science research. Scand. J. Inf. Syst. **19**(2), 4 (2007)
13. Clark, R.C., Kwinn, A.: The New Virtual Classroom: Evidence-Based Guidelines For Synchronous E-Learning. Wiley, San Fransisco (2007)
14. Acedo, C., Hughes, C.: Principles for learning and competences in the 21th-century Curriculum. Prospects **44**(4), 503–525 (2014)
15. Blaschke, L.M.: Heutagogy and lifelong learning: a review of heutagogical practice and self-determined learning. Int. Rev. Res. Open Distance Learn. **13**(1), 56–71 (2012)
16. Dabbagh, N., et al.: Learning Technologies and Globalization. SECT. Springer, Cham (2016). https://doi.org/10.1007/978-3-319-22963-8
17. Thinyane, H., Mufeti, K.: Google docs and skype for a low bandwidth virtual classroom for developing countries. Int. Inf. Mgmt. Corporation 1–7 (2010)
18. Rios, A.P., Callaghan, V., Gardner, M., Alhaddad, M.J.: The interreality portal: a mixed reality co creative intelligent learning environment. In: International Conference on Intellelligent Environments IEEE Computer Society Press (2012)
19. Jiang, Z., Guo, X.: A miniature e-Learning portal of full teaching and learning capacity. IEEE Computer Society Press, Los Alamitos (2012)
20. Repman, J., Zinskie, C., Carlson, R.: Effective use of CMC tools in interactive online learning. Comput. Sch. **22**(1/2), 57–69 (2005)
21. Keramidas, C.G., Ludlow, B.L., Collins, B.C., Baird, C.M.: Saving your sanity when teaching in an online environment: lessons learned. Rural Spec. Educ. Q. **26**(1), 28–39 (2007)
22. Valaitis, R., Akhtar-Danesh, N., Eva, K., Levinson, A., Wainman, B.: Pragmatists, positive communicators, and shy enthusiasts: three viewpoints on web conferencing in health sciences education. J. Med. Internet Res **9**(5) (2007)
23. Wickens, C.D., Hollands, J.G., Banbury, S., Parasuraman, R.: Engineering Psychology & Human Performance. Psychology Press, New York (2015)
24. Aditya, B.R., Permadi, A.: Implementation of utaut model to understand the use of virtual classroom principle in higher education. J. Phys. Conf. Ser. **978**(1), 012006 (2018)
25. Pirkkalainen, H., Pawlowski, J.: Global social knowledge management: from barriers to the selection of social tools. Electron. J. Knowl. Manage. **11**(1) (2013)
26. Baird, D.E., Fisher, M.: Neomillennial user experience design strategies: utilizing social networking media to support "always on" learning styles. J. Educ. Technol. Syst. **34**(1), 5–32 (2005)
27. Kurniasih, N., Riyadhsyah, T.: Virtual Ethnography Study Inter-lecturer Communication in Nation Young Lecturers Forum WhatsApp Group. In: Proceedings of the 8th International Conference of Asian Association of Indigenous and Cultural Psychology (2018)

Computer Application for the Evaluation of Mathematical Competence in Secondary Education: A Case Study

Lara Orcos[1(✉)], Rosario Arias[3], Alberto Magreñán[3], Juan Antonio Sicilia[2], and Íñigo Sarría[2]

[1] Facultad de Educación, Universidad Internacional de La Rioja (UNIR), 26002 Logroño, La Rioja, Spain
lara.orcos@unir.net

[2] Escuela Superiot de Ingeniería y Tecnología, Universidad Internacional de La Rioja (UNIR), 26002 Logroño, La Rioja, Spain

[3] Departamento de Matemáticas y Computación, Universidad de La Rioja (UR), 26004 Logroño, La Rioja, Spain

Abstract. The main purpose of this work is the development of an application that allows compulsory secondary education teachers the assessment of the students' maths competence. An equation of prediction is obtained in a pilot study through the multivariate technique of multiple regression using for its analysis, by means of SPSS, the results gathered throughout speaking tasks, tests and works done by students in 2nd, 3rd and 4th course of compulsory Secondary Education of a state school in Spain. This equation of prediction is introduced in the program in order to make the calculation that provides the result of the assessment. The software is set up by means of interfaces. The source of information consists of a series of activities designed on the basis of liberated, national and international diagnostic tests taking into account the three key dimensions related to the maths competence: procedures, contents and context.

Keywords: Assessment · Competences · Maths competence · Computer application · Diagnostic tests · Multivariate analysis · Multiple regression · Secondary education

1 Introduction

As discussed by [1] at their Formal Discipline Theory, mathematics helps in the development of generic skills such as logical thinking, the ability to analyze basing on reasoning and the concern of how to establish underlying assumptions can affect conclusions and decision making. The notion of mathematical competence is the central axis of evaluation in PISA tests and has marked the line that educational institutions and laws have followed to establish the pedagogical frameworks for the teaching and learning of mathematics in recent years. However, the development of the curriculum by the administrations does not effectively guide the teachers on how to incorporate, integrate and evaluate the competences in the curriculum [2].

L. Uden et al. (Eds.): LTEC 2019, CCIS 1011, pp. 162–173, 2019.
https://doi.org/10.1007/978-3-030-20798-4_15

In [3], author states that the competency approach is considered today as an educational proposal that goes beyond content learning by the international community. The DeSeCo (Definition and Selection of Competencies) project of the OECD [4], developed a list of key competences that has been used for subsequent curricular reforms throughout Europe in Primary and Secondary Education being the Tuning project the basis for curricular modifications in University Education for a competency-based approach [5–8]. [3] concludes that there is no consensus on the notion of mathematical competence and neither concrete structure to explain the teaching and learning of mathematics based on a competency-based approach. The quality criteria in competency assessment can be found in [9].

The resources that teachers have for the evaluation of mathematical competence in Secondary Education are scarce and are based on most of the activities that can be developed in the tests released from the different editions of PISA and in the national diagnostic tests, since the materials provided by the publishers and applicable in a session adapted to the daily educational needs are also based on these tests.

In the educational field, there have been developed some research to try to predict the performance of students from different points of view. Authors such as [10] provide information on the different applications made from the multivariate analysis to the field of psychology and psychometrics. [11] carried out a work in which they used statistical segmentation techniques in the analysis of the data of an evaluative investigation in order to evaluate the academic performance. The main objective of this work was to design a predictive model of performance in these subjects and analyze the possibilities of multivariate techniques for data analysis in evaluation research and communication of results.

In terms of computer tools related to the subject, there are numerous applets developed in Java for carrying out specific mathematical tasks, in which the objective is that students have a tool to practice these contents. An interesting example is the software developed by [12] to make descriptive geometry exercises. Another interesting tool is the one developed by [13] that provides exercises on elementary geometry, trigonometry, vectors and complex numbers. The Gauss project, of the National Institute of Educational Technologies (INTEF), provides teachers with hundreds of GeoGebra didactic and applet items that cover all the contents of Primary and Secondary mathematics [14].

Although these types of resources have a considerable potential from the point of view of their use in the practice of specific contents, they do not have the necessary characteristics to serve as an evaluator of the mathematical competence of the students.

The main objective of this work is to help students in the acquisition of mathematical skills through the support of a software that collects the results of the different activities that can be performed in order to evaluate the evolution of students in the acquisition of mathematical competences and thus, to be able to predict the influence of the different variables that take place in the process of mathematical skill acquisition by students through a prediction equation obtained by multiple regression. The software developed in which the prediction equation obtained by means of multivariate techniques is applied for the evaluation is based on these quality criteria, providing a solid pedagogical base that provides reliability to the results.

2 Application Design

Application to evaluate of the students' math's competence. The only limitation we had in this project was the one related to financial costs. For that reason, we needed to use low-cost and freeware devices and languages. Then, the system had to be implemented with the Eclipse IDE (Integrated Development Environment) and Java was used as programming language to develop the graphic user interface.

It has been selected the Java language, based on object-oriented programming (OOP), because it is a multiplatform language that allows the creation of great robustness, power and complexity programs. Therefore, the graphical user interface has been developed according to its AWT (Abstract Window Toolkit) and SWING libraries, whose development is more active and with fewer platform limitations when not using a native code [15, 16].

The application consists of a series of interfaces that show the user the set of activities to be faced to perform the competency assessment test. As it is an application that has to be used in a limited time, the duration of the test and, therefore, the number of questions and interfaces has been adapted to the characteristic time spaces in the Secondary Education sessions. The interface might comply with the WCAG 2.0 (Web Content Accessibility Guidelines) accessibility norms, including icons, fonts, images and color schemes that are easy to learn, use and remember. Additionally, due to the different level of knowledge of users, an easy-to-understand errors system might be developed to ease the use of the platform to all the actors. The implementation of the application has been based on the clarity in the presentation of the tasks, the simplicity and functionality in the navigation, as well as in the protection of the rating system, based on accumulators. The entire application has been programmed following a common and intuitive user interface (UI).

3 Methodology

3.1 Sample, Variables and Information Collection Tools

The population on which the application design has been implemented is made up of a sample of 22 students of mathematics of the 2nd, 3rd and 4th courses of Secondary Education due to the fact that this is a pilot study. The dependent variable is the mathematical competence which is quantitative as all the independent ones. The initial values of the dependent variable are obtained by performing diagnostic tests released by PISA for students of secondary education which can be found in [17]. The independent variables have been the average score resulting from different tests of mathematical competence assessment, the final average grade of the previous two courses and the dimensions of Numbers, Algebra, Geometry, Functions and Statistics of several exercises on which the qualification in the three evaluations has been based. The instruments used for the collection of information have been very varied: test, exams, analysis of work done, rubrics for the assessment of the use of mathematical tools, etc.

3.2 Data Analysis

The data of the qualifications obtained from the application has been analyzed through multivariate analysis techniques: factor analysis to simplify data and multiple linear regression to find the prediction equation through the statistical package SPSS.

In Factor analysis [18] we use the symmetric correlation matrix with the variance of all the standardized analysis variables and the Pearson coefficients, with the unilateral critical level (unilateral Sig) associated, between each pair of variables. A critical level less than 0.05 indicates that the correlation between the pair of variables can be considered significantly different from zero. To assess whether the correlation matrix can be factored, it is necessary to use the Bartlett sphericity test and the KMO indicator (Kaise-Meyer-Olkin). Once the pertinence of the factorization can be justified, it is used the principal components method to extract the maximum variance of the study variables.

For the linear regression in this analysis [18], we have used the Mathematical Competence as dependent variable and the four dimensions Algebra, Geometry, Functions and Statistics as independent variables. Algebra note is obtained as the arithmetic mean of the Numbers and Algebra columns. The multiple regression model is obtained with SPSS software after having check the principle of parsimony, the linearity, the ANOVA, the Durbin-Watson statistic, the normal distribution of the residuals, variance influence factor (VIF) and the tolerance (1/VIF) and the homoscedasticity.

4 Results

4.1 Factor Analysis Results

Table 1 shows the correlation matrix between the variables Numbers, Algebra, Geometry, Functions and Statistics. We can see that the correlations are very strong between almost all the variables since the values of the Pearson correlation coefficient are close to 1. In addition, the level of significance is less than 0.05, so it can be established that there is correlation between the variables.

Table 1. Correlation matrix.

		ComMat	Geomet	Function	Statistics	NumAlg
Pearson coefficient	ComMat	1	0.63	0.627	0.706	0.737
	Geomet	0.63	1	0.843	0.756	0.906
	Function	0.627	0.843	1	0.723	0.827
	Statistics	0.706	0.756	0.723	1	0.748
	NumAlg	0.737	0.906	0.827	0.748	1
Sig. (unilateral)	ComMat		0.001	0.001	0	0
	Geomet	0.001		0	0	0
	Function	0.001	0		0	0
	Statistics	0	0	0		0
	NumAlg	0	0	0	0	

Table 2 shows the data of the KMO test and the Bartlett sphericity test. As it can be seen, the level of significance obtained in the Bartlett test is less than 0.05 and the KMO value is close to 1 (0.806), so both tests allow us to conclude that we can factorize.

Table 2. KMO and Bartlett sphericity tests.

KMO value		0.806
Bartlett sphericity test	Aprox. Chi-Square	380.409
	gl	28
	Sig.	0

As mentioned, to extract the factors, the principal component method is used. In Table 3 there are the communalities initially assigned to the variables by factorial extraction. All the variables explain the variance with very high percentages, the variable Algebra, for example, explains 94%.

Table 3. Principal components analysis.

	Initial	Extraction
ComMat	1	0.641
Geomet	1	0.877
Function	1	0.784
Statistics	1	0.733
NumAlg	1	0.939

The extracted factors are shown in Table 4. As it can be seen, the first factor explains 82.44% of the variance, so the principal component method only extracts one factor to perform the analysis. In addition, the matrix of components, in Table 5 also corroborate that a factor has been extracted.

Table 4. Variance explained by the factors.

		Initial autovalues	
Component	Total	% of variance	% accumulated
1	6.595	82.439	82.439
2	0.512	6.396	88.835
3	0.396	4.953	93.789
4	0.246	3.076	96.865
5	0.117	1.464	98.329
6	0.069	1.111	99.44
7	0.045	0.560	100
8	2.232^{E-6}	2.952^{E-5}	100

Table 5. Component matrix and component's score coefficients matrix.

	Component matrix	Component's score coefficients matrix
ComMat	0.801	0.121
Geomet	0.937	0.142
Function	0.886	0.134
Statistics	0.856	0.130
NumAlg	0.969	0.147

It can be concluded that the factorial analysis corroborates the fact that all the dimensions that have been taken into account in the initial data table, all the variables, including the mathematical competence and the average grade of the previous courses can be explained with a single factor.

4.2 Prediction Equation Through Multiple Linear Regression

The program selects all the variables for the model and Table 6 shows that R is sufficiently high, R = 0.790, to ensure that Linearity exists. In the summary of the model we can see that although the coefficient of determination is not very close to 1, R2 = 0.624, the model allows predicting the mathematical competence of an individual chosen at random, having a certain uncertainty. That is, if we have information on the independent variables, average score in the 4 dimensions, the model allows us to predict Mathematical Competence with an uncertainty reduced by 62.4% with respect to the original.

Table 6. Summary chart of the regression model.

R	Square R	Adjusted square R	Estimation standard error	Durbin-Watson
0.790	0.624	0.535	1.09737	1.580

The typical estimation error (square root of the unexplained variance) is acceptable, sufficiently low. The Durbin-Watson statistic with a value of 1, 58 informs us that the residuals are independent, they do not fit any pattern for the four independent variables. Values less than 1.5 indicate a negative correlation. In Fig. 1 there are the graphs of the dependent variable vs the independent ones to study the linearity.

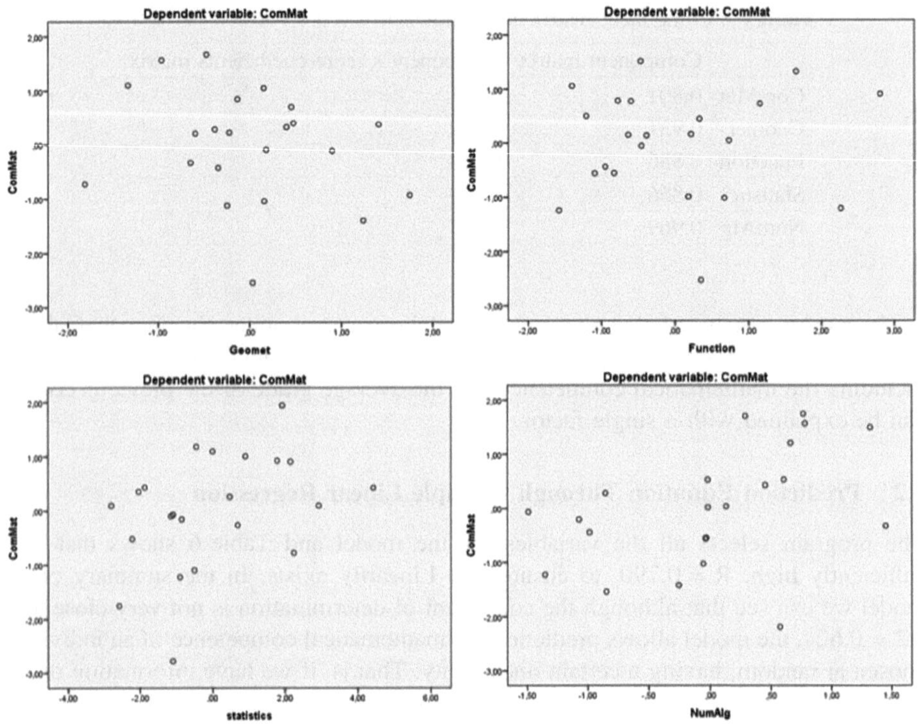

Fig. 1. Partial regression graphs of the dependent variable vs the 4 independent ones respectively.

The variance analysis test (ANOVA) in Table 7 shows that the model is significant (p is approximately 0, Sig = 0.002). Therefore, the null hypothesis is rejected and the Mathematical Competence is explained by the other variables. The obtained statistic F is smaller than the tabulated one for the level of significance chosen.

Table 7. Variance analysis (ANOVA) test results.

Model 1	Sum of squares	gl	Root mean square	F	Sig.
Regression	33.922	4	8.480	7.042	0.002
Residual	20.472	17	1.204		
Total	54.393	21			

In the second row of Table 8, we see that the residuals have a mean of cero and standard deviation 1, so this hypothesis is fulfilled.

Table 8. Residuals statistics.

	Min.	Max.	Mean	Standard deviation
Predicted value	3.3481	8.0186	5.8509	1.27095
Standard predicted value	−1.969	1.706	0	1
Standard error of the predicted value	0.254	0.758	0.509	0.122
Corrected predicted value	3.2969	8.1881	5.8884	1.32046

In Fig. 2 there is the diagram P-P of the normal distribution of the residuals diagram, the histogram and the scatter plot of the study of homocedasticity. The P-P graph shows the linear relationship between both probabilities that indicates that the residuals are normally distributed. In the histogram of the frequencies of the typified residuals, the expected cumulative probability is plotted against the cumulative probability observed. The scatter lot of the homocedasticity shows a constant variance of independent variables. As it can be seen, there is not a funnel shape in the fan and the typified residuals are very separated from the rest.

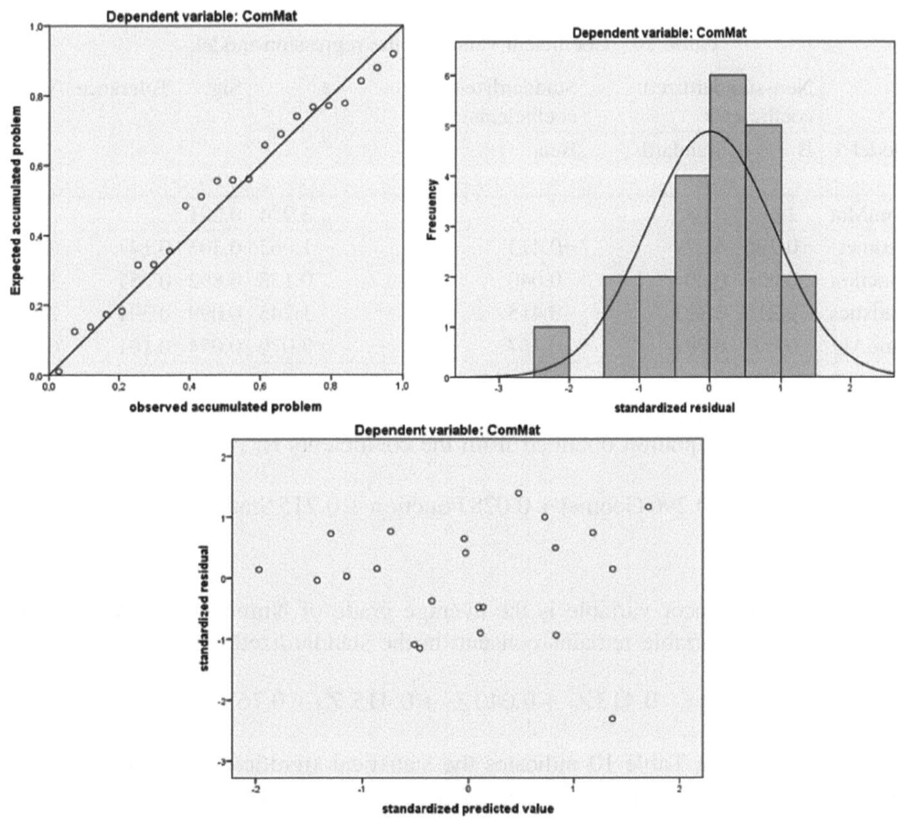

Fig. 2. P-P diagram of the residuals (top left), histogram of the residuals (top right), Scatter plot of type residuals vs predicted values (bottom).

Table 9 shows the values of the Cook distance and the centered influence value (Leverages). In the case of Cook distance, the reference value is 1 if this value is exceeded, this is an influential case. There is no value in the table that exceeds 1. In the case of the centered influence value, the reference value is a function of the return variables and the sample size: 2 (return variables + 1)/number of observations, in our analysis 2 * (4 + 1)/22 = 0.4545, as the maximum is 0.431 there is no observation that influences our model.

Table 9. Cook distance and centered influence value.

	Min.	Max.	Mean	Standard deviation
Cook distance	0	0.462	0.076	0.117
Centered influence value	0.008	0.431	0.182	0.106

The values of the coefficients obtained by the model are shown in Table 10.

Table 10. Coefficient values of the regression model.

	Non-standardized coefficients		Standardized coefficients	t	Sig.	Tolerance	VIF
Model 1	B	Standard error	Beta				
ComMat	2.695	0.685		3.934	0.001		
Geomet	−0.296	0.279	−0.413	−1.063	0.303	0.147	6.825
Function	0.028	0.204	0.040	0.138	0.892	0.257	3.886
Statistics	0.215	0.123	0.415	1.745	0.099	0.391	2.557
NumAlg	0.603	0.291	0.767	2.070	0.054	0.161	6.209

The prediction equation obtained from the coefficients is:

$$\text{ComMat} = 2.695 - 0.296\,\text{Geomet} + 0.028\,\text{Function} + 0.215\,\text{Statistics} + 0.603\,\text{NumAlg}, \tag{1}$$

The most influencer variable is the average grade of Numbers and Algebra. The influence of each variable remains constant in the standardized regression equation:

$$Z = -0.413\,Z_1 + 0.040\,Z_2 + 0.415\,Z_3 + 0.767\,Z_4, \tag{2}$$

The "t" value on Table 10 indicates the statistical significance of the coefficients being the maximum value the one Note of Numbers and Algebra. This greater influence can only have an origin and it is the fact of a greater temporary dedication to these contents which possibly influences higher qualifications among the students.

The tolerance although it not close to 1, is not zero for any of the variables, so we can say that they are not linear combination. Although the results are not excellent, we know that these variables are related in the sense that a bright student in algebra probably is also in the rest of the dimensions. The results are acceptable and the model can be used for a predictive purpose. In order to improve the model taking into account this result and subsequent ones, some modifications have been made to the prediction equation that will be explained later. In summary, the model obtained meets all the requirements necessary to constitute an excellent predictive model.

4.3 Results Obtained After the Application of the Prediction Equation

There have been carrying out several test with the prediction equation using the software with the aim of analyzing the results in comparison with those obtained in the evaluation per items. The results Apt or no Apt have been the same using both calculations but certain differences have been observed when the weight in the Geometry variable is high, decreasing the note obtained in the regression equation with respect to the one obtained in the evaluation per items. As can be seen in the equation, the coefficient of the variable Geometry is negative:

$$\text{ComMat} = 2.695 - 0.296\,\text{Geomet} + 0.028\,\text{Function} + 0.215\,\text{Statitics} + 0.603\,\text{NumAlg}, \quad (3)$$

This fact entails a penalty for students who answer correctly all questions of Geometry. It is also observed a deviation produced by the high value of the coefficient of the variable Algebra, for reasons already explained. Table 11 shows the comparison between the results obtained for the prediction equation when it is assigned the same value to the four independent variables.

Table 11. Comparison between the average mean and prediction equation.

0	1	2	3	4	5	6	7	8	9	10
2.69	3.24	3.79	4.34	4.89	5.44	5.99	6.54	7.09	7.64	8.19

The central values can be considered acceptable but the deviations that occur at the ends have to be corrected. Basing on the tests carried out and the results obtained in the multivariate analyses, the equation is modified in such a way that the influence produced by the aforementioned aspects is reduced, the algebra variable has excessive weight due to temporalization or penalties in correct answers in geometry. The correct equation is as follows:

$$\text{ComMat} = 0.69 + 0.15\ \text{Geomet} + 0.13\ \text{Function} + 0.22\ \text{Statistics} + 0.4\ \text{NumAlg}, \quad (4)$$

Table 12 shows the values obtained with this new corrected equation. The values obtained are considered very adequate and the tests carried out with the application corroborate it.

Table 12. Comparison between the average mean and the corrected prediction equation.

0	1	2	3	4	5	6	7	8	9	10
0.7	1.6	2.5	3.4	4.3	5.2	6.1	7	7.9	8.8	9.7

5 Conclusions

The main objective of this work was to help students in the acquisition of mathematical skills through the support of a software that collects the results of the different activities that can be performed in order to evaluate their evolution in the acquisition of mathematical competences and thus, to be able to predict the influence of the different variables that take place in the process of mathematical skill acquisition by students through a prediction equation obtained by multiple regression. The main objective has been fulfilled and the results obtained have been very positive.

Through the factorial analysis, it has been carried a simplification of the data obtained through the application of PISA diagnostic test. It has been shown that the predictive nature of the multiple regression multivariate technique is adapted to the research framework that has been developed, and the model proposed is effective from the statistical point of view, fulfilling the necessary requirements. The corrections made in the formula obtained correct the deviations that the characteristics of the educational data and praxis had reflected in the multivariate analysis. The final results of the scores obtained by both methods of evaluation, ordinary number of correct answers and by using the prediction equation coincide except for small deviations that do not influence the final grade of APT or NOT APT.

The developed application complies with current regulations on education regarding the evaluation and the way of carrying out teaching and learning based on key competences. It perfectly fulfils the function for which it was designed, and no insurmountable problem is found through the practice in the use of the tool by the students. The interface has been friendly and motivating for the users, so we consider important the extension of the application with more tests.

As already indicated, the software developed can be extended in future versions with the implementation of new interfaces that provide new tests for different educational levels so that the teachers can have a tool that can be used throughout the academic year as a usual resource. It is also considered necessary to include an interface from which the teachers can determine the percentages corresponding to each block of content, adapting it to the characteristics of the students and to the temporary spaces dedicated to the teaching of these blocks.

The compilation of more numerical data from test performed in other groups could provide a deeper analysis from the multivariate point of view, since the number of cases studied, although enough has been enough for the obtaining of the prediction equation, has been limited. It is the intention of the researchers to continue working in this sense in later courses with the aim of checking if there are variations in the initial equation with different groups.

References

1. Inglis, M., Attridge, N.: Does Mathematical Study Develop Logical Thinking? Testing the Theory of Formal Discipline, 1st edn. World Scientific, London (2016)
2. Rial, A.: Diseño Curricular Por Competencias: El Reto De La Evaluación. Universitat de Girona, Girona (2007)
3. Solar, H., Espinoza, L., Rojas, F., Ortiz, A., González, E., Ulloa, R.: Propuesta metodológica de trabajo docente para promover competencias matemáticas en el aula, basadas en un Modelo de Competencia Matemática (MCM). Universidad Católica de la Santísima Concepción, Chile (2011)
4. Definition and Selection of Competencies: Theoretical and Conceptual Foundations. http://deseco.ch/. Accessed 15 Oct 2018
5. Estructuras educativas europeas. La respuesta de la universidad mediante el proyecto «Tuning». http://www.eees.es/es/eees-estructuras-educativas-europeas. Accessed 15 Oct 2018
6. Sarría, Í., González, R., Magreñán, Á.A., Narváez, S.P., Orcos, L.: Games math. adaptive video game to evaluate basic mathematic concepts. In: Uden, L., Liberona, D., Liu, Y. (eds.) LTEC 2017. CCIS, vol. 734, pp. 27–35. Springer, Cham (2017). https://doi.org/10.1007/978-3-319-62743-4_3
7. Orcos, L., Magreñán, Á.A.: The hologram as a teaching medium for the acquisition of STEM contents. Int. J. Learn. Technol. **13**(2), 163–177 (2018)
8. Orcos, L., Hernández-Carrera, R.M., Espigares, M.J., Magreñán, Á.A.: The Kumon method: its importance in the improvement on the teaching and learning of mathematics from the first levels of early childhood and primary education. Mathematics **7**, 109 (2019)
9. Berrocoso, J.V., Revuelta, F.I., Fernández, M.R.: Modelos de evaluación por competencias a través de un sistema de gestión de aprendizaje. Experiencias en la formación inicial del profesorado. Revista Iberoamericana De Educación **60**, 51–62 (2012)
10. Closas, A.H., Arriola, E.A., Kuc, C.I., Amarilla, M.R., Jovanovich, E.C.: Análisis multivariante, conceptos y aplicaciones en Psicología Educativa y Psicometría. Enfoques **25**, 65–92 (2013)
11. Lizasoain, L., et al.: El uso de las técnicas de segmentación en la evaluación del rendimiento en lenguas. Un estudio en la Comunidad Autónoma Vasca. Revista de Investigación Educativa **21**, 93–111 (2003)
12. Toledo, E.: Un applet java^{TM} para hacer disponibles ejercicios de Geometría Descriptiva en Internet. Proceedings of II Congreso Iberoamericano de Expresión Gráfica en Ingeniería y Arquitectura, Salta, Argentina, pp. 141–146, September 1999
13. Mathematik. http://www.walter-fendt.de/math.htm Accessed 20 Sept 2018
14. Gauss project. http://geogebra.es/gauss/. Accessed 10 Oct 2018
15. Pavón Mestras, J.: Estructura de las Aplicaciones Orientadas a Objetos. Interfaces gráficas de usuario. Dpto. Ingeniería del Software e Inteligencia Artificial, Universidad Complutense, Madrid, Spain. https://www.fdi.ucm.es/profesor/jpavon/poo/2.11.GUI.pdf
16. Sznajdleder, P.A.: Java a Fondo: Estudio del lenguaje y desarrollo de aplicaciones, 2nd edn. Buenos Aires, Argentina, Alfaomega (2013)
17. National Institute of Educational Evaluation. http://educalab.es/inee/evaluaciones-internacionales/preguntas-liberadas-pisa-piaac/preguntas-pisa-matematicas
18. Gil, J.A.: Metodología Cuantitativa en Educación, 1st edn. Universidad Nacional de Educación a Distancia, Madrid (2015)

E-learning and MOOCS

Teachers' Beliefs Towards Blended Learning in Higher Education: A Mixed-Methods Study

María Cruz Sánchez-Gómez(✉), Antonio V. Martín-García(✉), and Juanjo Mena

University of Salamanca, Paseo Canalejas 169, 37008 Salamanca, Spain
{mcsago, avmg, juanjo_mena}@usal.es

Abstract. The objective of this paper is to analyse the main beliefs, expectations and attitudes of university teachers regarding the acceptance and adoption of blended learning (BL) methodologies using a quantitative and qualitative approach. A mixed-method design (DEXPLIS sequential explanatory model) was applied to lead the empirical analysis. A total of 982 teachers from different Spanish universities (quantitative part) and a subsample of 86 (for the qualitative study) participated in the study. The results identify a series of beliefs (advantages and disadvantages), as well as the main demands of these teachers related to the implementation of BL.

Keywords: Blended learning · New technologies · Mixed methods · TAM · DEXPLIS

1 Introduction

Experts from all over the world agree that education based on blended learning (B-learning or BL) methodologies has characteristics that make it an excellent opportunity to introduce a paradigm shift in higher education [1–4]. In fact, BL has been highlighted in the international reports of recent years as the education model of the 21st century [5]. The improvement of learning management systems (LMSs) or learning content management (LCM) has no doubt contributed to the interest and expansion of BL, as well as the progress in the development of new teaching methodologies that allow for the effective combination of certain technological resources with renewed pedagogical approaches. Some examples of this include the current expansion of flipped learning (which proposes new teaching approaches involving practices based on just-in-time teaching, peer tutoring, gamification, etc.), the creation of microworlds, learning by simulation, e-mentoring, etc. All of this added to other more consolidated methodologies based on computer-supported collaborative learning (CSCL), project-based learning, scenario-centred learning, constructivist learning environments, situated learning, learning communities, etc. As a result, many universities and higher education institutions are designing strategic plans and taking diverse actions to implement and spread the use of BL methodologies [6–8]. This growing interest of educational organizations is reinforced by the development of an important line of

L. Uden et al. (Eds.): LTEC 2019, CCIS 1011, pp. 177–188, 2019.
https://doi.org/10.1007/978-3-030-20798-4_16

theoretical and empirical research related to the acceptance of BL in higher education contexts [9–12].

Most of these theoretical approaches analyse individual acceptance based on assumptions of behavioural decisions centred on cognitive aspects such as the beliefs that a subject has about a specific technology or innovation, the intention or not to use it, the pressure of the social environment, etc. For example, in an international study on Information and Communication Technologies (ICT) and change in schools conducted by the OECD, in which 94 schools from 23 countries around the world were analysed, it was found that the rate of adoption of ICT in schools followed the traditional rhythms of diffusion of innovation, affected mainly by the personal characteristics of the individuals [13]. Thus, the dimension relative to the adopter involves considering the internal characteristics of people, such as their belief systems, behavioural aspects, feelings, etc., which would affect the decision or intention to use technology [14].

In this context, one of the most widespread models that analyses the role of the attitudes and beliefs over behaviours – or the intention to perform actions – has its origin in the Theory of Reasoned Action proposed by Fishbein and Ajzen in the mid-70 s and in the Theory of Planned Behavior (TPB) proposed by Ajzen [15]. Both state that a large part of human behaviour has a rational basis, determined by attitudes (favourable or unfavourable feelings of subjects towards a given object). In turn, the attitude is the result of a set of behavioural beliefs that refer to the subjective assessment of the consequences of performing an action. The application of this basic scheme to the field of technology originated a line of research around the so-called Technology Acceptance Model (TAM). The TAM was originally proposed by Davis [16] clustering beliefs into two types: perceived usefulness (PU) and perceived ease of use (PEOU) (Fig. 1).

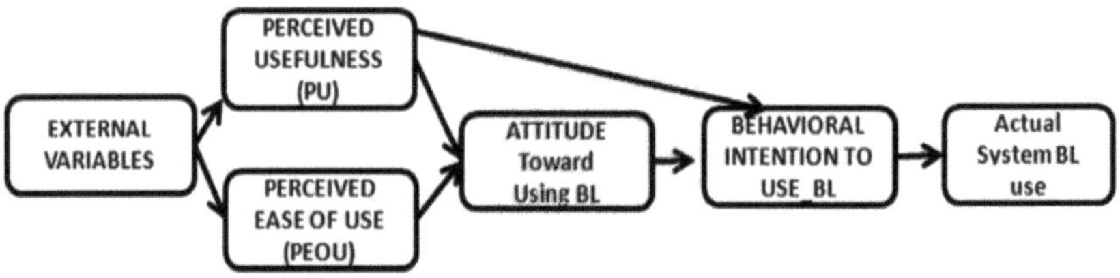

Fig. 1. The TAM (Davis 1989; David et al. 2003).

The successive empirical replication of the TAM, particularly in companies, has led to new extensions of the model, the TAM2 [17] and the TAM3 [18], which analyse different contexts and normative behaviours (in particular complex systems in which the technological component is important, but not the only one), and exploring new variables related to organizational support, self-efficacy in the use of ICT, expertise, degree of satisfaction with the task, learning style of the students, perception of anxiety in the use of technological systems, perception of external control, personal characteristics, etc. [19–21]. Thus, different explanations appear on a similar theoretical basis, although with different explanatory factors.

The methodological basis on which all these models are based has a strong quantitative component, based on multivariate techniques such as causal models or classic inferential techniques [22, 23]. Only a few studies are inclined to use qualitative approaches [24]. Specifically, in our work, we propose a study that combines both methodologies to analyse the main beliefs and expectations of university teachers regarding the use of training systems based on BL.

2 Method

2.1 Study Design

A sequential equivalence status mixed design was conducted by following quantitative and qualitative methods [25–28]. More specifically, the sequential explanatory model DEXPLIS was used, where in the first phase, quantitative data is collected and analysed, and in the second phase, qualitative data is processed. The connection between the methodologies occurs when the initial quantitative results are used to collect qualitative data. Therefore, the second phase is built upon the results of the first phase, and both are jointly integrated in the conclusions, enabling the researcher to address the research problem in a comprehensive manner. In the quantitative analysis, a non-experimental design (ex post facto) was conducted following the TAM. In the qualitative approach, the phenomenological theory was used to scrutinize the participants' feelings about their initial teacher education and experience to seek the meaning given to their university teaching.

The answers were analysed using content analysis through the software NVIVO12. The analysis allowed us to reduce the information (e.g., units of information), as well as to organize it in a conceptual map (e.g., categories, dimensions and integrating concepts), which, ultimately, led us to generate theory from practice (Fig. 2).

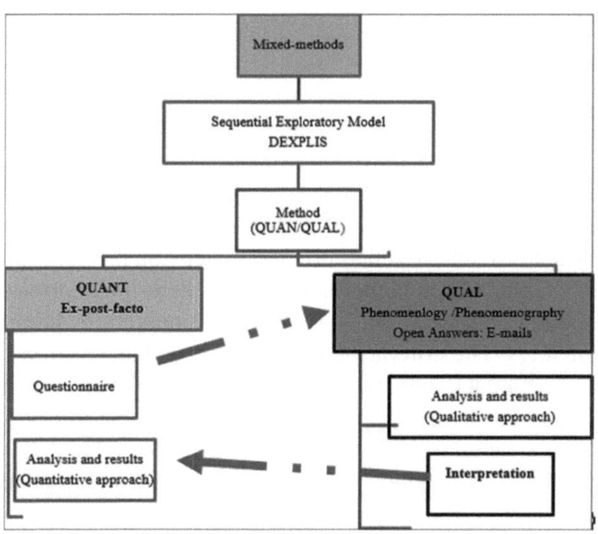

Fig. 2. Sequential explanatory model (DEXPLIS) [39].

2.2 Participants and Data Collection

Incidental and voluntary non-probabilistic sampling was applied through an online survey of active professors from Spanish public universities, resulting in a sample of 980 university teachers. Descriptive analysis of the data indicated, according to sex, that 49.1% of the sample were male professors and 50.9% were female professors. Regarding the age of the participants, 36.5% were under the age of 44, 38.1% were between 45 and 54 and the remaining 25.4% were older than 55. By academic rank, the most numerous were tenured professors of universities (and CEU Centres for University Studies), at 35.2%, followed by assistant professors and others (16.7%), university principals and temporary lecturers (19.8%) and university professors (10%). By area or branch of knowledge, the sample was divided into social sciences and humanities (55.5%), health sciences (15.7%) and physical sciences and engineering (28.8%). Of the sample of professors, 28.3% had less than 10 years of teaching experience, 28.1% had between 11 and 20 years and the remaining 43.7% had more than 20 years of experience. Lastly, 41.0% of the sample claimed to have received training courses on B-learning, while 48.7% explicitly indicated not having received specific training on this subject.

Regarding the instruments applied, a questionnaire adapted to the context of this study was constructed from the literature reviewed on the subject. For the measurement of TAM variables, PU and PEOU reactives adapted from the specialized literature on the subject [16, 29–32] were taken. For the measurement of attitude towards BL (AT_BL), a 6-point semantic differential scale (pleasant-unpleasant, cumbersome-simple, bad-good, useful-useless, beneficial-harmful, etc.) was produced, and, lastly, for the measurement of the "Decision-Intention" variable, a 7-point Likert scale from "extremely probable" to "extremely improbable" was used ("How often do you use a combined teaching system – face-to-face + virtual – in your teaching activity?"; "I combine face-to-face activities with online activities and vice versa"; "I use BL in different contexts and training programs"). All the listed scales were recommended by [29, 33, 34], etc.

3 Analysis and Results

3.1 Quantitative Study

The statistical package SPSS (V.25) and AMOS (V.25) were then used to conduct an initial exploratory analysis of the reliability and dimensionality of the scales (taking as criteria Cronbach's alpha values higher than 0.7 and item-total correlation greater than 0.3) and a confirmatory factorial analysis under the maximum likelihood estimation (multivariate normality). The criteria were loads greater than 0.5 of all the items in the corresponding factor for each dimension and total extracted variance of at least 50% in each scale. The analysis of the reliability and validity of the scales used showed the following Cronbach's alpha values: PU = .90, PEOU = .841, AT = .086 and BI = .819. On the one hand, the suitability of the indicators in the latent variables was assessed, that is, the reliability of the items by imposing a restriction on each of the standardized loads to a value of 0.7 or more. In order to analyse convergent validity, the average variance extracted (AVE greater than 0.5 and factorial loads with values greater than 0.7 for composite reliability, FCC) was taken into account (AVE: UP = .71, PEOU = .57, AT = .59, BI = .60; FCC: UP = .90, PEOU = 0.84, AT = .81, BI = .88). Finally, in order to analyse the discriminant validity, it was verified that the square root of the AVE for each construct was superior to the correlations between it and the other variables of the model (model fit: $\chi 2/df$ [CMIN/DF] = 3.26; CFI = 0.953; TLI = 0.943; IFI = 0.954; PCFI = 0.777; NFI = 0.934; RMSEA = 0.048).

The main results obtained in the empirical model show that the use of the BL system is clearly determined by the intention variable (BI) ($\beta = .677$, $p = .000$). On the other hand, intention is mainly determined by the expectations of results or PU when implementing a BL system ($\beta = .519$) and by the perception of relative effort involved in the use of this type of system ($\beta = .391$).

3.2 Qualitative Study

Once the questionnaire was handed out, statistical analyses were carried out. To delve into some topics and obtain relevant meanings of the responses obtained from the Likert scale, confirmatory emails were sent to respondents, inviting teachers to report or openly add reflections on B-learning teaching from their experience. A total of 86 teachers responded and further commented on the difficulties, advantages and/or improvements.

The emails were content analysed, and seven categories were extracted. In the first phase of the qualitative analysis (categorization), core ideas expressed by university teachers were identified. Secondly, the ideas from the analysis were backed up by theoretical studies on B-learning in order to confirm the final categories of analysis were finally established.

In the second phase of the analysis, axial and selective coding was carried out. Subsequently, the NVIVO12 software was used to organize, classify and code the textual entries. Quality criteria for research were guaranteed along the analysis [28, 35–38]: (1) the coding was carried out by several members of the research team for credibility (internal validity); (2) a descriptive manual with the categories was drawn up to conduct the coding (dependence or reliability); (3) the teachers were provided with verbatim fragments of their discourse (objectivity or confirmability). From the main constructs and indicators of the theoretical models, the categories were identified in the fragments (codification process). Finally, in the third phase of the analysis, the results of the teachers' opinions (content analysis) on the use of B-learning were described.

Below, we present the results obtained from the content analysis of the 86 emails received from the teachers who had answered the questionnaire. The themes that came up revolved around the advantages, disadvantages and demands of B-learning (Fig. 3).

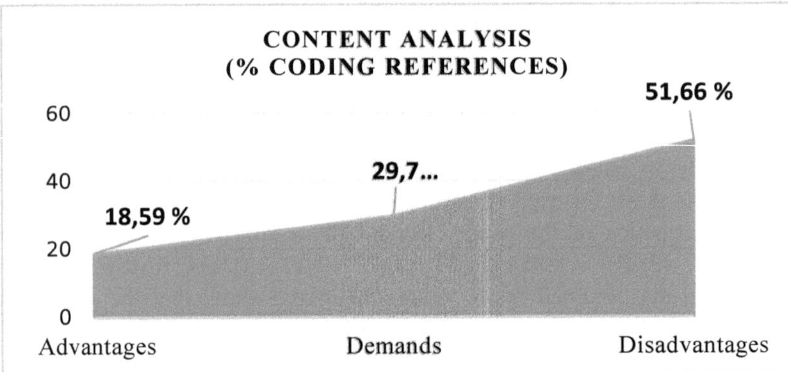

Fig. 3. Content analysis of beliefs about BL

Advantages (18.59% of the Comments)

In the emails, the teachers reflected that teaching using a B-learning methodology has positive effects on the teaching-learning process, especially because the future of education will rely on it. Furthermore, they believe that it facilitates teacher-student interaction, easy access to study cases, better management of documents and files (e.g., subjects, readings, tasks), decision-making in formative evaluation and selection of content, better accessibility to the content, greater autonomy of the students and increased responsibility in the tasks. In short, the teachers think that this new methodology improves the quality of teaching. The following are some examples: *"Bring real case scenarios to the students and link them to the theory"* (Reference 1); *"It facilitates learning and communication"*; *"It is indispensable at present in higher education"* (Reference 13); *"My idea has always been to combine ICT to improve learning so that it would be meaningful and long-lasting, not relying on the memorization of content but on the acquisition of competences"* (Reference 20); *"It improves the quality of the teaching, and, if there is time, it helps the students to stay interested in the subject"* (Reference 24).

Disadvantages (51.66% of References or Comments)

More than half of the teachers' opinions show that BL is difficult to implement in tertiary education mainly because of current conditions of teacher recruitment, absence of incentives or recognition, high number of students in the classrooms and lack of time to prepare the lessons. They also believe that high classroom ratios impede using this methodology. They think that students do not have enough competences for the completion of the required online activities, there is no coordination among teachers of the same course, teachers lack training in BL, evaluations are difficult and students lack motivation. In addition, some think that face-to-face teaching is irreplaceable and BL should only be used as a complementary teaching methodology: *"The use of B-learning has many positive aspects for teaching, but for the teachers, it greatly increases the workload since there are many hours devoted to preparing this type of teaching. This activity is not recognized in any way by the institutions. In addition, the use of ICT in the classroom often leads to technical problems. It is necessary to improve technical resources (e.g., network speed, up-to-date computers, etc.)"* (Reference 27); *"The students' motivation is a complicated issue. For the students, in general, final marks are often a priority over learning"* (Reference 25); *"I would like to highlight the additional workload that it implies for the teaching staff, which, given the limitations of material and current resources in the current context, does not seem acceptable"* (Reference 30); *"Often, the students do not show interest in the use of B-learning. If the teaching activities are not compulsory, they do not wish to participate"* (Reference 33); *"There is no control over the reliability f the students' use of this methodology. This implies that the students should be responsible for their own learning"* (Reference 38); *"While B-learning facilitates teaching and the participation of many students who have difficulty attending the face-to-face lessons, it is true that it leads to isolated learning. The dehumanizing factor can be considered an issue to be addressed"* (Reference 43).

Demands (21.75% of the Comments)

Approximately a quarter of the teachers' comments (24.41%; 21 of 86) suggest substantial changes in the plans of Spanish higher education institutions in order to optimally implement B-learning methodologies in their classrooms. Among the most frequent requests were those related to the conceptualization and implementation of this methodology, for instance, greater institutional support focused on the design of transition strategies leading from face-to-face teaching to BL, higher quality technological tools, more financing or specific regulations and support for open educational resources. In addition, they argue that greater recognition of the time and effort required for the teaching tasks involved in its type of teaching is necessary. They feel that they are saturated "with so many reforms of the university syllabus". Fewer students per classroom, more teacher training and greater student involvement are also highly demanded. *"There is a wrong association in many universities that virtual means less work than face-to-face. Therefore, there is less recognition of the teaching work and a greater increase in the teaching load to the teaching staff. In reality, the opposite is true; virtual teaching requires more work than face-to-face teaching, and if the number of students is high, more teachers are required"* (Reference 1); *"We have been changing plans in my university for a few years, which reduces the motivation to incorporate methodological innovations, which always implies additional efforts"* (Reference 5); "*It is necessary to improve the infrastructure (network speed, updated computers, etc.)"* (Reference 17); *"We have used the virtual campus a lot (Moodle), but basically to submit tasks, upload resources for the students, and do evaluations. The subjects I teach are entirely face-to-face; some subjects use a combined methodology, but they are few. It would be very useful to train the teachers to gradually incorporate this type of tool, but sometimes training is scarce and impractical"* (Reference 21).

If we pick some of the teachers' comments according to the subject of knowledge, the majority of them refer to the difficulties in the use of B-learning. Science, engineering and architecture degrees are perceived as having more limitations in the use of this new methodology than health sciences, social sciences and law.

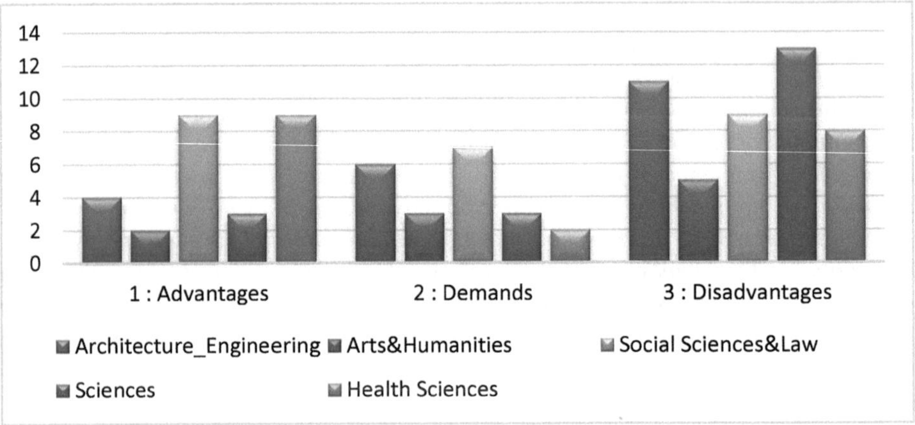

Fig. 4. Content analysis (Coding references by subject knowledge)

Figure 4 shows that most of the teachers found it difficult to implement B-learning in their classrooms, except in the fields of social sciences, law and health sciences.

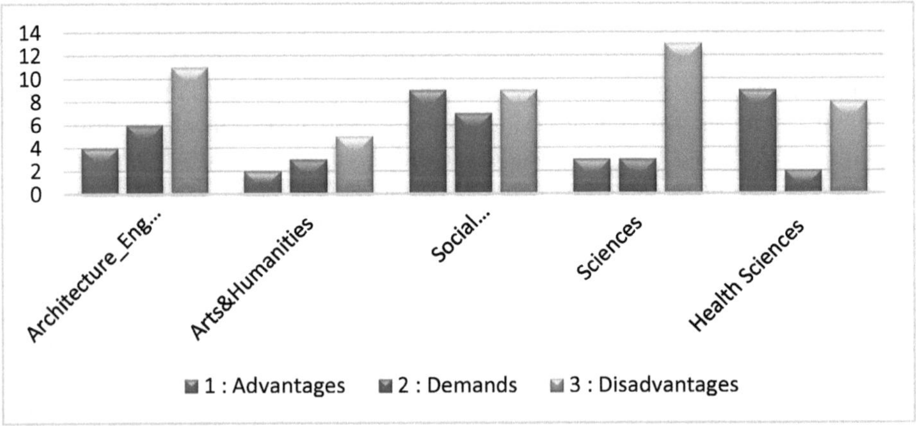

Fig. 5. Content analysis (Coding references by subject knowledge).

These qualitative results coincide with the items of the questionnaire related to the outgoing beliefs about teachers' perceptions of the use of the BL methodology. They are basically related to the consequences (advantages and disadvantages) for the teachers in their habitual teaching activity (Fig. 5 and Table 1).

Table 1. Main beliefs about the use of B-learning.

Advantages	Item	SD	Quite/strongly agree	No. Teachers
It would make my subjects more interesting and enjoyable	3.61	1.08	63.9%	627
It would make the learning of my students easier	3.61	1.02	59.8%	588
It would speed up the organization and presentation of the content to be learned	3.63	1.02	61.7%	606
It would speed up the organization and presentation of the content to be learned	3.46	1.06	52.9%	519
It would increase the motivation of my students	3.46	1.06	52.9%	519
It would make my teaching work more efficient	3.46	1.04	54%	530
Disadvantages				
It would require more work on my behalf	3.20	1.13	40.9%	401
I would need more time	3.20	1.13	59.0%	570
There is a need for knowledge of ICT resources	3.20	1.13	66.1%	649
There is a need for pedagogical knowledge	3.20	1.13	61.2%	591

The ANOVA analysis shows differences among the teachers according to the subject knowledge (F = 6.574, p = .000). Thus, science teachers are the ones who present lower evaluations of the utility of the BL methodology. On the other hand, there are no significant differences between teachers according to their academic category (ANOVA, F = .751, p = .585).

4 Conclusions

The positive factors highlighted by the teachers belonging to social sciences, law and health sciences are the following: better approach to social reality, more accessibility to practical cases and management of information, strengthening of digital competences, increase of students' autonomy and cooperative work, greater teacher-student interaction and meaningful learning. In addition, BL enhances communication and improves the evaluation processes. *"Nowadays, it is a basic element in higher education"* (law teacher); *"I consider it essential to develop digital competences, to improve students' autonomy and collaborative work"* (science teacher); *"It represents a better way to assess students and use the resources"* (health sciences teacher); *"The use of virtual methodology in the university enables this institution to respond to society's needs and the daily life of our citizens"* (health sciences teacher).

The disadvantages highlighted by the science teachers relate mainly to issues related to the high ratio of students, more time and personal effort, importance of face-to-face contact, poor coordination among teachers, personality impersonation, difficulty counting the hours in the activities that the student develops in a non-face-to-face manner, difficulty of integrating these activities in the evaluation process and the low motivation and high percentage of students dropping out. *"It gives you more work and nobody recognizes it"* (science teacher); *"A very high percentage of my students attend private academies to help them to pass the subject exams. It is an endemic problem. That is why many teachers abandoned the idea of using BL methodologies in the classroom as support for continuous Education. I have handed out a self-assessment questionnaire (of course, its resolution does not have any impact on the final grade), and the results have not been good"* (science teacher).

As for the demands, the engineering and architecture teachers demand better institutional policies, support in infrastructure and training. Social sciences and law teachers also demand specific regulations and teacher training initiatives from the faculty: *"The use of these methodologies cannot be left to the good will of each teacher. It must be an institutional policy, properly designed and financed, with a development plan correctly devised. The changes that are usually made in the Spanish university, in case someone wants to do something different, are upon a voluntarily basis, without coordination, etc."* (engineering professor); "*In my case, all the innovations in my classroom have been based on my will to do it. The teacher training courses are also not remunerated. This methodology option is voluntary and thus leads to disparity in both the offer and the assessment of teacher activity, subsisting the idea that (a) those who undertake this do so because there is time, (b) those who develop this teaching system devote fewer hours than those who use the traditional system, and, therefore, their teaching dedication is penalized"* (engineering professor); *"Institutional support is needed without half measures. If the student decides not to do the virtual work part, the teachers should not necessarily be blamed for it because it is not really their fault"* (engineering teacher); *"Shortage of resources and infrastructure for the use of the methodology"* (engineering teacher); *"Much more interest on the part of the universities in developing this type of methodology and explaining to the teachers what can be done and how teaching can be improved with this methodology and others"* (engineering professor); *"The absence of any institutional strategy for (a) the transition from face-to-face to B-learning; (b) the lack of institutional support for the development of B-learning through higher-quality technological tools; (c) the financing of educational innovation projects linked to teaching teams and specific titles related to B-learning; (d) the adaptation of the institutional organization to this modality (regulations); and (e) supporting the design, use and dissemination of open educational resources (OERs)"* (social sciences and law teachers).

Acknowledgements. Funding: This work was supported by the European Regional Development Fund (ERDF) and the Spanish Ministry of Economy and Competitiveness. I+D+i Plan. Project Ref. EDU2015-6721-R.

References

1. Bonk, C.J., Graham, C.R.: The Handbook of Blended Learning: Global Perspectives, Local Designs. Pfeiffer, San Francisco (2005)
2. Garrison, D.R., Vaughan, N.D.: Blended Learning in Higher Education: Framework, Principles, and Guidelines. Jossey-Bass, San Francisco (2007). https://doi.org/10.1002/9781118269558.fmatter
3. Margulieux, L.E., McCracken, W.M., Catrambone, R.: A taxonomy to define courses that mix face-to-face and online learning. Educ. Res. Rev. **19**, 104–118 (2016)
4. Dziuban, C., Graham, C.R., Moskal, P.D., Norberg, A., Sicilia, N.: Blended learning: the new normal and emerging technologies. Int. J. Educ. Technol. High. Educ. **15**(1), 3 (2018)
5. Becker, S.A., Cummins, M., Davis, A., Freeman, A., Hall, C.G., Ananthanarayanan, V.: NMC Horizon Report: 2017 Higher Education Edition, pp. 1–60. The New Media Consortium (2017)
6. Lim, C.P., Wang, L.: Blended Learning for Quality Higher Education: Selected Case Studies on Implementation from Asia-Pacific. UNESCO, Bangkok (2017)
7. Porter, W.W., Graham, C.R., Bodily, R.G., Sandberg, D.S.: A qualitative analysis of institutional drivers and barriers to blended learning adoption in higher education. Internet High. Educ. **28**, 17–27 (2016)
8. Ciabocchi, E., Ginsberg, A., Picciano, A.: A study of faculty governance leaders' perceptions of online and blended learning. Online Learn. **20**(3), 52–73 (2016)
9. Duarte Hueros, A., Guzmán Franco, M.D., Yot Domínguez, C.R.: Aportaciones de la formación blended learning al desarrollo profesional docente. RIED Revista Iberoamericana de Educación a Distancia **21**(1), 155–174 (2018). https://doi.org/10.5944/ried.21.1.19013
10. Ellis, R.A., Steed, A.F., Applebee, A.C.: Teacher conceptions of blended learning, blended teaching and associations with approaches to design. Australas. J. Educ. Technol. **22**(3), 312–335 (2006). https://doi.org/10.14742/ajet.128
11. Jokinen, P., Mikkonen, I.: Teachers' experiences of teaching in a blended learning environment. Nurse Educ. Pract. **13**(6), 524–528 (2013)
12. Martín García, A.V., Sánchez Gómez, M.C.: Modelo predictivo de la intención de adopción de Blended learning en profesores universitarios. Universitas Psychologica **13**(2), 601–614 (2014)
13. Venezky, R.L., Davis, C.: Quo vademus? The transformation of schooling in a networked world. Version 8c. OECD Centre for Educational Research and Innovation, Paris (2002). www.OECD.org/pdf/M00027000/M00027107.pdf
14. Eickelmann, B., Vennemann, M.: Teachers' attitudes and beliefs regarding ICT in teaching and learning in European countries. Eur. Educ. Res. J. **16**(6), 733–761 (2017)
15. Ajzen, I.: The theory of planned behavior. Organ. Behav. Hum. Decis. Process. **50**(2), 179–211 (1991)
16. Davis, F.D.: Perceived usefulness, perceived ease of use, and user acceptance of information technology. MIS Q. **13**(3), 319 (1989). https://doi.org/10.2307/249008
17. Venkatesh, V., Davis, F.D.: A theoretical extension of the technology acceptance model: four longitudinal field studies. Manage. Sci. **46**(2), 186–204 (2000)
18. Venkatesh, V., Bala, H.: Technology acceptance model 3 and a research agenda on interventions. Decis. Sci. **39**(2), 273–315 (2008). https://doi.org/10.1111/j.1540-5915.2008.00192.x
19. Al-Busaidi, K.A.: An empirical investigation linking learners' adoption of blended learning to their intention of full e-learning. Behav. Inf. Technol. **32**(11), 1168–1176 (2013). https://doi.org/10.1080/0144929X.2013.774047

20. Chen, J.L.: The effects of education compatibility and technological expectancy on e-learning acceptance. Comput. Educ. **57**, 1501–1511 (2011)
21. Konak, A., Kulturel-Konak, S., Nasereddin, M., Bartolacci, M.R.: Impact of collaborative work on technology acceptance: a case study from virtual computing. J. Inf. Technol. Educ. **16**(1), 15–29 (2017)
22. Teo, T.: Comparing pre-service and in-service teachers' acceptance of technology: assessment of measurement invariance and latent mean differences. Comput. Educ. 83, 22–31 (2015). https://doi.org/10.1016/j.compedu.2014.11.015
23. Venkatesh, V., Thong, J.L., Xu, X.: Unified theory of acceptance and use of technology: a synthesis and the road ahead. J. Assoc. Inf. Syst. **17**(5), 328–376 (2016). https://ssrn.com/abstract=2800121
24. Porter, W.W., Graham, C.R.: Institutional drivers and barriers to faculty adoption of blended learning in higher education. Br. J. Educ. Technol. **47**(4), 748–762 (2016). https://doi.org/10.1111/bjet.12269
25. Hernández Sampieri, R., Fernández Collado, C., Baptista Lucio, P.: Metodología de la investigación, 6a edn. Editorial Mc Graw Hill, México (2014)
26. Creswell, J.W., Clark, V.L.P.: Designing and Conducting Mixed Methods Research. Sage Publications, Thousand Oaks (2017)
27. Tashakkori, A., Teddlie, C. (eds.): Sage Handbook of Mixed Methods in Social & Behavioral Research. Sage, Thousand Oaks (2010)
28. Sánchez-Gómez, M.C., García, A.V.M.: Convergence between quantitative and qualitative methodological orientations: mixed models. In: Costa, A.P., Reis, L.P., Souza, F.N., Moreira, A. (eds.) ISQR 2017. AISC, vol. 621, pp. 341–357. Springer, Cham (2018). https://doi.org/10.1007/978-3-319-61121-1_29
29. Fishbein, M., Ajzen, I.: Predicting and Changing Behavior: The Reasoned Action Approach. Psychology Press, New York (2011)
30. Venkatesh, V., Morris, M.G., Davis, G.B., Davis, F.D.: User acceptance of information technology: toward a unified view. MIS Q. **27**(3), 425–478 (2003). https://doi.org/10.2307/30036540
31. Brown, S.A., Dennis, A.R., Venkatesh, V.: Predicting collaboration technology use: integrating technology adoption and collaboration research. J. Manage. Inf. Syst. **27**(2), 9–54 (2010). https://doi.org/10.2753/MIS0742-1222270201
32. Teo, T., Fan, X., Du, J.: Technology acceptance among pre-service teachers: does gender matter? Australas. J. Educ. Technol. **31**, 235–251 (2015)
33. Pynoo, B., Devolder, P., Tondeur, J., Van Braak, J., Duyck, W., Duyck, P.: Predicting secondary school teachers' acceptance and use of a digital learning environment: a crosssectional study. Comput. Hum. Behav. **27**(1), 568–575 (2011)
34. Šumak, B., Šorgo, A.: The acceptance and use of interactive whiteboards among teachers: differences in UTAUT determinants between pre-and post-adopters. Comput. Hum. Behav. **64**, 602–620 (2016)
35. Lincoln, Y.S., Guba, E.G.: Naturalistic Inquiry, vol. 75. Sage, Thousand Oaks (1985)
36. Guba, E.G., Lincoln, Y.S.: Fourth Generation Evaluation. Sage, Thousand Oaks (1989)
37. Sánchez Gómez, M.C., Delgado, M.C., Santos, M.C.: El proceso de la investigación cualitativa. Manual de procedimiento: ejemplificación con una tesis doctoral. Editras, Salamanca (2012)
38. Palacios Vicario, B., Sánchez Gómez, M.C., Gutiérrez García, A.: Evaluar la calidad en la investigación cualitativa. Guías o checklists. In: Actas del 20 Congreso Nacional sobre Metodología de la Investigación en Comunicación, vol. 3, pp. 581−596 (2013)
39. García-Peñalvo, F.J., Moreno López, L., Sánchez-Gómez, M.C.: Qual. Quant. **52**, 2427 (2018). https://doi.org/10.1007/s11135-018-0808-4

Motivating Engineer Students in E-learning Courses with Problem Based Learning and Self-Regulated Learning on the apT^{2}CLE4'Research Methods' Environment

Foteini Paraskeva[1], Aikaterini Alexiou[1], Hara Bouta[1](✉), Sofia Mysirlaki[1], Dimitrios J. Sotiropoulos[2], and Aikaterini-Maria Souki[1]

[1] Department of Digital Systems, University of Piraeus, Pireas, Greece
fparaske@unipi.gr, katialexiou@gmail.com, bouta.hr@gmail.com, smysirlaki@gmail.com
[2] Department of Computer Science, University of Thessaly, Volos, Greece
sotiropoulosdimitris@gmail.com

Abstract. More and more university programs try to establish an understanding of research methodology with relevant courses at undergraduate schools. Engineer students should have adequate academic training and experience to gain knowledge on such research content, should be able to thrive in research, to source valid and credible information by sorting out the best solution of a problem. Due to their complexity, these courses are usually unpopular with students. To this end, we propose an educational well-designed conceptual framework based on PBL and SRL, as an orchestrated educational scenario with the design, the development and the evaluation of the learning process, customized on Moodle for engineer students to motivate them in the field of scientific research. The analysis of the results reveals that our proprosed scenario fosters motivation, equips students with learning strategies, supports them to understand and apply the principles of PBL method as they acquire concepts of research methodology.

Keywords: Problem Based Learning · Self regulation learning · Motivation · Engineering education

1 Introduction

More and more university programs seek to establish an understanding of research methodology at undergraduate schools, expecting students to cultivate knowledge of research methodology. As said before, such courses are usually unpopular with students. Eg. engineers will confront problems and will need to devise innovative and practical solutions by sorting out the optimum. In order to gain insight in such research content, students should be able to thrive in research, in other words to source valid and credible information to formulate feasible solutions. These are vital skills that all

L. Uden et al. (Eds.): LTEC 2019, CCIS 1011, pp. 189–201, 2019.
https://doi.org/10.1007/978-3-030-20798-4_17

engineers are required to have for research cases and activities in their every day practice. Engineer students should have adequate academic training and experience to address future cases as professionals.

On the other hand, research has shown that in order to reinforce students' involvement in learning and developing practical skills, Problem-Based Learning (PBL) is of upmost importance [1]. Within the learning process, the PBL is able to develop mastery related to problem solving, to enhance self-efficacy beliefs as well as time management and other self-regulated skills [1, 2]. Consequently, the PBL has a constructive influence on enhancing students' motivation for self-learning while they work in teams. Solving lifelike problems is among the basic elements of the educational process [3].

Moreover, Self-regulated learning (SRL) is acknowledged as a valid forecaster of the student's academic motivation and accomplishments. In teaching students to be more self-regulative, numerous factors have been pinpointed as essential in students' active role in their learning process: cognition, metacognition, motivation, behaviour and context [4, 5]. Between those, context is regarded the central factor in encouraging or not self-regulated learning [6]. This notion refers to a fundamental process for students, in order to obtain academic skills for goal-setting, discerning and forming strategies, and supervising their own efficiency [4]. Therefore, students must be equipped with the SRL competence, in order to become in charge of their own learning and inwardly orientated.

Based on the above, as learning is intricate and academic training is not satisfactory on these research cases, we propose PBL as an educational well-designed conceptual framework and SRL as learning process, in order to narrow the gap between the theoretical and practical knowledge for engineer students as prospective educators and professional engineers in the future. Problem-based learning (PBL) as an instructional model and Self-Regulated Learning (SRL) as a model for the learning process were suggested for students' comprehension of research methodology at the university course. By utilizing the conceptual framework on (PBL), students were asked to build online activities on a Learning Management System (LMS) system as the center project complying with all the SRL processes, so as to become independent learners.

More explicitly, this paper describes the apT^{2}CLE environment, designed along the lines of PBL and SRL, to reinforce motivation, learning strategies and bring about learning results. A case of Research Methods for engineer students in the context of an e-learning course.

2 Theoretical Background

2.1 LMS and Educational Challenges for PBL and SRL

As society needs professionals with complex skills, learning has to comply with the new demands. Consequently, the educational system must make sure that students gain skills like team- working, organizing team-work, communicating ideas and concepts and administrative techniques [7]. This translates to a change in traditional class dynamics as collaborative learning paradigms are becoming more and more noticeable both in traditional and online learning. One of these paradigms, Problem Based Learning (PBL), has been in the educational field for a long time with confirmed results in developing situated learning as well as involving students in ill-structuring learning problems [1, 7].

Modern LMS offer a broad range of possibilities that promote the synthesis of PBL and other communal paradigms in class dynamics. Wikis, databases, glossaries, class or group forums and chat-rooms are a few tools to mention that teachers have at their disposal to endorse collaborative pedagogical methods in the most popular LMS (e.g. Moodle, Sakai, Blackboard, etc.) [7]. Several higher educational institutions have started to apply web-based learning platforms in a position to deliver online education on an incorporated learning academic background. Moodle, a free open-source software package, is used by educators to create online courses [8]. The use of Moodle has been cited by several literatures as an effective tool for teacher course administrative tasks, for improving student inquiry and critical analysis skills, inducing self-directed learning and promoting collaborative activities [9, 10].

Moreover, research shows that students should be capable of modifying their cognitive, affective, contextual and behavioral states to apply SRL. It seems that a few cognitive and metacognitive strategies should be applied by learners, in order to upgrade their learning experience and goals. These cognitive strategies could be experimenting, developing, arranging, processing information and thinking critically. In addition, students can adapt their thinking by managing their self-efficacy beliefs which, in turn, influence diverse processes like self-control and self-monitoring. The great social aspect of SRL is pinpointed here, as learners are motivated to deploy their peers as a source of interaction and knowledge (work well with peers) [11]. Taking into consideration all the above, Moodle can support and enhance the integration of PBL theory. Students will collaborate and create online activities along the line with all the SRL processes in order to become independent learners and also involve in research process. As a result, they will find motivation and build learning strategies.

2.2 PBL and SRL in Engineering Education

Studies suggested that the engineering curricula are too focused on engineering science and technical courses without providing sufficient integration of these topics, therefore such programs do not provide sufficient design experiences [12].

PBL is currently used in many of the top engineering programs. From those that extensively use PBL, students graduate with strong design and team skills [12]. PBL facilitates SRL because it sets the student to be responsible for discovering information, coordinating people and operations, monitoring understanding and being effective [13]. The different models of Self-Regulated Learning (SRL), share the same theory on students' driving motives and behaviour in order to have greater performance. Zimmerman [14] created a cyclical model of SRL which applied to education. Zimmerman's cyclical model of SRL includes three phases: 'Forethought phase', 'Performance Control' and 'Self-Reflection'.

Having said that, the pedagogical approach of PBL and the figurative manner of SLR in self-learning both support the construction and application of engineering curricula by successfully integrating science engineering relevant topics. This can be accomplished due to the fact that PBL runs through the process of raising a question, then researching, reasoning by using logical constructions, testing and developing a hypothesis by juxtaposition of evidence. Both co-students and teachers can come up with meaningful approaches [15]. The three main phases are:

(a) Project or problem launch, (b) guided inquiry and product/solution creation, and (c) project or problem conclusion [15, 16].

When the PBL and the SRL are implemented together students are guaranteed sufficient design experiences. Graduate engineering students interact uniquely as each different phase of PBL provides the ground for distinct self-regulatory processes; To this effect, the self-regulated learning procedure boosts student's performance during the three phases of PBL [16].

Moreover, in PBL environments, engineering students cooperate to conduct research in groups, put logic and reasoning into practice, and derive solutions to complicated problems. The necessary Project/Problem Launch (PBL) is achieved through SRL processes while establishing the roles of individuals in a team, or organising plans. In consequence, communication skills are improved and teamwork experience is enriched as the students accomplish tasks that must be acknowledged in the real world. Along with the students' involvement in solving multiple-solution problems (ill-structured problems), all the above foster a deeper understanding of social, economic, environmental, and legal nature matters [12].

On the grounds that engineering curricula teaching and learning strategies are not student-centered, they need to be updated [12]. The PBL pedagogical approach meets the criteria as it is student-oriented and inquiry-based. It develops the necessary real-world skills through promoting critical thinking, effective communication and cooperation [17]. Under the PBL approach students acquire a new role as active learners and develop self-regulated learning (SRL) skills. This means they are intrinsically motivated to set a goal, plan the course of action, select the appropriate strategies, self-monitor their learning, and self-evaluate their performance. What they report is high self-efficacy [18].

In our study, the proposed framework describes the specific learning environment features (SRL process) and teaching practices (PBL workflow) on a case of 'Research Methods' by a customization of Moodle features, in order to engage engineering learners in practical-based experience and ill-structured problems.

3 Methodology

This paper proposes the development of an e-learning course for 'Research Methods' for engineer students. In detail, the paper describes an orchestrated educational scenario with the design, the development and the evaluation of a conceptual framework based on Problem-based learning (PBL) and Self-Regulated Learning (SRL), through a learning management (LMS/Moodle) to motivate and support engineer students in the field of scientific research, as discipline. The proposed framework describes specific learning environment features (SRL process) and teaching practices (PBL workflow) on a case of 'Research Methods' by a customization of Moodle features, in order to engage learners in practical-based experience and ill-structured problems.

The objectives of the educational scenario were to provide learners skills in understanding research approaches, research inquiry, scientific thinking, following an instructional design model (PBL) in correlation with an autonomous learning path and responsibility, (SRL) gaining skills (setting goals, monitoring, reflecting, and sustaining their motivation from the beginning of a problem until the end) to perform effectively in an inquiry process as engineers (survey design, strategic manner, data management, statistical analysis, optimization techniques in real-world examples, problem solving skills).

We conducted a quasi-experimental research within a sample of 40 students of a university of computer science department, throughout a course entitled apT2-CLE4'Research Methods' on Moodle.

The objectives of the study were following the research questions:

In what extent, the design and implementation of e-learning 'Research Methods' course orchestrated along the lines of Problem-based Learning method combined with the processes of Self-Regulated Learning

RQ1: fosters Motivations and Learning strategies

RQ2: supports students to understand and apply principles of PBL method in every day educational practices

RQ3: supports students to acquire concepts of Research methodology

The sample of the study consisted of 40 undergraduate students, who participated voluntarily in the apT2CLE4'Research Methods'. Within the same group, the experimental group (N = 40) followed the process of implementing the proposed workflow of the e-course based on of PBL & SRL, in order to enhance students' self-regulated learning skills (motivation and learning strategies), problem solving skills (PBL scenario) and learning outcomes (research skills & scientific thinking skills).

Within a criterion-based system (rubric objectives criterion/included tutor assessment, self-assessment, peer-assessment) the students and teachers completed the tests to render the measurement of the students' perception and abilities to solve the case-problem. The measurements were conducted by the following rubrics:

(i) The 'SRL Questionnaire', as an adapted version of MSLQ [19] with two parts). The first part measured the 'motivation scale', (value components, expectancy components, affective components). The second part measured 'the learning strategies' (cognitive and metacognitive learning strategies, Resource Management Strategies. The questionnaire was formed on 1-7 Likert scale.
(ii) The 'PBL script Rubric', was used to evaluate the students' adequate involvement in the PBL framework and activities (evaluation of the final deliverables after the experimental procedure, including a 4-degree Likert scale, with the sub-factors: the problem, learning goals, interdisciplinarity, reflection, evaluation). The questionaire is based on Combs thesis [20].
(iii) The 'Cognitive and Metacognitive Evaluation' is an adaptive Rubric of 20 questions aimed at assessing whether students acquired the concepts they were taught, with the following sub-factors: research articles, research design, statistical criteria and analysis. The questionnaire tested with Cronbach's a for internal reliability.

The ApT^2CLE4'Research Methods' environment: many university programs seek to improve an understanding of research methodology at the undergraduate schools, requiring students to develop knowledge of research methodology content. Unfortunately, research methods courses are typically unpopular with students because the course material is complex and technical in nature. Within engineering education, engineers will be faced with problems that require to devise innovative and practical solutions judging the best one. For gaining knowledge on this research content the students should engage in research, be able to source valid and credible information in order to formulate viable solutions. These are important skills that all engineers need in research cases and activities in everyday practices.

As engineer students will be faced with research cases in their every day professional life the apT2CLE4'Research Methods' aim to equip them with the skills needed to conduct valid research in academic or industrial practices in ICT science, computer engineering etc. To this end, as learning is complex and academic training is not sufficient on these research cases, we propose the apT2CLE4'Research Methods' based on PBL as an instructional well-designed conceptual framework and SRL as learning process in order to bridge the gap between the theoretical and practical knowledge for engineer students as potential educators and engineers in action in the future. Thus, supplement e-courses, such as the apT2CLE4'Research Methods' on the traditional lecture classes with active learning experiences, are emerging for academic courses (CLE: Collaborative Learning Environment).

The apT2CLE4'Research Methods' aimed at representing students' understanding of research methodology by facilitating the SRL learning process in goal setting, goal orientation, performance control in writing research activities, producing research cases and articles and submitting all this research proposal on the LMS/Moodle system. The research activities were conducted within the conceptual PBL framework and the research investigations were chosen on authentic problems, according to the nature of Research Methods, setting the research problem, objectives of investigation, scopes and research evidence for these problems.

3.1 The apT^2CLE4'Research Methods' as Experimental Design and Learning Procedure

We introduce apT2CLE4'Research Methods' environment, which is based on the open source learning management system, Moodle (Modular Object-Oriented Dynamic Learning Environment). As Moodle is open and customizable, it provided us a with a flexible toolset as well as an extensive plugins directory for apT2CLE4'Research Methods'.

The aim of the experimental design was the development of the apT2CLE4 'Research Methods' to implement a research project as part of the CLE academic course on TELE based on PBL and applying the principles of SRL within a learning management system of Moodle. In an academic Department of Digital Science the apT2CLE4'Research Methods' environment on Moodle was designed, developed and implemented for a group of 40 students.

Specifically, students got involved with the following case: "As graduating students at the university and new researchers, please prepare your thesis. What steps will you follow to deliver a robust scientific work?"

In particular, the educational goals were: (a) understanding the process of Problem Based Learning (b) strengthening the Self-Regulated Learning Skills, (c) understanding and applying the subject of 'Research Methodology'.

The learning process structure is based on the model of self-regulated learning of Zimmerman [14] and the model of problem solving according to the seven phases (plus phase 0) [1, 21]. The whole educational intervention is structured in a way that consists of the 3 phases of self-regulated learning which incorporate the PBL phases from the method of problem solving as shown below in the Fig. 1.

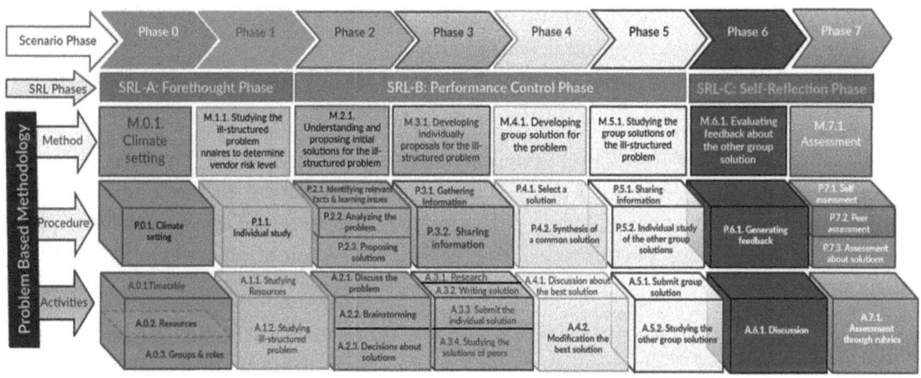

Fig. 1. The apT2CLE4'Research Methods' as a conceptional model for the orchestrated educational scenario

Analytically, students get involved in each phase of the workflow so as to solve the ill-structured problem (See Fig. 1):

SRL Phase A: 'Forethought' Phase: Students enter the SRL cycle for planning their learning efforts. The primary aim of the initial phase is focused on learners' preparation, with regard to the learning process schedule, their assignment to teams, the clarification of their roles within their teams and their registration to the apT2-CLE4'Research Methods'. In this phase students organize their learning path for understanding the principles of research methodology and implementing it on their research project. Each student, hence, gets involved in specific activities, including: goal setting and strategic goal planning and studying the ill-structuring problem. The educational scenario as an instructional design setting is divided into 2 phases:

- PBL Phase 0: includes learners' preparation for the learning procedures (PBL climate setting) onto the apT2CLE4'Research Methods'
- PBL Phase 1: includes studying about the ill-structured problem via resources uploaded onto the apT2CLE4'Research Methods'.

SRL Phase B: 'Performance Control' Phase: Students proceed to the second phase of SRL where they gather and elaborate on information that complements their learning efforts. In this phase, students explore their learning path and attempt to create and structure their research project. Students (individual and group mode) also get engaged in specific learning activities such as familiarizing with learning strategies and identifying the SRL process. The educational scenario is divided into 4 phases as instructional design procedures:

- PBL Phase 2: includes a thorough understanding and proposing of initial solutions for the ill-structured problem (identifying relevant facts, chunking and analyzing the problem, proposing solutions)
- PBL Phase 3: Developing individual proposals for the ill-structured problem (gathering information, sharing information).
- PBL Phase 4: Developing group solution for the problem (select the solution, synthesize the common optimal solution).
- PBL Phase 5: Studying the group solutions of the ill-structured problem (sharing information, individual study of the other groups).

SRL Phase C: 'Self-Reflection' Phase: While in the third phase, students reflect on the learning activities performed to evaluate their performance. In this phase, students evaluate their research project, their performance and their collaboration. This phase includes self-judgement performed along with a self-evaluation and self-monitoring questionnaire.

- PBL Phase 6: Evaluating feedback about the other group solution (provide mutual feedback between 2 teams with regard to the team solution proposals for the ill-structured problem, generate feedback).
- PBL Phase 7: Assessment Includes learners' reflection on the learning process by virtue of completing self-report questionnaires (self-assessment, peer assessment, knowledge assessment).

Within the end of the educational scenario, the students were able to apply the process of instructional design and learning on a digital environment, incorporating appropriate solutions (cases) and to propose the best solution in situative learning through reflective thinking in action.

4 Data Analysis

A t-test paired – samples test was carried out to reveal significant differences between the pre-test and post-test results for both Motivation and Learning Strategies scales of MSLQ questionnaire. Table 1 describes the results of the t-test for the Motivation scale and Table 2 describes the results of the t-test for the Learning Strategies scale.

The analysis of the results (Table 1) reveals a statistically significant difference in average values for each of the sub-scales and the total of the Motivation scale before and after the intervention, since all relevant levels are less than 0.05. A significant improvement has therefore emerged following the intervention based on the results of the Motivation scale before and after the intervention.

Table 1. Motivation scale. Results of t-test for the sub-scales and the total scale

Pairs	Sub-scales	Mean	Std. deviation	Std. error mean	95% Confidence		t	df	Sig. (2-tailed)
					Lower	Upper			
Pair 1	Intrinsic goal orientation	−.800	1.205	.191	−1.185	−.415	−4.198	39	.000
Pair 2	Extrinsic goal orientation	−.431	.969	.153	−.741	−.121	−2.815	39	.008
Pair 3	Task value	−1.175	.928	.147	−1.472	−.878	−8.005	39	.000
Pair 4	Value component	−1.135	.824	.130	−1.399	−.872	−8.718	39	.000
Pair 5	Control beliefs	−.663	1.240	.196	−1.059	−.266	−3.380	39	.002
Pair 6	Self-efficacy	−.341	.950	.150	−.645	−.037	−2.267	39	.029
Pair 7	Expectancy component	−.492	1.313	.208	−.912	−.072	−2.371	39	.023
Pair 8	Affective component	−.612	1.347	.213	−1.043	−.182	−2.876	39	.006
Pair 9	Motivation total	−.916	.807	.128	−1.174	−.659	−7.186	39	.000

Table 2. Learning strategies. Results of t-test for the sub-scales and total scale

Pairs	Sub-scales	Mean	Std. deviation	Std. error mean	95% Confidence		t	df	Sig. (2-tailed)
					Lower	Upper			
Pair 1	Rehearsal	−.338	.991	.157	−.655	−.020	−2.153	39	.038
Pair 2	Elaboration	−.380	1.044	.165	−.714	−.046	−2.301	39	.027
Pair 3	Organization	−.564	.940	.149	−.864	−.263	−3.792	39	.001
Pair 4	Critical thinking	−.901	1.256	.199	−1.303	−.500	−4.538	39	.000
Pair 5	Metacognitive self - regulation	.065	1.106	.175	−.288	.419	.374	39	.710
Pair 6	Time management	.589	.980	.155	.275	.902	3.797	39	.000
Pair 7	Effort regulation	−.652	.939	.148	−.952	−.352	−4.395	39	.000
Pair 8	Peer learning	−.248	1.044	.165	−.582	.086	−1.502	39	.141
Pair 9	Help seeking	.487	.882	.140	.205	.770	3.494	39	.001
Pair 10	Resource management strategies	−.472	1.050	.166	−.808	−.136	−2.844	39	.007
Pair 11	Cognitive and metacognitive learning strategies	−.450	.803	.127	−.707	−.193	−3.542	39	.001
Pair 12	Learning strategies	−.271	.769	.122	−.518	−.025	−2.231	39	.031

The analysis of the results (Table 2) reveals a statistically significant difference between mean values in almost all sub-scales and the total of Learning Strategies scale. The difference before and after the intervention is statistically significant, since almost all the relevant levels are less than 0.05. The exceptions are the sub-scales: Metacognitive Self–Regulation and Peer Learning, where there is no statistically significant difference before and after the intervention, since the corresponding levels of significance are greater than 0.05. A significant improvement has therefore emerged following the intervention based on the results of the Learning Strategies scale before and after the intervention.

Table 3 describes the results of the t-test which was applied to the "PBL script Rubric" before and after the intervention in order to determine whether the average values found are substantially greater than 2. The analysis of the results (Table 3) reveals significantly higher values than 2 in the: Problem, Learning Objectives, Role of learners, Role of teachers and in Cross-curricular/Interdisciplinarity sub-scales.

Table 3. Results of t – test applied to the "PBL script Rubric" after the intervention.

	t	df	Sig. (2-tailed)	Mean difference	95% Confidence	
					Lower	Upper
Problem	7.369	40	.000	1.073	.78	1.37
Learning objectives	11.246	40	.000	1.415	1.16	1.67
Learners role	14.863	40	.000	1.317	1.14	1.50
Teacher role	4.913	40	.000	.878	.52	1.24
Activities	−1.817	40	.077	−.244	−.52	.03
Collaboration	−4.901	40	.000	−.488	−.69	−.29
Interdisciplinarity	3.296	40	.002	.415	.16	.67
Reflection	−9.242	40	.000	−.805	−.98	−.63
Evaluation	−8.315	40	.000	−.756	−.94	−.57

Table 4 shows the results of t-test applied to questionnaire "Cognitive and Metacognitive Evaluation" after the intervention. The analysis of the results reveals that the average values of both sub-scales and total are substantially less than 1.5, because all the relevant levels of Sig (2-tailed) are less than 0.05. So the whole educational process can be judged to be a learning success.

Table 4. Results of t – test applied to questionnaire 'Cognitive and Metacognitive Evaluation'.

Sub-scales	t	df	Sig. (2-tailed)	Mean difference	95% Confidence	
					Lower	Upper
Research and kind of research	−10.907	36	.000	−.275	−.33	−.22
Research design	−7.188	36	.000	−.257	−.33	−.18
Statistical analysis - Criteria	−10.714	36	.000	−.264	−.31	−.21
Total	−13.479	36	.000	−.265	−.30	−.23

The questionnaire tested with Cronbach's a for internal reliability with a total degree of reliability: 0.823, that is considered very good value for that indicator [22].

5 Discussion – Suggestions for Further Research

This paper describes the apT2CLE4'Research Methods' environment designed along the lines of PBL and SRL to enhance motivation, learning strategies and learning outcomes in a case of Research Methods, part of the content of CLE course in Technology Enhanced Learning Environment (TELE), by exploiting multiple student-developed mini cases of research projects.

Statistical analysis (Tables 1 and 2) of the completed questionnaires (based on an adaptive version of MSLQ) showed positive results in all cases of the subfactors studied. Statistically significant were the most of the results in the field of Learning Strategies where only two sub-factors out of eleven, were found not to be statistically signifigant.

The t-test paired – samples (Table 1) revealed the environment motivating students to set goals and to seek ways to solve problems/cases. Improvement exists in all subfactors contributing to it such as the: Task Value, Extrinsic Goal Orientation, Self-Efficacy, mentioning some of the sub-factors of Motivation Scale that are fully reffered to Table 1. And it is well known that motivation is one of the most important values in learning.

Regarding the t-test for the Learning Strategies (Table 2), these findings reveal that the use of the proposed methodology along with the apT2CLE4'Research Methods' environment indeed tend to enhance learner's skills in the appropriate use of learning strategies.

Through the use of SRL phases, learners have the ability to monitor and regulate their learning process thus achieving organizational and meta-cognitive skills. In parallel other factors such as Critical Thinking, Resource Management and Time which are related to the learner's motivation to learn, tend to improve through the use of the SRL methodology implemented in the instructional design workflow.

Improvement, but not statistically important, is also present in subfactors of Metacognitive Self - Regulation and Peer Learning. We should pay attention to these subfactors and set out to improve them. This could happen if appropriate activities were added to the apT2CLE4'Research Methods' environment to this direction. To this end, Moodle data related to time and used in certain pages and the kind of communication between learners and their posts within the platform could be used.

From Table 3 we easily derive the conclusion that the principles and methodology of PBL as perceived by students leads them to use the PBL method in the best possible way. Furthermore, the findings from the last questionnaire given, revealed that what the students of apT2CLE4'Research Methods' environment learned from the whole process was what the case had put as learning results. This is an important element that reproves the coherence of the methods and the complementarity of procedures within the course. Overall we can claim that findings suggest that this blended Learning environment, designed along the lines of PBL and SRL, could enhance students' skills for an active participation in the problemsolving process of ill-structured problems and the reinforcement of their 21st century skills (collaboration, self-directed learning and critical thinking), as depicted in the four tables.

Acknowledgements. The publication of this paper has been partly supported by the University of Piraeus Research Center.

References

1. Barrows, H.S.: Problem-based learning in medicine and beyond: a brief overview. New Dir. Teach. Learn. **1996**(68), 3–12 (1996)
2. Hmelo-Silver, C.E.: Problem-based learning: what and how do students learn? Educ. Psychol. Rev. **16**(3), 235–266 (2004)
3. Surif, J., Ibrahimb, N.H., Mokhtarc, M.: Implementation of problem based learning in higher education institutions and its impact on students' learning. In: PBL Across Cultures, p. 66 (2013)
4. Zimmerman, B.J.: Investigating self-regulation and motivation: historical background, methodological developments, and future prospects. Am. Educ. Res. J. **45**(1), 166–183 (2008)
5. Zumbrunn, S., Tadlock, J., Roberts, E.D.: Encouraging self-regulated learning in the classroom: a review of the literature. In: Metropolitan Educational Research Consortium (MERC), pp. 1–28 (2011)
6. Agina, A.M., Kommers, P.A., Steehouder, M.F.: The effect of the external regulator's absence on children's speech use, manifested self-regulation, and task performance during learning tasks. Comput. Hum. Behav. **27**(3), 1118–1128 (2011)
7. Sancho, P., Torrente, J., Marchiori, E.J., Fernández-Manjón, B.: Enhancing Moodle to support problem based learning. The nucleo experience. In: 2011 IEEE Global Engineering Education Conference (EDUCON), pp. 1177–1182. IEEE (2011)
8. Estacio, R.R., Raga Jr., R.C.: Analyzing students online learning behavior in blended courses using moodle. Asian Assoc. Open Univ. J. **12**(1), 52–68 (2017)
9. Perkins, M., Pfaffman, J.: Using a course management system to improve classroom communication. Sci. Teacher-Wash. **73**(7), 33 (2006)
10. López, G.A., Sáenz, J., Leonardo, A., Gurtubay, I.G.: Use of the Moodle platform to promote an ongoing learning when lecturing general physics in the physics, mathematics and electronic engineering programmes at the University of the Basque Country UPV/EHU. J. Sci. Educ. Technol. **25**(4), 575–589 (2016)
11. Alexiou A., Paraskeva, F.: Triggering students' ability to influence their motivation and affect through a self-regulated career oriented ePortfolio. In: AERA Annual Meeting: The Dreams, Possibilities, and Necessity of Public Education, New York, pp. 13–17 (2018)
12. Hitt, J.: Problem-based learning in engineering, Center for Teaching Excellence. United States Military Academy, West Point, New York (2010)
13. Paris, S.G., Paris, A.H.: Classroom applications of research on self-regulated learning. Educ. Psychol. **36**(2), 89–101 (2001)
14. Zimmerman, B.J.: Attaining self-regulation: a social cognitive perspective. In: Boekaerts, M., Pintrich, P.R., Zeidner, M. (eds.) Handbook of Self-regulation, pp. 13–39. Academic Press, San Diego (2000)
15. Mergendoller, J.R., Maxwell, N.L., Bellisimo, Y.: The effectiveness of problem-based instruction: a comparative study of instructional methods and student characteristics. Interdisc. J. Prob.-based Learn. **1**(2), 5 (2006)

16. English, M.C., Kitsantas, A.: Supporting student self-regulated learning in problem- and project-based learning. Interdisc. J. Prob.-Based Learn. **7**(2), 6 (2013)
17. Duch, B.J., Groh, S.E., Allen, D.E.: The Power of Problem-Based Learning: A Practical "How to" for Teaching Undergraduate Courses in Any Discipline. Stylus Publishing, LLC, Dulles (2001)
18. Zimmerman, B.J., Kitsantas, A.: The Hidden Dimension of Personal Competence: Self-Regulated Learning and Practice (2005)
19. Pintrich, P.R., De Groot, E.V.: Motivational and self-regulated learning components of classroom academic performance. J. Educ. Psychol. **82**(1), 33 (1990)
20. Combs, L.M.: The design, development and evaluation of a problem-based learning module: implications for teaching digital technology skills to middle school students (Doctoral dissertation, Virginia Tech) (2008)
21. Hoidn, S., Kärkkäinen, K.: Promoting Skills for Innovation in Higher Education: A Literature Review on the Effectiveness of Problem-based Learning and Teaching Behaviours, OECD Education Working Papers, No. 100 OECD Publing (2014). http://dx.doi.org/10.1787/5k3tsj671226-en
22. George, D., Mallery, P.: SPSS for Windows Step by Step: A Simple Guide and Reference. 11.0 Update, 4th edn. Allyn & Bacon, Boston (2003)

Developing a MOOC to Foster Information Literacy (IL) by Means of a Conjecture Map

Sabine Seufert, Josef Guggemos, Luca Moser(✉), and Stefan Sonderegger

Institute of Business Education and Educational Management, Digital Learning & Corporate Learning, University of St. Gallen, 9000 St. Gallen, Switzerland
{sabine.seufert,josef.guggemos,luca.moser, stefan.sonderegger}@unisg.ch

Abstract. Teachers feel often insecure when handling digital media pedagogically and therefore need tools to support them. The present contribution shows how to develop an easy-to-use digital learning design to foster information literacy [IL] – the development of a Massive Open Online Course [MOOC]. This open form of digital learning setting is necessary to foster IL effectively as the handling of digital information is the main concern of IL at present. The Educational Design Research is conducted by means of conjecture mapping, what allows for a combined study of learning and teaching and its interdependence in a given learning setting. Derived from our high level conjectures, (I): IL consists of several interdependent competences, (II): a digital learning environment is crucial to foster IL, (III): an open and learner centered design is necessary, and (IV): a good MOOC follows defined principles, the MOOC has been developed. The MOOC lays ground for the yet to follow measure and improvement of the learning design.

Keywords: Conjecture map · Information literacy · MOOC · Open education

1 Introduction

In an increasingly interconnected knowledge economy and society, competent handling of information (information literacy [IL]) is decisive: The UNESCO (2013) considers IL as a key competence necessary for participating in the 21st century society. IL might also be a precondition for lifelong learning [8].

In the information age, children and pupils are being exposed to and have to deal with digital media and information, starting from early childhood [9] Consequently, the current generation of students is often referred to as "digital natives" [23]. This means they are familiar with digital devices as they have been using them their entire life. Promoting IL, therefore, may seem unnecessary because digital natives are information literate anyway. In this light, we have carried out two research projects with Swiss students on the upper secondary level [29, 30]. Our findings reveal deficits on students' IL. Furthermore, teachers systematically overestimated their students' IL. Against this background and considering the high importance of IL, we think it is crucial to foster

L. Uden et al. (Eds.): LTEC 2019, CCIS 1011, pp. 202–213, 2019.
https://doi.org/10.1007/978-3-030-20798-4_18

upper secondary students' IL on a large scale and to raise teachers' awareness about students' IL deficits. Moreover, there is a lack of research that focuses on IL on the upper secondary level [3, 16, 29, 30].

Even if there is consensus that IL should be fostered at school [1, 16], it has not been sufficiently incorporated in instruction [13]. Reasons may be a lack of theoretical founded and empirically validated IL models, which are necessary for effectively fostering IL [10], and a shortage of adequate IL learning material. Teachers need support and clarity how to evaluate IL in their subjects [17]. Moreover, the ability of teachers to use digital media in a classroom is of the utmost importance to teach IL. Many teachers, however, still lack a sufficient level of competences to design digital learning settings on their own [20] that combine the new requirements of digital, open, learner-centered settings with the fixed timetables.

In order to support teachers fostering IL with their students, our goal was to develop a learning design to raise awareness for IL and capably teach IL on the upper secondary level. Our Main research Question derives from this goal.

How to develop a Massive Open Online Course [MOOC] to foster information literacy skills in high school (upper secondary education) by means of conjecture mapping?

The content of the paper is structured as follows: the next section elaborates on the rationale of our research project: (1) why a MOOC is a fitting tool to foster IL (2) why the conjecture map is a favourable tool to design the MOOC; the third section explains the applied research methodology; the fourth section provides an overview of the findings: (1) the 7i framework for conceptualization and measurement of IL (2) the conjecture map of the created learning design; and the last section concludes the paper by discussing the results and providing recommendations for future research.

2 Rationale of the Research Project

Why We Develop a MOOC. The rapid change of technological advances forces to think about new ways how to develop information literacy and how to support teachers in classroom [23]. Using digital devices and performing online search is an important facet of IL [29, 30]. This is the reason for our focus on a digital learning design. As teachers show deficits coping with digital learning designs [23], we provide them with a ready-to-use course that does not require advanced digital skills. Students should be able to complete the MOOC without technical support. Hence, teachers can focus on supporting the students learning process without worrying about technical challenges.

For IL is considered a set of skills, attitudes and knowledge necessary for students to acquire information in all sorts of courses, the collaboration with teachers is crucial to foster IL [20]. Open educational resources constitute a new digital approach to learning designs that fulfil this need. The openness is crucial to use the potential of digital learning and break with closed platforms that limit the interconnected development and the dissemination of new and promising approaches [5]. Open educational resources allow for new forms of cooperative learning and co-creation-processes [25]. Co-creation-processes involving researchers, teachers, and students, enable the concurrent development, evaluation and optimization of a learning design. The digital learning design allows for the immediate collection of data during the learning process. In this light, design research may be conducted as a collaborative co-creation-process where researchers, teachers and users (e.g. students) improve the learning design by using the collected data [5]. A MOOC provides an open digital platform facilitating the aforementioned co-creation-process and the therefore required data collection [4].

To promote IL, we regard a MOOC that covers all IL facets [29, 30] as a solid method, because major disadvantages of MOOCs do not apply to our learning design. The acceptance of MOOCs, highly depends on the reputation of the institution that created it [15]. In this context, we may benefit from the standing of the University of St. Gallen (HSG) [12]. A main disadvantage of MOOCs - high dropout rates - should not be a major issue in our case. Firstly, MOOCs with a clear target group - Swiss high school students in our case - show higher completion rates [22]. Additionally, students are enrolled by their teacher(s) and therefore are in most cases obliged to finish the course. A MOOC that is combined with in-class interaction provides teachers with a learning design that allows fulfilling the new requirements of an open, learner-centered learning design notwithstanding the fixed timetable [32]. Hence, we regard a MOOC to be the ideal learning environment to foster IL.

Why We Use Conjecture Mapping to Develop The MOOC. The educational design research [EDR] developed by McKenny and Reeves that we apply here, consists of three phases that are conducted iteratively [21, 31]:

1. *Analysis and exploration of the learning goals*: In order to be able to plan and design suitable measures for teachers, the required skills initially have to be discussed and formulated [24]. In a two year research project with a Swiss school of the upper secondary level we refined the recent IL concepts and measures and formulated the required skills [26–30].
2. *Design and construction of the learning setting*: To develop the MOOC we use conjecture mapping. Conjecture mapping is a proven way to design digital learning settings [31]. Its focus lies on the conjectures (main hypothesis), explicating the set of relationships and thereby facilitating the traceability of the applied rationale [24, 31]. This second part of the EDR process constitutes the main part of this paper.
3. *Evaluation and reflection*: The conjectures that lead to the learning design have to be evaluated and, if necessary, to be adjusted [31] in order to further optimise the MOOC. Moreover, a general insight, concerning the IL learning on the upper secondary level, may be derived and enables us to contribute to filling the lack of research in this area. This paper cannot address the third step of the EDR process, for the necessary data has yet to be collected.

The conjecture mapping is of great value to the second and third step of the EDR, and has already been successfully applied to a similar design research (e.g. [31]). In order to launch an ongoing co-creation-process with teachers and students to further improve the MOOC, the advantage of the conjecture map to explicate the rationale behind the learning setting [23], was decisive for our decision to apply it.

3 Research Methodology

We discussed why we regard the design of a MOOC by conjecture mapping an adequate way to foster IL. In this section, we describe how this task is tackled.

3.1 Educational Design Research

Design Research combines the development of innovative practical solutions with the concurring development of relevant theories [6, 7, 26]. The Methodology of the EDR conducted, follows the three phases of EDR according to McKenney and Reeves [21] for it has successfully been applied to create digital learning settings using a conjecture map by Wozniak [31].

3.2 Analysis and Exploration of the Learning Goals (Phase 1)

Before developing the MOOC, we first had to adapt the concept of IL to schools at the upper secondary level and develop a practicable measure for this concept of IL. In order to achieve this goal, a two-year research project has been established in cooperation with a secondary school in the German speaking part of Switzerland. The project was based on a methodological combination of literature analysis, model development and empirical model testing: (1) To get an overview of existing IL research, a systematical literature analysis has been performed [28]. (2) Based on the findings of the literature research, and by combining and extending existing models, the 7i framework for measuring IL has been created. (3) The 7i framework for measuring IL has been tested in five classes at a Swiss school on the upper secondary level.

The results of the literature analysis and model development are presented in detail in [29, 30]. However, the most important results are outlined in this paper to clarify the learning goals that build the foundation of the designed MOOC.

3.3 Design and Construction of the Learning Setting (Phase 2)

In order to advance in the field, it seems to be crucial to examine both, the teaching and the learning process and the existing interdependence inherent to a given learning design. The research of teaching and learning as isolated processes cannot grasp the complexity of the subject [4]. The Conjecture map allows for conducting research that includes the learning and the teaching dimension and its interdependence in a given learning design [23] and is therefore a valuable tool to do research in the described way.

In the conjecture map, the researcher reveals three different types of conjectures of the created learning design. The *high level conjectures* (1) are the base a learning design is built on – the applied concept of the learning goals and additionally the understanding of the relevant learning and teaching processes [24]. Derived from the high level conjectures the *embodiment* of the learning design – materials, tasks, participant structure – is developed. *Design conjectures* (2) reveal how the embodiment shall lead to *mediating processes* – observable by means of student artefacts and interactions – that are supposed to induce the learning goals. Finally, the *theoretical conjectures* (3) on the third level show how the mediating processes are supposed to lead to the desired *outcomes* [24] Fig. 1.

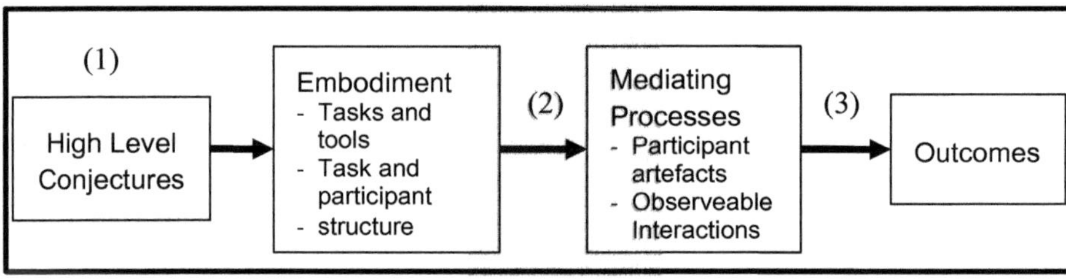

Fig. 1. The elements of a conjecture map. Adapted from [24]

The main advantage of the conjecture map is, that it puts the focus on the different levels of conjectures that require studying [24] and hence guides phase 3 of the EDR.

3.4 Evaluation and Reflection (Phase 3)

In Phase 3, the conjectures that led to the learning design are to be examined [31]. Do they apply in the constructed learning design? Are there crucial factors missing to explain the functioning of the learning design?

In this contribution, the focus lies on the MOOC-development and, therefore, the applied design research method of conjecture mapping. In autumn 2019, data will be available of the first 40 to 60 classes that will have completed our MOOC. Then, we will start refining the MOOC, our conjectures and the learning design as a whole.

4 Results

4.1 Teaching Information Literacy Skills in Secondary Education Based on the 7i Framework

The starting point for teachers' professional development in the field of information literacy (IL) must be to clarify the required learning outcomes. Therefore, we developed an IL framework to provide a basis for teachers on questions such as how to scaffold students' learning processes, give feedback or how to evaluate and grade the IL performance [27, 29].

The developed 7i framework (Fig. 2.) contains seven sub-competencies comprising knowledge, skills and attitudes: (1) Information needs; (2) Information sources; (3) Information access and seeking strategy; (4) Information evaluation; (5) Information use; (6) Information presentation; (7) Information process & finding reflection.

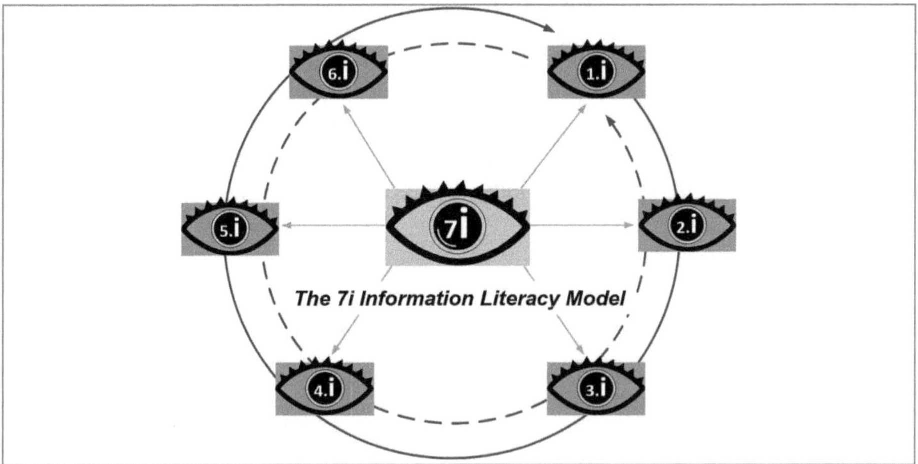

The Student who is information literate knows:
(1.i) Information needs: How to determine information needs in the context of a given problem, i.e. to determine information needs in a problem-driven manner
(2.i) Information sources: Identification of relevant information sources which information sources apply best to the identified information needs
(3.i) Information access & seeking strategy: Identification of search strategy for identified information sources which methods and search strategies suit best to access the selected information sources
(4.i) Information evaluation: Evaluation of information sources and resulting information how to evaluate whether the sources and information are valid and reliable
(5.i) Information use: Appropriate and problem-oriented use of the found information. This might also include understanding in general ethical, legal and socio-political issues of the information or subject- or problem-specific understanding of information how to use the information appropriately in order to solve the problem
(6.i) Information presentation: Present the information geared to defined target groups how to present the information geared to a specific target group
(7.i) Information process & finding reflection: Reflect upon the information search and processing procedure and upon the information resulting from it and learn how to reflect the applied information search and processing procedure and the information resulting from it and to learn for future information search processes

Fig. 2. 7i framework – students' information literacy [28]

The 7i measurement model results in two different scores of IL: one objective score based on a performance test, and one, rather subjective score, based on self-assessment. The results show a discrepancy between the self-assessed IL score and the objective IL. In the self-assessed test, the students averagely hold high scores for all of the seven sub-competences, whereas the objective test unveils substantial differences among the seven sub-competences [27]. Consequently, a main challenge will be, to sensitise and support students for the handling of online-based information.

4.2 The Conjecture Map of the i-MOOC to Foster IL in High Schools

The conjecture map of the i-MOOC (Fig. 3.) is explained along four major categories of our learning design: *High level conjectures*, *embodiment*, *measures*, and the *desired outcome*. Additionally, the *design conjectures* explain how we expect the embodiment to induce the mediating processes. The *theoretical conjectures* explain why the mediating processes are assumed to induce, the desired outcome.

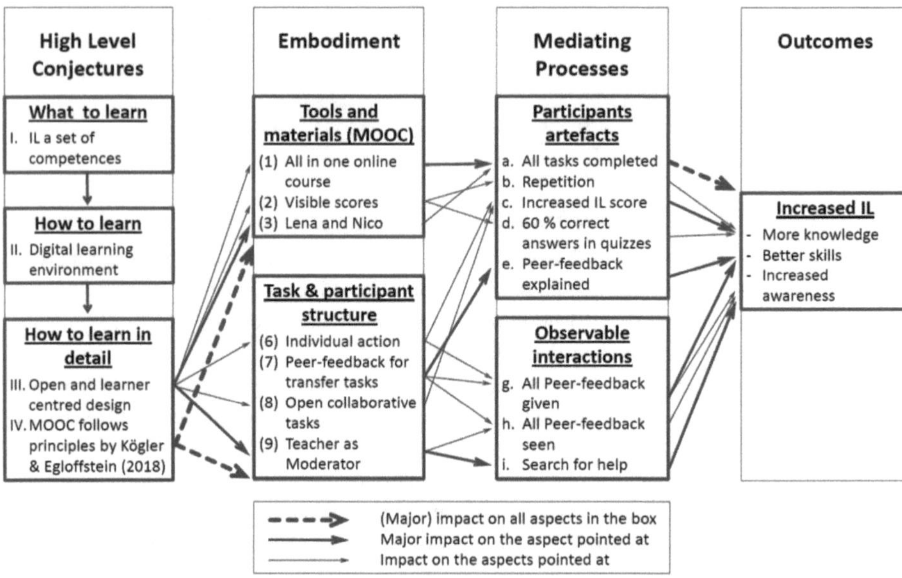

Fig. 3. Conjecture map of the i-MOOC. Own figure

Desired Outcome. The desired *outcome* equals in our case the learning goals and therefore entails the increase in IL that the participants should achieve. The knowledge, skills and attitudes defined in the 7i model [28] are the three facets of IL competences we want to foster.

High Level Conjectures. The *high level conjectures* follow from our research and define our understanding of what to learn and how to learn.

What to Learn. The content of the i-MOOC bases on the premise that IL consists of a set of competences (I) that include knowledge, skills and attitudes [28] which all should be fostered. The interdependence of the competences detected in the 7i model, has a major impact on the i-MOOC design, e.g. the scaffolding of the tasks in order to increase the complexity of the tasks gradually [27].

How to Learn. The second high level conjecture relevant for the i-MOOC entails, that a digital learning environment is crucial to foster IL (II) in theory and practice [28]. Considering the poor competences of many teachers to include digital learning designs in their instruction [20], the i-MOOC is designed for students to master without technical support provided by the teacher.

How to Learn in Detail. We acknowledge the idea, that an open and learner centred design is necessary to use the potential of digital learning environments (III) [5]. Even if a MOOC entails the potential to realise these advantages, MOOCs rarely manage to unleash their full potential [18]. Deficits may be the lack of authentic problems, activation of participants, and differentiation according to the personal skill levels [15]. Therefore, we design our MOOC in correspondence with the principles developed by Merrill [15] (IV):

- *Structure and clarity* – Every module of our MOOC entails an overview containing the structure of the module, the learning goals and the estimated time necessary to complete the module.
- *Merrill criteria* [15] – Together with the protagonists of the i-MOOC, Lena and Nico, the students discover one problem after the other (Problem centeredness). The story telling approach, following Nico's and Lena's journey to find out "why some videos go viral", allows us to demonstrate (Demonstration) solutions and encourage reflection of the acquired competences (Integration).
- *Further pedagogical principles* – Practical problems solved by Nico and Lena ensure the principle of authenticity. The two are real high school students themselves and thereby help the learner to identify themselves with the protagonists. Besides the created short movies, Nico and Lena also take part as animated characters in many of the Furthermore, students give and receive peer-feedbacks and participate in collaborative exercises.

Embodiment. The conjecture map includes only the tools, tasks, and materials of the i-MOOC, that we directly expect to induce the mediating processes seen the most important to reach the desired outcome. The vast majority of tasks and materials of the i-MOOC, not part of the conjecture map shown, derive from the high level conjectures too. It would exceed this papers' scope to explain every one of them and render the conjecture map too complex to give a good overview – its main purpose [4, 24].

Tools and Materials (i-MOOC). The all in one online course (1) allows for a clear structure according to the Merrill criteria [15] and allows the learner to be flexible in time and place, respecting the needs of a learner centred approach, consistent with high level conjecture III. The personal test scores are visible for the learner (2), not only in the pretest and posttest, whereby learners are activated (Merrill criterion) and can transparently track their progress. The scores as game elements may also rise the motivation level [14]. Among the most important decisions was the choice of the story telling approach with two actual high school students, Lena and Nico[1] (3), as the main characters guiding the students through the course. They underline the learner centrism and support the peer-learning, additionally implemented in the collaborative tasks and peer-feedbacks.

[1] Lena and Nico are not the real names of the two actors, leading through the i-MOOC by taking part in the learning movies that are part of the i-MOOC.

Task and Participant Structure. The combination of individual tasks (4), peer-feedbacks (5) and open collaborative tasks allows the asynchronous tackling of tasks as much as social learning, and thereby uses the potential of digital learning settings to create a flexible course for the participants. The peer-feedback is mainly applied in the transfer tasks. In order to induce integration (Merrill criterion), the learners reflect on their newly acquired skills by discussing their challenges and solutions with classmates and teacher(s). Moreover, they perform a substantial amount of peer-feedback tasks where they are able to perform social learning. The teacher's role as moderator (6) is decisive in this flexible and asynchronous learning setting. As the students have the possibility to adapt according with their own capacity, the teacher should be the one to assure the professional embedding of the process, to guarantee sustainable learning.

Mediating Processes. The students may complete a major part of the i-MOOC aside from the regular schedule. This flexible and learner centred design has one major disadvantage regarding the EDR. Many actions are not observable for the research team. However, the research team intends to interview all teachers participating in the first round of the i-MOOC design optimisation. This way, it is possible to identify interactions between the teachers and the students, too. Besides this disadvantage, the collection and analysis of the students' artefacts is facilitated by the digital learning environment provided by the i-MOOC setting and allows for capturing the mediating processes.

Participants Artefacts. In order to benefit from the learning design, the students should complete all tasks (a). Considering that MOOCs suffer from high dropout rates [19], despite the all in one online course (1), the school setting should prevent a high number of dropouts. However, the responsibility for taking the whole course lies, respecting the learner-centred approach, with the students. Lena and Nico as well as the visibility of the test scores should help to incentivize the students to complete all tasks and thereby prevent the lack of motivation often seen concerning IL [23]. Moreover, the content is straightforward and the storytelling may induce curiosity similar to a telenovela, where the viewers want to know how it continues. The students take an IL test at the beginning and at the end of the i-MOOC. Hence, might become aware of their learning potential and their progress is honoured. The diverse tasks including a lot of practical application and reflection in the transfer tasks, should lead to a higher IL score (c) and therefore to an increased IL. The validated IL test [2, 27] has repeatedly proven to measure the actual increase in IL and therefore raises the actual IL with a high probability in our learning design, too. The visibility of the scores and the possibility to repeat quizzes and tasks, should lead to at least 60% correct answers in the quizzes (d), as we defined this threshold to pass the course and students are likely to be motivated by this game-element [14] of collecting points to succeed. Repeating the quizzes strengthens and evaluates the IL knowledge alike. If students add reasonable explanations to their peer-feedback, they not only allow the peer to learn better but demonstrate higher involvement that may lead to higher skill levels and an increased awareness [11]. The artefacts are collected in the i-MOOC and therefore allow for an efficient handling and evaluating in the latter phase of the EDR.

Observable Interactions. The exchange with peers in the open collaborative tasks and the peer-feedbacks (f, g) build the main part of the interactions during the MOOC. The more the students appreciate and therefore conduct the peer-feedback the more likely it is for them to increase their IL skills and awareness [11]. The seeking for help (h) indicates the awareness of personal IL deficits, for poor performers often do not realize their own deficits in a specific field [6]. Therefore, it might be evidence for an increased awareness for the challenges of IL.

5 Discussion and Future Perspectives on Developing Information Literacy in a Digital Ecosystem

This paper addresses the problem of "fit" between new requirements in terms of digital skills such as IL and prevailing conditions of the schooling system – classroom and fixed timetables. The need for open learning settings, that include a broad number of participants and allows for co-creation of the learning setting [5], is a challenge. Especially in the light of teachers lack of competences concerning the use and development of digital learning settings [20], supporting tools have to be developed. The i-MOOC fulfils this requirement as, on the one hand, it provides teachers with an easy-to-use tool to foster IL, and on the other hand, allows for co-creation-processes to further develop the learning design.

The described EDR focuses on fostering IL in the Swiss school system. Not all aspects may be transferrable to other contexts. Furthermore, in light of the EDR, the quality and adequate use of the i-MOOC are yet to be optimized. The evaluation of the i-MOOC and its use are to follow as soon as the first approximately 600 students have completed the course. Testing the main conjectures and adjusting the learning design in accordance with the findings will be the next step of the EDR process [21, 31] to refine the i-MOOC. We are hoping to improve the learning design gradually. If we succeed in keeping up with this ongoing co-creation process by holding further webinars and encouraging the exchange between researchers, teachers and students, the building of an open educational ecosystem could be initiated.

References

1. Argelagós, E., Pifarré, M.: Improving information problem solving skills in secondary education through embedded instruction. Comput. Hum. Behav. **28**, 264–270 (2012). https://doi.org/10.1016/j.chb.2011.10.024
2. Balceris, M.: Medien- und Informationskompetenz: Modellierung und Messung von Informationskompetenz bei Schülern. Dissertation, Freie Universität Berlin (2011)
3. Çoklar, A.N., Yaman, N.D., Yurdakul, I.K.: Information literacy and digital nativity as determinants of online information search strategies. Comput. Hum. Behav. **70**, 1–9 (2017). https://doi.org/10.1016/j.chb.2016.12.050
4. Deng, R., Benckendorff, P., Gannaway, D.: Progress and new directions for teaching and learning in MOOCs. Comput. Educ. **129**, 48–60 (2019). https://doi.org/10.1016/j.compedu.2018.10.019

5. Dillenbourg, P.: The evolution of research on digital education. Int. J. Artif. Intell. Educ. **26**(2), 544–560 (2016). https://doi.org/10.1007/s40593-016-0106-z
6. Dunning, D.: The Dunning–Kruger effect: on being ignorant of one's own ignorance (Chap. 5). In: Advances in Experimental Social Psychology, vol. 44, pp. 247–296 (2011). https://doi.org/10.1016/b978-0-12-385522-0.00005-6
7. Euler, D.: Wirkungs- vs. Gestaltungsforschung – eine feindliche Koexistenz? Zeitschrift für Berufs- und Wirtschaftspädagogik **107**(4), 520–542 (2011)
8. Gapski, H., Tekster, T.: Informationskompetenz in Deutschland - Überblick zum Stand der Fachdiskussion und Zusammenstellung von Literaturangaben, Projekten und Materialien zu einzelnen Zielgruppen. Landesanstalt für Medien Nordrhein-Westfalen, Düsseldorf (2009)
9. Gust von Loh, S., Henkel, M.: Information and media literacy in kindergarten. In: Kurbanoğlu, S., Špiranec, S., Grassian, E., Mizrachi, D., Catts, R. (eds.) ECIL 2014. CCIS, vol. 492, pp. 253–262. Springer, Cham (2014). https://doi.org/10.1007/978-3-319-14136-7_27
10. Hartig, J., Jude, N.: Empirische Erfassung von Kompetenzen und psychometrische Kompetenzmodelle. In: Hartig, S., Klieme, E. (Eds.) Möglichkeiten und Voraussetzungen technologiebasierter Kompetenzdiagnostik. Eine Expertise im Auftrag des Bundesministeriums für Bildung und Forschung, pp. 17–36. Bundesministerium für Bildung und Forschung (BMBF), Berlin (2007)
11. Hattie, J., Timperley, H.: The power of feedback. Rev. Educ. Res. **77**(1), 81–112 (2007). https://doi.org/10.3102/003465430298487
12. HSG (University of St. Gallen) Homepage. https://www.unisg.ch/ueber-uns/portraet/rankingsundakkreditierungen/rankingresultate. Accessed 03 Jan 2019
13. Jones-Kavalier, B., Flannigan, S.: Connecting the digital dots: literacy of the 21st century. Educause Q. **2**, 8–10 (2006)
14. Kapp, K.: The gamification of learning and instruction: game-based methods and strategies for training and education. Essential resources for training and HR professionals. Pfeiffer, San Francisco (2012)
15. Kögler, K., Egloffstein, M.: Didaktische Qualität von Massive Open Online Courses im bereich Business & Management – Ergebnisse einer Pilotstudie. Presentation at: Jahrestagung der Sektion Berufs- und Wirtschaftspädagogik 2018, Frankfurt (2018)
16. Koltay, T., Špiranec, S., Karvalics, L.: The nature of information literacy (Chap. 2). In: Research 2.0 and the Future of Information Literacy. Chandos Information Professional Series. IMPACT Learning, pp. 61–110 (2016)
17. Lanning, S., Mallek, J.: Factors influencing information literacy competency of college students. J. Acad. Librariansh. **43**(5), 443–450 (2017)
18. Li, Q., Baker, R.: The different relationships between engagement and outcomes across participant subgroups in massive open online courses. Comput. Educ. **127**, 41–65 (2018)
19. Liyanagunawardena, T., Parslow, P., Williams, S.: Dropout: MOOC participants'perspective. EMOOCs 2014, the Second MOOC European Stakeholders Summit, 10–12th February 2014, Lausanne, Switzerland, pp. 95–100 (2014)
20. Maybee, C.: Three essentials for integrating information literacy (Chap. 10). Chandos Information Professional Series. IMPACT Learning, pp. 133–143. Chandos Publishing, Cambridge (2018)
21. McKenney, S., Reeves, T.: Conducting Educational Design Research. Routledge, Oxon (2012)
22. Paton, R.M., Scanlan, J.D., Fluck, A.E.: A performance profile of learner completion and retention in Australian VET MOOCs. J. Vocat. Educ. Training **70**(4), 581–599 (2018). https://doi.org/10.1080/13636820.2018.1463278
23. Prensky, M.: Digital natives, digital immigrants, vol. 9, no. 5, pp. 1–6. MCB University Press (2011). https://doi.org/10.1108/10748120110424816

24. Sandoval, W.: Conjecture mapping: an approach to systematic educational design research. J. Learn. Sci. **23**(1), 18–36 (2014). https://doi.org/10.1080/10508406.2013.778204
25. Seufert, S.: Berufsbildung 2030. Flexibilisierung der Berufsbildung im Kontext fortgeschrittener Digitalisierung. Gutachten im Auftrag des SBFI. Bern: Staatssekretariat für Bildung Forschung und Innovation (2018)
26. Seufert, S.: Potenziale von Design Research aus der Perspektive der Innovationsforschung. Zeitschrift für Berufs- und Wirtschaftspädagogik, Beiheft **2**(27), 79–96 (2014)
27. Seufert, S., Scheffler, N.: Developing digital competences of vocational teachers. Int. J. Digit. Literacy Digit. Competence **7**(1), 50–65 (2016)
28. Seufert, S., Stanoevska-Slabeva, K., Müller, S., Scheffler, N.: The design of Personal Learning Environments (PLE) with scope on information literacy in high school. In: Uden, L., Liberona, D., Welzer, T. (eds.) LTEC 2015. CCIS, vol. 533, pp. 148–163. Springer, Cham (2015). https://doi.org/10.1007/978-3-319-22629-3_12
29. Stanoevska-Slabeva, K., Müller, S., Seufert, S., Scheffler, N.: The 7i framework – towards a measurement model for information literacy. In: Proceedings of the American Conference on Information Systems (AMCIS), pp. 1–14, Fajardo, PR (2015)
30. Stanoevska-Slabeva, K., Müller, S., Seufert, S., Scheffler, N.: Modelling and measuring information literacy in secondary education. In: International Conference on Information Systems (ICIS), pp. 1–20, Fort Worth, Texas (2015)
31. Wozniak, H.: Conjecture mapping to optimize the educational design research process. Australas. J. Educ. Technol. **31**(5), 597–612 (2015). https://doi.org/10.14742/ajet.2505
32. Yousef, A.M.F., Chatti, M.A., Schroeder, U., Wosnitza, M.: A usability evaluation of a blended MOOC environment: an experimental case study. Int. Rev. Res. Open Distrib. Learn. **16**(2), 69–93 (2015). https://doi.org/10.19173/irrodl.v16i2.2032

Variations in Self-Regulation of Learning On-Line Versus On-Campus

Jonathan Kaplan[1,2](✉)

[1] Institut des Sciences et Pratiques d'Éducation et de Formation, Université Lumière Lyon 2, Laboratoire Éducation Cultures & Politiques, (EA 4571), 86 rue Pasteur, 69365 Lyon, France
jonathan.kaplan@univ-lyon2.fr

[2] Laboratoire Cognitions Humaine et Artificielle, Université Paris Nanterre, (EA 4004), 200 avenue de la République, 92000 Nanterre, France

Abstract. This paper describes the results of a study that compared self- and co-regulation perceived strategy use of Master's in Education students learning in two distinct learning environments. One cohort of students was studying predominantly face-to-face on-campus while the other studied predominantly on-line. Comparing the two cohorts enabled to contrast perceived regulation of learning strategy use. Subjects were postgraduate students in Educational Sciences studying in a French university during the academic year 2017–18. Data was collected using ERICA [12] which is a scale intended for measurement of six macro-level strategies of regulation of learning. The study found that two strategies differed in perceived frequency of use by students. The strategies were Individual Anticipation of materials and References (IAR) and Individual Tracking and Monitoring (ITM). Environmental conditions, instructional cues and group characteristics are discussed as potential explanations for the found similarities and differences. Future research directions are suggested to further explore the interplay between the ways students learn and environmental characteristics.

Keywords: Self-regulation · Co-regulation · Self-regulated learning · e-Learning · Anticipation · Monitoring · Learning environment

1 Context

The field of Self-Regulated Learning (SRL) has gained momentum since Zimmerman and Martinez Pons [23] explored how learners regulated their learning in the mid nineteen eighties. Researchers have taken interest in regulation of motivation, some have focused on regulation of cognition or on both, while others have also explored regulation of affect. Regulation of cognition or cognitive regulation, has been explored both as trait and as event, i.e. as a disposition to self-regulate as well as by observing the fine-grain details of how individual learners self-regulate as they work toward a specific learning goal. Some measurement instruments are suitable to measure the former "aptitude measures" while others are more suitable as "event measures" [1, 22].

L. Uden et al. (Eds.): LTEC 2019, CCIS 1011, pp. 214–223, 2019.
https://doi.org/10.1007/978-3-030-20798-4_19

ERICA, a scale designed to measure self- and co-regulation of learning [12] is suitable for aptitude measures. The strategies to regulate learning that can be measured with ERICA are deployed by learners before, during and after the cognitive activity aimed at gaining specific knowledge, though the strategies together are part of the learning process. Two sub-scales measure strategies that are classified as occurring before the aforementioned cognitive activity. They take place during the Anticipation phase. One strategy is classified as taking place during the cognitive action, named Monitoring. The phase taking place after the cognitive action is named Assessment. Two types of strategies are measured with ERICA pertaining to this phase. One is a strategy which is individually carried out; the other, a strategy that is carried out with other learners. A fourth phase was introduced in the theoretical model of regulation of learning phases [6, 7]. This phase, which is labeled Decisions, is measured with ERICA in its collective form. Decisions that are measured pertain to a change in methods used by learners to develop their knowledge. Strategies measured with sub-scales in ERICA should be considered as macro-level strategies. Learners deploy a vast number of micro-level strategies that are specific to not only the learner but also to the study field, motivation, goal orientation [16], situation, including environmental conditions, and social context. These micro-level strategies can be observed with event measures. ERICA is an instrument intended as a trait measure. It enables to depict a general picture of regulation strategies of a population of learners.

Research using ERICA is an ongoing exploration in an attempt to identify tendencies or patterns of regulation characteristic of learners in different environments. Comparisons of regulation that emerge in different environments need to also take into account other variables such as those related to demographic trends, topics being studied, instructional designs, support materials and teacher cues. In parallel to the exploration of relations between contextual variables, situational ones, population attributes and regulation strategies, the research program has begun testing the substantive validity of the theoretical Regulation of Learning Phases Model [9, 10]. Digitally based environments for learning are of particular interest as they enable educational staff to easily modify appearance through software choice, software parameters, configurations, graphic design, choice of software modules and their arrangement, interfacing with other software, services, tools, etc. The ways some of these choices could modify, hinder or support self- and co-regulation of learning should be of interest to educators as well as other stakeholders committed to promoting successful learning.

Environments can enable learners to use different kinds of learning strategies. Not giving the means for enacting certain strategies may lead to adaptations in the ways learners regulate the learning process. For example, a case of not using a strategy because it is not braced by the design of an e-learning environment may lead to the use of another means or strategy to increase the effectiveness of the learning; or, it could adversely prevent the learner from enacting a regulation strategy that would have otherwise improved learning. Strategies may manifest themselves in some environments either because they can possibly be deployed in them and students choose to, perhaps also because learners are encouraged to; or, because they are used as compensation for the impossibility or the inadequacy to use other, perhaps preferred, strategies that the learners are accustomed to use. The complexity of the interplay between environmental conditions and individual variability in strategy use does not lend itself to attempt generalization from studies of the processes as events. On the other hand, a general understanding of the interplay between the environment and strategy use for effective learning can be attempted by studying learners' perceptions. Through repeated measurements in different environments and varying situations, researchers can compare learners' regulation strategies in relation to the way learners engage and use the resources available to conduct and manage the learning process. Researchers can then study similarities and differences while taking into account contextual variables to learn about environments that are supportive of effective learning, student well-being and outcomes. The fields of cognitive ergonomics and the study of affordance, as the perceived possibility for action in a given e-learning environment [4], is the backdrop for the study presented in this paper.

2 Theory

Self-regulated learning has been the focus of researches for four decades with the more recent incursion into co-regulation becoming the focus of some authors during the last decade [10, 11]. Co-regulation in learning refers to strategies used by learners that involve interaction with peers. Interactions can take place both face-to-face and through the use of mediating technologies. The most common of these mediating technologies are general use text-based applications such as messaging and e-mail as well as specific services such as forums which are integrated in Learning Management Systems (LMSs). Exchanges can also take place using audio (phone calls or vocal messages) and through the use of audio-visual software or services (video calls, video-conferencing, video-recordings) that are sometimes integrated in or linked to LMSs.

ERICA can be used to determine perceived frequencies of strategy use. The scale measures six macro-level self-regulation strategies among which two are categorized as co-regulation strategies. The measured strategies are mapped to the theoretical model of regulation of learning phases [12] (refer to Table 1).

Table 1. Phases and learning regulation strategies measured with ERICA [12]

Phase	Code regulation strategy	Item example
Anticipation	IAR Individual Anticipation of materials and References	At the beginning of a course I look into of various documents to know what learning is required to succeed in my education
	IEC Individual Environmental Control	I set myself up in a place where I will not be distracted when I am learning
Monitoring	ITM Individual Tracking and Monitoring	I keep track of my learning activities in a logbook or a journal
Assessment	CEC Collective Evaluation of Content	I discuss the state of progress in my studies with other learners
	IEM Individual Evaluation of Method	I wonder about my learning method
Decisions	CDM Collective Decisions for Method change	The learning methods I use are the result of a choice made with others in which I took part

The study presented in this paper compared regulation strategies of graduate students learning in a distance education program on-line with graduate students learning on-campus. Students in the two cohorts were not enrolled in the same program, although both were preparing a Master's degree in educational sciences. The on-line cohort was made up of two groups taking a statistics course during their first-year of post-graduate studies while students on campus were made up of two groups taking a course in digital humanities on approaches in psychology and ergonomics applied to digital learning. The latter courses were provided to second-year post-graduate students in educational sciences.

Several previous studies using ERICA had explored various facets of Self- and Co-Regulation (SCoR). Laurent and colleagues [13] studied links between SCoR and executive functions. Simonian and colleagues studied links between affordance and SCoR of e-learning students [20] and studies of links between SCoR and interpersonal relationships of online students [8] as well as the study of a model of self-evaluation of the learning process [10] had been carried out. However, no known study using ERICA has yet compared regulation strategies used by on-line learners with those used by on-campus students. The research presented here sought to compare precisely that i.e. similarities and differences in regulation of learning strategies within these two educational formats.

3 Method

Data was self-reported. On-line students used an online version of the ERICA questionnaire. It was administered via a server using DrupalTM software and an installed Webform module. Students were asked to respond over a period of one week at the end of their courses which took place during the second semester of the 2017–18 academic year (February 5–11, 2018). On-campus students responded during a class session (first week of December 2017) using a printed version of the questionnaire. All student were free to provide their responses if so they wished. Both online and paper-based responses were provided anonymously.

The LMS used with the on-line students was BlackBoard LearnTM. Online students were respondents from two groups, each studying with a separate instructor. Students who had chosen to major in social work and health-care education plus those majoring in adult education were in group A with one instructor. Students who had chosen to major in the formal education professions were in group B with another instructor. On-campus respondents were students from two groups too. One was a group made up of students in a regular program while those in the other were students in a shortened program. Both groups were preparing the same Master's degree in adult education. The shortened program was catered to adult learners who were health-care instructors working in higher-education institutions providing health-care and nursing qualification training. On-line group A and both on-campus groups had the same instructor. On-line group B had a separate instructor.

Instruction in all groups combined classroom sessions with independent small-group tasks to be carried out by students. Cues given to students in online group A and and on-campus courses followed cooperative learning guidelines [5].

For comparisons to be made in order to consider similarities and differences in regulation strategies, data was described then analyzed. To begin, a multivariate analysis of variance (MANOVA) was performed to determine if similarity in variances between perceived strategy frequency use of learners in the two on-line groups was such as to consider collating the date to form the on-line cohort. Likewise, similarity in variances between the two on-campus groups was sought. To the degree to which the mean differences within each learning realm would be statistically insignificant, comparisons of variances between the on-line and the on-campus learners' data were to be sought. A detailed description of this process and the resulting findings follow.

4 Results

Analyzes were performed using R, version 3.5.2 [17]. A MANOVA was performed on each set of the two groups. The first set of groups was made up of the on-line students ($n = 70$). The second set of groups was made up of the on-campus students ($n = 35$). Results for the set of the on-line groups were previously computed [10]. Analyzes were run again for the purpose of this study with identical results [F (1, 55) = 1.22; $p = .310$]. Results for the set of the on-campus groups indicated no significant differences in perceived regulation frequencies either [F (1, 33) = .91; $p = .504$]. Between-subject effects on each variable were also tested with no significant differences between groups within each set.

Once consistency and homogeneity of data from each environment – on-campus and on-line – was established, descriptive statistics were calculated and internal consistency analyzes of the measures were carried out to estimate reliability for each cohort. Results were satisfactory for all dimensions representing macro-level strategy frequency of use (see Table 2). Analysis of similarities and differences in perceived frequency of use of regulation strategies between the on-line and the on-campus cohorts was carried out next. First, a MANOVA was carried out. It did not reveal a significant difference [F (1, 90) = 2.03; $p = .070$], however between-subject effects on each variable did uncover differences between on-campus and on-line perceived frequency of use for two macro-level strategies. The strategies for which differences were found were Individual Anticipation of materials and References (IAR) and Individual

Table 2. Internal consistency and descriptive statistics of measured regulation strategies

Strategy	On-Campus					On-Line				
	α	Min	Max	*M*	*SD*	α	Min	Max	*M*	*SD*
IAR	0.77	0.8	4.0	2.58	0.80	0.77	1.2	4.0	2.88	0.64
IEC	0.90	0.6	4.0	2.81	0.97	0.84	1.0	4.0	2.94	0.75
ITM	0.74	0.0	3.2	1.15	0.92	0.81	0.0	4.0	1.61	1.00
CEC	0.88	0.8	4.0	2.35	0.81	0.78	0.6	3.4	2.12	0.72
IEM	0.82	1.0	3.6	2.29	0.65	0.73	1.0	3.2	2.18	0.56
CDM	0.85	0.0	3.4	1.35	0.85	0.86	0.0	3.0	1.19	0.82

Note: Values for measured regulation strategies span from 0 to 4.

Tracking and Monitoring (ITM). An *F* test for equal variance in unrelated samples was first used to check homogeneity of variance for IAR ($F = 0.65$, $p = .138$) and for ITM ($F = 1.37$, $p = .316$). Following, a true t-test was performed to compare the means of scores for these strategies from on-campus and on-line subjects. IAR scores were statistically significantly higher for on-line students ($M = 2.88$, $SD = 0.64$) than for on-campus students ($M = 2.58$, $SD = 0.80$), $t(100) = 2.02$, $p = .046$, $d = .42$. ITM scores were statistically significantly higher too for on-line students ($M = 1.61$, $SD = 1.00$) than for on-campus students ($M = 1.15$, $SD = 0.92$), $t(100) = 2.13$, $p = .035$, $d = .45$. Figure 1 illustrates these differences.

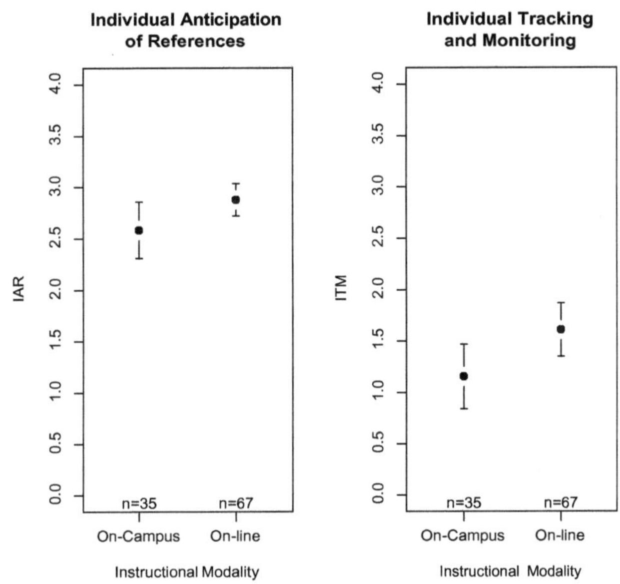

Fig. 1. Means with confidence intervals of IAR and ITM strategies On-Campus and On-line

5 Discussion

Comparing perceptions of degrees to which regulation of learning strategies were used in terms of their frequencies, requires taking contextual and situational variables into account. The research method and measurement instruments that were used are not intended for fine-grained observation of individual processes; they are intended to detect general dispositional tendencies across groups. Past personal sociohistorical experiences of respondents were hence not accounted for. On the one hand social environmental conditions that served as the back- drop of the study needed to be accounted for as they inform on the conditions that surrounded the learners. These conditions could have been constraining or enabling to varying degrees. They form the circumstances or situational variables that may have played a role in the way students perceived their ability to successfully conduct their assigned learning tasks. On the other hand, regulation strategies that were measured as similar among the studied cohorts can be considered as invariable within the academic environment of studies in the specific academic field, time, culture and place they took place in. Differences in measured regulation between cohorts could be the result of varying situational characteristics, such as the course topic, instructional design, learning materials and instructional cues that were given.

Given the similar results for four out of the six strategies, one can assume these results were due to shared contextual elements among the two cohorts. Differences found between the cohorts for the remaining two strategies can perhaps be attributed to perceptions students had of other environmental features, in particular those pertaining to perceptions of instructor proximity.

Measurements that did not reveal significant differences in their perceived frequency of use were Individual Environmental Control (IEC), Collective Evaluation of Content (CEC), Individual Evaluation of Method (IEM) and Collective Decisions for Method change (CDM). Two of the six strategies were significantly different, these were Individual Anticipation of materials and References (IAR) and Individual Tracking and Monitoring (ITM). Both these strategies were perceived to be used more frequently by students studying on-line. Both these strategies were carried out individually and are considered crucial to effectively self-regulate learning. The importance of monitoring was demonstrated in Greene and Azevedo's [3] study while anticipation strategies were previously demonstrated to be associated with higher grades [8].

The question that needed to be addressed was: what differences existed between on campus groups and on-line groups that could have contributed to differentiated perceptions? Data for control variables were not gathered from on campus students. These would be valuable for comparisons. Nevertheless, in line with the design of the research, it is reasonable to regard differences in regulation strategies as also attributable to differences in students' instructional environments.

In previous research [8] IAR scores were higher when students were assumed, based on age, to be more experienced. The on-line students in education sciences attending the university were perhaps more experienced which would explain the higher scores. This will need to be corroborated in future studies. It is hypothesized that more experienced students both as learners and generally, have developed more systematic use of anticipation strategies. It has been demonstrated that high prior knowledge students were more prone to engage in planning and monitoring [15]. Constraints on older students such as managing work-related contingencies and family contingencies may be higher. These older adults are presumably those who chose to study on-line as on-line modes offer more flexibility to accommodate work and family constraints.

Individual Tracking and Monitoring (ITM) is key to effectively regulate learning [8, 21] in particular when complex topics are being studied [3]. The assumption is that the absence of face-to-face guidance transfers the perceived responsibility for regulating learning to the learner. The learner may feel a heightened demand to self-regulate as the transactional distance [14] grows. To self-regulate effectively the learner needs to refer to past learning episodes that may be somewhat segmented when learning on-line. In absence of tracking and monitoring, segmentation and episodic learning for perhaps relatively short spurts of cognitive activity directed at the learning topic and perhaps spaced episodes of longer duration, make tracking more arduous, thus necessitating greater attention to tracking and more frequent monitoring.

To the question were challenges different for learners in each environment, the answer is without doubt that they were. For one, the transactional distance for learners was different and so the perceived relative presence of the instructors may have challenged learners differently. An earlier study had uncovered that the way learners perceived the Reference Person to the Field of Study (RPFS) affected co-regulation strategies [6]. The amplitude of anticipation of group processing was significantly higher and the assessment process of co-evaluation was more frequent when no RPFS was assigned to the group of learners in that study. In the present study, the frequency of perceived use of the IAR strategy may have similarly been affected, as students had probably perceived themselves to be primarily in charge of organizing and managing their learning. Tracking and monitoring was perhaps also perceived to be under the helm of the students. These assumptions would need further studying as indeed it would be possible to study RPFS perceptions of students in conjunction with self- and co-regulation.

6 Conclusion

In this study perceived frequency of use of SCoR strategies of first-year graduate students learning in a distance education program on-line in two groups were compared with SCoR strategies of second-year graduate students learning on- campus in two other groups. Each pair of groups formed a cohort, the former of on-line students, the latter of on-campus students. Students in the two cohorts were not enrolled in the same program though both were enrolled at the same university in the same institute and shared some of the teaching staff. A series of MANOVAs confirmed that the pairs of groups did not present statistically significant mean differences in measured SCoR strategy use within each cohort. Cohorts did however present differences in perception between on-line and on- campus students for two self-regulation strategies. Significant differences were found for Individual Anticipation of materials and References (IAR) and for Individual Tracking and Monitoring (ITM). Both these strategies were statistically significantly higher for on-line learners.

To explain the differences that were found, transactional distance theory [14] and self-determination theory can prove useful [2, 19]. The transactional distance is assumed to be perceived by the students as greater in the on-line learning environment [14], though this would merit checking in future studies. The greater transactional distance requires students to be more autonomous while at the same time contributing to a stronger feeling of autonomy [18]. If learners feel able to accomplish the learning task in an environment perceived as generating increased learner to instructor distance, this would lead to fuller engagement in the task, effectively self-regulating learning and a keen pursuit of the learning activities.

Students who had perceived that responsibility was more theirs for successful learning outcomes, may have led to stronger proactive engagement in the learning process, in particular regarding tracking and monitoring progress. Both strategies for regulating learning that were perceived to be higher by on-line learners were carried out individually (IAR and ITM). Co-regulation strategies were not perceived to be statistically different, nor was Individual Environmental Control (IEM). The co-regulation strategies Collective Evaluation of Content (CEC) and Collective Decisions for Method change (CDM) were not perceived differently by the two cohorts, perhaps as in both environments the learning tasks were organized similarly, based on small group team learning with a collective task to be carried out and a group report to be completed.

Repeated measures with other on-line and on-campus cohorts should enable to ascertain that differences found in IAR and ITM perceived strategy use do indeed follow a similar pattern. If indeed IAR and ITM are more frequently reported in on-line environments, measuring perceptions of the RPFS as a surrogate for transactional distance as well as perceptions of autonomy would enable to test the relation between the perceived transactional distance, autonomy as a mediator and the frequency of use of self-regulation strategies.

References

1. Cleary, T.J., Callan, G.L.: Assessing self-regulated learning using microanalytic methods. In: Handbook of Self-Regulation of Learning and Performance (Chap. 22), pp. 338–351. Educational Psychology Handbook Series, Routledge (2018)
2. Deci, E.L., Ryan, R.M. (eds.): Handbook of Self-Determination Research. University of Rochester Press, Rochester (2002)
3. Greene, J.A., Azevedo, R.: A macro-level analysis of SRL processes and their re- lations to the acquisition of a sophisticated mental model of a complex system. Contemp. Educ. Psychol. **34**(1), 18–29 (2009)
4. Hammond, M.: What is an affordance and can it help us understand the use of ICT in education? Educ. Inf. Technol. **15**(3), 205–217 (2010). https://doi.org/10.1007/s10639-009-9106-z
5. Johnson, D.W., Johnson, R.T., Smith, K.A.: Cooperative Learning: Increasing College Faculty Instructional Productivity, ASHE-ERIC Higher Education Reports, vol. 20. George Washington University, Graduate School of Education and Human Development, 2 edn (1991)
6. Kaplan, J.: L'autodirection dans les apprentissages coopératifs - Le cas des Cercles d'Étude [Self-Direction in Cooperative Learning - The Case of Study Circles]. Ph.D. thesis, Paris 10 University, Nanterre (2009)
7. Kaplan, J.: Co-regulation in technology enhanced learning environments. In: Uden, L., Sinclair, J., Tao, Y.H., Liberona, D. (eds.) LTEC 2014. CCIS, vol. 446, pp. 72–81. Springer, Cham (2014). https://doi.org/10.1007/978-3-319-10671-7_7
8. Kaplan, J.: Learning strategies and interpersonal relationships of students learning cooperatively online. In: Uden, L., Liberona, D., Feldmann, B. (eds.) LTEC 2016. CCIS, vol. 620, pp. 103–111. Springer, Cham (2016). https://doi.org/10.1007/978-3-319-42147-6_9
9. Kaplan, J.: Coévaluation entre pairs apprenants comme échafaudage de la régu- lation du processus de l'apprentissage. Symposium: Apprentissage autorégulé et régulation des apprentissages: le rôle de l'évaluation, Les rencontres internationales du Réseau de recherche en éducation et en formation (REF 2017), CNAM, Paris, July 2017

10. Kaplan, J.: Putting to test a model of self-evaluation of the learning method in an e-learning environment. International Conference on Technology and Innovation in Learning, Teaching and Education (TECH-EDU 2018), Aristotle University of Thessaloniki, June 2018
11. Kaplan, J.: Les stratégies d'autorégulation collective des apprenants adultes en e-formation. In: Jézégou, A. (ed.) Traité de la e-Formation des adultes, chap. 11, pp. 263–286. De Boeck Supérieur, Louvain-la-Neuve (2019)
12. Kaplan, J., de Montalembert, M., Laurent, P., Fenouillet, F.: ERICA - An in- strument to measure individual and collective regulation of learning [ERICA - Un outil pour mesurer la régulation individuelle et collective de l'apprentissage]. Euro- pean Review of Applied Psychology - Revue Européenne de Psychologie Appliquée **67**(2), 79–89 (2017). https://doi.org/10.1016/j.erap.2017.01.001
13. Laurent, P., Fenouillet, F., Kaplan, J., de Montalembert, M.: Apprentissage au- torégulé et fonctions exécutives. Journée d'Hiver de la Société de Neuropsychologie de Langue Française, Espace de conférence des Diaconesses, Paris (2014)
14. Moore, M.G.: The theory of transactional distance. In: Moore, M.G. (ed.) Handbook of Distance Education, pp. 66–85. Routledge, London (2013)
15. Moos, D.C., Azevedo, R.: Monitoring, planning, and self-efficacy during learning with hypermedia: the impact of conceptual scaffolds. Comput. Hum. Behav. **24**(4), 1686–1706 (2008)
16. Pintrich, P.R.: The role of goal orientation in self-regulated learning. In: Boekaerts, M., Pintrich, P.R., Zeidner, M. (eds.) Handbook of Self-Regulation, pp. 451–502. Academic Press, San Diego (2000)
17. R Core Team: R: A Language and Environment for Statistical Computing. R Foundation for Statistical Computing, Vienna, Austria (2018). https://www.R-project.org/
18. Reeve, J., Ryan, R., Deci, E.L., Jang, H.: Understanding and promoting au- tonomous self-regulation: A self-determination theory perspective. In: Schunk, D.H., Zimmerman, B. J. (eds.) Motivation and Self-Regulated Learning: Theory, Research, and Applications, pp. 223–244. Lawrence Erlbaum Associates, New York (2008)
19. Ryan, R.M., Deci, E.L.: Self-determination theory and the facilitation of intrinsic motivation, social development, and well-being. Am. Psychol. **55**(1), 68–78 (2000)
20. Simonian, S., Chaker, R., Kaplan, J.: Affordance en e-formation et régulation de l'apprentissage: une exploration dans un contexte d'études universitaires. Actes du Colloque e-Formation 2018, Université de Lille, Villeneuve d'Ascq, March 2018
21. Steffens, K.: Self-regulated leaning in technology-enhanced learning environments: lessons of a european peer review. European J. Educ. Res., Dev. Policies **41**(3–4), 352–379 (2006)
22. Winne, P.H., Perry, N.E.: Measuring self-regulated learning. In: Boekaerts, M., Pintrich, P. R., Zeidner, M. (eds.) Handbook of Self-Regulation, pp. 531–566. Academic Press, San Diego (2000)
23. Zimmerman, B.J., Martinez Pons, M.: Development of a structured interview for assessing student use of self-regulated learning strategies. Am. Educ. Res. J. **23**(4), 614–628 (1986)

Let's Digitize It: Investigating Challenges of Online Education

Stephan Schlögl(✉), Christian Ploder, Teresa Spieß, and Franziska Schöffer

Department Management Communication & IT, MCI Management Center Innsbruck, Universitätsstraße 15, 6020 Innsbruck, Austria
stephan.schloegl@mci.edu

Abstract. This paper focuses on the challenges education providers face when trying to offer different types of online education formats as an extension to their already existing course portfolio. We investigated generic challenges concerning both small and closed as well as big and open online courses, where challenges include the development as well as the integration of new online content into course structures. Our analysis is based on an interview study with representatives of 14 Universities in the German speaking area. Results yield six concrete problem areas education providers have to deal with. Those include cost, and increasing student base, drop-out rates, teaching quality, certifications and legal challenges. While the penetration of online education in the investigated area is surely too small to realistically construct best practice examples, the presented work represents a snapshot of today's challenges in offering online education, and therefore may be seen as a valuable starting point to work on future improvements.

Keywords: Online education · MOOC's · Technology supported learning · Digitalization challenges · Interview study

1 Introduction

Although the online education market has been struggling with a number of challenges in the past years, its application fields today reach areas that go well beyond the common student–professor relationship usually found within university settings – especially at postgraduate level. One particularly interesting application example may be found in the use of online learning as an enabler for 'lifelong learning' alongside existing part and/or full time working contexts. Here, an integrated mix of online learning and traditional training methods offer an efficient setting [1]. That is, technology may greatly support individual learning processes, which are usually very divers in different workplaces and moreover have to adapt to employees' day-to-day business [2]. Clear examples, which would illustrate best practices on how to approach this new type of employee training using online education and various other types of learning technologies, are however still missing, so that companies usually follow their very own strategies when tackling this topic - although education is not necessarily

L. Uden et al. (Eds.): LTEC 2019, CCIS 1011, pp. 224–233, 2019.
https://doi.org/10.1007/978-3-030-20798-4_20

their core competence [3]. Many universities, on the other hand still see online education best targeted at young students and not so much at companies interested in 'upgrading' their in-house staff. This is where we see a clear gap – a space that requires additional exploration and a better understanding of the relevant challenges that impede a better supply of online education.

2 E-Learning as a Game Changer

Online education, in particular the trend towards Massive Open Online Courses (MOOCs), whose success is *"build on the engagement of learners who self-organize their participation according to learning goals, prior knowledge and skills, and common interests"* [4], has led to a significant change in the academic landscape. Today, universities not only in the United States but increasingly also in Europe and Asia, use Internet platforms such as Coursera, Udacity, iTunesU or edX to offer their course content online. While consumers of these lectures may usually be found in students who aim at broadening their individual university curricula, we also see a demand coming from high school scholars wanting to verify whether their existing skillset is sufficient for enrolment in certain college degrees [5], or employees aiming to increase their chances for promotions and 'job upgrades'. In particular the latter, may be seen a user group, which would significantly benefit from online education.

A main challenge, however, remains in the integration of these as well as other, less 'massive' and thus more focused online resources with more traditional offline content so as to provide a coherent and overall efficient education package. The constant push towards a digitalization of learning does not only affect institutions of higher education and their potential students, but also enterprises, as they increasingly recognize the value of online education as a means to replace more traditional forms of employee training. Hence, we believe that companies should adapt their training strategies to these new conditions, the goal being to combine online lectures taught by well-known and esteemed experts in the field with company-specific personalized employee trainings. So far, however, universities often fail to recognize this potential of offering their core competences to companies rather than to high school graduates.

3 E-Learning – Why Even Bother?

While one may find several reasons, why universities should join the cause and offer at least some of their courses online, we see two particularly important aspects: (1) online education as a means to acquire potential future students, and (2) online education as an opportunity to boost an institution's reputation both on an international level as well as with its existing (offline) students.

3.1 Online Education to Acquire Potential Future Students

Acquiring customers is a core challenge for each and any business. Universities, and here especially business schools, are not different in this aspect, except for the fact that their customers, i.e. students, usually come with an expiry date. Consequently, one may argue that education providers are in constant search for customers. Given that some of their potential customers may have great time restrictions (due to work arrangements) or are simply not at ease to follow a more traditional, full-time, in-class study program, online education may be seen a promising path to expand the potential customer base. That is, from a marketing perspective MOOCs and other forms of online education may very well be used as a way of reaching out to new customer segments [6]. And even with the more traditional 'just out of high school' type of scholar, the availability of online content can be seen as a great advantage. That is, although some senior students may say that they have always known what and where they wanted to study and therefore did not really struggle with their choice of program, many high school graduates are often swamped by the heterogeneity of a given educational landscape. Offering online content in the form of so-called 'college readiness courses' can be of significant help here, as it supports potential students in their selection of an appropriate career path. Moreover, these learnings not only help these students select a field they are interested in, but also allow them to evaluate whether they meet the required skill level for their program of choice. Finally, for study domains where it is foreseeable that students may not bring in the required qualifications, it can further be wise to extend those 'college readiness courses' and convert them into so-called 'college preparation courses' in which graduates from different institutions, with different backgrounds, are aligned and brought together so as to up-skill them to the required level.

In summary, we argue that the availability of online education (either in the form of MOOCs or in smaller settings) has great value in acquiring future students because on the one hand it offers an accessible study format to those who cannot participate in more traditional face-to-face engagements, and on the other hand because it can be used to expand existing in-class education and consequently support those that need additional help or guidance in fulfilling relevant study requirements.

3.2 Online Education as an Opportunity to Boost an Institution's Reputation

The second advantage education providers should see in offering online courses concerns their positive effect with respect to an institution's reputation. This reputation plays not only an important role with its students but also with its faculty members and partner institutions, as well as with sponsors such as industry and alumni networks.

Offering online content that features a university's core competence subjects would thus not only increase an institution's potential reach and possibly attract an international audience, but it would also show that it is capable of mastering upcoming trends in education. Such can be seen as a key variable influencing an institution's overall reputation [7]. In addition, the promotion of faculty members via these type of online programs may further contribute to this reputational boost [8]. That is, if for example Stephen Hawking would have featured an online course on gravitational physics it would likely have influenced his university's positive reputation – even if in this example the institution may not even require additional glory.

Hence, it can be argued that online education not only supports universities in acquiring new students but may also help them boost their institutional reputation.

4 An Investigation of Challenges

In order to explore challenges accompanying the two above stated motivations for online education, we researched and contacted German, Austrian and Swiss universities and education providers which, according to their website offer online courses, and asked for an interview summarizing their experiences with the topic. A total of 14 potential interview partners replied and signalized their availability for the study. All of them were either personally working on online learning topics or in charge of online learning supplies at their institution. Respondents included both experts from institutions that offer MOOC-like education as well as representatives from institutions that have not yet started greater online initiatives but have some online course available to take by their students. In order to give the discussions some structure, the above highlighted motivations served as a starting point. The goal was to identify respective challenges and how they may potentially be shouldered. All discussions were recorded and fully transcribed. To analyze the data, Mayring's Qualitative Content Analysis [9] was used, where initially categories were defined according to previous work and later on refined through inductive, content-driven reasoning. Below we summarize the results of this analysis, structured along the identified categories.

5 Discussion of Results

Overall, the analysis of our 14 interviews yielded six key challenges education providers face when offering online courses: (1) increasing cost, (2) an increasing student base, (3) the handling of the drop-out rate, (4) keeping up the teaching quality, (5) certification and its link to evaluation, and (6) dealing with legal challenges.

5.1 The Cost Factors

The high financial resources required for creating and consequently offering online course formats are commonly seen as one of the main challenges for education providers. Covering production and distribution, these costs may lie between 39,000 and 325,000 USD, depending on direct cost factors such as the size of the course, the number of staff involved in the creation process, the required technical equipment, and indirect costs caused by marketing efforts or necessary improvements of the university infrastructure [10]. This issue was confirmed by the interview study. Interviewees report that existing experiences help with the creation of online material, but that such is not always sufficient to offer content on a large scale. Furthermore, it is not only the creation of a course but also the operation of an online platform and its accompanying need for technical personnel which is perceived as a great challenge. Also, the analysis of upcoming technological trends (e.g. mobile learning) is seen as a significant cost factor, which needs to be considered if one wants to survive in the online market. Know-how exchange with partner institutions can help tackle this challenge, yet these types of collaborations may require complex legal requirements, covering use cases such as for example a server outage.

In addition to technical resources, it is also the lack of available personnel that concerns institutions. This does not only affect production and maintenance but also the commercialization of online courses or the management of potential partners. On top of that one also has to find qualified faculty members that agree to integrate with or even replace offline lectures by corresponding online classes. Often, they would see the potential benefit of boosting their reputation and thus opt-in prematurely. When, however, confronted with the required additional workload, they quickly loose interest. Offering high quality online education usually needs new teaching material (i.e. different slide sets, a new course structure, additional evaluation metrics, etc.), which drastically increases the lecturer's workload (at least on a one-time effort level). Specialized support systems may help with these tasks – yet again, those systems are expensive. Many of our interviewed universities thus feel that online education is simply not cost-efficient at present. Limited budgets would not allow for the production and maintenance of high-quality material. Consequently, the online part is kept rather small and usually financed by a small portion of the institution's overall budget. This is also owed to the impression, that online education is supposed to be offered free of charge for which relevant expenses cannot be covered by incoming tuition fees – an impression which was mainly formed through the open availability of MOOCs offered by renowned schools such as the MIT or Stanford University.

Education providers would need to think about different business models so as to make their efforts put in online content profitable. For example, in countries where advanced education is perceived a national matter, the creation of online content is often subsidized. Consequently, some of the content providers we talked to use these funding schemes to leverage their internal budgets. Usually, however, those funds are earmarked to kick-start a pilot project and only available throughout the initiation phase. After this, institutions are back to relying on their limited budgets. Other, more realistic financial concepts are, however, barely available.

One possible revenue stream may be seen in additional benefits that go beyond the actual course offering. According to our interviewees, this could include additional coaching classes, individualized learning analytics that help push the learning success, as well as official diplomas and certificates. Also, it may be possible to bring in sponsors and industrial partners, which would cover at least part of the expenditure. In return they could, for example, provide real-world problem settings to be worked on during class, up to the point where the education provider would offer an entire MOOC in close collaboration with a company (incl. jointly branded course material and potentially visiting lectures given by industrial experts). Yet finding suitable partners for these types of collaboration may be difficult. Particularly, as companies often have their very own agenda of why they would sponsor such a course, which might lead to serious conflicts of interest.

Finally, it was mentioned that costs could also be covered through selling licences to other education providers i.e. an online course could be created by one institution but licences to be used by others as well [11, 12]. All in all, the interviews highlighted that the cost aspect still represents the greatest challenge that has to be overcome if some day online education should be more than a simple side product.

5.2 An Increasing Student Base

While we see the chance to enter into new customer segments as one significant advantage of online education, the institutions we talked to offer their online courses without the dedicated need of increasing their student base. They rather focus on improving the interaction with their existing students by offering a modern (sometimes additional) channel of interaction. External, potentially interested parties usually do not know about these offers and although other institutions may see here a potential for boosting their student numbers, they often find it difficult to justify the required marketing effort. Also, as some of our interviewees highlighted, the effort of entering new customer segments is not to be underestimated as it requires for different strategies to be adapted to different target groups. Solely, the cooperation with already existing partner institutions, national as well as international, is seen as a feasible and relatively cost neutral way of increasing an existing student base.

We may thus note that, while the institutions we talked to see the contribution online education might bring to the increase of student numbers, they also see a great danger in using this as a main argument for the investment.

5.3 Handling the Drop-Out Rate

"Moving to e-learning increases student drop-outs" – this or similar statements keep many institutions from entering the online education market. The evidence is further supported by studies, which show that not more than approx. 10% of enrolled MOOC students complete their course [5, 8]. Reasons for such low conversion rates are often seen in the high number of enrolments (note: given that MOOCs usually refrain from charging tuition fees the entry barrier is rather low) and its resulting didactical difficulties. With respect to the latter, it is particularly the limited contact time with faculty, which can influence both learning success and learning satisfaction [13]. The low entry barrier on the other hand offers a means to satisfy a certain level of curiosity. That is, people often register for a course because they show a certain interest in the topic. In this case, however, course completion is secondary and rather seen as a 'hobby' [14].

In addition, it needs to be clarified how drop-out rates are actually calculated. With MOOCs they are usually based on the total of registered students. However, a significant number of these students never even consume the course's initiation video i.e. they never come to 'class' for which they should not be counted as active students. Rather, one should compute drop-out rates based on students who (at least for some time) actively engaged in the course. Taken these figures, a study in France, for example, showed that drop-outs in online learning are almost comparable to those happening with traditional (offline) university courses [15]. Given that most of the institutions we talked to consider their current online course portfolio as an add-on to in-class teaching, drop-out rates seemed secondary. Yet, all of them agreed that these numbers need to be taken seriously in case the effort spent in online courses should increase in the future.

5.4 Keeping up the Teaching Quality

One aspect our interviewees consider critical in moving from physical lectures to an online course structure is the potential drop in teaching quality. While those institutions which already have experience with online education usually do not perceive this to be a challenge, it seems to be a great fear of those who have not yet moved to this type of knowledge transfer. From a didactic perspective, it is particularly large courses (e.g. MOOCs) that are considered a limitation, as they usually do not offer personalization features and thus lack the support for different learning types. Consequently, it may be difficult to offer the same learning quality as offline. More experienced e-learning providers counter this concern with the need for a reasonable and well-defined mix of online teaching tools and methods with which even the difficulty of personal supervision can be tackled. In any case, teaching quality is considered a great challenge; although one that can be overcome given sufficient training and experience.

5.5 Certification and Its Link to Evaluation

Many online education providers offer their participants some sort of certificate, which attests the successful completion of a course and consequently aims at providing a certain learning outcome. Whether this type of quality control is a nice-to-have feature or rather an important demand often depends on the course's target group. One of our interviewees spoke of a course which was offered relatively open, aimed both at junior level students as well as anybody interested in the topic. In such a case, the certification plays a rather minor role. However, if the course is restrictive and targeted at a distinct group of students, the availability of a certificate, which assures a defined learning outcome, may become a key requirement.

An aspect tightly linked to certification is the evaluation of said learning outcome. That is, a participant's learning outcome has to be measured so as to evaluate whether the defined learning goal was achieved. Such makes the problem of online examination and performance evaluation a distinct challenge to programs that offer certifications. It seems particularly difficult to find a suitable examination procedure, which is in line with the didactical concept of online education and at the same time guarantees the authenticity of a participant. Highlighting the statement of one of our interviewees *"if you can't guarantee the identity of the person taking the exam, the potentially gained certificate is not worth the paper it is written on"*. Consequently, providers often issue certificates only in cases where the final evaluation is performed in person and at their premise. According to our interviewees, this is also the only way to gain ECTS credit points, which may then be used to demonstrate already achieved learnings when applying for an academic degree or entrance into an academic degree program; although here participants may face an additional challenge. That is, while some European universities may accept ECTS points gained through online courses held at other education providers, the majority of institutions would only accept those points which were gained from participating in their very own courses. While this may be seen a very important challenge for online education, as it certainly contradicts one of its main advantages (i.e. one should be able to choose from a variety of providers and take the course which best fits one's needs and expectations), it may also be seen a more general problem of the European academic education landscape. That is, while in theory ECTS credit points gained at one European institution should, in case they are comparable in content and effort, be recognized at other European institutions, the reality often greatly deviates from this concept. This goes as far as that sometimes they are not even recognized within the same country. Thus, one may argue that before the problem of recognizing ECTS points can be solved on an online level, the general compatibility of this concept has to be implemented in the offline world. The increased propagation of online programs and education providers may, however, trigger relevant discussions.

5.6 Facing the Legal Challenge

Online education also poses some legal challenges that have to be tackled. For example, due to national data protection and privacy regulations it might not even be possible to track the (virtual) attendance of course participants. Consequently, in these countries the successful completion of a course (and further the potential issuing of a course certificate) cannot be subject to a defined level of course attendance. Course providers rather need to think of alternative solutions that would motivate students' virtual availability. Also, given that the currency for achieved learning, i.e. ECTS credit points, is connected to the time and effort spent, it is further important to balance the online and offline activities of participants. That is, in online education, the percentage of 'in-class time' is usually smaller than it is in traditional offline courses.

Another legal aspect concerns the workload of the lecturer and his/her assistants. Similar to the ECTS currency used to quantify the learning effort of students, lecturers have a defined number of teaching credits or contact hours written in their contracts. Thus, it is important to clarify how online teaching is measured. For example, in case of an asynchronous course structure, i.e. where lectures are recorded and students watch them whenever they have time to do so, it is not always clear how the lecturer's contact hours are calculated. This becomes a particularly important issue in cases where the course is given by an external lecturer, as this may directly affect his/her income. Here it needs to be defined whether the lecturer is paid once per academic year/term, or anytime the course is accessed. Alternatively, institutions may negotiate some sort of license fee to be paid to the lecturer, similar to licenses paid to other content providers such as musicians or filmmakers. In cases where the institution's in-house employees, i.e. its contracted lecturers, are holding online courses, it further needs to be clarified how the creation of the online material (i.e. structure, video lectures, online exams, etc.) is compensated.

Finally, the offered online content itself may be subject to legal disputes, in particular with respect to the potential violation of copyright. Multiple interviewees highlighted this problem and pointed to the difficulties they have had staying within legal boundaries. According to one interviewee, approximately 80% of the slide sets used in their offline courses had to be adapted so as to not infringe copyright. This usually concerns used graphics but sometimes also content, for which in both cases it has to be clarified whether the material can be made accessible to 3rd parties, i.e. course participants. While copyright infringement is not necessarily a problem of online education, but should rather be considered a challenge to be tackled with any type of teaching, it is the prolonged appearance of online courses that triggered the discussion. It almost seems that in the past, when lectures where still held within the protected walls of academic institutions, nobody thought about potential copyright violations in slide sets. Now, however, that the problem is out in the open, some offline institutions circumvent it by refraining their students access to lecture material. That is, students who physically attend the course are able to visually follow the slide set presentations. Access to those slides is, however, not granted. Yet, in the world of online education such an approach would not be appropriate, and so the copyright problematic needs to be faced and adequately handled.

6 Summary and Concluding Remarks

The discussions put forward in this article aimed at identifying challenges of online education, focusing on universities and other types of education providers. The literature highlights examples such as a high drop-out rate [8] or the assurance of required teaching qualities [16]. The discussion with a number of education providers in Germany, Austria and Switzerland has, however, shown that these aspects are currently less of a problem. A more pressing issue concerns the evaluation and certification of learning goals and performances and the dealing with potential copyright infringements. In particular the authentication of participants is perceived as a difficult challenge, which if not guaranteed may in the worst case even void the potential value of an issued certificate [17]. This type of valid measurement also influences the acceptance of study credits gained through online learnings. To this end, our research has shown that often credits are only recognized if they have been gained at the same institution. Credits gained from other institutions may, however, be rejected.

Another important aspect often named in connection with online education concerns its cost and its need for adequate business models. At this point education providers see online education as a way to expand their customer base, although the yielded reach is not yet sufficient so as to justify a complete channel switch. Consequently, the production cost is often cross-financed by other offline generated income streams. An alternative to this is seen in the customized provision of staff trainings. That is, companies as paying customers may help expand the online education landscape. Here universities and other education providers should offer their skillset. They would be able to draw from their existing teaching know-how and experiences and be able to procure the technical resources necessary to transfer this profession into a virtual setting. Furthermore, it may be seen as an additional motivation for the teaching personnel, for they might find satisfaction in designing lectures that are not targeted at traditional junior year students but rather at professionals.

In summary, this article highlighted a number of challenges Universities have to deal with when thinking about online-education. It is, however, limited by the fact that it is based on only 14 different institutions, all of which are located in German speaking countries. Consequently, it is not meant as a general reference but should rather serve as a starting point for more in-depth discussions on the challenges of propagating the use of learning technologies and online education.

References

1. Kaur, M.: Blended learning - its challenges and future. Procedia. Soc. Behav. Sci. **93**, 612–617 (2013)
2. Witt, C.: Mobile Learning. Springer Fachmedien Wiesbaden GmbH, Potenziale, Einsatzszenarien und Perspektiven des Lernens mit mobilen Endgeräten (2013)
3. Sauter, W., Sauter, S.: Workplace Learning. Integrierte Kompetenzentwicklung mit kooperativen und kollaborativen Lernsystemen. Springer Gabler, Imprint (2013)
4. McAuley, A., Stewart, B., Siemens, G., Cormier, D.: The MOOC model for digital practice (2010)
5. Brahimi, T., Sarirete, A.: Learning outside the classroom through MOOCs. Comput. Hum. Behav. **15**, 604–609 (2015)
6. Hollands, F.M., Tirthali, D.: MOOCs: expectations and reality. Full Report Center for Benefit-Cost Studies of Education Teachers College, Columbia University, Hrsg, New York (2014b)
7. O'Connor, K.: MOOCs, institutional policy and change dynamics in higher education. High. Educ. **68**(5), 623–635 (2014)
8. Hew, K.F., Cheung, W.S.: Students' and instructors' use of massive open online courses (MOOCs): motivations and challenges. Educ. Res. Rev. **12**, 45–58 (2014)
9. Mayring, P.: Qualitative content analysis: theoretical foundation, basic procedures and software solution (2014). http://nbn-resolving.de/urn:nbn:de:0168-ssoar-395173
10. Hollands, F.M., Tirthali, D.: Resource requirements and costs of developing and delivering MOOCs. Int. Rev. Res. Open Dist. Learn. **15**(5), 114–133 (2014)
11. Dellarocas, C., van Alstyne, M.: Money models for MOOCs. Commun. ACM **56**(8), 25–28 (2013)
12. Kalman, Y.M.: A race to the bottom: MOOCs and higher education business models. Open Learn. J. Open. Dist. e-Learn. **29**(1), 5–14 (2014)
13. Wulf, J., Blohm, I., Leimeister, J.M., Brenner, W.: Massive open online courses. Wirtschaftsinformatik **56**(2), 127–130 (2014)
14. Sandeen, C.: Integrating MOOCS into traditional higher education: the emerging "MOOC 3.0" era. Chang. Mag. High. Learn. **45**(6), 34–39 (2013)
15. Loya, A., Gopal, A., Shukla, I., Jermann, P., Tormey, R.: Conscientious behaviour, flexibility and learning in massive open on-line courses. Procedia. Soc. Behav. Sci. **191**, 519–525 (2015)
16. Margaryan, A., Bianco, M., Littlejohn, A.: Instructional quality of massive open online courses (MOOCs). Comput. Educ. **80**, 77–83 (2015)
17. Cooper, S., Sahami, M.: Reflections on Stanford's MOOCs. Commun. ACM **56**(2), 28–30 (2013)

Implementing Blended Learning in Mathematics Classrooms: Perspectives of Two South African Educators Working in an International School in Saudi Arabia

Ilhaam Abrahams(✉), Lawrence Meda(✉), and Eunice Ivala(✉)

Cape Peninsula University of Technology, Cape Town, South Africa
abrahams.ilhaam@gmail.com, medalawrence@gmail.com,
ivalae@cput.ac.za

Abstract. Blended learning is one of the modalities used to enhance students' learning experiences in the 21st century. South African educators who migrate to countries overseas have mixed feelings about their teaching using technology in schools. This paper presents findings on implementation of blended learning in mathematics classrooms from the perspectives of two South African educators working in an international school in Saudi Arabia. The study was done using a qualitative case study within an interpretivist paradigm and it was guided by the Technology Acceptance Model. Two South African educators teaching at an international school in Saudi Arabia were purposively selected to participate in the study. Data was collected using semi-structured interviews and document analysis. A significant contribution of the study was the development of a model which shows that perspectives of the educators on blended learning hinges on two entities: technology acceptance and educators' self-efficacy.

Keywords: Blended learning · Technology · Saudi Arabia · Learning experiences · Technology Acceptance Model

1 Introduction

The year 2007 saw the Kingdom of Saudi Arabia (KSA) establish an educational policy known as "the King Abdullah Public Education Development Project", better known as the "Tatweer" project. This project was aimed at improving teaching and learning within the KSA through the implementation of educational technologies into classrooms (Tayan 2017). Alyami (2014) described this project as an opportunity for schools to shift from traditional teaching and learning methods to an approach that incorporates blended learning.

Xakaza-Kumalo (2017) indicated that there were no universal approaches that an educator may take in implementing educational technologies in teaching and learning that would ensure learners' academic success. Opposing this opinion, Dziuban et al. (2018) argued that "blended learning" was fast becoming the standardised mode of teaching and subsequently contributed to improved learner academic success. Yushau (2006) concurred that the term blended learning had grown to represent an improved

L. Uden et al. (Eds.): LTEC 2019, CCIS 1011, pp. 234–244, 2019.
https://doi.org/10.1007/978-3-030-20798-4_21

array of teaching and learning approaches where traditional teaching and learning methods were fused with educational technologies or online learning. Furthermore, Dlamini (2018:1) stated that a study completed in 2015 showed that blended learning had improved student engagement by 69%, content retention by 39%, and test scores by 28%.

Despite the recognition of blended learning for student success, Alahmari and Kyei-Blankson (2016) stated that the integration of educational technologies in the KSA teaching and learning was welcomed with mixed reactions by educators. Some educators were eager to integrate educational technologies into their classrooms, with others not fully geared for the implementation because of factors such as ineffective training. Oyaid (2009) contended that to have educators successfully integrate educational technologies into their teaching, their pedagogical approaches may need to be altered. These changes may vary between educators based on their disposition to the use of technology. These personal dispositions affect the perspectives educators have regarding the implementation of educational technologies into their classes. As the KSA schools are in the process of evolving, the approach of blended learning is preferred as it is believed to increase efficiency, while allowing learners the opportunity to acquire modern learning skills (Bukhari 2016).

Additionally, there is a dearth of scholarship regarding South African educators' perspectives on the implementation of educational technologies within Saudi Arabian schools (Alahmari and Kyei-blankson 2016), and specifically in mathematics classrooms. A lack of scholarship in the area of educational technology, particularly blended learning in the Saudi Arabian context, is what this paper seeks to contribute to. This paper presents perspectives on implementing blended learning in mathematics classrooms from two South African educators working in an international school in Saudi Arabia.

1.1 Blended Learning Conceptualised

There is no one universally accepted definition of blended learning. Siyepu (2018) conceptualised the term as a systematic process of linking the worlds of traditional teaching and learning with educational technologies. Pierce (2017) echoed the same sentiments by defining blended learning as the combination of E-Learning alongside traditional classroom teaching and learning methods, additionally mentioning that blended learning may not look the same in every classroom.

Schwuchow (2018) states that there are three blended learning approaches: Firstly, the enriched approach, where classroom interaction is pivotal and technology is used to enhance the lesson. Bralić and Divjak (2016) concurred that the enriched approach allowed learners to have access to digital resources that supplement their learning while having the benefits of access to face-to-face classes. Secondly, the integrative approach, where learning environments created are of an equal part traditional classroom learning as well as virtual (Schwuchow 2018). Saxena (2017) contended that the integrative blended learning approach involves gamification where learners learn educational concepts through digital play spaces. These educational concepts are then expounded upon when learners are in class. The third is the Virtual approach, where the learning environment is entirely virtual and face-to-face interactions between educator and learner occur as and when requested (Fox et al. 2018). While the aforementioned illustrates three defined blended learning approaches, it should be noted that these are not the only methods of blending teaching and learning (Bralić and Divjak 2016).

2 Theoretical Framework

Grant and Osanloo (2014) interpret a theoretical framework to be the foundation upon which knowledge is constructed for a research study. This means that a theoretical framework comprises of a theory (or theories) that supports how the researcher approaches the study in terms of epistemology, philosophy, methodology, and analysis. A study can be guided not only by a theory but also a model (Sokolowski 2018:6). This study used the Technology Acceptance Model (TAM) as a theoretical framework. Huang and Liaw (2018) maintained that TAM has two principles: perceived usefulness (PU) and perceived ease of use (PEOU) of technology. Perceived usefulness is the extent to which a user feels implementing technology will better their performance (Davis 1989), for example, whether the educator feels that using a smartboard betters the teaching and learning experience of learners as opposed to using a whiteboard. PEOU is when an educator is convinced that technology makes work easy and more efficient (Huang and Liaw 2018). Masrom (2007) postulates that PEOU affects PU based on the principle that when one perceives something as easy to use, one would consequently feel that it is useful. The model was selected as it inter-relates the topic of technology usage and the perspectives of those making use of the technology.

3 Methodology

The study in which findings are presented in this paper was done using a qualitative approach within an interpretive paradigm. Both qualitative and interpretive were chosen as they are compatible and they allow researchers to interpret and understand the perspectives of people (Cohen et al. 2017). The study was done as a case study of an international school in Saudi Arabia where two South African educators are teaching mathematics. A case study was selected for this study as it allowed the researcher to gain an in-depth exploration of the educators' perspectives (Yin 2014). The school offers Grades K-12. As an international school, the curriculum used is an amended American curriculum whereby educators are encouraged to actively incorporate educational technologies into their teaching and learning of their students. Two South African educators teaching Grade 10 mathematics using blended learning at the school were purposively selected to participate in the study. Data was collected using semi-structured interviews and documentary analysis. Ethical clearance was sought from the school and district office in Saudi Arabia.

4 Findings and Discussion

4.1 Educators Perspectives on Blended Learning

The data indicated that the educators defined blended learning as a mixture of traditional and modern teaching methodologies. Educator 1 (E1) stated:

> I use the traditional whiteboard with working out calculations, for making notes or explanations but I also provide my learners with additional support and information via electronic means by displaying presentations or 3D shapes or having the smart-board generate graphs or to solve matrices. When the students purchase their textbooks, they are subscribed to the digital textbook which they use at home to go through the lessons before class and I will direct them to additional enrichment exercises in the digital book after the lesson.

Similarly, Educator 2 (E2) explained blended learning as:

> Simultaneously using technology and regular teaching tools. In my class we use the learners' textbooks and workbooks along with the smart interactive board. The learners have their textbooks on the desk and I will display something related to the lesson on the smartboard like a video, animation or interactive game where learners need to solve questions, select the correct answers or draw their graphs on the smartboard which will automatically synchronise to the shared OneDrive and update the lesson notes which will be available for the students online after the lesson. I also do calculations or explanations on the whiteboard in the same lesson.

From these findings, the authors deduce that both educators shared the opinion that blended learning was when the worlds of traditional teaching and modern teaching methodologies are used simultaneously in a teaching situation. This is in agreement with Pierce (2017), who defined blended learning as the combination of E-Learning alongside traditional classroom teaching and learning methods. Similarly, Al-Sharqi, Hashim and Ahmed (2015) conceptualised blended learning as the harmonious integration of learning strategies through the combination of face-to-face interaction and ICT, allowing for a more enriched learning experiences.

Furthermore, Schwuchow (2018) mentioned that blended learning in a class will take the form the educator feels comfortable with. Al Jaser (2017) highlighted a study conducted at the Princess Norah University in Saudi Arabia, where blended learning has taken the form of a flipped classroom. Sommer and Ritzhaupt (2018) described a flipped classroom as a learning situation where learners are given access to course content ahead of time so that when they get to class they are informed and ready to engage on the content. Findings of this study showed that the respondents selected to employ a flipped classroom approach to their blended learning. E1 explained: "When the students purchase their textbooks, they are subscribed to the digital textbook which they use at home to go through the lessons before class." Similarly, E2 stated:

> The digital text book is a great help as students go through the chapters before the lesson because they get participation points on the Learning management System (LMS) and that means the content is a little more familiar when I formally introduce topics in the class time.

Data showed that the flipped classroom format was employed by these educators. Firstly, the educators have the learners peruse the chapters ahead of the lessons. When the learners arrive for the formal lesson to be taught, the educators capture their interest through digital means, for example playing a video, animation, or warm-up game via the interactive smartboard. Educator two (E2) explained how his lessons are flipped:

> Before the lesson, I will upload information linked to the topics we are covering. During the lesson will have the textbook exercises open on the smartboard and when students go to the board to work out their answers or if I add any additional notes, these inputs will be directly uploaded to the shared drive which students will have access to, for revision, as soon as they check their devices. After the lesson I will upload information pertaining to the next lesson.

Furthermore, the learners are encouraged to revisit the lesson as well as engage with the content provided for the next lesson out of the classroom.

4.2 Technology Acceptance

Both educators reflected on how they had initially come from South African schools when describing the teaching technology and training being made available for them in Saudi Arabia. E1 felt that there was no real need for them to integrate the available technologies into their teaching in the South African school he worked in. Additionally, E1 stated that once he emigrated from South Africa to KSA, there was a greater need to integrate the teaching technologies made available and that he had to accept the technologies. Educator one (E1) stated:

> I really enjoy using technology to teach now. It makes things much easier, more manageable and content engaging especially for my Mathematics and Physical Science students. Initially, it was a big shock for me, coming from South Africa where there was one computer lab in the building with 20 computers that 48 students needed to share, unlike here in KSA where each student has a tablet, all classrooms have projectors with smart boards with Wi-Fi and you are expected to use these resources on a daily basis. Since being in KSA for the last 5 years, it has really shifted my opinion on using technology with my teaching. Back in SA the school would make the educators attend workshops where we would be shown how to use programs, but I would never pay attention. I took it for granted because I was at a poor school where the students outnumbered the resources and if I needed something done there was always a younger educator or one of my children I could ask to do these things for me. When I moved to KSA for the first time I was alone. I had to figure all these things out for myself. My livelihood depended on whether or not I was able to integrate these technologies into my classroom. I had to accept that I needed to use this technology in order to do my job successfully.

Alharbi and Drew (2014) discussed TAM, in light of a study conducted at Shaqra University in Saudi Arabia, stating that an educator would deem a technological tool to be useful depending on the degree to which this technological tool would enhance their performance as an educator. In this instance, it was evident that E1 previously had little motivation to make use of the technology at the South African school. This educator previously felt that the use of the available educational technologies made no real difference to their teaching and therefore deemed the use of these technologies useless. Based on the TAM model, E1's decision not to accept technology for teaching and learning was influenced by the fact that the educator viewed the technology as not needed. In contrast, when E1 emigrated to KSA there was a greater need to accept the technology as it was expected of him to integrate it in his teaching and learning of his learners. The educator expressed that he enjoyed using technology in his teaching and that the technology enhanced the lessons. This indicates that the educator viewed the use of technology as being useful.

Along with the need to view a technological teaching tool as being useful, TAM takes into account how easy a technological tool is for the user. Moukali (2012) posits that when considering the acceptance of technology, TAM connects the perception of perceived usefulness of technology and the perceived ease of use for a user. Educator two (E2) reiterated the points made by E1 regarding the implementation of technologies being useful to the teaching and learning of mathematics among other subjects. Furthermore, E2 highlighted that the use of these technologies was initially challenging but it had become easier to use with practice. Educator two (E2) reported:

> It was challenging at first, but with anything when you practice you do better. Being a South African educator, coming from a teaching environment where there was little to no blended teaching and learning or even incorporating any technology into lesson. I had to do quite a bit of learning on the job when I emigrated to KSA but that really allowed me the opportunity to discover things that were not taught in the workshops being offered by the school. Now I enjoy preparing my lessons, accessing the different functions on my smartboard and making my Mathematics and Computer Aided Drawing (CAD) lessons interactive and creating learning situations where students look forward to my lessons. For me a really motivating factor was that I have a family that I need to provide for back in SA, so I had to do what I could to make a success of working in KSA. I had to adapt my traditional teaching methods to the way teaching and learning takes place in KSA.

Based on the above results it is once again evident that the educator had a necessity to accept the usefulness of the technology they were presented with, moreover, the educator expressed the fact that the technology has become easier to operate, manipulate, and implement. This supports Moukali's (2012) explanation of TAM that if an educator perceives a technological tool as easy to implement, they would deem the technology to be useful and therefore the educator is more likely to accept and implement the technology.

4.3 Utilisation of Technology

When asked about the teaching and learning resources in their classes, E2 had this to say: "Smart board, Pearson digital textbook, YouTube, ClassEra, MS-office, presentation tool or laser pointer, data projector, tablets for learners, Wi-Fi enabled classroom, desktop computer, personal laptop and Khan Academy. We use the LMS and smartboard extensively." From this results it is evident that the educators have well-resourced classrooms. When asked about how the LMS (ClassEra) works, E1 explained:

> It is a learner management system that allows for communication between the educator, students, parents or guardians and the principal. It is fully online. The educator will upload lessons, class announcements, additional information or slides connected to topics, monitor student behaviour with the points system, parents can track the progress of their kids with weekly reports that are generated from self-marking quizzes and we can set up class groups for the students to discuss work while we, as the educators, monitor the discussions. It is a really great system and it serves as a storage bank for our lessons.

The above findings are in agreement with Alghamdi (2018), who indicated that technologies are selected for blended learning based on three factors, namely; the communication between learner and educator being direct and immediate, that the resources are cost effective, and that the need for continual teaching and learning is met.

Additionally, with blended learning, E2 spoke about the smart interactive board, stating:

> We use the smart board extensively; we have the board generate graphs, do calculations, play presentations, video and animations, display the textbook and make notes to slides to upload later or synchronise to the LMS. The smartboard is also an easy way of keeping the faster students busy with additional questions while I walk around assisting other students or checking if the students have any questions. The kids also enjoy it when I let them generate the graphs or writing their answers on the smartboard when we do final calculations.

Alghamdi (2018) articulates that successful integration of smartboard technology can transform a learning space into an interactive and dynamic learning environment and enhances the classroom environment. This encourages learner participation and confidence building. E2 has accepted the available technology and was reaping the benefits of utilising the smartboard in the class.

Both educators unequivocally stated that they enjoy being able to blend their lessons. When asked about the future of blended learning, E1 expressed:

> I do not see blended learning going away anytime soon. I think more educators will come on board with this method of teaching and I see younger educators coming up with better and more innovative methods of blending learning as a whole.

Similarly, E2 stated:

> I know that program developers will improve on educational technologies and the educational systems will get better. Learning will be more accessible to more students and become even more cost effective. If we expose our students to these educational technologies, the students may be inspired to create the changes we are speaking about.

The above findings show that both educators believed that blended learning will stand the test of time. Jonker et al. (2018) discussed educator identity in lieu of blended learning, indicating that there are a number of factors that affect an educator's professional identity and in turn affects their stance on their utilising of blended learning in a classroom situation. One of the factors Jonker et al. (2018) put forward was that when educators experience a shift in educational contexts, this affects educators professional identity.

4.4 Educators' Self-efficacy and Blended Learning

When speaking about professional development, the educators expressed that the current school they were teaching at offered continuous, consistent, and relevant professional development. Educator one (EI) explained that the school provided training workshops for the facilitation of blended learning: "Fortunately, the school had a really great educator program that trains you on all of the systems and they have a designated person you can ask any questions if you have any problems."

Echoing the same sentiment, E2 stated:

> The school provided lots of training where the LMS, the smartboard and the textbook companies all sent a representative to the school to offer educators specialised training. The school even had someone come in to show educators the best ways to set up their classrooms to gain maximum benefit from all of the technological resources.

Alghamdi (2018) suggested that correct, sufficient and appropriate professional development positively impacts the teaching strategies of educators and their self-efficacy. On the point of self-efficacy, both E1 and E2 seemed to have self-belief and confidence in the training they received. Educator one (E1) felt equipped enough to make a success of implementing blended learning within the classroom:

> As a mathematics and physical science educator, my subjects are generally difficult for students to grasp. Had it not been for the extensive and regular training we have to do at school, I do not think I would be as confident as I am with implementing all these teaching technologies into my lessons or rather blending my lessons. In life if you have the right tools it is easy to be sure of what you are doing. For me, I needed the confidence boost because my subjects are so heavy and there is a big language barrier between myself and my students.

Self-efficacy is conceptualised in this study as an individual's belief that he/she can achieve specific goals in a particular area of performance (Lisbona et al. 2018). Bandura (1977) concurs that self-efficacy has something to do with one's judgement and belief that he/she can do something. It (self-efficacy) has something to do with a people's intrinsic motivation and belief that they can achieve certain goals regardless of how difficult the task may be. It is essential to point that a person's self-efficacy is boosted when he/she was trained to do something. This is in accordance with findings of this study where educators felt highly motivated and geared to experiment teaching mathematics using blended learning in Saudi Aribia. It was through educators' self-efficacy that implementation of blended learning in mathematics was producing desirable results. Masitoh and Fitriyani (2018) argue that one of the main factors which makes students achieve greater results in Mathematics is self-efficacy. If students lack self-efficacy in challenging subjects like Mathematics, they are likely to perform poorly.

When speaking about how comfortable the educators are with implementing blended learning into their lessons, E1 stated that blended learning was "something that is relatively easy to implement." On the issue of seeking additional information, E1 admitted that they are always seeking new ways of improving their teaching and looking for better ways to implement what was being taught:

> I like to make use of the functions that allow me to be the best educator I can be. I am always looking at YouTube videos to see how I can improve my skills or tricks to better the way I use the systems.

As every learner is different, so are the educators. This exposure to new teaching methodologies and tools, E2 not only felt confident in his/her ability to blend their lessons, but also inspired to seek additional professional development on his/her own. Educator two (E2) stated:

> I am currently doing some studies with the University of Cape Town. A Post Graduate Diploma in Emerging Educational Technologies. This course is really enhancing my work and how I

conduct my lessons. I never thought I would be studying again at my age but this exposure to these teaching methodologies at school has opened my eyes.

Building on the work of Alamri et al. (2018) it was evident that these educators are taking full advantage of a professional development programme that not only encourages educators, but also inspires them to better themselves. It was evident that both E1 and E2 had engaged and embraced the blended learning style. These educators have become immersed in the blended learning approach and were actively seeking new and improved ways of teaching using educational technologies.

5 Conclusion

Framed on TAM, the study from which findings are presented in this paper was aimed at understanding the implementation of blended learning in mathematics classrooms from the perspectives of two South African educators working in an international school in Saudi Arabia. This study concludes that educators view technology as an enabler to quality teaching and learning at the school. The educators understand blended learning as a combination of online learning and face to face learning. A significant contribution emanating from the findings is a model on the educators' perspectives on blended learning as shown on Fig. 1. The model shows that perspectives of the educators on blended learning impacts on two entities, namely: technology acceptance and educators' self-efficacy and blended learning. When educators have adequate academic support and motivation, their perspective to the implementation of blended learning will become positive. If they are given enough support and motivation, they accept teaching utilising technology and develop self-efficacy about blended learning which ultimately result in optimisation of technology and positive perceptions of blended learning. If educators are not supported nor motivated, they have negative views about using technology in general and blended learning in particular.

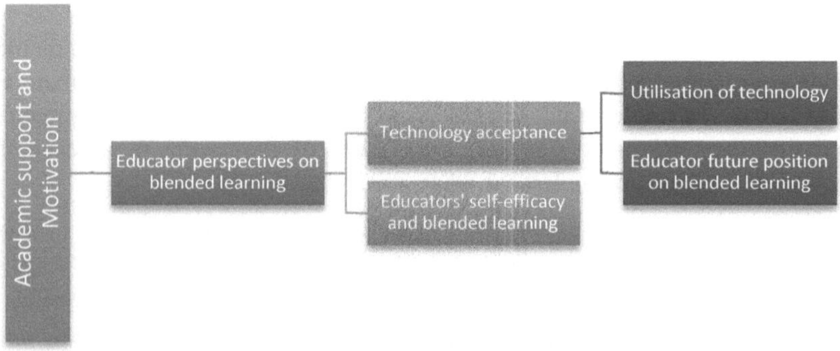

Fig. 1. Model of the educators' perspectives on blended learning

Focusing on the educator's self-efficacy and blended learning, this study comes to a conclusion that educators' perspectives influence their confidence, self-belief, and comfort when implementing teaching technologies and strategies such as blended learning. Thus, this paper provides insights which can be useful towards the successful implementation of blended learning in mathematics.

References

Al-Sharqi, L.M., Hashim, K., Ahmed, P.S.: Improving the learning environment at a university in Saudi Arabia: identifying factors that impede or motivate learning. Int. J. Sci. Basic Appl. Res. (IJSBAR) **19**(2), 234–249 (2015)

Alahmari, A., Kyei-blankson, L.: Adopting and implementing an e-learning system for teaching and learning in saudi public k-12 schools: the benefits, challenges, and concerns. World J. Educ. Res. **3**(1), 11–32 (2016)

Alamri, N.M., Aldahmash, A.H., Alsharif, K.M.: Emerging trends in research on math teacher professional development. Int. J. Instr. **11**(3), 91–106 (2018)

Alharbi, S., Drew, S.: Using the technology acceptance model in understanding academics' behavioural intention to use learning management systems. Int. J. Adv. Comput. Sci. Appl. (IJACSA) **5**(1), 143–155 (2014)

AlJaser, A.M.: Effectiveness of using flipped classroom strategy in academic achievement and self-efficacy among education students of Princess Nourah bint Abdulrahman University. Engl. Lang. Teach. **10**(4), 67 (2017)

Alyami, R.H.: Educational reform in the Kingdom of Saudi Arabia: Tatweer Schools as a unit of development. Literacy Inf. Comput. Educ. J. (LICEJ) **5**(2), 1424–1433 (2014)

Bandura, A.: Self-efficacy: toward a unifying theory of behavioral change. Psychol. Rev. **84**(2), 191–215 (1977)

Bralić, A., Divjak, B.: Use of moocs in traditional classroom: blended learning approach. Eur. J. Open, Dist. E-Learn. **766**(9), 250–259 (2016)

Bukhari, E.G.: Blended learning implementation in secondary education for girls: case study Tatweer Project in Saudi Arabia. Int. J. Acad. Res. Reflection **4**(7), 25–39 (2016)

Cohen, L., Manion, L., Morrison, K.: Research Methods in Education, 8th edn. Routledge, London (2017)

Davis, F.D.: Perceived usefulness, perceived ease of use, and user acceptance of information technology. MIS Q. **13**(3), 319–339 (1989)

Dlamini, K.: How the blended learning concept refines Education (2018). https://lcibs.co.uk/how-the-blended-learning-concept-refines-education/. Accessed 20 Aug 2018

Dziuban, C., Graham, C.R., Moskal, P.D., Norberg, A., Sicilia, N.: Blended learning: the new normal and emerging technologies. Int. J. Educ. Technol. High. Educ. **15**(1), 1–16 (2018)

Fox, J., Pittaway, L., Uzuegbunam, I.: Simulations in entrepreneurship education: serious games and learning through play. Entrepreneurship Educ. Pedagogy **1**(1), 61–89 (2018)

Grant, C., Osanloo, A.: Understanding, selecting, and integrating a theoretical framework in dissertation research: creating the blueprint for your "House". Adm. Issues J. Educ. Pract. Res. **4**(2), 12–26 (2014)

Huang, H.M., Liaw, S.S.: An analysis of learners' intentions toward virtual reality learning based on constructivist and technology acceptance approaches. International Review of Research in Open and Distance Learning **19**(1), 91–115 (2018)

Jonker, H., März, V., Voogt, J.: Teacher educators' professional identity under construction: The transition from teaching face-to-face to a blended curriculum. Teaching and Teacher Education **71**, 120–133 (2018)

Lisbona, A., Palaci, F., Salanova, M., Frese, M.: The effects of work engagement and self-efficacy on personal initiative and performance. Psicothema **30**(1), 89–96 (2018)
Masitoh, L.F., Fitriyani, H.: Improving students' mathematics self-efficacy through problem based learning. Malikussaleh J. Math. Learn. **1**(1), 26–30 (2018)
Masrom, M.: Technology Acceptance Model and E-learning. Technology **21**(24), 1–10 (2007)
Moukali, K.H.: Factors that affect faculty attitudes toward adoption of technology-rich blended learning. Unpublished PhD thesis. University of Kansas, Kansas (2012)
Pierce, D.: What effective blended learning looks like. J. Technol. Horiz. Educ. **44**(1), 18–21 (2017)
Saxena, N.: A study of proliferation of digital literacy in Indian higher education. Int. Educ. Res. J. [IERJ] **3**(4), 127–128 (2017)
Schwuchow, B.: Activity orientation in engineering education. In: Research in Technology Education: International Approaches. Germany: Waxmann Verlag GmbH: 195–205 (2018)
Siyepu, S.W.: Blended learning in a mathematics classroom: a focus in Khan Academy. In: ICMET 2018: 20th International Conference on Mathematics Education and Teachers Conference, London (2018)
Sokolowski, A.: Scientific Inquiry in Mathematics - Theory and Practice: A STEM Perspective - Andrzej Sokolowski - Google Books. Springer, Cham (2018)
Sommer, M., Ritzhaupt, A.: Impact of the flipped classroom on learner achievement and satisfaction in an undergraduate technology literacy course. J. Inf. Technol. Educ. Res. **17**(1), 160–182 (2018)
Tayan, B.M.: The Saudi Tatweer education reforms: implications of neoliberal thought to Saudi education policy. Int. Educ. Stud. **10**(5), 61 (2017)
Xakaza-kumalo, S.: Pedagogical issues arising from the introduction of educational technology at two South African universities of technology: a comparative study. Unpublished DTech thesis. Cape Peninsula University of Technology, Cape Town (2017)
Yin, R.K.: Case Study Research Design and Methods, 5th edn. Sage, Thousand Oaks (2014)
Yushau, B.: The effects of blended e-learning on mathematics and computer attitudes in pre-calculus algebra. TMME **3**(2), 176–183 (2006)

Learning Practices

Context Analysis of Teachers' Learning Design Practice Through Activity Theory, Distributed Cognition, and Situated Cognition

Leandro M. Queiros[1], Carlos J. P. Silva[1], Alex S. Gomes[1], and Fernando Moreira[2,3](✉)

[1] Informatics Center (CIn), Federal University of Pernambuco (UFPE), Recife, Brazil
{lmq, cjps, asg}@cin.ufpe.br
[2] REMIT, IJP - University of Portucalense, Porto, Portugal
fmoreira@upt.pt
[3] IEETA - University of Aveiro, Aveiro, Portugal

Abstract. The objective of this work was to analyze how different theoretical frameworks encompass the teachers' learning design practice. We compared the use of Activity Theory, Distributed Cognition, and Situated Cognition theoretical frameworks to deal with data analysis and interpretations and compared them. The Activity Theory is useful to study technology in activities since the unit of analysis is an activity, and it is always instrumentally mediated. The use of Distributed Cognition framework lies in exploring how mental schemas of the mind can represent structures outside the mind. Finally, Situated Cognition is focused on analyzing the continuous relationship integrating teachers and environmental instruments to act on class planning to understand the flow of the activities involved in this real scenario. The analysis from different theoretical points of view gave the designers a better understanding of the activity structure, how the artifacts support distributed cognitive activities and finally how the artifact is embodied in the planning activities. The present work aims to have contributed to a better understanding of teachers' planning practices to influence the design of lessons planning software services to be integrated into teaching practice.

Keywords: Lesson planning · Teacher practice · Learning design

1 Introduction

The technological advancement of hypertextual environments makes possible the presence of interactivity, which allows users to create, modify and share content from the consolidation of Web 2.0 [1]. This collaborative environment fosters new services and the development of innovative tools.

This context, the user starts acting as a protagonist in multimedia production, for example, blog creation, wiki, Instagram, Google docs, YouTube among other services and tools, providing content and files online where access is made anywhere at any time and in any device [1].

L. Uden et al. (Eds.): LTEC 2019, CCIS 1011, pp. 247–259, 2019.
https://doi.org/10.1007/978-3-030-20798-4_22

In view of the aforementioned scenario, we can see new ways of relating to information and knowledge in learning in school environments through digital technologies. Free access to this range of services that generate knowledge through a few clicks on the Web brings a reflection on how the use of technology can aid the teaching practices of the teacher in the classroom.

Today we are still faced with the traditional process of learning that involves students and teachers in the same confined classroom format and using the classic didactic materials [2]. Therefore, a survey is urgently needed that encompasses a new look at the user as a teacher with the possibilities of Web 2.0 services and tools.

Many online courses already use material production with the interactive and collaborative proposal of web 2.0, enabling the creation of open educational resources, used in distance and classroom education, available to any teacher [3].

Innovating and experiencing new challenges to transform practices into the day-to-day work of the teacher often come up with how to do and develop the idea that is on your mind. To do this, several systems may arise that articulate the teacher's need to produce material for the classroom. For example, a collaborative system for planning classes with educational resources is the case for this research proposal that would help teachers develop lesson plans with other teachers. It is characterized by the reuse and adaptation of lesson plans as an opportunity to improve the quality of teaching [4].

Thus, we can see the urgency of this proposal for the three spheres of the importance of research: market, academia, and society in general. To conceptualize this proposal, it follows the theoretical concepts that underlie this research.

2 Activity Theory, Situated Action, and Distributed Cognition

2.1 Activity Theory

The activity theory, despite its complexity, aims at understanding the phenomenon of the practice of the activity carried out by man in the social and cultural dimension that can change according to the conditions of the environment or the objective of the activity [5].

The main set of concepts of activity theory is fundamental to the study of technology since the unit of analysis is an activity. Actions are processes oriented to accomplish and fulfill the proposed objectives based on the components of the activity: subject, object, action, and operations [6] (see Fig. 1). The operations performed on a particular action to reach the object may be different, because they derive from the subject's creativity, since the operations become routine and often unconscious with the practice of day by day.

The application of activity theory gives us important insights into the notion of the context of the activity: the teacher's lesson planning activity and the artifacts that are the educational resources he uses to form the context. The author [6] presents the typical characteristics of this type of study, as described below:

People consciously and deliberately generate contexts (activities) in part through their objects; therefore, the context is not just "out there." The context is internal to

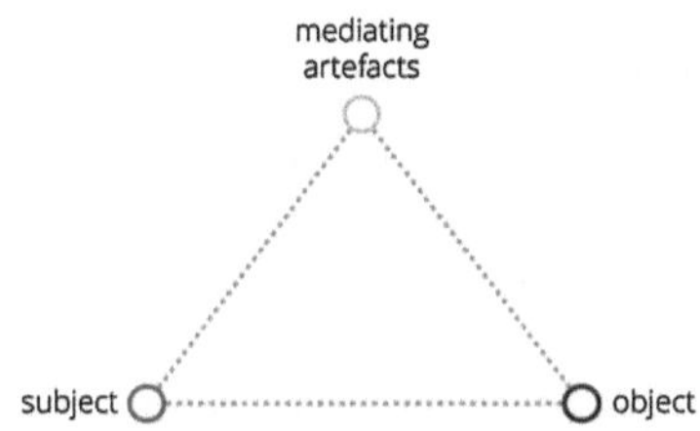

Fig. 1. Model of the theory of activity in the first generation. Source: Adapted from [7].

people – involving specific objects and objectives – and, at the same time, external to people, involving artifacts, other people, and specific settings.

Internal and external are merged, unified in activity theory, we cannot limit the number of teachers and artifacts, but the specific transformation of the relationship between teachers and these artifacts.

The second generation of the diagram, Engeström [7] proposes a model that enriches the relationship between subject and object, considering all the systemic relations existing between the individual and the context found in the activities (see Fig. 2).

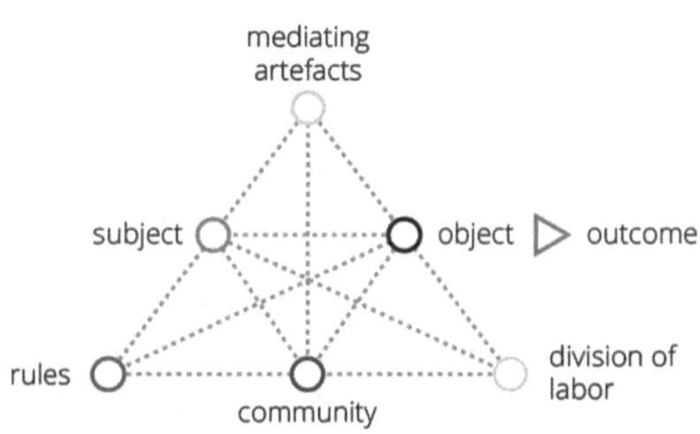

Fig. 2. Model of activity theory in the second generation. Source: Adapted from [7].

The third generation of the diagram aims to present the process of social transformation (Fig. 3).

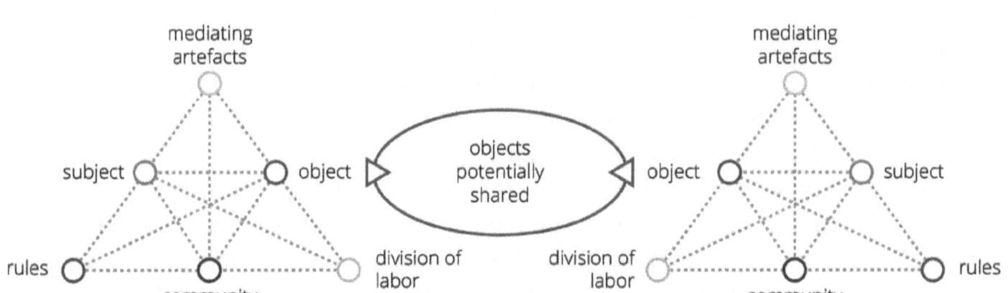

Fig. 3. Model of activity theory in the third generation. Source: Adapted from [7].

2.2 Situated Action Models

The situated action models are a property that results in temporary interaction between users; and between users and action environments. In this model, the central unit of analysis is the relationship between the individual and the environment [6, 8], as described below:

An important aspect of "people's activity - acting in configuration" as a unit of analysis is that it forces the analyst to pay attention to the flow of continuous activity.

According to [6, 8], the situated action model is focused on the study of the daily practical activities of the people that act in a certain context, being the application of this model to analyze the relationship between the teacher and the lesson planning act to understand the flow of the activities involved in this real scenario. This analysis will provide a detailed and sequential observation of the actual behavior in real situations of the rigid mental representations responsible for the planning activity by the teacher [9].

2.3 Distributed Cognition

Second [9], favor a reorientation in the way of thinking and conducting techniques of human-computer interaction for the analysis and extraction of information from the internal and external cognitive processes of individuals' heads. These new branches of cognitive science as a source of guidance to support the understanding of interactions between people and technology. The unit of analysis is a system composed of individuals and the artifacts they use [3].

Distributed cognition is concerned with the structural representations inside and outside the head - and the transformations these structures undergo. The concern of distributed cognition is how these inner schemas in mind can represent out-of-mind structures such as teachers and the educational resources and transformations these structures undergo throughout planning are the focus of our interest.

It will be a guide in designing the collaborative system for planning educational resources, taking into account the internal schemes in their minds in planning lessons with short, medium and long-term impact.

3 Methodology

The present study adopts qualitative research, identified by a case study. Given that the present research has as main objective to study the mental model of the teacher in the class planning activity, an intrinsic case study was performed, because it seeks representation of particular traits of the individual [10], and also by the "interest of the researcher to understand more about a particular case, i.e. there is a desire on the part of the researcher to learn more about that case." [11].

The case study was carried out with 04 teachers of a public school of integral education using traditional pedagogic methods. The teachers are here called A, B, C and D, where teachers A and B are from the same school and C and D from the same school. The systematization of the work carried out was organized as follows: (a) study and planning meetings for the collection; (b) visit in locus; (c) collection and organization of materials for studies through semi-structured interviews (questionnaire in appendix), which were recorded in videos); (d) analysis and description of the results obtained from the collection and the bibliography.

4 Results

From the perspective of the Theory of Activity, the data collection was carried out in two meetings, because it was necessary to understand more broadly the objects used by the teachers from activity patterns, instead of only recording fragments.

Thus, two semi-structured interviews were carried out, wherein the first interview a questionnaire was applied and also questions based on the answers given by the teacher (s). In the next section will be described the objects, operations performed by the teacher (s) interviewed from the perspective of the task analysis.

4.1 Activity Theory

In order to better analyze the data from the theory of the activity, we use the dimensions present in the diagram of [7].

The analysis I: activity based on its components, individual planning.

Subject: Professor A, who teaches chemistry.

Mediator Artifacts: Smartphone for storing digital books, searching the web during the class, searching for exercises and subjects related to the class, and finally registering the lessons in the SIEPE system (Educational Information System of Pernambuco). Proof of entrance exams, proof of the National High School Examination (ENEM). Whiteboard and pencil to the whiteboard, specific chemistry lab, experiments, exercise list, and stimulate student research on the web by the smartphone in the classroom.

Object: To work the program content present in the official document of the school unfolding in bimester to the planning of the classes according to the needs of the students and rules of the direction.

Results: To work the planned contents according to the need of the students and the availability of resources.

- Short term: The teacher takes into consideration the class level moments before entering the classroom, which guides the actions in relation to the depth of the subject being addressed. Moments before class the teacher usually takes a superficial look at digital chemistry books.
- Medium term: The teacher uses a continuous line in his/her logical reasoning to interconnect the continuation of the classes with the next ones by means of evaluation exercises to be delivered by the students.
- Long term: The teacher uses the official school document containing the programmatic content of the chemistry subject for each semester.

Communities: Teachers use an official school document containing the syllabus content of all subjects, focusing specifically on chemistry and dismembering units throughout each two-month period.

Rules: Mandatory use of content in accordance with management's instructions. Using the previous lesson plan with possible updates. Take into account the needs of the class.

Division of work: Individual lesson planning (class to class). Receives steering content requirements. Students seem to influence long-term planning.

Analysis II: activity based on its components, individual planning.

Subject: Professor B, who teaches biology.

Mediating artifacts: School notebook to carry out the planning, create and teach using software for presentation, storage (temporary) and organization of the folders of the 1st, 2nd and 3rd year biology classes with their respective educational resources. USB flash drive: organized by folder according to classes, classes, proof files, text activities and videos. Single and main storage without any other form of external storage, for example, cloud computing system. Other forms: notebook with class notes, data show and sound box. And finally, registration of the classes in the system SIEPE (Educational Information System of Pernambuco). Educational resources used: school computer, textbook, draft notebook, internet (sometimes personal) and presentation software.

Object: To work the programmatic content present in the official document of the school unfolding in bimester for the planning of the classes according to the dynamics of the classes and rules of the direction.

Results: To work the planned contents according to the need of the students applying educational resources.

- Short term: The teacher takes into account the resources, class level and dynamics that influence and guide the type of approach to the subject of the lesson moments before entering the classroom.
- Medium term: The planning is fitting as the teacher gets to know the class more. The teacher uses a notebook with class notes. The teacher uses the official document of the school that contains the programmatic content of the subject of biology and dismembers in units throughout each bimester.
- Long term: The teacher uses the official school document containing the programmatic content of the biology subject for each semester.

Communities: Teachers use an official school document containing the syllabus content of all subjects, focusing specifically on chemistry and dismembering units throughout each two-month period. Rules: Mandatory use of content in accordance with management's instructions. Using the previous lesson plan with possible updates. Take into account the needs and the dynamics of the class. Division of work: Individual lesson planning (class to class). Receives steering content requirements. Reuse of the plans that were recorded in the previous year's notebook serves as the basis for planning the following year only in the aspect of content, because changes always occur in planning based on the characteristics of the class and what went right or wrong.

Analysis III and IV: activity based on its components, here the teachers always plan together.

Subject: Teachers C and D, who teach physics and physical education.

Mediator Artifacts: Government Notebook: It is the starting point for planning and storing the (main) plan, USB flash drive: storage of lesson plans, (secondary) a form of redundancy. Search the web during class for exercise searches and related and correlated subjects. Registration of classes in the SIEPE system (Education Information System of Pernambuco).

Educational resources used: High school textbook, videos, interdisciplinary projects, researches, textbooks, experiments and computer lab.

Object: Work content present in the lesson plan according to student needs and school objectives.

Results: Work the planned contents according to the students' needs and availability of resources in the classes and interdisciplinary projects.

- Short term: Moments before class, planning is always revised because the teacher has time to research the school because it is a full-time school. separates didactic material from class. The pace of the class is a factor taken into consideration. Another aspect that impacts on planning is aspects outside the school, for example, the lack of water in the neighborhood.
- Medium term: The teacher focuses on interdisciplinary projects
- Long-term: Teachers from correlated areas come together to do semester planning.

Communities: Teachers use an official school document containing the syllabus content of all subjects. The bimester is planned collectively between teachers of the same subject and correlated subjects.

Rules: Compulsory use of content in accordance with the goals and objectives of the direction for the school. The reuse of planning is always applied reflecting what went right or wrong for next year. And with regard to texts and experiments worked on in the classroom, they are always updated based on the current context.

Division of work: Individual lesson planning (class-to-class) collectively based on the content requirements of the official school document.

4.2 Distributed Cognition

From the distributed cognition approach, we analyze the Planning of the teachers:

Teacher A: All chemistry lesson planning is in the mind of the teacher and his/her smartphone thus forming a unique cognitive system with the aim of giving an inspiring and fluid lesson to generate abstract reasoning and to have a greater understanding of the subjects discussed in the classroom.

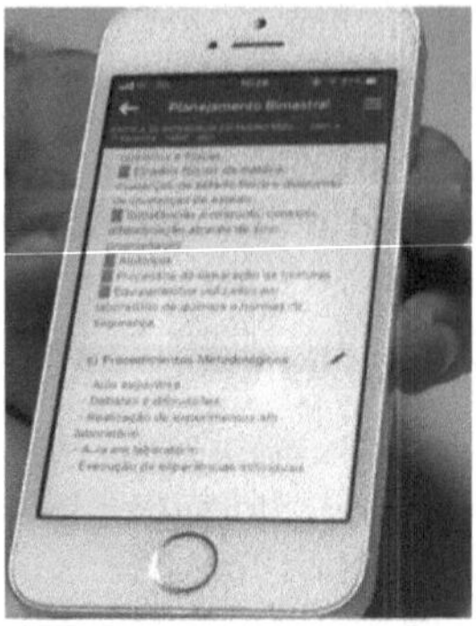

Fig. 4. SIEPE used on the smartphone to externalize the process initiated in mind.

Figure 4 expresses the process of externalizing the planning process that begins in mind and passed to SIEPE.

Teacher B: All planning of biology classes is distributed among the notebook, computer, textbooks, thus forming a single cognitive system with the purpose of giving a class to help the students to fix the content/subjects approached in the classroom through the educational resources used (Figs. 5, 6 and 7).

Fig. 5. Artifact used in planning.

Fig. 6. Mediating artifacts used to externalize the process initiated in the mind.

Fig. 7. Artifacts used in planning and conducting classes.

Teachers C and D: The notebook is used as a digital artifact to record the planning of the disciplines because it is how the schematics of the initial planning materialized that is in the mind of the teacher thus forming the cognitive system.

A very peculiar aspect with this teacher and the school is that the planning of the classes is always done collectively among the teachers of the correlated areas, so the schemas of each teacher are distributed externally in this planning (Figs. 8 and 9).

Fig. 8. Mediating artifacts used to externalize the process initiated in mind.

Fig. 9. Artifacts used in planning and conducting classes.

4.3 Situated Action Models

From the action model we analyzed, we analyzed the Planning of the teachers:

Teacher A: In the teacher's daily life, the flow of his/her lesson planning activities is measured every time before the class of the day, taking into account some aspects:

- First, the subject to be addressed is compared to the level of commitment of the students at the expense of wanting to learn.
- Secondly, in school, there are no monitors/chemistry technicians to assist you in the practice classes, which ends up not happening.
- Thirdly, the teacher has as a source of inspiration the way of teaching his teachers using only a whiteboard brush and an eraser to give an excellent lesson that leads students to abstract reasoning.

The teacher does not use any technological resources in the classroom by observing that a class using a data show, for example, provides sleepiness in the students (Fig. 10).

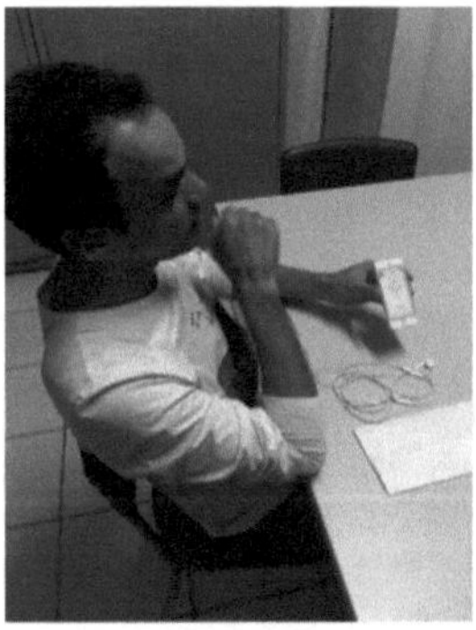

Fig. 10. Interview conducted at the place of natural and in the workplace.

Teacher B: According to the daily routine of the teacher who carries out the planning of the classes in the school, we have the configuration of the unit of analysis of the lesson planning within the context of the activities, in which the quality of your lesson/planning is due to the dynamics of students in relation to the subjects and which approaches can be used (Fig. 11).

The teacher makes use of technological resources in the classroom to stimulate the absorption of the subjects by the students.

Teachers C and D: An important aspect of the activity of teachers to carry out long-term lesson planning in a multidisciplinary setting as a normal practice for them. Each teacher with his or her particular habits and way of teaching his class contributes collectively to each other's daily lives within the context of a school that thinks lives and encourages collaboration more broadly (Fig. 12).

Fig. 11. Interview conducted at the place of natural and in the workplace.

Fig. 12. Interview conducted at the place of natural and in the workplace.

There is a reflexive practice regarding the progress of classes, when a class interacts more than others, impacting on short-, medium- and long-term planning, but that the teachers find it normal from their day to day and even like it to happen.

5 Conclusions

Analyzing the collected data, it was possible to highlight patterns and intersections between the actions of the teachers (a) s research.

Even with this similarity, teacher A showed less flexible actions than teacher B regarding the organization of classes and the use of educational resources in planning. The actions of teacher B appear to be more open to external factors according to the class dynamics in relation to the content expected to be addressed at that moment. Teacher B will have a greater facility to adapt or use lesson planning with educational resources in a collaborative system.

Teachers C and D already make use of strongly distributed cognitive aspects in class planning activity with educational resources, even with the limitation of technological knowledge and traditional pedagogical practice, are strong candidates to use a collaborative classroom planning environment which has educational resources. An important fact to be taken into account in all teachers is the fact that currently they do not use any cloud storage service, only use the USB flash drive, technological artifact susceptible to read/write failures, thus compromising the aspect of memory and reuse of lesson plans and resources used. It was perceived that external resources such as the internet service of schools were ineffective and had a direct impact on class planning.

Even so, the studies carried out have demonstrated the use of technologies to support the teacher in the act of planning his classes in a very simple way, only with regard to the research of auxiliary contents, integrating media and technologies to some extent already available. The present work believes to have contributed to a better understanding of teaching practices, with a view to influencing the elaboration of a collaborative system of class planning that integrates and contributes to a teaching practice more adequate to the current requirements of educational training, even traditional, based in innovation in the analysis of the context in relation to the theoretical references used here.

Acknowledgment. Leandro Marques Queiros is PhD student and receive a scholarship from CNPq. Carlos José Pereira da Silva is M.D. student and receive scholarship from FACEPE. We are also very grateful to all participants for dedicating their time and attention to our research.

References

1. Blattmann, U., Da Silva, F.C.C.: COLABORAÇÃO E INTERAÇÃO NA WEB 2.0 E BIBLIOTECA 2.0. **12**(2), 191–215 (2007). http://www.repositorio.furg.br/bitstream/handle/1/1005/Colaboraçãoeinteraçãonaweb.pdf?sequence=1. Accessed 15 Nov 2018
2. Balakrishnan, R., Dahnil, D.P.B., Ben Mubarak, M.A.A.: Mobile learning, effective integration of new technologies into existing models. In: Luaran, J.E., Sardi, J., Aziz, A., Alias, N.A. (eds.) Envisioning the Future of Online Learning, pp. 317–331. Springer, Singapore (2016). https://doi.org/10.1007/978-981-10-0954-9_28
3. Massaro, G.: Recursos Educacionais Abertos e Aprendizagem Colaborativa: Novas Perspectivas na Construção e Utilização de Materias Educacionais. **8**(31), 1519–8529 (2014). http://pead.ucpel.tche.br/revistas/index.php/colabora/article/viewFile/279/193. Accessed 13 Nov 2018
4. Zhu, X., Chen, M., Du, X., Li, H.: Research on model of collaborative lesson planning for primary teachers based on online environment. In: 2015 International Conference of Educational Innovation through Technology (EITT), pp. 213–215. IEEE (2015). http://ieeexplore.ieee.org/document/7446180/. Accessed 13 Nov 2018
5. Alquete, T., Campello, S.B.: A Contribuição Da Dimensão Social Na Análise Da Atividade Mediada Por Computador. https://www.academia.edu/32260733/A_Contribuição_da_Dimensão_Social_na_Análise_da_Atividade_Mediada_por_Computador. Accessed 17 Nov 2018
6. Nardi, B.A.: Action models, and distributed cognition. In: Proceedings East-West Conference on Human-Computer Interaction, pp. 352–359 (1993)
7. Engeström, Y.: Aprendizagem por expansão na prática: em busca de uma reconceituação a partir da teoria da atividade. Cadernos de Educação Universidade Federal de Pelotas, ano. **11**(19), 31–64 (2002)

8. Roth, W.M., Jornet, A.: Situated cognition. Wiley Interdisc. Rev. Cogn. Sci. **4**(5), 463–478 (2013). https://doi.org/10.1002/wcs.1242
9. Hollan, J., Hutchins, E., Kirsh, D.: Distributed cognition: toward a new foundation for human-computer interaction research. ACM Trans. Comput.-Hum. Interact. **7**(2), 174–196 (2000). https://www.lri.fr/~mbl/Stanford/CS477/papers/DistributedCognition-TOCHI.pdf. Accessed 5 Nov 2018
10. Marconi, M., Lakatos, E.M.: Técnicas de Pesquisa: planejamento e execução de pesquisas, amostragens e técnicas de pesquisas, elaboração, análise e interpretação de dados, 5th edn. Atlas, São Paulo (2002)
11. Correia-neto, j.S., Albuquerque, C.R., Silva, C.R., Souza, E.P.: Metodologia da Pesquisa em Computação, v. 2, Recife (2010)

Opening Spaces for the Development of Human Agency with Problem Based Learning in Palestinian Higher Education

Karl Royle(✉)

University of Wolverhampton, Wolverhampton, UK
k.royle@wlv.ac.uk

Abstract. This paper appraises the impact of Problem Based Learning (PBL) implementations within the (2016-19) Erasmus Plus "Methods" Project (Modernization of Teaching Methodologies in Higher Education: EU experience for Jordan and Palestinian territory) which introduced a range of learning modalities into formal learning contexts in higher education settings in Jordan (4 Universities) and Palestine (4 Universities). The project was jointly led by the Universities of Jordan and Birzeit, Palestine and there were six European partner universities. The paper focuses on the impact of PBL approaches on learners and university teachers through an analysis of semi-structured group interviews with students and individual staff interviews across a range of courses in the arts and sciences within the Palestinian context. The results of this small-scale research study are presented within a thematic framework focusing on participation, collaboration, agency, knowledge creation, problem solving and identity modification. It explores how far the adoption of student-centred PBL designs can open spaces for the development of human agency and capabilities within an existing orthodoxy of practice in Higher Education Settings in Palestine. It locates these student-centred practices within the context of higher education under occupation and examines what contribution they make to developing individuals' capacity to act effectively for change within the power dynamics and limits of their context.

Keywords: Problem based learning · Human agency · Participatory practice

1 Introduction

The Methods project's overarching objective was "To raise the competencies of individual learners to become active members of the knowledge society by enhancing the learning process of students acquiring 21st Century competencies to become autonomous learners through EU experience". The project was initially concerned with introducing educational technology and e-learning approaches to augment existing practice based on Moodle learning management systems. To balance this approach a professional development programme was co-designed to introduce different learning "modalities". The phrase "EU experience" was problematised and reformed into a knowledge exchange, co-production framework based on equality of experience rather than knowledge transfer based on a perceived gradient of expertise. Three main

L. Uden et al. (Eds.): LTEC 2019, CCIS 1011, pp. 260–278, 2019.
https://doi.org/10.1007/978-3-030-20798-4_23

modalities were adopted, PBL, flipped learning (that was problem based) and the creation of learning resources to support Massive Open Online Course (MOOC) development. The project introduced different collaborative learning approaches within the confines of an orthodox system that was, like its European counterparts, predicated upon standardisation of outcome, lectures and knowledge tests. The paper focuses on the response of learners and teachers to the introduction of problem-based learning within four Palestinian universities across 12 courses ranging from teacher education to computer engineering. It draws briefly on two online surveys (the subject of a separate paper) which highlighted an attitudinal shift in preferred learning approaches amongst participating students which prompted a further qualitative study (the subject of this paper) comprising a series of semi-structured group and individual interviews with staff and students at each university. These were conducted to answer the research question: What evidence is there that PBL and Flipped PBL methodologies give rise to a range of behaviours that can develop autonomy and agency within and outside the learning environment? The Palestinian development context is characterised by low graduate employment and outsourced working, coupled with restrictions on travel both into and out of the West Bank and also within the West Bank itself. This can result in very localised university populations as travel, even over relatively short distances, can take many hours due to checkpoints and other restrictions, (Yaha 2016). The exercise of power over the Palestinian people by the occupation permeates directly and indirectly into the lives and activities of students and lecturers. Learning designs that create agency and autonomy of thought are arguably crucial within this dynamic to actively develop Palestinian society.

2 Background and Context

Defining PBL in the Methods Project

PBL was a chosen methodology within the project because of its ability to shift learning designs from the didactic to more student-centred approaches. As such it invites students to become self-organising and to work together on "authentic" problems. Outcomes, in the most agentic forms of PBL can be divergent and are not predetermined. They also have an emphasis on process as much as product, how people engage and participate is often as important as the solution arrived at. The key principles employed in the Methods project, were based on the work of (De Graff and Kolmos 2003). This includes a problem definition process coupled to learner self-direction; activity based learning and decision making based on interdisciplinary 'real world' complex problems; and group based activities so that personal competencies are developed and students learn to handle the process of co-operation in all its stages, (p. 658). Introducing PBL in the Palestinian context entailed a fundamental shift in learning design from objective led, content heavy approaches to looser, more open patterns of student engagement and participation. The training element for Palestinian Lecturers was delivered by the University of Aalborg see Fig. 1 below after Magnussen (2016) (Methods Project Documents). The framework was very adaptive to the Palestinian context because it stressed that PBL can be more or less student controlled

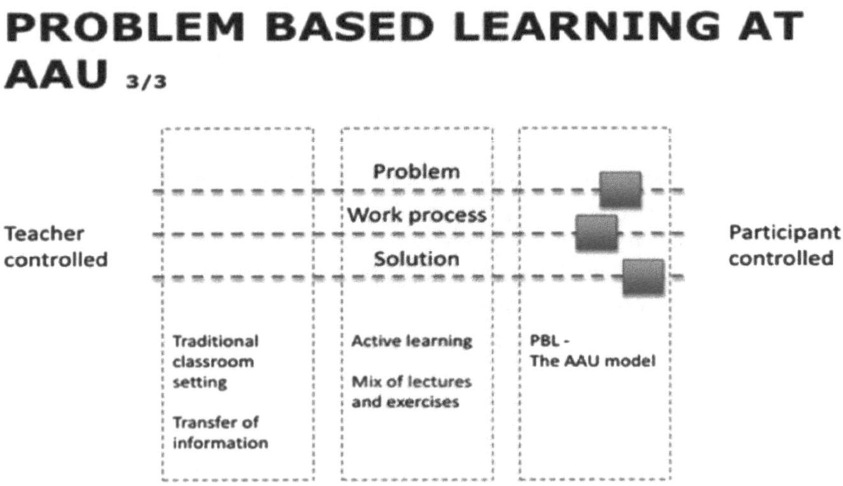

Fig. 1. Problem based learning design model.

and more or less group oriented. The Aalborg model allowed a range of approaches to be adopted by lecturers that could be readily adapted to fit their particular learning context.

Opening Space for Change

Palestinian education is bounded by the power relationships with the occupier and it is understandable that conforming to academic norms and 'standards' is important, especially where comparisons may be drawn with others. Change in any environment comes with risk and this is perhaps why methodologies become fixed/orthodox in spite of the fact that other forms of education may address the context of occupation more effectively. Deleuze and Guattari (1987) notion of smooth (nomad) and striated (state) spaces is useful for thinking about the effect of pedagogies such as PBL on an institution's instructional norms. Bayne (2004) puts it most succinctly: "Smooth space is informal and amorphous, striated space is formal and structured. Striated space is associated with arboreal, hierarchical thought, … opposed to rhizomatic thought – non-hierarchical, underground, multiply-connected." (Bayne 2004, p. 303).

In this case, the existing practice of a lecturer mediating knowledge in an ordered way with pre-determined outcomes is representative of striated space whereas participatory approaches such as PBL can be considered to possibly open a space within which learners can explore a variety of directions and collaborations (smooth space) resulting in diverse outcomes. However, one might equally argue that PBL just replaces one striation with another, "smooth space is constantly being translated, transversed into a striated space; striated space is constantly being reversed, returned to a smooth space (Deleuze and Guattari 1987, p. 474).

It is the 'stent' like quality of PBL formats and frameworks, to open space for flows of difference, criticality and creative thought within the striated orthodoxy, that is attractive. Savin-Baden (2014) describes PBL practices and proposes an ontology of five curriculum types ranging from type one - Striated – highly bounded and controlled, which might in this case represent the orthodoxy where the type of learning is "routine, preparation and rehearsal" and moves to type five Connectivist (learning through making connections). Types two, Borderland- control with open endedness and three, Smooth- open, flexible and contested spaces and four Troublesome, where learning is based on dealing with disjunction and uncertainty, perhaps best summarise the how PBL models can and do affect change in learning design and the nature of student engagement. Savin-Baden (2014), also supports the notion that PBL methodologies can open spaces that scaffold the release of personal and collective agency through self-organisation. According to Den Bossche et al. (2006) students work together in such spaces to develop solutions to emerging problems through co-construction of meaning, convergent and divergent discussions, listening and negotiation. It is interesting in some cases to note how the activities and behaviours enabled by the methods project became physically manifest. In the before and after (PBL) photographs (Fig. 2) below of a classroom layout we can see on the left a scene that is not out of place in any University. The lecture chairs in rows, designed for listening and writing and increasing classroom occupancy, explicitly illustrates what Monahan (2002) calls "built pedagogy." A classroom with neat rows of desks embodies pedagogies or "tacit curricula" of discipline and conformity, whereas spaces personifying flexible properties … can be said to embody pedagogies of freedom and self-discovery". (Monahan 2002, p. 5).

Fig. 2. Before and after PBL at Birzeit University, Ramallah, Palestine: Electronic Engineering Group.

Agency in the Context of Power Relationships

In the Palestinian context, developing human agency, (Bandura 2001), through learning designs that give people a measure of control over their own functioning and environmental events, are arguably to be valued above those that are directed and managed monocratically with little room for diversity of approach or outcome. Agency, is often aligned in educational terms with the notion of perceived self-efficacy, defined by

Bandura (1982) as being concerned with judgments of how well one can execute courses of action required to deal with prospective situations. Cauce and Gordon (2013) note those with a strong sense of self-efficacy are most likely to persist in the face of failure. Therefore, it follows that self-efficacy can be brought about by practice and by putting people into situations where failure and overcoming failure through perseverance are part of success in any endeavour. Within any context, there are limits within which agency can be applied. Sen's (1985) notion of agency freedom refers to "what a person is free to do and achieve in pursuit of whatever goals and values he or she regards as important" (Sen 1985, p. 203) and this greater resonance within the context of occupation. Tobias (2005) rightly cautions against adopting a liberal acceptance of "freedom to choose". "The reification of agential freedom abstracts from the concrete context and conditions under which chosen ends can be effectively pursued." (Tobias 2005, p. 70).

Whilst the spaces within which we work, live and learn are striated, education that allows us to critically assess the fabric of those rules and striations is valuable in developing individuals who are inventive in the face of adversity and are open and responsive to constructing a change in possibilities and circumstances. Palestinian students are resilient when faced with the random restrictions of the occupation, as a lecturer at Bethlehem University (2018 Interview transcript.) notes, "In Palestine you are going to have days where movement is very difficult, but we need to continue. We live in a precarious environment." Students from Birzeit University (Methods Project Report) also voice similar issues: "Sometimes they (Israel) close the roads so we can't go (to the university). Last year, because of the intifada … Those that come from Jerusalem could not reach the campus safely." A constraint on agency is arguably connected to the constructs of power and control that pervade any context. Foucault's discussion of power and agency is highly relevant here. Foucault's (1975) notion of education as being part of the extension of social control whereby we police ourselves through our own institutions and we fabricate docile citizens through education would seem to obviate the very notion of human agency. As Palestine is constantly surveilled and has been described by Pappe (2018) as the 'Biggest Prison on Earth' it is particularly difficult to counter this through notions of agency freedom, Sen (1985). As Leask (2012) notes, Foucault likens education to the panopticon of the prison where there are "processes for controlling space, for programming and scheduling time, for compiling data and records, and for employing ever-improving methods of surveillance." (Leask 2012, p. 58) Foucault's later work however, according to (Leask 2012), advocates that there is always the possibility for change in the dynamics of power and that that change is brought about by the agency of individuals.

"The possibility now emerges that it can also be the theatre of subjects' creation of new 'practices of self', new kinds of relations—especially via continued resistance to domination. (…) Teachers and students alike can now be regarded as creative agents, capable of voluntary and intentional counter-practices, and always able, in principle, to resist aspects of the kinds of managerialism, instrumentalization and commodification they face daily, and to construct strategic interventions." (Leask 2012, p. 67).

Further, one can note after Foucault (2000), that whilst we are never free of power relations and cannot jump outside them, - the Palestinian is not free from occupation, the student (and teacher) are not free from examination and grading, - these things can always be changed. As Leask (2012) notes, quoting Foucault, "'We are always free'; we can always resist; our ongoing task is to construct 'arts of living' that might counter the manifold expressions of 'fascism' that lurk throughout institutions, systems, relations, and even ourselves," (Leask 2012, p. 67). The following sections will detail how far PBL interventions in the Methods project have created change within the confines of the institutions involved.

Method. A mixed methods approach, using survey responses as a catalyst for further qualitative group and individual interviews (Mertens 2018) was used to gain further insight into the effect of PBL across a range of stakeholders and their accumulated body of knowledge about their lived experience of the intervention/learning design. (Chilisa 2005). The validity of the qualitative research process is constrained in part in that participants in semi structured group interviews were selected by the course leaders as members of the courses that included PBL for the first time. Equally, because of the distributed nature of participants and travel restrictions (see previously) little co design of the research could be undertaken. However, most students had completed their courses so were under no pressure to report favourably and were assured of anonymity of response by the research team. Staff were also interviewed separately using semi-structured interviews. Although most participants had a good standard of English two researchers were engaged in the process so that Arabic could be used to elaborate points and as the primary medium where required. Semi-structured group interviews were therefore conducted bilingually. The researchers were also aware of the cultural context of education in Palestine and the continuing occupation and history of the Palestinian people. The researchers were aware that the voice of students was particularly important in this project so that future policy might be set with their contributions in mind.

Initial Surveys. Two online surveys were used with all participants in both Jordanian and Palestinian Universities, these were a "Digital Habits" survey/single time point, see (Ozdamar-Keskin et al. 2015) and an impact evaluation survey after Kirkpatrick (1996) which had two time points. Time point one involved questions about reactions and learning, whereas timepoint two looked at changes in behaviour and longer lasting impacts (results). These surveys are the subject of a later paper and so only the initial findings that prompted this further investigation are reported here. The impact evaluation surveys also focused on students' direct experience of the methods courses and their learning preferences and any change in learning preferences as a direct result of a methods course. Numbers of respondents: Time point 1: Total respondents = 1433 (Jordanian Universities = 997, Palestinian Universities = 436). Time point 2. Total respondents = 1407 (Jordanian Universities = 1179, Palestinian Universities = 228). The time points were 3 months apart and although the cohort was the same the number of respondents had fallen because they were no longer taking the same courses and were only reached by email. This was particularly true of Palestinian participants who had mostly taken electives or who had been final year students.

Students from Palestinian Universities seemed to express more confidence, competence, and utilisation of independent learning skills through these self-report suvbeys than Jordanian Students. Using descriptive statistics only the Jordanian result showed a shift between T1 and T2 of $\approx 5\%$ from individualised learning behaviours to a preference for more structured and lecture-led learning. Contrastingly, the Palestinian responses showed a decrease in these behaviours and an increase of ≈20% towards more collaborative learning behaviours. This suggested that the greater emphasis placed on problem-based learning/teaching methodologies by Palestinian Universities (605 students)/Jordanian Universities (190 students) may have influenced this change and as such was worthy of further investigation through qualitative interviews.

Forming the Framework for the Focus Groups and Interviews. The initial three learning modalities were developed and adapted to the varied contexts for learning and teaching in Jordan and Palestine. These modalities were further defined through conversations with colleagues and through monitoring visits and project meetings. The following modalities were evident within practice.

E learning. Courses that used on line learning with online discussion and occasional face to face contact were concerned with compulsory courses with high numbers (250+) of students.
Flipped learning was defined as tasks set outside of class and then discussed face to face in class. This involved the provision of online materials within the Virtual Learning Environment system or on You Tube that students would review at home before coming to class. This was a departure from previous classes which would involve lectures and practice.
MOOC: The MOOC concept was primarily used as a form of online learning that sought to incorporate the best aspects of collaborative face to face learning but more often than not fell into the arena of content with tests in a behaviourist style.
Flipped/PBL. Here the modality gave students challenges in terms of group-based research where they were directed to online resources in order to solve a problem which was more open ended. This was quite a radical departure for many lecturers and it often required a change in assessment methods. This was classified as the "challenge based" flip.
PBL: Where PBL was used this required greater student autonomy. It was purely, group and challenge led but was facilitated with varying degrees of scaffolding by the tutors involved. It invariably needed a change in assessment to facilitate the change in pedagogical approach. Students tended to choose their own way of communicating and used their own devices.

These modalities were placed onto a revised SAMR, (Puentedura 2006) model in order to project how the learning modalities might affect teaching practice and engagement. The SAMR model has been revised by others (Hamilton et al. 2016) and aligned with other models such as Bloom's Digital Taxonomy by the originator, (Puentedura 2014). The model itself is appealing in its simplicity but is essentially based on the effects of technology integration into teaching and learning. Other approaches such as Technology, Pedagogy, Content, Knowledge (TPCAK) (Koehler and Mishra 2009) focus on the teacher's relationship with a variety of variables. What we create here is an attempt to place the methods modalities at the centre of the learning transformation and focus on what effect that might have on student engagement. The original SAMR model (Fig. 3) places the focus on what kind of learning can be created by introducing digital technology whereas we looked at the anticipated levels of engagement, agency, creativity and collaboration produced by the learning design where digital technology was seen as an integral tool but not central to learning change. The 'technology' in this case was the learning design itself (Royle and Nikolic 2016).

The revision below (Fig. 4) (constructed with colleagues at a project meeting: (Jordan 2018)) was used as a working model to describe the learning designs and their possible effects in the Methods Project. Whilst the emphasis in the original SAMR model is on the position of technology as the change agent here we look at the teaching and learning modality, its relationship to technology and its possible effects on learning.

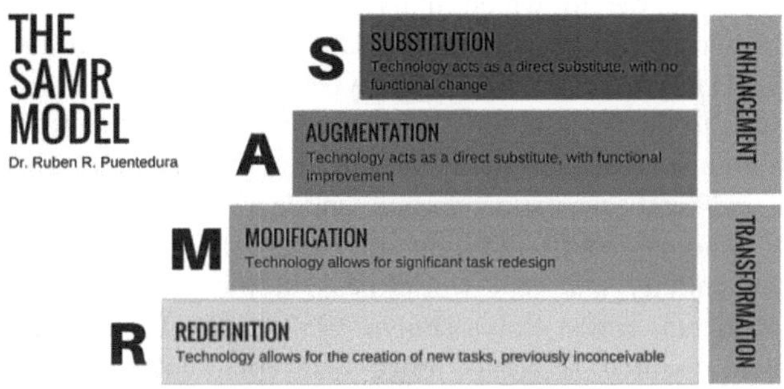

Fig. 3. The original SAMR model: CC by Attribution-ShareAlike 4.0 International

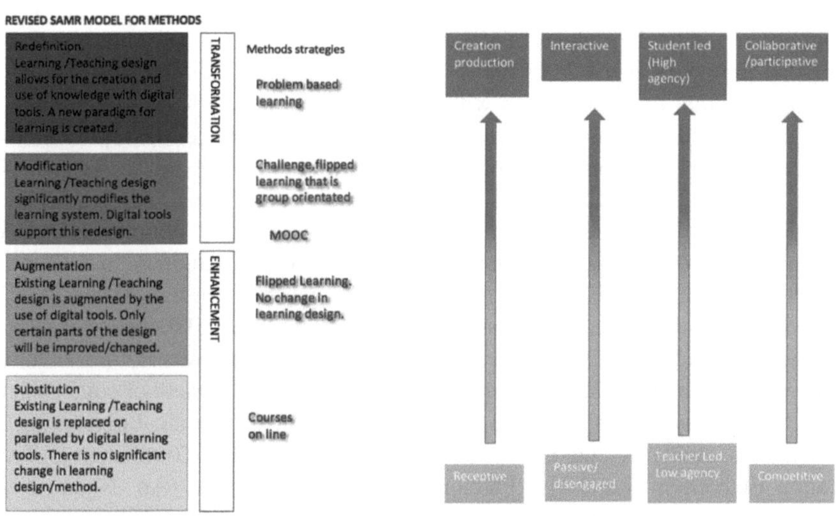

Fig. 4. Revised SAMR model focusing on learning design and learner engagement.

This revised model proposes that PBL and Flipped PBL methodologies can be transformational in developing a range of behaviours that develop autonomy and agency within and outside the learning environment. Autonomy is used here an overarching "label" for a range of behaviours one would expect to be present (according to the literature) within problem-based learning. This is not to say that digital technology is not important in enabling pedagogical change and in some instances in the Palestinian context it is also vital to mitigate structural issues around physical attendance in a precarious security situation.

Group Interviews. This consensus mapping in the diagram above prompted the design of an interview framework based on the following themes. Agency: defined as, the ability to exert control or freely make decisions based mainly on Bandura's (2006) definition of four core properties of human agency. Collaboration: the basis for this was the range of skills needed for effective collaboration after Roselli (2016). Participation or taking part: the degree to which individuals discussed or engaged with more knowledgeable others, tutors or with peers. (Lee and McLoughlin 2007), (Leadbetter and Wong 2008) (Hampson et al. 2011). Knowledge creation and transfer: As a part of the PBL process is to devise solutions to problems it was pertinent to interrogate the degree to which both students and tutors thought this had occurred. This could include, content creation and synthesis, metacognition, and learning from others. With problem-based strategies, (Thomas 2000), (Trilling and Fadel 2009), (Bransford 2004), all note the need for authenticity and real worldliness in the problems that are given or established by students, whilst Polya (Pólya 1957) refers to some form of structure being used to plan, research, set goals, reflect and replan collectively. Finally, identity formation for both lecturers and students was considered as Osterlaken (2015) notes, when we change a learning design, we may also affect identities and roles.

Students from a range of Palestinian courses took part in semi structured group interviews based on a bespoke interrogative framework. Lecturers were interviewed individually to gauge their views on the effects of PBL. Students were interviewed over a three-day period in April 2018 and as such the sampling method was that of convenience. Although there are issues with this type of sampling it could be argued that the sample was a homogenous group and consisted of a mix of gender representative of the overall university populations of around 60% female, 40% male. Twenty seven students from different courses at four different Universities, Birzeit University (BZU) (Ramallah) five students, An Najah University (ANU)(Nablus) eight students, The Palestinian Polytechnic University (PPU) Hebron eight students and Bethlehem University (BU) six students, were interviewed in groups. These were cross subject groups in ANU and PPU and single subject groups in BZU and BU. Ten staff were also interviewed individually. Communication between the groups was not possible and it was interesting to note the similarities of response despite the variety of courses that the students were drawn from. Students and teachers from: Electronic Engineering (Birzeit); Systems Analysis and Computer Systems Engineering (Bethlehem); Teacher Education Bethlehem, Land Use Planning, Ecology, Literature, (An -Najah, Nablus) Methods of Scientific Research (Hebron), were interviewed and all courses were undergraduate. Initial responses were transcribed and then coded against the framework sections above carried out by the author. Secondary analysis was then undertaken where further subthemes were identified within each main framework theme.

Findings

Agency is at the heart of PBL. Its properties as defined by (Bandura 2006) include, intentionality (planning), forethought (goal setting), self-reactiveness (reacting to developments and ensuring plans are enacted and achieved - self-regulatory behaviour), and self-reflectiveness (how are we doing). Sub themes that emerged from student responses were: confidence; ownership of the process of learning and any consequent control that students felt they had over proceedings; collaboration; knowledge creation; authenticity; and sustainability.

Confidence

(By)Making applications in the real world not just doing something for the course, we saw the output. We are more confident because we can do stuff now. When I walk into a room now I can look at anything and understand how it works. BZU Student 1

In Bethlehem, confidence was equated with doing things rather than passive reception. This seemed to confirm the premise of the SAMR modification from passivity to engagement and a transfer of control to the student. "*Didn't feel like students it made us more confident - we do things not receive them. I have become more confident in presentations and how to work with people.*" BU Student2. In Nablus (ANU) students spoke of "self confidence in my own abilities" and *–Before this course I did not have the powers to stand and discuss with students. Now I can speak and discuss with others. We are more confident, we felt proud because we had achieved something. ANU Student 3.* This feeling of increased confidence was also expressed in Hebron (PPU) where students felt more engaged and confident in their interaction with the subject. In terms of engaging with an 'active learning process' students spoke of the way in which technologies were used to enable the "new" way of learning.

The main point for me was to get rid of paper and use technologies. To use video was important for me not just to sit in the class and listen and write. We worked mostly face to face but also online, we used gdocs and, Facebook/WhatsApp. PPU Student 2

Others spoke more about their own personal control and freedom in the process of learning: acting and thinking in new ways and for themselves. A movement from teacher control to student control was expressed and students saw their experience as one of learning as much as being taught.

Systems analysis taught me research skills... I should look for information myself and not depend on teachers. This was really important for me. To think and build something on your own is important. BU Student 6 This way gave me higher grades and. I was able to be more effective when researching on other courses. My methodology of researching got better. BU Student 6. We see the lecturers as guides and this way we have more control and power. ANU Student 5

A theme related to self-regulatory behaviour, adapting to change and a test and learn mentality were evidenced in some responses. *The point is applying and testing. It works- great you can apply it, if it doesn't work then okay, we will try something else. BU Student 6.* In one case a student referred to their work in teaching literature in Palestinian schools by remarking that the PBL process had made them realise that. *"Literature is not a smooth subject, it is rigid, and we try to open it and make it more accessible".* Whilst this alludes to Deleuze and Guattari (1987) notion of smooth (nomad) and striated (state) space and whilst perhaps only coincidental, it does illustrate that students are reflecting about the fabric and nature of their subject and testing how different approaches might open them to others.

Self-advocacy and voice were also evidenced across the PBL classes at different universities, the PBL learning design seemed to open space for speaking up and speaking out within the bounds of the subject.

In this kind of class, you do things, you give your voice, you write your opinion, you suggest, you make something, you say what you think and then if you think it is true you have to prove it through practice. BU Student 3. Inside the class you could speak freely. You can discuss and explore anything you want. Express yourself and give your opinions. ANU Student 4

Learning through failure and belief in one's own self efficacy and in not giving up at the first obstacle was also evident. There was an acceptance of "failure" as part of learning and as part of the process. *We tested hypothesis as we practised so failure is part of the plan. BU Student 2. We didn't think about the grade only that we shouldn't quit. PPU Student 5.*. Equally, an increase in perseverance emerged and a realisation that with a willingness to try and discover what worked in their context students could achieve results. *We changed our output 5 times... either because we were giving the wrong solutions or the wrong causes for the problem. So we had to revise and do it again. BU Student 3 It was stressful in the beginning and it was a lot more work. When we understood what we were doing in this way it got better and less stressful. ANU Student 5*

Collaboration and Participation in the Learning Process

Teamworking and collaboration as a result of PBL also led to opportunities for negotiation, conflict resolution and mutual support. Students talked of negotiation and bringing other students up to speed with their ways of working. This also made them active participants in the learning process. *We had discussions about what to do and all agreed after negotiation - We learned a new set of skills around practical and communication skills, we had to adapt to having a new partner who we had to train.* BZU Student 1. New insights were gained into working collaboratively in teams and the students realised that they had to solve any problems that arose and use soft skills to do so. *The team is most important and sometimes some members don't work but we solved it. You should try to choose your team well. – We had some issues but we made each other work.* BU Student 6 *(We learned)- By working in a team on a project we have to deal with many opinions. Dealing with others respectfully.* PPU Student 4. However, team working was a mixed experience: *Working with a group was harder than working by myself. ANU Student 8* Mutual support was also evident. *For me this course improved my personality ...how to work with others...communication, conflict solving, co-operation. This made us more effective in group work- we learned more because we worked together...we helped students who were not advanced.* ANU Student 2

As well as participating through collaboration in teams students also commented on how much more involved they were in classes. Increased participation (how far students take part and engage in class through discussion with peers and the lecturer and other points of connection, online or through research and texts) is a key aspect of pedagogical change. When a space for co-production is created, student generated knowledge which extends both their own learning and the lecturer's is key. Students also voiced perceived differences between other methods and the PBL experience.

In a regular class you just take whatever the teacher says, you don't understand the whole thing ... you only get about 70% of the information that you need to actually comprehend everything. You just sit in class and listen. In the methods project we contributed. ANU Student 5

We were more active as students and less passive. We are not receivers we are producers. PPU Student 6 They also commented on discussions and the benefits of working with the lecturers and students. *We benefitted from every side. We worked with the lecturer and the students. We discussed the lecture with the students and solutions and causes. ANU Student 6 Each stage of the problem-based learning was discussed, and we got feedback from her (lecturer). Difficulties and improvements. It's the only class where I never felt bored. BU Student 3.* There was also an expression of feelings. "It's fun" was mentioned regularly in the transcripts. *It was fun, we had fun, it's a fun way to learn,* across all the Universities and courses. *Great* also featured as an expression of feeling several times alongside *"amazing"*. Sic:

It was really amazing, we had fun.

Knowledge Creation

This was evidenced through project outputs. Presenting and publishing results were seen as positive learning experiences as part of PBL. Making - that could be applied to social needs was a positive outcome for computer engineering students.

We are developing power supplies for every school for them to do stuff with it. It costs 115 dollars normally. To power up computers and projectors. We take the power supplies from old PC CPUs and convert them. Low cost and allows the school to use a power supply for different things. So we make this initiative for the people as a social obligation so we can give something back. To help them. BZU Student 5

One of the lecturers noted that students came up with several different solutions to a problem which wasn't the normal practice. *At the end they all came with different solutions to the same problem which was great and unusual. Lecturer 3, BU.* Ways of thinking were also purported to have changed:

We started to use critical thinking and started to think like an analyst to solve problems. BU Student 6

Authenticity

A key effect of PBL was the authenticity of the tasks, (De Graff and Kolmos 2003), that were used which engaged students in the learning process. Birzeit students reported that they had extended their learning and skills to developing a start-up making power supplies for community organisations effectively transferring their knowledge from the classroom to a wider context. Even the act of co-ordinating activity became an authentic learning experience that replicated the world of work. *It is difficult when you are cross disciplinary to get time together to complete projects. We used technology but we had to be together physically as a group too. PPU Student 1.* Students scaffolded their work by planning and replanning and setting goals themselves. *We had a plan and if things go wrong, we replan. – Yes, I got frustrated but then I carried on.* BU Student 4. They remarked on the motivational aspects of having an authentic purpose. This was a theme throughout the interviews. Projects were grounded in the Palestinian context and had real outcomes. The theory became live and practice was hypothesised and tested.

We had a problem at the beginning of the course itself and we had to make a work plan. So this was based on actual general life problems and we had to make a work plan for how to solve it. Then from this point we had to make work plans for other problems related to the course.

We looked at global warming issues, so they were real. We looked at biodiversity and we came up with a good solution. BU Student 6

The realisation or theory through practical application also led to a degree of authenticity in that applying theory was seen as an effective learning strategy. *I did not understand the concepts but when it was done in the practical sense it became easier for me. Getting knowledge about what you can't understand theoretically through practical work. This broke the barrier for me.* BZU Student 5. Even subjects that are not really noted for their practical application were related to the Palestinian context of living in a pluralist society. *The poems we studied - Blake and Wordsworth we looked at how people lost trust in religion and related this to our context. How the political system uses this to achieve their aims. And we can see that now. ANU Student 7*

Sustainability

One of the most positive drivers for change was that grades improved, and several lecturers expressed "pride" in their students' achievements and how much the students enjoyed the approach.

Grade averages came up from C+ to B+ . I was shocked that they understand so well and... I have become a good teacher. The biggest change for me is how to overcome student's disengagement from the material.

Ways to increase motivation. The results were great, so I focus on that.

When you see the results, you forget everything. BU Lecturer 1

The students were amazing, and their work was a very high standard. They related their solutions to the context of Palestine and chose the best one. Hebron Lecturer 2.

All lecturers interviewed felt they could spread the PBL method to other courses and some had already done so.

It's becoming a way of teaching in other areas too, not structurally but it is spreading. ANU Lecturer 3. However, all said it was hard work and could not be done with large groups. This will probably be the next challenge to face - how does PBL become scaled and more importantly, does it need to be scaled?

It's hard for us, it takes a lot of work. It's easier for me to be a mono transmitter rather than a facilitator. You are involved in several projects and you are more involved in them and with the students. It's not easy for classical teachers to convert to this method. ANU Lecturer 3

Conclusions and Discussion

Undoubtedly, where PBL was implemented it resulted in greater student engagement and agency. However, Bayne's (2001) notion of smooth space as being informal and amorphous and striated space being formal and structured does not quite fit with problem-based learning. Although PBL does open a space it appears to be more successful where it is scaffolded and control is released to students incrementally.

All lecturers without exception used some form of scaffolding of the experience. Some were more controlled than others. Some were content with providing a problem-solving rubric, materials and regular meetings for discussion where others created detailed assessment frameworks and project plans.

I then used PBL... gave structure to students and they worked in groups and each month they presented their work. Each group had a use case given by me and they applied it in their group. After 1 month they have to present the progress. They thought it was a lot of work. BU Lecturer 3.

Another lecturer used clearly defined stages to scaffold the work of the students.

It was a lot of work for them, trying to identify problems, going into the community trying to test your solutions. They did it in three stages.

Stage 1 was id problems, stage 2 was finding solutions and testing them out, stage 3 was presenting what happened. I was able to meet them at each stage and guide them through...I also told them it was okay to fail. BU Lecturer 1

Each tutor had a different way of structuring the learning which were more or less "striated":

I give them directions to convert the problem definition into evaluation criteria for their solution at the end, (support the structure of the learning). BU Lecturer 3 This is much better for them. I had regular classes but only for project discussion. I advised them in these sessions. ANU Lecturer 1

Identity

In some cases, the PBL ethos extended the curriculum into the community where students were solving authentic needs. Students had practised and acquired a range of soft skills and in some cases claimed that they were thinking differently rather akin to Gee's (2005) conceptualisation of 'authentic professionalism' where experience transforms individuals into 'becoming' researchers or engineers or teachers. Students took on more professional positions in regard to how they thought of themselves and also around how they worked with their lecturers. Students said that they felt like *"researchers or engineers* and *real teachers"*. They thought the lecturers were friendly and approachable, like team leaders or colleagues. Barriers seemed to disappear, and communication became easy. The lecturers also articulated their revised orientations. *My role changes from a teacher, (I act as) a supervisor and as a consultant when they design something, I advise them to review their solutions. ANU Lecturer 2*

Biggest change is that you are closer to the students, friendlier...in the classical one the students are far from you but in this you are sitting with them, talking, close face to face, discussing and you are like a friend rather than a teacher.. ANU Lecturer 3.

Changing One Thing (Pedagogy) Ultimately Means Changing Everything

Staff responses to working with PBL were a mixture of both positive and negative. Whilst all interviewees said that they enjoyed working in this way they mostly all agreed it was a lot more work and higher risk. The broad framework presented in the Aalborg model was easy to conceptualise and follow, it was, a 'sticky' method, *the framework we used is from the Aalborg PBL training in UK and when you are a practitioner it just clicks. Lecturer 1 PPU* but required more thought and structure than was at first realised. As the curriculum broadened to include practical applications and became process driven through the PBL approach, assessments also needed to be rethought. Lecturers remarked that the quality of work and engagement had increased but several realised they had to change the mode of assessment.

I also tweaked the assessment to ask them if they wanted to be evaluated as a team or individually. Also, peer evaluation and we discuss the assessment, so we introduced democracy to the grading process. ANU Lecturer 1. I changed the assessment so less writing and more technology-based products and presentations. PPT, videos. BU Lecturer 3. Group working was problematic in some groups but groups that worked well together did better. It was the first time that I noticed students enjoying the work. PPU Lecturer 3

Power Relationships

The PBL classes gave rise to a flatter structure where learning was negotiated. In some cases, the lecturers felt it was more democratic and the power dynamic in classes shifted. *We loved the way that the student and the teacher are the same level. ANU Lecturer 3* It could also be argued that this change in pedagogical approach was a movement towards "constructing arts of living" by developing skills within students that resist being passive reception and create actors within society. Teaching people how to be 'agentic' within the bounds of their freedoms is always problematic but teachers realised the value in developing 'agentic' soft skills within their students. *Seeing them collect data, engage with the texts, complain to me and fight sometimes with each other…that was a transformative experience for them. PPU Lecturer 2. They were structured around team work and dynamics and negotiations. It's worth it even if it fails. BU Lecturer 1* Some lecturers also saw the use of different spaces as a way of changing the footing of pedagogy (after Monahan 2002) and the dynamics of power in the classroom.

Class space is used for discussion… we have a round table, so I moved them to this room so that the space is different, so we are discussing the subject, they are free to talk and discuss. ANU Lecturer 1 However, PBL methods in Palestine as in other countries are working within a results based, content driven system. Barriers to implementation are systemic and revolved mainly around the difference in approach and whether students were receptive to it.

We get an inflow of students that are very traditional with this type of lecturing - indoctrination, exam based. This continues in the university. The students put high pressure on their teachers against any new approach. It's challenging to move the students from teacher centred to student centred. It's not easy to change existing learning habits and expectations. Learning is harder this way. They expect you to transmit knowledge and when you flip the roles it's a bit of a shock. BU Lecturer 1

The PBL methodologies and cases at play in Palestine were broadly representative of the range within the Aalborg model. PBL also seemed to align with the needs and concerns of practitioners Royle and Hadfield (2012) where a technology (See Royle and Nikolic 2016) for a discussion of Technic (Teaching methods as Technology) is more likely to be adopted if it is aligned with teaching and learning concerns of practitioners. In this event there were four key attributes that PBL was able to tap into. The first was its simplicity, applicability and adaptability across a range of contexts. The simple Aalborg model asks lecturers to problematise existing courses rather than make courses anew, as such it is a bit of a 'Trojan Horse' as once started, other aspects of learning design require change as well. Second, there was a genuine desire to engage students who were demotivated. Lecturers were pleased by the increased levels of engagement. Third, there was a conscious need to develop critical thinking and collaborative skills within learners. *I think it's a must in our education system because we need students who are problem solvers. I think it's a national thing… we need to create a nation of problem solvers. ANU Lecturer 3.* Fourthly, the digital aspects and how PBL integrates them into practice (technology as tools for change) were useful in mitigating structural issues.

In a country like Palestine, because of the political situation for example Jerusalem on Tuesday there will be no transport and no classes, so we need alternatives so that education is not disrupted. In Palestine you are going to have days where movement is very difficult, but we need to continue. We live in a precarious environment and that's where technology plays a role. BU Lecturer 2

It can be seen that PBL is a pedagogy that opens space for change within previously orthodox practices in which students and lecturers can be actors and agents for change and it seems to promote deeper learning, (Fullan 2014), than the previous transmission models. Where PBL does initially open a 'smooth space' this space is quickly striated by scaffolding, however it is a loosely assembled striation with smoothness within it. As Allen (2009) notes,

There is no freedom without discipline, no vision without a form…If there were no lines painted on the road, you wouldn't be free to let your mind wander and be creative while you drive. You'd be too busy hoping no one hits you. But if there were too many lanes and restrictions and rules, you'd have traffic moving much slower than it should, as everyone was paying attention to being in the right place. (Allen 2009, p. 56).

At present however, PBL only opens small spaces within the greater confines of the orthodoxy, and it cannot get beyond this without a rethinking of curriculum at system level. Further work might use Savin Baden's ontology to position PBL as a cross discipline curriculum development or whole university initiative. This curriculum needs to link to the social context of Palestine directly and its young minds need to be directed to both thinking through and taking actions that solve the problems that are inherent within the developing society. If our ongoing task is to construct "arts of living" (after Foucault) it would seem that quite by accident rather than design in the Methods project, the manifold varieties but basic simplicities of PBL have chimed with the Palestinian spirit of collaborative endeavour and perhaps it is a potential Pedagogy for Palestine. As Gibson (1999) notes "That which is overdesigned, too highly specific, anticipates outcome; the anticipation of outcome guarantees, if not failure, the absence of grace." (Gibson 1999, p. 133).

Co-Funding. This research study was co-funded by the Erasmus+ Programme of the European Union, Erasmus+ Programme – METHODS Project number: 561940-EPP-1-2015-1-JO-EPPKA2-CBHE-JP, project title: **M**odernization of **T**eaching **M**e**tho**dologies in **H**igher Educati**o**n: EU Experience for Jor**d**an and Pale**s**tinian Territory (METHODS).

Disclaimer. This research project has been co-funded with support from the European Commission. This publication reflects the views only of the author, and the Commission cannot be held responsible for any use which may be made of the information contained therein.

Acknowledgments. The author is grateful to Dr Wasel Ghanem (Birzeit University) who assisted with data collection in Palestine, the staff and students of Birzeit, Bethlehem, An Najah and Palestine Polytechnic University, Prof. Ahmed Al-Salaymeh the project General Coordinator-The University of Jordan and his assistant Lina Al-Marashdeh and all members of the project steering committee who added their insights and feedback.

References

Allen, D.: Making it all Work: Winning at the Game of Work and the Business of Life. Penguin Books, New York (2009)

Bandura, A.: The assessment and predictive generality of self-percepts of efficacy. J. Behav. Ther. Exp. Psychiatry **13**(3), 195–199 (1982). https://doi.org/10.1016/0005-7916(82)90004-0

Bandura, A.: Social cognitive theory: an agentic perspective. Annu. Rev. Psychol. **52**(1), 1–26 (2001). https://doi.org/10.1146/annurev.psych.52.1.1

Bandura, A.: Towards a psychology of human agency. Perspect. Psychol. Sci. **1**(2), 164–180 (2006). https://pdfs.semanticscholar.org/4c53/0339369cff0093101ba611b28e48620f3493.pdf. Accessed 28 Dec 2018

Bayne, S.: Smoothness and striation in digital learning spaces. E-Learn. Digital Media **1**(2), 302–316 (2004). https://doi.org/10.2304/elea.2004.1.2.6

Bransford, J.D.: How People Learn: Brain, Mind, Experience, and School. National Academies Press, Washington, D.C. (2004)

Cauce, A.M., Gordon, E.W.: Toward the measurement of human agency and the disposition to express it (2013). https://www.ets.org/Media/Research/pdf/cauce_gordon_measurement_human_agency.pdf. Accessed 19 Dec 2018

Chilisa, B., Preece, J.: Research Methods for Adult Educators in Africa. UNESCO Inst. for Education, Hamburg (2005)

Deleuze, G., Guattari, F.: A Thousand Plateaus: Capitalism and Schizophrenia. Continuum, London (1987)

Den Bossche, P.V., Gijselaers, W.H., Segers, M., Kirschner, P.A.: Social and cognitive factors driving teamwork in collaborative learning environments: team learning beliefs and behaviors. Small Group Res. **37**(5), 490–521 (2006). https://doi.org/10.1177/1046496406292938

De Graff, E., Kolmos, A.: Characteristics of Problem-Based Learning. Int. J. Eng. Educ. **19**(5), 657–662 (2003)

Edwards, A.: Working collaboratively to build resilience: A CHAT approach. Soc. Policy Soc. **6**, 255–265 (2007)

Foucault, M.: Discipline and Punish: The Birth of the Prison. Random House, New York (1975)

Foucault, M.: Ethics. In: Rabinow, P. (ed.): Essential works of Foucault, 1954–1984, vol. 1 (R. Hurley et al., trans.). Penguin, Harmondsworth (2000)

Fullan, M., Langworthy, M.: A Rich Seam: How New Pedagogies Find Deep Learning. Pearson, London (2014)

Gee, J.P.: What would a state of the art instructional video game look like? Innovate **1**(6) (2005). http://www.innovateonline.info/index.php?view=article&id=80

Gibson, W.: All Tomorrows Parties. Penguin, London (1999)
Hamilton, E.R., Rosenberg, J.M., Akcaoglu, M.: The substitution augmentation modification redefinition (SAMR) model: a critical review and suggestions for its use. TechTrends **60**(5), 433–441 (2016). https://doi.org/10.1007/s11528-016-0091-y
Hampson, M., Patton, A., Shanks, L.: Ten Ideas for 21st Century Education. London, Innovation Unit (2011). https://www.innovationunit.org/wp-content/uploads/2017/04/10-Ideas-for-21st-Century-Education.pdf. Accessed 28 Dec 2018
Kirkpatrick, D.L.: Evaluating Training Programs: The Four Levels. Berrett-Koehler, San Francisco (1996)
Koehler, M.J., Mishra, P.: What is technological pedagogical content knowledge? Contemp. Issues Technol. Teacher Educ. **9**(1) (2009). https://www.citejournal.org/volume-9/issue-1-09/general/what-is-technological-pedagogicalcontent-knowledge
Leadbeater, C., Wong, A.: Learning from the Extremes: A White Paper. Cisco Systems Inc., San Jose (2010). http://charlesleadbeater.net/wp-content/uploads/2010/05/LearningfromExtremes_WhitePaper.pdf. Accessed 28 Dec 2018
Leask, I.: Beyond subjection: notes on the later foucault and education. Educ. Philos. Theor. **44**, (2012)
Lee, M.J.W., McLoughlin, C.: Teaching and learning in the Web 2.0 era: empowering students through learner- generated content. Int. J. Instruct. Technol. Distance Learn. **4**(10), 21–34 (2007). http://itdl.org/Journal/Oct_07/article02.htm. Accessed 28 Dec 2018
Magnussen, R.: Methods Project Documents (Unpublished) (2016)
Mertens, D.M.: Mixed Methods Design In Evaluation. Sage, Los Angeles (2018)
Monahan, T.: Flexible space & built pedagogy: emerging IT embodiments. Inventio **4**(1), 1–19 (2002)
Ozdamar-Keskin, N., Ozata, F.Z., Banar, K., Royle, K.: Examining digital literacy competences and learning habits of open and distance learners. Contemp. Educ. Technol. **6**, 74–90 (2015)
Osterlaken, I.: Technology And Human Development. Routledge, Oxford (2015)
Pappe, I.: Biggest Prison on Earth: A History of the Occupied Territories. Oneworld Publications, London (2018)
Pólya, G.: How to Solve it: A New Aspect of Mathematical Method. Doubleday & Company, Garden City (1957)
Puentedura, R.R.: The SAMR Model (2006). http://hippasus.com/resources/tte/. Accessed 13 Dec 2018
Puentedura, R.: Building transformation: an introduction to the SAMR Model [Blog post] (2014). http://www.hippasus.com/rrpweblog/archives/2014/08/22/BuildingTransformation_AnIntroductionToSAMR.pdf. Accessed 4 Feb 2019
Roselli, N.D.: Collaborative learning: theoretical foundations and applicable strategies to University. J. Educ. Psychol.-Propositos Y Representaciones **4**(1), 251–280 (2016). https://eric.ed.gov/?id=EJ1126307. Accessed 28 Dec 2018
Royle, K., Hadfield, M.: From 'posh pen and pad' to participatory pedagogies. Int. J. Mobile Blended Learn. **4**(1), 1–17 (2012). https://doi.org/10.4018/jmbl.2012010101
Royle, K., Nikolic, J.: A modern mixture, agency, capability, technology and 'Scrum': agile work practices for learning and teaching in schools. J. Educ. Soc. Policy, **3**(3), 37–47 (2016). https://www.researchgate.net/publication/309764033_A_modern_mixture_Agency_Capability_Technology_and_'Scrum'_Agile_Work_Practices_for_Learning_and_Teaching_in_Schools. Accessed 19 Dec 2018
Savin-Baden, M.: Using problem-based learning: new constellations for the 21st century. J. Excellence Coll. Teach. **25**(3&4), 197–219 (2014)
Sen, A.: Well-being, agency, and freedom. The Dewey lectures 1984. J. Philos. **82**, 169–221 (1985)

Sen, A.: Inequality Re-examined. Oxford University Press, Oxford (1992)
Thomas, J.W.: A Review of Research on Project Based Learning (2000). http://www.newtechnetwork.org.590elmp01.blackmesh.com/sites/default/files/dr/pblresearch2.pd
Tobias, S.: Foucault on freedom and capabilities. Theory Cult. Soc. **22**(4), 65–85 (2005). https://doi.org/10.1177/0263276405053721
Trilling, B., Fadel, C.: 21st Century Skills: Learning for Life in Our Times. Jossey-Bass, San Francisco (2009)
Yahya, A.H.: Tools for internationalizing higher education in developing countries. In: Fardoun, H.M., Downing, K.J., Mok, M. (eds.) The Future of Higher Education in the Middle East and Africa, pp. 87–103. Springer, Cham (2018). https://doi.org/10.1007/978-3-319-64656-5_9

Facing a Digital Challenge at a Traditional University

Viktorija Florjančič(✉)

Faculty of Management,
University of Primorska, Cankarjeva 5, 6000 Koper, Slovenia
viktorija.florjancic@fm-kp.si

Abstract. This article presents the challenges that teachers of the youngest Slovenian public university are facing in introducing ICT into the pedagogical process. The introduction of ICT into pedagogical practice requires the support of the school management and also impacts on the quality of education. Thus, within the framework of the InoTeZ project, we conducted group interviews with representatives of the faculty management and those responsible for the quality assurance system. The analysis of the group interviews content revealed that the differences in faculties' development are also evident in the fields of e-learning understanding and in the processes of ICT implementation into the pedagogical process. Some faculties are more systematic, and changes are planned accurately, while others leave it to individual enthusiasts. The interviewees showed support for the establishment of unified technical and pedagogical-didactic support at the university level with the desire to retain partial local support. The support needs to be set up as an infrastructure center, taking into account the specificities of the study programs and the needs of individual faculties and teachers.

Keywords: E-learning · Open education · Higher education · Digital transformation · InoTeZ project

1 Introduction

Information and communication technology (ICT) offer the possibility to learn anything, anytime, and from anywhere. Therefore, it was recognized as an enabler for lifelong learning [15]. Widely open access to different resources and learning contents help people achieve the contemporary skills and knowledge demanded from the knowledge society.

The revolution of higher education, as some call it [6, 9], started with so called Massive Open Online Courses (MOOCs) in 2012, even though the abbreviation MOOC was created in 2008 [9]. The impact of MOOC rates is evident through statistics showing that in the year 2017 MOOCs included 81 million students [13]. MOOCs are offered by more than 800 universities, some of them in cooperation with companies, especially in the field of information technology [13]. MOOCs are gaining in quality and therefore in recognition. According to Goodman [4], 14% of American students acquired knowledge only through online studies in 2015. In the same period,

L. Uden et al. (Eds.): LTEC 2019, CCIS 1011, pp. 279–291, 2019.
https://doi.org/10.1007/978-3-030-20798-4_24

an additional 15% were included in at least one online course. In response to the opening of universities in the USA, the European Commission (EC) in September 2013 adopted the Opening up Education (EC 2013) initiative. The initiative to opening up education focuses on three areas [1]:

- Creating opportunities for organizations, teachers, and learning to innovate;
- Increased use of Open Educational Resources (OER); primarily those resources that are publicly funded; and
- Improving ICT infrastructure and connectivity in schools.

Former European Commissioner Androulla Vassiliou underlines the importance of opening minds to new learning methods that make persons more employable, innovative, and creative [1]. Implementing new teaching methods is crucial to the creation of an innovative and interconnected society of the 21st century. Digitization of the society changes the learning resources, the way of education, and the education experience. As emphasized in the initiative to open up education, policymakers and teachers should be introduced by the changes rather than by making changes only to coincidence and enthusiastic individuals.

Opening education is only one area that has a significant impact on education. Education is becoming more and more adapted to the learner; different learning technologies are involved in the learning process, making learning more varied, more interesting and playful which all motivate students even more (e.g., gamifications, game-based learning) [7]. The shorter learning content (microlearning) and learning done through social interaction and collaboration (ibidem) is taking place more and more. Virtual reality and intelligent assistants (ibidem) come into education too. Many universities, with the aim of increasing student progressions in their study path, achievement of learning outcomes, and a better understanding of the whole learning process, have increasingly been including learning analytics that link all the available data at the institution with understandable and useful reports [14].

Presented trends and initiatives are being pursued by the Slovene Ministry of Education, Science and Sport (MESS). In the *Strategic Guidelines for the further implementation of ICT in the Slovenian education by 2020* [10], MESS supports the development of open, creative, and sustainably sustainable learning environments, which should be supported by ICT. In the field of higher education, e-education is highlighted as goal 5 [10]. E-education has to be promoted in formal education as well as supporting lifelong learning and as an opportunity to tackle the shortage of students' knowledge in the transition from secondary to higher education. Goal 5 should be realized with the development of study programs where individual courses, parts of the program, or the whole study program are carried out online and to assist higher education institutions to increase the supply of open content.

In Slovenia there are four universities: University of Ljubljana,[1] University of Maribor,[2] University of Primorska[3], and University of Nova Gorica.[4] The first three are public universities; the University of Primorska (UP) is the smallest and youngest of them.

In 2018, based on strategic national and European documents, MESS launched a bid for a public university with the aim of promoting ICT usage in higher education pedagogical processes. The projects are financed by European Social Funds (80%) and by MESS (20%). The University of Primorska succeeded with the *InoTeZ project – Innovative with Knowledge Technology*. One of the goals of the InoTeZ project is to set up central e-learning support (technical and pedagogical-didactic) for the whole university. The second important goal is related to setting up the minimum standards for the integration of ICT into the pedagogical process. The basis for carrying out all planned activities is a good state of art and becoming familiar to contemporary trends in the higher education field. Implementing ICT in organizations depends highly on management support [12]. Therefore, we tried to find out how supported these trends are by the leading university staff members. We performed interviews with vice deans for education/study activities and representatives of individual university members (faculties) in the field of quality assurance.

2 Information and Communication Technology in Slovenian Higher Education

ICT in Slovenian public universities is most commonly used to support administration processes and less to support instruction. This is despite the fact that ICT is already universally presented in society. In 2018, there was the same portion (89%) of Slovenians who used internet in the last 3 months daily as it was in EU 28 countries [2]. In the last 3 months there were 1% Slovenians who did not use the internet at least once a week. In the EU 28, there were 2%. Slovenian internet users (72%) interacted more with public authorities in 2018 than an average EU 28 citizen (59%). In 2015 there were slightly more individuals in the internet users' group that used the internet for looking up information about education, training, or offered courses in Slovenia (43%) than in the EU 28 (41%), but fewer than those who were doing online courses in 2017 (Slovenia 7%, EU 28 9%). In 2017, there were more Slovenian (19%) internet users that used the internet for online learning materials than in the EU 28 (17%), but fewer of them (Slovenia 7%, EU 28 10%) that used internet for communicating with instructors or students using educational websites or portals.

The use of ICT in the educational process, modeled in the business world, where the term e-business is used, is called e-education or e-learning [3]. E-learning is used for partial support of the pedagogical process or for delivering courses/study programs

[1] https://www.uni-lj.si/eng/.

[2] https://www.um.si/en/Pages/default.aspx.

[3] https://www.upr.si/en.

[4] http://www.ung.si/en/.

online. Understanding the concept of e-learning, despite its long presence in the Slovenian educational space, is still different. Some people under this concept understand the use of programs for presenting/illustrating learning material (for example, PowerPoint), while for others e-learning means online delivered courses. The understanding of the concept of e-learning was also investigated in the interviews presented later on. Having a common understanding of e-learning is crucial for further project activities.

Although the strategic MESS document encourages the implementation of study programs online, this has not been adopted by public higher education institutions yet. A quick look to the "Call for enrollment in undergraduate and unified master's study programs in the academic year 2018/2019" [11] shows that e-learning/e-study is offered by:

- Faculty of Public Administration, University of Ljubljana, where the e-learning method is mentioned as information support for organized forms of study and in part-time studies call where e-studies are mentioned in the context of distance learning.
- Faculty of Management, Business and Informatics, Novo mesto, publishes a call for e-study as a way of conducting part-time studies.
- E-study, as a way of conducting part-time studies, is also offered by GEA COLLEGE – Faculty of Entrepreneurship.

In the call for enrollment in 2018/2019, there were 17,388 places for regular and part-time studies has been opened. For part-time studies (3,249 places), there were only 7.1% places for e-learning students.

3 Understanding and Acceptance of ICT in Higher Education – A Qualitative Study

3.1 University of Primorska

The University of Primorska (UP), the youngest and smallest Slovenian public university, was founded in 2003. Upon the establishment of UP, the previously established higher education institutions joined together under the umbrella of the university:

- High School of Tourism and Hospitality Portorož (established in 1994), since 2008 the Faculty of Tourism Studies – Turistica (UP FTŠ – Turistica);
- High School of Management (1995), which has been working as management faculty (UP FM) since 2007;
- Faculty of Humanities (2000) (UP FHŠ); and
- High School of Health (2002), since 2011 as the Faculty of Health Sciences (UP FVZ).

In 2003, the Faculty of Education (UP PEF) was established and in 2006 the Faculty of Mathematics, Science and Information Technologies (UP FAMNIT). The UP is thus joined by six pedagogical members offering study programs at all three

Bologna levels. In the academic year 2016/2017, 5,103 students studied at the UP, representing 8.6% of the student population of Slovenian universities.

Different fields of study in which UP members carry out their study activities as well as differences in development are also evident in the introduction of ICT in the pedagogical process. While some faculty are quite conservative and traditional in introducing innovations, and also referring to the inappropriateness of the ICT field of study, others are much more determined and innovate easily.

3.2 Methodology of Data Collection and Processing

As in business organizations, ICT in education was firstly implemented to support the administration processes – from general administration to students and staff administration, and for research purposes. The teaching and learning processes finally were supported [5]. ICT implementation in business organizations need to have the backing and commitment of management at various levels [8]. The same is needed in educational organizations. The introduction of ICT into education institutions cannot succeed without the acceptance/affection of all stakeholders. The InoTeZ project activities are based on the state-of-the-art report. The state-of-the-art report consists of a review of existing hardware, software, and networks that exist at the university and data analyses about ICT usage among teachers and students. The data was collected with two e-questionnaires, one for students and one for academic staff. Although the last one included a question about ICT support and management support, we try to make an overview of understanding and acceptance of ICT from the management structure (vice deans for education or academic affairs) and those who are in charge of quality assurance (the faculties' representatives for quality assurance). We decided to lead the interviews in two separate groups, although both interviews were conducted on the same day, January 31, 2018. First, a group interview was conducted with vice deans responsible for the study matters. We conducted the interview during a meeting of the Committee for Academic Affairs at the university. There were four of the six vice deans and a vice rector for academic affairs present. The author of the paper and the interviewer came from the faculty with missing representatives and are familiar with the situation at the faculty. The second group involved five representatives of the university members (faculty) who are in charge of quality assurance for their faculties. Each interview lasted 90 min. In both groups, we proceeded from the same set of questions:

1. Understanding e-learning for faculty and how/why e-learning is involved in the pedagogical process.
2. How is e-learning included in the normative acts (rules, instructions, policies) and curricula? How do you evaluate the work of teachers who perform e-learning?
3. Who is responsible for technical and pedagogical-didactic support for teachers and (technical) students? How is teacher training provided?
4. How should be the e-learning support and training organized in the future? Centralized for all university members or decentralized? What are the expectations for e-learning support?

5. Opening education – what are they thinking about? Would faculty be willing to open some of their content? Under what conditions? Where do members see opportunities/barriers for opening up?

Presented research questions were used for orientation to collect all needed information. For example, the representatives for quality assurance were not asked to answer a question about how the e-learning support is regulated for the faculty if the vice-dean had already responded to this question. We asked this question to the representative of the faculty whose vice dean was not present at the meeting.

The interview in both groups was conducted in the same way: the interviewer asked the question and the interviewees answered in the order in which they were sitting, in the same sequence for each question. They were free to add some additional explanation or opinion, depending on the flow of conversation. Conversations in both groups were recorded, to which participants were informed before the beginning of interviews. The transcript of the audio recording was processed using MS Office 2016. All words that were related to the question were marked with comments. The comment included the abbreviation of the faculty and the code defining the content/summary of the text. Using the Word macro,[5] we transferred all highlighted text with comments to a new text document. The table in the word document was transferred to Excel, where we classified the records, merged duplicate records, and classified records into categories that tracked the content of the questions by encoding:

- Understanding e-learning (Code: Concept)
- Management's commitment (Code: Leadership)
- Integrating ICT into the pedagogical process (Code: Integration)
- Existing support and training of teachers (Code: Support)
- Future support and training of teachers at the university level (Code: Center)
- Opening education (Code: Open).

In the analysis of the transcript, two new categories appeared that we thought were worth adding:

- Barriers to greater use of ICT in the pedagogical process (Code: Obstacles)
- Suggestions for improvements (Code: Suggestions).

Data were processed in such a way that an overview by category and by individual faculty could be presented.

3.3 Discussion

Through interviews, we wanted to gather the views of the vice deans responsible for academic affairs and from core persons for faculty quality assurance in order to find out what their understanding of e-learning is for each faculty member, and what is the opinion about the integration of ICT into the pedagogical process and other topics included in the research questions.

[5] https://www.thedoctools.com/word-macros-tips/word-macros/extract-comments-to-new-document/.

Table 1. Understanding e-learning and leadership

Category/Code	Description
Understanding e-learning (Concept)	– There is no single understanding at the facility – Understanding is up to the individual teachers – Lectures at a distance – Using ICT to support lecturing (presentations) – Delivering a course in a virtual environment – Use multimedia content – Uploading a study material to a LMS is not e-learning – ICT is a tool for improving teaching
Management's commitment (Leadership)	– Support is related to the personal experience of the faculty representative and the course subject s/he is teaching

As we forecasted, there is no uniform understanding of e-learning in university (Table 1). The representatives' understanding of e-learning varied from using ICT only to support lectures face-to-face (e.g., PowerPoint presentations) to teaching a course online. Differences in understanding also occur within the faculty. Therefore, the understanding of e-learning is largely left to teachers who use ICT as they decide. It is obvious that we will need to achieve some kind of common agreement regarding the proper naming, as it affects e-learning models, the setting of minimum standards, as well as the processes of monitoring the quality of e-learning.

The initiators of the introduction of ICT in the pedagogical process are at UP FM. ICT is intensively included at the UP FTŠ–Turistica, where teachers and students from Slovenia collaborate intensively with their colleagues from the USA. Video-conferencing systems are used for synchronous collaboration and an online learning environment for asynchronous communication. The field of humanities studies is more conservative about using ICT, but the interview discovered that the leading position and personal experience of this person may influence better attitudes toward ICT among academic staff. For now, ICT is integrated only into two fields of study – geography and some languages.

According to interviewees, all subject areas are not equally suitable for the intensive use of ICT. As we will see below, the specific features are also reflected in the support and training proposals, as this should be adapted to subject-specific requirements and needs.

At all facilities, Moodle, named e-classroom, is used as the official learning management system. The technical administrative support for Moodle is offered by UP FAMNIT, but some additional administrative activities are done by some faculty too, mostly by IT staff or by some of advance and enthusiastic user of Moodle. Support for Moodle in not officially organized at any of the facilities. Assistance and training is mostly carried out in a collegial way; much of this is so called 1:1 counseling, where a teacher with experience helps a beginner.

Table 2. The integration of ICT and the existing support

Category/Code	Description

Integrating ICT into the pedagogical process (Integration)	• Using e-classrooms (Moodle)
	  • To support the absence of a teacher
	  • A non-compulsory complement to the classic course; decision about how and how much is left to a teacher
	  • A compulsory supplement – students take a part of their obligations online (at distance)
	• Intensity of integration depends on a teacher (personal affection and/or content of the subject) or the department
	• Intensity of Moodle usage differs from basic to advanced functions; depending on an individual teacher and on faculties' decisions
	• ICT is used to support teaching, searching for information
	• Use of other technologies (Google Drive, interactive whiteboard at UP PEF)
	• Different approaches at opening courses and encouraging teachers to do it
	• Different ways of presenting how ICT is included in curricula; teacher work is evaluated differently
	• At UP FM teachers have to define ICT usage in course delivery plan, others do not. For one member, a minimum of content (information) and activity (e.g., a forum) is set, which must be included in Moodle; in others, the use and method of use are left to a teacher
	• The use of Moodle is not specifically monitored (supervised); the concern that it is not used for teachers' inactivity
	• UP FM deliver some courses online
	• Teachers at UP FM should deliver online at least a small part of the course (students' homework)
	• UP FTŠ-Turistica co-operation with the USA university, joint online lectures in one course

Existing support and training of teachers (Support)	• Mostly technical support of IT or enthusiastic ICT user (teacher)/colleague at the faculty • Content support is rare • Training on demand, as it is needed (do not have all the same needs), tailor-made training 1:1 consulting on the use of ICT

The intensity of Moodle usage varied from faculty to faculty. For some faculty, each course has a space in Moodle (e-classroom) opened, but generally there is no control over how this space is used. Therefore, there are fears among the interviewees that the e-classroom can be used to hide teacher non-activity. The use of the e-classroom is mostly left to individual teachers, with the exception of UP FM, where at least a part of undergraduate courses at a professional study program should be delivered online. Monitoring how this is realized is not yet regulated. Interviewers agree that other faculty should follow the UP FM practice, though it may be slightly less rigorous. The impact of MOOCs is also noticed; teachers who attended these courses often regulated their courses in a similar way – courses are organized by topics, students have to do different weekly activities, etc. At UP FM, peer grading is used in some courses as well.

Teachers also use other ICTs, especially cloud services (e.g., Google Docs). Smart or interactive boards are in use for three faculty groups; their use depends on individual teachers and the course they are teaching. The interactive boards are usually used only for the presentation of the topics and less in the way that they should be used.

Interviewers exposed a potential barrier for greater integration of ICTs in the pedagogical process – a teacher's work online is not evaluated in the same way as a classical work is. An hour of lecture is equal two hours of working online. Therefore, teachers prefer to have classic lectures. Evaluation of teachers' work online will undoubtedly have to be unified and organized in a way that will not inhibit the introduction of ICT into the pedagogical process. The collected comments on the integration of ICT into the pedagogical process and the existing support on the member are shown in Table 2.

In addition to the aforementioned evaluation of teacher work, the interviewees also highlighted other obstacles (Table 3), which makes it more difficult to integrate ICT into pedagogical practice. Interviewees stressed the burden of teachers with other work, which makes it difficult to attend training or workshops where they will get acquainted with modern, ICT-supported, working methods. At some facilities it is pointed out that older teachers do not want changes, though that was not noticed at other facilities. ICT is introduced by both younger and older teachers. It is true, however, that some teachers find it difficult to convince themselves of the change if they are sympathetic to the classical forms of teaching. It was highlighted that it would be useful to present examples of good practice in order to inform teachers about the possibilities and benefits of using ICT in pedagogical practice. Therefore, an annual conference named University Swallow was organized for this purpose – to present examples of good use of ICT in pedagogical processes and to motivate teachers to change the pedagogical paradigm of teaching and learning.

Outdated ICT equipment and a concern over how ICT might compensate a teacher in a pedagogical process was highlighted in Table 3. The UP PEF points to the prudence of the use of ICT, or that the use of ICT must be designed and thought-out. A student's inclination toward personal contacts would be checked with surveys in the continuation of the project.

Interviewees supported the planned centralized support (technical and content) at the university level (Table 4). They also expressed the financial part of such a center. The center should be financed by a university and the service offered for free for all university members. Despite the centralized support at the university level, interviewees want to maintain a part of the support on the faculty itself, as such support would be more adapted to specific needs and faster. During the discussion with both groups of stakeholders, the diversity of study areas was emphasized that should also be taken into account in support and training.

Table 3. Obstacles for ICT in the pedagogical process

Category/Code	Description
Obstacles to the increased use of ICT in the pedagogical process (Obstacles)	• Teachers are overloaded with other activities that prevent the acquisition of new teaching methods • The inadequacy of the study area (content) or the way in which the subject is to be carried out (e.g., the subject/course needs to be taught face-to-face) • Teachers favor classical techniques/forms of teaching; some teachers find it hard to accept innovations or stubbornly insist on classical work • Teachers are not particularly motivated to integrate ICT • In one faculty group, the age of teachers is an obstacle, but not at others • Evaluation of teachers' workload • Fear that ICT may substitute a teacher • ICT should be used with prudence • Inadequate infrastructure and equipment • Students want personal contact

In the interviews, we talked about the topic of open education, which everyone, like the concept of e-learning, understands different. Teachers are generally in favor of opening at the principle level, but they pointed out a number of problems – copyright protection, missing resources for the development of open content (teacher overload, financing issue for development of open content), the time of implementation of these contents, etc. The open approach is seen as the possibility to promote faculty as well as promoting teachers.

The interviews highlighted the inadequate students' digital skills, so they suggested the preparation of learning content that would fill the missing gaps while at the same time being accessible to all students at the university, regardless of the faculty they come from. Open content in the field of ICT use should also be freely available to teachers.

After the interviews, we tried to visualize the state of the faculty in terms of the integration of ICT (intensity of ICT usage) in the pedagogical process and the expressed support (affection) of the management (Fig. 1). The faculty's position in the matrix is based on the author's subjective assessment.

We placed a single faculty based on the analysis of the interview transcripts. As we discuss later on in the project team, where the representatives of all faculties participate, there is often high declarative support, but in practice it is not demonstrated and realized. Therefore, we decided not to include faculties' full names in the matrix.

Table 4. Support and open education

Category/Code	Description
Support and training (Center)	• Supported by all faculties • Central and uniform services for all faculties • Center has to be financed by university, services for faculties need to be free • Part of the support should be decentralized (for the faculty) • Fair and correct evaluation of teachers' work that offer pedagogical-didactic support • Teacher training has to planned in advanced and so it is easier to cope with other teachers' activities • Training has to be tailored to study fields • Advantage of 1:1 counseling

Opening Education (Open)	• Internal mobility is the way to open a member's education
	    • Obstacle: internal billing of ECTS
	    • Obstacle: coordinating schedules
	• Ready to prepare open content; Lectures are already public, so e-content can also be public.
	• Obstacles for opening a content:
	    • Necessarity of development resources
	    • The course ought to have a beginning and the end
	    • Tutor support for the participants (who/how)
	    • Evaluating a teacher's work for the course preparation and for monitoring the participants
	    • The copyright issues
	• Open content as an opportunity for promoting the faculty and professors

Suggestions for improvement (Suggestions)	• PowerPoint ought to be banned • Introduce examples of good practices • Use MOOCs structure and teaching paradigm in universities courses • Using and planning online delivery similar as it is at UP FM • ICT can be an element of quality of teaching – transparency; integrate ICT usage indicator in the quality assurance system • Students learn better with ICT, although study still has to a hard work

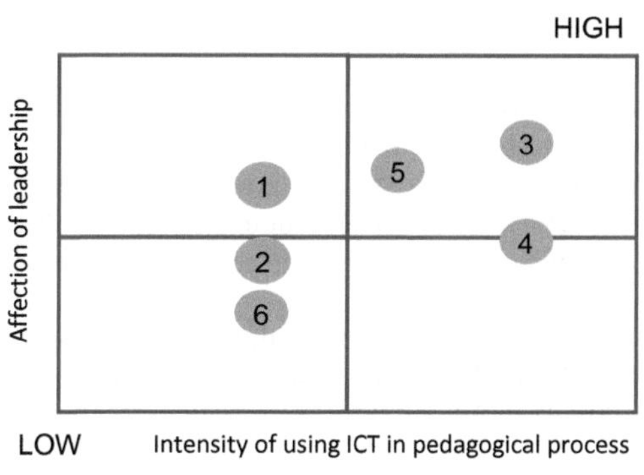

Fig. 1. Support and intensity of using ICT

4 Conclusion

In the article we present the challenges that we faced at the university when introducing ICT into the pedagogical process. Prior to the start of the InoTeZ project, at least three attempts were made (appointment of working groups for the elaboration of the strategy and/or introduction of e-studies), which, due to the lack of support from the management structures, were unsuccessful. The InoTeZ project team has set ambitious goals, which were mostly directed from the ministry bid. The results of the interviews presented in the paper are only a part of the project activities, which already show a partial picture of the challenges that we are facing at the university, starting from different understandings of e-learning, different ICT adoption levels, and also different leadership support and commitment. The last one mostly depends on personal characteristics and experiences with ICT and e-learning. If some faculties treat e-learning as more organized and planned, then the introduction of ICT into the pedagogical process is still left to individual enthusiasts. The organization of support activities at the faculty as well as the university differs a lot. Among the teachers who participated in the discussions, the uniform regulation of technical and pedagogical-didactic support at the university level is supported, by the subject-specific and different needs of individual teachers need to be taking into account. Teachers draw attention to the need for a uniform curriculum for the evaluation of a teacher workload, which should not constitute an obstacle to more intensive integration of ICT into pedagogical practice. Among the participating teachers there is an awareness of the trends in the field of higher education in the world and the desire to follow them. Opening education and greater integration of ICT in the pedagogical process might be a positive challenge for the university, faculties, and the academic staff as well. Teachers, however, are aware that ICT does not change the pedagogical paradigm itself, and that these challenges must be addressed by teachers with the support of management and also by taking into account students at the university.

References

1. EC – European Commission. European Commission – Press release: Commission launches 'Opening up Education' to boost innovation and digital skills in schools and universities (2013). http://europa.eu/rapid/press-release_IP-13-859_en.htm
2. Eurostat. Digital Economy and society (2018). http://ec.europa.eu/eurostat/web/digital-economy-and-society/data/main-tables
3. Florjančič, V.: E-študij v slovenskem visokošolskem prostoru. Didactica Slovenica – Pedagoška obzorja. **3**(4), 139–155 (2014)
4. Goodman, J., Melkers, J., Pallais, A.: An elite grad-school degree goes online: can georgia tech's virtual master's increase access to education? Educ. Next (2018). http://educationnext.org/elite-grad-school-degree-goes-online-georgia-tech-virtual-masters-increase-access-education/
5. Keengwe, J., Kidd, T., Kyei-Blankson, L.: Faculty and technology: implications for faculty training and technology leadership. J. Sci. Educ. Technol. **18**(1), 23–28 (2009). https://doi.org/10.1007/s10956-008-9126-2

6. Kolowich, S.: The MOOC ‘Revolution’ May Not Be as Disruptive as Some Had Imagined. The Chronicle of Higher Education, 8 August 2013. https://www.chronicle.com/article/MOOCs-May-Not-Be-So-Disruptive/140965
7. Kumar, S.: 9 eLearning Trends For 2018. eLearning Industry (2017). https://elearningindustry.com/elearning-trends-for-2018-9
8. Laudon, K.C., Laudon, J.P.: Management Information Systems: Managing the Digital Firm, Global Edition, 15/E -. Pearson Education, Harlow (2018)
9. León-Urritia, M., Cobos, R., Dickens, K.: MOOCs and their influence on higher education institutions: perspectives from the insiders. J. New Approaches Educ. Res. **7**(1), 40–45 (2018). https://doi.org/10.7821/naer.2018.1.252
10. MESS – Ministry of Education, Science and sport. Strategic guidelines for further implementation of ICT in the Slovenian education until 2020 (2016). http://www.mizs.gov.si/fileadmin/mizs.gov.si/pageuploads/URI/Slovenian_Strategic_Guidelines_ICT_in_education.pdf
11. MIZŠ – Mininistrstvo za izobraževanje, znanost in šport. Razpis za vpis v dodiplomske in enovitev magistrske študijske programe v študijskem letu 2018/2019, Univerze v Ljubljani, Univerze v Mariboru, Univerze na Primorskem, Univerze v Novi Gorici in samostojnih visokošolskih zavodih (2018). http://portal.evs.gov.si/documents/10157/5a0f4152-a937-46a9-8f76-790171f031d5
12. Oz, E.: Management Information Systems, 6th edn. Course Technology, Cengage Learning, Boston (2009)
13. Shah, D.: By the numbers: MOOCS in 2017 (2018). https://www.class-central.com/report/mooc-stats-2017/
14. Sclater, N., Mullan, J.: Learning analytics and students success – assessing the evidence (2017). http://repository.jisc.ac.uk/6560/1/learning-analytics_and_student_success.pdf
15. UNESCO – United Nations Educational, Scientific and Cultural Organization. Leveraging Information and Communication Technologies to Achieve the Post-2015 Education Goal. Report of the International Conference on ICT and Post-2015 Education (2015). https://www.icde.org/assets/RESOURCES/report_qingdao_web.pdf

Math Anxiety Analysis in Indonesian Elementary School

Nurhayati[1(✉)], Dina Anika Marhayani[1], Chih-Hung Chang[2], and Marja Naaranoja[3]

[1] STKIP Singkawang, Singkawang 79251, Indonesia
nurhayati@stkipsingkawang.ac.id
[2] National University of Kaohsiung, Kaohsiung, Taiwan
[3] Vaasa University of Applied Sciences, Vaasa, Finland

Abstract. The starting point of the research was the fact that the math results in the region were low according to the international evaluation. The paper also aims to make new math anxiety questionnaire since the existing math anxiety inquiries focus mainly on feelings of learners and we wanted to study psychological, physiological and social elements of math anxiety using the viewpoints of Dacey and Fiore (2000). This questionnaire is compared to existing ones and the comparison shows that the questionnaire has new viewpoints. The results show that the anxiety level of the 1–6 graders was mostly low. The developed math anxiety tool needs further development.

Keywords: Math anxiety · Learning mathematics · Math anxiety questionnaire · Elementary school

1 Introduction

This study assesses whether elementary school 1–6 graders (7–13 year old children) in primary school 03 Sajingan Besar have math anxiety. The school is near to the Indonesia-Malaysia border where the mathematical ability of students has been assessed to be low (Syachrumsyah 2017). We want to understand whether the poor math skill results (Mullis et al. 2008; Mullis et al. 2012) are outcomes of math anxiety that starts already in elementary school. One of the interesting viewpoints is that Sukmadinata (2004) revealed that anxiety and worry also have a positive value, as long as the intensity of the anxiety is not too strong, because high, medium, and light anxiety can be a motivation. We need to be aware that the math anxiety is not always bad.

The other reason for this study is to create math anxiety questionnaire by using Dacey and Fiore (2000) reasoning that anxiety has psychological, physiological and social elements. The focus of the earlier anxiety questionnaires is mainly a bit narrower since they focus on feelings of the learners. We aim to compare the created anxiety questionnaire with the existing math anxiety questionnaires.

Learning mathematics requires abstract, axiomatic and deductive skills (Hamzah and Squares 2009). However, abstract thinking of children in elementary school is still evolving. Because of this, elementary school teachers are forced to connect pupils understanding from the concrete to abstract.

L. Uden et al. (Eds.): LTEC 2019, CCIS 1011, pp. 292–301, 2019.
https://doi.org/10.1007/978-3-030-20798-4_25

According to Ramirez et al. (2013a) a self-report measure of math anxiety is associated with math achievement in children as early as first and second grade. According to them math anxiety measure is not related to children's reading achievement, suggesting it is not just a proxy for general academic anxiety.

2 Math Anxiety

2.1 Math Anxiety and Its Results

According to Mohd Nordin et al. (2013) the math anxiety is due to the past life experience; social force and family expectations; negative attitudes and thoughts towards mathematics; method of teaching; influence of peers; situation and instrumentality of test or examination; poor curriculum; repressed emotions and physical causes and also myths related to mathematics, for example believing that mathematical skills are born naturally or there is a magic key to solve mathematic problem or girls don't learn mathematics.

Math anxiety can be a real fear, the root of which can be affective and cognitive, with people's belief influencing the way they think about mathematics and subsequently affect their learning (Jackson 2008): p. 41. Math anxiety may cause children to fear mathematics. The anxiety may hinder a child's ability to make math a relevant part of their everyday life (Rossnan (2006: p. 1).

Working memory is linked to math anxiety. The more working memory capacity one has, the better the performance on academic tasks such as problem solving and reasoning (Engle 2002) and the better they are at regulating their emotional experiences (Schmeichel and Demaree 2010; Schmeichel et al. 2008). However when they are in a stressful situation when the working memory capacity cannot be used normally their results are more poor. But a person who has low working memory has learned to use the reasoning and other strategies than memorizing. This explains that when a low working memory people are in stressful situation they still rely on the other skills than memorising they will perform better than a person who normally can rely on working memory (Ramirez et al. 2013a).

Willis (2010) claims that elementary level pupils with math anxiety do not develop higher-order thinking skills. Higher-order thinking comprises creative problem solving and emotional response control that are needed to solve math problems and manage complex technology (Willis 2010).

2.2 Math Anxiety Questionnaires for Elementary Level Pupils

There are not many researchers who have examined math anxiety of young children. There are three main scales available to assess math anxiety of pupils in elementary school. The 22-item Mathematics Anxiety Scale for Children (MASC; Chiu and Henry 1990) is based on the MARS (that was aimed for older students) but shortened for use with children in upper elementary grades. The MASC uses a 4-point Likert-type scale and has good evidence based on internal structure ($\alpha = .92$) and strong evidence based on relations to other variables (i.e., test anxiety and school achievement motivation).

The Mathematics Anxiety Survey (MAXS; Gierl and Bisanz 1995) is a 14-item assessment using a 5-point Likert-type scale also based on the MARS but included pictoral depictions of anxiety to clarify the response options for children. The MAXS also has good evidence based on internal structure (α = .85 for third grade and α = .87 for sixth grade) and strong evidence based on relations to other variables (i.e., test anxiety and math attitudes). Finally, the 26-item Suinn Mathematics Anxiety Rating Scale, Elementary Form (MARS-E; Suinn et al. 1988) uses a 5-point Likert-type scale and also has good evidence based on internal structure (α = .88) and strong evidence based on relations to other variables (i.e., standardized math subtest scores). Ramirez et al. (2013b) and Jameson (2013) created their own math anxiety questionnaire for elementary school children using the above mentioned questionnaires. Both of them focused on psychometric measures like the earlier math anxiety questionnaires.

Jameson (2013) created a pool of 20 items based on academic content standards for elementary math. The pool of items was revised by five experts who suggested minor rewording and independently confirmed the items' appropriateness. A pilot test of the 20-item Children's Anxiety in Math Scale (CAMS) revealed that four items were not functioning similarly to one another or to the other items on the scale. Those four items were removed, leaving the current 16-item scale. The questionnaire expresses 16 issues like "When solving math problems I feel" and "When teacher calls me to answer math question I feel".

Ramirez (et al. 2013a) made questions that evaluated the math anxiety attitudes of 1–2 graders in elementary school. Children were asked what they felt when solving a particular problems that were drawn from mathematics-teaching workbooks for children in the early elementary grades (e.g., "There are 13 ducks in the water, there are 6 ducks on land, how many ducks are there in all?"). Other items asked children about specific situations they might be confronted with at school concerning math (e.g., "being called on by a teacher to explain a math problem on the board"). They asked children to make their responses about each question using a sliding scale that featured a calm face on the far right, a semi nervous face in the middle, and an obviously nervous face on the far left. The researchers encouraged all children to use the full continuum of the scale. The questionnaire highlighted that already in early elementary school level children faced math anxiety that potentially effected on math achievement (Ramirez et al. 2013b).

In addition, it is possible to evaluate the anxiety level by someone who is trained to see physiological signs of anxiety and the actions associated with them. Psychiatrists and psychologists are the experts who are trained to diagnose such a problem and can give a third party opinion. This is seen as a must issue when the anxiety is serious (Shishigu 2018).

2.3 How to Reduce Math Anxiety

The researchers have found following methods that either prevent or minimize the effect of math anxiety

1. Parents learn to believe that their children have enough good mathematics abilities, to express normal expectations, and avoid comparing the mathematics abilities or achievement of one child with that of another (Mohd Nordin et al. 2013).
2. Psychological Techniques like anxiety management, desensitization, counseling, support groups, bibliotherapy, and discussions.
3. Once a student feels less fearful about math, he/she may build their confidence by taking more mathematics classes.
4. Most research shows that until a person with math anxiety has confronted this anxiety by some form of discussion/counseling no "best practices" in math will help to overcome this fear (Furner 2007).
5. The teachers should emphasize problem solving in mathematics learning and practicing cooperative learning in small groups (Ma and Jiangming 2004). Make the learning fun since students who consider mathematics as enjoyable usually show good performance (Deci and Ryan 2002). Take into consideration the ability to think in abstract level. Relate math to real life as often as possible. Encourage critical thinking, engaged in exploring, thinking, practicing, and using knowledge, rather than listening to verbal descriptions of concepts. This can be done for example by games (e.g. Geist 2010). Practice math problems daily since this supports the confidence development needed to solve mathematical problems (e.g. Freedman 2010). There are also tools that help to teach math like Geogebra (Furner and Marinas 2012)

3 Method

3.1 Research Approach and Strategy

The research is qualitative and quantitative research. The pupils assessment of their experienced math anxiety is verified by asking the teachers opinion of the observed math anxiety.

The qualitative part is the part how we created the questionnaire.

The actual analysis of the answers when using the questionnaire was quantitave.

3.2 Research Aim

The aim of this study is to create a math anxiety questionnaire that studies feelings, physiological symptoms, and social elements of math anxiety. The aim is also to use the questionnaire in order to find out what are the 1–6 graders math anxiety levels in elementary school 03 Sajingan Besar.

3.3 Developing the Questionnaire

Questionnaire was developed based on the interviews of children and teachers. Math anxiety questionnaire divides different angles of anxiety.

Data reduction aimed to simplify and transform the raw data that was got when interviewing the pupils at school. Data was first summared, encoded, themes were searched, groups made, memos written and finally the aim was take away (reduce) the data/information that is not relevant

The following table describes the statements that were formulated based on the interviews and the expert finally validated statements and formulated them as is seen in the Table 1:

Table 1. Statement before and after validation

No.	Statement before validation	Statement after validation
1	Fear to get it wrong when completing math assignments	I am afraid to get a wrong answer when completing math assignments
2	Worry not to be able to complete the math assignment	I am worried not to be able to solve a math problem
3	Increased tense when the math task completion time is almost over	I become anxious when the time to do math is almost over
4	Nervous when completing math assignments	I am nervous when facing a math problem
5	Pale when solving math problems	I become doughy when I am solving a math problem
6	Hand is shaking when I am solving math problems in front of the class	Hand is shaking when I am solving math problems in front of the class.
7	A cold sweat when going to present to the class a math assignment	I am sweating when presenting exercise during math class
8	Knee was shaking when answering questions of the teacher	The knee is shaking when I answer to the questions of the teacher
9	Body is stiff due to the tension when I am learning of mathematics	The body is tensioned when I am in the math lesson
10	Irregular heart beats when completing math assignments	My heart is in my moth when completing a math problem
11	I don't focus when learning mathematics	I have difficulties to pay attention to the teacher while studying mathematics
12	Raised their hands to answer a teacher's question	I don't raise hand to answer a teacher's question
13	Not going to class when learning of mathematics	I don't go to class when we have math lessons
14	Late collect math assignment	My math assignments are overdue
15	No matter the math assignment	I don't mind to do the math assignments
16	Avoid math	I avoid math

The problem of data reduction, data presentation, and conclusion/verification into the image contained a series of activities. Furthermore, the data was analyzed, described and interpreted in the form of words to describe the facts.

Based on the information that has been described previously, each stage in the process is carried out to obtain the validity of the data by examining all the data available from various sources.

Comparing the Questionnaire With the Existing Ones:
There are similar questions related to feelings in this questionnaire psycholocal symptoms. But the psychological symptoms are lacking in the existing questionnaires as well some of the sociological symptoms are lacking. This questionnaire is narrower when we think about feelings but there are four questions related to feelings classes of are there. However they seem to have stronger expressions example:

- The following question "I am afraid to get a wrong answer when completing math assignments" is formulated by Jameson (2013) "When I solve math problems I feel" and by
- The following question "I am worried not to be able to solve a math problem" is formulated by Jameson (2013) "When I think about doing math I feel"

The questions like 5, 6, 7, 8, 9 that are related to physiological reactions were not mentioned in other math anxiety questionnaires but might be seen as questions related to feeling.

- The question 6 "Hand is shaking when I am solving math problems in front of the class" While in the other questionnaires they are formulated "If I have to add up numbers on the blackboard in front of the class, I feel" Jameson (2013)
- The questions that have sociological viewpoint like Question 11 "I don't raise hand to answer a teacher's question" are visible in other questionnaires in form of asking feelings Jameson (2013).

4 Result Math Anxiety Interviews

90 pupils were interviewed. 60 answers were possible to be analysed. The teachers evaluated separately their pupils.

The questionnaire summary gives anxiety level points. The data obtained can be seen in Table 2 below:

Table 2. Results anxiety level math pupils

Interval	Category	Number of Pupils
$71.46 < x \leq 80$	Very High	0
$54.4 < x \leq 71.46$	High	2
$41.6 < x \leq 54.4$	Medium	13
$24.53 < x \leq 41.6$	Low	38
$16 < x \leq 24.53$	Very Low	7

The Table 2 shows the results of math anxiety level. The result show that math anxiety level is low for 38 pupils, high for 2, medium for 13, and very low for 7 pupils none of the had very high math anxiety Fig. 1.

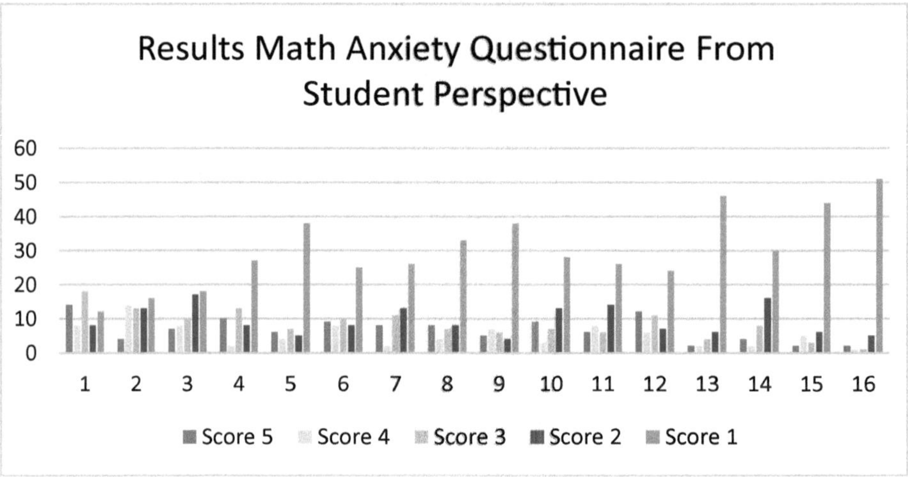

Fig. 1. Graph results math anxiety questionnaire from the perspective of pupils

1. A total of 16 pupils are sometimes afraid of getting a wrong answer when completing math assignments.
2. 17 pupils had not been worried about failing to solve a math problem
3. 20 pupils had not been anxious when the time to do math is almost over.
4. 28 pupils had not been nervous when they faced a math problem.
5. 39 pupils never felt doughy when doing the math exercises.
6. 26 pupils have never experienced hands trembling when they solved math problems in front of the class.
7. 27 pupils never were sweating during math classes.
8. 35 pupils have never experienced knee shaking when they answered math teacher questions.

9. 39 pupils never felt increased tension when doing math exercises
10.30 pupils never felt heart in their mouth when solving a math problem.
11.26 pupils were always able to pay attention to the teacher while studying mathematics.
12.24 pupils were always able to pay attention to the subject during math lessons.
13.46 pupils always go to math lessons.
14.30 pupils were never returned late their math assignment.
15.45 pupils don't mind to do their math excesses.
16.53 pupils never avoid mathematics.

The math anxiety of elementary school 03 Sajingan Besar is at a low level since the total points of pupils is between 24, 5 and 41. In addition, researchers also gave the questionnaire to the teachers of the pupils who evaluated their pupils' math anxiety. The data of teachers can be seen in the chart below Fig. 2:

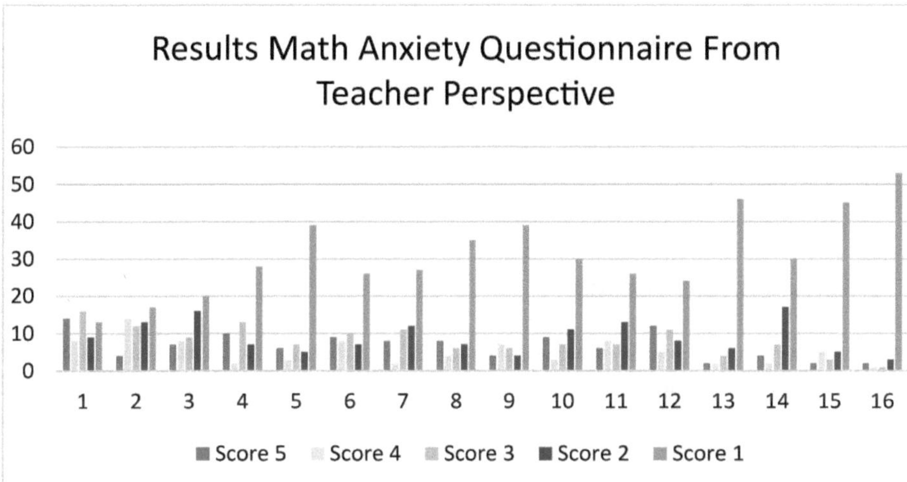

Fig. 2. Graph results math anxiety questionnaire from teacher perspective

1. A total of 16 pupils are sometimes afraid giving wrong answer when they are solving math problem.
2. 17 pupils had not been worried about failing to solve a math problem.
3. 20 pupils had not been anxious when the time to do math is almost over.
4. 28 pupils had not been nervous when they faced a math problem.
5. 39 pupils never felt doughy when they were doing the math.
6. 26 pupils have never experienced hands tremling when solving math problems in front of the class.
7. 27 pupils were never sweating during math class.
8. 35 pupils never experienced knee shaking when they answered questions from the teacher.
9. 39 pupils never felt increased tension when they were doing math exercises
10.30 pupils never felt heart in their mouth when they were solving a math problem.
11.26 pupils were always able to pay attention to the teacher while studying mathematics.
12.24 pupils always raise their hands to answer the question of the teacher.
13.46 pupils always go to math lessons.
14.30 pupils never returned late their math assignment.
15.45 pupils don't mind to do their math exercises.
16.53 pupils never avoid mathematics.

The previous statements allow us to conclude that pupils anxiety of elementary school 03 Sajingan Besar according to the viewpoint of the teachers are at a low level. We analyzed the responses to the questionnaires in order to find the error score. This error score serves as a benchmark of how valid the used instrument is.

The calculated error is:

$$Error\,score = \frac{28}{60} = 0.46$$

The score of questionnaire data errors is 0.46, meaning that the math anxiety questionnaire related to the experienced and observed anxiety of elementary school pupils can be declared valid. In conclusion, pupils' math anxiety questionnaire can be used for research related to the math anxiety of pupils.

The math anxiety questionnaire was created in order to have other viewpoints than only feeling based viewpoint in math anxiety evaluation.

5 Discussion and Results

Results show that the anxiety level of the pupils was mostly low both from pupils and teachers perspective. The developed math anxiety questionnaire results are not possible to be compared with the earlier results. This might mean that however the math anxiety is higher than the anxiety in the previous studies.

The study revealed that math anxiety questions have earlier focused on psychological feelings but the more serious anxiety symptoms like shaking hands or sweating due to physiological anxiety or social fears linked to math anxiety were not possible to be found in the earlier math anxiety questionnaires. The developed math anxiety questionnaire is unique since it studies psychological, physiological and social elements of math anxiety. However, we have to admit that the translated questionnaire might need further editing before it can be used in other countries.

The math anxiety can be really fatal for pupils and students in later education. It is important to find out who need help, and how the teachers support and discuss of the importance of parents support as well as teachers role in minimizing anxiety.

References

Dacey, J.S., Fiore, L.B.: Your Anxious Child: How Parents and Teachers Can Relieve Anxiety in Children. Jossey-Bass Publishers, San Francisco (2000)

Chiu, L.-H., Henry, L.L.: Development and validation of the mathematics anxiety scale for children. In: Measurement and evaluation in counseling and development (1990)

Engle, R.W.: Working memory capacity as executive attention. Curr. Dir. Psychol. Sci. **11**(1), 19–23 (2002). https://doi.org/10.1111/1467-8721.00160

Freedman, E.: Ten Ways to Reduce Math Anxiety. http://www.mathpower.com/reduce.htm. Accessed 2010

Furner, J.M., Berman, B.T.: Review of research: math anxiety: overcoming a major obstacle to the improvement of student math performance. Childhood Educ. **79**(3), 170–174 (2003)

Furner, J.M., Marinas, C.A.: Connecting geometry, measurement, and algebra using GeoGebra for the elementary grades. In: Twenty-Fourth Annual International Conference on Technology in Collegiate Mathematics, pp. 63–72 (2012)

Gierl, M.J., Bisanz, J.: Anxieties and attitudes related to mathematics in grades 3 and 6. J. Exp. Educ. **63**, 139–158 (1995). https://doi.org/10.1080/00220973.995.9943818
Hamzah, U.B, Squares, M.: Managing Intelligence in Learning, Earth Literacy, Jakarta (2009)
Jackson, E.: Mathematics anxiety in student teachers. Pract. Res. High. Educ. Univ. Cumbria **2**(1), 36–42 (2008)
Jameson, M.M.: The development and validation of the children's anxiety in math scale. J. Psychoeducational Assess. **31**(4), 391–395 (2013). https://doi.org/10.1177/2912470131
Ma, X., Jiangming, X.: The causal ordering of mathematics anxiety and mathematics achievement: a longitudinal panel analysis. J. adolesc. **27**(2), 165–179 (2004)
Mohd Nordin, N.A., Md Tahir, H., Kamis, N.H., Khairul Azmi, N.N.: Students' perception and relationship between confidence and anxiety in teaching and learning mathematics: a case study in Sekolah Kebangsaan Bukit Kuda, Klang. In: AIP conference proceedings, vol. 1522, no. 1, pp. 396–399. AIP (2013)
Mullis, I.V.S., et al.: TIMSS 2007 International Mathematics Report: Finding From IEA's Trends in International Mathematics and Science Study at the Fourth Mac Eighth Grades. TIMSS & PIRLS International Study Center, Boston College, Newton (2008)
Mullis, I.V.S., Martin, M.O., Foy, P., Arora, A.: TIMSS 2011 International Results in Mathematics. TIMSS & PIRLS International Study Center, Chestnut Hill (2012)
Nevid, J.S., Spencer, A.R., Greene, B.: Abnormal Psychology, Publisher, Jakarta (2005)
Ramirez, G., Gunderson, E.A., Levine, S.C., Beilock, S.L.: Math anxiety, working memory, and math achievement in early elementary school. J. Cogn. Dev. **14**(2), 187–202 (2013a)
Ramirez, G., Gunderson, E.A., Levine, S.C., Beilock, S.L.: Math anxiety, working memory, and math achievement in early elementary school. J. Cogn. Dev. **14**(2), 187–202 (2013b). https://doi.org/10.1080/15248372.2012.664593
Rossnan, S.: Overcoming math anxiety. Mathitudes **1**(1), 1–4 (2006)
Schmeichel, B.J., Demaree, H.A.: Working memory capacity and spontaneous emotion regulation: high capacity predicts self-enhancement in response to negative feedback. Emotion **10**, 739 (2010)
Schmeichel, B.J., Volokhov, R.N., Demaree, Ha: Working memory capacity and the self-regulation of emotional expression and experience. J. Pers. Soc. Psychol. **95**(6), 1526–1540 (2008). https://doi.org/10.1037/a0013345
Sukmadinata, N.S.: The Foundation of Psychology Education Process. PPB FIP UNY, Yogyakarta (2004)
Suinn, R.M., Taylor, S., Edwards, R.W.: Suinn mathematics anxiety rating scale for elementary school students (MARS-E): psychometric and normative data. Educ. Psychol. Meas. **48**(4), 979–986 (1988)
Syachrumsyah, S.: Kebijakan Pemerataan dan Peningkatan Mutu Pendidikan di Wilayah Perbatasan (equity and improvement policy of education quality in border area Cendekia. Jurnal Pendidikan dan Pengajaran **1**(1), 25–45 (2017)
Willis, J.: Learning to love math: teaching strategies that change student attitudes and get results. Alexandria, US: ASCD (2010). http://www.ebrary.com

Co-creation Workshops for Work Life Oriented ICT Education

Anne-Maria Aho[1(✉)] and Jane Sinclair[2]

[1] School of Business and Culture, Seinäjoki University of Applied Sciences, Seinäjoki, Finland
anne-maria.aho@seamk.fi
[2] Department of Computer Science, University of Warwick, Coventry CV4 7AL, UK
j.e.sinclair@warwickac.uk

Abstract. ICT Companies in Finland today are facing problems in recruiting the right skilled workforce to meet their needs [1]. There is particular shortage of application developers, application designers, web professionals and coders in the South Ostrobothnia area of Finland [2]. Typical degree courses offered by universities would not work because there is a mismatch between the university degrees offered and the needs of these companies. There is a need to develop a new approach to address this shortage. In response to this, local University of Applied Sciences has developed a new ICT education programme using co-creation methods. The new approach is based on the concepts of co-creation of value from service science. This paper discusses the importance of this new approach in education and how it can be implemented. Empirical data is gathered through observation of and reflection on the development of the ICT programme which follows the principles of co-creation.

Keywords: Co-creation · Work life orientation · Educational planning

1 Introduction

Taking care of the quality and know-how of working life will be more challenging in the future and will require more attention. Changes in the micro and macro environments also create new opportunities. Knowledge requirements increase and diversify, challenging both management and employees.

The concept of co-creation is about working co-operatively to produce better results. It has emerged as a management initiative in which different parties (such as a company and their customers) work together. This allows different perspectives and ideas to be contributed and can result in enhanced value for all concerned. The theoretical basis for the concept of co-creation is examined in Sect. 2. In business terms, the benefits of co-creation are seen in terms of advantage (ultimately financial) to the company and an enhanced, tailored product for the customer. However, co-creation can apply in a similar way in other contexts as well, notably to the creation of knowledge [3] where students and teachers are recognised as contributors to the knowledge creation process. Regardless of context, six elements can be identified in the process of

L. Uden et al. (Eds.): LTEC 2019, CCIS 1011, pp. 302–312, 2019.
https://doi.org/10.1007/978-3-030-20798-4_26

co-creation, the contents and roles of which should be defined as part of the process of facilitation [4].

- A role-free community involving both problem-definition and decision-makers. Users and other external actors act as developers and traditional producer-consumer roles are faded in the process. (The platform structure and transparency of the community is emphasised)
- Neutral environment in which to operate. This underlines the openness of the operating environment, i.e., in principle, it is not delivered behind one of the closed doors of one company or operator, but serves more operators and in a common space. (The openness and innovativeness of the space are highlighted)
- Co-creation is both problem-solving and solving problems in a collaborative way for all parties involved. Because of this, it is important to identify and define the roles of the client, the problem solver, and other community members; who is involved in the process and in what way, and how are they motivated to participate? (The openness and innovativeness of the community are highlighted)
- Value creation has been thought and recognized in the development process, i.e. how working together increases the value of the activity and how the different parties benefit from the process. (The innovativeness and originality of the community are highlighted)
- The innovation process has been defined and timed at least to some extent within the framework of the platform, so that the customer can identify it. The beginning of the process, the milestones, the ways of interaction, the end and the form of the end result must be defined. (The innovativeness and platform structure of the community are highlighted)
- Repeatability is a key element of the platform model, i.e. scalability is possible if demand is sufficient and can be created. Repeatability means that you can continuously or repeatedly bring new problems to the platform. However, the co-creation process itself should also be reproducible in other environments. (Platform structure and openness of the community are highlighted.)

Knowledge creation in the context of a subject such as ICT is more complex than a simple two-party interaction. Universities are involved in developing, accrediting, delivering and assessing courses, providing accredited levels of assurance. A purely teacher-centric model of education is giving way to a more collaborative model in which students are recognized as being part of the knowledge creation process [5]. This is particularly valuable in the case of mature students with knowledge of working in industry. Thirdly, companies themselves have direct knowledge of the challenges of the workplace and the issues they face in a real business context as opposed to a purely academic learning environment. Hence, they are ideally placed to be part of the co-creation process.

So far, there has been little investigation of this type of three-way co-creation of knowledge, or of the impact on the different parties involved (for example, the work-life balance of the students). This paper consider a practical case study of the implementation of a programme based on the principles of co-creation and reflects on the issues arising and experience gained from the initiative.

2 Theoretical Background of Co-creation

Taking Co-creation has emerged as a new business management paradigm and is based on value creation in interaction between the company and the customer. The theoretical background of co-creation is largely based on the literature of the service business, although research on innovation management, marketing and consumer behaviour has also provided new insights into the co-creation of value [6]. The discussion of co-creation presented here is largely in the context of business as this is where the majority of current literature is focused.

Co-creation refers to a common, communal, concurrent, equal process that generates new, either tangible or symbolic value [7]. Prahalad and Ramaswamy [8] presented the concept of co-creation in recognizing the change of roles in the market: interaction and co-operation between customers and suppliers increasingly influenced on market mechanisms than the traditional supply-demand relationship.

The changing operating environment of companies and the widening of the service business require a service dominant logic, in which services are playing a key role instead of products and production. The company's entire business aims to create value for its customers and their role is central. Interaction is active both between the company and the customer, and in the relationships between the customers. Co-creation is one of the basic elements of this perspective, which enables the company to develop its service offering. [9, 10]. Today, interaction is increasingly taking place through social media channels and the Internet. Product and service advisers are given an ever-increasing value and, for example, when choosing a destination, many are looking for social media channels to support other consumers and industry enthusiasts in their decision-making.

Co-creation offers benefits to both the company and the customer, for example through better consumer and user experience [11, 12]. Co-creation can promote product and service innovations [13, 14]. In addition, it can also be explored from a cultural perspective in consumer research. Consumption can be regarded as a highly symbolic and culturally related activity where consumers give subjective meaning to products and services. [15, 16]. Consumers and the meanings they create have a key role to play in creating value for products and services, as symbolic and cultural-related meanings have a significant impact on the attractiveness of products and services [17]. From the point of view of innovation research, cooperation and open processes of the company and users are central to co-creation [18–21].

The changing environment in business may be compared to the evolving context in higher education. Institutions which were once regarded as the main creators of knowledge and providers of learning are now recognising the benefits of an approach in which students contribute to the generation of knowledge [22] and external bodies such as industry partner in the development of the curriculum [23]. However, there has been little evaluation of these approaches. Further, initiatives which embed students' learning in their work practice, such as work-life oriented Masters in Finland [24] and degree apprenticeships in the UK [25], involve a three-way relationship which has received little attention.

3 Case Study

In this paper we report a preliminary study in which empirical data is based on observations of a practical development process of ICT education. The case study was conducted at the University of Applied Sciences, in Finland between May 2018 and October 2018. Following the principles of "value creation" the development of the education was informed by "co-creation workshops" with local industrial partners, combining action research with a case study approach.

3.1 Research Methodology and Data Collection

According to Yin [26], case research is appropriate to answer the questions "how" and "why", which aim to explain causal connections or a series of events that happened during a longer period. It is also appropriate to answer the explorative "what" question and evaluate and describe the research. So, the initial task is to clarify rigorously the nature of the study questions [27].

Susman and Evered [28] describe action research with six properties, as follows. Action research is future oriented and collaborative, implies system development, generates theory grounded in action, is agnostic and situational. The typical action research process has a cyclical nature. Susman [29] distinguishes five phases to be conducted within each research cycle. Initially, a problem is identified and data is collected for a more detailed diagnosis. This is followed by a collective postulation of several possible solutions, from which a single plan of action emerges and is implemented. Data on the results of the intervention are collected and analyzed, and the findings are interpreted in light of how successful the action has been. At this point, the problem is re-assessed and the process begins another cycle. This process continues until the problem is resolved.

The research methodology of this study is an action case study, which is a combination of case specific analysis and action research methods [30]. The main purpose of the case study is to understand and interpret, whereas action research aims to change the object of research.

3.2 Description of the Development Process

The needs of ICT competence of the South Ostrobothnia region have been studied in close cooperation with the local ICT and industrial companies.

The process started with a joint business meeting on the needs of ICT skills (10 companies) in May 2018. The invitation to the starting meeting was sent to key ICT and industrial companies. After this, the ICT competence survey was conducted for the ICT and industrial companies in the region (49 companies) in June 2018. In the web survey willingness to participate in the development process was asked. The invitations to the workshop were sent to those who were interested to participate. Based on the analysis of the survey, the co-creation workshop was arranged with the local companies (12 companies) in September 2018. This was further elaborated by the companies participating through online connections. In addition, strong company involvement will be continued during the forthcoming implementation phase including the memberships in the advisory board, visiting lectures and real development projects in the companies.

Need Analysis of ICT Competences

In the starting meeting, it was discussed the ICT needs of the region. Companies highlighted the need for ICT education and it was decided to launch a web survey about the needs and education mode. The survey was widely distributed through various regional networks for ICT and industrial companies.

The survey explored the importance of the need for know-how related to information technology and digitalisation as well the preferred way to meet the competence needs. They were identified in the following areas: Software Engineering, Information Networks, Information Security, Information Systems and Server Management, and Embedded Systems and Electronics.

As a result of the survey, 76% of respondents in South Ostrobothnia consider the IT and digital skills shortage to be significant. For most companies, the expertise needs are related to software technology (56%) and to the management of information networks, systems and servers (65%). The need for software engineering is immediate for 64% of companies and 36% of companies say they need more experts within 1–2 years. The need for networking, systems, and server management is an immediate need for 56% of companies and 34% for this competence within 1–2 years. The need for embedded systems is immediate for 43% of companies and 43% say they need this expertise within 1–2 years.

Businesses preferred recruiting new graduates to meet their skill needs. 48% of companies announced they were hiring a newly graduated software engineer. Recruitment of experienced experts was felt to be preferable to embedded systems and electronics.

The e-mail survey carried out in the design workshop and thereafter specified the content of the training, its implementation and the role of the companies in the planning and implementation of the training.

The planned training has been developed in cooperation with the companies and is thus an excellent response to the region's need for expertise in producing software engineering, information networks, systems and server management.

Planning Process of the ICT Education

This section describes the content of the workshop and the implementation of the principles of co-creation. The workshop was planned based on the principles of co-creation and the preliminary study plan has prepared before the workshop based on web survey.

The co-creation workshop was organized in collaboration with company representatives/ICT professionals from twelve local ICT and industrial companies. Their role was to present the needs of ICT competence and the understanding of working life into the workshop. The teaching staff brought pedagogical skill and knowledge about curriculum development.

In the beginning of the workshop, a preliminary study plan was presented and participants were introduced. In the workshop, participants attended a wide-ranging and in-depth discussion of both today's and future ICT competence needs and contributed to the study plan. They presented ideas about content and approaches of it.

As well, ideas about learning styles were considered. Participants highlighted practical perspectives on the quality and need for ICT skills.

After the workshop, the study plan was further elaborated by online workshop, which clarified companies' interest in participating in the implementation phase. New kind of company involvement was developed. Three companies expressed their interest in engaging in a steering group. All companies, except one, were ready to provide teaching in the form of guest lectures. One company was also interested in teaching larger study modules and courses. As well, an option to run some of the courses in the premises of the company was discussed. The companies were willing to offer work life projects, internships and company visits.

4 Discussion

In this section the results of the co-creation method will be described and discussed. At the moment, a deeper analysis only about the development process is possible, because the education programme will be implemented after the publication of this article. In the following sub-chapters, the added value produced by the co-creation methods will be analysed. The analysis is divided to the content and the development process of the ICT education. As well some of the potential features of the implementation are presented.

4.1 Work Life Oriented ICT Education

The name of the programme is *The Study Programme of Software Developer* and it is a type of conversion/updating education. According the admission criteria students are eligible if they have a higher education degree in the field of engineering or business. Length of the studies is 60 ECTS Credits and it will be implemented in one year (Table 1).

Table 1. Study programme (60 cr) of software developer

Pre-assignment and Complementary studies					
Programming Skills (22 cr)					
Basics of programing	Object-oriented programing	Data structures and algorithms	Software engineering	Interfaces	Embedded systems
Data Competence (18 cr)					
Databases	Communication technology and information security		Virtualization methods	Cloud services	Data analytics
Orientation Option 1: Industrial Internet (15 cr)					
Basics of industrial Internet	Web programming		Server programming	Browser programming	Basics of artificial intelligence
Orientation Option 2: Data Analytics (15 cr)					
Data analytics tools	Big data and NoSQL databases		Data analytic tools	Machine learning	Statistical methods
Work Life Project (5 cr)					

The programme aims to increase student's ICT competency and it is for those looking for a career in ICT or wishing to improve their professional ability.

Training is carried out in a multidisciplinary way in close cooperation with companies. Multimodal learning methods are used. It includes contact sessions and online studies. The emphasis of learning is on independent work as well as solving distant learning assignments and studying online. The work life project is an essential part of the studies.

The study programme will be ensured by personal study guidance. At the beginning of the training, students are interviewed and their learning abilities and motivation are surveyed. Individual study plans are prepared for students. Possible learning difficulties are taken into account through structured guidance. In the middle of the training, the progress of the studies is discussed with each student and the necessary steps are taken.

4.2 Co-creation Workshops in the Development of ICT Education

In the development process of ICT education co-creation workshops were arranged. The primary co-creation workshop was organised by face to face and the secondary workshop was organized by online. In each workshop, a preliminary study plan produced on the basis of previous steps was under discussion (Fig. 1).

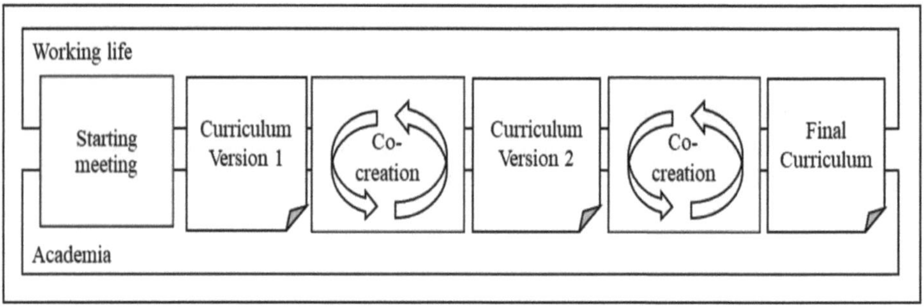

Fig. 1. Co-creation model in ICT education

Next, the implementation of co-creation principles in the primary workshop will be described and analysed according to the following prerequisites for successful co-creation [31].

1. Equal participation
2. Identifying different goals
3. Concrete work
4. Appropriate space and guidance
5. Transparency for new ideas

Co-creation requires equal participation. The company participants were invited by personal invitations and by the web survey. Various representatives of the ICT and industrial companies were included in the workshops. At the beginning of the workshop, the participants presented themselves. Everyone had equal opportunities to participate and all participants were listened to. The benefits of participation were also made visible and the participants' contribution was appreciated. The atmosphere of the workshop was sought to be open and to encourage participation.

The work should identify the different goals of the participants and find a common goal and a shared topic of interest. Participants had their own goals, but the common interest was to find a solution to the shortage of ICT competences in their companies. The co-creation workshops were successful in bringing together different perspectives.

Co-creation should proceed by doing, that is, ideas should proceed quickly to concrete action and everyone should be allowed to experiment and fail and at the same time learn. The curriculum has been developed step by step and participants have contributed to it during the planning process. Communication and transparency play a key role in co-creation, and therefore evaluation data was structured and visualized and dealt with by entrepreneurs after the workshops.

Co-creation needs the right spaces and guidance. The facilities were chosen to provide a good framework for presentations and joint discussions. The aim was to create an environment and atmosphere that supports cooperation as much as possible. The time was carefully designed and manuscripts were prepared in advance for the workshops.

Collaboration can also create a variety of emotions in the participants. Various emotions are essential in all development work. Thus, it is important to create open and transparent atmosphere where participants feel themselves valued.

4.3 Analysis of Added Value for Different Parties

The benefits of the co-creation, methods can be characterized from three different perspectives: regional business life, students' learning process and university teaching (Table 2).

Table 2. Added value of co-creation for different parties

Regional business life	Students' learning	University teaching
Better recruitment opportunities Outputs of work life project and assignments Professional input from the university faculty Opportunity to influence in content and learning methods	Work life oriented content Authentic learning environment New learning methods Opportunity to get company knowledge, feedback and experience Better opportunities for employment	Genuine cooperation with work life Better employment opportunities for students More diverse teaching resources Well-functioning industrial relations Support from work life

For regional business life the ICT education developed by co-creation methods offers customized expertise and better recruitment opportunities. During the training process companies can get valuable outputs from students' work life projects and assignments and expertise from professors. In addition, the close co-operation with education can offer teaching opportunities for the staff of ICT companies. In turn, these companies are able to influence the learning content and methods in the university teaching.

For the student's learning process this model offers work life oriented content and an authentic learning environment in a real company context. Students have good opportunities to gain company knowledge and experience during the training process. This can lead to better opportunities to find employment. New kinds of learning methods are applied and students are able to get genuine feedback from working life and have ICT professionals as teachers.

For the university teaching process, it is valuable to arrange education in genuine cooperation with work life and get more diverse teaching resources. Well-functioning industrial relations lead to better quality of education.

We can conclude that the described co-creation of ICT education can at least partly, solve the shortage of ICT skills in regional companies. The companies start to get skilful software developers and they can influence the subject knowledge and learning process for their forthcoming work force.

For students, the ICT programme offers genuine, working-based, real life experiences. From the perspective of the university, co-operation with real businesses helps faculty to gain first-hand experience of the needs of the company. This allows faculty to develop research that helps companies to innovate.

5 Conclusions and Future Work

The case study shows that a co-creation approach to the development and delivery of ICT education has resulted in the successful development of an education programme. Further, the participation of industry from the earliest stages has resulted in a curriculum in which all parties are invested and see themselves as meaningful stakeholders and contributors (rather than just consumers in response to us as providers).

Analysis of the co-creation process shows that the early and continued involvement of industry resulted in a syllabus which met their needs and which they had confidence would foster the graduate skills they need. Students benefit through closer integration of their studies with industry, with greater consideration to the work-life balance.

This paper considers the process of development and outlines important issues for successful co-creation. The next stage is to assess the delivery of the programme, to monitor the on-going co-creation process and to evaluate both students' experience of the course and the feedback from industry assessing the process from their perspective.

References

1. Ministry of Education and Culture Homepage. Osaavan työvoiman saatavuutta turvataan uusilla 10 miljoonan euron muuntokoulutuksilla (2019). https://minedu.fi/. Accessed 15 Jan 2019
2. Regional Council of South Ostrobothnia Homepage. Regional Strategy (2019). https://www.epliitto.fi/. Accessed 10 Jan 2019
3. Trencher, G., Terada, T., Yarime, M.: Student participation in the co-creation of knowledge and social experiments for advancing sustainability: experiences from the university of Tokyo. Curr. Opin. Environ. Sustain. **16**, 56–63 (2015)
4. Raunio, M., Nordling, N., Ketola, T., Saarinen, J., Heinikangas, A.: Avoin innovaatioalusta kaupunkikehittämisen lähestymistapana. Käsikirja kehittäjille (2018). https://avoimetinnovaatioalustat.files.wordpress.com/2016/09/alustajohtamisenkc3a4sikirja_pc3a4ivitetty.pdf
5. Lorenzo, G., Oblinger, D., Dziuban, C.: How choice, co-creation, and culture are changing what it means to be net savvy. Educause Q. **30**(1), 6 (2007)
6. Galvagno, M., Dalli, D.: Theory of value co-creation: a systematic literature review. Managing Serv. Qual. **24**(6), 643–683 (2014)
7. Gröönroos, C., Voima, P.: Critical service logic: making sense of value creation and co-creation. J. Acad. Mark. Sci. **41**(2), 133–150 (2013)
8. Prahalad, C.K., Ramaswamy, V.: Co-opting customer competence. Harv. Bus. Rev. **78**(1), 79–90 (2000)
9. Vargo, S.L., Lusch, R.F.: Evolving to a new dominant logic for marketing. J. Mark. **68**(1), 1–17 (2004)
10. Prahalad, C.K., Ramaswamy, V.: The Future of Competition: Co-creating Unique Value with Customers. Harvard Business School Press, Boston (2004)
11. Gentile, C., Spiller, N., Noci, G.: How to sustain the customer experience: an overview of experience components that co-create value with the customer. Eur. Manag. J. **25**(5), 395–410 (2007)
12. Payne, A.F., Storbacka, K., Frow, P.: Managing the co-creation of value. J. Acad. Mark. Sci. **36**(1), 83–96 (2008)
13. Sawhney, M., Verona, G., Prandelli, E.: Collaborating to create: the internet as a platform for customer engagement in product innovation. J. Interact. Mark. **19**(4), 4–17 (2005)
14. Bitner, M., Ostrom, A.L., Morgan, F.N.: Service blueprinting: a practical technique for service innovation. Calif. Manag. Rev. **50**(3), 66–94 (2008)
15. Holbrook, M.B., O'Shaughnessy, J.: On the scientific status of consumer research and the need for an interpretive approach to studying consumption behavior. J. Consum. Res. **15**(39), 398–402 (1988)
16. Belk, R., Wallendorf, M., Sherry Jr., J.F.: The sacred and the profane in consumer behavior: theodicy on the odyssey. J. Consum. Res. **16**(1), 1–38 (1989)
17. Arnould, E.J., Thompson, C.J.: Consumer culture theory (CCT): twenty years of research. J. Consum. Res. **31**(4), 868–882 (2005)
18. von Hippel, E.: Lead users: a source of novel product concepts. Manag. Sci. **32**(7), 791–805 (1986)
19. von Hippel, E.: Democratizing Innovation. MIT Press, Cambridge (2005)
20. Chesbrough, H.W.: Open Innovation: The New Imperative for Creating and Profiting from Technology. Harvard Business School Press, Boston (2003)
21. Chesbrough, H.W.: Open Business Models: How to Thrive in the New Innovation Landscape. Harvard Business School Press, Boston (2006)

22. Kotze, T.G., Du Plessis, P.J.: Students as "co-producers" of education: a proposed model of student socialisation and participation at tertiary institutions. Qual. Assur. Educ. **11**(4), 186–201 (2003)
23. Ferns, S., Russell, L., Kay, J.: Enhancing industry engagement with work-integrated learning: capacity building for industry partners. Asia-Pac. J. Coop. Educ. **17**(4), 363–375 (2016)
24. Aho, A.-M., Sinclair, J.: Blended learning as a tool for work-life oriented master courses. In: Uden, L., Liberona, D., Liu, Y. (eds.) LTEC 2017. CCIS, vol. 734, pp. 110–121. Springer, Cham (2017). https://doi.org/10.1007/978-3-319-62743-4_10
25. Rowe, L.: Managing degree apprenticeships through a work based learning framework: opportunities and challenges. In: Enhancing Employability in Higher Education through Work Based Learning, pp. 51–69. Palgrave Macmillan, Cham (2018)
26. Yin, R.K.: Case Study Research. Design and Methods, 2nd edn. Sage Publications, Inc., Thousand Oaks (1994)
27. Järvinen, P., Järvinen, A.: Tutkimustyön metodeista. Opinpajan Kirja, Tampere (2000)
28. Susman, G.I., Evered, R.D.: An assessment of the scientific merits and action research. Admin. Sci. Q. **23**, 582–603 (1978)
29. Susman, G.I.: Action Research: A Socio-technical Systems Perspective. In: Morgan, G. (ed.). Sage Publications, London (1983)
30. Järvinen, P.: On Research Methods. Opinpajan Kirja, Tampere (2001)
31. Aaltonen, S., Hytti, U., Lepistö, T., Mäkitalo-Keinonen, T.: Yhteiskehittäminen, kaikki siitä puhuu, mutta mitä se on ja miten siinä onnistua. University of Turku Homepage (2018). https://www.utu.fi/fi/. Accessed 21 Aug 2018

Developing Entrepreneurship Education: Case of the University of Žilina

Anna Závodská[✉], Veronika Šramová, and Vladimír Konečný

University of Žilina, Univerzitná, 8215/1, 01026 Žilina, Slovakia
anna.zavodska@gmail.com, nika.sramova@gmail.com,
vladimir.konecny@uniza.sk

Abstract. The recent growth and development in the curricula and programs devoted to entrepreneurship have been remarkable. Nowadays, there is more than thousand courses all over the world related to entrepreneurship. It is because innovativeness and entrepreneurship are seen as key factors to achieve economic growth. European Union as well as Slovak government recognized this importance of an entrepreneurial education and prepared Action plans to support it. However, a restricting factor is on one hand the implementation of the proposed Action plans and on the other hand the availability of competent individuals to generate innovative ideas, establish and grow their business based on those ideas. Universities can help by increasing competences of young entrepreneurs so they are able to uncover untapped opportunities and establish profiting businesses. This paper describes the development of an entrepreneurship education at the University of Zilina, Slovakia. There was used a case study method for describing experiences with building an entrepreneurship program at the University of Zilina. The case study shows that entrepreneurship education focuses less on traditional lecture-based teaching of individuals and more on experiential learning activities. Learning-by-doing was analysed as best approach to entrepreneurial education in contrary with traditional development of business plans. However, the study also showed that continuous modification of the curriculum is required. Therefore, recommendations how to develop entrepreneurship programs were proposed.

Keywords: Entrepreneurship education · Startup program · Learning-by-doing · Inquiry-based learning · Experiential learning

1 Introduction

Until 1970, very few universities offered entrepreneurship courses. Entrepreneurship education was pioneered by Shigeru Fijii, who started teaching in this field in 1938 at Kobe University in Japan. Courses in small business management began to emerge in the 1940s and in 1947 Myles Mace introduced the first course in entrepreneurship in USA at Harvard Business School. The Harvard Business School introduced an entrepreneurship course, apparently in response to students who were returning from World War II military service to an economy that was in transition due to the collapse of the weapons industries. Only half a century later did this phenomenon gain a more universal recognition [1, 35]. Entrepreneurship courses are taught at nearly every

L. Uden et al. (Eds.): LTEC 2019, CCIS 1011, pp. 313–324, 2019.
https://doi.org/10.1007/978-3-030-20798-4_27

American Assembly of College Schools of Business (AACSB) accredited institution, at over 1400 postsecondary schools, and enjoy considerable world-wide growth [18].

A coherent framework for entrepreneurship education was presented in the Entrepreneurship 2020 Action Plan and the Communication on Rethinking Education. As education policies are the competence of EU countries, the European Commission acts mainly as a catalyst and a facilitator for the promotion of entrepreneurship education [9].

In 2015 the Slovak government introduced a document related to the support of the Slovak entrepreneurial ecosystem called the Concept for Supporting Startups and Startup Ecosystem in the Slovak Republic and since that the Slovak ministries have been working on its implementation but we have not experienced most proposed governmental measures to be implemented so they could jump-start the development of business startups to help drive the country's economy as promised.

Currently, universities are expected to play a new role in society, in addition to research and teaching, by applying a 'third mission' of economic development [8].

University of Zilina (UNIZA) and Science and Technology Park Zilina (VTP) recognized that expected role and proposed development of the entrepreneurship ecosystem at University. One of the main activities that laid the foundation of the ecosystem was creation of a unique whole-university entrepreneurship education in 2010.

Entrepreneurship education mostly takes very traditional routes. However, the traditional approach which usually contains development of business plans does not reflect the current global entrepreneurship challenges and therefore teachers need to consider new approaches for entrepreneurship education.

Teachers play a key role in the realisation of goals for entrepreneurship education [4, 6, 31]. Since there are no clear-cut pedagogical guidelines for entrepreneurship education, teachers are largely responsible for the integration of entrepreneurship education into their teaching and finding the best and most useful practices. Many researchers have found that teachers face difficulties in finding contents and methods to implement entrepreneurship education [13, 30, 34].

UNIZA and VTP Zilina face the same problems when creating the entrepreneurship education. Finding the right curriculum and connect it with right methods of teaching was and still is the hardest part of the development of the entrepreneurship education.

This paper analyses entrepreneurship education at UNIZA called Startup program which is the only whole-university entrepreneurship education in Slovakia.

This paper begins with description of the term entrepreneurship education, methodology and research approach is described in the following chapter. Next chapter deals with case study of development of an entrepreneurship education at the University of Zilina. Subsequent part proposes concept for creating an entrepreneurship education and last chapter concludes with recommendations for further research.

2 Theoretical Background to Entrepreneurship Education

Nowadays, entrepreneurship education is one of the fastest growing fields of education globally [34]. This is an indication for the importance of entrepreneurship for the economy of any society. There is a tacit assumption that links between providing entrepreneurship education and promised economic growth, generating employment opportunity and enhancing economic development at large. This assumption was examined by many researchers and some evidence were found to support it [7].

The popularity of the term "entrepreneurship" has also propelled its application as an adjective. The term "entrepreneurial" has found a widening application, connoting innovativeness, initiative, job creation, creativity, ambition, perseverance, achievement, and success [24, 35].

2.1 Entrepreneurship Education and Teaching Methods

Rae and Carswell define entrepreneurial learning as an individual's ability to apply his or her skills to identify and develop surrounding opportunities. According to them, learning is a dynamic process which enables the activation of entrepreneurial behaviour [28]. The purpose of the working methods chosen is to develop learners' knowledge and skills [14, 25]. The working methods should promote students' active participation, interaction and social skills and problem-solving abilities [5, 19, 20].

According to Gibb, the pedagogy applied to entrepreneurship education should be built on the active role of learners in the learning process, and thus, on non-traditional teaching methods [16, 17]. Information is created collaboratively, and failure is accepted as a part of the learning process. Methods for such purposes include, for example, cooperative learning, team learning, project work, learning by doing, learning journals, drama pedagogy, practice enterprises, workplace guidance and enterprise visits.

Shepherd has identified a wide range of teaching methods, such as role-play, learning diaries, guest speakers, case studies and simulations. However, all these methods were applied in the classroom [32]. Solomon encourages exploring teaching pedagogies employed both inside and outside of the classroom setting as it can improve the outcomes of teaching [34].

Many researchers have reported positive learning outcomes and teaching experiences in projects carried out in close cooperation with businesses [5, 15, 26, 29].

The most common approach used by universities is the creation of business plans. Yet, there is little research that indicates that the creation of a business plan is an effective approach to teaching entrepreneurship. To date, there is not much research describing the impact or effectiveness of different methodologies for teaching entrepreneurship [36].

Entrepreneurship education includes all activities aiming to foster entrepreneurial mindsets, attitudes and skills and covering a range of aspects such as idea generation, start-up, growth and innovation [12].

The study by Solomon et al. highlighted that the most popular teaching methods in entrepreneurship education are creation of business plans, case studies and lectures [33].

Experiential Learning as the Core Teaching Method of an Entrepreneurial Education

Kolb described learning as "the process whereby knowledge is created through the transformation of experience." Experiential learning is any knowledge gained through experience. Experiential learning actually occurs when students engage in some activity, reflect upon the activity, derive insight from the analysis, and incorporate the result through a change in understanding [21].

A learning-by-doing programme enriches the student experience and thereby enhances the development of their entrepreneurial skills and knowledge [27].

Entrepreneurship education therefore is one particular answer to designing curricula closer to the 'reality of life'. Teaching entrepreneurship implies moving away from traditional theoretical approaches in favour of a learning-by-doing approach. The closer it gets to real-life experiences, the better the learning results are. That is why many practice examples in education take the form of creating "mini-companies" or company visits. Entrepreneurship education can also take place outside the classroom in non-formal and informal settings, for instance, with volunteering activities and community projects.

2.2 Reflective Practice in Teaching Entrepreneurship Education

Reflection is an important process by which knowledge is developed from experience. When reflecting, one considers an experience that has happened and tries to understand or explain it, which often leads to insight and deep learning—or ideas to test on new experiences. Reflection is particularly important for perplexing experiences, working under conditions of high uncertainty, and problem-solving. As a result, it should not be a surprise that reflection is an integral component of entrepreneurship education and also a way of practicing entrepreneurship.

Given the nature of entrepreneurship as a continuous cycle of action, learning, testing, and experimenting, developing students as reflective entrepreneurs requires reflection-on-practice and reflection-in-practice as part of a pedagogy portfolio.

An entrepreneurship method is teachable and learnable, but it is not predictable. Starting businesses help students "feel" what it is like to assume the role of an entrepreneur. Serious games and simulations allow students to play in virtual worlds that mirror reality. Designed-based learning encourages students to observe the world through a different lens and create opportunities. Finally, reflective practice gives permission to our students to take time, think, and absorb the learning of their practice-based curriculum.

Feeling, playing, observing, creating, and thinking are all important components of the entrepreneurship method. Learning a method is often more important than learning specific content, and it requires practice. In an ever-changing world, we need to teach methods that stand the test of dramatic changes in content and context.

2.3 Objectives of Entrepreneurial Education

Entrepreneurship education covers a wide variety of audiences, objectives, contents and pedagogical methods [11]. The most commonly cited objectives of entrepreneurship education by previous studies are: to acquire knowledge germane to entrepreneurship, to acquire skills in the use of techniques, in the analysis of business situations and in the synthesis of action plans, to identify and stimulate entrepreneurial drive, talent and skill, to undo the risk-adverse bias of many analytical techniques, to develop empathy and support for the unique aspects of entrepreneurship, to revise attitudes towards change, to encourage new start-ups and other entrepreneurial ventures, to stimulate the 'affective socialization element' [2].

The objectives of entrepreneurship education could be classified into three categories: raising awareness, teaching techniques, tools and how to handle situations and supporting project bearers [10]. Generally, entrepreneurship education aims to increase the awareness of entrepreneurship as a career option, and enhance the understanding of the process involved in initiating and managing a new business enterprise [22].

There are many ways to offer entrepreneurship education, depending on the objectives of such education. If the objective of the education is to increase the understanding of what entrepreneurship is about, the most effective way to accomplish the objective is to provide information through public channels such as media, seminars, or lectures. These methods are effective in terms of sending the relevant information to a broader population in a relative short time period. If the objective is to equip individuals with entrepreneurial skills, which are applicable directly to work, the best way is to provide education and training that enable individuals to involve directly in the entrepreneurial process, such as industrial training. Lastly, if the objective of the education is to prepare individuals to act as entrepreneurs, the most effective technique is to facilitate experiments by trying entrepreneurship out in a controlled environment, for instance through business simulation or role playing [3].

3 Research Methodology

Qualitative research was used as the main method for data collection and their subsequent analysis. The following three methods were used: **a case study** of an entrepreneurship education at the University of Zilina called Startup program (analysing and evaluating the current curriculum, stakeholders involved to creation of the program, students enrolled to this program, their motivation and background to entrepreneurship, motivation of University of Zilina to support this program).

To be able to develop a case study, various methods were used: **semi-structured interviews** with stakeholders involved in this course (enrolled students, UNIZA management, successful entrepreneurs, various governmental agencies supporting improvement of entrepreneurship in Slovakia, etc.). Interviews were used in order to map the requirements of each stakeholder involved in the Startup program.

Content analysis was used so the secondary data from websites and scientific articles related to entrepreneurship education evaluating methods used in creating entrepreneurship education, approach to teaching entrepreneurship education, topics covered in entrepreneurship education, objectives of the entrepreneurship education were evaluated. Based on the evaluated data curriculum, teaching methods and topics of the Startup program were compared.

The main question of our research was: *What is an ideal concept for entrepreneurship education at the University of Zilina?*

4 Case Study of an Entrepreneurship Education at the University of Zilina

Startup program is an entrepreneurial course, which offers university students invaluable experience with real business. Course started at UNIZA in 2010. Course was created in cooperation with VTP Zilina (legal part of the University of Zilina) and Junior Achievement organization. Authors have been teaching this course since 2012.

The first version of the program was implemented at UNIZA according to high school model developed by Junior Achievement. This model contained establishment of a simulated joint-stock company and its liquidation at the end of program. Students gained real experiences with: establishment of the company, fundraising the first capital, selling of their manufactured products, collecting money for their sold products which at the end needed to cover costs and also students had to return money to their investors with interest.

Despite the uniqueness of the program even after the implementation of the first and second phase (described in our previous papers) the expected results in terms of increased number of established new innovative start-up companies were not achieved. It was because students had to liquidate their simulated businesses and were scared to establish real business afterwards as they realized that simulated company is not the same as the real company [23, 37].

Based on authors' own knowledge and experience in the preparation and implementation of the Startup program, results from students' and UNIZA management feedback, feedback from entrepreneurs who gave lectures to students, updates of the program are developed each year.

There were introduced new innovative teaching methods at classes. These teaching methods included learning-by-doing method and problem-based learning. Most of the classes are taught in classroom, however, some of the work has to be done outside the class. Students have also possibility to participate in events such as Startup Weekend ("hackathon-like" event) where they can experience totally different approach to development of innovative ideas then in our course.

Startup program is two-semester course and students can get 3 ECTS credits each semester. Usually around 80 students enrol to this course each semester. Students are either bachelor or master, rarely doctoral. They are from various UNIZA faculties but the most interest is mostly from students attending Faculty of Management Science and Informatics. Other Faculties that are offering this course are Faculty of Electrical Engineering, Mechanical Engineering, Civil Engineering, Humanities and lastly Operation and Economics of Transport. The ratio of students from Faculty of Management Science and Informatics and other faculties is 70 to 10.

The first semester results in business model creation and its verification with customers. At the end of second semester students should have verified prototype and finetuned their marketing, sales, and financial strategy. They know how to use various tools for development of their ideas, team communication, project management, designing, etc. They know various methodologies such as validation of business ideas, lean startup, customer development, design thinking, business modelling, etc. When students understand these methods, they can use them even if they decide to change their business idea. The aim of the course is to provide information to students and let them experience the real business world by validating and developing their ideas with real customers and help of business mentors so after they finish Startup program they are able to establish and run their businesses. However, the success rate is still very low and only few students were able to establish real businesses and run them successfully.

We took a design thinking approach to the development of Startup program. This approach has following phases:

- Emphasize: lecturers identify problems with stakeholders experienced during each semester and academic year as whole.
- Define: lecturers analyse observations and synthesize them in order to define the core problems the group of stakeholders have identified so far.
- Ideate: lecturers think outside the box to identify new solutions to the identified problem that was most crucial in each semester.
- Prototype: lecturers prepare concept of the Startup program for the following academic year.
- Test: lecturers test concept during the first semester and make amendments to second semester if needed.
- After testing, the whole phase of design thinking process starts again before the next academic semester.

Lecturers ask stakeholders to articulate their problems and requirements for Startup program so it reflects their needs as well as needs of the market.

Identified needs are following:

- University of Zilina authorities need to have as much students as possible enrolled to this course so financing of this course will be justified.
- Companies need to have students who have business skills and entrepreneurial spirit.
- Successful entrepreneurs are willing to join the program and provide lectures. They usually come pro bono and their motivation is transfer of their experiences that they have gained throughout their entrepreneurial journey.
- Various governmental agencies supporting improvement of entrepreneurship in Slovakia are co-organizing and also co-financing some events for Startup program. Their motivation is fulfilment of the project KPIs.

We always contact each stakeholder at the beginning of each semester, collect their requirements and try to build the program based on them. After the competition of the program we present summarization of the fulfilled requirements to stakeholders.

5 Results of Case Study Analysis

Based on our experiences and analysis of the presented case study, we identified several groups of aspects that have the biggest impact on the Startup program curriculum creation:

1. Students' aspects:
   - Number of enrolled students,
   - Level of skills and experiences of enrolled students,
   - Study majors,
   - Family background (parents are entrepreneurs or have entrepreneurial mindset and skills),
   - Financial background of students and their parents,
   - Variety of business ideas they want to develop throughout the program,
   - Motivation and drive of students,
   - New generation and its characteristic (change from Generation X to Z).
2. Lecturers' aspects
   - Working experiences,
   - Lecturers – time availability, number of lecturers teaching Startup program, experiences, etc.
   - New trends in teaching,
   - New theories in entrepreneurship education.
3. Stakeholders' aspects
   - Level of support of stakeholders in organization of events and their financing (e.g. Agencies that have projects to support entrepreneurship in Slovakia) and the way how they are involved into the Startup program,
   - Fundraised money for the program from stakeholders,
   - Support of the University management and their level of engagement in the program,
   - Market conditions (trends, stability, financing, capacity, competition, etc.)

We found out that after 8 years of teaching this program it is necessary to constantly build new curriculum based on above mentioned factor that have impact on it. We found out that this continuous update of the program is:

- Time-consuming,
- Financially demanding,
- Physically and mentally challenging for both students and lecturers.

Therefore, we suggest that for future success of this program it is crucial:

- to transfer knowledge and know-how to younger lecturers,
- better engage stakeholders and community to the program creation,
- and ensure stable financial stream from various sources.

6 Discussion

Based on the previous analysis it is not disputable that the curriculum of an entrepreneurship program has to be changed over the years.

Our previous study revealed that Startup program is developed in cooperation with other regional actors and is highly dependent on support from these actors. Moreover, the initiatives mapped in our previous study utilise a large amount of voluntary resources, such as experienced business people, young start-uppers and successful entrepreneurs who are willing to contribute as mentors, consultants, and lecturers of students and their companies [38].

This is a very important contribution for many reasons. First, the voluntary support makes it possible to offer higher quality and quantity of education without the need of extensive financial resources from UNIZA. Second, stakeholders contribute with real-life experience, which is especially important in such field like entrepreneurship. Third, these stakeholders also provide their own network, thus helping the participants to build their own networks and relate to external contacts. Fourth, external entrepreneurs are considered as idols or influencers and can contribute significantly to move the student projects forward. Fifth, successful entrepreneurs can act as investors and help student companies to grow.

There is a considerable need for public and private funding in order to facilitate the development of innovative entrepreneurship education in contrary to traditional. In Slovakia, this funding is provided via government agencies such as SIEA (supporting innovations) or Slovak Business Agency (supporting start-ups). Both agencies are cooperating with us and thus supporting young entrepreneurs. The question is, what kind of support will follow when the implementation of projects of these agencies finish.

Entrepreneurship education is an integrated part of the activities at UNIZA. With more than 100 student start-ups during a period of 9 years, this could be viewed as an implementation of a successful entrepreneurship education, where learning-by-doing, problem-based learning and student active involvement is the core activity.

Having access to sufficient infrastructure, finances, stakeholders and mentoring capacity, it has been possible to build a stable education activity and to give many students the opportunity to explore and develop their entrepreneurial skills.

The main contribution of Startup program is that it plays a key role as facilitator for entrepreneurship.

Our study revealed that developing learning-by-doing entrepreneurship education is dependent on many factors, is very resource consuming and mentally and physically exhaustive.

However, we believe that by involving students, volunteers and other relevant stakeholders to development and implementation of an entrepreneurial education we can help to decrease the physical, mental and financial burden of UNIZA and its lecturers.

We proposed model how the entrepreneurship education should be created. Each year it has to be revised based on students' feedback. This process should be following the logic of lean start-up methodology (customer development and co-creation of value) and build-measure-learn loop. It means that once we build the program, we have to implement it and see students' reactions. We will measure them and learn from the results. This knowledge will be considered in development of new program next year which will be again measured.

It is very important to take into consideration students and their level of skills, experiences, maturity of their business ideas, motivation, drive and other factors when creating the program. Therefore, each semester there are only topics that we as lecturers want to cover, however, those might be slightly modified and form of teaching of those topics will depend on students and external consultants. During the semester we always have to adjust topics as the progress of students cannot be foreseen.

The best approach how to teach young people to become entrepreneurs depend solely on two factors:

- Do they want to be entrepreneurs or do they only want to broaden their knowledge?
- Do they have idea or not?

If they do not have idea and want to only inspire and broaden their knowledge, different approach is followed such as providing information through public channels such as media, provide education and training that enable individuals to involve directly in the entrepreneurial process, such as industrial training.

If students have ideas and also want to become entrepreneurs, the most effective technique is to try entrepreneurship out in a controlled environment with a help of mentors and lecturers.

7 Conclusion

The recent growth and development of entrepreneurship initiatives including education have been significant. Not only in USA but also in Europe as well as Slovakia the importance of an entrepreneurial education was recognized. However, attempts of European union and Slovak government did not bring substantial change in entrepreneurship ecosystem.

On the other hand, universities can help by increasing entrepreneurial skills of young entrepreneurs. A role of universities is to provide education for entrepreneurs and they have been doing so for decades. However, the insufficient traditional approach to entrepreneurship education has not been changed until now when the traditional approach was supplemented by new innovative approach characterised as learning-by-doing. The case study indicates that this approach to entrepreneurship education can be accomplished in many different ways depending on many factors.

Although it has been questioned whether it is possible to educate entrepreneurs, the case study shows that teaching entrepreneurship can be very challenging but the success can be measured by the number of companies started by the participants.

This paper described the development of curriculum of an entrepreneurship education at the University of Zilina, Slovakia.

The study showed that continuous modification of the curriculum is required. We believe that our recommendations can help many universities in shifting mindset from traditional teaching methods to new methods they can implement and changing the way how to look at the process of entrepreneurship education development.

Acknowledgements. Made as a part of the project: University of Žilina Enhancing Quality of Education based on Internationalization, project Nr.: 004ŽU-2/2016, supported by the Ministry of Education, Science, Research and Sport of the Slovak Republic.

References

1. Aleberti, A., Sciascia, B., Poli, A.: Entrepreneurship education: notes on an ongoing debate. In: 14th Annual IntEnt Conference, University of Napoli Federico II, Italy, p. 4 (2004)
2. Alberti, S., Bohse, K., Arndt, V., Schmitz, A., Hohfeld, J.: The cochaperone HspBP1 inhibits the CHIP ubiquitin ligase and stimulates the maturation of the cystic fibrosis transmembrane conductance regulator. Mol. Biol. Cell **15**, 4003–4010 (2004)
3. Ahmed, M.M.M., El-Hag, F.M.: Degradation characteristics of some Sudanese forages and tree pods using in sacco and gas production techniques. Small Rumin. Res. **54**(1–2), 147–156 (2004)
4. Birdthistle, N., Hynes, B., Fleming, P.: Enterprise education programmes in secondary schools in Ireland: a multi-stakeholder perspective. Educ. + Train. **49**(4), 265–276 (2007)
5. Cooper, S., Bottomley, C., Gordon, J.: Stepping out of the classroom and up the ladder of learning: an experimental learning approach to entrepreneurship education. Ind. High. Educ. **18**, 11–22 (2004)
6. Deakins, D., Glancey, K., Menter, I., Wyper, J.: Enterprise education: the role of the head teacher. Int. Entrepreneurship and Manag. J. **1**(2), 241–263 (2005)
7. Dzisi, S.: Entrepreneurial activities of indigenous African women: a case of Ghana. J. Enterprising Communities: People Places Glob. Econ. **2**(3), 254–264 (2008). https://doi.org/10.1108/17506200810897231
8. Etzkowitz, H., Webster, A., Gebhardt, C., Terra, B.R.C.: The future of the university and the university of the future: evolution of ivory tower to entrepreneurial paradigm. Res. Policy **29**(2), 313–330 (2000)
9. European Commision. Policies, information and services. Internal Market, Industry, entrepreneurship and SMEs. Commission's actions on entrepreneurship education. Source 13 December 2018. https://ec.europa.eu/growth/smes/promoting-entrepreneurship/support/education/commission-actions_en
10. Fayolle, A.: Handbook of Research in Entrepreneurship Education: Contextual Perspectives, vol. 2, p. 304. Edward Elgar Publishing, Cheltenham (2007)
11. Fayolle, A., Gailly, B.: From craft to science: teaching models and learning processes in entrepreneurship education. J. Eur. Ind. Train. **32**(7), 569–593 (2008). https://doi.org/10.1108/03090590810899838
12. Fayolle, A.: Entrepreneurship education in Europe: Trends and challenges. OECD LEED Programme, universities, innovation and entrepreneurship: good practice workshop (2009)
13. Fiet, J.O.: The theoretical side of teaching entrepreneurship. J. Bus. Ventur. **16**(1), 1–24 (2000)
14. Fiet, J.O.: The pedagogical side of entrepreneurship theory. J. Bus. Ventur. **16**(2), 101–117 (2000)
15. Frank, A.I.: Entrepreneurship and enterprise skills: a missing element of planning education? Plann. Pract. Res. **22**, 635–648 (2007)
16. Gibb, A.: The future of entrepreneurship education–determining the basis for coherent policy and practice? The Dynamics of learning entrepreneurship in a cross-cultural university context. Kyrö, P., Carrier, C. (eds.) University of Tampere, Research Centre for Vocational and Professional Education (2005)
17. Gibb, A.: Concepts into practice: meeting the C development of entrepreneurship educators around an innovative paradigm: the case of the International Entrepreneurship Educators' Programme (IEEP). Int. J. Entrepreneurial Behav. Res. **17**, 146–165 (2011)
18. Honig, B.: A contingency model of business planning. Acad. Manag. Learn. Educ. **3**(3), 258–273 (2004)

19. Jones, C., Iredale, N.: Enterprise education as pedagogy. Educ. C Train. **52**, 7–19 (2010)
20. Joyce, B., Weil, M.: Models of teaching. PrenticeHall International, London (1980)
21. Kolb, D.A.: Experiential Learning: Experience as the Source of Learning and Development, vol. 1. Englewood Cliffs, Prentice-Hall (1984)
22. Lee, J.T., Connor-Appleton, S., Haq, A.U., Bailey, C.A., Cartwright, A.L.: Quantitative measurement of negligible trypsin inhibitor activity and nutrient analysis of guar meal fractions. J. Agric. Food Chem. **52**, 6492–6495 (2004)
23. Lovecek, T. et al.: Currently required competencies of crisis and security managers and new tool for their acquirement – the eSEC portal, In: 13th IEEE International Conference on Emerging eLearning Technologies and Applications (ICETA 2015), Article Number: 7558492 (2016)
24. Lumpkin, G.T., Dess, G.G.: Clarifying the entrepreneurial orientation construct and linking it to performance. Acad. Manag. Rev. **21**, 135–172 (1996)
25. Neck, H.M., Greene, P.G.: Entrepreneurship education: known worlds and new frontiers. J. Small Bus. Manag. **49**, 55–70 (2011). https://doi.org/10.1111/j.1540-627x.2010.00314.x
26. Pittaway, L., Cope, J.: Simulating entrepreneurial learning: integrating experiential and collaborative approaches to learning. Manag. Learn. **38**, 211–233 (2007)
27. Rae, D., Carswell, M.: Using a life-story approach in researching entrepreneurial learning: the development of a conceptual model and its implications in the design of learning experiences. Educ. + Train. **42**(4/5), 220–228 (2000)
28. Rae, D., Carswell, M.: Towards a conceptual understanding of entrepreneurial learning. J. Small Bus. Enterprise Dev. **8**(2), 150–158 (2001)
29. Richardson, I., Hynes, B.: Entrepreneurship education: towards an industry sector approach. Educ. C Train. **50**, 188–198 (2008)
30. Seikkula-Leino, J.: Advancing entrepreneurship education in the Finnish basic education – the prospect of developing local curricula. In: Fayolle, A., Kyro, P. (eds.) The Dynamics Between Entrepreneurship, Environment and Education, pp. 168–190. Edward Elgar Publishing, Cheltenham (2008)
31. Seikkula-Leino, J., Ruskovaara, E., Ikavalko, M., Mattila, J., Rytko, L.T.: Promoting entrepreneurship education: the role of the teacher? Educ. Train. **52**(2), 117–127 (2010)
32. Shepherd, G.: The human sense of smell: are we better than we think? PLoS Biol. **2**, 146 (2004)
33. Solomon, M., Bamossy, G., Askegaard, S.: Consumer Behaviour; A European Perspective, 2nd edn. Prentice Hall Europe, New Jersey (2002)
34. Solomon, G.: An examination of entrepreneurship education in the United States. J. Small Bus. Enterprise Dev. **14**, 168–182 (2007). https://doi.org/10.1108/14626000710746637
35. Vesper, K.H., Gartner, W.B.: Measuring progress in entrepreneurship education. J. Bus. Ventur. **12**(5), 403–421 (1997)
36. Winslow, E.K., Solomon, G.T., Tarabishy, A.: Empirical investigation into entrepreneurship education in the United States: Some results of the 1997 National Survey of Entrepreneurial Education. USASBE Conference Proceedings (1999)
37. Zavodska, A., Sramova, V., Rybovic, A.: Developing Entrepreneurial Education at the University Focused on Start-ups. KMO 2016, 25–28 July 2016, Hagen, Germany. Article No. 37 (2016)
38. Zavodska, A., Sramova, V.: Collaboration and knowledge sharing as a key to success of entrepreneurial ecosystem. In: International Conference on Knowledge Management in Organizations KMO 2018: Knowledge Management in Organizations, 128–139 (2018)

The Digital Literacy of Business Students with Evidence from Poland and Slovenia

Viktorija Florjančič[1](✉) and Łukasz Wiechetek[2]

[1] Faculty of Management, University of Primorska, Cankarjeva 5, 6000 Koper, Slovenia
viktorija.florjancic@fm-kp.si

[2] Faculty of Economics, Maria Curie-Skłodowska-University, Plac Marii Curie-Skłodowskiej 5, 20-031 Lublin, Poland
lukasz.wiechetek@umcs.pl

Abstract. The purpose of this article is to explore digital literacy levels and better understand the main differences in ICT competences among business students from Slovenia (n = 229) and Poland (n = 258). Our research was divided into three steps: a literature review, quantitative research based on an online survey for young business students and a statistical analysis in SPSS. In exploring ICT literacy, we identified the types of IT tools used, the frequency of their use, and the main differences in ICT literacy between Polish and Slovenian business students. We also investigated the relationships between time spent online, one's study year and the level of competencies in the area of using basic tools (text editors, spreadsheets, presentation tools) and more advanced computer applications used for business purposes like database management systems and graphics editors. Our analysis shows that business students mainly use their mobile devices for education and communication. The developed normalized index of usage skills (NIUS) indicates that the students involved had the highest level of knowledge and skills in the area of using word processors, business presentation tools and mail services. The lowest index value was measured for database management systems, photo editors and spreadsheet applications. In our opinion, growing up with ICT is not enough to develop the digital skills necessary for the digital economy in the field of business and, therefore, the ICT curricula (even basic level courses) offered by business schools should be revised in order to better prepare future business graduates for the needs of a digital society.

Keywords: Digital literacy · Business students · Comparative study · ICT education · Polish students · Slovenian students

1 Introduction

Literacy is defined as the ability to acquire, communicate, connect and create meaning in the world [1]. Thus, the world is changing and, nowadays, the concept of literacy is different from the traditional view of literacy as the ability to read and write. Not only is data media changing, but society is also changing rapidly. Our digital society demands

L. Uden et al. (Eds.): LTEC 2019, CCIS 1011, pp. 325–336, 2019.
https://doi.org/10.1007/978-3-030-20798-4_28

different (new) abilities in order to acquire knowledge and to actively participate in a technologically-driven society.

In theory, different terms are used to describe the abilities of using information and communication technologies (ICT) in everyday life. The words "information" and "digital" are combined with the words "skills" and "literacy" and depend on the term used to describe today's society. JISC[1] [11], with a vision of the UK as the most digitally-advanced higher education, defines digital literacy as the capabilities that help an individual to live, learn and work in a digital society. Glister [8] connected digital literacy to digital resources. Becker [2] differentiated information literacy from digital literacy. While information literacy existed before the digital era, digital literacy is closely related to ICT usage [2]. The American Library Association [2] defines a digitally literate person as a person who is able to find, understand, evaluate, create and communicate digital information in different formats. For these purposes, a digitally literate person is able to use different technologies effectively and able to understand the relationships between technology, lifelong learning and personal privacy. It is important that a digitally literate person understands how ICT and its usage impact on way we live and do things (ibidem). It is assumed that the digital natives, young people that became familiar with ICT from an early age, are digitally literate by default. Becker [2] claims that no one is born digitally literate and that digital literacy is an incomplete process because ICT is changing immensely.

Digital literacy covers a range of skills – from the purely technical to cognitive skills. A digitally literate person has to use all of these skills to communicate and collaborate with others and to actively participate in society [2]. These technical skills are the foundation for digital literacy or literacies (as we will discuss later on) and are much easier to identify, gather and compare among different groups. This was the reason why the comparison study between Polish and Slovenian business students was based solely on a comparison of technical skills.

2 The Theoretical Background

2.1 Digital Literacy

A digitally competent person is a confident, critical and creative ICT user that is able to achieve goals related to work, learning, leisure and societal participation [6]. A digitally skilled person has no problems in succeeding in the labor market (ibidem). Digital competence is a transversal 21st century key competence that supports the acquisition of the other key competences needed for employability, social inclusion and active participation in society. Researchers see the digital competence as a basis for functioning in society [8] or even as a survival skill in the digital era [5].

In theory and practice, different terms are used to describe digital literacy: digital competencies, eLiteracy, e-Skills, eCompetence, ICT skills, etc. [7]. Some even discuss "new literacies" [4] and presents definitions of literacies used in different environments and circumstances: computer and internet literacy, media literacy and information

[1] https://www.jisc.ac.uk/about.

literacy [7]. Eshet-Alkalai [5] discusses photo-visual literacy, reproduction literacy, branching literacy, information and social literacy. ICT literacy, as the ability to use computers and related technologies [7], is needed to participate in technology-facilitated learning environments and facilitates lifelong learning [13]. Facing the numerous ubiquitous web resources and the pervasive growth of web-based learning [12], students should be able to use computers, various networks, and much more. They should be digitally literate.

Digital literacy includes a large number of complex cognitive, motor, sociological and emotional skills [5]. Digital competence is tools (applications) dependent and not user dependent (Livingstone 2003 in Ferrari et al. 2012). Using online resources engaged users more than any other offline resource. Users create, participate and share content online while other skills are needed in the "offline" world [7]. There is more than "one" literacy. Goodfellow [9] discusses many different literacies as well as media literacy as the most expansive and interesting concept for educators.

There are many various types of framework that consider different skills and attitudes related to the digital competence [7]. Based on the 15 frameworks' comparison study, Joint Research Centre (JRC) formed a working definition of digital competence [7]:

> *"Digital Competence is the set of knowledge, skills, attitudes, abilities, strategies and awareness that is required when using ICT and digital media to perform tasks; solve problems; communicate; manage information; behave in an ethical and responsible way; collaborate; create and share content and knowledge for work, leisure, participation, learning, socializing, empowerment and consumerism."*

JRC research digital skills from 2005. Based on different studies, they form the Digital Competence Framework for Citizens, known as DigComp [3]. The last version of the framework is labelled DigComp 2.1 [3]. The first version of DigiComp introduced four proficiency levels: foundation, intermediate, advanced and the highly specialized level. DigComp 2.1 expanded the initial levels to eight proficiency levels [3] (see Fig. 1). Users with basics skills (Foundation level in DigComp 1.0 – Fig. 1)

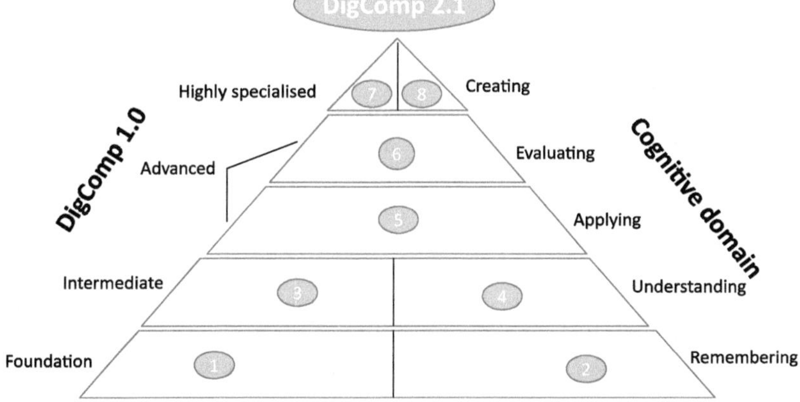

Fig. 1. DigComp 1.0 vs DigComp 2.1. Source: Carretero [3].

develop skills that only recall the cognitive domain (Levels 1 and 2 in DigComp 2.1 – Fig. 1). Only advanced and highly specialized users are able to develop skills at higher cognitive levels (Fig. 1).

3 Research

The digital transformation barometer [10] reports that only 53% of 4,164 information technology, security and business executives, managers and professionals from different global industries and company sizes, are digitally literate. Our business students are studying ways to adapt companies to such new challenges. We wonder if they are prepared for global changes and if there are any differences between Polish and Slovenian business students. The questionnaire was prepared in Slovenian and then translated into the English language. Polish students filled in a survey in the English language and the Slovenians in Slovenian. Google Forms was used to deliver the questionnaire online. The survey (28 questions divided into five sections) was launched during the last quarter of 2017. Students of both business schools were invited via announcements in their online learning environments to fill in an online survey.

The data gathered by the online survey helps us to answer the following research questions:

1. What applications are the most frequently used for creating digital content and network communication?
2. What activities are mainly performed by students online?
3. What groups of IT tools and what functionalities of these programs are best known to students?
4. What are the main differences in the area of using basic components of office suits?
5. What are the main differences in online activity among Polish and Slovenian students?
6. What are the dependencies in terms of time spent online, study year, second school grade and digital literacy?
7. Are there any correlations between digital literacy and students' school success?

3.1 Data Analysis

The questionnaire had been sent between September and December 2017. During that time, 487 business students from Poland and Slovenia completed the survey. The survey was completed by 258 respondents from Poland (53%) and 229 from Slovenia (43%), however, some data such as gender, second school grade was not collected in a group of Slovenian students. Most of the respondents were management students (55%). All Slovenian respondents studied management, while almost a half of the Polish respondents (43.4%) studied logistics. The majority were students of the first-year bachelor's program (81.7%), the second largest group consisted of the first-year master's program (12.5%). Almost all students (97.3%) were full-time students.

Frequency of Using ICT Hardware

Students were asked about the frequency (1–never, 5–always) of using different types of hardware. The most frequently used piece of hardware was the smartphone (always used by 87% Slovenian and 84% Polish respondents) and laptop computers (always used by 48% Slovenian and 49% Polish respondents). The least used were desktop computers and tablets (often or always used by 13% Polish and 13% Slovenian students). There was only one statistically significant difference in using different types of hardware. Polish students more often reported using desktop computers than their Slovenian counterparts (p = 0.008). There were no significant differences between the frequency of using laptop computers, tablets and smartphones.

Types of Computer Tools Used

In order to uncover the students' knowledge and skills (from 1– beginner to 5– advanced) in the area of types of basic IT tools, students were asked to give their opinion on eight categories. Students illustrated that they are most skilled at web searches (M = 4.10), similarly good in the area of general computer use (M = 3.90), communication tools (M = 3.71), word processors (M = 3.70) and a bit less in presentation programs (M = 3.66). However, they are less skilled users of spreadsheets (M = 3.24) and have little knowledge in the area of applications for editing photos (M = 2.51) and database management systems (M = 2.19).

The statistically significant differences were identified in five categories of tools. Slovenian students reported that they are more skilled in the area of communication tools (p = 0.002), word processors (p = 0.011) and presentation programs (p = 0.000). The respondents from Poland reported that they are more skilled in programs for editing photos (p = 0.044) and database management tools (p = 0.001).

Using Basic Computer Applications

In order to explore the students' opinions on the frequency of using specific office applications (1 = never, 5–always), we asked them to report how often they use certain applications.

Students both from Poland and Slovenia used mostly Microsoft Word (M = 4.01), Microsoft Excel (M = 3.10), Microsoft Power Point (M = 3.29) and Google Documents (M = 2.89). The least frequently used included applications for editing graphics and audio such as GIMP, Blender, Corel Draw, Audacity (all M <=1.35).

The data analysis shows statistically significant differences in using basic Microsoft Office components and GIMP. Slovenian students reported a more frequent use of Word (p = 0.000) and PowerPoint (p = 0.000), while respondents from Poland used Excel (p = 0.000) and GIMP (p = 0.000) more often.

Normalized Index of Usage Skills

To compare the students' self-esteem with specific skills, respondents were asked about the given functionalities of basic IT tools. We examined 35 functions in the area of word processors, 31 functions in the area of spreadsheet programs, 15 functions of presentation applications, 13 tasks on the web, 13 functions in the area of database management systems, 10 functions of photo editors and 9 functionalities of mail web services.

In order to compare skills in the area of the usage of certain functionalities of basic IT tools, the *normalized index of usage skills* (NIUS) was developed. The NIUS was calculated as a point average to show knowledge of a specific function of the program (see Eq. 1):

$$NIUS = \frac{\sum_{i=1}^{n} u_i}{n} * 4 + 1 \tag{1}$$

Legend: NIUS – normalized index of usage skills (its value is in [1,5], u_i – ability to complete the i task (its value is 1 – able or 0 – unable), n – number of explored tasks.

The value of the NIUS index for respondents able to perform all of the tasks concerning the given tool was 5. Student that did not know how perform any tasks received a NIUS index of 1.

The NIUS index was higher for web services (M = 4,26), word processors (M = 4,22) and presentation applications (M = 4,18). Slightly lower values were obtained for spreadsheet applications (M = 3,64) and photo editors (M = 3,33). Students were the least skilled in the area of database management systems (M = 2,68). The results are similar to answers given for the question concerning abilities in terms of basic IT tools (Fig. 2).

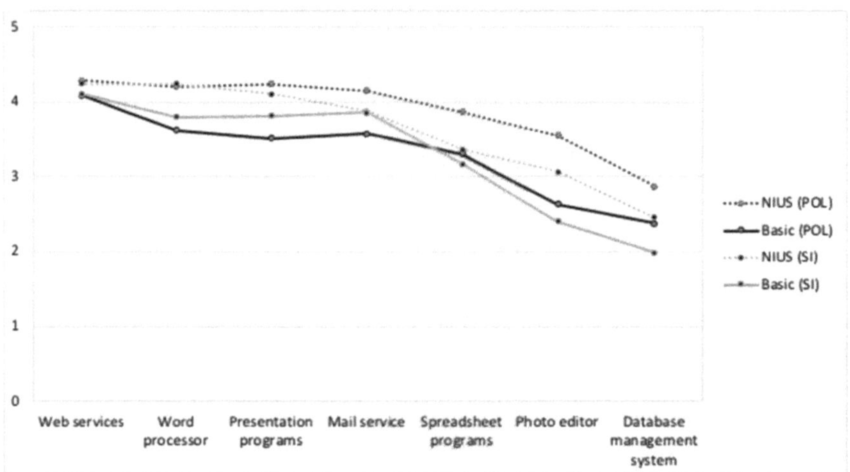

Legend: POL = Polish students, SI = Slovenian students; NIUS = Normalized index of usage skills, Basic = an average of self-assessment IT tools usage

Fig. 2. NIUS index and self-assessment IT tools comparison

Statically significant differences were identified in the area of mail service usage (p = 0.005), spreadsheet applications (p = 0.000), photo editors (p = 0.000) and database management system skills (p = 0.002). There were no statistically significant differences between Polish and Slovenian students in the field of simple applications for web browsing, text editing and business presentation development.

Polish students were more skilled in business specific areas such as spreadsheet applications, photo editors and database management system skills (Fig. 2); this is based on the NIUS index and on self-assessment.

Access to the Internet

In the area of online activity, the respondents were asked to indicate the places where they most often (1–never, 5–always) connect to the Internet.

The majority of students both from Poland and Slovenia tend to access the internet from home (*always* was indicated by 79% Polish and 90% Slovenian respondents) and by means of mobile data transfer (*always* indicated by 45% Polish and 56% Slovenian respondents). The least popular places included transportation and university libraries (*often* and *always* indicated by less than 22% of Slovenian and 24% of Polish respondents).

We observed six significant differences in the frequency of using different places for Internet access. Slovenian students were more likely to connect to the internet from home ($p = 0.002$), internet cafes ($p = 0.000$), from school ($p = 0.008$) and places with Wi-Fi access ($p = 0.000$). Polish students used library internet connections more often ($p = 0.003$).

Students' Online Activity

The research allowed us to identify the main activities performed by students on the Internet. The respondents could assess 11 different activities on a scale from 1 to 5 (1–never, 5–always).

Most students spent time sharing data with friends ($M = 4.03$), searching for jobs ($M = 3.37$), sharing data with family ($M = 3.31$), using e-banking services ($M = 3.16$), following national news and watching TV (both $M = 3.15$), following foreign news ($M = 3.00$) and watching video courses ($M = 2.60$). The least frequently performed activities included using e-government services, tax services and participating in massive open online courses ($M <= 1.78$).

Statically significant differences were observed in six out of eleven categories. Polish students used the internet for e-banking services ($p = 0.000$), watching TV ($p = 0.001$), using e-government services ($p = 0.000$), taxes office services ($p = 0.000$) and participating at MOOCs ($p = 0.000$) more frequently. Respondents from Slovenia watched video courses ($p = 0.028$) more often.

Applications Used for Communication

In order to identify the preferences in the area of communication tools, students specified how often they used popular applications and communication channels (1–never, 5–always).

The most popular tools were Facebook Messenger, email and Skype ($M > 2.4$). Significantly less popular were MSN Messenger, Google Chat, and Google Hangout ($M < 1.4$).

The Mann-Whitney test showed significant differences in the use of three tools: Viber, FaceTime and MSN Messenger. Respondents from Slovenia were more likely to use Viber ($p = 0.000$) and FaceTime ($p = 0.000$) while surveyed students from Poland used MSN Messenger more often ($p = 0.000$).

Social Media

Social media plays a significant role nowadays, not only in entertainment, but also in education and business. Therefore, students were asked about how often (1–never, 5–always) they use popular social media platforms. The most frequently used were Facebook (M = 4.75), YouTube (M = 4.68) and Instagram (M = 4.25). Other social media platforms were much less used.

The least popular included Ask.fm, LinkedIn, MySpace, and Flickr (M < 1.2). The analysis showed significant differences in the frequency of use in five out of ten social media portals. Respondents from Slovenia were more likely to use YouTube (p = 0.036), Instagram and Pinterest (both p = 0.000) while surveyed students from Poland used Ask.fm (p = 0.000) and LinkedIn (p = 0.015) slightly more often.

Shopping Online

The students' online activity in the area of shopping is very important for the future business graduates. Respondents indicated how often (1–never, 5–always) they buy goods and services online.

Online shopping is not a popular online activity as the total mean was 2.06. The majority of students (both from Poland and Slovenia) stated that they purchased clothing and shoes (M = 3.09), tickets (M = 2.90), tourist services (M = 2.62) and electronic devices (M = 2.19). The least frequently bought goods were digital music or movies (M = 1.62), music, movies or programs on CD\DVD (M = 1.54) and e-books (M = 1.30).

The Mann–Whitney U test showed 7 statistically significant differences ($p < 0.05$) out of 10 examined services and goods. Polish students bought clothing and shoes, tickets, electronic devices, food and drinks, paper books, music, movies or programs on CD and e-books more often. Online shopping was the area where the authors observed the greatest differences between the students from Poland and Slovenia.

Factors Influencing Digital Literacy

The Pearson correlation coefficient (r) was calculated to identify the relationship between the level of knowledge of different types of software and the relationship between the time spent online and knowledge of the software (Table 1).

Table 1. Pearson correlations between time spent online and application knowledge

Variables	1	2	3	4	5	6	7
1. Word processor NIUS							
2. Spreadsheet NIUS	.606**						
3. Business presentation NIUS	.642**	.573**					
4. Web services NIUS	.592**	.486**	.524**				
5. Data bases NIUS	.302**	.509**	.343**	.341**			
6. Photo editing NIUS	.262**	.352**	.327**	.374**	.268**		
7. Mail NIUS	.533**	.505**	.524**	.586**	.394**	.271**	
8. Time spent online			–.095*			.094*	

** Correlation is significant at the 0.01 level (2-tailed).
* Correlation is significant at the 0.05 level (2-tailed).

There are two statistically significant relationships a variable time spent online with a variable Photo editing NIUS ($r = 0.094$) and Business presentation NIUS ($r = -0.095$). The correlations were very weak but statistically significant ($p < 0.05$) (Table 1).

A significant correlation has been found between possessing skills in the area of different applications. A moderate dependence was observed between email services and knowledge of both word processors, spreadsheet programs, presentation programs and web searching engines ($r > 0.5$). Students skilled in the area of word processors claimed to also have more skills in the area of using basic office suit components, spreadsheets, business presentation applications. In this area, we observed a moderate positive relationship ($r > 0.6$).

To identity the correlation between the second school grade, study year and possessing the knowledge of basic types of software, the Spearman's rho was calculated (Table 2).

Table 2. Spearman's correlation (rho) between year of study, second school grade and application knowledge

Variables	1	2	3	4	5	6	7	8
1. Word processor NIUS								
2. Spreadsheet NIUS	.643**							
3. Business presentation NIUS	.643**	.596**						
4. Web services NIUS	.580**	.487**	.496**					
5. Data bases NIUS	.339**	.505**	.349**	.345**				
6. Photo editing NIUS	.329**	.389**	.366**	.425**	.293**			
7. Mail NIUS	.540**	.527**	.562**	.585**	.391**	.326**		
8. Second school grade	.204**	.238**	.181**	.154**	.107*	.233**	.175**	
9. Study year	.116*	.311**	.129**		.223**		.169**	.099*

** Correlation is significant at the 0.01 level (2-tailed).

* Correlation is significant at the 0.05 level (2-tailed).

The analysis showed a weak positive relationship between the study year and knowledge of Excel (rho = 0.311), a weak correlation was also observed between the study year and knowledge of database systems (rho = 0.223). We also observed a slight positive relationship between the second school grade and knowledge of word processors, spreadsheets and business presentation tools (0.203 <=rho <=0.238).

The correlation analysis also showed weak positive relations between the study year and performing online actions. Older students more often make e-payments, use e-government services and tax office services (rho = 0.308, rho = 0.246, rho = 0.216). Older students also made online purchases more often particularly physical books (rho = 0.270), music, movies or programs on physical media (rho = 0.175), tickets (rho = 0.185) as well as food and drinks (rho = 0.304).

4 Conclusion

In this article, we explored digital literacy among young business students from Poland and Slovenia. The conducted literature review and quantitative analysis showed that teaching in the area of digital literacy is very demanding because it covers a range of skills from the purely technical to cognitive skills and needs continuous development. However, a well-trained, digitally competent person is able to act more efficiently in the areas of work, learning or leisure. Digital literacy can be explored on four main levels: basic, intermediate, advanced and highly specialized. Many study programs stress the two highest levels, but, as the analysis showed, there are many gaps and room for improvement even at the basic levels. These basic ICT skills need to be developed especially among non-IT users like business students and older members of our digital society.

Our research showed that young people mainly use mobile devices for education communication and leisure. Therefore, the offered courses should be prepared in a "mobile friendly" way. We observed that respondents were very skilled in Microsoft Office but had less knowledge and skills in the area of other office suits or more demanding applications for multimedia creation (graphics, audio and video content). So, when preparing course framework, teachers should stress the multimedia aspect and introduce up-to-date, interesting and easy to use tools for creating multimedia content. The normalized index of usage skills developed by the authors (NIUS) showed that there were some gaps between the students from Poland and Slovenia, especially in the area of using spreadsheets, photo editors and database management systems. Therefore, it is worth comparing the Polish and Slovenian study programs to find sources of those differences.

The main activities performed online by students included sharing data with friends and family members, searching for jobs and using e-banking services. The least frequently performed activities were using e-government services, tax services and participating in massive open online courses. To support these less frequently performed activities, syllabi should contain more content in the area of e-government and e-learning. Teachers should also stress the capabilities and advantages of MOOC courses. Young students like to use social media like Facebook, YouTube, Instagram. Facebook Messenger, email or Skype that are widely used for communication purposes. These tools should be incorporated to courses in order to make the learning process more enjoyable, interactive and fresh.

The performed analyses indicate that teaching in the area of ICT basics is necessary for students, can affect both education, leisure and professional areas of life. Nowadays, IT tools are widely accessible and easy to use especially those in software as a service form (SaaS). They can increase the effectiveness of the learning process and make it more enjoyable but also require constant (sometimes rapid) development and improvement from the ICT teachers/trainers. So, both students' and teachers' ICT literacy should be researched and developed/improved according to changing market requirements.

Future Research

ICT tools have many areas of usage and are increasingly used to support educational and business processes. Therefore, ICT literacy should be an important area of research. There is a need to prepare new courses for business students with the use of IT solutions. In order to prepare good courses, teachers should know students' knowledge, skills and needs in the area of IT tools usage. The research presented was limited to students at the Faculty of Economics MCSU and business students at the Faculty of Management, University of Primorska that may limit the findings generalizability. Therefore, future research will be conducted in two directions to compare the obtained findings with the opinions of students of different fields: strongly IT related, medium IT related and not related to IT. The authors also wish to co-examine students from different countries that are developing, developed and highly developed in order to identify the main differences. The results of future research will be used to prepare better quality e-learning courses for foreign students such as participants of the Erasmus program.

References

1. Alberta Education: Literacy – Definition, Components and Elements of the Progressions (2015). https://education.alberta.ca/media/3069627/definition-components-and-elements-literacy.pdf. Accessed 26 Dec 2018
2. Becker, B.W.: Information literacy in the digital age: myths and principles of digital literacy. Sch. Inf. Student Res. J. **7**(2) (2018). http://scholarworks.sjsu.edu/slissrj/vol7/iss2/2. Accessed 26 Dec 2018
3. Carretero, S., Vuorikari, R., Punie, Y.: DigComp 2.1: the digital competence framework for citizens with eight proficiency levels and examples of use. European Union (2017). http://publications.jrc.ec.europa.eu/repository/bitstream/JRC106281/web-digcomp2.1pdf_(online).pdf. Accessed 25 Dec 2018
4. Coiro, J., Knobel, M., Lankshear, C., Leu, D.J.: Handbook of Research on New Literacies. Routledge, New York-London (2008)
5. Eshet-Alkalai, Y.: Digital literacy: a conceptual framework for survival skills in the digital era. J. Educ. Multimedia Hypermedia **13**(1), 93–106 (2004)
6. EU Science Hub. Project Background – EU Science Hub – European Commission, 23 June 2017. https://ec.europa.eu/jrc/en/digcomp/project-background. Accessed 28 Dec 2018
7. Ferrari, A., Punie, Y., Redecker, C.: Understanding digital competence in the 21st century: an analysis of current frameworks. In: Ravenscroft, A., Lindstaedt, S., Kloos, C.D., Hernández-Leo, D. (eds.) EC-TEL 2012. LNCS, vol. 7563, pp. 79–92. Springer, Heidelberg (2012). https://doi.org/10.1007/978-3-642-33263-0_7
8. Glister, P.: Digital Literacy. Wiley, New Jersey (1997)
9. Goodfellow, R.: Literacy, literacies and the digital in higher education. Teach. High. Educ. **16**(1), 131–144 (2011). https://doi.org/10.1080/13562517.2011.544125
10. ISACA. ISACA Research Report on Emerging Technologies. Digital Literate Leaders Are Essential for Business Transformation (2017). http://www.isaca.org/SiteCollectionDocuments/2017-Digital-Transformation-Barometer-Report.pdf
11. JISC. Developing students' digital literacy (2015). https://www.jisc.ac.uk/guides/developing-students-digital-literacy

12. O'Brien, M., Verma, R.: How Do First Year Students Utilize Different Lecture Resources? Higher Education, April 2018. https://doi.org/10.1007/s10734-018-0250-5
13. Oliver, R., Towers, S.: Benchmarking ICT Literacy in Tertiary Learning Settings (2000). https://pdfs.semanticscholar.org/97ec/125a3ade74c85ecbae627627bba4aaed55a9.pdf

Using Digital Resources to Boost English Writing Development

Ângela Musskopf[1], Débora Nice Ferrari Barbosa[2(✉)], Patrícia Brandalise Scherer Bassani[2], and Amanda Jefferies[3]

[1] Instituto Ivoti, Ivoti, RS, Brazil
angela.musskopf@institutoivoti.com.br
[2] Universidade Feevale, Novo Hamburgo, RS, Brazil
{deboranice,patriciab}@feevale.br
[3] University of Hertfordshire, Hatfield, Hertfordshire, UK
a.l.jefferies@herts.ac.uk

Abstract. Official documents from the Brazilian Government stress the importance of including technological issues for teacher training. Also, programmes to promote teachers' digital literacy were created. Yet, recent surveys in the country show low relevance of the pedagogical use of ICTs in classrooms. This research describes a practice developed with undergraduates being prepared to become teachers of English as a Second Language in the south of Brazil. The practices were developed in a subject aimed to develop the students' proficiency in English. The experiment proposed the use of educational digital resources to develop the writing skill. The main objective was to develop pedagogical practices, which include digital educational resources for students preparing themselves to become English teachers and to verify their influence in the linguistic knowledge of the students. According to the theories of Second Language Learning, interaction, meaningfulness and task-essential form must be considered to achieve success. These features were explored through the digital resources. It is possible to state that there was an improvement in the writing skill of the participants.

Keywords: Teacher training · Digital tools · Writing development

1 Introduction

The Base Nacional Comum Curricular[1] [1], the normative document that defines the organic and progressive set of essential learning that all students must develop throughout the stages and modalities of Elementary Education in Brazil, mentions explicitly in four of the ten general competencies the usage of digital resources in education. In addition, another official document, the Resolution No. 2 of July 1, 2015 [2], which defines the National Curricular Guidelines for initial training at the Higher Level (undergraduate courses, pedagogic training for graduates and second degree) and

[1] Available at http://basenacionalcomum.mec.gov.br/wp-content/uploads/2018/02/bncc-20dez-site.pdf.

L. Uden et al. (Eds.): LTEC 2019, CCIS 1011, pp. 337–348, 2019.
https://doi.org/10.1007/978-3-030-20798-4_29

continuing education, stresses the importance of including technological issues for teacher training.

However, according to Mapelli's research [3], even though technological subjects are part of the trainee teachers' curriculum, the author concluded that they do not subsequently develop practices with digital resources in their professional planning. Furthermore, not only did the participants mention their unfamiliarity with educational software, they also said they were unaware of apps for mobile gadgets and websites with online activities supporting education. Those few who used online materials were unable to propose any innovative activity from the perspective of education in cyberculture, according to Mapelli [3].

The recent report, "ICT in Education, a Survey on the Use of Information and Communication Technologies in Brazilian Schools 2017" offers evidence to corroborate this. It mentions that whilst the Brazilian Government has created programmes to promote teachers' digital literacy, "recent surveys show that the relevance of the pedagogical use of ICTs in classrooms is still very low" [4] even when infrastructure is not an issue. Despite the fact that the use of ICT allows a wide range of opportunities, these are directly connected to the teachers' capacity for planning in accordance to their didactic objectives. According to this report, it continues to be a challenge to promote digital literacy to teachers.

From this starting point, it is possible to conclude that there is a potential gap between the guidelines and teacher training programmes. Considering this context, our research question is how to promote the use of digital resources in pedagogical practices for second language acquisition? Thus, as an educator preparing students to become English teachers, this is a major personal concern and the main motivation for developing pedagogical practices in my classes which include digital resources for second language acquisition. At the same time as creating opportunities for the students to become familiar with technology use, from an English teacher's point of view, the activities are aimed to integrate digital resources and the learning of the English language. This paper is part of a larger work which has been developed for researching across two semesters. The main objective was to develop pedagogical practices which include digital educational resources for students preparing to become English teachers and to verify their influence in the linguistic knowledge of the students. To check changes in the proficiency levels the scales of the CEFR are mentioned.

The specific objectives were (a) analyse the role of technology in teacher training courses in the region; (b) investigate if the theories of second language acquisition support the use of digital resources in the curriculum; (c) describe innovative practices through the choice of digital resources so that students feel confident in using them in other contexts, hopefully in their own practice as teachers; and (d) find indications of improvement in the proficiency level. After two semesters of experimenting with pedagogical practices using technology to promote appropriate use by the students, to develop linguistic awareness and to increase the linguistic level of future English teachers during their training, this third article aims to join the resources used in the two previous semesters, so that the undergraduates reinforce their use of digital resources, as well as motivating them to incorporate ICT in their proposed pedagogical practices. The first practice was described in an article that presented the activities proposed using Edmodo (https://edmodo.com/) to create a closed social environment in which students would have access to suggestions and feel comfortable expressing themselves openly in writing posts without worrying about possible mistakes and criticisms [5]. The second practice linked second language learning theories and the improvement in the students' writing skill [6]. Through the use of freely available resources, the study showed significant improvement in the students' vocabulary level. At the end of this period, the students mentioned some difficulties when they were asked to produce a text, a reality that was already expected, mainly because of two reasons: (a) the basic English level of the undergraduates and (b) writing competency is not usually developed in schools, especially academic writing, which was the kind of skill students were being required to use.

Therefore, this present practice aimed to join those resources used previously, which are Edmodo, the Thesaurus (https://thesaurus.com/), the English Profile (http://www.englishprofile.org/) and Write and Improve (https://writeandimprove.com/). It proposed pedagogical practices on the social educational network focusing on improving the students writing skill. This practice is based on the premium version of the Write and Improve platform, permitting access to more features than the free version. The intention is to verify what features are available in the paid version and their influence on the students' development. The two previous articles presented the reasons for choosing these resources, but the key rationale is that the institution in which the practices occurred is a Preparation Centre for the University of Cambridge proficiency tests and both, the English Profile and the Write and Improve are supported by Cambridge. There are two main differences from the present practice to the second [6]: firstly, before the final written production, students had a writing class, following a lesson plan specifically for this skill, and secondly the teacher subscribed to the Write and Improve platform, allowing the creation of a workbook for this group of students. As a result, they could access more features than the 'freemium' version used before, such as a feedback box. Thus, the participants had the opportunity to experience a condition that most of the resources provide: free and premium versions to improve their writing level in the English language. In this third practice, the written proposals were linked to topics discussed in class while in the previous one this did not happen, as the written assignment was chosen among the platform suggestions simulating the situation of a proficiency test. Also, the premium version would allow the teacher to follow the students' submissions through a progress chart and, most importantly, to write individual feedback to each student through it.

2 Literature Review

The literature review presented below offers theoretical support to the research undertaken and the larger project of which it is part. Researchers who defend connectionism believe that our brain works similarly to a computer hence it consists of neural networks which are 'complex clusters of links between information nodes' [7]. One of the claims of this theory is that stimulus-response associations are strengthened through repetition and this enhances learning. Repetition is also a key feature on the use of technology, Time is needed to learn how to deal with technology, especially when people have not used yet. It is important to deal with it continuously, especially if it offers more possibilities to be explored.

Practice is a key component in language learning. According to Lourdes Ortega [8], there are three principles that should be met when practicing inside classrooms: (a) interactivity, (b) meaningfulness and (c) focus on task-essential forms. The first two are largely self-explanatory but this third one is related to the essential forms and structures required by the designed activity. For example, in developing their written assignments, students must be able to structure their ideas into paragraphs, choose suitable transition words from one to another, and use appropriate vocabulary and language, as an essay is a formal paper. Keeping this in mind this practice was revisited and joined the use of resources already valued by the participants to promote more opportunities to deal with their specific writing issues, seeking to acquire a good level of mastery and, at the same time, paying attention to their language development.

According to Lightbown and Spada [9], all researchers of language acquisition are trying to understand and explain how human learners are able to acquire language, taking into consideration various social and instructional environments. Either from a linguistic or a psychological point of view, digital resources can address the basic principles of language learning and contribute to the students' personal development.

Besides language development, the practices also involved new ways of using the resources. By inviting students to post their own understanding of specific content, they could now produce, distribute and share, interactive and collaborative features that were only possible because of Web 2.0 technologies which enable people to use social media. In this study, this was the educational social media platform, Edmodo. According to Bassani and Barbosa [10], this allowed students to find and share information in multiple digital ways as well as to communicate and collaborate. They define social software as a subset of the Web 2.0 tools that support social interaction and collaboration e.g. wikis. The authors also state that 'the Web 2.0 applications are the ones that highlight the possibilities of this platform through a participative architecture among the members' (subjects of interaction - Version by the author) [10]. In our opinion, even when designing activities in which students are the authors of content, it is very important not to forget that meaning should be integrated with features such as decision making, sharing, and socializing to enhance learning experiences, as stated by the theories of second language acquisition [7–9].

According to Musskopf and Barbosa [5], newly qualified teachers still join schools without apparently knowing how to use digital resources, especially those designed for educational contexts, a situation also acknowledged by Mapelli. The challenge is to change this current situation so that undergraduates and future teachers will be exposed to apps, platforms, resources, and websites created to be used in schools for language teaching and learning, thus promoting improvements to linguistic levels. Their initial unfamiliarity of these options impoverishes pedagogical practices of teachers in both cognitive and linguistic development since there are resources which promote the improvement of them concomitantly.

Paiva [11] wrote about incorporating the use of digital technologies into general teacher training in Brazil. According to her, the Brazilian government has been promoting some initiatives, but she still states that it is necessary to think about adding ICT as an essential element in teacher training courses [11]. She continues by sharing her own experience, since the 1990s, by asserting that her biggest source of information is now the web itself, mentioning some of the websites used in this study, such as the Centre for Learning and Performance Technologies.

Therefore, it is possible to conclude that there is a potential gap between the guidelines and teacher training programmes. This point is a focus of our research.

3 Methodology

Due to many features, the cartographic method seemed to be very suitable to be applied in the pedagogical practices involved in this research. It has been used in field research in which subjectivity is a component of the context being studied. The cartographic method [12] aims to follow processes, not represent an object. Therefore, while the research is being undertaken, the path must be built, adapted, creating its own movements.

It was clear that many forces surround the research territory inhabited by the researcher and the students, provoking not only a change in the reality around them, in knowledge acquisition, but also a change in themselves as learners during the process. As odd as it might seem, objectivism and subjectivism can coexist, completing each other. The practices developed by following this methodology searched for data. At the same time, the participants considered the adaptation and reorganization of the territory while performing the practices. At times the subjects involved in the process analysed aspects from inside, although there would be times they would proceed as if they were hovering and observing from above. For example, students reorganizing their ideas while involved in the process of rewriting would be considered from inside; when finished, they reflected about the entire process would be considered from above, analysing what was already done. When processes are followed, there is a necessity of registering them, which was achieved by writing a regular research diary, to assure that details would not be lost in the long run. This may cause a change in describing the experiences, a different shape so that the results would not be lost along the way. While finishing one pedagogical practice, it was important to reflect about this part, to evaluate whether it indicated any swerve to the right, or left, or continuing straight ahead. Hence, the proposal of the final product was to put together three papers which were conducted by a thread which passes throughout all practices and though described separately, are part of one complex piece of structured research.

4 Learning Practice

4.1 The Research Context

The following practices were developed with four undergraduates preparing to become teachers of English as a second language. Due to the objectives and methodology of this research, which require a period of time to apply the processes in the context of the clues, the practices were developed from August 2017 to December 2018, that is three semesters during which students enrolled in subjects named English II, English III, and

English IV, respectively. The focus in these subjects was to improve the students' proficiency level so that they would be able to reach an intermediate level defined as B1 according to the Common European Framework of Reference (CEFR) [13]. So, when students enter the course, they have basic knowledge and are expected to follow classes taught in English from the first semester.

In the last semester, August to December 2018, which is the focus of this paper, pedagogical practices are joined with the digital resources used in the previous semesters. The practice promoted students as authors of content which was posted on Edmodo and was used to produce an essay, one of the requirements of the students' semester. Throughout the two first practices, students continued to use Edmodo to share interesting pieces they found outside the classroom, surfing on the web randomly or finding suggestions on YouTube channels they signed up for. As this environment showed it was a place where the students felt comfortable, wrapping up the three-semester pedagogical practices led to a proposal linking Edmodo to a writing assignment. This may raise a question: why test more writing? Two main reasons can answer this: (a) students were very motivated after the second practice and considered they improved their writing skill as well as reporting that the digital resources used were extremely helpful and (b) as a famous proverb states 'practice makes perfect': students were longing for more time and further opportunities to continue developing their writing.

Experiences and improvements are elements which demand time and require careful observation of processes which in this case could not be controlled by the proposer since the path was clear but would not be pre-established due to the fact that the group would be in charge of directing the study. Thus, the cartographic method [12] was adopted to carry on the research. In brief, cartography considers there is no separation between theory, practice, reflection and action all of which happen at the same time, being built by the subjects involved while they are working.

4.2 The Practice

As these students had mentioned their concerns about certain aspects of writing which they considered difficult, the first step of this practice was to determine what they were. With this in mind, the idea of creating a word cloud came up. To build it, Mentimeter (https://www.mentimeter.com/) was used, since according to Centre for Learning & Performance Technologies (http://c4lpt.co.uk/) it occupies the 56th position in the 2018 Top Tools for Learning. Students had to type three aspects they consider difficult when they have to produce writing. The result of the activity was the words: preposition, better structure, verbs, punctuation, vocabulary, connectors, support ideas, etc. Looking at the results, the teacher asked each student to choose one of the topics to research: vocabulary, punctuation, verbs, connectors, and prepositions, the last one being taken by the teacher. Students were asked to look for information about each topic, decide on a way to present it, add some exercises to practice and post all of it to the class page at Edmodo, which is an education network page similar to Facebook, created in the first practice to become a place for the students to discuss issues, post suggestions, activities. By doing this, students were in charge of reading, thinking about their topic, summarizing the information they considered relevant, and deciding what and how they were going to share this with their classmates.

An interesting aspect to be pointed out here is that one participant decided to look for a new resource to present her topic. While her classmates decided to use a power point presentation to express their ideas, she searched and found Genial.ly (https://www.genial.ly.com/). She learnt how to use it and expressed her views on the topic she was responsible for, through using this new resource, standing out among the group. She did not ask the teacher about any suggestions, on the contrary, she decided to look on her own, showing entrepreneurship. Later on, students were asked to do more research about their topic on books available at the library of the institution and write a post adding a tip or a piece of information they had not previously mentioned. They were also asked to read and comment on it. Figure 1 shows a post from one of the students.

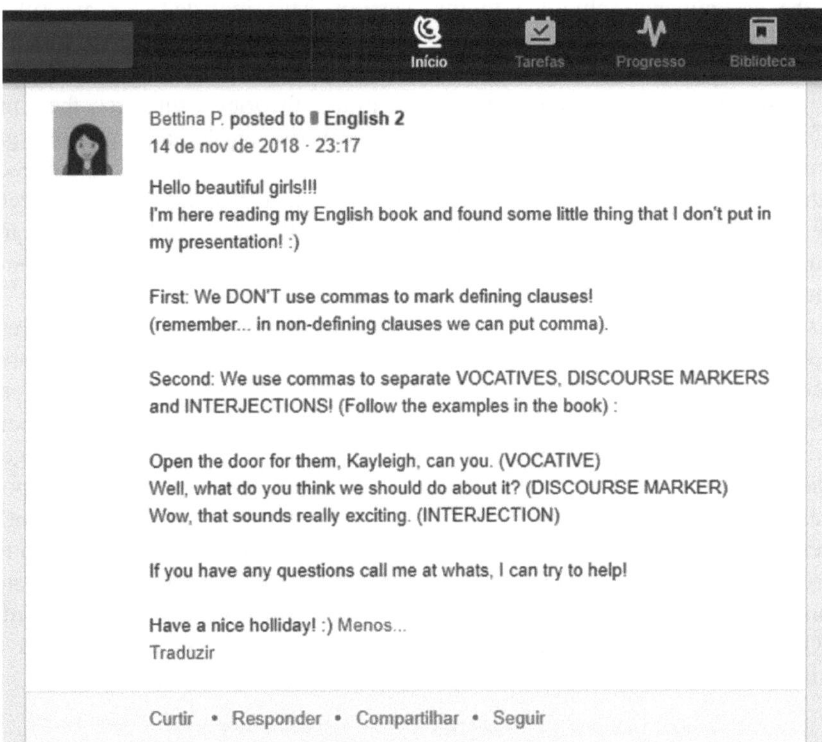

Fig. 1. Edmodo post

All of them used a very friendly tone and none of them repeated information posted in their first task. Students were able to extend their topic content with significant pieces such as including new pieces of advice as well as expanding knowledge. As they were supposed to read these posts at home, the teacher asked in class if they had any questions or comments, so that it would be possible to check the meaning.

The next step was to follow a writing lesson plan from the students' textbook used in class, which suggested an essay titled 'The environment we live in will change dramatically in the next 50 years'. The class steps raised some topics to discuss, build vocabulary connected to the topic, promote some exercises, leading to a written production. To produce it, students were asked to refer to Edmodo's postings whenever they felt necessary and to access the Thesaurus and the English Profile if required. Participants had another opportunity to use the digital resources as helpers while developing their tasks.

Finally, the teacher inserted the writing proposal in the Write and Improve platform, the students accessed it and wrote their essay. Throughout the time they were working, access to the other resources used was allowed (Edmodo, Thesaurus, English Profile). As this proposal was part of their grades, students had 45 min to complete the task.

Having subscribed in advance, the platform permitted them to access more details about the assignments submitted to this version. This included, for example, the number of times each student submitted their work and their progress forward or backward, according to what changes they made in each submission. This feature is really interesting since language acquisition theories support the model write/feedback/rewrite for written production. The Write and Improve platform grants this opportunity: after the first submission, besides the platform feedback, the teachers have the opportunity to write comments for each student, helping them to reflect and decide what to change to improve their work. This feature is only available in the premium version of the platform and there was an enormous difference from the previous practice in which the freemium version was used.

Also, the premium version generates a chart showing the students' progress. It allowed the teacher to give each student individual feedback. Such features are not available in the free version of this platform; therefore, this is a substantial difference between this practice and the previous ones. The progress chart is helpful as it permits following each student's progress as well as giving a visual of all students altogether. Yet, the possibility of writing feedback to the students is considered the most important feature of this version because it allows teachers to interact with the students about their production, leading them to reflect, check and decide changes they can make to move forward. As students submit their texts, teachers are able to make suggestions related to structures and form demanded by academic writing. Such features are in accordance with Ortega's principles stated previously: interactivity, meaningfulness and task-essential form.

5 Results

During all the time, the principal author kept a diary in which she wrote down observations, such as the students' reaction and their own comments. When they experimented in the activity with Mentimeter, they were amazed by the opportunities which technology could promote in the classroom. Most of them considered it a user-friendly resource, though one of the students did not realise there were three boxes for three options, and she typed her options all in one. As a consequence, when we looked at the result and she realised what she had done, she asked to redo it, which was promptly accepted by the others. As previously said, it is not easy and sometimes the resources can raise doubts not always asked by the students.

Through the pedagogical practices proposed, students had to interact with each other and the teacher, receiving feedback from their peers and the teacher, using language for a communication purpose in a social context as Lightbown and Spada [9] and Mitchell and Myles [7] state as necessary to support a meaningful learning process. Tasks performed always had an objective and the resources were a mechanism to mediate communication between all the agents involved, inside and outside of the classroom, so that the geographic space was not a barrier. Language acquisition can take more time for some students so the fact that the practices were developed over three semesters allowed students to experience the resources more than once, giving them time to become familiar with them, making their brain store to embed information from the short-term memory to the long-term memory [7]. The writing assignments in the activities stimulated students to respond to the proposals promoting the strength of associations through repetition, [7] as well as promoting interaction, meaningfulness and focus on task-essential form [8]. The data collected showed that the theories of second language acquisition mentioned, support the use of digital resources in the curriculum for both language and cognitive development. Yet, more than once, the undergraduates mentioned they were using some tools in other classes and accessed resources such as the Thesaurus to help in the tasks they had as homework.

Related to the activity completed, after recognising the topics they elected as difficult, only one of the students chose a new resource to build her presentation. When asked about it in the following class, she said she wanted something new and then googled and found Genial.ly suitable and accessible. She was able to integrate other media resources in her presentation, such as a video and two other links. The other three students chose the ubiquitous Powerpoint™. It is interesting to notice that the innovative student is also the one who has the best English level of the four. This may suggest some questions for a further study: were the others more worried about language accuracy than about the tool? Does a better (higher) level of English competence influence the students to broaden their scope and take some risks, allowing them to spend more time trying to figure something out because language is not an issue? Or is this just related to a personality trait?

Students were engaged in the activities and had no trouble in adding information to their topics. Unfortunately, none of them posted any comments. They said they had forgotten to do it. Even so, it was possible to check that they read their classmates posting as they made some comments about them in class. Despite this fact, undergraduates used features of Web 2.0 technologies to share content in social media [10], becoming confident as authors from the posts on Edmodo, a safe environment where they feel comfortable in sharing freely with students from their own closed group.

Related to the writing assignment based on the class textbook, students found the topic interesting and participated confidently in the discussion. They also received regular input of new vocabulary to enhance their production. The writing assignment of each student was subjected to the English profile text analyser, which showed that the vocabulary level of the students is still in development as all of them reached some words in high levels of the CEFR[2], such as B2, C1 and some of them even C2. Nonetheless, to determine the level of the text as a whole, another digital resource called Text Analyzer[3] was used this time. This tool showed that only one text was classified as B1 while the others reached the B2 level. Before the practices, undergraduates were categorised as A2 level.

The last activity developed was the final written assignment of the semester using the Write and Improve resource. The students were already used to the resource; therefore, they could concentrate on their text. Surprisingly, the result shown was not as good as expected: one student achieved level A2 of the CEFR while the other three achieved the level B1. According to observation by the principal author during the students' performance, at least three reasons can be suggested: (a) as the activity was done on the chrome books, students did not realise they could have used other possibilities to plan their writing, such as a Word™ file, or an online mind map or even taken some draft paper; (b) timing is still a difficult issue for the students to deal with; (c) the pressure of a grade made them nervous and insecure. Even so, none of these reasons were directly related to digital resources.

These pedagogical practices are the third part of a three-semester sequence, the other two practices having already been published under the titles of (1) Edmodo: Experiencing a Global Education Network and (2) ICTs and Second Language Learning. To conclude this study, the institution in which the practices were developed organised a meeting to address internal interests. The participants shared their acquired knowledge about the digital resources with the English staff.

For this meeting, the students prepared a presentation using the new digital resource one of the students had found. This presentation was created outside the classroom through collaborative tools.

Students then created a 10-question quiz afterwards and they made the teachers answer a question, creating a word cloud with the same digital resource they experienced in class. All were the students' initiative; when they were invited to do it, they were allowed to decide what they were going to say and how they were going to present. This shows, at least, that they decided to explore more than one tool without being motivated or guided by their teacher.

This meeting also provided a fantastic opportunity for the students to communicate with an audience combining their writing and speaking skills. It was the first time they had the chance of performing a presentation speaking in English, which made them a little nervous. Another reason is that the audience was made up of English teachers and the students were worried about making mistakes. These feelings and conflict were naturally expected since the majority of people would feel stressed about such a situation. Even so, the undergraduates managed to present their written assignment and engage in communication in both presenting and answering the audience's questions.

[2] CEFR relates to the Common European Framework of Reference, a set of descriptors to describe levels of proficiency in languages from A1 to C1.

[3] Available at: http://www.roadtogrammar.com/textanalysis/.

6 Conclusion

This study joined aspects of second language acquisition and applied them to the usage of digital resources allowing future English teachers to experience ICTs and, at the same time, develop their English language proficiency. Even though it is hard to determine if results were connected to the platform or the teacher feedback, it is possible to state that there was an improvement in the writing production of each of the students. And, in the authors' point of view, both teacher and technology support had a share, because as good as the platform is, there were some issues which students were able to solve only after receiving the teacher's feedback. Therefore, any digital resource is exactly what the word means: a resource, it is something that can be used to achieve an aim and provide information for teachers and students. It does not replace the teacher, but it may help the student greatly. Nevertheless, features from the premium version such as the possibility of written feedback and the progress chart, facilitate the students' assessment and feedback by the teacher. It also respects the pace of each student, since they submit their tasks when they feel ready to do so; they may also receive the teacher's comments asynchronously.

Two contrasting aspects can be outlined in this study: (a) authorship and (b) stress while being accessed. On the one hand, students showed they felt comfortable in choosing a different digital resource than the ones used in class and explored it to build a presentation and a quiz on their own. On the other hand, the level of their final writing may strongly be related to the stress of being assessed, which was the only new element introduced in this task.

In addition, the opportunity that undergraduates had to engage in oral communication during the meeting with the English teachers of the institution at the end of the semester was the perfect event to end the three-semester practices. Students were able to explain the resources, answer questions about them, inspire the teachers to experience two possibilities of usage (quiz and word cloud) and demonstrate knowledge about the digital educational resource and linguistic competence to convey their points of view. For future trends research, it is important to investigate the learning effectiveness. For this, it will be necessary more time for study and analyses.

Acknowledgment. We would like to thank Feevale University for the scholarship throughout the master's course which enabled the three semestres of research, practices, and knowledge. The authors are also grateful to CNPq (National Council for Scientific and Technological Development) by their support in the development of this research.

References

1. BRASIL. Ministério da Educação. Base Nacional Comum Curricular (BNCC). Educação é a Base. Brasília, MEC/CONSED/UNDIME. Disponível em (2017). http://basenacionalcomum.mec.gov.br/images/BNCC_publicacao.pdf. Accessed 20 Oct 2018
2. BRASIL. Ministério da Educação. RESOLUÇÃO No 2, DE 1º DE JULHO DE 2015. Define as Diretrizes Curriculares Nacionais para a formação inicial em nível superior (cursos de licenciatura, cursos de formação pedagógica para graduados e cursos de segunda licenciatura) e para a formação continuada. Brasília, Disponível em. http://portal.mec.gov.br/index.php?option=com_docman&view=download&alias=17719-res-cne-cp-002–03072015&category_slug=julho-2015-pdf&Itemid=30192. Accessed 20 Oct 2018
3. Mapelli, N.: Formação inicial docente e o uso de tecnologias digitais de informação e comunicação: levantamento de práticas educativas no ensino fundamental. 2018 Dissertação (Mestrado) – Universidade Feevale, Novo Hamburgo, RS (2018)
4. PESQUISA SOBRE O USO DAS TECNOLOGIAS DE INFORMAÇÃO E COMUNICAÇÃO NAS ESCOLAS BRASILEIRAS [livro eletrônico]: TIC Educação 2017. Survey on the Use of information and Communication Technologies in Brazilian Schools: ICT in education 2017/Núcleo de Informação e Coordenação do Ponto BR, [editor], Comitê Gestor da Internet no Brasil, São Paulo (2018)
5. Musskopf, Ângela, Barbosa, Débora Nice Ferrari: EDMODO: experiencing a global education network. In: Uden, Lorna, Liberona, Dario, Ristvej, Jozef (eds.) LTEC 2018. CCIS, vol. 870, pp. 131–141. Springer, Cham (2018). https://doi.org/10.1007/978-3-319-95522-3_12
6. Musskopf, Â., Barbosa, D.N.F., Bassani, P.B.S.: ICTs and Second Language Learning. RENOTE, vol. 16, no. 2 (2018). https://seer.ufrgs.br/renote/article/view/89295/51534
7. Mitchell, R.; Myles, F.: Second Language Learning Theories. Hodder Arnold, p. 228 (2004)
8. Ortega, L.: Meaningful L2 practice in foreign language classrooms: a cognitive-interactionist SLA perspective. In: DeKeyser, R. (ed.), Practice in a Second Language: Perspectives from Applied Linguistics and Cognitive Psychology, pp. 180–207. Cambridge University Press (2007)
9. Lightbown, P., Spada, N.: How Languages are Learned, p. 324. Oxford University Press, Oxford (2013)
10. Bassani, P.B.S.; Barbosa, D.N.F.: Ensinar e aprender na rede: criando ambientes de aprendizagem na web. In: MEIRELLES, Mauro et. al. Repensando o lugar da sociologia e o uso das novas tecnologias, p. 444. CirKula, Porto Alegrep (2015)
11. Paiva, V.L.M.O.: A formação do professor para uso da tecnologia. In: Silva, K.A.; Daniel, F. G.; Kaneko-Marques, S.M.; Salomão, A.C.B. (Orgs) A formação de professores de línguas: Novos Olhares, vol. 2, pp. 209–230. SP: Pontes Editores, Campinasvol (2013)
12. Passos, E., Kastrup, V.E.: Liliane da. Pistas do método cartográfico. Pesquisa-intervenção e produção de subjetividade, Porto Alegre, Sulina (2009)
13. Council of Europe. Common European framework of reference for languages: learning, teaching, assessment: companion volume with new descriptor, February 2018. https://rm.coe.int/cefr-companion-volume-with-new-descriptors-2018/1680787989. Accessed 10 Dec 2018

Social Media Learning Tools

Using Social Media to Enhance Learning and Motivate Students in the Higher Education Classroom

Eva Lahuerta-Otero[1,2(✉)], Rebeca Cordero-Gutiérrez[3,4], and Vanessa Izquierdo-Álvarez[5]

[1] Business Administration, University of Salamanca, Salamanca, Spain
eva.lahuerta@usal.es
[2] IME, University of Salamanca, Salamanca, Spain
[3] Faculty of Computer Science, Pontifical University of Salamanca, Salamanca, Spain
rcorderogu@upsa.es
[4] School of Languages and Education, Nebrija University, Madrid, Spain
[5] University of Salamanca, Salamanca, Spain
vizquierdo@usal.es

Abstract. Since the advent of the Internet and the web 2.0 technologies, the world has changed profoundly. While academics and professionals call for a deeper integration of social media technologies in the classroom, millennials and generation z students come to university. These students are social, mobile, global, digital and visual in nature, so it is imperative to establish digital mechanisms in the classroom that enhance learning by helping students to co-create, collaborate and participate using technology. This research explores the challenges of facing digital native students in the classroom by conducting a practical experiment using social networks in different universities, courses and subjects. Results show that students enjoy integrating social network practices in the classroom, as they perceived them as a tool to increase collaboration, active student participation and collaborative learning. The findings of the paper can be used to propose effective teaching-learning strategies to improve students' performance and satisfaction in higher education.

Keywords: Social networks · Collaborative · E-learning

1 Introduction

The power of social networking is transforming the world. With 2.62b worldwide users in 2018, this number is expected to reach 3.02 by 2021, which means a third of the entire population [50]. 85% of Spanish Internet users use social networks; Facebook and WhatsApp are still the most popular, followed by Youtube, Instagram and Twitter. However, by age, generation Z (16–23 years) prefers to use Instagram, WhatsApp and Youtube, and Millennials (24–38 years) prefer WhatsApp and Facebook [21]. This major usage, combined with the arrival of the millennials to the university classrooms,

L. Uden et al. (Eds.): LTEC 2019, CCIS 1011, pp. 351–361, 2019.
https://doi.org/10.1007/978-3-030-20798-4_30

raises the teaching challenge to adapt the traditional master class to transform the teaching-learning process and adapt it to the new requirements of this digital era.

Following the implementation of the European Higher Education Area (EHEA) and the adoption of the ECTS (European Credit Transfer System) philosophy, universities adopted a methodology in which both the hours of work in the classroom and everything that happens outside of it becomes important from the point of view of the teacher. With this paradigm, universities reduced classroom hours of a master class, in favor of more hours devoted to the acquisition of skills that will support students in their professional future. Besides, the student becomes an active agent of their own learning, with special attention to the skills they must acquire, becoming a proactive and active student, immersed in an environment that fosters know-how and self-initiative [22]. This context favors the use of Information and Communication Technologies (ICT), an issue that universities have not been slow to implement in university teaching [56]. These media provide an efficient environment to develop the fundamental competences that the European Higher Education Area implies, in matters relevant to professional life such as critical thinking, autonomy or the collaborative work of students [13]. This new generation of students has modified the relationship with the world around them and with their learning. They use ICT in formal, non-formal and informal learning contexts, which require teachers to change their strategies [8, 35]. That is why many different ways of involving students in their teaching-learning processes arise in recent years, especially those linked to the use of participatory and collaborative networks such as Facebook, Twitter or Instagram.

Most university students have grown up in a generation dominated by the use of Internet and new technologies. Terms like Net Generation, Millennials or Digital Natives [42, 53] assume that students, because of early exposition to 2.0 technologies, have superior digital skills that change the way they learn. As a result, social media gives learners an opportunity to adapt their learning environment to get more involved in it [20], promoting self-learning and the collaborative creation of knowledge [38]. Consequently, a growing number of research is focusing on the use of social media as a learning tool in higher education [7, 18, 45, 54].

However, there are still challenges and opportunities in the use of social network sites in the learning environment that need further investigation [15, 34]. For example, more studies are needed to incorporate and exploit social networking practices into teaching, or to include geographical or gender differences that could affect to the implementation and use of these sites [44]. Junco [24] consider that there is still little research on the effects of Facebook usage among college students. Consequently, the present research tries to contribute to this research gap by analyzing the use of three different social media tools (Facebook, Twitter and Instagram) in different university courses and subjects both of public and private universities. The empirical results of this study contributes to the literature investigating the effectiveness of using 2.0 technologies in the higher education classroom.

2 Literature Review

The boom in the use of social networks in higher education environments and other educational levels leads researchers to wonder if the practices developed are fostering meaningful learning. This implies that social media can help to build significant relationships through learning communities that encourage the construction of knowledge, thus developing reciprocity in the contribution of new ideas [39], which ultimately allow students to assimilate new knowledge along with others. A large group of researches in recent literature look at the opportunities that social networks offer for the development of the students' teaching-learning process [17, 33, 34, 54]. Other studies emphasize students' use of networks at universities [6, 10, 25, 40]. Studies aimed at understanding the reality of what happens in the classroom are scarcer [31], although teachers are strengthening the use of these practices in their daily lives, both in their personal and professional dimensions [37]. There are several studies that confirm the favorable opportunities that social networks have [15, 33, 34, 44, 54] for the development of knowledge. This research focuses on the contributions of social networks to learning processes in higher education.

In particular, Gao, Luo and Zhang [15] affirmed that microblogging services have a high potential to generate "participation, commitment, reflective thinking, collaborative learning and to expand learning content in different formal and informal ways". Manca and Ranieri [33] acknowledged the potential of Facebook as a technology-enhanced learning environment. Manca and Ranieri [32] showed that most teachers use social media to improve the quality of teaching, to share content or to increase student's motivation and [23] found significant differences in GPA and engagement scores of students using Twitter in the classroom. Alwagait, Shahzad and Alim [1] showed that an increased use of social network does not decrease students' performance. Roblyer et al. and Sturgeon and Walker [43, 52] carried out research to analyze aspects related to the use of Facebook by students and teachers, obtaining revealing data on the interest shown by students in the possibility of using Facebook for educational purposes, issues not found in the research by [30]. Wang et al. [58] showed in their research that most of their students preferred the use of Facebook to the traditional classroom system. Kirschner and Karpinski [27] conducted research with 219 undergraduate and graduate students and found GPAs averages in Facebook users compared to non-user students. In this study, it also became apparent that Facebook users spend fewer hours studying per week as, in general terms, the use of Facebook is considered by students to be fun and informal tool [28]. Moreover, Charlton, Devlin and Drummond [9] found Facebook to be an excellent tool for student collaboration between two different universities with similar modules in order to develop software for a common course project. Other authors, such as [12], used Twitter to share resources and comment on news related to the subject matter of the course, making the students consider this experience as something positive. Tobias [55] wrote about college instructors using Twitter as an extension of the classroom and [59] reported a positive experience on eight students using this microblogging tool to reflect on teaching practices. Silver and Kassens-Noor [26, 49] also introduced Twitter in the higher education classroom with positive results.

Despite the benefits highlighted in the literature, a high number of teachers in universities resist the normalization of the use of these tools in their subjects or do not succeed in making use of them as a method to evaluate students [11, 17]. Other educators, because of the importance of social media in our lives, have studied ways to find partnerships with technology to improve their teaching practices and put students in an active role in learning [2, 36, 48]. Therefore, it is necessary to have different roles in social networks that allow the generation of informal learning [41], with a significant use [29]. Consequently, students are now a proactive agent of his own learning [5, 20], selecting what makes them learn [3, 46], generating his own content as a result of the learning process thanks to the networks [16].

This is one of the most important challenges of today's education, for students to be able to orient their learning to the changing environments we face [47]. It is a challenge to promote "self-directed learning" in the formal educational context mediated by social networks [57]. As is well known, networks not only allow us to generate content in an individualistic way, but also favor the group creation of knowledge [38]. For example, Gikas and Grant [16] highlighted social networks as environments through which students can increase their understanding of what they are creating. Immersion in their own learning facilitates the assimilation of knowledge and makes social networks a catalyst for learning. Millennial students are used to having access to a large amount of information, but sometimes they are not necessarily trained to process it correctly. Barnes, Marateo and Ferris [4] agree with this idea and highlight the benefits of this learning style, emphasizing the need to train our students in issues such as critical thinking because social media without structure can have negative impacts on student learning [16].

Taking all these issues into account, the purpose of this study is to assess the effects of the use of social networks in university classrooms. The aim is to ascertain the effectiveness of the tools based on social networks and to gather the opinions and experiences of university students of four degrees and five different subjects in both public and private universities in order to provide answers to the following questions:

- RQ1: Do students have a willingness to use social media for academic purposes?
- RQ2: Do students in higher education accept this new way of learning through social networks?
- RQ3: Does the use of social media in the class facilitate knowledge sharing?
- RQ4: Do students enjoy using social networks in class for learning purposes?
- RQ5: Does the previous use of social networks in academic contexts predispose students to use them more frequently in class?
- RQ6: Are students willing to use these types of platforms with more intensity in the academic field?

3 Methodology

3.1 Description of the Activity

In order to gather the students' perception of the use of social networks in the teaching field, we designed a practical activity that would be developed in the three main horizontal social networks (Facebook, Instagram and Twitter).

Those responsible for the subjects coordinated a practice with the same structure for each course that was explained to the students in one of the practical classes of it. Thus, the student had to give an opinion on a current topic through the social network selected. For a better localization of the content that the student was publishing in social networks and the reactions he was getting, we requested the use of a specific on each subject. The evaluation of the practice took into account the dissemination of the content obtained (number of likes, number of times shared, etc.), the quality of the content, the reflections in relation to the current topic, the comments from other colleagues, etc.

3.2 Selection of the Sample and Questionnaire

In the present study we analyzed data related to the survey of students in four subjects (mandatory and elective), four degrees and two different undergraduate courses at two universities (one public and one private), with a total of 191 participants out of which 146 answered the questionnaire. Regarding the descriptives of the sample, 76.7% of students were women and the age ranged from 18 to 27 years old. In addition, 92.5% of the students who responded to the questionnaire used social networks daily. We chose such a varied sample of individuals to give robustness to the results of this work.

Table 1. Questionnaire item.

Concept	
Social_Network_perception	1. I find it interesting to exchange academic information on the social network with my teachers 2. The use of social networks for academic purposes is positive 3. The use of social networks is a tool with which you can learn much more 4. The use of social networks promotes social relationships with my classmates 5. The participation of my classmates in the social network has been good 6. The use of social networks is a way of making teaching more participatory 7. The use of social networks encourages students' participation among themselves and with teachers 8. The use of social networks has allowed me to deepen my knowledge in topics that I did not know about 9. Using social networks in the course is innovative

(*continued*)

Table 1. (*continued*)

Concept	
Experience_perception	10. The experience was satisfactory to me 11. In practice, it has been easy to synthesize the idea I wanted to transmit through the social network 12. I think I have communicated the message I wanted to transmit well 13. I liked the comments of my classmates 14. Practice has increased my knowledge of the subject 15. Finding the content of other classmates has been easy 16. I have researched the subject in the accounts of other people outside my class 17. Commenting on other classmates' publications has been rewarding 18. Commenting on other classmates' publications has allowed me to learn more 19. Practice helps me to draw important conclusions on the subject 20. The reward of practice motivates me
Previous_use	21. I had used social networking before in some other university subject
Dependent variables	22. I would like social networks to be used in other subjects/courses as well 23. Global satisfaction with the experience

We collected students' answers by means of an online questionnaire from 14 to 25 May 2018, once the experience with social networks was over. The items can be seen in Table 1. On the one hand, we asked students about their previous attitude or opinion about social networks in the academic context and, on the other hand, we asked questions about the student's opinion about their own experience with social network practice, their overall satisfaction and their willingness to carry out more teaching activities on these platforms.

4 Results and Conclusions

We used IBM SPSS Statistics Version 23.0 software to carry out the methodological analysis of this research. We performed an exploratory factorial analysis of main components with Varimax rotation with the aim of checking whether there were underlying concepts that lead students to develop a satisfaction with the fact that they were carrying out teaching activities on social networks and to develop a future intention to repeat. We selected those items with self-values greater than 1 [19].

In this way, we introduce items 1 to 9 (related to the student's previous perception of social networks in teaching) together and we obtained a single dimension in which all items had a factorial load greater than 0.5 (minimum factorial load: item 4 = 0.678) and a variance extracted of 59.878%. On the other hand, we loaded items 10 to 20 (items related to the student's opinion of the experience made in the subject through social networks) obtaining a minimum factorial load of 0.697 and an extracted variance of 58.443%. These results largely exceed the minimums established in the literature [14, 51]. We performed an additional factorial analysis to verify that the combined load of all independent items of the concept to be tested resulted in two subdimensions. This was the case indeed and these dimensions coincided with those previously mentioned.

We propose the following linear regressions to test whether the concepts raised in the factorial analysis and the previous use of social networks in teaching explained student satisfaction and their future desire to use social networks in the education sector.

$$S_i = \beta_0 + \beta_1 SNP_i + \beta_2 EP_i + \beta_2 PU_i + e_i$$

$$ER_i = \beta_0 + \beta_1 SNP_i + \beta_2 EP_i + \beta_2 PU_i + e_i$$

We observe that the perception of social networks in teaching (beta = 0.23, p = 0.020) and the experience with them in the classroom help explain satisfaction. Thus, we obtain an explanation of this variable with an adjusted R square of 0.609 (p = 0.000). In the case of the student's desire to perform more tests in a social network environment, we observe that all variables are significant in the explanation of the dependent one (R square = 0.621, p = 0.000). Thus, it is the perception of the experience with a beta = 0.433 (p = 0.000) that provides the greatest explanation of the variable, followed by its perception of social networks (beta = 0.347, p = 0.000) and finally, the fact of having already used these platforms in the teaching field (beta = 0.125, p = 0.020) (Table 2).

Table 2. Regressions results

Dependent variable	Independent variable	Beta (sig)	Adjusted R square
Satisfaction (S)	Social_Network_perception (SNP)	0.230 (0.020)	0.609 (0.000)
	Experience_perception (EP)	0.579 (0.000)	
	Previous_use (PU)	−0.058 (0.288)	
Experience_repeat (ER)	Social_Network_perception (SNP)	0.347 (0.000)	0.621 (0.000)
	Experience_perception (EP)	0.432 (0.000)	
	Previous_use (PU)	0.125 (0.020)	

As we can see in the results and in relation to the first research question of the study, we can see how students show a good predisposition to carrying out activities in the teaching field through social networks. In addition, higher education students accept the use of new forms of learning through social networks, so we provide empirical support to answer research question 2. As participants point out, previous contact with these type of platforms facilitates the exchange of knowledge and the active learning of the students (RQ3). But also, students enjoy the experience carried out in these online environments (RQ4) since it mixes the relaxed atmosphere of a social network with the social recognition of the individual and also the learning itself. Consequently, these features make social networks an ideal learning environment in the 21st century.

We have also seen that user's previous experience with social networks in the academic context predisposes him/her to continue using them in the same field (RQ5), which leads us to suppose that those who have already had contact with these online tools have enjoyed or have had a positive memory of them and want to continue using them, which reinforces even more the conclusions obtained for RQ4.

Finally, in terms of students' willingness to increase the intensity of the use of these tools in an academic context, it can be observed that this is indeed the case, thus confirming our RQ5. Moreover, we can also affirm that this fact is motivated by the predisposition towards social networks themselves, the positive feeling in relation to the learning experience of the classroom and the previous contact with this type of social environment in an academic context.

5 Limitations and Future Research Lines

This paper presents some limitations that should be mentioned. On the one hand, the sample used in spite of representing two universities, different degrees and educational levels, should be extended in order to make the model and conclusions more robust. We can easily overcome this limitation by replicating the research methodology in other institutions in Spain or other countries.

On the other hand, the questionnaire used in this paper is not fully tested in the previous literature. This problem lies in the novelty of the work, which has made it difficult to find previous research that completely adapts to this work. However, it should also be noted that the results obtained at the methodological level allow us to ensure that the scales are reliable and consistent. They could therefore be replicated in other studies to propose a new measurement scale.

Future lines of research in this regard focus primarily on overcoming the limitations of the present work. In addition, other experiences will be considered in the context of social networks in order to identify what kind of activities best promote learning in these academic contexts.

References

1. Alwagait, E., Shahzad, B., Alim, S.: Impact of social media usage on students' academic performance in Saudi Arabia. Comput. Hum. Behav. **51**, 1092–1097 (2015)
2. Anderson, P.: What is Web 2.0?: Ideas, technologies and implications for education, vol. 1, no. 1. JISC, Bristol (2007)
3. Attwell, G.: The Personal Learning Environments - the future of eLearning? ELearning Papers **2**(1) (2007)

4. Barnes, K., Marateo, R., Ferris, S.: Teaching and learning with the net generation. Innovate 3 (2007)
5. Bautista, G., Borges, F., Forés, A.: Didáctica universitaria en Entornos Virtuales de Enseñanza-Aprendizaje. Narcea, Madrid (2006)
6. Bennett, S., Bishop, A., Dalgarno, B., Waycott, J., Kennedy, G.: Implementing Web 2.0 technologies in higher education: a collective case study. Comput. Educ. **59**(2), 524–534 (2012)
7. Bosch, T.E.: Using online social networking for teaching and learning: Facebook use at the University of Cape Town. Communication **35**, 185–200 (2009)
8. Calderón, C., Escalera, G.: La evaluación de la docencia ante el reto del Espacio Europeo de Educación Superior. Educación **XX1**(11), 237–256 (2008)
9. Charlton, T., Devlin, M., Drummond, S.: Using Facebook to improve communication in undergraduate software development teams. Comput. Sci. Educ. **19**, 273–292 (2009)
10. Cooke, S.: Social teaching: student perspectives on the inclusion of social media in higher education. Educ. Inf. Technol. **22**, 255–269 (2015)
11. Crook, C.: The 'digital native' in context: tensions associated with importing Web 2.0 practices into the school setting. Oxf. Rev. Educ. **38**(1), 63–80 (2012)
12. Dunlap, J.C., Lowenthal, P.R.: Tweeting the night away: using Twitter to enhance social presence. J. Inf. Syst. Educ. **20**, 129–136 (2009)
13. Esteve, F.: Bolonia y las TIC: de la docencia 1.0 al aprendizaje 2.0. La Cuestión Universitaria **5**, 58–67 (2009)
14. Fornell, C., Larcker, D.F.: Evaluating structural equation models with it unobservable variables and measurement error. J. Mark. Res. **18**, 39–50 (1981)
15. Gao, F., Luo, T., Zhang, K.: Tweeting for learning: a critical analysis of research on microblogging in education published in 2008e2011. Br. J. Educ. Technol. **43**(5), 783–801 (2012)
16. Gikas, J., Grant, M.: Mobile computing devices in higher education: student perspectives on learning with cellphones, smartphones and social media. Internet High. Educ. **19**, 18–26 (2013)
17. Greenhow, C., Askari, E.: Learning and teaching with social network sites: a decade of research in K-12 related education. Educ. Inf. Technol. **22**, 623–645 (2015)
18. Gupta, A.: Scope and implications of social media in the context of higher education: review of researches. MIER J. Educ. Stud. Trends Pract. **4**(2), 231–253 (2014)
19. Hair, J.F., Anderson, R.E., Tatham, R.L., Black, W.C.: Multivariate Data Analysis. Prentice Hall Iberia, Madrid (2010)
20. Hrastinski, S.: A theory of online learning as online participation. Comput. Educ. **52**(1), 78–82 (2009)
21. IAB Spain: Estudio Anual de Redes Sociales 2018. https://iabspain.es/wp-content/uploads/estudio-redes-sociales-2018_vreducida.pdf. Accessed 21 July 2018
22. Joint Quality Initiative: Shared 'Dublin'descriptors for short cycle, first cycle, second cycle and third cycle awards. In: Draft 1, Working Document on JQI Meeting in Dublin (2004)
23. Junco, R., Heiberger, G., Loken, E.: The effect of Twitter on college student engagement and grades. J. Comput. Assist. Learn. **27**(2), 119–132 (2011)
24. Junco, R.: The relationship between frequency of Facebook use, participation in Facebook activities, and student engagement. Comput. Educ. **58**, 162–171 (2012)
25. Karvounidis, T., Chimos, K., Bersimis, S., Douligeris, C.: Evaluating Web 2.0 technologies in higher education using students' perceptions and performance. J. Comput. Assist. Learn. **30**(6), 577–596 (2014)
26. Kassens-Noor, E.: Twitter as a teaching practice to enhance active and informal learning in higher education: the case of sustainable tweets. Act. Learn. High Educ. **13**(1), 9–21 (2012)

27. Kirschner, P.A., Karpinski, A.C.: Facebook and academic performance. Comput. Hum. Behav. **26**, 1237–1245. J. College Stud. Dev. **50**(6), 683–706 (2010)
28. Lewis, J., West, A.: 'Friending': London-based undergraduates' experience of Facebook. New Media Soc. **11**(7), 1209–1229 (2009)
29. Light, D.: Do Web 2.0 right. Learn. Lead. Technol. **38**(5), 10–15 (2011)
30. Madge, C., Meek, J., Wellens, J., Hooley, T.: Facebook, social integration and informal learning at university: it is more for socializing and talking to friends about work than for actually doing work. Learn. Media Technol. **34**, 141–155 (2009)
31. Manca, S., Ranieri, M.: Facebook and the others. Potentials and obstacles of Social Media for teaching in higher education. Comput. Educ. **95**, 216–230 (2016a)
32. Manca, S., Ranieri, M.: Yes for sharing, no for teaching!: social media in academic practices. Internet High. Educ. **29**, 63–74 (2016)
33. Manca, S., Ranieri, M.: Is it a tool suitable for learning? A critical review of the literature on Facebook as a technology-enhanced learning environment. J. Comput. Assist. Learn. **29**(6), 487–504 (2013)
34. Manca, S., Ranieri, M.: Implications of social network sites for teaching and learning. Where we are and where we want to go. Educ. Inf. Technol. **22**, 605–622 (2015)
35. Martínez, P., Echeverría, B.: Formación basada en competencias. Revista de Investigación Educativa **29**(1), 125–147 (2009)
36. McLoughlin, C., Lee, M.J.W.: Personalised and self regulated learning in the web 2.0 era: international exemplars of innovative pedagogy using social software. Australas. J. Educ. Technol. **26**(1), 28–43 (2010)
37. Moran, M., Seaman, J., Tinti-Kane, H.: Blogs, wikis, podcasts and Facebook: how today's higher education faculty use social media. Pearson Learning Solutions and Babson Survey Research Group (2012)
38. Moskaliuk, J., Kimmerle, J., Cress, U.: Wiki-supported learning and knowledge building: effects of incongruity between knowledge and information. J. Comput. Assist. Learn. **25**(6), 549–561 (2009)
39. Ovelar, R., Benito, M.: La transformación tecnológica de los entornos de aprendizaje. Observatorio de eLearning. Universidad del País Vasco (2005)
40. Peruta, A., Shields, A.B.: Social media in higher education: understanding how colleges and universities use Facebook. J. Mark. High. Educ. **27**(1), 131–143 (2017)
41. Preece, J., Nonnecke, B., Andrews, D.: The top five reasons for lurking: improving community experiences for everyone. Comput. Hum. Behav. **20**(2), 201–223 (2004)
42. Prensky, M.: Digital natives, digital immigrants. In: On the Horizon, vol. 9, no. 5. En MCB University Press (2001)
43. Roblyer, M.D., McDaniel, M., Webb, M., Herman, J., Witty, J.V.: Findings on Facebook in higher education: a comparison of college faculty and student uses and perceptions of social networking sites. Comput. Educ. **13**, 134–140 (2010)
44. Rodríguez-Hoyos, C., Haya-Salmon, I., Fernández-Díaz, E.: Research on SNS and education: the state of the art and its challenges. Australas. J. Educ. Technol. **31**(1), 100–111 (2015)
45. Romero, O.C.: Social Media as learning tool in higher education: the case of Mexico and South Korea. Revista Electrónica Sinéctica **44**, 1–15 (2015)
46. Schaffert, S., Hilzensauer, W.: On the way towards Personal Learning Environments: Seven crucial aspects. elearning papers Nº 9 (2008). ISSN 1887-1542
47. Schmitz, B., Schmidt, M., Landmann, M., Spiel, C.: New developments in the field of self-regulated learning. J. Psychol. **215**, 153–156 (2007)
48. Selwyn, N.: Looking beyond learning: notes towards the critical study of educational technology. J. Comput. Assist. Learn. **26**(1), 65–73 (2010)

49. Silver, D.: Twitter Meets the Breakfast Club. The Chronicle of Higher Education (2011). http://chronicle.com/article/Twitter-Meets-the-Breakfast/127379/
50. Statista: Number of Social Media Users Worldwide from 2010 to 2021 (in billions). https://www.statista.com/statistics/278414/number-of-worldwide-social-network-users/. Accessed 30 Oct 2018
51. Steenkamp, J.B.E.M., Geyskens, I.: How Country Characteristics affect the perceived value of a website. J. Mark. **70**(3), 136–150 (2006)
52. Sturgeon, S.M., Walker, C.: Faculty on Facebook: confirm or deny? Paper presented at the 14th Annual Instructional Technology Conference, Murfreesboro, TN (2009)
53. Tapscott, D.: Growing Up Digital: The Rise of the Net Generation. McGraw-Hill, New York (1997)
54. Tess, P.A.: The role of social media in higher education classes (real and virtual) e a literature review. Comput. Hum. Behav. **29**(5), A60–A68 (2013)
55. Tobias, S.P.: College professors find Twitter a useful educational tool. The Wichita Eagle (2009)
56. Uceda, J., Barro, S.: Las TIC en el Sistema Universitario Español: UNIVERSITIC 2008. Conferencia de Rectores de las Universidades Españolas, CRUE, Madrid (2008)
57. Väljataga, T., Fiedler, S.: Supporting students to self-direct intentional learning projects with social media. Educ. Technol. Soc. **12**(3), 58–69 (2009)
58. Wang, Q., Woo, H.L., Quek, C.L., Yang, Y., Liu, M.: Using the Facebook group as a learning management system: an exploratory study. Br. J. Educ. Technol. **43**, 428–438 (2012)
59. Wright, N.: Twittering in teacher education: reflecting on practicum experiences. Open Learn. J. Open Distance E-Learn **25**, 259–265 (2010)

Fostering Foreign Language Learning Through a Telecollaborative Social Media-Based Tandem Language Learning Approach

Alberth[1(✉)], Yun Wang[2], and William Yu Chjung Wang[3]

[1] Department of English Language Education, Universitas Halu Oleo, Kendari, Indonesia
alberth@programmer.net

[2] Department of Fashion Design and Management, National Pingtung University of Science and Technology, Pingtun, Taiwan

[3] Waikato Management School, University of Waikato, Hamilton, New Zealand

Abstract. Traditional tandem language learning (involving two students learning each other's mother tongue) is not a new concept. In fact, it has long been practiced in foreign language classrooms. However, a tandem approach involving learners of different countries using social media is something that has not been fully understood. Theoretically speaking, language acquisition occurs when rich comprehensible input is provided to language learners. Unfortunately, not all language learning contexts can provide this vital input, primarily owing to an inadequate language proficiency level of both teachers and students. In fact, this situation is not uncommon in the English as a Foreign Language (hereafter EFL) context. As a result, foreign language learning is hampered or impeded and little learning can occur, if at all. This paper argues that employing a telecollaborative social media-based tandem language learning approach could help to provide the missing input. With this approach, language learners of different linguistic backgrounds (i.e. native English speakers learning Indonesian and native Indonesian speakers learning English) work collaboratively using social media and assist one another in their learning - following the principle of mutual benefit and reciprocity. Teachers of both groups work together to design learning activities for the students with the aim being to provide ample opportunity for language learners to interact with native speakers of the target language and receive comprehensible input accordingly. Thus, a tandem approach by means of social media, such as Facebook, could help provide input critical to foreign language learning at times when input from the language learning environment is so inadequate. More importantly, a tandem language learning approach is compatible with and attuned to contemporary language learning theories such as Language Acquisition Theory and Constructivism. Finally, a tandem approach also promotes a fruitful collaboration among a wide array of educational institutions worldwide which, in turn, foster an international collaboration and networking.

Keywords: Tandem language learning · Social media · Facebook

L. Uden et al. (Eds.): LTEC 2019, CCIS 1011, pp. 362–368, 2019.
https://doi.org/10.1007/978-3-030-20798-4_31

1 Introduction

Tandem language learning involves students from different linguistic backgrounds, working together and helping each other to learn the target language [1]. During tandem language learning, language learners are paired with native speakers of the target language. For example, native Arabic speakers learning English are paired with native English speakers learning Arabic. These students take turn assuming the role of native speaker of their mother tongue. Successful tandem language learning observes two principles; principles of reciprocity – both groups should support each other equally – and the principles of autonomy – both groups should take control of their own learning [2].

Traditionally, tandem language learning takes place in a conventional face-to-face classroom. The advent of Web 2.0 has brought about new possibilities because its nature of emphasizing on the user-generated content, ease of use, participatory culture and interoperability with various platforms for end users [3].

Thus, it fosters an environment for tele-collaborative tandem language learning and for language learners from different parts of the globe can now learn in-tandem by means of social media. Based on the literature, this paper argues that social media-based tandem language learning (herein after SMB-TLL) offers at least two benefits. First, it fosters language acquisition through the provision of 'comprehensible input' [4] and, second, it promotes fruitful international collaboration and networking among educational institutions across the globe. Throughout the discussion, it is also argued that SMB-TLL is compatible with, and is grounded on, contemporary learning theories, which further justifies its merits.

2 Language Acquisition and SMB-TLL

Ample research evidence shows that language acquisition occurs especially effective when language learners are exposed to sufficient 'comprehensible input' [4] and 'comprehensible output' [5] in the process of negotiation of meaning [6]. In other words, in order for language acquisition to come to pass, language learners should be provided with sufficient time to be exposed to the target language (either through listening or reading), but they should also be provided with adequate time to practice using the target language in the classroom. One of the objectives of any language classroom should, therefore, include optimizing both comprehensible input (opportunity to listen and to read in the target language) and comprehensible output (opportunity to practice the target language) as they are critical to language learning. However, in a conventional face-to-face classroom with the brick and mortar context, the opportunity for being exposed to the target language is so limited due to time constraint available in such a classroom [7]. To make matters worse, use of mother tongue by the teacher is not uncommon in such a classroom and, when the target language is used either by the teacher or the students, at times, there are problems with the grammar or the pronunciation resulting in invalid input. This could, in turn, hamper language acquisition.

This paper argues that introducing SMB-TLL program could potentially overcome the above constraints of linguistic learning processes. To begin with, there is currently a wide range of social media, but for the sake of discussion, this paper will focus on Facebook and all its facets, as this social media is one of the most widely used in the world. One of the by-products of Web 2.0, Facebook is the largest multi-language site on the net [8]. Facebook enables internet users to communicate across different continent, language, and culture. Since Facebook enables users to communicate using different languages, both oral and written, such social networking has great potential to offer in the language classroom [9–11], especially for the teaching and learning of second and foreign languages [12], such as English and Arabic. Thus, use of SMB-TLL could potentially foster language acquisition through dynamic interaction with native speakers of the target language.

As far as SMB-TLL is concerned, Arabic students learning English as a Foreign Language, for example, can be paired with native English speakers learning Arabic, so that students of both nationalities can help each other learn the target language and provide each other with comprehensible input using Facebook as a platform. To do this, teachers of both cohorts should work together to design the learning activities for their students. A simple example to begin with could be to get students interview each other using the target language, either synchronously (chat) or asynchronously (bulletin board/threaded discussion). In the above example, Arabic-speaking students learning English will interview their counterparts – English-speaking students learning Arabic using English and vice-versa. They subsequently report the results of their interview back to their conventional classroom for discussion. In this way, each student is provided with abundant opportunity to receive valid comprehensible input from his or her native speaker partner. More importantly, the context of communication is more authentic, as the language is used for real communication purposes without being constrained by time and space. With effective SMB-TLL, equipped with teacher's good facilitation skills, the problem of limited exposure to the target language in a conventional classroom can be addressed more effectively.

In addition to providing rich comprehensible 'input' and 'output', this paper also argues that use of SMB-TLL is compatible with one of the major tenets of Constructivism [13–15] – the contemporary learning theory. Constructivism postulates that, as far as learning is concerned, social interaction is critical simply because knowledge is constructed through social interaction. This implies that language classroom should promote social interaction among the students and between the students and the teacher. However, again, in a conventional classroom, promoting such interaction is not always easy to achieve, primarily due to time constraints and sometimes the cultural issues. Also, at times, large classes make it difficult for the teacher to organize effective group discussion. What is more, some students are occasionally reluctant to participate in a conventional face-to-face language classroom because they do not want to make mistake in the presence others [16]. In the end, fostering effective and efficient social interaction in a conventional language classroom could be a challenging task for both the teacher and the students.

Empirical evidence suggests that, using online media, language learners are inclined to participate in the social interaction processes. For example, previous research confirms that online discussion among language learners attract more participation than its counterpart face-to-face discussion and that language learners feel more comfortable to participate in such learning milieu [17]. Thus, since one of the important goals of language classroom, as far as Constructivism and Language Acquisition theories are concerned, is to promote social interaction among language learners, it becomes immediately apparent that tandem language learning is compatible with these contemporary learning theories. As far as Constructivism is concerned, social interaction that takes place during tandem exchanges serves as both 'a means to an end' and 'an end in itself'. In other words, social interaction is both an instrument for learning the target language and the goal of learning itself. It is not surprising that the web is often referred to as "a vehicle for constructivist approaches in language learning" [18, p. 2]. However, as noted earlier, successful e-tandem language learning observes two principles; principles of reciprocity – both groups should support each other equally – and the principles of autonomy – both groups should take control of their own learning [2].

In a nutshell, SMB-TLL should be seriously considered when teaching foreign languages in this century, as dynamic interaction with native speakers afforded by the media could potentially provide the learners with rich 'comprehensible input' and 'comprehensible input', thus enabling language acquisition to occur. This is especially promising since research studies indicate that students enjoy using Facebook [8, 19, 20]. Needless to say, more research is needed to better understand how to effectively and efficiently use Facebook as a platform for tandem language learning program.

In the following section, the second benefit of SMB-TLL is discussed – promoting international collaboration among educational institutions around the world.

3 Promoting International Collaboration

A part from the benefit related to improved language proficiency, another benefit of SMB-TLL is that it could potentially promote fruitful collaboration among educational institutions across the globe [2, 7]. Needless to say, in order for a tandem language learning program to occur, teachers of two institutions, or more, should work together to design the learning activities that need to be included and to decide on their own roles as teachers during tandem exchanges. Intensive collaboration between teachers and students from different educational institutions worldwide could potentially foster tighter collaboration between these institutions, especially when such a program is perceived to be mutually beneficial by all parties concerned. Thus, again, in order for a tandem language learning program to develop into more formal partnership and collaboration, it is extremely important that all parties ensure that each is benefitted from such a program.

A tandem language learning program can easily be followed up by the signing of MoU between interested institutions on a wide range of collaborative programs such as teaching, research, student and staff exchange, just to name a few. In the long run, tandem language learning initiative can be regarded as the seed of, or the stepping stone towards, international collaboration among educational institutions in the world on the basis of mutual-benefit partnership. In the following section, we will discuss how SMB-TLL is relevant to language learning in the 21st century.

4 SMB-TLL and Foreign Language Learning in the 21st Century

The turn of the 21st Century is heralded by the omnipresence of social media such as Facebook and Twitter, just to name a few. As argued previously, this social media has a great potential to offer in foreign language classroom through SMB-TLL programs. Interestingly, the advent of this social network coincides with significant changes in the principles of foreign language teaching and learning. For example, it has been argued that grammar is no longer the focus of language education in the 21st century [21]. Instead, language learners are encouraged to use the target language for communication purposes. Thus, the ability to communicate using the target language becomes the main priority of foreign language classroom in this century. In this case, the advent of social media is a welcome coincidence simply because of its capability to support communication and social interaction between language learners and native speakers of the target language around the world. This paper argues that SMB-TLL is especially important not only because of the changes in the principles of foreign language teaching and learning in this century, but more importantly, because of the classical shortcomings associated with foreign language classroom today. These limitations will be discussed one after the other and this paper will show how SMB-TLL could potentially help reduce, if not get rid of, such limitations.

To begin with, language learners are afforded with limited exposure to the target language [7] during ordinary foreign language classroom and this is particularly true when the target language is taught along with other distinct subjects in the curriculum. To make matters worse, during this very limited time, it is not uncommon that use of the target language by the teacher is also so limited. As a result, language learners receive so little 'comprehensible input' [4] during regular meeting in the classroom. Nor are they afforded sufficient time to experiment with their 'comprehensible output' [5]. In the end, language acquisition is barely possible in such a learning environment. As noted earlier, SMB-TLL in the curriculum could help provide language learners with ample opportunities to be exposed to both 'comprehensible input' and 'comprehensible output' through social interaction with native speaker partners, thus optimizing language acquisition. What is more, such communication is not constrained by time and space.

The second limitation of a typical foreign language classroom concerns language proficiency of the teacher [7]. At times, the teacher himself does not have sufficient language proficiency or has limited understanding of the culture of the people speaking the language (of course, teacher's language proficiency varies; some teachers are more proficient than the others). As a result, language learners are exposed to inaccurate forms, expressions, or pronunciation. Without appropriate feedback, the learners will keep producing the same errors in the future. Again, SMB-TLL is so helpful when it comes to providing feedback. A native speaker partner could provide corrective feedback on any unacceptable forms, expressions, or pronunciation in such a way that both speakers could improve their language proficiency. Of course, these students should discuss right from the very beginning how they should provide feedback to each other under the auspices of the teachers.

Foreign language teaching and learning in the 21st century is benefited immensely by the advent of social media and it appears that use of this social network in language classroom will soon gain popularity. For one thing, social media appears to be able to address most, if not all, of the classical shortcomings associated with conventional foreign language classroom. However, it is important to bear in mind that the roles of the teacher in facilitating tandem exchanges will remain vital and cannot be replaced by technology. SMB-TLL requires that teachers be familiar with technology and, in the end, it is every institution's responsibility to provide on-going training and support to foreign language teachers. Only then, can we expect fruitful SMB-TLL.

5 Concluding Remarks

The turn of the 21st century has seen the ubiquity of social media and this paper argues that SMB-TLL offers at least two benefits. First, it could potentially foster language acquisition through the provision of both 'comprehensible input' and 'comprehensible output' and, second, it may well promote fruitful collaboration among educational institutions across the globe through tandem language learning initiatives. Whereas the examples discussed in this paper focus exclusively on SMB-TLL, it is important to emphasize that, strictly speaking, tandem exchanges are not limited to language learning only. Use of tandem exchanges is also appropriate for the teaching and learning of other subjects. This research notion has some limitation related to the learner's personal characters, cultural issues and the context of a certain type of social media. Therefore, future research may investigate the confirmation of the notions mentioned in the paper and bring in more parameters in investigating their influences to the learning motivation and outcome. In sum, despite the potential benefits of SMB-TLL, teachers still need to decide for the classes how to whether or not to opt for SMB-TLL and how to do so in their teaching in order to meet the demands.

References

1. Alberth, A.: Technology-enhanced teaching: a revolutionary approach to teaching English as a foreign language. TEFLIN **24**(1), 1–13 (2013)
2. Little, D., Ushioda, E.: Designing, implementing and evaluating a project in tandem language learning via e-mail. ReCALL **10**(1), 95–101 (1998)
3. John, N.A.: Sharing and Web 2.0: the emergence of a keyword. New Media Soc. **15**(2), 167–182 (2013)
4. Krashen, S.D.: The Input Hypothesis: Issues and Implications. Longman, London (1985)
5. Swain, M.: Three functions of output in second language learning. In: Cook, G., Seidhofer, G. (eds.) Principles and Practices in Applied Linguistics: Studies in Honor of H.G. Widdowson. Oxford University Press, Oxford (1995)
6. Gass, S.M., Varonis, E.M.: Variation in native speaker speech modification to non-native speakers. Stud. Second Lang. Acquisition **7**, 37–58 (1985)
7. Cziko, G.A.: Electronic tandem language learning (eTandem): a third approach to second language learning for the 21st Century. CALICO J. **22**(1), 25–39 (2004)

8. Grosseck, G., Bran, R., Tiru, L.: Dear teacher, what should I write on my wall? A case study on academic uses of Facebook. Proc. Soc. Behav. Sci. **15**, 1425–1430 (2011)
9. Chartrand, R.: Social networking for language learners: creating meaningful output with Web 2.0 tools. Knowl. Manag. E-Learn. Int. J. **4**(1), 97–101 (2012)
10. Godwin-Jones, B.: Emerging technologies: web-writing 2.0: enabling, documenting, and assessing writing online. Lang. Learn. Technol. **12**(2), 7–13 (2008)
11. Kabilan, M.K., Ahmad, N., Abidin, M.J.Z.: Facebook: an online environment for learning of English in institutions of higher education? Internet High. Educ. **13**, 179–187 (2010)
12. Reinhardt, J., Zander, V.: Social networking in an intensive English program classroom: a language socialization perspective. CALICO J. **28**(28), 326–344 (2011)
13. Allen, K.: Online learning: constructivism and conversation as an approach to learning. Innov. Educ. Teach. Int. **42**(3), 247–256 (2005)
14. Boudourides, M.A.: Constructivism, education, science, and technology. Can. J. Learn. Technol. **29**(3) (2003)
15. Schcolnik, M., Kol, S., Abarbanel, J.: Constructivism in theory and in practice. Engl. Teach. Forum **4**, 12–20 (2006)
16. Alberth: How effective are technology-enhanced teaching techniques in the EFL classroom? Curtin University of Technology, Perth (2012)
17. Freiermuth, M.R.: Native speakers or non-native speakers: who has the floor? Online and face-to-face interaction in culturally mixed small groups. Comput. Assist. Lang. Learn. **14** (2), 169–199 (2001)
18. Felix, U.: The Web as a vehicle for constructivist approaches in language teaching. ReCALL **14**(1), 2–15 (2002)
19. Madge, C., Meek, J., Wellens, J., Hooley, T.: "Facebook", social integration and informal learning at university: "It is more for socialising and talking to friends about work than for actually doing work". Learn. Media Technol. **34**(2), 141–155 (2009)
20. Pempek, T.A., Yermolayeva, Y.A., Calvert, S.L.: College students' social networking experiences on Facebook. J. Appl. Abilityal Psychol. **30**(3), 227–238 (2009)
21. Eaton, S.E.: Global Trends in Language Learning in The Twenty-First Century. Onate Press, Calgary (2010)

Social Media Services Ecosystem for Marginalized Youth to Access Adult Education

Kai Pata[1(✉)] and Sille Paas[2(✉)]

[1] School for Digital Technologies, Center for Educational Technology, Narva Road 25, 10120 Tallinn, Estonia
kpata@tlu.ee

[2] Education Technology Centre, Tallinn University of Technology, Ehitajate tee 5, 19086 Tallinn, Estonia
sille.paas@taltech.ee

Abstract. This paper discusses the development of the reference interaction model for enhancing young marginalized adults (16–30) from various vulnerability backgrounds to access adult education opportunities by social media-based services' ecosystem. The paper drives from H2020 project EduMap case studies' data conducted with young people in different European countries: with migrant background (Turkey, Germany, Austria, UK), NEET and special education background (Estonia, UK, Finland, Austria), prison education background (Finland), roma background (Romania, Spain) and homeless youth (Greece). The qualitative reports were analysed for interaction patterns using concept mapping approach, and the reference model of interactions was developed. Based on the reference model, six interaction scenarios were developed as comics, which were evaluated formatively by focus group and 15 stakeholders. The design guidelines for social media services ecosystem were developed, to support using the reference interaction model and the scenarios for developing supportive social media ecosystems in countries that support the access to adult education for marginalized adults.

Keywords: Marginalized young adults · Vulnerable · NEET · Migrant · Homeless · Social media services ecosystem · Access to adult education

1 Introduction

This paper proposes an empirical study based design solution how to support marginalized groups of young adults to be part of society, enhancing their access to adult education (AE) opportunities with social media based ecosystem of services. Research literature of the marginalized adults' communicative interactions in educational domain is not substantial. In the European Council report (Bellardi et al. 2018) about spaces of inclusion highlights the role of virtual and face-to-face networks in affording social capital with regard to problem solving (administrative procedures, access to health care and social welfare, housing etc.). It suggests to multiply visibility and access to media content and training through partnerships with civil society

L. Uden et al. (Eds.): LTEC 2019, CCIS 1011, pp. 369–380, 2019.
https://doi.org/10.1007/978-3-030-20798-4_32

organisations, local institutions, public service and commercial media. Our study was undertaken under H2020 research and innovation project EduMap, that aimed at decreasing the gap in the knowledge how to make AE best accessible to the vulnerable groups. Our design research targets particularly the opportunities and issues summarized by EduMap project in the Communicative ecologies report (Tacchi and Sabiescu 2019) about the communicative ecologies of marginalized young adults' groups: (i) Potential of social networks for information access: Social networks are the most effective ways of passing on educational information to young people and heightening chances of follow-up. Social networks refer to personal and professional contacts that are close to young people, and whom young people trust. Communication among these networks can be direct or mediated, diversely by voice services, digital and social media. In most instances, it is the human factor and direct contact with young people that makes them valuable for enhancing young people's access to AE information. (ii) Potential of blending social networks and digital media: Digital media can be an effective means to reach out to young people if used in conjunction with direct communication through personal and professional networks close to young people. (iii) Access to digital media and Internet: Mobile device ownership is most wide spread, though in some cases (like the Romanian Roma) they can be shared in the family. WhatsApp is the most used and preferred application among some groups, also Facebook and YouTube are more used. The use of Instagram, well established in some contexts, appears to be popular especially among the younger people, 16 to 18. (iv) Communication challenges: Some young adult groups are difficult to reach. Many young adults in vulnerable situations lack the capacity to navigate social services. Young people's digital practices tend to be more focused on entertainment than on active information research about AE opportunities. Accessing AE requires active mediation by advisers using blended channels. Language barriers often prevent young refugees and migrants from accessing AE information.

The main research question in our design research was: *How can access to Adult Education (AE) programmes be improved for vulnerable marginalized groups using blended face-to-face and social media and supportive services?*

2 Service Based Social Media to Support Marginalized Young Adults

A possible approach using ecosystem principles in the society domain is a service-based ecosystem approach. The service is generally defined as a flow of logically combined products (units, inventories, activities) between the service providers and the users through the operating level management, in accordance to the outlined processes, rules or definitions (Sipina 2011). Services comprise the following components: attributes (inventories, units, monetary and nonmonetary sources), provider, service manager, service user, activities (necessary for delivering service to the user), and accompanying rules and/or processes how user will consume the service. In the society, we may define different stakeholders that can be viewed as the kind of species within ecosystem. For example, we may view young marginalized adults, adult educators, social advisors, employers as the relevant stakeholder groups when exploring the vulnerability of young adults that lack opportunities for active citizenship. Secondly, the service ecosystem for young marginalized adults contains processes that take place between different stakeholder groups in the society. The types of services within the adult learning ecosystem will cover not only the services that directly provide access to the AE, but also the social or legal services that enable access to AE by removing constraints the young adults may experience: age range to fit to certain educational level, education level to access certain AE, language and citizenship, location, family- and economic situation, employability status- and disability. Services mutually constrain or extend the opportunities for specific stakeholder groups. They may be considered as ecosystem potentialities that could be validated by the actualization of services from the specific stakeholders' point of views. However, young adults from the service receiver groups cannot be unified under the limited number of category types. Rather every person is unique and has unique combination of characteristics that all together build the constraints and service needs for the young adults to become active and participatory citizen. Desjardins and Rubenson (2011) provide a model of characteristics that influence participation in AE: (i) Individual characteristics: social background, being immigrant, age, gender, education and qualification, competences, experiences, actual competences; (ii) Work-related characteristics: job context, job tasks, need for competences, usage of competences, organizational structures, innovation and adaptation level of organizations, career opportunities, training opportunities, work safety, salary, effectiveness, flexibility of work; (iii) Environmental characteristics: socio-cultural norms and practices, trade unions role, political context.

In the social media-based ecosystem that aims to bring young marginalized groups to AE there is the need to identify and provide support to different aspects that constrain young adults. This requires personal approach to discovering what the constraints in every person's case are, and proposing how similar persona types have benefitted from supportive services. We propose considering the vulnerability through the set of characteristics presented in the service target group model. Such a model allows describing any young adult at risk as unique a combination (Downes 2014).

3 Methodology

Sites and sampling: In EU FP project Edumap (http://blogs.uta.fi/edumap/), partners conducted the research in AE environments, and within selected groups of young people at risk of social exclusion in seven EU countries (Finland, Germany, Greece, Hungary, Romania, Spain, UK) and Turkey. These case reports, and the summarized findings presented in the report (Tacchi and Sabiescu 2019) were analyzed using concept-mapping of interaction paths. The interaction scenarios for enhancing dialogue between AE providers and vulnerable young adults were developed taking the following steps: The reference conceptual model was developed from different concept maps of the cases. Guided by the reference model, six possible generalized interaction paths were extracted that focus on advisory practices at different support organizations, social media, social networks, and digital social innovation services. Based on these interactions the generalized stories were developed using comics storytelling approach. The evaluation of scenarios by survey was conducted with 12 persons (mainly in the role of counsellers and adult educators from UK, Estonia, Greece, Finland, Germany, Taiwan); and by interviews 3 persons (social workers from Estonia). The survey asked the following aspects: Where does the scenario work? Could the stakeholder use it? What needs to be changed in the scenario? Could you provide new scenario ideas? The findings were summarized as the design framework.

4 Results

4.1 Conceptual Reference Model of Interactions Within the Social Media-Based Service Ecosystem to Promote Young Adults to Access Adult Education

We built our interaction scenario elements on essential elements that enable young people to reach out to information, identify suitable opportunities and engage in AE programmes that make a difference for their lives: (i) the capacity to aspire and construct goals; (ii) access to social networks and hubs; (iii) access to relevant content and information; (iv) access and use of relevant media and platforms; and (v) possession of needed information and communication competences and literacies (Tacchi and Sabiescu 2019). We developed a conceptual reference interaction map (Fig. 1) that summarized different case studies' results of focus group interviews.

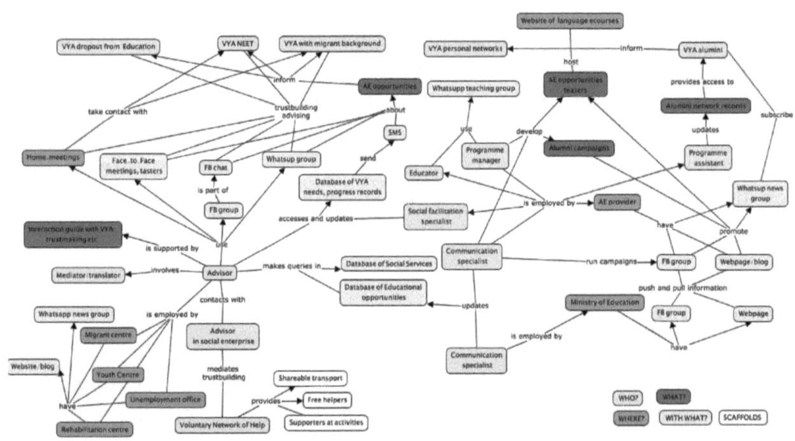

Fig. 1. Reference framework for interactions in social media-based service ecosystem to support young marginalized adults to access Adult education

4.2 The Interaction Scenarios for Social Media-Based Service Ecosystem to Support Young Marginalized Adults to Access Adult Education

In the second phase of the design study we developed based on the conceptual reference map of interactions the interaction scenarios (S1–S6). We used the visual cartoon-based storytelling approach (with software Pixton.com) to depict the interaction patterns. This approach enabled to generalize the roles and places visually.

Scenario 1. Communication ecosystem with social media (S1[1])
Problem/issue: Different stakeholder organizations that target young adults' active citizenship as a goal separately run distributed social media sites in Facebook, blogs, Instagram, Youtube to conduct social media campaigns for accessing youth and bringing them to education, job and social services'. There is the need to effectively prompt information across such media, so that it reaches potentially to all.

Audience/Context: Central AE policy organizations at regional and local level, AE providers, youth-, employment-, migration- and rehabilitation centres that provide counselling, specialists' networks and associations run their own web pages to share news and specific information about AE and additional services. The web-pages have the blogs, that can be pushed/pulled to social media such as Facebook or WhatsApp groups, monitored by personal aggregators or shared across platforms. Some of these Facebook pages are monitored by thousands of youth, adult educators and counselling specialists. They incorporate also Youtube for sharing videos about the learning facilities, and best practice cases in AE, and the Instagram or Snapchat for sharing visual materials about vocational competitions or job-related designs etc. The Facebook pages may be used for promotion campaigns, such as winning the access tickets to the training events, selecting the best specialists based on videos. Campaigns and competitions prompt visits and sharing of media content about jobs, practices, careers and learning opportunities.

Solution: Seamless access to information across social media between the coordinating organizations for young adults. The interconnected social media will provide more relevant content to young adults independent of their access points.

Discussion/consequences/implementation: Orchestrating social media of different organizations into the communication ecosystem where information can be pushed and pulled across partners may increase information visibility and prompt education-, job- and social services-directed informedness and engagement among young adults. It also makes up the cohesive secondary communicative ecosystem where different organizations can be aware of each others' initiatives and approaches.

Related patterns: S1 scenario links with the S3 (social facilitator): the Facebook pages are used for providing immediate contact with advising persons. While already at the place young adults may become aware of more information and take part of other offered engagement. S1 scenario associates with the S4 (alumni network).

Purpose: Media layer augmentation to embed Information layer elements, such as hidden advisor mediated prompting to promote AE.

Scenario 2 - Hidden advisor (S2[2])
Problem/issue: Often young adults from vulnerable background have few interests except hanging around in social media interest groups or playing various multiplayer games with virtual friends. This is the community they may trust more than official advisors. It is difficult to identify such young persons, to get familiar with their problems to offer adequate help to return to learning or work.

[1] https://www.pixton.com/schools/storyboard/e6ieff80.

[2] https://www.pixton.com/schools/storyboard/97ek6mj1.

Audience/Context: There are cases when youth centres have organized projects where as part of the project young adults from vulnerable background are engaged into the interest groups or gamified activities that are no related directly to studies or work. In the interest group or game settings the youth workers who participate in the game become more familiar with the young people, they get trusted relationships and often young people mention the problems they have in life. This augmented to settings advisory practice is the leverage that may be built on to invite young people to receive more guidance in their life.

Solution: Scenario S2 describes the approach of augmented (hidden) advising. Often young adults develop passions and interests around social media groups, multiplayer games, e-sport activities etc. These activities may be used as entry points to gain access to young adults, develop trusted relationships, and open up for them new opportunities in AE programmes.

Discussion/consequences/implementation: This scenario requires situation augmented trained advisors as trustees, that do not violate young persons' privacy and rights in deciding about their needs and consider all ethical principles.

Related patterns: The scenario may be combined with S3 (social advisor), as the problems and needs of the person have been identified, some more formal forms of advising may be following to find suitable AE opportunities and supportive services. The scenario may be combined with scenario S5 to discover the opportunities for voluntary network of support. Finally, the S4 (alumni network) may be used also for recruiting new players to the game using the snowball methodology.

Scenario 3 - Social facilitator (S3[3])

Problem/issue: Bringing young adults from vulnerable background to organizations where they get advice and guidance in the career, job, or can discover AE that fit for their needs, as well as, helping them to discover supportive services that enable the access is difficult, because young vulnerable people do not have sufficient self-drive and communication competences to set up visits to official places they are not familiar with. The drawback of digital media is that young people do not know where to look for AE, so they first need to find out about and follow up on leads and tips from contacts. There is lack of knowledge about the local AE system and opportunities among young adults from vulnerable groups, and lack of support structures for turning information into decisions. Another issue is that while young people are falling out from educational institutions, they lose contact with the institutional advisors, and are not transferred smoothly to the next coaches in their life path. There are no complete track records of life paths of vulnerable young adults, because the data from advising events are kept in different data systems.

Audience/Context: The scenario (S3) targets young adults that have low communication skills for setting up meetings in official organizations they are not familiar with (rehabilitation centres, educational advisory centres, unemployment centres etc.). The scenario depicts the key advisory role of professional figures such as community and social workers, local administration youth contact points etc. in mediating AE

[3] https://www.pixton.com/schools/comic/3epp70kk.

information to young adults from vulnerable groups. Advising typically is accompanied by using different databases to track down the records of interviewed people for further sharing among different advisory bodies and organizations, searching for AE that fit the profile of young adults from vulnerable groups, and the accompanying services to scaffold access to the AE and compensating the lack in young adults from vulnerable groups agency.

Solution: The different advisory practices (at schools, vocational places, rehabilitation centres, youth centres) should have connections across social media (S1). The initial contact with young people can be developed through lightweight chat such as Facebook Messenger, Instagram or others that young people use in their everyday practice. The young adults can be invited to talk with different advisors, before the face-to-face meeting is set up. In order to have track records of young persons' life paths towards educational and vocational opportunities, the advisors in organizations may fill in the records of young adults in shared databases, or by using linked data approach, they should easily access earlier records made by different advisors. The anonymized track records may be used for intelligent decision support systems to discover gaps and predict needs and successful vocational and educational choices in for specific young adult types. The advisors should also use the educational information and social service systems in combined searches to make relevant offers to young adults in need. Blending different advice forms is useful and promotes discovering and engaging better with young adults.

Discussion/consequences/implementation: This scenario was found to be the most relevant one, since advising is the main access channel of young adults to AE. The young adults from vulnerable groups are characterized by very rarely purposefully looking for AE. The use of digital and social media for personal browsing and entertainment is not an indication that these are also used for accessing information about AE. The tracking of young adults' records has been implemented in some countries, however privacy concerns apply, as well as the equality reasons. The tracking methods should not be used for specific vulnerable groups only. It has also been argued that real advising should happen in secure settings, not in social media, that is controlled by international corporations. e-mail is not very reliable with young adults from vulnerable groups as a communication channel, it is problematized by many users who admitted they do not check it regularly.

Related patterns: S3 scenario relates with S1 (communication ecosystem), since the Facebook groups of AE or associations providing advising services often use live chat (Facebook Messenger) for first immediate information sharing. The best way for AE information to reach out to youth is through blended channels that merge direct information provided through contacts, organizational mediators and social networks, with information provided through a variety of digital and social media.

Scenario 4 – Alumni network (S4[4])

Problem/issue: Many adults with migrant background hardly use other channels of information than trusted inner community groups in Messenger or WhatsApp. Access these persons in need for education may be gained by the alumni, who already

4 https://www.pixton.com/schools/storyboard/xjixt5am.

experienced how education might change their life. Educational organizations have not managed to build up access and information sharing to inner networks of migrants with the help of the alumni. Sustaining post-course alumni communication has challenges – the lack of resources; formal impediments to maintaining contact (privacy, data protection); transiting from informal to structured practices.

Audience/Context: The audience of this scenario is particular migrant and cultural groups who keep their identity by communicating mainly with their inner communities. In such communities, the trust is built by the members who have experienced success in their life path and may advice others. While educational institutions are successfully communicating with their students, they lose the track of them after graduation. The study groups created with social media may be used to build alumni networks. The task of communicating with alumni may be transferred from educators to communication specialists who can develop targeted campaigns through social media of institutions, also in WhatsApp and Messenger chat.

Solution: S4 provides the ways of accessing an inner community or group focus using personal social media in WhatsApp. The scenario creates the linkage between trustworthy acquaintances from AE, associations, community centres or social care centres and inner social networks cultivated informally among friends and family.

Discussion/consequences/implementation: There needs to be motivational elements to promote such alumni channels and post-studies information sharing to the inner networks.

Related patterns: Scenario relates with S6 (Learning with WhatsApp). Scenario makes use of the fact that the value of social networks increases exponentially when young people benefit from the support of a cohesive community or group, young vulnerable adults appreciate above all personal contacts as sources for information, including when it comes to finding out about learning or job opportunities.

Scenario 5 – Voluntary help network (S5[5])

Problem/issue: Young adults with vulnerable background often face several obstacles to access AE. They need additional social services, but often the services they need are not available in their localities (such as while living in remote areas, they need transport, or babysitting help). Other young adults have issues with self-directing their studies and work, or communicating in formal settings and they might benefit from study peers, or mentors.

Audience/Context: While the young person may access centrally several services that facilitate AE, there may still be the need for tailored services to remove all the constraints to facilitate persons' agency. Such constraints may be related with their lack of self-organization or communication literacy, disability or inexperience in new situations where the person may need to find the more experienced study-body or friend. Alternatively, the persons may need the lift with the car, or caretaking of their children or relatives at home while they are studying. In the best cases, such voluntary help networks should be mediated to young adults from vulnerable groups by the advisors at different advisory related centres.

[5] https://www.pixton.com/schools/storyboard/4iqo27t4.

Solution: S5 depicts the emerging social enterprise based opportunities to extend the support to young adults from vulnerable groups using the active participatory citizen based approaches to get support and scaffolding.

Discussion/consequences/implementation: The voluntary help network is a new sharing-economy based service, that enables the young adults from vulnerable groups themselves and the alumni of AE (former young adults from vulnerable groups) to offer services also to others, such as mentoring, language support or the lift with car.

Related patterns: This pattern relates with S3 (advising practices).

Scenario 6 – WhatsApp learning group (S6[6])

Problem/issue: The persons from informationally isolated or culturally constrained communities primarily use social media such as WhatsApp for communicating with inner communities. They do not have digital tools to learn other than mobiles. The group's specific cultural and social norms and values may also shape possibilities to use social media for learning. Even educated women access some information via their male relatives rather than from direct contact with the institutions. Their agency to develop autonomous communication and information practices is severely restricted by their domestic and care responsibilities.

Audience/Context: Characteristic to communicative dialogues in informationally isolated or culturally constrained communities are that word of mouth and social networks are among the most important ways of accessing information about AE; information is delivered locally through trusted information sources such as community centres, local foundations or informal community leaders; key mediators such as support organizations, foundations, or caretakers have a central role. These places may be used for offering learning opportunities.

The persons from informationally isolated or culturally constrained communities who already access AE, also use the social context of their courses to develop WhatsApp networks that may offer information about future opportunities. Persons appreciate if WhatsApp or Messenger are used for personalized help and advice either from tutors or advisors at the college, or from within their social networks, because information available on the internet can be confusing and unclear. The follow-up after-course communication of WhatsApp course may range from maintaining relationships and networks, with a general purpose of connecting, sharing and keeping in touch, to supporting people in their personal lives and preventing set-backs.

Solution: This scenario S6 depicts the WhatsApp engagement with the young adults belonging to informationally isolated or culturally constrained communities. In general, the solution to the cultural isolation problem is social layer repurposing, such as social media study groups may be developed for sharing information within informally isolated communities.

Discussion/consequences/implementation: Some groups of young adults may be digitally disconnected, having access to Internet only in the care facility they regularly attend, where their agency is enhanced by their own knowledge and motivations to communicate, computers, WIFI and the social workers who manage the centre, among other factors. Persons may be sharing mobile phones and Facebook profiles.

[6] https://www.pixton.com/schools/comic/ja6n1tcb.

Related patterns: This scenario relates with S4 (alumni network), since the social media based learning groups may be transformed to alumni networks.

4.3 The Evaluation of Interaction Scenarios

The interaction scenarios were shared publicly at EduMap blog post, EPALE post in Estonia, Helpific.com social network, in the network of Youth centers (Noorte tugila) in Estonia and among the Edumap partners by email. The feedback to the scenarios was collected using online survey. The scenarios were viewed online by many persons. The scenarios were evaluated in the survey by 12 persons, and in focus groups by 3 persons. The cartoon-based interaction stories were found useful in discussing the scenarios with different stakeholders (advisors, adult educators, young adults with different level of literacies). The critical issues:

S1: The new social media approaches to enhance marginalized young adults' groups to access AE would also require training; there aren't free human resource to help marginalized young adults with social media; there are better ways of sharing information between AE institution than social media; social media does not necessary represent the whole spectrum of services different support service organizations provide; young people do not use Facebook; Protecting anonymity was considered a concern in the communication using social media.

S2: Ethically problematic, as it invades to personal space and violates marginalized young adults privacy; linguistic issue may emerge in hidden advising; gaining trust while being hidden is a method used by online perpetrators; It is important to consider the willingness of young persons to be advised; It is important to reveal the intention and presence of embedded advisor roles from the beginning if such are used; pitfalls of using multiplayer games as medium were related with the lack of interaction between players and the facilitator; to contact the marginalized young adults rather in their activity places than in social media.

S3: Several marginalized groups may benefit from the advisor mediated AE access scenario, while others cannot be accessed so easily; the inadequacy in advising may emerge from the lack of suitable offers for marginalized young adults' group; It would be important that the advisors have access to dynamically updated databases to AE; distrust and data privacy concerns related with personal lifelong data; need for smooth transitional phase; need for the Information Sharing Protocol across social workers; not sharing personal information with third parties; using interview guidelines, that would be more immersive and closer to the communication forms of young people.

S4: There aren't such follow up tools of alumni; the data protection and privacy.

S6: Using WhatsApp requires different course design.

Beyond specific scenarios some general concerns emerged with the comics based visual scenario approach: Overall, the graphics for scenarios need to avoid stereotypization that might invoke stereotypization (racial, ethnic, gender, behavioral); The facial expressions and the body postures may cause mood and motivation related stereotypization). The scenes at cartoons may show too speedy and optimistic progress, and do not show the trust building as a lengthy process.

5 Discussion

The findings from the scenarios were summarized to the key principles. Interaction scenarios must consider some critical problems: access to different marginalized young adults' groups, ethical implications of suggested interaction behaviors, data protection and privacy, linguistic issues, stereotypization of stakeholders at scenarios regarding racism, digital equality, gender equality but also stereotypization about their roles, motivations and behaviors. Scenarios may serve as the reference architecture to develop communicative ecosystems for enhancing the access of youth to AE.

The vulnerable groups cannot be described by official categories such as NEET, migrant, or refugee, but vulnerability associates with complex combination of cultural, educational, social, economic background, the passiveness to take part of active life, regional, literacy or language constraints and disabilities, gender constraints and digital equality and literacy. For each country, the target groups must be specified and their communicative patterns described. The communicative ecosystems of similar marginalized young adults' groups vary. The trends that affect access to marginalized young adults' groups associate with their accessibility: in specific places (like refugee camps, schools); difficulties in identifying their localities (like school drop-outs, long term migrants); according to the services they are accessing (such as people who get social services) and needs (passive young adults, with low communication competences, self-regulation and literacy, young adults in remote locations, homeless). For tailoring different needs the communicative ecosystem requires several interaction paths. Other important roles are advisor, communication specialist and educator. In the regional communicative ecosystem several complementary roles may be needed to support different marginalized groups.

The main organizations providing advice, education, support should be identified. Similar interaction practices with media must be introduced across complementary roles. The data of vulnerable needs to be updated in databases. Guiding young adults transitionally between advising, supporting and teaching stakeholders is needed.

The data about AE and services must be harvested dynamically. The data of young adults (if tracked along life path) must be protected, the linked data approaches should be used across different data recording systems to enable also the application of future intelligent decision support engines to be used in providing relevant and tailored AE advice.

The tailored to marginalized groups media content should be developed about AE, that can be used across platforms. There could be motivational packages to scale up the access young adults (e.g. gamified approaches to collect badges, points, achieving small successes through different personalized life paths). One of the future features in educational and supportive services' databases is the intelligent recommendation tailored to personal needs but also predictive data models.

The growing dependency of corporative controlled social media is predicted. Corporative media layer defines the interaction (free and payed) that can be used for advertising AE with games, campaigns or other means. Separate empirical studies are needed to define the successfulness of such campaigns and games. For example, the harvesting of data from communicative interactions in the regional communicative ecosystem could be useful to make evidence based decisions.

Agency: The emerging social sharing economy potential in providing educational and supportive services through help networks models also the active participatory citizenship competences among marginalized young adults, develops informal networks and increases social cohesion.

6 Conclusions

The design research results can be used in the countries to develop and orchestrate the communicative ecosystem of services for vulnerable youth. An effective system requires developing the national database of social services, database of AE, databases of linked and lifelong records of educational and employment paths and specific needs and accessed services. Using linked records' data would require decisions and regulations at the data access and privacy level. Our analysis demonstrated that there is the need for stabile and payed advisor roles to promote mediated access AE for the youth from vulnerable minority groups. Advisors are at present at different organizations such as in educational-, rehabilitation-, youth-, unemployment-, and migrant centers. A common procedure for tracking and advice mediation needs to be developed in each country context that enables different stakeholders in the country to be mutually informed while advising a person, and the person should to be guided to the advisors and to the AE by their preferred ways (such as in physical centers and places, in public social media groups, in personal social media groups, in gamified digital environments).

Acknowledgement. The Edumap research was supported by EU Grant 693388 in Research an Innovation actions YOUNG -3-2015.

References

Bellardi, N., Busch, B., Hassemer, J., Peissl, H., Scifo, S.: Spaces of inclusion – an explorative study on needs of refugees and migrants in the domain of media communication and on responses by community media. Council of Europe report. DGI (2018)01. Commit Community Media Institute (2018)

Desjardins, R., Rubenson K.: An analysis of skill mismatch using direct measures of skills. OECD Education Working Papers No. 63 (2011)

Downes, P.: Access to Education in Europe: A Framework and Agenda for System Change Series: Lifelong Learning Book Series, vol. 21. Springer, Dordrecht (2014). https://doi.org/10.1007/978-94-017-8795-6

Sipina, N.: Universal Service Definition in the Context of Service Catalog Design. BPTrends (2011)

Tacchi J., Sabiescu, A.: Communicative ecologies report. Edumap Deliverable 4.1. (Published at Edumap project website) (2019)

The Effect of Social Media on the Emotional Intelligence of Teachers in Indonesia

Andi Mursidi[1(✉)], Yudi Darma[2(✉)], Rustam[2(✉)], Suherdiyanto[2(✉)], T. Yani Achmad[3(✉)], and I-Hsien Ting[4(✉)]

[1] STKIP Singkawang, Singkawang, Indonesia
andimursidi@gmail.com

[2] IKIP PGRI Pontianak, Pontianak, Kalimantan Barat, Indonesia
yudidarma@ikippgriptk.ac.id, rustammunif@gmail.com, her.lien2009@gmail.com

[3] Universitas Tanjungpura, Pontianak, Kalimantan Barat, Indonesia
ahmad.yani.t@fkip.untan.ac.id

[4] National University of Kaohsiung, Kaohsiung, Taiwan
iting@nuk.edu.tw

Abstract. The purpose of this study was to present information and an overview of the influence of social media on the emotional intelligence of prospective teachers in Indonesia with aspects of competence to understand: (1) The use of by social media prospective teacher, (2) Emotional intelligence of prospective teacher and (3) The relationship between social media activity and the emotional intelligence of prospective teacher in Indonesia. The research method used in this study is Ex Post Facto with correlational forms and theoretical discussions. The sampling technique is used in this study is the quota sampling area intended for prospective teachers. The technique of data collection is indirect communication and documentation. The data analysis technique used is the analysis prerequisite testing which consists of a normality test and continued with a product trial hypothesis test, a coefficient of determination and influence to see the agreement between variables. Based on the results of research obtained that the use of social media has a significant relationship to emotional intelligence with a contribution of 53.63%, as for specific conclusions in this study as follows: The use of social media and intelligence of prospective researchers obtained average teachers of 3.14 and 3, 28 with good categories; There are a significant influence and relationship between the use of social media and the emotional intelligence of prospective student teachers; and facilitation of online learning and teaching spaces in the industrial revolution era 4.0 requires technology synergy and human society.

Keywords: Social media in education · Use of social media by prospective teachers · The emotional intelligence of prospective teachers

L. Uden et al. (Eds.): LTEC 2019, CCIS 1011, pp. 381–390, 2019.
https://doi.org/10.1007/978-3-030-20798-4_33

1 Introduction

Today a paradigm shift, daily patterns, activities and almost all aspects of life are continually undergoing changes. It is very quickly felt is the development and rise of technology, not even a little that the role of humans itself has been replaced by technology and information.

The more rapid development and progress in the IT sector is certainly one proof of the rapid development and progress of world human resources. However, not all of the progress that occurs is directly proportional to the increase in human resources in several countries.

Not a few people have not been able to place technological development and progress in accordance with their roles, such as the rise of hoax news, the occurrence of social disputes, and even the impact on health which are some negative activities caused by misuse of technology and information.

The use of social media itself has become a kind of trend or lifestyle in Indonesia [1]. Based on a survey of Global Web Index Data in 2014, Indonesia is the country that has the most active social media users in Indonesia, which is 79.7% compared to other countries such as the Philippines 78%, Malaysia 72%, and China 67%. This confirms that social media users in Indonesia 15% of the total population and the average time used by users to access social media is 2 h 54 min per day.

In which access mobile using a smartphone or tablet. While the most widely accessed social media is Facebook, around 62,000,000 users, followed respectively are Twitter and Instagram. Social media provides easy access to cheap information and communication to be able to connect with anyone in the world, including teenagers. Teenagers are a period of transition or transition from the age of children to adulthood. In this transition period, various changes occur including changes in attitude and behavior. Consumption of social media is one of the behavioral changes experienced by adolescents caused by the development of the internet [1].

In addition, facebook and youtube are social media accounts that can be used by all operating systems in mobile phones and computers as well as social media that are very often used by the public, as stated by [2, 3] which states "54% or as many as 71, 6 million people use Facebook, 11% or 14.5 million people use YouTube, while the rest use other applications such as Instagram, Google+ , Twitter and Linkedin".

The success of a person is not determined solely by knowledge and technical skills (hard skills) but by the skills of managing themselves and their relationships with others (soft skills) and aspects of character education [4], [5].

Moreover, the essence of education not only educates one's life but also directs a person or learner to become a person who knows the truth and wants to do right. To obtain quality human resources, a person is not only required to have hard skills, but also soft skills. Furthermore, the results of social psychology research show that successful people in the world are determined by the role of science at 18%. The rest, 82% is determined by emotional skills, soft skills and the like [6].

This opinion is in line with [7], that emotional intelligence refers to the ability to recognize one's own feelings and other people's feelings, the ability to motivate themselves and the ability to manage emotions well in themselves and in relationships with others. The main problem that needs to be observed from the explanation above is that prospective teachers do not only master science, technology, or art in certain fields, but also need to master additional skills, such as abilities or emotional intelligence as mentioned above.

This research will present an actual activity and become a global habit today, namely social media activity and relationships and their influence on emotional intelligence. The information extracted by the researcher is important because it can provide an overview that can be used as a reference in the framework of returning the principle of benefit from each aspect. The sample that will become the object of this research is prospective teacher.

Given that prospective teachers are agents of change who are expected to be able to play a role and take advantage of opportunities to knit the future. Based on some of the above explanations, researchers are interested in knowing more about the influence of social media on student emotional intelligence, so that it is expected to be a joint evaluation or view for managers, lecturers, and institutions about social media and emotional intelligence.

2 Methodology

The research method used in this study is a survey with correlational techniques, namely to determine the relationship of variables, namely the independent variable (use of social media) with the dependent variable (emotional intelligence). The reason researchers use survey methods is that the survey method is research conducted on large or small populations, but the data studied is data from samples taken from the population so that relative events, distribution, and relationships between sociological and psychological variables are found.

The reason the researchers used survey methods with correlational techniques because correlation research is “research that tries to see the relationship between several variables” [8]. Is it possible to change one variable related to changes in other variables? The survey method with the correlational approach will provide an overview of the relationship between the independent variables (X = use of social media) and the dependent variable (Y = emotional intelligence).

2.1 The Scope of Research

The content in the scope of this research is related to the research variable. The independent variables in this study are the use of student social media related to content indicators, community, communication, the collaboration that is directed at the limitations of the view of the role of social media in learning or lectures. While the dependent variable in this study is emotional intelligence that is associated with indicators of self-awareness, empathy, self-management, and self-motivation.

2.2 Population and Samples

The research population is an accurate data source that is needed in research; therefore, its role is very important in determining the population that will provide the necessary data information. According to [9], that: "the population is the whole of the object of research which can be in the form of humans, animals, plants, air, symptoms, values, life attitudes and so on".

Whereas according to [10] "the sample is part or representative of the population to be studied. Whereas [11] says: "Samples as part of the number and characteristics possessed by the population". In connection with this, because the researcher determines the sample for a specific reason, the sampling technique used in this study is the sampling area quota, which is where 10 (ten) people from each class represent a sample of 40 prospective teachers.

2.3 Technique and Data Collection Tool

A study requires certain techniques to facilitate the research process and the technique must be in accordance with the achievement of the research objectives. Determining the right techniques in research will have a positive impact and have a strategic importance, because everything that will be recorded, analyzed and interpreted will be right. Data obtained through research activities is a very important factor in efforts to solve research problems. Therefore, the data obtained must be accurate and scientifically accountable.

The data collection technique used in this study is indirect technique. Indirect communication techniques are the main techniques used to collect data. [12] argues that: "Indirect communication techniques are techniques in which researchers collect data by communicating with research subjects through intermediary tools, both those already available and special tools made for this purpose."

A similar opinion was expressed by [13] who argued that: "Indirect communication techniques are ways of collecting data carried out by holding indirect relationships or with intermediaries, both tools that are already available and special tools made for that purpose."

So, indirect communication techniques are a way to collect data about the object of research with the intermediary of a particular tool that is in the form of a data collection tool. The technique is used to obtain data related to the use of social media and the emotional intelligence of prospective teachers.

2.4 Data Collection Tool

Based on the data collection techniques used, the data collection tools that are in accordance with the techniques or used in this study are questionnaires. Questionnaire is used to obtain information data about the variables studied by prospective teachers.

The questionnaire used is in a closed structured form, meaning that a number of questions have been provided by a number of alternatives that will be chosen by the respondent, so that the respondent only gives a cross (X) or check (pada) on one of the alternative answers that are appropriate or appropriate.

To obtain data relating to the purpose of the study, the data collection technique that the researcher chooses is an indirect communication technique, with a data collection tool in the form of a questionnaire. Questionnaire contains statements, which are indicators of the use of social media and student emotional intelligence in the form of choice questions with 4 alternative answers or likert scale.

2.5 Data Analysis Technique

The data collected then the researchers examined one by one, to find out whether there were errors in filling out the research questionnaire. Furthermore, the results of the problem solving ability test are calculated according to the assessment indicators. The recapitulation carried out is then analyzed according to the problem statement. "Correlation analysis is a set of statistical techniques used to measure the closeness of the relationship between two variables with the main goal of determining how closely the functional relationship between variables" [10].

The calculations carried out include testing the analysis prerequisites in the form of a normality test and continued with testing the hypothesis of the product moment correlation test and the determination coefficient to see the contribution of relationships between variables. The interpretation of contributions according to [11] is as follows:

$0,00–0,199$	:	Very low
$0,20–0,399$	:	Low
$0,4–0,599$	:	Middle
$0,6–0,799$	:	High
$0,8–1,00$	:	Very High

3 Discussion

On this occasion will be presented about the results of the research that has been carried out. The results of the research that will be presented are descriptions of research data, data analysis and discussion of research results.

3.1 Data Description

Because this research is a de facto expost research, while the research data used in this discussion is social media usage data directed at aspects of use as a medium/facilitation of learning or lectures, and data on emotional intelligence of prospective teacher prospective teachers. From the data on the use of social media and student emotional intelligence, a measure of central tendency was found which included the average, median and mode, and measures of data variability including minimum data, maximum data, and standard deviation. The description of the data is presented in Table 1 as follows:

Based on Table 1 above, the following data for each variable in Tables 2 and 3 match the measurement indicators which are survey descriptions of this study:

Table 1. Use of social media and emotional intelligence

Kelompok	N	Tendensi			Variabilitas		
		$\bar{X}$	Mo	Me	Min	Maks	Sd
Media Sosial	40	3,14	3,17	3,17	2,58	3,67	0,25
Emotional Intelligence	40	3,28	3,36	3,32	2,73	3,64	0,24

Table 2. Use of social media

Statement	Mean	Category
Finding interesting topics for me is very easy in the "search" menu on social media	3,50	Good
The features in the Application and social media technology are very clear in their use	3,25	Good
In application and technology social media allows me to create topics related to learning/lectures	3,35	Good
I will ask for help from the group on social media if I find a problem in learning/lecturing	2,85	Enough
Social media gives me the topic of learning/lectures to be discussed	3,25	Good
Social media helps me to do self-introspection through sharing fellow users	2,93	Enough
Social media can broadcast the latest information to all members	3,23	Good
Social media provides an opportunity to be able to share knowledge as user services via email and live chat	3,38	Good
Social media can provide motivation to anyone who joins the same community	3,18	Good
I can study with fellow users in applications and social media technology	2,95	Enough
I can discuss learning/lecture material through social media	2,90	Enough
Social media provides an opportunity to work in groups	2,95	Enough

3.2 Data Analysis

Normality Test

The normality test is done to find out whether the sample comes from a population that is normally distributed. The test statistic used in the normality test is Kolmogrov Smirnov by using Minitab assistance services. In this study the normality test was carried out based on the variable use of social media and student emotional intelligence. A summary of the results of the normality test data is presented in Table 4, while the full calculation is presented in the appendix.

From the table above it appears that all H0 test decisions are not rejected. This means that for each sample both the categories of social media usage and emotional intelligence of prospective teachers come from populations that are normally distributed.

Tabel 3. Emotional intelligence

Statement	Mean	Category
I know my weaknesses and I develop the abilities that	3,30	Good
I have without covering up those weaknesses	3,48	Good
I know what I can do and what I can't do	3,05	Good
I can still calm even when I'm angry or panic for something	3,53	Very Good
I always consider the feelings of others in resolving conflicts. I am sometimes selfish in giving opinions	3,18	Good
When I was stressed, I turned my attention to doing positive things	3,43	Good
When I'm experiencing failure, I'm not easily discouraged	3,43	Good
I can feel what others are feeling	3,23	Good
I am always open to others about my condition	3,05	Good
I can reconcile the conflicts between my colleagues	3,18	Good
I can be a good listener when my coworkers complain	3,30	Good

Table 4. Summary of normality test results

Team	Test	P (α = 0.05)	Result
Sosial media	H_0accepted	>0,150	Normal
Emotional intelligence	H_0accepted	0,122	Normal

Hypothesis Test

The purpose of the product moment correlation test is to find out the value of r (correlation) as the significance of the relationship between free and bound variable, namely the use of student social media and emotional intelligence. The results of calculations are presented in Fig. 1, below:

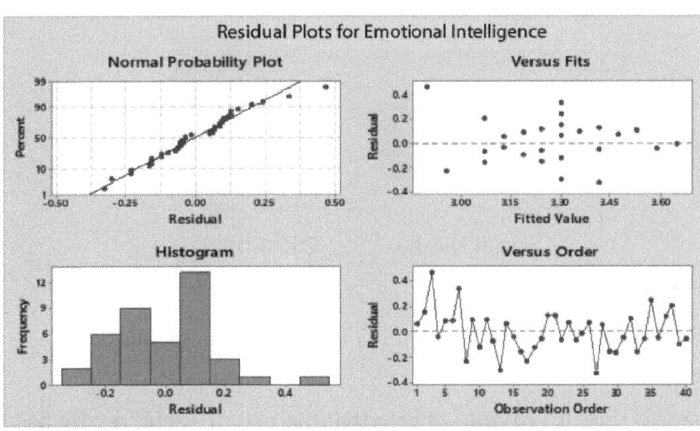

Fig. 1. Analysis S = 0.1645; R-Sq = 53.6%; R-Sq(adj) = 52.4%

$$\text{Emotional intellligence} = 1,106 + 0,6933\,\text{Media Sosial}$$

3.3 Significant Test and Contribution

Based on the product moment correlation calculation, it is obtained that r count = 0.733 and r table = 0.312 with a significance of 5%. Because rcount > rtable is obtained that H0 is ejected and Ha is accepted which states that there is a high relationship of social media use to emotional intelligence, this refers to the criteria [14].

To answer the second sub-problem with regard to the contribution of social media use to prospective teacher's emotional intelligence were analyzed using a coefficient of determination and then adjusted to the existing interpretations. Based on the calculation, it is found that rxy = 0.733, so that contributions can be obtained as follows:

$$\begin{aligned}(r_{xy})^2 \times 100\% &= (0,733)^2 \times 100\% \\ &= 0,5363 \times 100\% \\ &= \mathbf{53,63\%}\end{aligned}$$

interval area 0.4 – 0.599 with **middle** category.

3.4 Discussion of Research Results

Based on the results of calculations on the correlational test and the coefficient of determination, it is found that there is a significant relationship between the use of social media and the emotional intelligence of prospective teacher, especially with regard to the use of social media in supporting learning. It can be seen that each aspect obtained a mean score of 3.14 and 3.28 with equally good categories (Fig. 2).

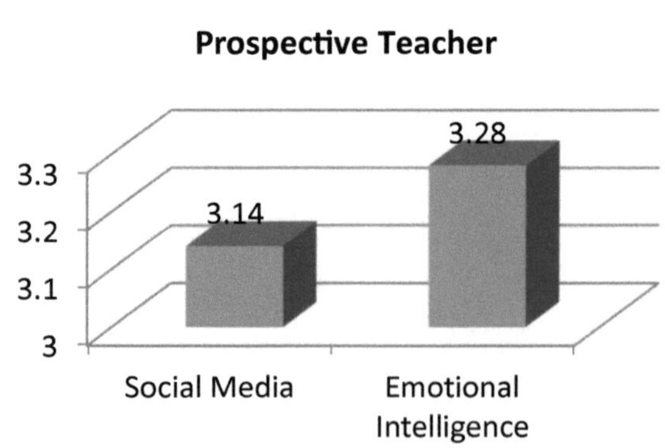

Fig. 2. Mean social media and emotional intelligence

With regard to this, it provides clarity that the use of social media has a significant relationship with prospective teacher's emotional intelligence. Based on the results of the research, the relationship between the use of social media and emotional intelligence is directly proportional or in other words positive (+), meaning that the higher the level of use of social media by prospective teachers in using learning media, the better emotional intelligence it has, because "media social present provides easy dissemination of information and communication among users" [1, 15].

In addition, based on the theory and research results obtained, it is known that the contribution of the relationship between the use of social media and emotional intelligence is 53.63% with the medium category, while the rest is influenced by other factors.

In line with these results it may also be of concern to educators, observers, especially in the education sector who are concerned with emotional intelligence, because future teachers must really be able to become problem solvers when in a school environment or wherever they work [16]. The emotional intelligence aspect becomes one of the important components as an inseparable part in achieving student learning outcomes, because it has a very important role in supporting the sustainability and success of students after taking higher education, in line with what was stated by [17] states that emotional intelligence provides influence on one's performance.

Furthermore, a review of various relevant aspects so that it can also be a consideration and basis as an effort to increase emotional intelligence in order to achieve national goals in helping Indonesian people as a whole, namely having competence and noble character.

4 Conclusions

In accordance with the research objectives and the results obtained that the use of social media has a significant influence and relationship to the emotional intelligence of prospective teacher in Indonesia with a contribution of 53.63% with reference to several conclusion indicators as follows:

1. The use of social media and emotional intelligence of prospective teacher obtained a mean of 3.14 and 3.28 in the good category.
2. There is a significant influence and relationship between the use of social media and the emotional intelligence of prospective teacher.
3. Facilitation of online learning and teaching spaces in the era of industrial revolution 4.0 requires a synergy of technology and human society.

Acknowledgment. Thank you to the IKIP PGRI Pontianak institution and STKIP Singkawang who have provided opportunities, moral and material support to the team in carrying out this research.

References

1. dan Aprinta, G., Dwi, E.: Hubungan Penggunaan Media Sosial Dengan Tingkat Kepekaan Sosial Di Usia Remaja. Jurnal Messenger **9**(1), 65–69 (2017)
2. Asosiasi Penyelenggara Jasa Internet Indonesia: Survey Pengguna Media Sosial. APJJ, Jakarta (2016)
3. Schwartz, H.A., et al.: Personality, gender, and age in the language of social media: the open-vocabulary approach. J. Pers. Soc. Psychol. **3**, 10–20 (2013)
4. Muqowim: Pengembangan Soft Skills Guru. Insan Madani, Yogyakarta (2012)
5. dan Darma, Y., Susiaty, U.D., Fitriawan, D.: Pendidikan Karakter dalam Pembelajaran pada Mahasiswa Calon Guru Matematika. Jurnal SAP **3**(2), 110–115 (2018)
6. Elfindri, R.J., Wello, M.B, Tobing, P., Yanti, F., Eriyani, Z.E., Indra, R.: Peningkatan Soft Skills Siswa SMP melalui Pembelajaran Generatif. Soft Skills untuk Pendidik. Baduose Media, Tanpa Kota (2010)
7. Goleman, D.: Kecerdasan Emosional. PT Gramedia Pustaka Utama, Jakarta (2002)
8. Kountur, R.: Metode Penelitian untuk Penulisan Skripsi dan Tesis. PPM, Jakarta (2004)
9. Bungin, B.: Metodologi Penelitian Sosial: Format-format Kuantitatif dan Kualitatif. PT Air Langga, Surabaya (2001)
10. Arikunto, S.: Prosedur Penelitian Suatu Pendekatan Praktik. Rineka Cipta, Jakarta (2010)
11. Sugiyono.: Metodologi Penelitian Kuantitatif. Kualitatif dan R & D. Bandung, Alfabeta (2011)
12. Surachmad, W.: Pengantar Penelitian Ilmiah Dasar: Metode dan Teknik. Tarsito, Bandung (2000)
13. Nawawi, H.: Metode Penelitian Bidang Sasial. Gajah Mada University Press, Yogyakarta (2003)
14. Arikunto, S.: Prosedur Penelitian (Suatu Pendekatan Praktis). Rineka Cipta, Jakarta (2005)
15. Fuchs, C.: Internet and Society, Social Theory in the Information age. Roudledge, New York (2008)
16. Saputra, G.W., et al.: Pengaruh Teknologi Informasi Terhadap Kecerdasan (intelektual, spiritual, emosional dan sosial) studi kasus: anak-anak. Jurnal Sistem Informasi **10**(2), 77–88 (2017)
17. Risma, D.: Pengaruh Kecerdasan Emosional Terhadap Kinerja Karyawan: Penelitian Eksperimen. Jurnal Educhild **1**(1), 86–97 (2012)

Machine Learning and Evaluation Support Programs

Design for System Change: Developing Digital Competences of Vocational Teachers

Sabine Seufert, Josef Guggemos, and Eric Tarantini(✉)

University of St. Gallen, Guisanstr 1a, 9010 St. Gallen, Switzerland
{sabine.seufert, josef.guggemos, eric.tarantini}@unisg.ch

Abstract. Digital transformation shapes the educational system in many ways. It has also far-reaching implications for teachers as their job description may fundamentally change in the future. In this light, it is important (1) to identify necessary digital competences of teachers and (2) to find ways to foster those competences in an efficient way. By means of a literature review and expert interviews, we developed a framework of teachers' digital competences. In line with Baumert and Kunter (2006) as well as Koehler and Mishra (2009), it comprises content knowledge, pedagogical content knowledge and pedagogical knowledge. However, these facets have extended meaning in the context of digital transformation. Moreover, our framework considers the official EU competence framework (Carretero et al., 2017) and hence covers instrumental skills and knowledge in handling digital media. We successfully validated our framework by means of structural equation modelling with a sample of 215 Swiss teachers. Utilising an Importance Performance Map Analysis, we identified competence facets that show the highest effects on the (self-reported) use of digital media and content. For efficiently fostering those facets, we established a webinar series in order to provide further education service regarding topics like digital teaching and learning.

Keywords: Digital competence of teachers · Formal learning · Informal learning · Systematic change

1 Introduction

One would be hard pressed to find a topic of current debate in education policy and educational practice that is as exhaustively discussed as the (proper) handling of the digital transformation (e.g. 'standing conference of the ministers of education and cultural Affairs' [KMK], 2016). A widely shared perception is that a more intensive use of digital media in the classroom will improve learning effectiveness, facilitate greater orientation to the future needs of learners, and support accompanied personality development in a digital society. The sweeping pressure to make changes is marked with a high degree of uncertainty regarding the use and benefits of digital media in schools [6].

L. Uden et al. (Eds.): LTEC 2019, CCIS 1011, pp. 393–407, 2019.
https://doi.org/10.1007/978-3-030-20798-4_34

Teachers addressing digital skills, such as the competent handling of online information, are often entering uncharted territory in their respective fields (media education). In this context, teachers are increasingly asking for inclusion of media-specific qualification objectives. However, the kind of competences teachers need to acquire remains somewhat vague and is largely limited to the use and operation of computer applications and digital content media [5, 6]. Furthermore, it is obvious that formal seminars, such as one-day training workshops on how to use ICT, are neither sufficient nor effective for developing teachers' digital competences. On the contrary, successful support initiatives to develop teachers' competence will have to be rooted in their particular context and simultaneously embedded in innovation strategies and quality development processes in their respective schools [33]. The conceptualisation and design of suitable training measures for teachers requires a systematic approach to the professional development of teachers at vocational schools. Developing professional communities among teachers to underpin the benefit of learning together and from each other is of central importance [19]. Learning communities that make use of the potential of digital information and communication are becoming increasingly important as a means of continuously fostering teachers' digital competences. However, there is a research gap in the promotion of digital competences for teachers [13, p. 15]. In this light, this paper focuses on three research questions:

(1) How can digital competences of teachers be defined and measured?
(2) How can measures and interventions to be designed and evaluated for developing teachers' digital competences?
(3) How can teachers' professional development be interlinked with school development for a systematic change?

The paper consists of three parts. In the first part, we consolidate relevant theoretical considerations. The second part outlines the research methodology and the results of the research conducted. The third and final section discusses the results of the study and presents a perspective for further research.

2 Review of the Literature

2.1 Digital Competences of Teachers

An important point of reference is a highly regarded model of professional teaching competence, which comprises professional knowledge, convictions in the sense of personally biased basic orientations, values, motivational orientations and self-regulation (for empirical findings on professional knowledge in the commercial sector, cf. [51]) [7, 23, 24]. Professional knowledge consists of content knowledge, pedagogical content knowledge and pedagogical knowledge. This division can be traced back to Shulman (1986, 1987). Koehler and Mishra (2009) added technological aspects to these facets of professional knowledge. They include technological knowledge as a new, disparate type of knowledge.

Current technological developments, such as artificial intelligence and cognitive computing, are flanked by fundamental questions about which digital competences teachers need to possess.

Moreover, approaches for developing media skills [3, 5, 6, 27, 34, 40] might be taken into account. In this vein, Blömeke's (2003) model is an approach that refers to teacher training. It distinguishes five areas of competence: 'didactic media competence', 'educational media competence', 'socialisation-related competence', 'school development competence', and 'personal media competence'. The demands faced by a vocational school in the light of ever-increasing digitalisation cannot be tackled through the efforts of single individuals. In such a case, the individual teachers would quickly feel overworked [36]. In the light of digital transformation, appropriate advisory and organisational knowledge regarding cooperation in teams and networks can thus be regarded as a relevant facet of competence for the joint development of teaching and schools.

For vocational education and training, the official EU competence framework [9] is leading the way because it defines cross-vocational digital competences (in the sense of "digital literacies"), which can be specified in the Europass European Skills Passport[1] in the form of self-evaluations. The KMK Strategy 2016 follows a similar path, identifying six areas of competence for education in the digital world – comparable to the EU competence framework [22]. However, the implications for professional teaching skills have remained (as yet) ambiguous.

Empirical findings on technology-mediated learning (TML) indicate that affective-motivational characteristics of the instructor are a decisive factor influencing the educationally effective use of digital media in the classroom [14]. Teachers have widely divergent views regarding the extent to which the lessons themselves should undergo digital change [32].

2.2 Professional Development of Teachers

Teacher training and its effectiveness is a field of research that has great untapped potential [39]. Currently, there are virtually no studies that demonstrate the effectiveness of measures for digital competence development [25] [26, p. 228]. According to Terhart et al. (2014, p. 517ff.), the efficacy of training measures must be considered on a case-by-case basis. Since this can be influenced by countless variables and contextual factors (class, teacher, setting, quality of training content, diverse and challenging learning opportunities for teachers, etc.), Terhart (2014) proposes that it is practically impossible to distinguish generally applicable quality standards.

Multiple studies have shown that teachers develop their skills mainly in the informal context of their professional practice, i.e. in exchange with colleagues or through individual, critical reflection [17, 21, 28]. As a result, international research literature on teacher education and training is especially focused on "integrated learning at the workplace", which is increasingly aimed at informal learning and reflective

[1] The Europass aims to provide a way to present qualifications and competences in a way that is transparent and understandable throughout Europe, cf. https://europass.cedefop.europa.eu/de.

dialogue among the teaching staff [28]. For this reason, strong learning environments are based on design principles from a socio-constructivist perspective in the context of informal learning theories. Team and community-based learning may be considered one of the most effective and predominant learning methods in this context and it is against this backdrop that the construct of the professional learning community should be mentioned. According to Hord (1997), PLCs involve groups of teachers or the entire teaching staff at a school that are jointly and constantly seeking ways to increase the effectiveness of their teaching, sharing what they have learned, attempting to put new ideas into actual practice, systematically testing these ideas and reflecting on them [18]. New competence requirements in the wake of increasing digitalisation necessitate ongoing (further) education that is marked by a high degree of speed and innovation dynamic. Teachers can no longer implement these changes individually and in isolation from one another in their day-to-day school routine. Bonsen and Rolff (2006, p. 170) therefore propose "the combination of community and professionalism" in times of turbulent change. In general, experimental testing of new approaches is risky. Hence, it requires continuity and a stable framework for developing common value patterns [7]. Effectiveness studies on PLCs have produced key success factors: Shared practice [19], reflective dialogue, deprivatisation of teaching (teaching is a personal, but not a private matter), common focus on students' learning (shifting the focus from teaching to learning), and fundamentally reinforced cooperation [29].

3 Method

3.1 Design

First, it is necessary to delineate professional competences of teachers in the context of the digital transformation. The resulting framework concept must then be systematically differentiated. For the subsequent test development phase, it is imperative to take into account the purpose of the measurement and the intended use of the results [1, p. 75f.]. The purpose of the measurement is to assess teachers' digital skills for formative purposes. The results should serve to identify potential for improvements and to design appropriate support measures. With this in mind, we have designed a self-assessment tool that has been validated using confirmatory factor analyses. Since the aim of our research is to identify adequate professional development measures, which is within teachers' own interest, we regard a self-assessment instrument as suitable. Finally, the research shall lead to measures in order to develop professional, digital competences of vocational teachers.

In collaboration with five partner schools from German-speaking Switzerland, we have developed items that capture the constructs described in Sect. 2.1, cf. Table 1. The items are measured on a 7-point rating scale. We have validated the instrument by means of 12 expert interviews. The experts show a diverse background: Training representatives of companies, researcher in the field of digitalization, school principals, educational policy makers and federation representatives. Moreover, we carried out five focus group discussions with teachers at every partner school.

We utilised an importance-performance map analysis (IPMA) [31] to assess teachers' competences and promising fields for improvement. This method, though not yet widely used in the PLS-SEM context, enables a clear and theoretically justified presentation of the results for a baseline evaluation. The first dimension (Importance [I]) of the importance-performance map depicts for each construct, cf. Table 1, or item its impact on a previously specified construct. In our case, we utilize frequency of use (measured on a 5-point rating scale) as the target construct, cf. Table 2. For instance, a value of 0.1 for "pedagogical knowledge" would indicate that an increase in this construct by one unit on the rating scale increases the expected frequency of digital media use by 0.1 units. IPMA also considers indirect effects. This enables us to identify measures that are potentially most beneficial in terms of increasing the frequency of use of digital media. The second dimension (Performance [P]) places each construct or item on a scale from 1 to 100, indicating how pronounced the construct or item is among the teachers studied. A value that is low compared to other constructs or in absolute terms may indicate a potential for improvement. When selecting interventions, the focus should be on constructs that have a comparatively strong impact on the target construct and are not (yet) close to the maximum. We discuss IPMA-results in focus group interviews with school administrations and specialist representatives from pilot schools.

3.2 Instruments and Data Analysis

The final instrument for capturing teachers' digital competence consists of 86 items covering 11 constructs (10 facets of digital competences, cf. Table 1 and frequency of use, cf. Table 2). 215 teachers at nine Swiss vocational schools act as a sample. 50% of them are female. On average, they are aged 45 (SD = 6) and have 18 (SD = 10) years of teaching experience. The lack of normal distribution for all items is noteworthy (Shapiro-Wilk test: $p < .05$). Overall, 3.9% missing values occurred. The absence of values does not follow any specific pattern. A Little's MCAR test performed taking into account all context variables was not significant ($\chi^2 = 3616$, df = 3297, p = 1). We also checked for outliers using Mahalanobis distances. However, we did not exclude any observation.

Table 1 provides an overview of the 10 competence facets measured by a seven-point rating scale: From "very low" to "very high" (content knowledge, pedagogical content knowledge) and from "does not apply at all" to "applies very strongly" for all other facets (see Table 1).

Table 2 shows the three elements of the target construct "frequency of use". They are measured on a 5-point rating scale: Never, infrequently (1–2 times per semester), occasionally (3–5 times per semester), frequently (every month), very frequently (every week).

Overall, we consider our instrument suitable for a comprehensive and valid formative assessment of digital competences as well as for competence development among teachers.

Table 1. Facets of teachers' digital competences including sample questions.

Professional knowledge (classroom level, school level) with respect to digitalisation	Instrumental skills and knowledge in handling digital media	Affective-motivational characteristics related to digitalisation
Classroom-oriented professional knowledge *Content knowledge:* (1) General knowledge about digitalisation (e.g. "My basic knowledge about decisive principles of digitalization is…") (2) Business knowledge about digitalisation (e.g. "My knowledge about digital value chains is…") *Pedagogical Content knowledge:* (3) Knowledge about digitalisation as a school subject, (e.g. "My knowledge about teaching digital value chains is…") *Pedagogical knowledge:* (4) General knowledge of digital media (e.g. "I am able to use digital assessment tools for students' summative assessment") (5) Promoting students' interdisciplinary digital skills (e.g. "I am able to foster my students' digital skills to use online information") (6) Media didactics (e.g. "I am able to select adequate learning videos for students' knowledge creation") Professional knowledge at the school level: (7) Advisory and organisational knowledge (e.g. "I am able to support my colleagues to improve professional practice in terms of digital content and digital media use")	(8) Digital skills: – handling digital information (e.g. "I can efficiently use search strategies to find online information"); – creating digital content (e.g. "I can create learning videos"); – digital collaboration (e.g. "I can efficiently use digital communication tools"); – ensuring digital security (e.g. "I regularly check my security settings of my digital devices and/or applications"), – digital problem solving (e.g. "I can regularly keep up-to-date my skills in handling digital media/tools); – specific applications (e.g. "I can use profession-specific applications (e.g. Office applications)"	(9) Positive attitudes (e.g. "I like using digital media/tools in my instruction") (10) Negative attitudes (e.g. "I am afraid of making mistakes when using digital media/tools in my instruction")

Table 2. Target construct 'frequency of use' including sample items.

Frequency of use	Sample items
Digitalisation as a class subject (professional, interdisciplinary)	How often do you consider digital related topics in your instruction?
Use of digital media for individualisation	How often do you foster students' competences when dealing with digital media (e.g. dealing with online information)?
General use of digital media	How often do you practice individualisation of your teaching according to the learning progress supported by digital media?
	How often do you practice individualisation of your teaching according to learning preferences supported by digital media?
	How often do you use blended learning scenarios (e.g. flipped classroom)?
	How often do you use digital learning arrangements in your instruction?

4 Results

4.1 Competence Facets and Data Analysis

Test validations by means of confirmatory factor analyses generally yielded good values for all eleven constructs (CFI > .974, TLI > .966, RMSEA < .093, SRMR < .036). Measurement invariance analyses demonstrate the instrument's suitability for assessing competence development as well as group comparisons in terms of gender, age and teaching expertise. Frequency of use can be adequately explained using the facets of digital competence (.36 > R^2 > .26).

It is important to view the facets of competence in context, and to systematically foster all of them. However, developing all facets of competence at the same time would likely overtax the teaching personnel. Therefore, the next step will be to concentrate on selected competence facets within the framework of an online PLC. In line with the IPMA (baseline evaluation), these would primarily encompass the following:

- **Media didactics** (CFI = .979, TLI = .970, RMSEA = .059, SRMR = .030). This facet of competence exhibits both a low self-assessment and a high level of effect on the frequency of use of digitalisation and on teaching with digital media; the findings show that digital media is primarily used for instructional knowledge acquisition (e.g. use of learning videos), but less for constructivist and cognitive processes, such as for discussion, reflection or for forms of action-oriented teaching and learning (e.g. simulations, multimedia applications).
- **Pedagogical knowledge** (CFI = 1.000, TLI = 1.000, RMSEA = .000, SRMR = .003): General, interdisciplinary knowledge of digital media also shows a rather high importance and a moderate performance. In this area, competence diagnostics with digital media in particular constitutes a knowledge gap for many teachers (this is accompanied by the relatively low values for formative and summative

self-assessments in the competence facet of media didactics, which basically represents the concrete implementation level);

- **Fostering students' digital skills** (CFI = .990, TLI = .982, RMSEA = .058, SRMR = .024). Teachers give the lowest rating to their ability to promote their students' knowledge acquisition of digital media. Against the requirements in vocational education and training, this finding is alarming and illustrates how pressing the need for action to develop the skills of teachers in this area is.
- **Instrumental skills and knowledge in handling digital media** (CFI = .974, TLI = .966, RMSEA = .069, SRMR = .036). This competence facet also has a relatively strong effect on the use of digital content and digital media. The importance of the inclusion of digitalisation related topics in the classroom is even higher than that of the use of digital media in the classroom. A teacher who seems to be more active in the 'digital world' is more likely to recognise the necessity and become familiar with concrete application possibilities in order to integrate digitalisation topics into the classroom in a didactic manner.

In sum, media didactics has a particularly positive influence on the use of digital learning arrangements. There is potential for improvement, particularly in the digital assessment of learners' competences (summative and formative).

The results show, that the average teacher is never or casually (Median = 1 and 3, respectively) actively working with digital media within his lecture (Blended Learning). This is an illustration for the trend that schools are at the very beginning of digital transformation (Fig. 1).

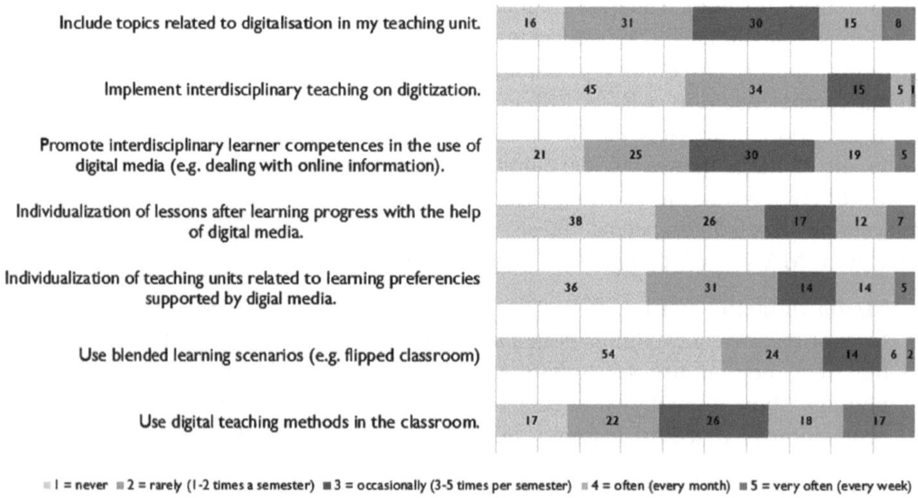

Fig. 1. Frequency of use (percentages).

4.2 Teacher's Professional Development in Formal and Informal Learning Settings

The following section focuses on the importance of the skills development of teachers in this context. Heise (2007) particularly emphasises the importance of largely self-directed further education in this professional field. To support and strengthen these desired informal learning activities, it might be vital to create an environment conducive to communication within the school organisation. The targeted encouragement of professional discussions before classes begin or during breaks and the use of free periods for detailed reflection, for example on critical practical situations, can make an important contribution to triggering and promoting informal learning among teaching staff [15]. However, not all teachers will be willing or able to collaborate with their colleagues on the preparation and follow-up of the classes. On the contrary, a certain proportion of teachers usually work alone, which might make a different kind of support necessary than would be required for teachers that already cooperate or collaborate with one another [17]. A concept to promote informal learning tailored individually to the aims and objectives of teachers could therefore generate benefit for curriculum and school development.

In the field of information literacy, for example, the pressure on teachers to seek further education has increased immensely due to the constant and rapidly advancing technological development (Fig. 2).

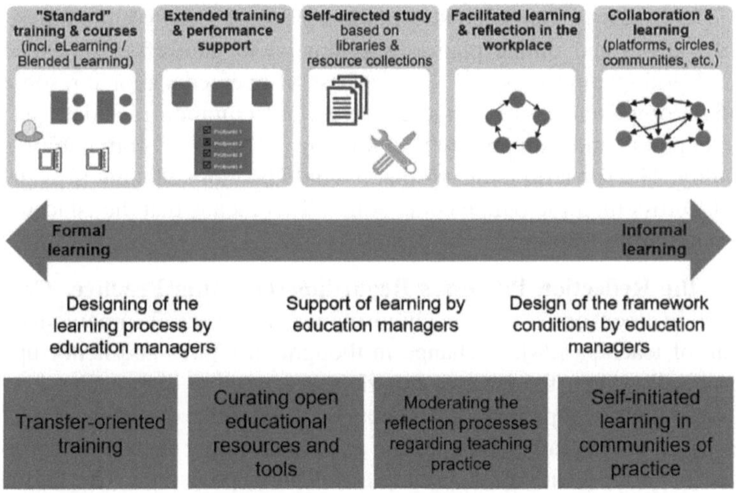

Fig. 2. Teacher's Professional Development in formal and informal learning settings.

A main question for schools to address can be summarized as follows: How might skills development measures for teachers that integrate learning in informal contexts be structured in practice? Some examples are outlined below (see following illustration):

Transfer-Oriented Training. School-based training services (SBT) are nothing new. However, it is now often combined more than was the case in the past with measures that support the transfer of what has been learned (such as preparatory phases and follow-ups). Effective results can for example also be achieved with more open learning environments, such as Engestrøm's Change Laboratory® [13]. In such a framework, it would be possible to re-design courses in a professional association and hence combine the skills development of teachers with innovative strategies for curriculum development in schools [18, p. 12]. Whether or not the transfer of training or further education into the everyday life of teachers succeeds, largely depends on individual factors [17]. An open mind towards new ideas and the willingness to adopt and implement innovative proposals is the prerequisite for initiating and implementing change processes in school routine. How teachers learn informally differs from one individual to the next [17]. This aspect should be considered when developing further education concepts and should lead to a sense of openness with respect to the curriculum, so that it is possible to adapt learning processes to the individual needs. One significant benefit provided by the required openness is the opportunity to obtain feedback on the learning progress. For example, Zwart et al. (2008) suggest providing teachers with a "peer coach", who can help them reflect upon what has been learned [17].

Curating Open Educational Resources and Tools. Open educational resources are defined as teaching, learning and research resources that "reside in the public domain or have been released under an intellectual property license" permitting their free use [3, p. 4]. It is important that educators have access to tools that highlight valuable resources [38, p. 240]. The adequate management of user communities, multiple information sources and online platforms is crucial to gain effective experiences in "digital-rich learning environments". The success of open educational resources lies in four essential components: The convergence toward common metadata, an adequate balance of experts' and community's definitions of quality, community input and interoperability. The last term indicates that it would be more efficient if "a single query could search across multiple online collections". This means that the educator does not have to visit multiple websites.

Moderating the Reflection Processes Regarding Teaching Practice. Critical, individual reflection upon one's own teaching represents a central impetus for the skills development of teachers [28]. A change in thought structures and hence upskilling is possible especially when the teacher experiences cognitive dissonance, i.e. inconsistencies between their own perception and how they actually experience critical teaching phases [38, p. 410]. This raises the question as to what extent such learning options can be promoted in order to initiate appropriate reflection processes. The findings of the group led by Zwart et al. (2008, p. 990) show that informal talks with students from the perspective of an observer offer a valuable learning option. Other examples involve mentoring programmes in which students act as trained mentors and assist the teacher in teaching with notebooks. "Reverse mentoring" is currently enjoying growing popularity even in business. Trainees who are familiar with and able to use digital media critically act as mentors for senior managers and help them find their way in the new digital world. It remains to be seen whether this is merely a short-term fad, or if it will become established as an element of a changing learning and management culture.

Reverse mentoring could also be an approach for the school learning environment to compensate for any lack of media skills on the part of teachers by using the potential of the digital natives. In this way, the students' resources could contribute to the informal skills development of the teachers.

Furthermore, other forms of mentoring, such as near-peer shadowing, are capable of triggering reflection processes among teachers and thereby promoting the informal skills development [28]. Experimenting with new teaching methods (whether adapting a theoretically recognised concept, copying a colleague's method or developing one's own new idea) and even the immediate feedback from a colleague contributes substantially to the informal learning of teachers [17] [28, p. 90]. In this regard, mentoring programmes can be orchestrated in different ways, i.e. the proportion of informal and formal elements of the learning process vary greatly [10]. The degree of refinement of the framework, such as the concrete learning setting, the place of learning or the general process, influences the "predictability of chance" in the further education for teachers and generates an added value for the school organisation and the learners.

Self-initiated Learning in Communities of Practice. The idea of the near-peer mentoring entails a practice-oriented community of people (community of practice according to Wenger [1998]), who are informally linked with each other, are faced with similar tasks and shape the practice in this community through a self-organised exchange. "Professional Learning Communities" in the teaching profession have long been a popular research field [19], but the effects of professional learning communities have yet to be researched in detail [38, p. 408]. The basic consensus in the literature seems to be that community-internal characteristics – such as high motivation for self-development and student focus – are required in order to address a deeper level of reflection in teachers as compared to a conventional training seminar [38, p. 408]. The literature on collegial reflection illustrates the added value of such working relations [17, 28]. Communities of practice increase the circle of possibilities for reflection and provided the aforementioned conducive group characteristics exist, are another instrument of informal skills development of teachers. A beneficial environment for the successful interplay within the community of practice, such as the time window for the professional exchange, must be provided by the school.

Not only networking internally within the teaching staff, but also the search for forms of more intensive cooperation between learning locations, is a field that is still relatively young in Switzerland and has yet to be implemented systematically [11]. Schneider and Mahs (2003) provide one example of a concept of continuous self-qualification and cooperative self-organisation for the skills development of teams of trainers (trainers, teachers, professional services). Here, team meetings represent an important measure in the course of which training modules and further education per se can take place in a self-organised way through the multiplier principle [33, p. 300]. More recent examples support learning cooperation using Web 2.0 to bridge the gap between learning locations [4]. However, experience with knowledge forums [33, p. 416] reveals that work within the forum has so far encountered considerable problems; there is often a lack of motivation to cooperate at the various locations. The formation of networks in relation to the outside world thus also has a bearing on the internal relationship between the participating organisations, ("which is why knowledge forums cannot become bridges between the organisations, yet bridges are built without ensuring the access," [33, p. 416]). Even when using Web 2.0 applications, the critical success factors are therefore not so much technological aspects. Rather, cultural factors determine the extent of participation in the community of practice. The above-mentioned promotion of a climate that is conducive to cooperation within the school influences the informal learning activities of the teachers [24]. The availability of time as well as virtual and real rooms fosters proactive action by the practical community [30].

4.3 Developing Teachers' Digital Competences as a Systematic Change Process

Teachers' professional development in the competent use of digital information therefore requires considerable efforts in the schools. Consequently, it is not enough to organise a new training course as a further education offer for teachers, which is usually held as a one-time event. The new further education course will continue to be out of place in the school. On the contrary, it appears more important that support initiatives for the skills development of teachers are based on this context and are simultaneously embedded in innovation strategies and quality development processes in schools [33, 35]. As a result, curriculum development, staff training and school development measures must be coordinated in order to implement education reforms [19]. The development of a school culture in which students and teachers alike attach great importance to learning together and from each other is of central importance [19].

New competence requirements in the wake of increasing digitalisation necessitate ongoing (further) education that is marked by a high degree of speed and innovation dynamic. Teachers can no longer implement these changes individually and in isolation from one another in their day-to-day school routine. Bonsen and Rolff (2006, p. 170) therefore propose "the combination of community and professionalism" in times of turbulent change. In general, experimental testing of new approaches is risky.

In this regard, the relevance of virtual and online learning communities in a learning organisation has become apparent through learning communities with the objective to enhance teachers` digital competences. The conditions for their success (such as coherence, transparency and quality of moderator performance) have been examined in numerous studies (particularly noteworthy is the meta study [comparison of 64 studies] by Wegener & Leimeister, 2012, cf. also [2, 6, 8, 12, 16, 36, 37]. Similar results have been obtained in studies that investigate professional learning community for the teaching profession supported by digital media [20].

5 Conclusion and Outlook

Our research project has produced a framework for the conceptualisation of digital competences of teachers in the field of business. In terms of professional knowledge, there are two building blocks of digital competences: (1) *Instructional level:* designing classroom situations, and (2) *School level:* shaping school development. Drawing on this framework model, we were able to operationalise the ten facets of digital competence in an instrument that we tested empirically in a pilot study with 215 teachers.

The fit values for the instrument are decent, allowing the results of the pilot study to be used as a baseline evaluation for subsequent research projects.

Furthermore, it was possible to acquire insight into how these digital competences can be continuously and effectively fostered among teachers by means of professional learning communities. The aim is not only to examine the effectiveness of the support models, but also to explore which factors influence teachers' use of digital learning opportunities. The skills development of teachers, in particular in order to test and learn new teaching concepts, is inextricably linked to curriculum and school development. As already stated in the introduction, school routine is currently dominated by traditional forms of teaching, in which innovative educational approaches are almost impossible to realise. Such teaching practices are therefore the central impediment to the integration of digital media in everyday school life [41, p. 38].

The main limitation of our study is the reliance on self-assessments. This could result in two different types of bias: Teachers deliberately give inaccurate answers or are not able to make a valid assessment. We regard the first bias as unlikely because the survey was voluntary and anonymous. Irrespective of this, based on the impressions gained during the qualitative phase of the research project, we can attest that the teachers are highly self-reflective. This indicates that the second type of bias may also be inapplicable.

References

1. AERA, APA, & NCME: Standards for educational and psychological testing. American Educational Research Association, Washington (2014)
2. Arnold, P.: Kooperative Lerngemeinschaften. Gestaltungsdimensionen und -prinzipien. In: Burkhard, L., Bloh, E. (Hrsg.). Online-Pädagogik, Band 3: Referenzmodelle und Praxisbeispiele, pp. 98–107. Schneider-Verlag Hohengehren, Baltmannsweiler (2005)
3. Atkins, D.E., Brown, J.S., Hammond, A.L.: A Review of the Open Educational Resources (OER) Movement. Achievements, Challenges, and New Opportunities. Mountain View: Creative Commons (2007)
4. Baumert, J., Kunter, M.: Stichwort: Professionelle Kompetenz von Lehrkräften. Zeitschrift für Erziehungswissenschaft **9**(4), 469–520 (2006)
5. Blömeke, S.: Neue Medien in der Lehrerausbildung. Zu angemessenen (und unangemessenen) Zielen und Inhalten des Lehramtsstudiums. Zeitschrift für Theorie und Praxis der Medienbildung, 1–29 (2003)
6. Blömeke, S.: Medienpädagogische Kompetenz. In: Frey, A., Jäger, R.S., Renold, U. (eds.). Berufspädagogik: Bd. 5. Kompetenzdiagnostik. Theorien und Methoden zur Erfassung und Bewertung von beruflichen Kompetenzen, pp. 76–97. Empirische Pädagogik e.V., Landau (2005)
7. Bonsen, M., Rolff, H.: Professionelle Lerngemeinschaften von Lehrerinnen und Lehrern. Zeitschrift für Pädagogik **52**(2), 167–184 (2006). Frankfurt am Main: Deutsches Institut für Internationale Pädagogische Forschung (DIPF)
8. Carlén, U., Jobring, O.: Perspectives on the sustainability of activities within online learning communities. Int. J. Web Based Commun. **3**(1), 100–113 (2007)
9. Carretero, S., Vuorikari, R., Punie, Y.: DigComp 2.1. The Digital Competence Framework for Citizens with eight proficiency levels and examples of use. European Union (EU), Luxembourg (2017)

10. Colley, H., Hodkinson, P., Malcolm, J.: Formality and Informality in Learning. Learning and Skill Research Centre, London (2003)
11. Dubs, R.: Schweiz. In: Euler, D. (ed.) Handbuch der Lernkooperation. Theoretische Fundierungen, vol. 1, pp. 564–579. Bertelsmann, Bielefeld (2003)
12. Dückert, S.: Treffpunkt Wissensnetzwerk. In: Wissensmanagement 8, 20–22. Büro für Medien Oliver Lehnert e.K., Neusäss (2003)
13. Engestrøm, Y.: New forms of learning in co-configuration work. J. Workplace Learn. **16** (1/2), 11–21 (2004)
14. Gupta, S., Bostrom, R.P.: Technology-mediated learning. A comprehensive theoretical model. J. Assoc. Inf. Syst. **10**(9), 686–714 (2009)
15. Heise, M.: Professionelles Lernen jenseits von Fortbildungsmaßnahmen. Zeitschrift für Erziehungswissenschaft **10**(4), 513–531 (2007)
16. Hew, K.F.: Determinants of success for online communities. An analysis of three communities in terms of members' perceived professional development. Behav. Inf. Technol. **28**(5), 433–445 (2009)
17. Hoekstra, A., Korthagen, F., Brekelmans, M., Beijaard, D., Imants, J.: Experienced teachers' informal workplace learning and perceptions of workplace conditions. J. Workplace Learn. **21**(4), 276–298 (2009)
18. Höfer, C.: Unterrichtsentwicklung als Schulentwicklung. In: Buchen, H., Rolff, H.-G. (eds.) Professionswissen Schulleitung, pp. 752–788. Beltz Verlag, Weinheim (2006)
19. Hord, S.M.: Professional learning communities. communities of continuous inquiry and improvement. Southwest Educational Development Laboratory, Austin (1997)
20. Huffman, J.B., Hipp, K.K.: Restructuring schools as professional learning communities. Scarecrow Education, Lanham (2003)
21. Jurasaite-Harbison, E.: Teachers' workplace learning within informal contexts of school cultures in the United States and Lithuania. J. Workplace Learn. **21**(4), 299–321 (2009)
22. KMK: Strategie der Kultusministerkonferenz "Bildung in der digitalen Welt" (2016). http://www.kmk.org/fileadmin/Dateien/pdf/PresseUndAktuelles/2016/Entwurf_KMK-Strategie_Bildung_in_der_digitalen_Welt.pdf
23. Kunter, M., Baumert, J., Blum, W., Klusmann, U., Krauss, S., Neubrand, M.: Professionelle Kompetenz von Lehrkräften. Ergebnisse des Forschungsprogramms COACTIV. Waxmann, Münster (2011)
24. Kunter, M., Klusmann, U., Baumert, J.: Professionelle Kompetenz von Mathematiklehrkräften: Das COACTIV-Modell. In: Zlatkin-Troitschanskaia, O., Beck, K., Sembill, D., Nickolaus, R. & Mulder, R. (Hrsg.). Lehrprofessionalität. Bedingungen, Genese, Wirkungen und ihre Messung, pp. 53–166. Weinheim, Beltz (2009)
25. Lipowski, F.: Lernen im Beruf. Empirische Befunde zur Wirksamkeit von Lehrerfortbildung. In: Müller, F. Eichenberger, A., Lüders, M., Mayr, J. (Hrsg.) Lehrerinnen und Lehrer lernen. Konzepte und Befunde zur Lehrerfortbildung. Waxmann, Münster (2010)
26. Lorenz, R., Bos, W., Endberg, M., Eickelmann, B., Grafe, S., Vahrenhold, J. (Hrsg.).: Schule digital – der Länderindikator 2017. Schulische Medienbildung in der Sekundarstufe I mit besonderem Fokus auf MINT-Fächer im Bundesländervergleich und Trends von 2015 bis 2017. Waxmann, Münster (2017)
27. Mayrberger, K.: Medienpädagogische Kompetenz im Wandel – Vorschlag zur Gestaltung des Übergangs in der Lehrerbildung am Beispiel mediendidaktischer Kompetenz. In: Schulz-Zander, R. (ed.) Jahrbuch Medienpädagogik, pp. 389–412. Springer VS, Wiesbaden (2012). https://doi.org/10.1007/978-3-531-94219-3_17
28. Meirink, J., Meijer, P., Verloop, N., Bergen, T.: How do teachers learn in the workplace? An examination of teacher learning activities. Eur. J. Teacher Educ. **32**(3), 209–224 (2009)

29. Newmann, F.M.: School-wide Professional Community. Issues in Restructuring Schools, 6, pp. 1–3 (1994)
30. Overwien, B.: Schulorte und Raumgefüge informellen Lernens. In: Böhme, J. (ed.) Schularchitektur im interdisziplinären Diskurs. Territorialisierungskrise und Gestaltungsperspektiven des schulischen Bildungsraums. Springer, Wiesbaden (2009). https://doi.org/10.1007/978-3-531-91868-6_3
31. Ringle, C.M., Sarstedt, M.: Gain more insight from your PLS-SEM results. Ind. Manage. Data Syst. **116**(9), 1865–1886 (2016)
32. Schmid, U., Goertz, L., Behrens, J.: Monitor Digitale Bildung. Die Schulen im digitalen Zeitalter. Gütersloh: Bertelsmann Stiftung (2017). http://www.bertelsmann-stiftung.de/digimonitor
33. Schneider, P., Mahs, C.: Kontinuierliche und Kooperative Selbstqualifikation und Selbstorganisation (KoKoSS) der Ausbilder. In: Euler, D. (ed.) Handbuch der Lernortkooperation. Band 2: Praktische Erfahrungen, pp. 298–312. Bertelsmann, Bielefeld (2003)
34. Schorb, B.: Gebildet und kompetent Medienbildung statt Medienkompetenz. merz **53**(5), 50–56 (2009)
35. Seufert, S., Lehner, M., Tödtli, M.: Didaktisierung des Informellen Lernens. In: Seufert, S., Metzger, C. (eds.), Kompetenzentwicklung in unterschiedlichen Lernkulturen. Festschrift für Dieter Euler zum 60. Geburtstag, pp. 487–507. Eusl, Paderborn (2013)
36. Seufert, S., Scheffler, N.: Developing digital competences of vocational teachers. Int. J. Digital Literacy Digital Competence (ILDLDC) **7**(1) (2016). ISSN: 1947-3944
37. Seufert, S., Lechner, U., Stanoevska, K.: A reference model for online learning communities. Int. J. E-Learning (IJEL) **1**(1), 43–54 (2002)
38. Porcello, D., Hsi, S.: Crowdsourcing and curating online education resources. Science **341** (6143), 240–241 (2013)
39. Terhart, E., Bennewitz, H., Rothland, M.: Handbuch der Forschung zum Lehrerberuf, 2nd edn. Waxmann Verlag, Münster/New York (2014)
40. Tuldoziecki, G.: Entwicklung von Medienkompetenz als Erziehungs- und Bildungsaufgabe. Pädagogische Rundschau **52**(6), 693–709 (1998)
41. Wilbers, K.: Entwicklung der Kompetenzen von Lehrkräften berufsbildender Schulen für digitale Medien. Berufsbildung in Wissenschaft und Praxis (BWP) **3**, 38–41 (2012)

Teaching Data Analytics to Sport Management Majors: A Practical Approach

Reneta P. Barneva[1(✉)] and Valentin E. Brimkov[2,3]

[1] The State University of New York at Fredonia, Fredonia, NY 14063, USA
barneva@fredonia.edu

[2] SUNY Buffalo State, Buffalo, NY 14222, USA
brimkove@buffalostate.edu

[3] Institute of Mathematics and Informatics, Bulgarian Academy of Sciences, Sofia, Bulgaria

Abstract. The growing sector of sport industry increases the demand of sport management specialists capable of using digital technologies in their work. Among the most important fields, in which they need to gain proficiency is data analytics, which is expected to revolutionize the sports in near future. This suggests developing and offering of relevant technology courses to sport management students. Various factors (briefly discussed in the sequel) make the design of such courses a challenging task. In this paper we share our experience of how one can overcome the possible obstacles. We present the main aspects and components of a course on Data Analytics in Sport Management at a small liberal arts college and explain how the educational process is organized. The course is offered by using mostly Open Educational Resources (OER) and other free sources which are described in the paper. This complies with the aspiration of many universities to achieve reduction of textbook cost for their students.

Keywords: Data analytics · Sport management · OER

1 Introduction

According to Forbes, The sports market in North America is expected to reach $73.5 billion by 2019; it was worth $60.5 billion in 2014 [4]. This is 21.5% growth since 2014, or on average 4.3% a year – almost twice the average US economic growth rate for this period, which is 12.8%, or yearly on average 2.56% [13]. It is also interesting to note that according to Forbes, one of the main reasons for such growth is that the "media rights sales will surpass gate revenues and will become the sports industry's largest segment" [4]. These media are not only the traditional TV, but also live streaming of events.

The growing sector of sport industry increases the demand of sport management specialists as it becomes increasingly important for them to be able to apply digital technologies in their work. One of the most important fields in which they have to get proficiency is data analytics. In fact, data analytics and big data are expected to revolutionize the sports [1]. Nowadays, for a team to be successful it is as important to have a good data analyst as to have a good coach [19]. Professional teams in baseball,

L. Uden et al. (Eds.): LTEC 2019, CCIS 1011, pp. 408–417, 2019.
https://doi.org/10.1007/978-3-030-20798-4_35

basketball, football, hockey, and soccer have established data analytics departments to support decision-making on and off the field. Data analyst in sports became a profession of high demand.

Data analytics is used not only to make important decisions for the team strategy and tactics; it is also applied to enrich fans experience, to attract more sponsors, and to increase the chances in sport betting. Although it may seem that data analytics is used only in professional sports, there is another large area of applications and this is the analytics of the data generated by the personal tracking devices. Thus, data analytics is valuable virtually in every area of practice and sciences related to physical activities.

Many universities started offering bachelor degree programs in sport management including specialized courses such as event and facility management, leadership in sports, psychology in sports, sport law, international sport, sport economic, etc. A recent study showed, however, that the use of computing technology within the sport management discipline is underutilized [2]. The reason, in part, is that there are no prepared sport management instructors proficient in technology. On the other hand, the computer science experts do not feel prepared to teach such courses.

Some schools such as Yale, Columbia, and New York University either offer the course on sport analytics as a half-semester course or as a seminar [9, 16, 17]. The used textbook is *Mathletics: How gamblers, managers, and sports enthusiasts use mathematics in baseball, basketball, and football* [21], which give some mathematical methods that could be applied in baseball, basketball or football. While the book is a pioneer in the field of data analytics in sports, it considers only three of the major sports and gives different mathematical solutions for each of them.

Students enrolled in our undergraduate Sport Management program usually find the courses on quantitative reasoning challenging. They have a preference for hands-on activities, service learning, projects and internships than for typical lecturing classes. The quantitative courses that they take are usually just part of the general education and do not go beyond the introductory level. While the knowledge of Python and R is considered as a necessity for any data scientist, sport management students almost never take any programming courses. Thus, it would be difficult for them to take courses on data analytics offered to other majors such as computer science or mathematics majors.

Some other factors play a prohibitive role in offering technology courses to sport management students. For example, technology courses in sport management definitely need to be offered in a computer labs, but computer lab are often considered as proprietary to computing departments and other instructors and students are not allowed to use them. Another factor is the lack of textbooks that could be used for such courses.

The objective of this paper is to share our experience at a small liberal arts college of overcoming the above obstacles and offering a course on Data Analytics in Sport Management. Our goal is to help the instructors who would like to develop such a course in the future. In the next section we describe how the course is organized and what material we cover. Further, following the university initiative of reducing the textbook cost, we offer the course using mostly Open Educational Resources (OER) and other free sources. In the sequel, we describe the resources we used. Finally, we conclude with a discussion and plans for future work.

2 The Course

Below we describe a case study of offering in two consecutive years a 3-credit one semester course (15 weeks of instruction; 45 class hours) on data analytics to sport management majors in the framework of a School of Business in a small liberal arts college.

2.1 Students' Background

The students are enrolled in a Sport Management bachelor degree program. The incoming freshmen usually have lower than college average Mean SAT-Math scores [12] and the courses in computing that they take are minimal. As part of their education, they have to pass only two mandatory quantitative courses:

1. A course on *Introduction to Microcomputer Software* including concepts of spreadsheets and database management systems. The course has a pre-requisite of three units of high school mathematics. It uses the textbook New Perspectives Collection MindTap [10], which covers the basics of MS Excel and Access.
2. Since the Sport Management major is offered by the School of Business, the students take a course on *Fundamentals of Statistics for Business Administration and Economics*, mandatory for all students in the School. It covers basic notions, models, and methods in statistics, such as frequency distributions, probability and probability distributions, sampling distributions, estimation, statistical inference, and simple linear regression [20]. Often the students perceive this course as the most challenging one in their study.

2.2 Course Content

The course on data analytics is offered at 400-level. The above two courses are used as prerequisites. No programming language knowledge is required; instead, various software systems are used. The students are taught to explore decision-making methods and software to measure performance and gain advantage in the competitive sports arena. The course aims at developing analytical skills from practical points of view, useful in sport management. The acquired knowledge aims at allowing the students solving typical sport management problems such as:

- predicting team performance;
- creating winning strategies;
- player analysis;
- player or team ranking, and others.

2.2.1 Case Studies

The course starts with reading articles and discussing the applications of data analytics in sports. Then the students watch videos discussing case studies of applying data analytics into various sports and the achieved improvement. The goal is to motivate the students and show them the endless opportunities data analysis offers. The topic finishes with an assignment: writing a paper how data analysis could be used – in sport management area of student's choice – to improve performance, increase revenue, reveal trends, or, in general, lead to advancement. This paper is extended step-by-step throughout the course and at the end of the course takes the form of a professional report.

2.2.2 Data Collection, Restauration, Storage, Protection

After the students become motivated and sketch a plan of further work, they have to move to the next step and start collecting data for their project. The instructor explains the different types of data, how they can be collected (automatically, through video-capturing or tracking devices; manually, through surveys; or extracted from data repositories), how they are stored in computer systems, how to organize big volumes of data, how to use cloud services, and how to protect the data. The students are also acquainted to approaches of performing data screening, filtering, integration of data from different data sources, and restoring of missing data. They perform several exercises of data gathering, integration, organization, and storage. As an assignment, the students collect data for their specific sport management project described during the first stage of the course.

2.2.3 Data Visualization

At the next phase of the course, the students are introduced to exploratory data analysis, in which the software tools are used to reveal some statistical characteristics or visualize the data, while the analysis is based on human intuition. For this purpose, MS Excel or another software system or language, such as Tableau, R, or SAS are employed. Various types of data filtering and visualizations, as well as their applications in sport management are discussed. More specifically, the students learn how to create some advanced charts such as:

- Band Chart
- Box and Whisker Chart
- Bullet Chart
- Gantt Chart
- Gauge Chart
- Heat Map
- Histogram
- Step Chart
- Pareto Chart
- Thermometer
- Waterfall Chart

and apply them for various tasks. At the end of this stage, the students use appropriate visualization for their projects. Figures 1, 2 and 3 depict some examples.

The visualizations evolve in dashboards, which allow to represent the data dynamically. The students add interactive controls such as scrollbars, option buttons, target lines, check boxes, and others.

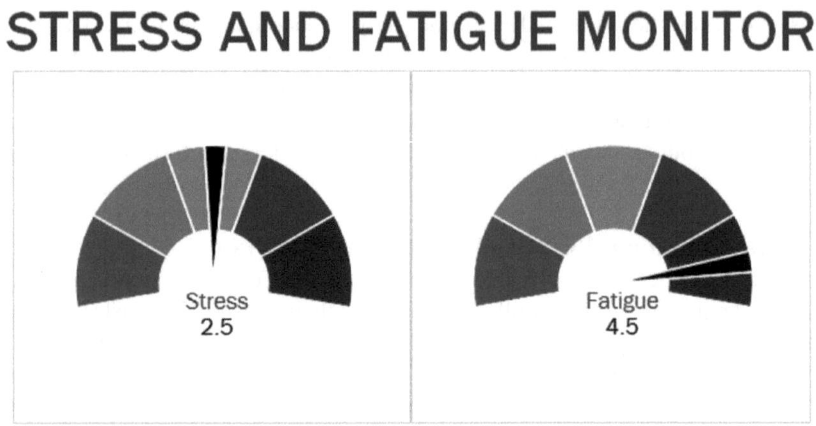

Fig. 1. Sample usage of advanced Excel data visualizations in sport management: a gauge chart for individual athlete monitoring.

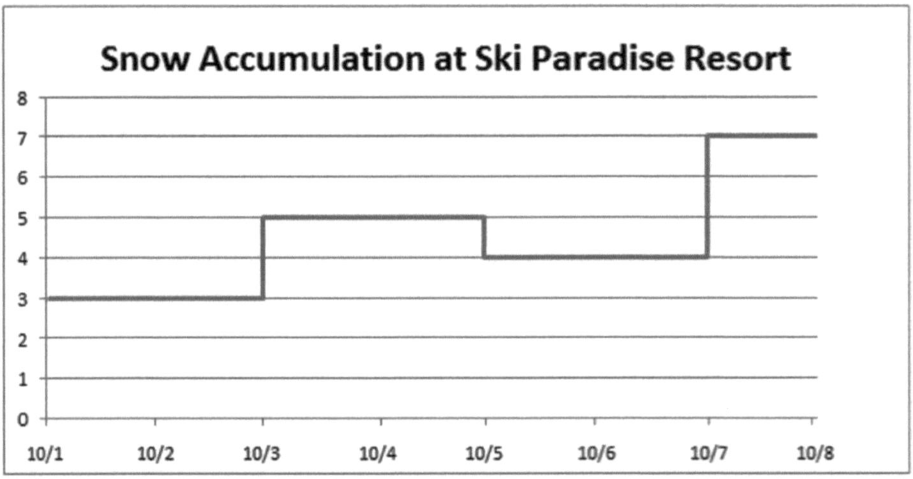

Fig. 2. Sample usage of advanced Excel data visualizations in sport management: a step chart for snowfall accumulation in ski resort.

2.2.4 Decision-Making

Further, the students are acquainted with approaches for data-supported decision-making. Articles in sport management decision-making are explored and the role of attention, anticipation and intuition are discussed. Specific case studies about perceptual information and associative knowledge are considered. Then software and models for decision-making are introduced. Our choice was the system *Knime*, which is a free, open-source platform for data analytics. We also explored *Excel's Solver* add-in to make decisions. It is a very powerful tool for solving linear and even non-linear programming problems, allowing finding the optimal solution given some set of conditions.

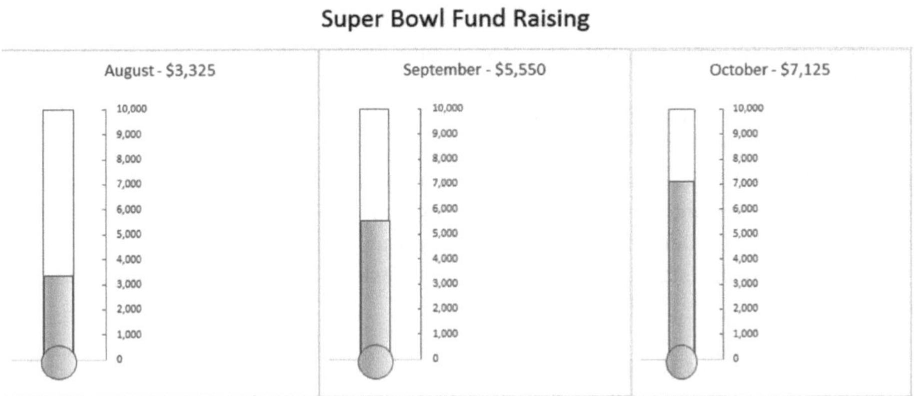

Fig. 3. Sample usage of advanced Excel data visualizations in sport management: a thermometer cart for fundraising for a group visit of the Super Bowl.

The efforts were directed towards learning how the software works and how to apply it for sport management problems. We do not try to cover systematically the entire functionality of these software systems, but rather to see what models and functions are applicable for our goals.

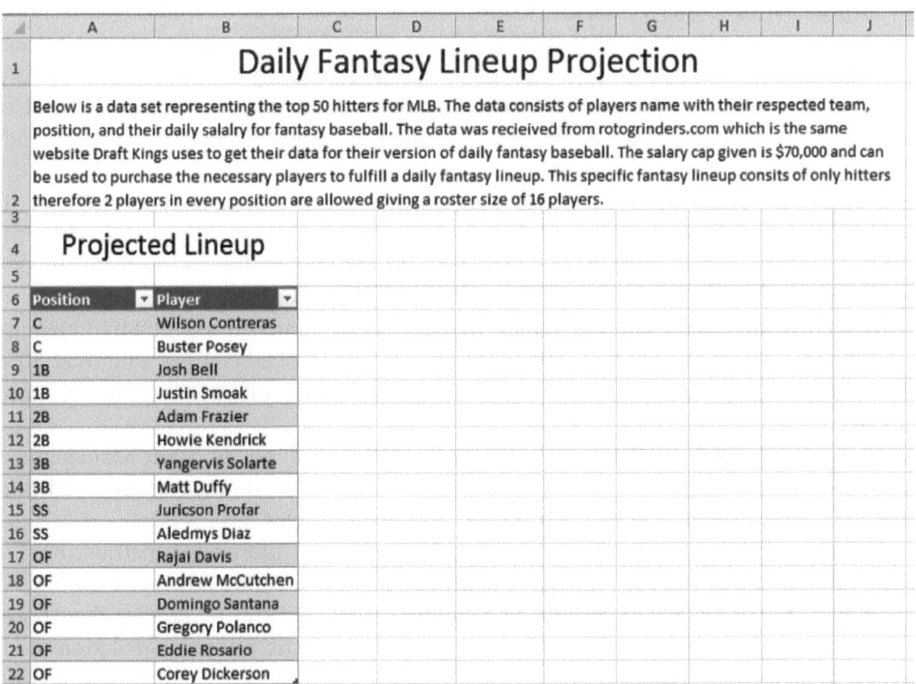

Fig. 4. Sample project for using Solver to make a decision about Daily Fantasy Lineup Projection.

For example, *Knime* is used to create a machine learning model for winning strategies. The students populate the model with existing data sets from sport events. Then they pre-process the data, as it was studied at the first stage. After that they use the pre-built block for creating a decision tree. Finally, they score the prediction model.

Solver could be used extensively in sport management for finding the best strategy, the maximal funding, the minimal expenses, the optimal lineup, and others. The course explains the model and gives the students examples of using it in sports. Figure 4 displays a sample student project of team lineup using *Solver*.

At the end of this stage, the students have to extend their projects using predictive analytics.

2.2.5 Evaluation of the Model

Next, the students learn various types of metrics, measurement, and their usage in predictive analytics. They are asked to research and find appropriate metrics related to various problems in sports and apply at least one metric in their project to evaluate the analytical model that they developed.

Finally, the projects are written in a professional manner, formatted accordingly, and presented in class.

3 Open Educational Resources

The rising cost of higher education world-wide is a concern to the public, legislators, and prospective students and their families. In response to this concern, about 10 years ago, a new movement started widely proclaiming the possibility of getting a completely free degree equivalent through MOOCs (massive open online courses). MOOCs, however, did not replace the traditional education, as many expected; the traditional education continues to be dominant.

Part of the college expenses, which is sometimes overlooked, goes for textbooks. In the USA, these expenses have increased nearly 8 times in the last 30 years (see Fig. 5). Recently, federal grants were given in the USA to the universities to lower the cost of the textbooks. The individual states also allocated funds for that.

Related to this, the State University of New York launched an initiative encouraging the instructors to use OER in their courses. The approved courses with over 50% OER material usage are marked as *low cost* in the course offering and attract more students.

Thus, we took the challenge to redesign the Data Analytics in Sport Management course as an OER-approved course. The sources that we used could be grouped into three main parts: open videos, open books, and open articles.

The open videos are mostly open tutorials, such as a tutorial for metrics [8], for using a decision tree [6], for regression analysis [15], for creating advanced charts [5], and others. Other videos represent case studies such as how to predict the sports winners using data analytics [7] or how to perform realistic golfing simulation [14]. Several general open books on data analytics and statistics exist, which can also be explored [3, 11, 18]. The books are released under Creative Commons BY-SA 3.0, which allow the instructors to not only share, copy, and redistribute the content, but

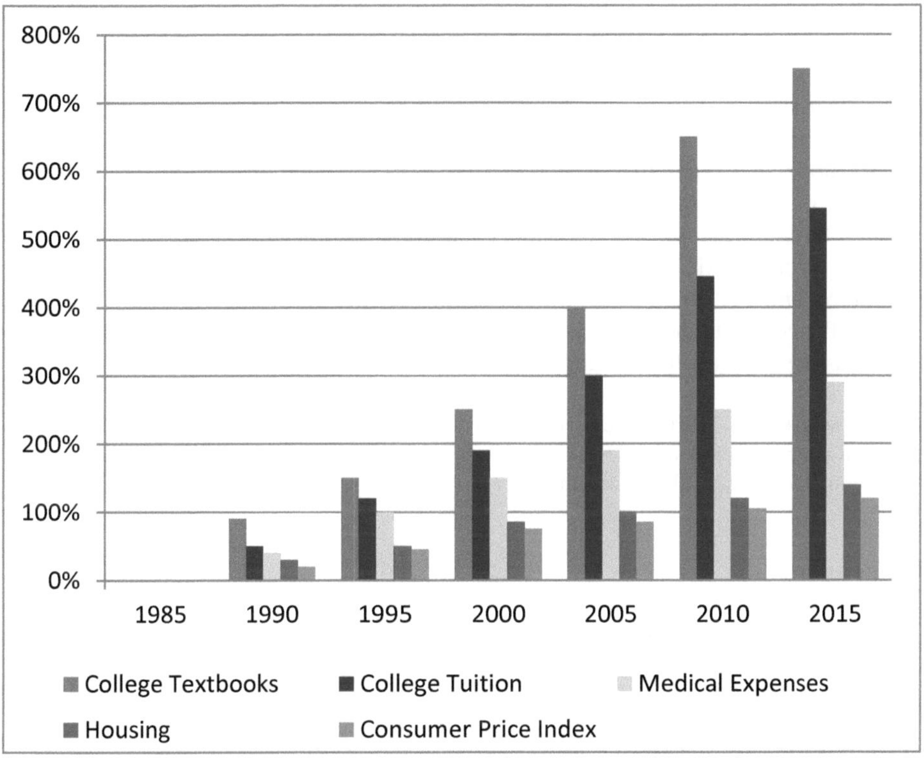

Fig. 5. Increasing cost of textbooks in the USA (*Data from the Bureau of Statistics*).

also to adapt and build upon the material. This is particularly useful in a dynamically developing discipline, where it is important to update the information at every offering. Finally, the open articles were given to students for read-at-home assignments and class discussion.

4 Conclusion and Further Work

In this paper we considered offering data analytics to sport management students in the framework of liberal arts education. Both disciplines are relatively new and there are no readily available textbooks that could be used for such a course. In addition, the preliminary preparation of the students in quantitative reasoning is quite light. In particular, they have not taken any programming course.

Hence, our approach is practical. We acquaint the students with models and methods through case studies and show them how to use software systems to solve various tasks. Throughout the entire course they work on specific individual projects, using sport data and make recommendations based on respective analytical models. Finally, the projects are professionally written and publicly presented. This hands-on approach proved to be beneficial for the students and they shared that they learned a lot.

After an initial offering of the course, we redesigned it using OER so that the cost of associated materials is zero. The benefit is not only lowering the cost, but also making it possible to easily update the content, which is important for fast-developing disciplines. Our studies showed that the students were comfortable with the OER and saw more benefits than disadvantages.

We hope that our experience could be used by other instructors teaching data analytics to students in social sciences or humanities.

As a further work we plan to conduct additional studies of the student perception of learning through exit surveys. We intend to get feedback from the students after graduation and poll them about the application of the knowledge and skills acquired through the course in their professional work. We also plan to develop a mechanism for formal assessment of the learning outcomes.

Acknowledgements. Part of the work reported in this article is supported by the 2019 Cooperative Research Project at the Research Center of Biomedical Engineering and the Research Institute of Electronics, Shizuoka University.

References

1. Ayers, R.: How big data is revolutionizing sports. Dataconomy. https://dataconomy.com/2018/01/big-data-revolutionizing-favorite-sports-teams/. Accessed 09 Jan 2019
2. Barneva, R.P., Hite, P.: Information technology in sport management curricula. J. Educ. Technol. Syst. (Sage) **45**(3), 326–342 (2017)
3. Data Screening. Wikiversity. https://en.wikiversity.org/wiki/Data_screening. Accessed 09 Jan 2019
4. Heitner, D.: Sports industry to reach $73.5 billion by 2019. Forbes, 19 October 2015. https://www.forbes.com/sites/darrenheitner/2015/10/19/sports-industry-to-reach-73-5-billion-by-2019/#195f2ce51b4b. Accessed 09 Jan 2019, 10 Mar 2019
5. How to make advanced charts. https://www.youtube.com/watch?v=HDNynLSQBRs. Accessed 09 Jan 2019
6. Introduction to using a decision tree. https://courses.lumenlearning.com/wm-principlesofmanagement/chapter/introduction-to-using-a-decision-tree/. Accessed 09 Jan 2019
7. Layton, R.: Predicting sports winners using data analytics with pandas and scikit– learn. https://www.youtube.com/watch?v=k7hSD_-gWMw. Accessed 09 Jan 2019
8. Lean startup key metrics. https://www.youtube.com/watch?v=o0t2dBkalDk. Accessed 09 Jan 2019
9. MGT 817 01 Sport Analytics – Syllabus. https://yale.instructure.com/courses/29304/assignments/syllabus. Accessed 09 Mar 2019
10. Mind Tap AC. New Perspectives Collection, Cengage Learning (2017)
11. Missing Data. Wikiversity. https://en.wikiversity.org/wiki/Missing_data. Accessed 09 Jan 2019
12. Office of Institutional Research, Planning & Assessment. University fact book fall 2017. SUNY Fredonia. https://www.fredonia.edu/about/offices/institutional-research-assessment/fact-book. Accessed 09 Jan 2019
13. Real gross domestic product (GDP) growth rate in the United States from 2012 to 2022 (compared to the previous year). Statista. https://www.statista.com/statistics/263614/gross-domestic-product-gdp-growth-rate-in-the-united-states/. Accessed 09 Jan 2019

14. Realistic golfing simulation. https://www.youtube.com/watch?v=biNrhvLI6q0. Accessed 09 Jan 2019
15. Simple linear regression with residuals – Excel. https://www.youtube.com/watch?v=lNXylS4ztfA. Accessed 09 Jan 2019
16. Sports Analytics: Half-Course Edition. https://www8.gsb.columbia.edu/courses/mba/2015/spring/b8131-00. Accessed 09 Mar 2019
17. Sports Analytics in Practice. http://w4.stern.nyu.edu/economics/docs/Syllabi/Sp17/Altman_%20Sports%20Analytics%20in%20Practice%20-%20Syllabus%20v2.pdf. Accessed 09 Mar 2019
18. Statistics/Data Analysis. Wikibooks. https://en.wikibooks.org/wiki/Statistics/Data_Analysis. Accessed 09 Jan 2019
19. Steinberg, L.: Changing the game: The rise of sports analytics. Forbes, 18 August 2018. https://www.forbes.com/sites/leighsteinberg/2015/08/18/changing-the-game-the-rise-of-sports-analytics/#300b71984c1f. Accessed 09 Jan 2019
20. SUNY Fredonia. 2018–2019 University Catalog. https://www.fredonia.edu/catalog. Accessed 09 Jan 2019
21. Winston, W.L.: Mathletics: How Gamblers, Managers, and Sports Enthusiasts Use Mathematics in Baseball, Basketball, and Football. Princeton University Press, Princeton (2012)

A Teaching-Learning Model of Collaborative Assessment in Computer Engineering Studies

Ana B. Gil-González(✉), Ana de Luis Reboredo,
Sara Rodríguez González, and Fernando de la Prieta Pintado

Department of Computing and Automation,
University of Salamanca – Sciences Faculty,
Plaza de la Merced s/n, 37008 Salamanca, Spain
{abg, adeluis, srg, fer}@usal.es

Abstract. The aim of this article is to highlight the benefits of implementing an active learning methodology in classes delivered to engineering degree students in Spain. The proposed teaching methodology has been designed for subjects with assessable practices and a high number of students in Computer Engineering degrees. The methodology is based on the redefinition of roles in the work assessment process where collaborative learning methods are incorporated. The idea of this approach is that students work closely together to learn from each other and that they are responsible for their own learning and that of fellow classmates. Moreover, they learn from participating in the process of assessing the work of their peers. This research describes the implementation of this technology and its promising results. Students increase their activity because they assume the role of solver of the proposed assignment in pair programming and also as evaluator of those of others due peers' protocol. The proposed methodology gives them a more enriching understanding of the contents of the subjects as well as the need for greater intensity in the acquisition of such knowledge in the subject.

Keywords: Pair programming · Computer science education · Collaborative learning · Project-based learning · Active learning methodology

1 Introduction

It is necessary to review traditional methods of evaluating the competences acquired by students within the framework of the current higher education system. The motivation behind this review is to create a new assessment paradigm in which not only the teacher but also the students are responsible for the task of assessing their work and learning. Lecture as a model of teaching is often considered an ineffective means of transmitting information. Experts have recognized skills such as critical thinking, innovation, problem solving, collaboration and communication, as key for any learner.

Peer assessment is a common scientific practice that has attracted considerable attention. Numerous assessment approaches have been developed in different areas of the academy, such as the arbitration system of specialized journals or the assessment of research projects. The use of several forms of peer, collaborative or cooperative

L. Uden et al. (Eds.): LTEC 2019, CCIS 1011, pp. 418–427, 2019.
https://doi.org/10.1007/978-3-030-20798-4_36

learning, has increased in university courses, helping students achieve a variety of learning goals, mainly in small groups. These goals include working collaboratively with others, being responsible for one's learning and deepening one's understanding of specific course content [3]. Moreover, collaboration is a requirement in the professional life of any Computer Science student. Teachers must help learners develop autonomy and creativity as part of academic excellence. Findings demonstrate that cooperative and collaborative pedagogies are of benefit to students [11, 12] as strategies for redesigning learning tasks. Collaborative aspects of Computer Science Education are compatible with student-centred learning but are also directly linked with the well-known constructivist pedagogy [1, 7].

The need for the continuous assessment of student competences has given rise to a more active role of the students in the learning process. This necessity will facilitate the integration of new assessment processes as mechanisms that validate the students' achievements and at the same time guide their learning process.

In the Computer Engineering Degree, a major part of the credits are obtained from practical experience as opposed to knowledge of the theory. However, the design of practices and their subsequent qualification is a complicated task, because there is no single solution and the assessment criteria of these practices constitute a competency training guide in themselves.

The research of Yacedjina et al. [13] examined, from the perspective of the students, the effectiveness of small-group work in a large lecture class. This study illustrates the ways in which small-group activities enhance the comprehension of course material, reduce the anonymity associated with large lecture classes, and promote student accountability.

The validity of the solutions proposed to Computer Engineering problems, can only be determined by their performance within a given context. The need for a technical interpretation makes the assessment of practical tasks difficult. As a result of this difficulty we have been motivated to develop a teaching-learning model, based on a series of teaching methods for the acquisitions of competences and their subsequent assessment. The proposed methodology allows Computer Engineering students to become actively involved in the collaborative construction of knowledge, together with the use of pair programming [4]. This approach redefines the roles in the assessment process and leverages collaborative learning methods for the Computer Engineering Degree. In this process, students work together to learn and are responsible for both, the learning of their peers and their own, then, they perform a supervised peer assessment of the practices they have conducted.

This research proposes and validates a model of assessment of practices by pairs that will be incorporated into the construction of knowledge through collaborative techniques of assessment, pair programming and learning through projects [2].

To develop this model a work team was formed, in included several teachers who taught subjects from the Computer Engineering Degree at the Faculty of Sciences in the University of Salamanca, Spain. Several subjects with a strong emphasis on the practical aspect have been chosen from different years of the Computer Engineering Degree.

This paper compiles a final summary of the main contributions and results. Section 2 presents the objectives of the work. Section 2.1 describes the development and generation of the methodology. Section 3 outlines the obtained results and the degree of success of the designed teaching models. Finally, Sect. 4 concludes the work and discusses future lines of research.

2 Objectives

The guiding principle for the development of this methodological approach is the concept of project-based learning or "learning by doing"; the main objective of the project is the development of a collaborative methodology that strengthens the traditional mechanisms of learning in subjects with high practical content and development of activities that can be evaluated by the students. The general objectives of this research are as follows:

1. Study the use of collaborative learning techniques as part of continuous assessment in the classroom.
2. Develop peer assessment and peer co-assessment techniques in evaluable practices in computer engineering degrees.
3. Involve the students in the tasks of assessment and acquisition of competencies within a model of exercise solving.
4. Determine the weight (their importance in the teaching-learning process) of different assessment techniques for different subjects of the degree.
5. Develop an execution model of collaborative assessment practices in Computer Engineering Degree subjects with high practical content, creating an active teaching-learning methodology in the classroom.
6. Generate specific materials for the practical work for subjects such as "Operating Systems", "Database Systems" and implement them in the Computer Engineering Degree.

2.1 Development of Activities. Methodology of Resolution and Assessment of Practical Assignments

For each subject, all the information related to the assessment process and its rules are published in the virtual Campus; the online Moodle-based teaching platform.

On the first day of class, the students are given a calendar with all the dates of (1) publication of the statements of the practices, (2) delivery a product as solution for the assignment and (3) defences.

One of the aspects of group work, that most concerns students and teachers, is the lack of involvement of some group members who leave the work to others. This problem arises mainly in groups made up of more than four people [6, 9]. The possibilities of this opportunist behaviour in group tasks, at higher education level, have been studied along some practical experiences [8, 10]. For this reason, in the model we developed, the students perform practical tasks in pairs, using the paradigm of pair programming [5]. The students decide who they are going to work with and remain in the same pair for the rest of the year. All students also choose a name for the team

```
FEBRUARY          (*) Group A1          (&)Groups A2, B2, B3    (#) Group A3, B1
 M    T    W
 13*  14&  15&    Session 1: 13-FEB     Session  1: 14-FEB      Session  1: 15-FEB
 20*  21&  22#    Session 2: 20-FEB     Session  2: 21-FEB      Session  2: 22-FEB
 27*  28&         Session 3: 27-FEB     Session  3: 28-FEB

    MARCH
  M    T    W
            1#                                                  Session  3: 01-MAR
  6*   7&   8#    1ª Pract: 06-MAR       1ª Pract.: 07-MAR      1ª Pract.:: 08-MAR
 13*  14&  15#    Session  4: 13-MAR    Session  4: 14-MAR      Session 4: 15-MAR
 20*  21&  22#    Session 5: 20-MAR     Session 5: 21-MAR       Session 5: 22-MAR
 27*  28&  29#    Session 6: 27-MAR     Session 6: 28-MAR       Session 6: 29-MAR

    APRIL
  M    T    W
  3*   4&   5#    2ª Pract.: 03-APR    2ª Pract.: 04-APR       2ª Pract.: 05-APR
  (...)
 17*  18&  19#    Session  7: 17-APR    Session 7: 18-APR      Session 7: 19-APR
 (24) 25&  26#                         Session 8: 25-APR       Session 8: 26-APR


    MAY
 M     T    W
 (1)  2&    3#                         Session 9: 02-MAY      Session 9: 03-MAY
  8*  9&   10#    Session 8: 08-MAY     3ª Pract.: 09-MAY     3ª Pract.: 10-MAY
 15*  16&  17#    Session 9: 15-MAY
 22*  23&  24#    3ª Pract.: 22-MAY

Delivery deadline:
          - 1ª Practice: Monday, 27-MAR
          - 2ª Practice: Tuesday, 25-APR
          - 3ª Practice: Tuesday, 31-MAY

Dates for defense:
         - 1ª Practice: [29-MAR to 5-APR]
         - 2ª Practice: [2-MAY to 17-MAY]
         - 3ª Practice: [5-JUN to 08-JUN]

-------------------------------------------------------------
```

Fig. 1. Sample calendar of practical sessions

and give it to the teacher. In addition, one of the students is the captain of the group. Throughout the year, the teams perform three voluntary practical assignments. The teacher keeps all the captains updated of schedules, appointments etc. through the virtual Campus.

2.2 Practice Instructions and Evaluable Aspects

Once a practical assignment has been given to the team, each team develops its solution and uploads it to the platform in the indicated format and before the deadline. The students defend their work in what we call triads (three teams). Once the deadline has closed, the teacher arranges the triads and publishes their list and the date and time of each. The groups that formed a triad were different in the three practices performed during the course.

A peer review will be conducted: each team should review the practical work of the other two teams, which make up the triad and complete a review form for both. Thus, the defence and assessment of the practices of the subject consists of several parts:

1. Each group will provide a solution to the practical work assigned to them.
2. The teacher chooses the groups to form the triads and plans the publication.
3. Assessment of the solutions of the other two teams and preliminary preparation of the defence task.

To perform this preliminary review, the involved teams are organized to facilitate collaborative work. Each team must assess the work of the other two teams of their triad in each of the three aspects:

a. A critical assessment of the practice
b. Determine if the execution is working correctly or not, to this end it is necessary to interpret the foreign code and to put it into operation.
c. If some part of the foreign practice in the assessment does not work properly, the assessment team has to identify how it should be solved correctly.

In the virtual campus, the students of the subject contribute to the revision process. The virtual campus provides a form with sections related to the practical work, each group must complete and submit those forms on the day of the defence. It is recommended to complete the form directly in the provided spaces, also print it after filling it out and sign it for delivery to teacher.

4. The students defend the proposed solution in a computer lab, in which all the members of the three teams (six people in three teams or triads) participate.
5. During the defence, each team will be asked questions related to the practical work of the other two teams and the information will be included in the practice form generated for this practice, which will be filled out and signed. They will also have to describe their practical work that they will have to defend.
6. The grade for the practical work is, nevertheless, given to each student individually because in the defence of their work, the teacher evaluates each member of the team orally and considers the student's assessment of the practical work of the other two teams.

A summary of other criteria in the qualification, which is important to take into account are the following:

- The teacher examines the group's assessment of the other two teams, if faults are detected in their assessment, the grade of the assessment group is lowered.
- On the contrary, if the assessment group detects and solves the errors of the other groups, the impact on the grade of the assessment team is positive.
- The team, whose practical work had errors that were detected by the assessment group, can improve its grade if it is able to provide a possible solution to these errors during the defence of their practical work.

The groups in the triad change in each practice, so that no team coincides throughout the defence processes. This allows to encourage a student with three practices to visualize at least the way of working of six teams and interact with twelve people in their group in the course of the course in addition to work in pairs.

Students are given a statement for each practice, as well as an itinerary to carry out this practice. Therefore, the summary of the protocol finally designed is the following:

1. Formation of student pairs for development of practical work
2. In time assignment delivery
3. Creation of triads
4. Publication of the names of group captains
5. Informing the captains of the triads for any communication
6. Peer review of the practice: each group will review the practices of the other two groups together with those forming the triad
7. Complete each group the review form for each evaluated practice
8. Defence of the practices
   a. Exposition of reasons and delivery of the signed assessment review form for each of the practices of the two teams
   b. Individual defence of the practice and replicas to the other teams and the teacher.

In the case of a study carried out in the subject Operating Systems, the practical work represents 30% of the final grade of the subject, with 70% of the final written exam. There were three voluntary practical assignments, which amounted to up to10% of the final grade of the subject.

In the case of the groups where the peer defence assessment protocol was followed, the practices were assessed according to three sections, shown at Table 1:

Table 1. Weighting of voluntary practices note

Activity	Score
Practice delivery	Up to 30%
Personal exposition	Up to 50%
Peer review	Up to 20%

3 Case Study and Results

In this project we have designed a collaborative assessment model in which the student can be evaluated objectively and participates in the process.

Our model redefines the student's role, who becomes responsible for their own learning and that of their classmates through the development of the practical assignments in pairs.

This teaching methodology is designed for subjects with a lot of practical workload and a large number of students and assessable practices in the Degree in Computer Engineering studies. Specifically, the case study conducted in this paper affects two different groups studying the same subject (Case 1 and Case 2). In this subject, 50% of their ECTS are of a practical nature, which makes them ideal for studying the proposed methodology (Fig. 1).

It was found that it could be useful if tools were generated in order to facilitate the students' assessment over the practices of their classmates. Figures 2 and 3 show how in the first attempt exams the groups that made a defence of practices with triads methodology had a greater number of approved (53.45%) compared with the groups with individual defence (38.96%). The resit exams did not generate hardly any differences.

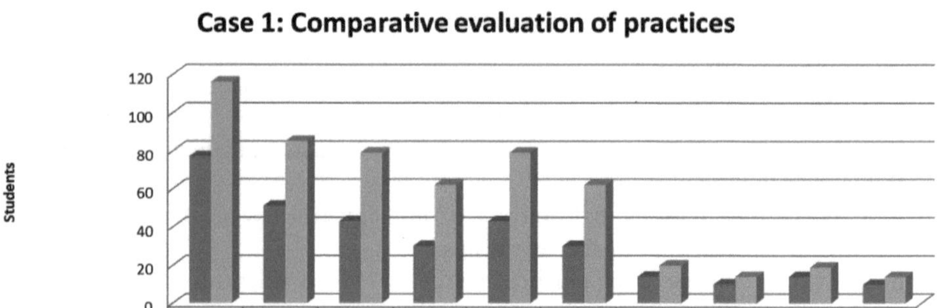

	Students	Practices Presented	Presented 1st call	Passed at 1st call	Presented 1st call with practices	Passed 1st call with practices	Presented 2nd call	Passed at 2nd call	Presented 2nd call with practices	Passed 2nd call with practices
Individual evaluation	77	51	43	30	43	30	14	10	14	10
Peer evaluation	116	85	79	62	79	62	20	14	19	14

Fig. 2. Comparative graph of the number of students who participate in the assessment tasks

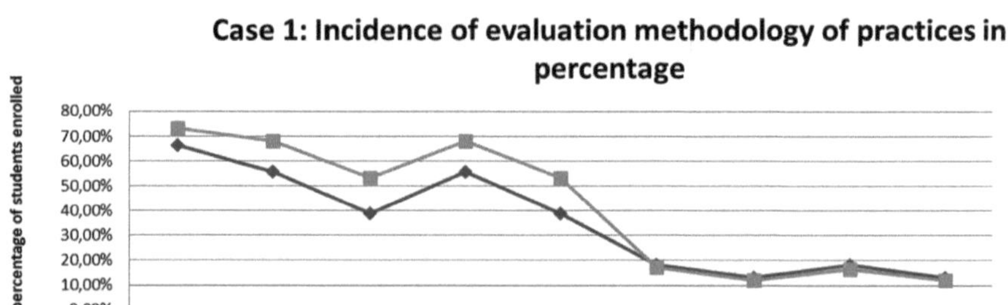

	Practices Presented	Presented 1st call	Passed at 1st call	Presented 1st call with practices	Passed 1st call with practices	Presented 2nd call	Passed at 2nd call	Presented 2nd call with practices	Passed 2nd call with practices
Evaluación individual	66,23%	55,84%	38,96%	55,84%	38,96%	18,18%	12,99%	18,18%	12,99%
Peer evaluation	73,28%	68,10%	53,45%	68,10%	53,45%	17,24%	12,07%	16,38%	12,07%

Fig. 3. A comparative of the percentage of students enrolled in the performed assessment tasks

Throughout the following academic year, called Case 2, work groups were created for the development of a teaching following the same methodology with light changes. A methodology of assessment of the practices by pairs has been established that has been applied in the two groups in the morning while for the two groups of the afternoon there was an individual defence of the practices that would allow their comparative assessment as a control group. Figures 4 and 5 show the results obtained in the first

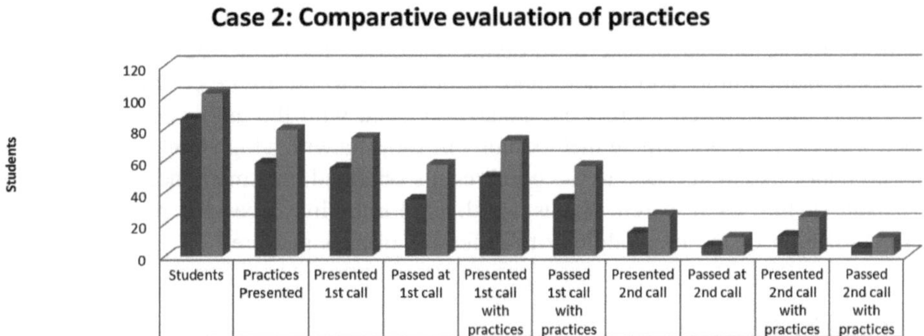

	Students	Practices Presented	Presented 1st call	Passed at 1st call	Presented 1st call with practices	Passed 1st call with practices	Presented 2nd call	Passed at 2nd call	Presented 2nd call with practices	Passed 2nd call with practices
Individual evaluation	86	58	55	35	49	35	14	6	12	5
Peer evaluation	102	79	74	57	72	56	25	11	24	11

Fig. 4. Comparative of the number of students who participated in assessment tasks (Case 2)

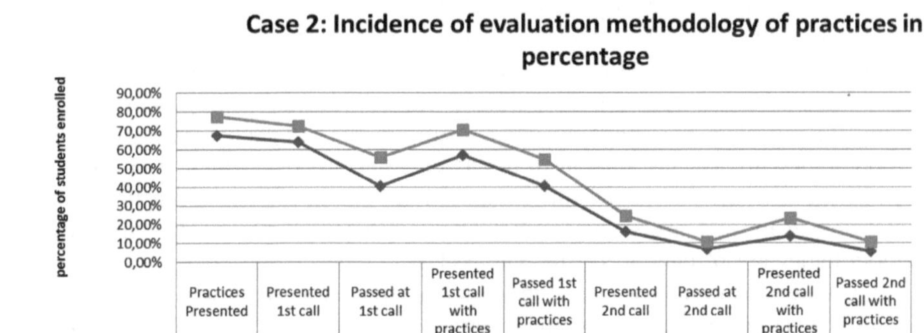

	Practices Presented	Presented 1st call	Passed at 1st call	Presented 1st call with practices	Passed 1st call with practices	Presented 2nd call	Passed at 2nd call	Presented 2nd call with practices	Passed 2nd call with practices
Evaluación individual	67,44%	63,95%	40,70%	56,98%	40,70%	16,28%	6,98%	13,95%	5,81%
Peer evaluation	77,45%	72,55%	55,88%	70,59%	54,90%	24,51%	10,78%	23,53%	10,78%

Fig. 5. Comparative percentage with respect to students enrolled for assessment tasks carried out (Case 2)

attempt exam of the subject. Again, the percentage of students who passed the subject is (55.88%) where voluntary practices were performed in pairs, while the percentage of students who have passed in a classroom with an individual learning approach was 40.70%.

Over the course of the described case study, the team of teachers studied and elaborated teaching strategies and methodologies applied to teaching, including collaborative assessment by peers, has been carried out jointly by the team of teachers. Practical materials and instructional designs have been developed for individual subjects that have been included and managed using the online teaching tools. For to evaluate the proposed methodology in context, four practice groups were coordinated, with four teachers and 188 students in the subject. This experience has allowed us to generate new materials and consider the scope of the proposed methodology. In this regard, the results are excellent.

To sum up, almost all the project objectives have been met. Once the project was finalized, the results encourage us to define objectives for further development of the proposed methodology and to add more assignments to the future courses.

Finally, the research team is particularly satisfied with the innovation work put in place with the peer assessment methodology in subjects with a high content of practices and number of students. Due to the good results obtained, this methodology allows us to ensure a line of research that is worth exploring in successive projects with a systematization of the methodology to different subjects and areas.

4 Conclusions

The research proposed in this article lays the foundations for the development of a teaching and assessment methodology for computer engineering subjects with a high practical workload. The large number of students in this type of assignments makes it very difficult to assess the progress of each student. The current teaching approach of the Spanish higher education system, in the case of engineering degrees, requires a greater number of teachers. However, due to the economic situation, this is not going to be possible in the coming years. The use of collaborative methodologies as a means of solving this problem has rendered good results in the conducted case study. Those methodologies involve the student in the assessment process, which is always supervised by the teacher. This allows the student to get good hold of the practical contents of the subjects through assessment with the help of their classmates. Thus, the proposed methodologies are of benefit for the whole class.

The student using the proposed methodology increases their activity by means of solving an exercise given to them and evaluating the exercises performed by two other student groups. This approach provides the student with a more global overview of the practical contents and according to the surveys completed by the students, this methodology has increased their speed of learning. Moreover, students stated that they have learned from the solutions of their peers, allowing them to correct their mistakes or to learn to develop more elaborate solutions.

As shown in Figs. 3 and 5, the classrooms that adapted this methodology had a higher student pass rate than those that followed an individual assessment methodology; there is a visible difference in the success rates of the two methodologies, especially in the first attempt exams. The difference in the performance of the two teaching methodologies is not as strongly reflected in the resit exams, although there is a slight improvement in the results of the students involved in the proposed assessment process.

The analysis of peer review methods and their application to teaching as a peer assessment methodology has made it possible to elaborate specific materials for the Operative Systems subject of the Computer Engineering Degree. The interviews with the students, teachers and colleagues from other universities, have provided us with different points of view, enabling us to develop a methodology that has improved in many aspects.

The experiences students gained from this methodology of learning have been excellent and its impact on the exam results of the students who of participated in the case study, corroborate the effectiveness of peer assessment.

Due to the above results, we arrive at the conclusion that this innovative teaching project has excellent prospects for the future and will likely be implemented in the computer engineer assignments in the coming years. The project has directly generated an action for improvement in the subjects involved because as a result it has allowed the adaptation of:

- The design of the subjects contemplated in the Curriculum,
- The program of the subjects in the teaching program and
- The development and assessment of the subjects in the teaching reality.

To sum up, the results of the case study are satisfactory and demonstrate the effectiveness of the proposed learning-teaching model.

Acknowledgments. This work was carried out under the partial frame of the innovation project ID10/147, supported by University of Salamanca.

References

1. Ben-Ari, M.: Constructivism in computer science education. J. Comput. Math. Sci. Teach. **20**(1), 45 (2001)
2. Blumenfeld, P.C., et al.: Motivating project-based learning: sustaining the doing, supporting the learning. Educ. Psychol. **26**(3–4), 369–398 (1991)
3. Boud, D., Cohen, R., Sampson, J.: Peer learning and assessment. Assess. Assess. High. Educ. **24**(4), 413–426 (1999)
4. Braught, G., Tim, W., Eby, L.M.: The case for pair programming in the computer science classroom. ACM Trans. Comput. Educ. **11**(1), 21 (2011)
5. Dybå, T., Arisholm, E., Sjøberg, D.I., Hannay, J.E., Shull, F.: Are two heads better than one? On the effectiveness of pair programming. IEEE Softw. **24**(6), 12–15 (2007)
6. Fruchter, R.: Dimensions of teamwork education. Int. J. Eng. Educ. **17**(4/5), 426–430 (2001)
7. Greening, T.: Emerging constructivist forces in computer science education: shaping a new future. In: Greening, T. (ed.) Computer Science Education in the 21st Century, pp. 47–80. Springer, New York (2000). https://doi.org/10.1007/978-1-4612-1298-0_5
8. Hsiung, C.M.: The effectiveness of cooperative learning. J. Eng. Educ. **101**(1), 119–137 (2012)
9. Kalliath, T., Laiken, M.: Use of teams in management education. J. Manag. Educ. **30**(6), 747–750 (2006)
10. Marin-Garcia, J.A., Lloret, J.: Improving teamwork with university engineering students. The effect of an assessment method to prevent shirking. WSEAS Trans. Adv. Eng. Educ. **5** (1), 1–11 (2008)
11. Slavin, R.E.: Using Student Team Learning. Baltimore, MD: Johns Hopkins University. Center for Social Organization of Schools (1994)
12. Slavin, R.E.: Cooperative Learning: Theory, Research, and Practice. Prentice-Hall, Englewood Cliffs (1990)
13. Yazedjian, A., Kolkhorst, B.B.: Implementing small-group activities in large lecture classes. Coll. Teach. **55**(4), 164–169 (2007)

Students Performance Analysis Based on Machine Learning Techniques

Alberto Rivas[1,2(✉)], Jesús M. Fraile[1], Pablo Chamoso[1], Alfonso González-Briones[1,2], Sara Rodríguez[1], and Juan M. Corchado[1,2,3,4]

[1] BISITE Research Group, University of Salamanca, Edificio I+D+i, Calle Espejo 2, 37007 Salamanca, Spain
{rivis,jezu1996,chamoso,alfonsogb,srg,corchado}@usal.es

[2] Air Institute, IoT Digital Innovation Hub, Carbajosa de la Sagrada, 37188 Salamanca, Spain

[3] Department of Electronics, Information and Communication, Faculty of Engineering, Osaka Institute of Technology, 535-8585 Osaka, Japan

[4] Pusat Komputeran dan Informatik, Universiti Malaysia Kelantan, Karung Berkunci 36, Pengkaan Chepa, 16100 Kota Bharu, Kelantan, Malaysia

Abstract. One of the main concerns of educational entities is improving the quality of teaching and the academic performance of students. As a result of this concern, countless studies have been performed to identify the factors that affect student's learning. These have helped to guide students in the correct direction and to change for the better their students' habits and personal situation. Since the appearance of virtual classrooms, the monitoring of the students' use of online resources has allowed teachers to identify their learning habits, analysing some of the reasons for their academic progress or the lack thereof.

This research analyses different machine learning techniques, including tree based models and different types of Neural Networks. The objective is to apply those models to a dataset containing data from a virtual environment and construct performance models that will allow to predict if a student is going to fail or pass the academic year. Finally, the factors that have a greatest influence on the performance of a student are identified and suggestions for the improvement of those factors are proposed in order to achieve an increase the pass rate among students.

Keywords: Machine learning · Neural network · Classification trees · Student performance · Virtual classroom

1 Introduction

Academically, the main objective of both students and teachers is to achieve the highest possible pass rate. Normally, the students who pay attention and are involved in the classes can get through their exams. The amount of study hours they dedicate and their reasoning capacity are essential. However, there have always been students who have had more difficulty and this fact, in most cases,

L. Uden et al. (Eds.): LTEC 2019, CCIS 1011, pp. 428–438, 2019.
https://doi.org/10.1007/978-3-030-20798-4_37

is linked to a series of social variables that directly affect poorly performing students. Families with economic problems, an inadequate circle of friends or low class attendance are clear examples of this.

As a result, many studies have been carried out in the field of education to identify the external factors that affect the academic performance of students. However, some positive factors have also been identified, such as the emergence of virtual classrooms like Moodle, which makes a lot of resources available to students online to encourage and accelerate the learning process [12,21]. Universities and colleges are therefore looking at how they can eliminate or minimise those negative factors for their students and try to maximise their students' performance; these studies help them decide how to go about doing this.

To perform a study in this area it is necessary to collect data about students. Underage students' data cannot be used for data protection reasons. As a result, higher education courses or universities are the best places for conducting a research because the students' legal age allows to process the collected information without any barriers. Once a sample of data from different student profiles has been obtained, it is possible to apply different techniques such as statistical studies or different machine learning techniques. The purpose of a statistical study can be very varied [17,22], although it commonly consists of identifying pass and fail rates versus other variables. On the other hand, applying machine learning techniques, it is possible to study a sample of data in order to identify the variables that most affect students. In addition, they give the opportunity to train a predictive model that allows anticipating and improve future cases [19].

This article relies on the use of Neural Networks to study what factors and how they affect academic performance in an online course and how the number of passers could be increased based on the factors studied.

The rest of the article is structured as follows: the background is shown below, detailing the main machine learning models most used when classifying data and how they can be applied in the field of education. The Neural Network designed is described in Sect. 3. In Sect. 4 the system proposed is presented and evaluated. Finally, in Sect. 5 the conclusion and the future lines of work are presented.

2 Background

In the field of data analysis, one of the most important aspects is the classification into different clusters or groups, either binary classification when there are two groupings, or multiclass in other types of cases. Statistical and probability techniques [27], as well as machine learning methods, can be used to carry out this process. Following an approach based on machine learning models, the most common classification techniques are tree-based models [7]. Thus, the following are the most popular:

Decision Trees: consists of grouping elements depending on the possible interactions that can be formed with explanatory variables. In each resulting category, the observed frequency is measured with respect to the target variable.

The branches are then opened according to the most relevant frequencies, repeating the process until categories are found in which the resulting frequencies are no longer relevant [25]. Focusing on the context in the field of education, there are numerous studies carried out with decision trees, such as the work presented in [27] which studies the satisfaction of university students from a series of opinion polls. On the other hand, [23] studies student dropout and achievement.

Random Forest: consists of an improved algorithm based on multiple decision trees [6]. In [2] the Random Forest Technique predicted students academic performance in a virtual environment using factors such as students interaction with the environment, their assessment grades, and previous knowledge of student data. In addition, [3] pointed out that the field of education is one of the areas that needs to gain more knowledge on how the classifications performed by this algorithm and therefore decides to apply Random Forest.

Extreme Gradient Boosting: is a more complex algorithm than Random Forest, which builds trees taking into account the error caused by variables classified by the previous tree [13].

It should be noted that many of the studies on classification algorithms are comparative, such as the study conducted in [26], which concludes that using a more complex model does not lead to better results.

Another fairly common classification technique is based on Neural Networks. Neural Networks are a simplified model that emulates the way the human brain processes information. A large number of interconnected processing units, that look like abstract versions of neurons, work simultaneously to process information. There are different models of Neural Networks depending on the way in which the neurons are grouped. The most prominent models are described above:

- **The Simple Perceptron** is a classifier, it assigns to a vector of N values a binary value, using a non-linear transformation. So each vector belongs to one of the partitions created by the perceptron [10,11].
- **Hopfield's network** is a monolayer network, meaning that it only has a single layer. Although it can also be represented as a two-layer network, where the first layer groups sensors and the second one is where the processing takes place.
- **The multi-layer Perceptron** has a number of very important limitations. The most important one is its inability to classify sets that are not linearly independent. This model is an extension of a perceptron to which series of layers are added to transform the input variables [14–16].
- **Competitive learning networks** differ from other Neural Networks in that instead of collaborating, their neurons compete with each other to represent patterns.
- **Convolutional Neural Networks** are a type of Artificial Neural Network where neurons correspond to receptive fields in a very similar way to neurons in the primary visual cortex (V1) of a biological brain. This type of network is a variation of a multilayer perceptron, however, because its application is made in two-dimensional matrices, they are very effective for computer

vision tasks, such as classification and segmentation of images, among other applications [24].
- **Kohonen Maps/Authorizing Neural Networks**. The Kohonen network belongs to the category of unsupervised networks, the difference with other networks is that neurons representing similar patterns appear together in the output space, this space can be one-dimensional, a line, two-dimensional, a plane or N-dimensional [5,9].

In the field of education, the most common approach when applying a Neural Network is to opt for a multi-layered perceptron. For example, this model was used to carry out a predictive study of the academic performance of students doing engineering [20]. In the study conducted in [28] Artificial Neural Networks were used to predict the students' grades. Another example is presented in [4] where a prediction model is applied to analyze patterns of general high school exam result and use them to predict future exam results.

Regarding the evaluation of the different models, there are several types of metrics that can be used to assess how good a classification is. Some of the most used models are precision and recall. In binary classification, the precision is the proportion of positive classifications that were correct, in the same way, the recall is the proportion of real positives that were correctly identified. With these two metrics, we obtain what is known as F1-Score which is the harmonic mean of precision and recall. Thanks to these measurements it is possible to know how the classifying model behaves. In addition, the so-called confusion matrix is used to evaluate the deficiencies of a model.

3 Neural Network Architecture

The proposed system architecture is based on a multi-layered perceptron with two hidden layers as shown in Fig. 1. The first layer is made up of six neurons, while the second layer is made up of four neurons. The activation function selected in both layers is a Rectified Linear Unit (ReLU), defined as Eq. (1):

$$R(z) = max(0, z) \tag{1}$$

This activation function allows all positive values to pass through, while negative values are assigned a value of 0.

On the other hand, the input layer has as many neurons as there are inputs in the data set, while the output layer has 2 neurons with a SoftMax activation function [8], ideal for multiclass classification as it scales actual values in the range of $[0, 1]$. The first neuron in the output layer is the probability that a student is going to fail, while the second is the probability that a student is going to pass the course.

To minimize the processing costs of the algorithm, an optimization method has been leveraged. Specifically, the Adam optimizer [18] designed to train Deep Neural Networks, has been used with 500 epochs and a batch size of 30.

Finally, the mean square error (MSE) has been used to evalaute the precision of the network.

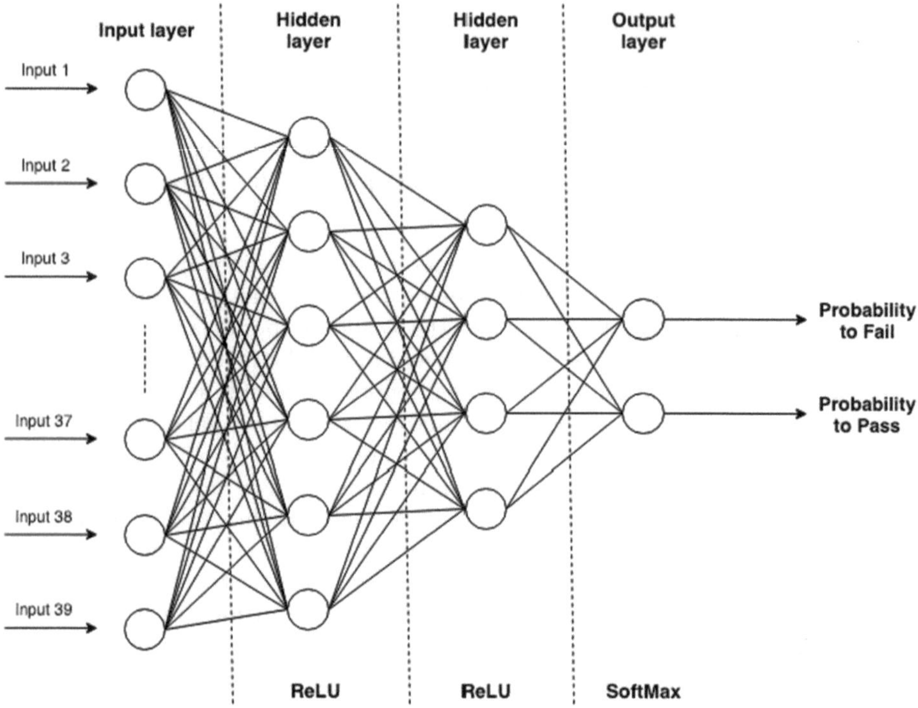

Fig. 1. Design of the multilayer perceptron

4 Proposed System

The objective of this paper is to increase the exams pass rate among student through the evaluation of an automatic learning model and its subsequent improvement. The system proposed in Fig. 2 has been designed for this purpose; the Neural Network is trained with data in order to make it capable of identifying patterns of behaviour. Subsequently, the initial data set is analyzed and the parameters that contribute to students failing their exams are minimized to increase the pass rate. Finally, the already trained network is used in order to predict if with the modifications made in the parameters are going to help students to pass their exams.

4.1 Dataset Analysis

Due to data protection, the processing of data may be a complicated process, as a result it was decided to work and apply a set of public data that can be accessed at [1].

The data that have been included in our dataset come from a group of students who have participated in a series of four online courses. Those who have taken the BBB module have been selected for the study, resulting in a total

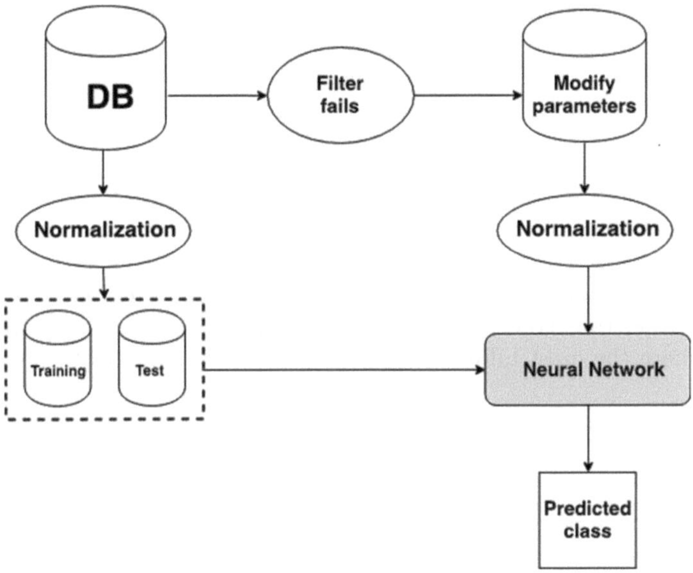

Fig. 2. System workflow

of 7909 students. The studentinfo.csv file (included in the dataset described), includes the students' personal data such as their identification code, the student's gender, region, educational level, age range, neighborhood crime rate (IMD), number of times they have previously participated in the course, enrolled credits, disability and the final exams result (passed/failed). In addition, the number of times the student clicked on any of the online course contents has been counted throughout the course; this data is obtained after making a simple analysis of the file studentVle.csv, also available in the mentioned dataset.

Most of these data are divided into different categories, therefore, we have proceeded to categorize the database finally obtaining 39 columns and 7909 rows. The objective is to predict whether a student, based on all the analyzed parameters, is going to pass or fail their final exams. In addition, it is intended to conduct a study on the students that failed their exams, to determine the key parameters that cause their low performance and to understand how to improve those parameters.

4.2 Results

To perform the training, the data set is divided into two parts: a training set and a test set. Prior to training, the data is subjected to a min-max standardization model to scale the attributes to an appropriate set of values, thus improving network processing. Once trained, the resulting model is applied to the test data set, resulting in an accuracy of 82.46% as seen in Table 1.

Table 1. Metrics obtained after training

	Precision	Recall	f1-score
Fail	0.88	0.74	0.80
Pass	0.77	0.89	0.83
Average	0.824	0.815	0.815

Moreover, Random Forest has been applied to the different parameters of the data in order to extract the variables with more weight. The result is shown in Fig. 3, where the most influential variable was the number of clicks.

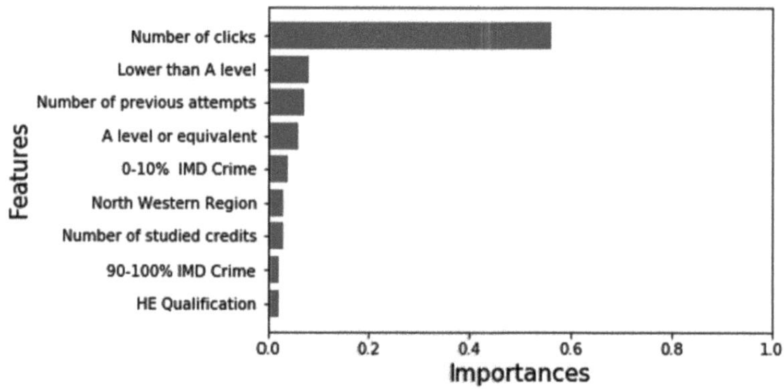

Fig. 3. Weight of parameters

Analyzing these results in detail, we represent the pass and fail rates as opposed to the number of clicks made by the students. The result is shown in Fig. 4 where two different groups are observed. In red, the students who have not managed to pass the course and whose number of clicks is very low. On the other hand, in green are represented the students who pass the course being their number of clicks usually quite high. Another relevant feature is some strange points, such as students who have not passed the course with a high number of clicks. In order to analyze these values, in future studies, it would be ideal to collect the time that the student remains in the different web resources, as it may have a high click rate but not remain barely time on the web.

Once the data have been analyzed and a behavior model has been generated through the Neural Network, the students that failed their exams are filtered out of the initial data set. The objective is to modify the parameters of these students on the basis of the previous study, and thus analyze whether the changes made to those parameters would allow students to pass their exams. Since the number of clicks has been determined as the factor with the greatest weight, we have proceeded to increase the number of clicks of students failures as Eq. (2):

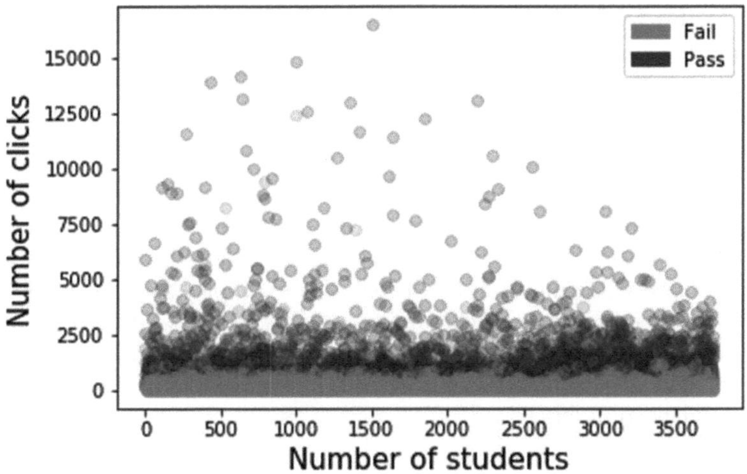

Fig. 4. Number of clicks and result rates.

$$\hat{y}_i = y_i + \alpha m \tag{2}$$

where $\hat{y}_i$ is the minimum number of clicks that the student should have to pass, y_i is the number of times a student clicked on the contents originally, m is the median of the times that the students who passed clicked on the contents and α is a variant factor. The closer the value of α is to 0, the new number of clicks will be closer to the original number of clicks.

For each possible value of α, the number of times students clicked on the contents has increased. The previously trained Neural Network has been used to predict if the students are going to pass or fail the course. In this way, varying

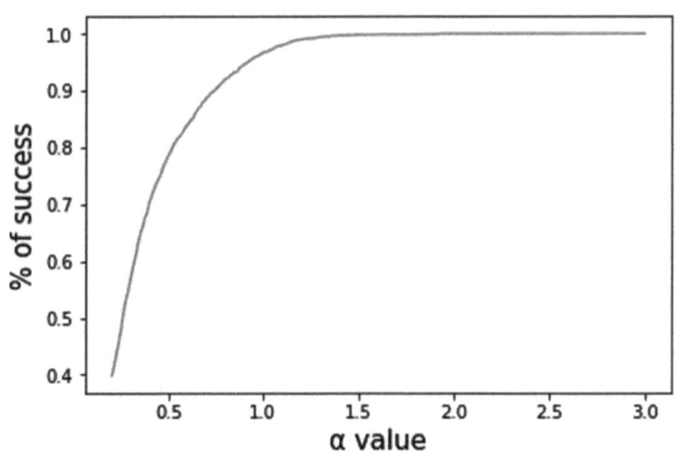

Fig. 5. Percentage number of passes as a function of α

the α parameter we have obtained the graph shown in Fig. 5. It is observed that when α approaches 0.75 approximately 90% of students pass.

Substituting the values in the equation to $\alpha = 0.75$ and replacing the value of the median, the number of clicks should be increased by 570 units per student as defined in Eq. (3).

$$\hat{y}_i = y_i + 570 \tag{3}$$

Note that the value of α could increase with the disadvantage that it would significantly increase the number of clicks that students would have to make, but the pass rate will remain fairly stable. For example, to get the 99.78% pass rate you would need to increase the number of clicks by 1140, which is an increase of 575 clicks to get only 9.78% more passes. Bearing in mind that the median number of clicks of passing students is 760, it is not worthwhile to increase the number of clicks so much.

5 Conclusions and Future Work

Different variables that affect academic performance have been studied using machine learning techniques and the variables with greatest weight have been identified, that is those that most affect the students' performance. In addition, the use of a Neural Network has been proposed to predict a behavioural model which is capable of improving academic performance. This work reflects the importance of interacting with a virtual classroom. However, it would be valuable if we could measure the time that students spend on interacting with a virtual environment, in order to be able to assess its benefits with certainty.

In a future work we are going to study the duration of students' participation in a virtual classroom, since frequent access for short time periods does not ensure success.

Currently, a system is being designed which, depending on the frequency with which a student uses references, positions the content in a virtual classroom differently.

Acknowledgments. This research has been partially supported by the European Regional Development Fund (ERDF) under the IOTEC project grant 0123_IOTEC_3_E and by the Spanish Ministry of Economy, Industry and Competitiveness.

References

1. Open learning analytics - knowledge media institute. The Open University 2019, 2019. https://analyse.kmi.open.ac.uk/open_dataset. Accessed 18 Jan 2019
2. Abubakar, Y., Ahmad, N.B.H.: Prediction of students' performance in e-learning environment using random forest. Int. J. Innovative Comput. **7**(2), 1–5 (2017)
3. Ahmed, N.S., Sadiq, M.H.: Clarify of the random forest algorithm in an educational field. In: 2018 International Conference on Advanced Science and Engineering (ICOASE), pp. 179–184. IEEE (2018)

4. Awad, M., Ewais, A.: Prediction of general high school exam result level using multilayer perceptron neural networks. Int. J. Appl. Eng. Res. **13**(10), 7621–7630 (2018)
5. Baruque, B., Corchado, E., Mata, A., Corchado, J.M.: Ensemble methods for boosting visualization models. In: Cabestany, J., Sandoval, F., Prieto, A., Corchado, J.M. (eds.) IWANN 2009. LNCS, vol. 5517, pp. 165–173. Springer, Heidelberg (2009). https://doi.org/10.1007/978-3-642-02478-8_21
6. Breiman, L.: Random forests. Mach. Learn. **45**(1), 5–32 (2001)
7. Breiman, L.: Classification and Regression Trees. Routledge, New York (2017)
8. Bridle, J.S.: Probabilistic interpretation of feedforward classification network outputs, with relationships to statistical pattern recognition. Neurocomputing. NATO ASI Series, vol. 68, pp. 227–236. Springer, Heidelberg (1990). https://doi.org/10.1007/978-3-642-76153-9_28
9. Corchado, E., Mata, A., Baruque, B., Corchado, J.M., Lancho, B.-P.: A topology-preserving system for environmental models forecasting. Int. J. Comput. Math. **88**(9), 1979–1989 (2011)
10. Corchado, J.M., Corchado, E.S., Aiken, J.: An IBR System to quantify the ocean's carbon dioxide budget. In: Perner, P. (ed.) ICDM 2004. LNCS (LNAI), vol. 3275, pp. 33–41. Springer, Heidelberg (2004). https://doi.org/10.1007/978-3-540-30185-1_4
11. Corchado, J.M, Rees, N., Fyfe, C., Lees, B.: Study and comparison of multilayer perceptron NN and radial basis function NN in oceanographic forecasting. In: Applications and Science of Artificial Neural Networks III, vol. 3077, pp 550–561. International Society for Optics and Photonics (1997)
12. Costa, C., Alvelos, H., Teixeira, L.: The use of moodle e-learning platform: a study in a Portuguese university. Proc. Technol. **5**, 334–343 (2012)
13. Freund, Y., Schapire, R., Abe, N.: A short introduction to boosting. J. Japan. Soc. Artif. Intell. **14**(771–780), 1612 (1999)
14. González-Briones, A., Chamoso, P., De La Prieta, F., Demazeau, Y., Corchado, J.M.: Agreement technologies for energy optimization at home. Sensors **18**(5), 1633 (2018)
15. González-Briones, A., Chamoso, P., Yoe, H., Corchado, J.M.: GreenVMAS: virtual organization based platform for heating greenhouses using waste energy from power plants. Sensors **18**(3), 861 (2018)
16. González-Briones, A., Prieto, J., De La Prieta, F., Herrera-Viedma, E., Corchado, J.M.: Energy optimization using a case-based reasoning strategy. Sensors **18**(3), 865 (2018)
17. Hanssen, T.E.S., Mathisen, T.A.: Exploring the attractiveness of a norwegian rural higher education institution using importance-performance analysis. Scand. J. Educ. Res. **62**(1), 68–87 (2018)
18. Kingma, D.P. and Adam, J.B.: A method for stochastic optimization. arXiv preprint arXiv:1412.6980 (2014)
19. Masci, C., Johnes, G., Agasisti, T.: Student and school performance across countries: a machine learning approach. Eur. J. Oper. Res. **269**(3), 1072–1085 (2018)
20. Oladokun, V.O., Adebanjo, A.T., Charles-Owaba, O.E.: Predicting students' academic performance using artificial neural network: a case study of an engineering course. Pac. J. Sci. Technol. **9**(1), 72–79 (2008)
21. Gabriela Carmen Oproiu: A study about using e-learning platform (moodle) in university teaching process. Procedia Soc. Behav. Sci. **180**, 426–432 (2015)

22. Perrotta, C., Williamson, B.: The social life of learning analytics: cluster analysis and the ‘performance’ of algorithmic education. Learn. Media. Tech. **43**(1), 3–16 (2018)
23. Quadri, M.N., Kalyankar, N.V.: Drop out feature of student data for academic performance using decision tree techniques. Glob. J. Comput. Sci. Technol. **10**(2) (2010)
24. Rivas, A., Chamoso, P., González-Briones, A., Corchado, J.: Detection of cattle using drones and convolutional neural networks. Sensors **18**(7), 2048 (2018)
25. Rokach, L., Maimon, O.Z.: Data Mining with Decision Trees: Theory and Applications, vol. 69. World Scientific, Singapore (2008)
26. Saltos, V.A.A., Flores, P.: Comparativa entre classification trees, random forest y gradient boosting; en la predicción de la satisfacción laboral en ecuador. Ciencia Dig. **2**(4.1), 42–54 (2018)
27. Thomas, E.H., Galambos, N.: What satisfies students? Mining student-opinion data with regression and decision tree analysis. Res. High. Educ. **45**(3), 251–269 (2004)
28. Umair, S., Sharif, M.M.: Predicting students grades using artificial neural networks and support vector machine. Encyclopedia of Information Science and Technology, 4th edn, pp. 5169–5182. IGI Global, Harshey (2018)

A Report on the Application of Adaptive Testing in a First Year University Course

Anna Maria Angelone and Pierpaolo Vittorini(✉)

Department of Life, Health and Environmental Sciences, University of L'Aquila, P.le S. Tommasi 1, 67100 L'Aquila, Italy
{annamaria.angelone,pierpaolo.vittorini}@univaq.it

Abstract. Assessment in education is a crucial task. The adoption of adaptive instead of classical testing poses questions from both a teacher and student perspective. According to the literature, teachers should experience shorter times to complete the assessment and obtain more precise evaluations, albeit at the cost of calibrating their questions. As for the students, adaptive testing does not allow to revise the already given questions, which is usually seen as a detrimental characteristic. On the other hand, adaptation seems to increase their engagement. Given these premises, the paper describes the system for online assessment currently under development in the University of L'Aquila and reports on the research questions mentioned above. The results are positive (i.e., no particular usability issues, no problems for the item calibration process), inline with the literature (i.e., FIT is considered easier than CAT, CAT is more efficient than FIT) even if we cannot confirm that CAT is more engaging than FIT. These results, in summary, show that CAT should not introduce issues in the assessment process and could be experimented by professors and students with reasonable safety.

1 Introduction

Assessment in education can be essentially divided into formative and summative assessment [10]. Formative assessment takes place during a course as a means of checking on student learning, by the teacher or by the students themselves. Summative assessment takes place at the end of a period of study and the results are used to determine the examination outcome. Within any assessment system, question types may vary. For example, questions may include short essay type questions, true or false type questions, or multiple-choice questions [8]. When limiting questions to have dichotomous or multiple-choice answers, they are usually called items and have been largely studied in psychometry. A test created according to the classical test theory (CTT) [6] assigns to an individual an observed test score given as the unweighted sum of responses to test items, plus a casual error component. On the other hand, the item response theory (IRT) [7] states that the individual's probability of giving a correct answer depends on the interaction between two elements, i.e., the individual's ability and the item parameters (like difficulty level, discrimination, and guessing).

L. Uden et al. (Eds.): LTEC 2019, CCIS 1011, pp. 439–449, 2019.
https://doi.org/10.1007/978-3-030-20798-4_38

By taking advance of IRT, Computerised Adaptive Testing (CAT) may provide important advantages over traditional Fixed-Item Tests (FIT) [9,24]. Studies show that CAT can measure the ability of different examinees with the same level of precision, higher than that of classical tests, by also reducing the number of administered items (e.g., [22,25]). Furthermore, CAT also provides an appropriate challenge for each examinee, so that low examinees are not discouraged whereas high examinees may enjoy receiving challenging items, which should result in an increased engagement [12]. As for the drawbacks, CAT requires calibration, i.e., the application of a complex procedure that takes in input a large data-bank of tests (administered using FIT and already corrected) and returns the values of the items' parameters. Furthermore, a CAT provides the items sequentially, until the examinee's ability is estimated within a certain precision, without the possibility to revise the answers previously given: such a limitation has been found to adversely impact students' reactions [20]. Moreover, if a student answers the initial items incorrectly, e.g., due to severe test anxiety, the test can correct itself only partially. However, according to the literature, test anxiety, as well as the overall experience, does not seem to vary in computerised adaptive tests with respect to classical tests [12,17].

Given these premises, the authors recently started the development of a system called UTS (Univaq Test Suite) [1] that implements, among the others, an engine for the administration of CAT, with the aim of integrating (or even substituting) the assessment system – based on FIT – currently used in the University of L'Aquila.

The system has been experimentally used with students learning Health Informatics in the degree course of Medicine and Surgery of the University of L'Aquila (Italy) to understand – from both the student and the teacher perspective – the impact of adaptive testing.

To this aim, the paper briefly describes the UTS system (Sect. 2). Then, it reports on the experimental use of the adaptive testing feature, and in particular:

- from the teacher perspective
  - describes the possible pros and cons of CAT, as discussed with professors that used FIT so far, and the item calibration process (Sect. 3),
  - investigates the expected better efficiency of CAT wrt FIT, by comparing the times, number of administered questions and time per question (Subsect. 4.3);
- from the student perspective
  - describes the user experience [21] in performing a FIT or a CAT assessment, through a slightly revised version of the After-Scenario Questionnaire [11] (Subsect. 4.4);
  - investigates whether differences in terms of engagement (using an adapted version of the User Engagement Scale [15]) exist between students assessed with FIT from those assessed with CAT (Subsect. 4.5).

The paper ends with a discussion on the findings and their possible impact in the adoption of CAT testing in the University of L'Aquila (Sect. 5).

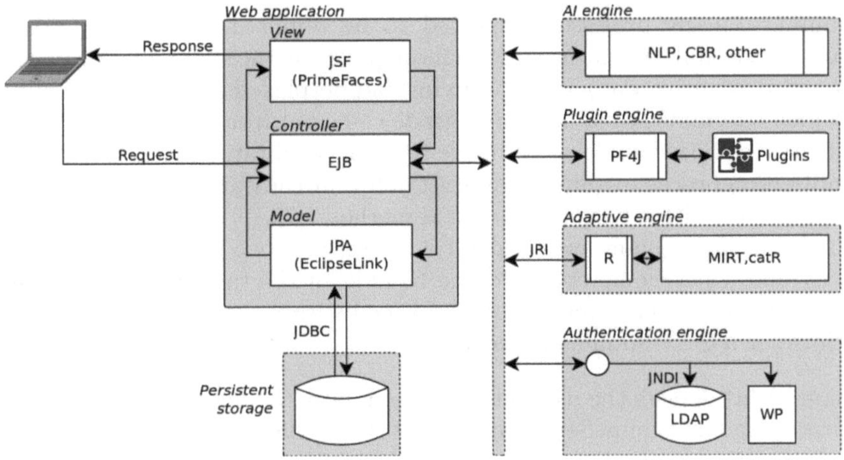

Fig. 1. UTS system architecture

2 The UTS System

The UTS system architecture [1] is depicted in Fig. 1. Its main blocks are (i) the actual web application, (ii) the artificial intelligence (AI) engine, (iii) the plugin engine, the (iv) authentication engine and (v) the adaptive engine. They are briefly discussed below, with more details on the adaptive engine:

Web application The web application follows the well-know MVC design pattern [2];

AI engine The AI engine is included in the architecture since artificial intelligence has a long tradition in education and we aim to include a feature about the automated grading of code snippets [14,16];

Plugin engine The plugin engine allows the system to be extended in terms of its functionalities, e.g., further types of questions;

Authentication engine The authentication engine allows the system to be more easily integrated into existing organisations (e.g., through LDAP and WordPress integration);

Adaptive engine The adaptive engine takes care of supporting all CAT functionalities within the system. Because of the need for fast calculations, we decided – similarly as in other projects (e.g., [23]) – to implement it as a wrapper to R and the MIRT/catR packages [4,13]. In particular, the MIRT package is used for test calibration, whereas the catR package is used for item selection and ability estimation.

3 CAT and Calibration

The project regarding the introduction of CAT assessment started with individual interviews with professors that used FIT for their assessments. It is worth noting that all professors using FIT are supported – during the assessment – by a technician, and only few of them are skilled in computer science and/or psychometry.

In summary, many professors reported to be tempted of switching to CAT (because of the ability to measure with more precision the students' ability, also in a faster and adaptive way), other were instead perplexed about the difficulty for the students to understand how their grade came out from the answers. Another perplexity was how complex could have been the calibration of their items, since the calibration process requires a large set of test already answered and evaluated, to be processed with advanced statistical methods [7].

As for the latest point, we decided to discuss with two professors (a computer scientist and a psychometrist) and the technician the task of item calibration. Figure 2 shows the main steps to be performed within the system to prepare the questions for a CAT administration:

- Figure 2-(a) depicts the user interface to import the questions. Firstly, a user must upload a Comma Separated Values (CSV) file. The file must contain, for each row, the questions to be imported, in terms of the following information: the question type (IRT in this case), question name (a unique identifier), question text, item type (either 1PL, 2PL or 3PL), number of correct answers, text of the possible answers. Once the file is uploaded, a user must parse it, verify how the system read the questions, before actually import them;
- Figure 2-(b) shows the user interface for the actual calibration. First, a user must upload a CSV file containing, for each row, the answers given by a student to a test. Each row must provide, for all the imported questions, if the answer was correct (1), incorrect (0) or missing (NA);
- Figure 2-(c) depicts the user interface that can be used to edit the items. Each row of the table contains a question, that can be opened to modify the text and the possible answers.

The computer scientist involved in the case study already had in a digital format circa ten years of exams, for a total of more than 1800 tests already answered, evaluated and stored in a database. He reported that exporting them into the aforementioned format was a straightforward task and that both the process of importing the questions into the system and the item calibration proceeded without issues. The psychometrist also had her data for the calibration process in the proper format and reported no particular issues in calibrating her test. Finally, also the technician expressed no technical problems in exporting the data into the required format for a potential CAT administration.

4 Adaptive Administration

To complete the study about the impact of a CAT assessment, we organised a randomised crossover study with the students learning Health Informatics at the first year of the Medicine and Surgery course of the University of L'Aquila (see Fig. 3).

In details, all students were casually and blindly assigned to two groups (A and B). The first group started with FIT, proceeded with the usability/engagement questionnaires, then ended up with CAT. The second group made the opposite, i.e., first CAT then FIT. We chose such a design because, for ethical concerns, we had to guarantee to all students the same workload and evaluation.

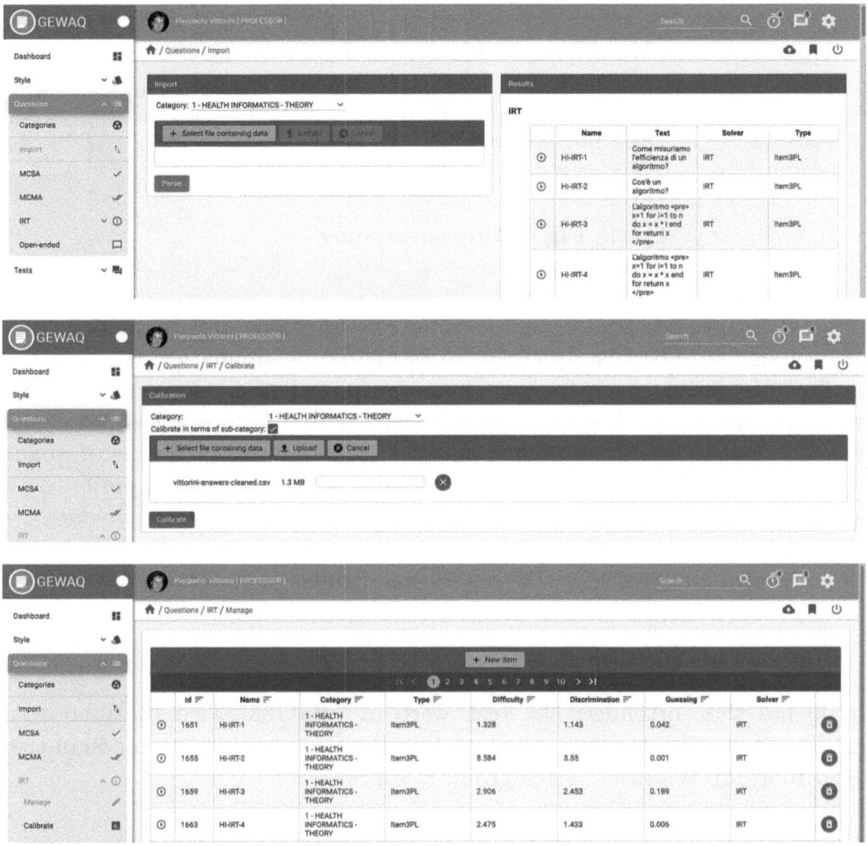

(a)
(b)
(c)

Fig. 2. Screenshots of the item calibration process, from the import (a), the actual calibration (b) and editing (c)

Furthermore, FIT was made up of 20 questions randomly extracted from a pool of more than two hundred questions. CAT was instead tailored to administer a maximum of 20 items (the same of FIT), to interpret an ability of −3.0 as 0/30 and an ability of 3.0 as 30/30[1] and to terminate when the ability is estimated with a standard error less than 0.4 (i.e., ±1 in Italian grade).

Finally, in order for the students to be equally committed to both tests, we used as final grade the maximum grade obtained from the two tests. the measures of performance, i.e., time to complete the test and number of administered questions, were recorded automatically by the system.

4.1 Methods

To analyse the data, we performed both descriptive and inferential statistics.

[1] In the Italian system, the grade is a value ranging from 0 to 30.

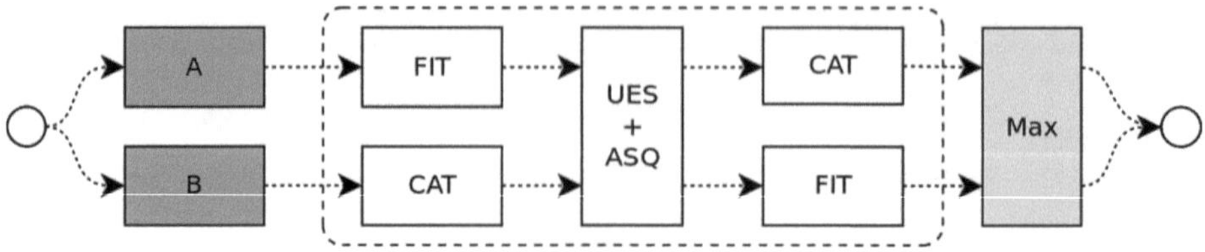

Fig. 3. Cross-over study

As for descriptive statistics, we used means, medians and frequency tables [19], as well as Chronbach's alphas [5] to estimate questionnaires' reliability.

As for inferential statistics, we investigated whether differences existed between FIT and CAT. The differences regarded the performances, user experience and engagement. Since performances were measured by means of quantitative data, we used t-tests. On the other hand, since the user experience and the engagement were investigated with questionnaires (i.e., qualitative data), we used Wilcoxon tests.

All statistical analyses have been performed through R version 3.5.2 [18].

4.2 Sample Description

The students that attended the test were in total 83. Two of them withdrawn. Therefore, 81 tests were successfully submitted to the system: 40 of them belonged to group A (49%), 41 to group B (51%).

4.3 Performances

On average, a FIT test lasted 1910 s (ca 32 mins), while a CAT test lasted 523 s (ca 9 mins). The difference is statistically significant ($p < 0.000$). Furthermore, the median number of questions administered in CAT tests was 9, which is significantly less than the 20 questions used in FIT tests. Also this difference is statistically significant ($p = 0.001$). Finally, by introducing as a further measure the time taken to complete a single question, we measured on average 95 s/questions in FIT tests and 37 s/questions in CAT tests. Also this difference was found statistically significant ($p = 0.0002$).

This latter measure is the most interesting one, since not affected by the test length. Furthermore, this finding is also coherent with the opinions collected from the students that reported that a CAT administration (i.e., with questions administered sequentially) allowed them to focus on the specific question and therefore better proceed throughout the test.

Such findings are in line with the existing literature (e.g., [22,24]). Therefore, since CAT offers an increased precision in estimating the examinee ability wrt to FIT [22,24], the better performances offer a further advantage especially when the assessment regards a large number of students.

4.4 User Experience

As mentioned in the introduction, we developed a slightly revised version of the After Scenario Questionnaire [11] to measure the students' user experience. We opted for the ASQ since it touches upon the three fundamental areas of usability (i.e., effectiveness with Q1, efficiency with Q2 and satisfaction with Q1, Q2 and Q3) with only three questions, each rated from 1 to 7 (e.g., from "strongly disagree" to "strongly agree"), where the higher the rating, the better the perceived usability.

Appendix A.1 lists the questions, slightly changed from the original version only to specifically mention the assessment rather than the abstract word "scenario". Its internal consistency was measured through the Cronbach's α: the obtained value of $\alpha = 0.86$ suggests that also this version of the questionnaire can be considered reliable.

On average (see Fig. 4), we obtained positive results for all the investigated areas, albeit the effectiveness of FIT was better than CAT ($p = 0.03$). This finding is inline with the literature, since students usually see the impossibility to revise the previous questions as a detrimental characteristic [20]. However, since the average rating for the CAT assessment is still high, we do not consider this result as a problem. Therefore, given these result, we can conclude that our system should not represent an impairment – in terms of usability – to perform a CAT with respect to a FIT assessment.

	FIT	CAT	p
Q1	6.0	5.8	0.03 *
Q2	6.2	6.3	0.68
Q3	6.1	6.1	0.16

Fig. 4. Results

4.5 Engagement

Engagement in a course is an attitude that seems to be positively related to learning outcomes [3]. With specific respect to the assessment activity, and in particular in terms of CAT versus FIT, little evidences exist. Nevertheless, a recent study suggests – at least for the mathematical abilities – that under certain constraints CAT results more engaging that FIT [12].

We then developed a specific tool for measuring the engagement during an assessment, reported in Appendix A.2. The developed questionnaire is a revised version of the short form of the user engagement scale short form (UEF-SF) [15]. The revision essentially consists in specifically mentioning the assessment process instead of the abstract "experience" word. The questionnaire is made up of twelve questions, divided into four subscales investigating the focused attention, perceived usability, aesthetic appeal and rewarding.

Similarly as for the ASQ questionnaire, we measured its internal consistency through the Cronbach's α [5]. The obtained value of $\alpha = 0.68$ is very close to the value of $\alpha = 0.7$, commonly considered as the threshold for a good level of reliability. Therefore, given such a small difference, we still considered this questionnaire as a reliable tool.

To score the questionnaire, the researcher should:

- reverse the answers for items FA-S1, PU-S1 and PU-S2;
- calculate the scores for each of the four subscales by adding the values of responses for the three items contained in each subscale and dividing by three;
- calculate the overall engagement score by adding all of the items together and dividing by twelve.

On average, we obtained a very limited higher level of engagement in the students that used the CAT assessment (4.04 vs 4.02). This difference was not statistically significant. Furthermore, also investigating the single subscales and questions, no differences were found statistically significant. All p-values were calculated with a Wilcoxon test.

Even if we would have aimed at finding an increased engagement in using CAT with respect to FIT, our findings at least do not indicate any drawback in introducing a CAT assessment.

5 Conclusion

The paper discussed – from both a student and teacher perspective – the possible impact of CAT in the assessment process.

From the professors' perspective, the paper suggests that the system does not introduce usability and technical issues (from the calibration and usability viewpoints) and can offer increased performances of CAT wrt FIT (i.e., reduced time, number of administered questions, time per question). Also from the students' perspective, the system does not seem to introduce usability problems to perform the assessment, even if the FIT was considered easier than CAT. Finally, the engagement in performing the assessment using CAT was not different than using FIT, our findings at least do not indicate any drawback in introducing a CAT assessment.

As for the limitations of the study, it is worth remarking that the sample is representative only of students coming from a specific course of study. Therefore, a generalisation of our findings should take into account this fact. Moreover, the user experience and engagement were measured through self-reported measures: it is possible that some student may have given answers to these questionnaires superficially, since focused on the exam.

However, our results in summary seem to suggest that CAT can be introduced in the assessment process, can improve the assessment performances, and could be experimented by professors and students with reasonable safety.

Acknowledgements. The authors thank prof. Dina Di Giacomo for her suggestions in revising the UES-SF scale.

A Appendix

A.1 After Scenario Questionnaire

Q1	Overall, I am satisfied with the ease of completing the assessment
Q2	Overall, I am satisfied with the amount of time it took to complete the assessment
Q3	Overall, I am satisfied with the support information (online-line help, messages, documentation) when completing the assessment

A.2 User Assessment Engagement Scale

Focused attention	
UAES-FA-S1	I felt lost during the assessment (neg)
UAES-FA-S2	The time I spent during the assessment just slipped away
UAES-FA-S3	I felt involved in the assessment
Perceived usability	
UAES-PU-S1	I felt frustrated during the assessment (neg)
UAES-PU-S2	I found the assessment confusing (neg)
UAES-PU-S3	The assessment carried out in this way was taxing
Aesthetic appeal	
UAES-AE-S1	The system was attractive
UAES-AE-S2	The system was aesthetically appealing
UAES-AE-S3	The system was captivating
Rewarding	
UAES-RW-S1	Using the system was worthwhile
UAES-RW-S2	Performing the assessment in this way was rewarding
UAES-RW-S3	I felt interested in the assessment

References

1. Bernardi, A., et al.: On the design and development of an assessment system with adaptive capabilities. In: Di Mascio, T., et al. (eds.) MIS4TEL 2018. AISC, vol. 804, pp. 190–199. Springer, Cham (2019). https://doi.org/10.1007/978-3-319-98872-6_23
2. Buschmann, F.: Pattern-Oriented Software Architecture: A System of Patterns. Wiley, New Jersey (1996)
3. Carini, R.M., Kuh, G.D., Klein, S.P.: Student engagement and student learning: testing the linkages*. Res. High. Educ. **47**(1), 1–32 (2006). http://link.springer.com/10.1007/s11162-005-8150-9
4. Chalmers, R.P.: mirt: a multidimensional item response theory package for the R environment. J. Stat. Softw. **48**(6), 1–29 (2012). http://www.jstatsoft.org/v48/i06/

5. Cronbach, L.J.: Coefficient alpha and the internal structure of tests. Psychometrika **16**(3), 297–334 (1951). http://link.springer.com/10.1007/BF02310555
6. DeVellis, R.F.: Classical test theory. Med. Care **44**(11), S50–S59 (2006). https://www.jstor.org/stable/41219505
7. Embretson, S.E., Reise, S.P.: Item Response Theory for Psychologists. L. Erlbaum Associates, Mahwah (2000). https://books.google.it/books?hl=it&lr=&id=9Xm0AAAAQBAJ&oi=fnd&pg=PR1&ots=Eb1_VwKO1k&sig=g1vYTBhWmp592aTYFpFEqIIf4BE#v=onepage&q&f=false
8. Gikandi, J., Morrow, D., Davis, N.: Online formative assessment in higher education: a review of the literature. Comput. Educ. **57**(4), 2333–2351 (2011). https://www.sciencedirect.com/science/article/pii/S0360131511001333
9. Hambleton, R.K., Jones, R.W.: Comparison of classical test theory and item response theory and their applications to test development. Educ. Meas. Issues Pract. **12**(3), 38–47 (1993)
10. Harlen, W., James, M.: Assessment and learning: differences and relationships between formative and summative assessment. Assess. Educ. Principles Policy Pract. **4**(3), 365–379 (1997). http://www.tandfonline.com/doi/full/10.1080/0969594970040304
11. Lewis, J.R.: Psychometric evaluation of an after-scenario questionnaire for computer usability studies. ACM SIGCHI Bull. **23**(1), 78–81 (1990). http://portal.acm.org/citation.cfm?doid=122672.122692
12. Ling, G., Attali, Y., Finn, B., Stone, E.A.: Is a computerized adaptive test more motivating than a fixed-item test? Appl. Psychol. Measur. **41**(7), 495–511 (2017). http://journals.sagepub.com/doi/10.1177/0146621617707556
13. Magis, D., Barrada, J.R.: Computerized adaptive testing with R: recent updates of the package catR. J. Stat. Softw. **76**(Code Snippet 1), 1–19 (2017)
14. McArthur, D., Lewis, M., Bishary, M.: The roles of artificial intelligence in education: current progress and future prospects. J. Educ. Technol. **1**(4), 42–80 (2005). http://www.imanagerpublications.com/article/972
15. O'Brien, H.L., Cairns, P., Hall, M.: A practical approach to measuring user engagement with the refined user engagement scale (UES) and new UES short form. Int. J. Hum.-Comput. Stud. **112**, 28–39 (2018). https://www.sciencedirect.com/science/article/pii/S1071581918300041
16. Penstein Rosé, C., et al. (eds.): AIED 2018. LNCS (LNAI), vol. 10947. Springer, Cham (2018). https://doi.org/10.1007/978-3-319-93843-1
17. Powers, D.E.: Test anxiety and test performance: comparing paper-based and computer-adaptive versions of the graduate record examinations (Gre©) general test. J. Educ. Comput. Res. **24**(3), 249–273 (2001). http://journals.sagepub.com/doi/10.2190/680W-66CR-QRP7-CL1F
18. R Core Team: R: A language and environment for statistical computing (2018). https://www.R-project.org/
19. Riffenburgh, R.H.: Statistics in Medicine. Elsevier/Academic Press, Cambridge (2012)
20. Tonidanel, S., Quinones, M.A.: Psychological reactions to adaptive testing. Int. J. Sel. Assess. **8**(1), 7–15 (2000). http://doi.wiley.com/10.1111/1468-2389.00126
21. Tullis, T.T., Albert, B.W.: Measuring the User Experience: Collecting, Analyzing, and Presenting Usability Metrics. Elsevier, Amsterdam (2013)
22. Vispoel, W.P., Rocklin, T.R., Wang, T.: Individual differences and test administration procedures: a comparison of fixed-item, computerized-adaptive, and self-adapted testing. Appl. Measur. Educ. **7**(1), 53–79 (1994). http://www.tandfonline.com/doi/abs/10.1207/s15324818ame07015

23. Vittorini, P., Michetti, M., di Orio, F.: A SOA statistical engine forbiomedical data. Comput. Methods Programs Biomed. **92**(1), 1–160 (2008)
24. Wainer, H., Dorans, N.J., Flaugher, R., Green, B.F., Mislevy, R.J., Dorans, N.J., Flaugher, R., Green, B.F., Mislevy, R.J.: Computerized Adaptive Testing. Routledge, New York (2000). https://www.taylorfrancis.com/books/9781410605931
25. Weiss, D.J., Kingsbury, G.G.: Application of computerized adaptive testing to educational problems. J. Educ. Meas. **21**(4), 361–375 (1984). http://doi.wiley.com/10.1111/j.1745-3984.1984.tb01040.x

Teaching Effectiveness: An Innovative Evaluation Model

Walter Orozco[1,2(✉)], Miguel Ángel Rodríguez-García[1], and Alberto Fernández[1]

[1] Universidad Rey Juan Carlos, Madrid, Spain
wa.orozco@alumnos.urjc.es,
{miguel.rodriguez,alberto.fernandez}@urjc.es
[2] Universidad Península de Santa Elena, La Libertad, Ecuador
worozco@upse.edu.ec

Abstract. The evaluation of teaching effectiveness is an important process of higher educational institutions. Having regulations, policies and procedures that guide the teaching activity strengthens the quality of teaching. There are several teaching effectiveness evaluation models that have been applied, each one with their own particularities, objectives and supporting tools. Furthermore, there are numerous studies about their validity, metrics, weighting, properties collection, among others. One of the main inputs for teaching evaluation is the student's achievement, in addition to the qualitative assessment done by expert peers. With this baseline, we intend to design a new evaluation model capable of evaluating teaching quality. The model focuses on the instructor's educational capacities that include innovative metrics that will allow the evaluation of his/her competences from a nonobjective perspective. To support the application of the model, we have designed an architecture where we integrate Semantic Technologies and Machine Learning algorithms for knowledge representation and information processing. As a result, we expect that the final system will be able to measure the effectiveness of the teaching activity of each professor and to identify potential problems in the applied teaching method.

Keywords: Education · Evaluation · Knowledge representation

1 Introduction

Currently, the implementation of evaluation systems at universities is especially important, not only for compliance with legal requirements but also for the assurance of institutional quality [1]. Professors, as a fundamental part of the educational process, must gather the necessary competencies for the fulfilment of their work. Furthermore, the institutions must implement the corresponding mechanisms to guarantee the success of the academic processes. Given that teaching activity is the main factor that determines student learning, the evaluation of teacher performance is defined as a strategy for improving educational quality [2].

The strategies and models that are used to evaluate professors depend on the goals of each institution. They seek to have procedures and tools to measure the quality of their work. In the same way, they assess the contribution professors in the students'

L. Uden et al. (Eds.): LTEC 2019, CCIS 1011, pp. 450–461, 2019.
https://doi.org/10.1007/978-3-030-20798-4_39

achievements to identify potential problems in time. Many countries have implemented their own evaluation models, each with its particularities, objectives and support tools for processing, e.g. Brazil, Japan, Germany, United States [1]. Historically, one of the main strategies used to measure teaching effectiveness is to apply students standardized tests on topics oriented to the development of the class [3]. In this strategy, it can be identified that the results will depend on the instrument quality and the actors' pre-disposition to give the answers of its application. The automation of the data collection process of the surveys should significantly contribute to the process. However, that does not solve the discretionality of the data obtained from the applied population [4].

Several models have been defined to evaluate the teaching performance. Generally, these models include new metrics that combine different types of data. Additionally, they incorporate innovative technologies for processing and generating timely results in the evaluated context. The basis for the evaluation of coaching activity is focused on student achievements and opinion polls [5]. Several studies have been carried out to prove their validity and propose other alternatives for doing it better. The studies have focused on verifying the importance of the variables used, the metrics and the correlation with other variables.

Measuring teaching effectiveness has given rise to the use of models based on statistical techniques that use data generated from the academic processes. Proposals such as the Value Added Model (VAM) [6] and Linear Hierarchical Model (HLM) [7], make use of these techniques to measure teaching effectiveness, taking student achievement as the basic variable for the process. In the scenario that VAM and HLM process, a question is posed: can the quality of the teacher really be measured by the results that the students obtain? [5]. There are several factors that may affect student's results such as origin location and context, professors of previous courses, number of students per group, classroom conditions for learning, among others. Thus, carrying out an evaluation based on a single variable is very ambiguous and it is necessary to incorporate new metrics [8].

Technologies have gained special importance in educational domain providing different tools for activities development [9]. The availability of different types of data allows us to use Knowledge Representation and processing techniques that can provide valuable information in order to take corrective actions even before the event occurs. Cases such as the strengthening of eLearning systems have received important contributions from techniques such as Knowledge Representation [10], Semantic Web [11] and Machine Learning [12]. Stojanovic et al. [11] present an approach for implementing the eLearning scenario using Semantic Web technologies. The proposed system mainly utilises ontologies to describe the content, context and structure of the learning materials improving their accessibility. Conversely, the work presented by [10] utilises ontologies to represent contents, exercises, evaluation elements, among others, to contribute to the systems of study. The studies noted above, allow to identify the potential of knowledge representation techniques and will be used to measure variables whose data are in the electronic portals.

In educational institutions, students' opinions and achievements are important variables [13] because they provide information from the direct beneficiary of the training process. Different analysis techniques can be applied to extract knowledge from such data. For instance, to study the satisfaction level, the approach proposed in

[14] utilises sentiment analysis techniques to measure opinions about the educational system implemented. In terms of student achievement, [12] uses Machine Learning techniques to predict students' grades considering their demographic characteristics with regression algorithms. From an objective point of view, the relationships between students and teachers are represented by students' achievements, therefore, those are data of interest that contribute to the measurement.

This paper presents a new evaluation model that incorporates metrics to evaluate teaching effectiveness from an objective perspective. We include four components that represent teacher's activity: teacher profile, academic processes, student achievements and support activities. To assess the model, we propose an architecture based on technologies such as Ontologies, Semantic Web and Machine Learning for data processing, as an alternative to current approaches.

The rest of the manuscript is organized as follows: in Sect. 2, some relevant works on evaluation models are analysed to identify their strengths and weaknesses. In Sect. 3, the proposed model is described based on its four components. The main technologies to be considered are described in Sect. 4. Finally, we analyse the conclusions and future lines of the proposed approach.

2 Related Works

Throughout history, higher education institutions have used different models to evaluate teacher effectiveness. Their approaches have a lot to do with the purposes and objectives of the exercise of evaluation. Here, we analyse some of the most extended teaching effectiveness evaluation models.

2.1 VAM: Value-Added Model

VAM [15] model uses a generic production function to estimate the differences based on student results. It has been widely used for the teaching evaluation when the techniques allow to incorporate measures of previous achievements and in some cases contextual characteristics of the students. Using VAM enables a more refined analysis of the student performance. Furthermore, it is more effective on identifying the effects of various factors that affect student progress.

There is a direct correlation between the student's achievements and variables such as professor experience, number of students, level of the subject, among others [7]. The model identifies and analyses the factors of associated variables and then it calculates the student's achievements towards the professor. The objective is, therefore, to process the students' achievements with their associated factors to be capable of generating more realistic information.

2.2 HLM: Hierarchical Lineal Model

HLM [7] is a regression analysis model that enables to estimate the relation among several variables. In particular, HLM utilises hierarchical regression equations systems to analyse how it affects variables in the lower level of the hierarchy and in the upper level contextual variables. For instance, [7] in his research, identifies the impact factor of variables such as the socioeconomic level and level of previous knowledge, in relation to the academic achievements of the students.

This model overcomes the weakness detected in VAM analysing the student achievement impact factor [16]. The numerical data processing generates results based on objective data, but it is also necessary to add qualitative data that allow a better definition of the teaching activity and incorporate other technologies for processing.

2.3 DOCENTIA

DOCENTIA [17] is a multicriteria evaluation model promoted by the National Agency for the Evaluation of Quality and Accreditation of Spain (NAEQA). It aims at satisfying the need of the Spanish educational system, guaranteeing the quality of university professors' performance and favouring their development and recognition. DOCENTIA defines a reference framework to evaluate professors considering the European Space for Higher Education learning and teaching model.

The model is organized by dimensions, criteria and indicators. For instance, the Teaching Planning and Training dimension is associated to the Teaching-related task criterion, and this, in turn, contains indicators such as participation in committees and conferences preparation. It consists of three dimensions and at least nineteen criteria; all oriented to measure the quality of teaching. Before its application, the system requires the previous establishment of weights for each indicator given by expert peers. The incorporation of qualitative data is an important advantage over the other models. It enables to measure the teaching work by incorporating new non-numerical variables such as: use of the virtual classroom, opinions of students, training course, among others. Peer evaluators are an essential element to be capable of executing this model.

2.4 NBPTS: National Board for Professional Teaching Standards

NBPTS [18] is a professor accreditation model that is dedicated to promoting excellence in education, strengthening the teaching process and learning from students. The model aims at improving the overall effectiveness of the educator, recognising and rewarding highly competent educators who meet high and rigorous standards.

The model is based on four inputs: three entries to outline the work done in the classroom and an entry to measure the professor's knowledge in the area to be certified. Classroom work includes: differentiation in instruction, teaching practice, learning environment, and reflective and effective practice; it is done in real work environments and it requires the participation of expert peers. In the case of the measurement knowledge levels, the professor must demonstrate knowledge and pedagogical practices for the teaching on the particular knowledge area.

2.5 Analysis/Model Discussion

The studied models aim at assessing the educational work to improve the performance of each teacher. In general, this improvement is reflected in the achievement of their students. Hence, each analyzed model defines a set of metrics to evaluate the teaching effectiveness. VAM and HLM work with quantitative data avoiding the problem of subjectivity since their main input is the students' grades achieved in each academic period. However, the used of limited number of metrics does not cover the complete context of the teaching activity providing the chance to emerge other assessment models. On the other hand, DOCENTIA and NBPTS include qualitative and quantitative data for their evaluation, which allow to emphasize: (i) the development of the class; and (ii) the results generated by the process. This is an important strength to consider since it enables to evaluate the work of the professor in a wider scenario with different types of variables. However, the academic peers participation in the evaluation of many variables needs to be analyzed. Table 1 shows a general concepts summary that covers the different evaluation reviewed models considering the high (H), medium (M) and low (L) scale that represents the relevance level of the concept in the generation of results.

Table 1. Main concepts of evaluation models

Concepts	VAM	HLM	DOCENTIA	NBPTS
Student achievements	H	H		M
Teaching practice			H	H
Factors influence student achievement	M	H		M
Peer reviewers			H	H
Content knowledge				H
Learning environment			L	M

The table includes a concept incidence level qualification generated from the results of each model. Key concepts are raised such as student achievement, teaching practice, factors that influence student outcomes, peer participation and knowledge of content. We observe that only NBPTS considers all concepts giving a greater level of importance in the Teaching Practice [19]. Teaching effectiveness evaluation requires paying attention to the entire academic process to analyze the generated results.

To evaluate the effectiveness instruction, one of the basic metrics that have been used is the students' achievement, tangible data that are the result of the academic process and are available in the institutional databases. The important point is to consider there are factors that may influence those achievements, so it is necessary to incorporate metrics that are related and contribute to the final result. In this regard, [6, 20] raise the need to incorporate factors related to the own teaching activity in such a way that it is possible to generate information for decision making.

The incorporation of new non-numerical metrics is an important feature of DOCENTIA and NBPTS. In these cases, the problem arises from the data availability of the selected variable, the used processing method and the way in which the data is obtained. Regarding the concept "Content Knowledge", the identification of this factor of each professor is valid if there is a standardized procedure. Semantic technologies can be useful here to reason on expertise profiles.

In summary, establishing which is the best model to evaluate professors, is ambiguous if we consider that each one has been defined to assess different teaching environments. Models such as VAN and NBPTS are highlighted by the use of metrics with numerical data. Consequently, their results have an objective basis. DOCENTIA and NBPTS consider the teaching activity more broadly, incorporating metrics that need to be measured with documented evidence and with peer experts participation including certain degree of subjectivity.

3 Proposal

Reaching educational objectives depends on a great extent on the implementation of processes that organize and harmonize the activities that each actor must fulfill in the education system [2]. The role of professors are essential to achieve the desired success and the evaluation of their activities is an ideal tool to achieve the desired objectives. The responsibility of the professor is not only summarized in the development of the class. He/she must also consider aspects that contribute to the fulfillment of their function such as preparation of the class, materials used, academic experience, among others, which are reflected in the achievements of the students. Therefore, there is a need to design a new model that not only builds on students' achievements but also incorporates metrics associated with the entire context of teaching activity. The model also has to define efficient measurement procedures capable of generating timely results to respond to the weaknesses detected in other models such as subjectivity, limited use of metrics and weights. Hence, we want to minimize the use of metrics that depend on a certain degree on subjective academic peers criteria and make use of existing data in institutional databases and other open access sources.

The implementation of the model is supported by an architecture that makes use of innovative technologies capable of processing the measured variables intelligently. Figure 1 shows the proposed evaluation architecture.

Two aspects are identified in the figure: (i) the measurement model that is implemented on the architecture represented by components: *Professor Profile*, *Academic Process*, *Student Achievements* and *Academic Support Activities*; and (ii) the proposed technologies to organize and analyze the data: Ontologies, Machine Learning, Semantic Web and Statistics.

The model organizes the activities developed by the professor into four components:

(i) *Student Achievements* component is focused on incorporating student achievement into the model as an input generated from the training process. There are factors that directly or indirectly influence the obtained results such as socioeconomic level, number of students, level of the subject, among others. The statistical and Machine Learning techniques approach the problem of processing this type of data to estimate the contribution of the teacher in the students as an input for the general evaluation. For example, the difficulties that professors have had in a work group to identify the reasons why student performance has not been as expected, determine behavior patterns of the dropout of students. The historical data of qualifications, teaching history, socioeconomic studies can be analyzed by techniques to measure teaching work;

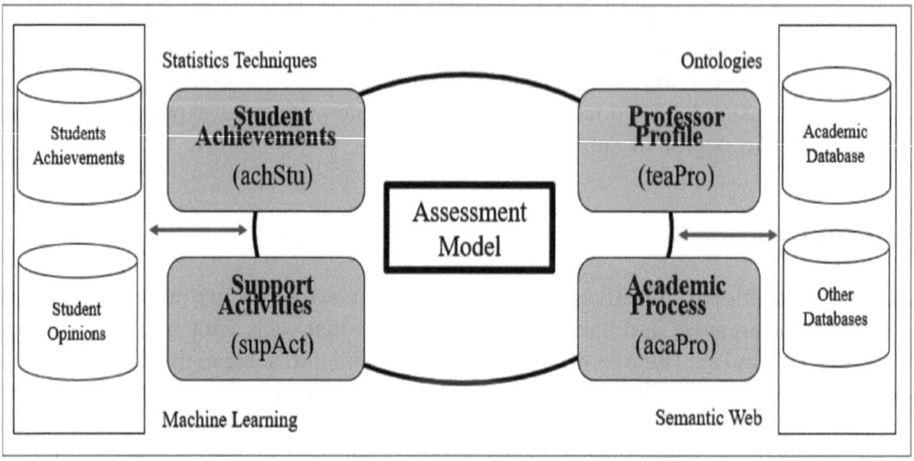

Fig. 1. Professor effectiveness assessment architecture.

(ii) *Professor Profile* component aims to measure professors' professional experience in the subjects they teach, identify the teaching experience in the subject and value the relationship between the requirements of the subject and teacher training. According to the studied models that consider the variable, this activity is carried out manually through verification of documentary evidence. It requires the use of technologies that allow modeling, representing and maintaining relationships between each modeled teaching entity. In this context, the use of ontologies as a knowledge representation technique provides the necessary elements for this purpose and therefore effective processing can be achieved. For instance: the teaching experience is one of the metrics to consider; aspects such as years of experience, work groups in which he/she has worked, instructor training and subjects, among others. Consequently, having a model that represents both the characteristics required for the subject and the requirements that the teacher must have, in such a way that the professor contribution can be measured from the available data.

(iii) *Academic Process* component contemplates activities that complement the academic process of the students. For instance, to support learning and therefore a better performance reflected in their achievements. Metrics such as academic planning, attention to students, compliance with responsibilities, learning environment, among others; they are validated through satisfaction surveys. Type of applied instrument, structure of your questions, population to which it is addressed, are just some factors that can determine the results that can be solved with statistical techniques. To enrich these results we will use technologies such as the Sentiment Analysis and Machine Learning so that from the data available in both public and private databases contribute to the assessment of the professor. The objective is to work with the variables that correspond to opinion criteria with inputs generated mainly by open questions that the student answers freely. Similarly, data obtained from public access databases (e.g. social networks) can be used to infer opinions of students.

(iv) *Support Activities* component evaluates additional activities that can affect student achievements, e.g. thesis supervision, participation in committees, postgraduate classes. These factors can be determined by the quality of the teaching work. To measure this component, statistical techniques will be used on the available data (hours of dedication).

The model aims at assessing the teaching work of each professor by the sum of the normalized partial results of each components. (See Eq. 1). All values are normalized in the range [0–1].

$$Utility = w_1 * teaPro + w_2 * acaPro + w_3 * supAct + w_4 * achStu \tag{1}$$

Where w_j is a weight to assign different importance to each component, with $w_1 + w_2 + w_3 + w_4 = 1$. Next, we will analyse each component in detail.

3.1 Professor Profile

It represents the level of compliance with the minimum requirements that must be met by the professor for the development of the class according to the academic institutions. It also includes the following metrics: Professor Training (*teaTra*) and Professor Experience (*teaExp*); each are normalized in the range [0–1] (See Eq. 2).

$$teaPro = w * teaTra + (1 - w) * teaExp \tag{2}$$

Professor Training (teaTra) measures the hours the professor has participated in professional training during the evaluation period. *Professor Experience* (*teaExp*): identifies the matching of the professor experience to the required knowledge (aspects such as: academic title, subjects, professor academic level, etc.).

3.2 Academic Process

The academic process represents the relationship between students and professors through the exercise of teaching. It seeks to identify relevant aspects that allow reaching high success rate. It includes the following aspects: academic tutelage, class development, success percentage, performance percentage and class hours (See Eq. 3).

$$\begin{aligned} acaPro = {} & w_1 * acaTut + w_2 * devCla + w_3 * perSuc \\ & + w_4 * perPer + w_5 * claHour \end{aligned} \tag{3}$$

Where:

- *Academic Tutelage (acaTut)*: identifies the professor's academic support with students during their academic period, with the purpose of improving their achievements. The value is generated by the level of student satisfaction.

- *Class Development (devCla)*: is the level of student satisfaction with the use of academics resources, teacher's competences, class methodology, evaluation system, achievement of academic objectives, academic planning, etc.
- *Success (perSuc)* and *Performance Percentage (perPer)* measure the results generated by the educative process based on the students who successfully complete the course. The success percentage is obtained from the relationship between the students who pass and students enroll. The performance rate, however, is defined as the relationship between the students approved and the students who pass the subject evaluated.
- *Class Hours (claHour)*: represents the number of hours of dedication to teaching activities at graduate and postgraduate level for an academic period.

3.3 Student Achievements

Students' achievements is an important element to evaluate teaching performance. It represents objectives and data generated by the educational process. They are factors that can influence the final result (See Eq. 4).

$$achEst = f(ratings) \tag{4}$$

Where *ratings* are the marks obtained by the students and *f* is a function of those marks. This value defines the level of impact of factors related to student achievement. The number of students per course, the type of subject, the professor experience, among other aspects, can influence the results. Studies like [16] provide a basis for the identification of these inputs.

3.4 Academic Support

It identifies the impact of additional tasks that teachers may have been assigned. The academic support activities include doctoral thesis supervision, participation in committees and preparation of academic guides (See Eq. 5).

$$supAct = w_1 * theDir + w_2 * comPar + w_3 * guiDev \tag{5}$$

Where:

- *Doctoral Thesis Supervision (theDir)*: identifies the amount of doctoral thesis that the professors has directed or tutored, with an upper limit.
- *Participation Committees (comPar)*: defines the amount of committees in which professors have participated.
- *Guides (guiDev)*: represents the academic planning of the professor as support for the teaching activity and which must include at least: competencies, objectives, contents, methodology, material, evaluation, bibliography and coordination criteria

4 Required Technologies

The presented architecture uses a set of innovative technologies that we will describe in this section. The purpose is to identify suitable strategies for processing based on different knowledge representation and processing techniques.

4.1 Semantic Web

Currently, web-based education has become a significant trend in educational institutions. The majority of resources created by professors are available on the Internet. In this environment, Semantic Web adds new relevant advantages to manage these contents [21]. For instance, it provides mechanisms to publish resources easily, semantic annotations to provide efficient tools to process and search for information. For example, in our application domain, teaching resources like books, assessments can be easily located.

Furthermore, Semantic Web also provides a standardised way to model and represent knowledge. Hence, the analysed academic inputs can be easily described by using the same semantic format to improve their management. We can also easily measure the e-learning platform usage by examining the student visits, among other variables.

4.2 Machine Learning

The use of machine learning techniques for educational purposes is a promising field aimed at developing methods to explore data from computational educational environments and discover meaningful patterns [12]. In his research, he presents a case study to predict students' grades considering the demographic characteristics of students using a regression method. This contribution is very important since in educational environments, data of similar characteristics are available that need to be processed to assess the work of the professor. In addition, based on historical academic data, we will try to identify early the chances of success of a professor in a new academic period. Variables such as student achievements will be analysed by this technology using regression algorithms to predict students' chances of success based on their historical records. Related data such as socioeconomic status, type of subject, students per course, among others, their inclusion will be analysed, considering the study proposed by [16] and [15], where these variables are incorporated and associated with student achievement.

4.3 Sentiment Analysis

The application of opinion surveys has historically been one of the most used techniques for professor evaluation [22]. As a case study, this technique has been used in the evaluation of the 2013 study plan of the Indonesian educational system where its implementation has generated diverse opinions among students, professors and the general public, especially in the social networks of Twitter [14]. This technique allows us to assess the opinions that the students give about the teaching activity in such a way that they constitute an important input for our purpose. Process unstructured content obtained from a planned opinion survey or from another public source, such as social networks, provide valuable information for decision making. The identification of student satisfaction levels in academic subjects is a variable that will be processed based on classification algorithms for Sentiment Analysis, so that the impact factors of these variables in others are quite real. It is necessary to identify aspects such as compliance with planning, academic support, the use of support materials, among others.

5 Conclusions

In this work, we have analysed the current situation of popular teaching evaluation models. During the analysis, we have pointed out several weaknesses related to metrics, subjective procedures or even data used to evaluate the teaching quality. In response, we propose an innovative model which combines new metrics and cutting-edge techniques to overcome such problems.

The new model incorporates four specific components oriented to deeply analyse the teaching performance: teacher's profile, academic process, student achievements and academic support activities. Furthermore, to facilitate the data integrability and analysis, we have integrated Knowledge Representation techniques to provide a standard data model; Machine Learning techniques to infer new knowledge from historical data and Natural Language Processing technologies that provide tools for efficiently analysing resources described in natural language.

To implement the architecture is one of the future lines that we plan to achieve. Furthermore, once we develop it, we would like to carry out different tests to evaluate the teaching performance and compare the results against other models. Last but not least, we would like to apply into a real teaching environment.

Acknowledgements. Work partially supported by the Autonomous Region of Madrid (grants "MOSI-AGIL-CM" (S2013/ICE-3019) co-funded by EU Structural Funds FSE and FEDER and Talent Attraction Program ("2017-T2/TIC-5664")), project "SURF" (TIN2015-65515-C4-4-R (MINECO/FEDER)) funded by the Spanish Ministry of Economy and Competitiveness, and through the Excellence Research Group GES2ME (Ref. 30VCPIGI05) co-funded by URJC-Santander Bank.

References

1. Wächter, B., Kelo, M.: University quality indicators: a critical assessment. European Parliament, Brussels (2015)
2. Astin, A.W., Lising, A.: Assesment for Excellence: The Philosophy and Practice of Assesment and Evaluation in Higher Education. Rowman & Littlefield Publishers Inc., Lanham (2012)
3. Berk, R.A.: Survey of 12 strategies to measure teaching effectiveness. Int. J. Teach. Learn. High. Educ. **17**, 48–62 (2005)

4. Duffy, B., Smith, K., Terhanian, G., Bremer, J.: Comparing data from online and face-to-face surveys. Int. J. Mark. Res. **47**(6), 615–639 (2005)
5. Alenoush, S., Cheryl, A.: Evaluating university teaching: time to take stock. Assess. Eval. High. Educ. **26**(4), 341–353 (2010)
6. Heneman, H., Kimball, S., Milanowski, A.: The Teacher Sense of Efficacy Scale: Validation Evidence and Behavioral Prediction. WCER, Wisconsin (2006)
7. Ita, G., Kreft, G.: Using multilevel analysis to assess school effectiveness: a study of Dutch secondary schools. Am. Sociol. Rev. **66**(2), 104–129 (1993)
8. Darling-Hammond, L., Amrein-Beardsley, A., Haertel, E., Rothstein, J.: Evaluating Teacher Evaluation. Phi Delta Kappan **93**, 8–15 (2012)
9. Bates, W.T., Sangrá, A.: Managing Technology in Higher Education: Strategies for Transforming Teaching and Learning. Jossey-Bass, San Francisco (2011)
10. Wang, S.: Ontology of learning objects repository for pedagogical knowledge sharing. Interdisc. J. E-Learn. Learn. Object. **4**, 39–57 (2008)
11. Stojanovic, L., Staab, S., Studer, R.: eLearning basad on the Semantic Web (2001)
12. Kotsiantis, S.: Use of machine learning techniques for educational proposes: a decision support system for forecasting students' grades. Artif. Intell. Rev. **37**, 331–344 (2012)
13. Dochy, F., Segers, M., Sluijsmans, D.: The use of self peer and coassessment in higher education: a review. Stud. High. Educ. **24**, 331–350 (2006)
14. Rizzo Irfan, M., Ali Fauzi, M., Tibyani, T., Mentari, N.D.: Twitter sentiment analysis on 2013 curriculum using ensemble features and K-Nearest neighbor. Int. J. Electr. Comput. Eng. **8**(6), 5409–5414 (2018)
15. Cunha, J., Trey, M.: Measuring value-added in higher education: possibilities and limitations in the use of administrative data. Elsevier **42**, 64–77 (2014)
16. Xin, M., Klinger, D.A.: Hierarchical linear modelling of student and school effects on academic achievement. Can. J. Edu. **269**, 41–55 (2000)
17. Galán, A., Amilburu, M.G., Muñoz, I.: The effects of implementing the ESHE on the assessment of teaching. Revista catalana de dret públic **44**, 349–370 (2012)
18. Yeh, S.: The Cost Effectiveness of NBPTS Teacher Certification. SAGE, Thousand Oaks (2010)
19. Standards, National Board for Professional Teaching, Guide to National Board Certification, Pearson (2017)
20. Goe, L., Bell, C., Little, O.: Approaches to Evaluating Teacher Effectiveness A Research Synthesis. National Comprehensive Center for Teacher Quality (2008)
21. Devedzic, V.: Education and the semantic web. Int. J. Artif. Intell. Educ. **14**, 39–65 (2004)
22. Ingvarson, L., Rowe, K.: Conceptualising and evaluating teacher quality: substantive and methodological issues. Australian Council for Educational Research ACEReSearch (2007)

Machine Learning for the Identification of Students at Risk of Academic Desertion

Leidy Daniela Forero Zea(✉), Yudy Fernanda Piñeros Reina(✉), and José Ignacio Rodríguez Molano(✉)

Universidad Distrital Francisco José de Caldas, Bogotá, Colombia
{ldforeroz,yfpinerosr}@correo.udistrital.edu.co,
jirodriguezm@udistrital.edu.co

Abstract. In Latin America, desertion rates in higher education range between 40% and 75%. There are many reasons for a student to deserted of their studies. However, the importance of identifying the level of risk related to such desertion is reflected in the socio-economic impact for the institutions as well as for the country. Technological advancements in database management and artificial intelligence have led to the development of techniques such as Machine Learning, which supports decision-making when facing a problem and adapts accordingly to the required conditions.

The following article shows a case study of the identification of students in Industrial Engineering at risk of dropping out in the Universidad Distrital Francisco José de Caldas from the 2003-1 to 2018-1 academic semesters. The algorithm is selected based on which is more suitable to the nature of data, through the comparison of automated learning techniques in Azure Machine Learning Studio.

Keywords: Academic desertion · Algorithm · Artificial intelligence · Machine Learning

1 Introduction

The approach for student desertion and retention involves variables on individual, institutional and family-related levels, which on top of that are classified in terms of psychological, economic, sociological, organizational and interactional aspects [1, 4]. This implies handling large amounts of information that require the use of technologies with high, medium or low complexity depending on the nature of the study. From this standpoint, Artificial Intelligence offers a variety of techniques for database management and analysis including Machine Learning.

Machine Learning, emerges as an artificial intelligence method derived from computing programs that access data and uses it to learn and predict results. These decision-making methods are assessed and receive feedback so that they can determine the algorithm that is more suitable for the type of data and response related to the research.

L. Uden et al. (Eds.): LTEC 2019, CCIS 1011, pp. 462–473, 2019.
https://doi.org/10.1007/978-3-030-20798-4_40

2 State of the Art

2.1 Academic Desertion in Colombia and Context of the Universidad Distrital

Academic desertion can be defined as the condition of those people enrolled in higher education that abandon the institution during two or more consecutive periods at the time of their studies [5].

According to data gathered in 2015 by the Colombian System for the Prevention of Desertion in Higher Education Institutions (by its acronym in Spanish SPADIES) in the statistical report of desertion and graduation of the Colombian Ministry of National Education and considering the desertion rate by cohort and by training level, the undergraduate students that deserted represent 41.60% out of the total number of students that enroll in an academic period on a national scale and 45.25% on a district scale [6].

On another note, the last report "Statistics of permanence, graduation and desertion of students in the Engineering Faculty in undergraduate programs from 2009 to 2017" carried out by the Consultant System Office in the Universidad Distrital Francisco José de Caldas (UDFJC), 53.8% of the faculty students between 2009 and 2017, either deserted or lost their student status [11]. Furthermore, specific information on desertion for the curricular program of Industrial Engineering indicates that the desertion percentage in the assessed periods is equivalent to 48% [11].

2.2 Machine Learning and Classification of Its Algorithms

Machine Learning is a form of artificial intelligence where large volumes of data are accessed and interpreted, the system is trained and new information is predicted through learning algorithms. These techniques are classified according to various criteria: the type of learning, the tasks dictated to the algorithm and the types of models used.

Classification is a task in which an individual of the system intends to determine to which class it belongs according to the process of learning characteristics, patterns and behaviors that other individuals have previously adopted and their documented records [10]. Thus, these algorithms are divided into two categories: binary classification and multiclass classification. Binary classification refers to those algorithms whose observation result must be catalogued as either positive or negative. Therefore, classification depends on a threshold used to compare the generated score for each iteration of the algorithm. The multiclass classification differs in the sense that it predicts the classes with the highest scores [3].

Binary Classification Algorithms. This article will use the binary classification learning algorithms, since the objective of the development of the case study is to predict a desertion or no desertion label for a student whose values of the variables allow their classification; these algorithms are Averaged Perceptron, Bayes Point Machine, Boosted Decision Tree, Decision Forest, Decision Jungle, Logistic Regression and Two-Class Neural Network [2, 9].

3 Methodology for the Application of Classification Models Using ML

3.1 Definition of the Computational Tool to Use

There are many options for commercial Machine Learning software. However, in this case, it is suggested that it is directed towards the predictive model as well as understandable and easy to use, which allows the manipulation of data and the types of results that it can generate.

Next, a comparative table is presented including the advantages, functionality and generalities of each tool keeping in mind the previously mentioned criteria (See Table 1).

Table 1. Characteristics of machine learning software. Source: Author.

Software	Description	Functions
Azure Machine Learning Studio	Collaborative solution with drag-and-drop interface developed to create and implement predictive analytics solutions in minutes. Designed for applied machine learning	Predictive Modeling
Google Cloud ML Engine	Engine Managed service that provides a balanced, scalable and automatic predictive training compiled in mathematical models that allow to understand the information extracted from the data set	Deep learning Model formation Predictive modeling
AWS	It allows to create, train technically and implement deep learning models quickly and easily, with high performance automatic learning algorithms; includes data storage, business intelligence, batch processing, transmission processing and organization of data workflows	Self-learning Machine Learning algorithm library Model formation

It is determined that the Azure Machine Learning Studio from Microsoft is used whose predictive model function is required based on the expected response and handled database. Additionally, it is code-free which facilitates the understanding of applied automated learning and includes a free trial version so any user can access it.

3.2 Used Database and Determination of Variables

Considering the concepts and trends mentioned in Machine Learning and the goal of identifying students at risk of Academic desertion of the Industrial engineering program of the District University Francisco José de Caldas, Bogotá, Colombia. The following sample was taken:

Sample Description. The software training process is done with a student status database of the program of Industrial Engineering between 2003 and 2018 (Active student, graduate, suspended, sanctioned, retired); which was provided by the UDFJC for academic purposes, and They do not contain personally identifiable information about people, as recognized by Habeas data. A database treatment was required, from which unnecessary, incomplete and inconsistent data were eliminated; Bearing in mind that the required information is specifically that of the students who left the university, either as a graduate student who is classified as not abandoned or by desertion or abandonment, leaving a total sample of 3201 data, each one 24 academic and social variables, which are presented below. (see Table 2).

Table 2. Description of the database variables. Source: Author.

Variable	Id.	Definition
Student code	CE	Identification number within the institution. Numeric character string
State	ES	Characterizes the student in the state Abandoned, which covers sus pended students, deserted or who did not pass academic test, or No Abandoned that refers to graduate students.
Sex	SX	Gender of the student: Male (M), Female (F)
Stratum	ST	Socioeconomic classification. Integer value between 0 and 6
Age of Entry	EI	The age at which the student enters the first semester
Type of Inscription	TI	Classification of the inscription: Normal, Displaced, Indigenous, External transfer.
Average	PR	Accumulated average of the career until the last semester taken. Value between 0 and 5.
Number of Academic Tests	PN	State at risk of losing student quality. Value between 0 and 4
Approved Subjects	EA	Number of subjects taken and passed. Whole value between 0 and the number of subjects in the academic program
Failed Subjects	ER	Number of subjects studied, but not approved
Score ICFES	PI	Total score obtained in the Saber test 11. Weighted average of the scores in the five (5) Areas. Value between 0 and 100
Biology	B	Score obtained in the Saber 11 test for each subject. Value between 0 and 100
Chemistry	Q	
Physics	F	
Social	S	
Verbal Aptitude	AV	
Spanish and Literature	EL	
Mathematics Abilities	AM	
Mathematical Knowledge	CM	
Philosophy	F	
History	H	
Geography	G	
Foreign language	IE	
Interdisciplinary	I	

The sample was submitted to a statistical analysis of independence and homogeneity on the average variable of students who deserted to verify the validity of the data, which were approved with a correlation index of 0.14 and 0,496 for test Kruskall Wallis with a confidence level of 95%, respectively.

Table 3. Pearson correlation coefficients. Source: Author.

CI Pearson	Average	Stratum	Age of entry	N. of Ac. Tests	Approved subjects	Failed subjects	Score ICFES	Math. Knowledge	Math. Abilities
Average	1.000	0.113	0.176	0.035	0.757	0.003	0.290	0.193	0.180
Stratum	0.124	1.000	0.058	0.057	0.096	0.056	0.087	0.021	0.004
Age of entry	0.176	0.057	1.000	0.080	0.179	0.076	0.174	0.042	0.036
N. of Ac. Tests	0.035	0.056	0.080	1.000	0.055	0.881	0.055	0.137	0.015
Approved subjects	0.757	0.087	0.179	0.055	1.000	0.033	0.285	0.148	0.136
Failed subjects	0.003	0.049	0.076	0.881	0.033	1.000	0.002	0.131	0.022
Score ICFES	0.290	0.060	0.174	0.055	0.285	0.002	1.000	0.041	0.467
Math. Knowledge	0.193	0.021	0.042	0.137	0.148	0.131	0.041	1.000	0.384
Math. Abilities	0.180	0.003	0.036	0.015	0.136	0.022	0.467	0.384	1.000

Based on the analysis of variables, their level of correlation is established through the Pearson coefficient assessed in the software. The highest correlation indexes delivered by the Pearson correlation can be seen in Table 3.

However, the algorithm that is more suitable to the needs of the case study is chosen with the purpose of predicting when a student is at risk of dropping out of the Industrial Engineering program of the UDFJC given that the term desertion includes those students that entered the program as such yet did not culminate their careers.

3.3 Determination of Performance Metrics of the Selected Algorithms

In order to validate the performance of the implemented algorithms, the crossed validation tool provided by the software used which generates assessment metrics (accuracy, precision, recall and F1 score) for binary classification algorithms. Additionally, the duration of the experiment is also considered as well as the factors generated by the confusion matrix which includes the percentage of true positives, true negatives, false positives and false negatives. These variables are understood as a whole to determine the assertiveness of the algorithms and then choose the best conditions to predict the classification of the status of students. Then (Table 4), the definition of these measures is presented.

Table 4. Definition of the assessment metrics. Source: Author.

Measure	Definition	Formula
Accuracy (A)	Is the ratio of true results to total cases. Measure the goodness of a classification model	$A = \frac{TP+TN}{\text{Total of cases}}$
Precision (P)	It is the proportion of true results on all positive results	$P = \frac{TP}{TP+FP}$
Recall (R)	It is the relation of all the correct results returned by the model	$R = \frac{TP}{TP+FN}$
F1 Score (F1S)	It is the weighted average of Precision and Recall. The summary of the evaluation is considered	$F1S = \frac{2*(R*P)}{R+P}$
Duration of the experiment (T)	It is the time it takes the model in the training of the database. It is measured in seconds	
True positives (TP)	Number of cases of No Abandonment, whose prediction was "No abandonment"	
Negative positives (TN)	Number of cases of No Abandonment, whose prediction was "Abandonment"	
False positives (FP)	Number of cases of Abandonment, whose prediction was "Abandonment"	
False negatives (FN)	Number of cases of Abandonment, whose prediction was "No Abandonment"	

3.4 Application of the Different Algorithms to the Case Study

Based on the objective of the case study, it is stated that according to the desired response the algorithm must be a binary (two-class) classification (supervised learning) since the program needs to choose between two response options: Desertion or Non-desertion. To determine the appropriated algorithm within the Binary Classification, a software test is performed as shown in Figs. 1 and 2.

The assessment scheme for the algorithms shown in Figs. 1 and 2 consists of a software tool that can find the value of the Assessment Criteria. Afterwards, the Select Columns module is used to choose the variables that will be a part of the software training. In Split Data, the proportion of data used for training is determined. The subsequent modules refer to the learning, training and result assessment algorithms. For the testing process, each algorithm is trained for the Two-Class Classification based on the status variable with a significant sample of 80% of the data and the remaining 20% is assessed later. The obtained results are shown in Table 5.

Using the previous results, it is determined that the learning algorithm that is more suitable for the nature of data and the type of response is a Two Class Boosted Decision Tree. Establishing an equitable weighing strategy for each criteria, this represents a larger set of characteristics that enable proper adjustment and minimization of prediction errors.

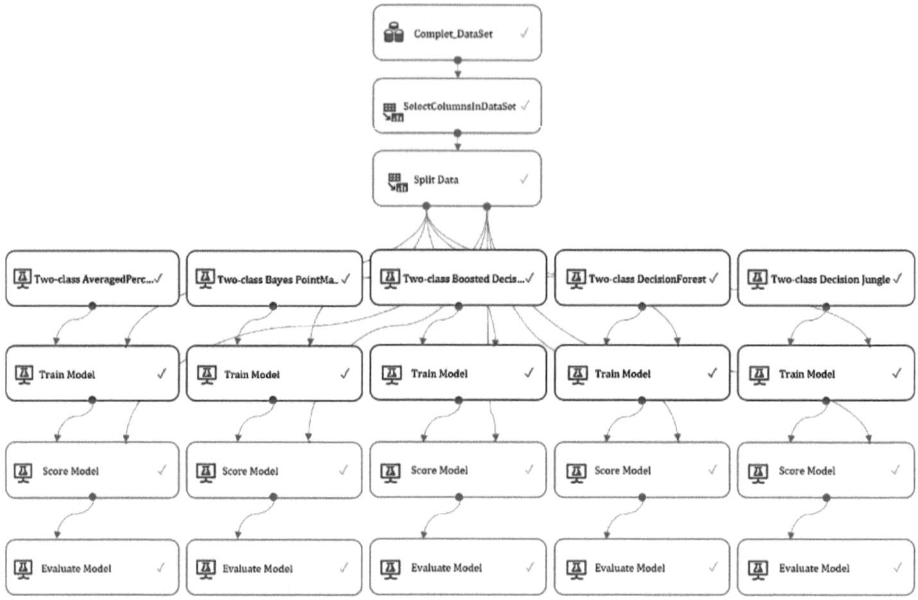

Fig. 1. Assessment structure of the algorithms. Part (a) Source: Author.

Fig. 2. Assessment structure of the algorithms. Part (b) Source: Author.

Table 5. Comparison of the measurements for the assessment of algorithms. Source: Author.

Algorithm	TP	TN	FP	FN	A	P	R
Averaged perceptron	0.879	0.955	0.121	0.045	0.919	0.879	0.947
Bayes point machine	0.852	0.963	0.148	0.037	0.908	0.852	0.958
Boosted decision tree	0.903	0.965	0.097	0.035	0.936	0.903	0.958
Decision forest	0.899	0.956	0.101	0.044	0.93	0.899	0.947
Decision jungle	0.891	0.982	0.109	0.018	0.938	0.891	0.979
Locally deep support vector machine	0.890	0.979	0.110	0.021	0.936	0.89	0.975
Logistic regression	0.850	0.963	0.150	0.037	0.906	0.85	0.958
neural network	0.870	0.975	0.130	0.025	0.923	0.87	0.972

3.5 Performance Assessment of the Chosen Algorithm

Aiming to improve the performance of the selected algorithm, five tests are carried out (See Table 6) with different groups of variables (Abbreviations Table 2), where the X represents the variables chosen from the database that are included in the algorithm. Since the status is the main variable used to train all algorithms, it is not included in the tests.

Table 6. Comparison matrix of attribute addition. Source: Author.

TEST	SX	ST	EI	TI	PR	NP	EA	ER	PI	B	Q	F	S	AV	EL	AM	CM	F	H	G	IE	I
1		X			x	x	x	x	x							x	x					
2	x	x	x		x	x	x	x	x							x	x					
3	x	x	x	x	x	x	x	x	x	x	x	x	x	x	x	x	x	x	x	X	x	x
4					x	x			x													
5	x		x	x	x	x		x	x							x	x					

Table 7 shows a summary of the Assessment Criteria per test, which is useful to identify the variables that have a significant impact on the results of Accuracy, Precision, Recall and F1Score.

Table 7. Test comparison of assessment criteria.

Test	Accuracy	Precision	Recall	F1Score
1	0.994	0.989	0.996	0.993
2	0.995	0.99	1	0.995
3	0.994	0.986	1	0.993
4	0.911	0.887	0.915	0.901
5	0.938	0.909	0.954	0.931

It was confirmed that the variables with the highest correlation such as Average (PR), Approved Status (EA) and Number of Tests (NP), Failed Subjects (ER) must necessarily be included in the test and generates the highest values in the assessment indexes. In contrast, other variables such as the areas of knowledge do not have a significant impact in the improvement of results.

4 Results of the Predictive Experiment

The chosen learning algorithm is used to create the Training Experiment (Fig. 3) which comes from the selection of the previous variables based on the determination of the status and the use of the Two-Class Boosted Decision Tree as an ordered set of systematic operations that the algorithm uses to determine the result.

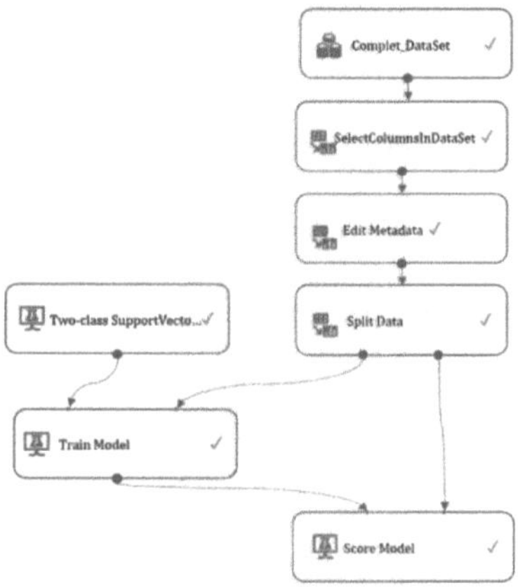

Fig. 3. Training experiment. Source: Author.

The Predictive Experiment (Fig. 4) shows the final structure of the software modelling trained with 80% of the data as well as the algorithm that is more suitable for the characteristics and the type of response. Additionally, the Web Service Input module requests information to the user to deliver the corresponding prediction. These requirements are the group of variables in test (Table 6) that are more appropriate according to the assessment criteria (Table 7).

With the prediction module created, an example can be tested with the data in Table 8.

Figure 5 presents the result of the practical example where the student deserts of the university under the given characteristics.

Fig. 4. Predictive experiment. Source: Author.

Table 8. Data for the practical example. Source: Author

Variable	Val.	Variable	Val.	Variable	Val.
Sex	M	Score ICFES	303	Mathematical knowledge	66
Stratum	1	Biology	51	Philosophy	0
Age of entry	20	Chemistry	61	History	0
Type of inscription	Normal	Physics	56	Geography	0
Average	3.0	Social	50	Foreign language	0
Number of academic tests	1	Verbal aptitude	57	Interdisciplinary	0
Approved spaces	42	Spanish and literature	56		
Failed spaces	15	Mathematics abilities	68		

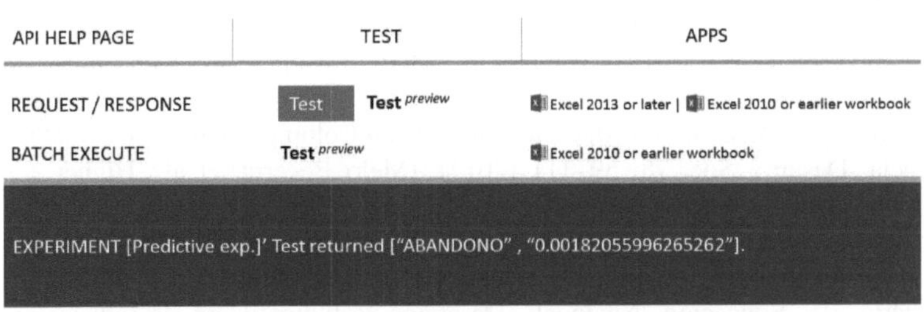

Fig. 5. Results of the practical example. Source: Author.

5 Conclusions

The data of the practical example is used to determine that the student deserts of university without specifying the academic or social variable that the student quits from. In this case, the student has passed 26% of the subjects in his syllabus and a GPA of 3.0, which classifies him as a student in academic probation. Since these variables have stronger weights within the prediction model, it is valid to state that the desertion is due to low academic performance of the student who decides to deserted. This analysis would lead to promote strategies that reduce the academic hardships of students by offering subjects during mid-year breaks, more scholarships to students with better GPAs, among others. It is noteworthy to highlight that there are many academic or social reasons that lead a student to deserted. However, the previous analysis of predictions establishes more effective retention mechanisms within higher education institutions. Learning techniques such as Machine Learning consider both the main and secondary variables, as well as their normal and abnormal values through previous training. In this scenario, the responses obtained are reliable with a precision of 90.3% and an accuracy of 93.6%.

At last after developing this case study, we identify Machine Learning tools that can be used in business, commercial, financial, industrial, academic, scientific and other fields. However, from an educational perspective and in order to predict whether a student will desert or not, with the use of Azure Machine Learning Studio; from the identification of the relevant variables; the treatment of the database is done by filtering the useful information for the study; the program is trained with the historical behavior of the variable (s) it seeks to predict; the current information is entered and the results are analyzed in order to make decisions and action against the possible scenarios. This algorithm can be replicated with different objectives and applied in multiple areas that require the prediction of random variable behaviors.

References

1. Chung, J.Y., Lee, S.: Desertion early warning systems for high school students using machine learning. Child. Youth Serv. Rev. (2018)
2. Copeland, M. et al.: Microsoft Azure Machine Learning. In: Microsoft Azure (2015)
3. Guides, A.M.D.: Amazon Machine Learning
4. Himmel, E.: Modelo de análisis de la deserción estudiantil en la educación superior. Calidad. en la Educación **17**, 91 (2018). (Himmel, E.: Model for the analysis of student desertion in higher education)
5. Melo-Becerra, L.A., et al.: La educación superior en Colombia: situación actual y análisis de eficiencia. Desarro. Soc. **78**, 59–111 (2017). (Melo Becerra, et al.: Higher education in Colombia: current situation and efficiency analysis)
6. Ministerio de Educación.: *Estádisticas de deserción y graduación. (*Colombian Ministry of National Education: Desertion and graduation statistics) (2016)
7. Ministerio de Educación Nacional: Deserción estudiantil en la educación superior colombiana. (Colombian Ministry of National Education: Student desertion in Colombian higher education.) (2009)

8. Ministerio de Educación Nacional.: Estadisticas de Educacion Superior, (Colombian Ministry of National Education: Statistics of higher education) (2016)
9. Sisodia, D., Sisodia, D.S.: Prediction of diabetes using classification algorithms. Procedia Comput. Sci. **132**, 1578–1585 (2018)
10. Tan, M., Shao, P.: Prediction of student desertion in e-Learning program through the use of machine learning method. Int. J. Emerg. Technol. Learn. **10**(1), 11–17 (2015)
11. Universidad Distrital: Estadística de la permanencia, graduación y deserción de los estudiantes en la Facultad de Ingeniería en programas de pregrado 2009–2017. (Universidad Distrital: Statistics on the permanence, graduation and desertion of students in the Faculty of Engineering in undergraduate programs 2009–2017). (2018)
12. Navarro, C.A.T., Neira, J.A.C.: Design of Expert System for Decision Making in Materials Purchasing (n.d.). http://www.scielo.org.co/pdf/cuadm/v30n52/v30n52a03.pdf
13. Hidalgo, L.A.: Artificial Intelligence (n.d.). https://doi.org/M-26913–2004
14. Alberto Ruiz Marta Susana Basualdo, C., Jorge Matich, D.: Cátedra: Informática Aplicada a la Ingeniería de Procesos-Orientación I Redes Neuronales: Conceptos Básicos y Aplicaciones. (Alberto Ruiz Marta Susana Basualdo, C., & Jorge Matich, D. Chair: Computer Science Applied to Process Engineering-Orientation I Neural Networks: Basic Concepts and Applications.) https://www.frro.utn.edu.ar/repositorio/catedras/quimica/5_anio/orientadora1/monograias/matich-redesneuronales.pdf
15. Gómez, J., Sánchez, J., William Restrepo, J.: Aplicación de Redes Neuronales en la Clasificación de Arcillas. Revista EIA (vol. 17). (Gómez, J., Sánchez, J., & William Restrepo, Application of Neural Networks in the Classification of Clays) (2012) http://www.scielo.org.co/pdf/eia/n17/n17a14.pdf
16. Garcia, M.R., Rodríguez, J.E.R.: Sistemas Basados En El Conocimiento. Revista Vínculos. (Knowledge-Based Systems. Vínculos Magazine) **1**(1), 37–44 (2004). https://doi.org/10.14483/2322939X.4070
17. Gorges, C., Öztürk, K., Liebich, R.: Impact detection using a machine learning approach and experimental road roughness classification (2019). https://doi.org/10.1016/j.ymssp.2018.07.043
18. Cai, J., Luo, J., Wang, S., Yang, S.: Feature selection in machine learning: a new perspective. Neurocomputing **300**, 70–79 (2018). https://doi.org/10.1016/j.neucom.2017.11.077
19. Kotsiantis, S.B., Zaharakis, I.D., Pintelas, P.E.: Machine learning: a review of classification and combining techniques. Artif. Intell. Rev. **26**(3), 159–190 (2006). https://doi.org/10.1007/s10462-007-9052-3
20. Badaró, S., Javier Ibañez, L., Agüero, M.J.: Sistemas Expertos: Fundamentos, Metodologías y Aplicaciones. (Expert Systems: Fundamentals, Methodologies and Applications) (n.d.). https://www.palermo.edu/ingenieria/pdf2014/13/CyT_13_24.pdf
21. Goldberg, D.E.: Genetic Algorithms in Search, Optimization, and Machine Learning. Addison-Wesley Longman Publishing Co., Inc., London (1989). https://dl.acm.org/citation.cfm?id=534133
22. Moreno-Eva, A. et al.: Aprendizaje automático (n.d.). www.edicionsupc.es
23. Kim, I., et al: A predictive model for high/low risk group according to oncotype DX recurrence score using machine learning (2018). https://doi.org/10.1016/j.ejso.2018.09.011
24. Patricia, S., Moreno, B., Támara, L.G.: Acercamiento a la deserción estudiantil desde la integración social y académica (Approach to student desertions from the perspective of social and academic integration). Revista de La Educación Superior **46**(183), 63–86 (2017). https://doi.org/10.1016/j.resu.2017.05.004

Evaluation of Computer Assisted Qualitative Data Analysis Software (CAQDAS) Applied to Research

M. C. Sánchez-Gómez(✉), M. V. Martín-Cilleros, and G. Sánchez Sánchez

Faculty of Education, University of Salamanca, Paseo Canalejas 169, 37008 Salamanca, Spain
{mcsago, viquimc, galo}@usal.es

Abstract. The recent increase in qualitative research has led to the production of software packages that help researchers process enormous amounts of data. Currently, several types of software are available depending on what they are intended for: data processing, text management, coding and recovery of data, building of theories or conceptual networks. This research introduces the different software allowing researchers to get an understanding of currently available tools. Moreover, it provides some guidelines to help researchers choose the most adequate tool. These programs offer valuable support in routine tasks, and conceptual and theoretical development. Nevertheless, no tool is ever going to substitute prior knowledge of methodological research.

Keywords: Software · CADQAS · Qualitative research

1 Introduction

From the 1990s onwards, the importance of qualitative research increased dramatically. There has been a definite trend in its use among researchers from different disciplines. As a result, there has been considerable rise in the number of qualitative researches in Spain and other countries [1]. This surge went hand in hand with the creation of a wide variety of software, known as Computer Assisted Qualitative Data Analysis Software (CAQDAS), whose objective is to assist researchers in performing qualitative analyses, but which in no way replace the creative, in-depth analyses done by researchers. The first programs appeared in the 1960s, but it wasn't until the 1980s and early 1990s that they were recognized in the field of qualitative analysis [2, 3].

Currently, there is a large variety of CAQDAS, aimed at specific tasks such as storage, integration and organization of data, performance of data searches, data structuring, information categorization, annotations, links, hyperlinks, graphs, maps, tables, memorandums and comments. Thus, their use during the analysis process is increasing. CAQDAS are being updated continuously offering new functions and possibilities, systematizing and optimizing the analysis of qualitative data. They maintain the quality of the analytical process without affecting the analyst's creativity, the plurality of analysis types or the core features of qualitative methodology:

L. Uden et al. (Eds.): LTEC 2019, CCIS 1011, pp. 474–485, 2019.
https://doi.org/10.1007/978-3-030-20798-4_41

flexibility, reflexivity. Again, programs cannot analyze the data by themselves, nor can they interpret or influence the type and quality of the analyses [4].

Whenever changes come about we are bound to meet with conflicting opinions. The use of a computer as an aid in qualitative analysis has been no different. Some claim that the use of software offers infinite possibilities while others continue advocating a manual analysis. The former approach CADQAS as a major area of specialization within analysis, as is statistics in quantitative analysis.

As soon as qualitative research became a trend among researchers, a debate began on the use of software in this area. There have been different concerns; the most prominent software packages had been developed in the context of a specific approach - codification according to grounded theory - and as a result, it was difficult to apply them to other approaches. If the programs do not follow a sequential analysis, should the researchers who use them ignore this? Does it change the way the data are analysed? [5]. Fielding and Lee [6] found in their empirical study of CADQAS usage that two-thirds of the reviewed projects had not used grounded theory, but did use software for qualitative research. This shows that software and grounded theory are not as closely related as some authors suggest.

Concern had been expressed over the risk of researchers moving their focus away from data as a result of the Ethnograph [7], a software designed by Seidel. This software initially involved a very laborious coding process, which meant that its users were trapped in code making and lost sight of the contextualization of data. Ten Have [8], however, shows how the Ethnograph can be applied to conversation analysis. Another concern is that computer programs implicitly force their logical and expository structure upon the researcher's data and analysis. The NUDIST software, for example, assists in the development of a hierarchical code structure in the form of a tree. A slight increase in tree-structured coding systems had been identified among its users. Seale [9] illustrates this problem well by applying NUDIST and ATLAS-ti to a grounded theory developed by Glaser and Strauss, and shows the differences in the presentation and structure of this theory in both programs.

There is fear that the attention attracted by the computer and the software will distract the researcher from the real analytical work: reading and understanding the texts, thinking contemplatively about what is in the texts and what underlies them, etc., [10]. Similarly, Richards and Richards [11], who have developed one of the most important programs (NUDIST), assert that the use of informatics in qualitative analysis can have contradictory implications for the process and results of research, from unacceptable restrictions on analysis to the unexpected unlocking of possibilities. Ultimately, however, it is the user that chooses how they use the computer and software in research, and how they reflect on the work they are doing. Thus, computers and software should be seen as a pragmatic tool that support qualitative research. Researchers must reflect on the impacts that qualitative research software has on their research. It is likely that much of the mistrust and misconceptions surrounding the use of these software is a product of low usage rates among researchers [12, 13].

2 Characteristics of CAQDAS

The computer is an invaluable aid with great potential for carrying out routine tasks and for supporting conceptual and theoretical development [14], but it cannot replace the researcher's capacity.

2.1 The Usefulness of Software

Publications on data analysis in computer-assisted qualitative research [9, 15] observe that the use of a computer aids in the management, search and display of data and related elements, such as codes or memos. It is worth the effort to choose a program, install it and learn how to use it (or even learn how to use the computer), since a considerable amount of time is gained when compared to the time it takes to perform a manual analysis.

Another benefit is that the use of a computer increases the quality of a qualitative research or at least it is easier to demonstrate its quality. Researches mention greater coherence in the analytical procedures [15] or the rigor added to the analyses [9]. Kelle and Laurie, [16] claim that the use of these software provides qualitative research with greater validity.

Flick [17] states that the use of these software increases the transparency of the research process and communication in a research team. Weitzman [15] also points to the consolidation of research, since the computer allows the researcher to have all the research documents (from the initial field notes to the final presentations, tables and writings on the discoveries) in one place: the computer's hard drive. Moreover, Seale [9] says that this software facilitate sampling decisions based on the current status of data analysis (according to theoretical sampling).

An important utility is that data management is made easier with computers. Some authors [16, 17] list various data management techniques supported by qualitative analysis computer software: (a) the definition of indicators containing keywords along with "addresses" of text passages that can be used to retrieve indexed text segments; (b) the construction of electronic cross-references with the help of so-called hyperlinks. which can be used to jump between text passages that are linked to each other; (c) functions for storing researchers' comments (-memorandums-), which can be linked to keywords or text segments; (d) features for defining links between keywords; (e) the use of variables and filters so that the search for text segments can be restricted by certain limitations; (f) functions for retrieving text segments with specific formal relationships between them (for example. (g) functions for recovering quantitative attributes from the database.

The first two functions are provided by all qualitative analysis software, while the other five are provided only by the most elaborate qualitative research software packages.

Pujol [13] in the same line of data management states that the CAQDAS can be used to: organize documents; segment and tag texts, sounds or images relevant to the researcher; facilitate coding and categorization and to theorize and abstract the meaning of codes and their rearrangement according to levels, if appropriate; increases speed and flexibility in coding; provide tools that ease the search for text in documents;

retrieve coded segments; study temporal aspects (integral narrative sequence); consult the database looking for relationships, similarities and differences between codes; provide a graphical way of looking at the relationships between different codes and fragments of text, through diagrams and tables; promote conceptual and theoretical reflection on the data; provide a formal structure to facilitate the writing and storage of memos, comments and annotations relevant in the development of the analysis; help write final results reports; make explicit the underlying analytical operations, making their audit possible (replication of an analysis by independent researchers).

2.2 Choice of Software

As we have explained before, to be able to use CAQDAS it is necessary to have prior knowledge of qualitative data analysis and the implicit processes [13]: type of planned analysis, e.g. Nvivo, Atlas it and Maxqda are very suitable for content [18, 19]; nature of data (text, sound, image); type of coding (hierarchical or not, or both); process of writing the final report (exportable to other applications) and other factors such as amount of information; affinity with computer environments, whether to work with quantitative data, available computer equipment, research equipment, etc.).

Fig. 1. CAQDAS software homepages

At least in theory, any form of qualitative analysis could be computer-assisted through CAQDAS software created for this purpose, which facilitates the manual handling of data: search, selection and organization. Figure 1 Homepage of several CAQDAS for qualitative analysis. Source Merino 2009. Programs such as ETHNOGRAPH, AQUAD, NVIVO or ATLAS-Ti, ATLAS.ti; DEDOOSE; HyperRESEARCH; MAXQDA and QDA Miner, whose interface can be seen in Fig. 1., are extremely useful in analysis, for operations such as marking and coding text, listing categories and subjects, preparing typologies or profiles, or counting, searching and retrieving coded units. They are particularly useful when working simultaneously with large amounts of information [20, 21].

To determine which program should be used in a given research, we must consider several authors [13, 22]. Moreover, the researcher must consider different points before deciding to use a computer or a specific computer software or the use of computers in general [23], which are summarized in Table 1.

Nonetheless, note that "no software has yet been considered the best" [17].

Table 1. Key points to consider before deciding which CAQDAS to use.

Aspects	Questions	Characteristics to consider
Ease of use:	Is it compatible with PC or MAC? What are the required network features (type of computer? RAM, hard disk. graphics card, screen.) or of the programs (software system, need of other programs). What specific and particularly technical skills does the program require of the user (programming skills, perhaps specific programming languages, etc.)?	Compatible with Windows, Macintosh and other environments. Simple software that can be used by novel users Clarity of the manuals
The types of documents it can analyse	What kind of data was the program designed for? Can it also be used to analyse different types of data? What types of data may not be used?	Text Sound Images Multimedia
Text review	Is it easy to work through the document?	Ability to mark relevant paragraphs and connect references Ability to search for specific paragraphs in the text
Memos	What can I access with this software?	Facilitate the preparation of notes, memos and reflections on the analysis Facilitate access to notes and memos
Codification	To interpret the text must it always be accessible (on the screen) or only the categories?	Options for the development of codes Easy to apply codes to text, images and multimedia Easy to display and visualize codes Ease to review and modify codes
Analysis and assessment capacity	What type of analysis is planned? How does the programme influence data management? Based on previous experience what role does the researcher or interpreter play in the analysis? What new possibilities did it offer? What has become more difficult or time-consuming in the interpretation process due to the software?	Data can be sorted according to specific codes Possibility of combining codes to perform a search Ability to generate maps, matrices, diagrams and relationships Facilitate the generation of hypothesis and theories
Connection with other programs	What conditions do the other programs require (SPSS, word processors, databases, etc.)?	Ability to import and export data, texts, materials, files and code systems with other programs.

(*continued*)

Table 1. (*continued*)

Aspects	Questions	Characteristics to consider
Interfaces between multiple projects	Can two or more researchers analyse the data and can these analyses be merged?	Possibility of sharing the analysis between different analysts
Cost	Can you afford to buy the program and/or the computer to use it? Are there any benefits of getting a license? How long does the license last?	Free of charge License provided by an institution Periodic License

2.3 Most Used Qualitative Analysis Software

The currently available software can be grouped into several types [9, 11, 15, 17, 24]:

(a) Word processors, which allow not only to write, but also to edit texts and search for words or sequences of words in a limited way.
(b) Text retrieval software, designed specifically for investigating, summarizing, enumerating, etc. certain sequences of words.
(c) Text database management to search, classify and sort text segments.
(d) Coding and recovery programs that separate text into segments, to which codes are assigned, and to retrieve or enumerate all text segments that have been marked with a code. Marking, sorting, classifying and linking texts and codes are the available features and both (text and code) are presented and managed together.
(e) Building theories based on codes: in addition, these programs support the building of theories by backing up steps and operations at the text level (assignment of one or more passages to a code) but also at the conceptual level (relationships between codes, upper categories and subcategories, networks of categories), always going back to the assigned text segments. Graphical editors are included in some programs. and it is possible to integrate video data.
(f) There are ample options for developing conceptual networks and category networks and numerous ways of visualizing relationships between individual parts of the network.

The coding and retrieval functions are prevalent in all CAQDAS, but there are no notable differences between them. Currently, there are three programs that are widely used by researchers. Some of them are available to students through universities and university networks [20, 24]. They are Atlas.ti*; Maxqda before were Winmax and Nvivo. All three share similar characteristics, although they have slight differences.

Nvivo: http://www.qsrinternational.com/other-languages_spanish.aspx
Software QSR, is an Australian company affiliated to the University of La Trobe (Australia). It specializes in the creation of software for the qualitative analysis of data. It has created the NUD*ist software and previous versions of Nvivo. The most recent version of Nvivo is already the 12th one. It started in version 2, being the improvement

of the well-known NUD*ist 6, and in the last years it has gone through its version with substantial modifications and improvements.

Nvivo is specifically designed for the analysis of qualitative data, coming from interviews, discussion groups, diaries, life stories…, but they have new functionalities that give it a unique position in the soft-ware landscape. QSR NVivo is a highly advanced and powerful program for the analysis of qualitative data in research projects. It has the capacity to manage large volumes of information (resources) and analyse textual documents, audio documents, spreadsheets, social networks, references, shared files, e-mails, interviews, videos and photographs. It also allows to operate with an almost unlimited number of categories and subcategories, which can be compared in an abbreviated way through intersection matrices [25]. With the NCAPTURE application, screenshots and comments can be incorporated into the program, especially useful for analysing data from virtual environments and social networks. It also has creative and flexible functions that facilitate the creation of analytical annotations, the integration of work and discussions through the use of links and hyperlinks. Establish different search possibilities with very flexible tools that allow multiple searches at the same time and access to reports or results.

The current version enhances several aspects: document management, coding, data management, modelling (graphical representation), reports, export to a large number of formats, facilitates cooperative work and the processing of social network data. Another noteworthy feature of this program is that it offers a wide range of possibilities for reports and presents results directly, without going through other programs. Reports, graphs and dendrograms can be edited. Until now, for example, other support programmes such as Cmaps, Excell or similar were used and are no longer needed.

One of the drawbacks is the complexity of using all of the software features. It may require training or initial mentoring, but this does not detract from its worth. The software uses RAM memory, and it is possible to have several options of a section open at the same time but located in different windows, this may make its use difficult. The internal database and the rich text format may cause slower navigation and search for information.

ATLAS.ti: http://www.atlasti.com/

It was developed by Muhr [26] as part of a research project at the Technical University of Berlin. The programme is based on a grounded theory and theoretical coding approach proposed by Strauss [27]. Its most recent versions can process not only text, but also images, graphics and sound. Most authors classify it in the category of "conceptual network builders" [15], but mainly in the group of "code-based theorists".

This program has several units, the most important one is called Hermeneutic Unit because it is an information storage; it stores all the operations that raw data undergo, the starting point of all the analysis. Within this hermeneutic unit we can find several basic components for analysis, such as primary documents, citations, codes, annotations, families, networks and relationships.

Pujol [13] describes it as a flexible program that greatly facilitates the systematic coding of the search and retrieval of texts and codes. At the conceptual level of analysis, its ability to organize and establish links between data coming from different sources, the grouping of categories, the hypertext and hypermedia system and the visualization of the results through graphics (networks) is very useful. It supports multimedia data analysis. The "Object Crawler" or extended search option provides a general or global view of the project and facilitates the retrieval of texts from primary documents, annotations or comments within a project. This author affirms that the latest versions maintain: (a) the format of complex documents (web pages) with each and every one of their elements (tables, images), (b) the line numbers used in methodologies such as narrative analysis, conversation analysis, revisions and comments of Word and Open Office documents, and segments the images included in the documents as independent graphic objects. Allows you to export your project to XLM, HTML or SPSS formats.

Saving and moving the project and the data is difficult in an external database structure. When moving the project to another space, the primary documents to which it is linked must also be moved, and when changes are made to the primary documents, the coordinates of the references change.

MAXQDA: http://www.maxqda.com/

MAXQDA is a powerful new program developed by the creators of WINMAX, for qualitative data text analysis. MAXQDA leverages the following qualitative methods and techniques: grounded theory, qualitative content analysis, field research methods and ethnographic methods. It analyses different types of texts: transcriptions of open interviews, in-depth, semi-structured and expert interviews, observations, field studies, group debates, speeches and documents, texts from the web, political speeches and therapeutic talks. This software is used in many disciplines or fields, such as sociology, educational sciences, economics, marketing, ethnology, architecture, urban planning, public health and medicine.

Pujol [13] states that the MAXqda interface is very user-friendly, simple, easy to understand and use, accurate, intuitive and tidy. Organized with windows of varying sizes that allow to customize and focus on the primary data in its context, allows to work with multimedia files and stores documents within the same project archive. It is a very suitable software to be taught to students. It has good writing tools and it is very easy to systematically retrieve the results and elements of the project, which is useful when working in teams (selects and shares elements for comparison or to continue working cumulatively). It works with flexible codes (they can be relocated or reassigned to other codes or subcodes) creating a maximum of 10 levels of code categories. Simple and advanced search functions are available (single or multiple codes (O) or intersection (AND) multiple codes) Self-coding elements are less flexible than in other programs. You can fragment images to encode them, but your video encoding capacity is limited. You can geolocate and transcribe audio/video in the application, inserting internal or external links to the original documents.

Free or Low-Cost Software

The programs described above can only be used with a license fee, other free or low-cost software can be found on the network, as indicated in Table 2, but with limited possibilities.

Pujol [13] regards ELAN to be the best free software for transcription, annotation and encoding of audio-visual files. It can be installed on any type of computer and operating system. The coding and visualization processes of the annotations are very

Table 2. Free or low-cost software

Software	Data type	Webpage
AnSWR	Textual data. Designed by the CDC	http://answr.software.informer.com/
Audacity	Audio editor (WAV, AIFF and MP3 archives)	http://audacity.sourceforge.net/
TAMS analyser	Textual data	http://tamsys.sourceforge.net/
ELAN	Audiovisual data	https://tla.mpi.nl/tools/tla-tools/elan/
Weft-QDA	Textual data	http://weft-qda.uptodown.com/
Transana	Audiovisual data	http://www.transana.org/
Aquad 7	Textual and audiovisual data	http://www.aquad.de/es/

simple and intuitive, it makes it possible to work with coding templates, it carries out multiple searches with regular expressions, and it can import and export with different formats and schemes coming from other CAQDAS. It is advisable to use it "to carry out behaviour, language and communication analyses or other lines of research that require an exhaustive, precise and synchronized control of each of the parts of the audio-visual material: audio, video and text".

TRANSANA is a free or open source software, created to analyse audio and video data. The video or audio and the transcription are displayed in a single window. Provides the ability to encode video and audio, transcribe, record clips, choose keywords and establish interrelationships. It can run on Windows and Mac and supports multiple users. It supports unprotected video formats such as AVI, MPG, MPEG and MP3 audio, supports WAV or WMV, but it is advised that the most compatible formats be used.

Weft-QDA is a free program that works with documents in (txt) or PDF format, allows to classify text segments into categories, add and update notes to categories or texts, search for words or sets of words, text segments with Boolean operators and export classified text or tables to Word or Excel. It's very easy to use. It has few and simple functions that are easy to manage, an intuitive and simple interface. It can run on Windows and Linux.

It is important to remember that free software grows thanks to the contributions and suggestions of all researchers. Functionalities can be added on the basis of the detected needs.

3 Conclusion

Qualitative data analysis is characterized by a series of procedures that can be systematized and optimized with the aid of computer programs. The use of computers allows researchers to apply different types of analyses and be creative while maintaining the quality of the data and ensuring the fundamental characteristics of the qualitative methodology: flexibility, reflexivity and inductive reasoning.

Attentive reading, or observation of contextualized data, is a prerequisite to any analysis process. It is not possible to analyse the data without first having read and reread it, listened to it or observed it repeatedly, until you are very familiar with it. This includes all data: full transcripts, field notes, quotations, audio data, videos and graphics.

CAQDAS enable researchers to effectively organize, store and manage large amounts of qualitative data and sustain a rigorous analysis process. They allow researchers to perform analyses in a precise and transparent manner that is also more agile, more systematic, exhaustive, creative and rigorous. However, no program can perform data analysis on its own, nor can it develop interpretation schemes that would express their true meaning. The real meanings of the analysis must be conveyed by the analysts.

Analytical capacity depends on the theoretical and methodological training of the researcher. The described software packages are only one more tool among many and they have their own limitations and strengths. Whenever we use any type of tool, we are always at risk of performing superficial analyses that lack rigour and depth. The use of technology does not have to increase this risk. CAQDAS are very useful in particular types of qualitative analysis, may be of help in some and be of no use in others. Qualitative researchers, once they are clear about what they want to do, should decide whether to use these programs, whether they meet their needs, and whether they are consistent with their epistemological budgets.

Training in the use of CAQDAS should be targeted at professionals with prior knowledge in qualitative data analysis or otherwise should include such training. In addition, it should promote the participants' critical thinking about the programs (methodological implications, advantages and disadvantages of their use and reading of research projects performed with them) and should not be limited to teaching basic skills for the use of those tools.

The majority of CAQDAS focus on the coding and recovery of coded texts or images without decontextualizing them, i.e. without losing information on where the text comes from. The Atlas.ti, MAXqda and NVivo packages also have text search functions, code search, memo writing and printing options, which are of great help in analysis. They also provide analysts with a variety of tools for examining traits and relationships in texts. Code searching can be used to examine patterns (using comparisons) and to test analytical judgments in the early stages of data analysis.

The great challenges faced by the creators of software include analytical modelling and visualization, the need to improve capabilities in the analysis of discourse, sound and audio-visual material, improve types of formats, improve graphic output types and concept maps, achieve greater flexibility in exporting models, improving transcription processes, creating lower cost or free software.

References

1. Sánchez-Gómez, M.C., Martín-Cilleros, M.V.: Implementation of focus group in health research. In: Costa, A.P., Reis, L.P., Neri de Sousa, F., Moreira, A., Lamas, D. (eds.) Computer Supported Qualitative Research. SSDC, vol. 71, pp. 49–61. Springer, Cham (2017). https://doi.org/10.1007/978-3-319-43271-7_5
2. Carvajal, D.: Las Herramientas de la Artesana. Aspectos Críticos en la Enseñanza y Aprendizaje de los CAQDAS. Forum Qualitative Sozialforschung/Forum: Qual. Soc. Res. **3** (2) (2002). Disponible en: http://www.qualitative-research.net/fqs-texte/2-02/2-02carvajals.htm
3. Richards, L.: Rigorous, rapid, reliable and qualitative? computing in qualitative method. Am. J. Health Behav. **26**(6), 425–430 (2002)
4. Chernobilsky, L.B.: El uso de la computadora como auxiliar del análisis de datos cualitativos. In: Vasilachis de Gialdino, I. (ed.) Estrategias de investigación cualitativa. Gedisa, Barcelona (2006)
5. Coffey, A., Atkinson, P.: Making Sense of Qualitative Data. Sage Publications, London (1996)
6. Fielding, N.G., Lee, R.M.: Computer Analysis and Qualitative Research. Sage Publications, London (1998)
7. Seidel, J.: Method and madness in the application of computer technology to qualitative data analysis. In: Fielding, N., Lee, R.M. (eds.) Using Computers in Qualitative Research. Sage, London (1991)
8. Have, P.: Doing Conversation Analysis: A Practical Guide. Sage, London (1999)
9. Seale, C.: Using computers to analysis qualitative data. In: Silverman, D. (ed.) Doing Qualitative Research: A Practical Handbook. Sage, London (2000)
10. Lee, R.M., Fielding, N.: Computing for qualitative research: options, problems and potential. In: Fielding, N., Lee, R.M. (eds.) Using Computers in Qualitative Research. Sage, London (1991)
11. Richard, T.J., Richard, L.: Using computers in qualitative research. In: Denzin, N.K., Lincoln, Y.S. (eds.) Handbook of Qualitative Research. Sage, Thousand Oaks (1994)
12. Sohn, B.: Phenomenology and qualitative data analysis software (QDAS): a careful reconciliation. Forum Qualitative Sozialforschung/Forum: Qual. Soc. Res. **18**(1), Art. 14 (2017). http://nbn-resolving.de/urn:nbn:de:0114-fqs1701142
13. Pujol, E.: Los programas informáticos en la investigación cualitativa. In: Calderón, C., et al. (eds.) Introducción a la Investigación Cualitativa. Máster de Investigación en Atención Primaria Barcelona, Sem FYC, Fundació Doctor Robert, Universitat Autònoma de Barcelona (2015)
14. Vallés, M.: Técnicas cualitativas de investigación social. Síntesis, Madrid (1997)
15. Weitzman, E.A.: Software and qualitative research. In: Denzin, N.K., Lincoln, Y.S. (eds.) Handbook of Qualitative Research, 2nd edn. Sage, London (2000)
16. Kelle, U., Laurie, H.: Computer use in qualitative research and issues of validity. In: Kelle, U. (ed.) Computer-aided Qualitative Data Analysis: Theory, Methods and Practice. Sage, London (1995)
17. Flick, U.: Introducción a la Investigación Cualitativa. Morata, Madrid (2004)
18. Muñoz Justicia, J.: Análisis cualitativo de datos textuales con Atlas-ti. Universitat Autónoma de Barcelona, Barcelona (2005)
19. Hwang, S.: Utilizing qualitative data analysis software: a review of Atlas.ti. Soc. Sci. Comput. Rev. **26**, 519–527 (2008)

20. Silver, C., Lewins, A.: Using Software in Qualitative Research: A Step-by-Step Guide, 2nd edn. Sage, London (2014). https://doi.org/10.4135/9781473906907
21. Willig, C., Rogers, W.S.: The SAGE Handbook of Qualitative Research in Psychology. Sage, London (2017)
22. Creswell, J.W.: Educational Research: Planning, Conducting, and Evaluating Quantitative and Qualitative Research, 2nd edn. Prentice-Hall, Upper Saddle River (2005)
23. Anguera, T., López, O.: Comparación de CAQDAS para la investigación psicosocial: atlas-ti versus Nvivo. XI CONGRESO DE METODOLOGÍA DE LAS CIENCIAS SOCIALES Y DE LA SALUD, pp. 224–228, Málaga (2009)
24. Gibbs, G.: El análisis de datos cualitativos en investigación cualitativa. Ediciones Morata, Madrid (2012)
25. Valdemoros, M.Á., Ponce De León, A., Sanz, E.: Fundamentos en el manejo del Nvivo 9 como herramienta al servicio de estudios cualitativos. Contextos educativos **14**, 11–29 (2011)
26. Muhr, T.: ATLAS/ti: a prototype for the support of text interpretation. Qual. Sociol. **14**, 349–371 (1991)
27. Strauss, A.: Qualitative Analysis for Social Scientists. Cambridge University Press, Cambridge (1987)

Author Index

Abdul Rani, Mohamad Firdaus Che 23
Abrahams, Ilhaam 234
Achmad, T. Yani 381
Aditya, Bayu Rima 151
Aho, Anne-Maria 302
Al-Azawi, Rula 3, 36
Albadi, Ali 36
Alberth, 362
Alexiou, Aikaterini 189
Al-Obaidy, Mohaned 3
Angelone, Anna Maria 439
Arias, Rosario 162

Barbosa, Débora Nice Ferrari 337
Barneva, Reneta P. 408
Bassani, Patrícia Brandalise Scherer 337
Berardi, Anna 93
Bilinkis, Julia 45
Bouta, Hara 189
Brimkov, Valentin E. 408

Canham, Niki 103
Chamoso, Pablo 428
Chang, Chih-Hung 292
Chua, Yi Han Victoria 125
Ciriaco, Mirelly Atanázio 58
Corchado, Juan M. 428
Cordero-Gutiérrez, Rebeca 351

Darma, Yudi 381
Dauwels, Justin 125
de Campos Filho, Amadeu Sa 58
de la Prieta Pintado, Fernando 418
de Luis Reboredo, Ana 418
de Souza Fantini, Webber 58
Della Ventura, Michele 14
dos Santos, Joelton 58

Farina, Ilaria 93
Fernández, Alberto 450
Florjančič, Viktorija 279, 325
Fraile, Jesús M. 428

Galeoto, Giovanni 93
Gil-González, Ana B. 418
Gomes, Alex Sandro 58, 247
González, Sara Rodríguez 418
González-Briones, Alfonso 428
Gorchakov, Yaroslav 45
Gromoff, Alexander 45
Guggemos, Josef 202, 393

Heričko, Marjan 114
Huang, Yun-Hsuan 139

Ivala, Eunice 234
Izquierdo-Álvarez, Vanessa 351

Jefferies, Amanda 337
Joe, Sebastin Antony 3

Kamišalić, Aida 114
Kaplan, Jonathan 214
Karampa, Vasiliki 67
Karra, Stavroula 67
Kasinathan, Vinothini 23
Konečný, Vladimír 313

Lahuerta-Otero, Eva 351

Magreñán, Alberto 162
Marhayani, Dina Anika 292
Martín-Cilleros, M. V. 474
Martín-García, Antonio V. 177
Meda, Lawrence 234
Mena, Juanjo 177
Moghaddas, Raziyeh 36
Molano, José Ignacio Rodríguez 462
Moreira, Fernando 58, 247
Moser, Luca 202
Mrdović, Saša 114
Mursidi, Andi 381
Musskopf, Ângela 337
Mustapha, Aida 23
Mysirlaki, Sofia 189

Naaranoja, Marja 292
Nurhas, Irawan 151
Nurhayati, 292

Orcos, Lara 162
Orozco, Walter 450

Paas, Sille 369
Paraskeva, Foteini 67, 189
Pata, Kai 369
Pattermann, Juliana 103
Pawlowski, Jan 151
Pizzi, Cecilia 93
Ploder, Christian 224

Queiros, Leandro M. 247

Rabl, Maria 103
Rajalingam, Preman 125
Reina, Yudy Fernanda Piñeros 462
Ribera, Juan M. 79
Rivas, Alberto 428
Rodríguez, Sara 428
Rodríguez-García, Miguel Ángel 450
Rotger, Lucía 79
Royle, Karl 260
Rustam, 381

Sánchez Sánchez, G. 474
Sánchez-Gómez, M. C. 474
Sánchez-Gómez, María Cruz 177
Sansoni, Julita 93
Sarría, Íñigo 162
Schlögl, Stephan 103, 224
Schöffer, Franziska 224
Seufert, Sabine 202, 393
Sicilia, Juan Antonio 162
Silva, Carlos J. P. 247
Sinclair, Jane 302
Sonderegger, Stefan 202
Sotiropoulos, Dimitrios J. 189
Souki, Aikaterini-Maria 189
Spieß, Teresa 224
Šramová, Veronika 313
Suherdiyanto, 381

Tan, Seng Chee 125
Tarantini, Eric 393
Ting, I-Hsien 381
Turkanović, Muhamed 114

Vittorini, Pierpaolo 439

Wang, William Yu Chjung 362
Wang, Yun 362
Westlake, Jonathan 3, 36
Wiechetek, Łukasz 325

Závodská, Anna 313
Zea, Leidy Daniela Forero 462

MIX
Papier aus verantwortungsvollen Quellen
Paper from responsible sources
FSC® C105338

If you have any concerns about our products,
you can contact us on
ProductSafety@springernature.com

In case Publisher is established outside the EU,
the EU authorized representative is:
Springer Nature Customer Service Center GmbH
Europaplatz 3, 69115 Heidelberg, Germany

Printed by Libri Plureos GmbH
in Hamburg, Germany